This Book Belongs To:

Ruth Triplett

1. PSA 2
2. Thomas Jefferson High School
3. 666 Dumont Avenue
4. Unity Houses
5. Van Dyke Houses
6. Zaids' supermarket
7. Public Library
8. Brownsville Community
   Baptist Church
9. Brownsville Recreation Center
10. Brookdale Hospital
11. Betsy Head Park
12. Tilden Houses
13. Brownsville Houses
14. Langston Hughes Houses
15. Howard Houses
16. Fiorentino Plaza
17. Cypress Houses
18. Pink Houses
19. Linden Houses

THE VILLE

THE VILLE

COPS AND KIDS IN URBAN AMERICA

GREG DONALDSON

ANCHOR BOOKS
DOUBLEDAY

NEW YORK   LONDON   TORONTO   SYDNEY   AUCKLAND

AN ANCHOR BOOK
PUBLISHED BY DOUBLEDAY
a division of Bantam Doubleday Dell Publishing
Group, Inc.
1540 Broadway, New York, New York 10036

ANCHOR BOOKS, DOUBLEDAY, and the portrayal
of an anchor are trademarks of Doubleday, a division of Bantam Doubleday Dell Publishing
Group, Inc.

The Ville was originally published in hardcover
by Houghton Mifflin Company in 1993. The Anchor Books edition is published by arrangement
with Houghton Mifflin Company.

Library of Congress Cataloging-in-Publication
Data
Donaldson, Greg.
The ville : cops and kids in urban America / Greg
Donaldson. — 1st Anchor Books ed.
        p. cm.
Originally published: New York : Ticknor &
Fields, 1993.
    1. Brownsville (New York, N.Y.) — Social
conditions. 2. Juvenile delinquents — New
York (N.Y.) 3. Police — New York
            (N.Y.) I. Title.
        [HN80.B87D66 1994]
306'.097477'1 — dc20   94-20510 ·
                                         CIP

ISBN 0-385-47545-4

For John and Constance Donaldson

ACKNOWLEDGMENTS

The Ville could not have been written without the complete cooperation of Sharron Corley and Gary Lemite. Above all, it is their book. I would like to thank them and their families.

I am indebted to the people of Brownsville and East New York, who treated my project with an open mind and in many cases welcomed me with real hospitality under extremely difficult circumstances, asking only that I "tell it the way it is."

I would also like to express my appreciation to Chief Joseph Keeney of the Housing police for allowing me to follow the activities of his officers at PSA 2, and the policemen there for letting me watch them work. I am grateful to the principal of Thomas Jefferson High School, Carol Beck, who trusted me enough to give me access to her teachers and students.

Acknowledgment is due to Alter F. Landesman and Gerald Sorin for their books on the history of Brownsville.

Special thanks goes to Ingrid Griffith for living with this project for three years, and my deep appreciation to Michael Fahey and Dave Young for their friendship and perspective.

Mercer Sullivan of the New School gave advice, and Sharon Zukin of Brooklyn College offered background on the history of Brownsville and criticism of segments of the manuscript. John Garvey and John Mogulescu of the City University supported me with optimism, ideas, and analysis throughout the process. Demographer Frank Vardi was a vital source of information. Thanks also to Alan Dichter, principal of the Satellite Academy High School, and Nathan Jackson for his fact checking.

The Ville also owes much to the photographs of Charlena

Berksteiner, Mitch Zykofsky, and Bruce Gilbert. I would like to thank Eli Reed, whose photos have added so much.

Dave Herndon and John Capouya, editors at *New York Newsday*, were early sources of advice and enthusiasm for my features on Brooklyn youth. Thanks to Rick Landau for his unstinting support.

Finally, credit goes to Matt Bialer, my agent, for suggesting the idea of approaching the story of Brownsville through its police officers and teenagers, and to Jane von Mehren, my editor at Ticknor & Fields. Only she and I know how mightily she labored to produce this book.

PREFACE

This book about Brownsville and East New York, isolated and troubled neighborhoods in Brooklyn, New York, is an attempt to bring the people behind the cardboard images of cops and inner-city African American teenagers to life. It is an effort to fill a gap in understanding that troubles this country deeply.

There are people in Brownsville, thousands of them living in city housing projects, who overcome the conditions there and continue to prevail. The private and public struggles go on. The East Brooklyn Congregations has built large numbers of affordable private homes that are pockets of stability. It plans to erect thirty square blocks more of housing. Activists such as Reggie Bowman, who founded the Community Coalition to Save Brownsville, continue to fight a system that is content to allow levels of joblessness, despair, and violence to persist in Brownsville (and communities like it) that are destroying a generation of African Americans. Bowman has spent the better part of the past decade battling to make New York City deliver on its promise to construct East Kings High School on an empty lot on Bristol Avenue. Symbolically, the city recently broke ground for a $35 million high-tech juvenile detention facility on the site.

The story of the political struggle for the future of Brownsville and the many lost battles is one that should be heard. Instead, I have chosen to write of day-to-day life in Brownsville through the eyes of police officers and teenagers who live there now. On that excruciating line between officers of the law and young men of the streets I hope to catch the soul of a community.

To write *The Ville*, I spent more than two years in Browns-ville and East New York. I accompanied the Housing police on every kind of call, from domestic disputes to shootings. Some-times I followed officers and suspects from the initial radio call through pursuit, arrest, and court case. I visited Thomas Jeffer-son High School regularly, sat in the classrooms, and traveled with the basketball team. I walked the streets of Brownsville, was a guest in people's homes, attended community and church events. Whenever and wherever I could, I followed the central characters, officer Gary Lemite and young Sharron Corley. The events in the book are real, based on my own observations or interviews. Nonetheless, I saw fit to change the names and identities of some of the characters portrayed and to disguise some locations. In some instances, I have shifted the time frame of an event to suit the narrative.

I chose to follow Gary Lemite, a Housing police officer, in-stead of a New York City policeman because of the close and constant contact Housing police have with the people in the pub-lic housing projects they patrol. The officers I depict in the book are the ones I met; it is incorrect to assume that they are repre-sentative of all police in inner-city neighborhoods. In fact, I ob-served distinct differences between the performance of Housing police and NYPD officers from precincts serving Brownsville and East New York.

Likewise, the young men I have focused on are not represen-tative of all black teenagers, even those in Brownsville itself. There are a number of two-parent households in the neighbor-hood that manage through herculean effort to guide their chil-dren past the dangers and on to productive lives.

I could have concentrated on one of those priceless victories, but instead I chose to tell the story of a young man from Brownsville who lives on the edge between success and disaster. Sharron Corley, who is the centerpiece of this book, does not have an impenetrable parental buffer. He is young and intelli-gent, sensitive and ambitious, and he is a living record of the relentless economic and social forces in his community and his country. To the extent that his travails reinforce negative ste-reotypes of black teenagers, the book has failed. To the measure that the story humanizes the struggle of inner-city black teen-agers to make sense of their lives, not only to survive but to make something special of themselves, it will have succeeded.

THE VILLE

I shall not listen.
I shall not listen
When they tell me
Life is sad and brief.

— Anonymous graffiti on a memorial wall in Brownsville, Brooklyn

PROLOGUE: LIKELY

The salty breeze that lifts off Jamaica Bay and drifts past the towering high-rises of Starrett City, over the roofs of the one-family houses in Canarsie, makes it only as far as Flatlands Avenue. From Linden Boulevard north, the air is dead still. This is Brownsville.

In their blue and orange patrol car, rolling through the midnight streets, the two Housing cops could be two buddies in that time between school and family — a bit too old to cruise for girls, too young for the burden of kids, two regular guys. But outside the windows of their sector car are the streets of Brownsville and East New York, where there have been 185 murders in the past twelve months. Where it is so dangerous the bars have been shut down for years, there are no movie theaters, and some newly renovated city-subsidized apartments on New Lots Avenue go unclaimed because of fear. Where the only establishment sure to be open is a narrow storefront on Rockaway Avenue flashing a neon sign, 24 HOURS, WE BUY GOLD. Outside the window of the patrol car is a red tide of rancor. The radio crackles. The radio tells that story.

Through a blizzard of static, the dispatcher jolts across with a message about a shooting. The words are laced with numbers, codes for conditions and offenses. One phrase is clear; it will be repeated again and again throughout the night, the season, and the year, words that are the mantra of Brownsville: "Shots fired." "Numerous calls," Central says. "One male shot at that location. K."

The Housing police of the PSA 2 do not customarily answer

1

OP (off-project) calls, but this is a shooting and car 9712 is close. The driver stomps on the gas pedal and rockets to the site, a schoolyard on Hopkinson and Pacific, near Saratoga. Across the darkened yard, a cluster of people consider a fallen human being.

The late spring night is thick and bright. A round of stars sits high above the rooftops. As is almost always the case in Brownsville, the body is that of a young black man. The cops kneel down next to the figure and fumble for a few moments. They have no medical supplies, will not give mouth-to-mouth unless a child is dying. Nor will they decide to carry the man to their patrol car and whisk him to Brookdale Hospital, the way they would if this were a 10-13, an officer shot. The crowd leans; a boy edges his bicycle forward and gapes. One officer reports over his radio that the young man is "likely," police jargon for either dead or soon likely to be.

The call for a bus (ambulance) was made several minutes ago, when somebody from a window high above made a 911 call. Somebody saw the youth fall, because no one in Brownsville would call an ambulance just because they heard shots fired. The cops crouch a moment longer, then straighten up. No sense pretending. In another half-minute, the orange and white EMS vehicle storms across the blacktop to the foot of the steps near the cornerstone of the school. An EMS technician in a green uniform hustles out and verifies the "likely" report. The boy is already dead. The medics prepare to load the body into the bus. The folks on hand exchange whispered information. "You know, the guy with the dreads. Nooo, dark skin, guy who *just got* the dreads."

The crowd swells. Here, murder is a curse laid on a people who have carried too many burdens, an unspeakable place where a segment of the African American population has found itself after a desperate journey.

In the first half of the century, Brownsville was a thriving Jewish enclave. But as viable a community as it was then, it was never a destination for the Jews who filled its roiling streets, looked out over its clothesline-crossed yards and ramshackle homes. It was, in Alfred Kazin's words, "a place that measured all success by our skill in getting away from it." The war provided the prosperity; the freeways and the automobile, the means.

Most of the buildings in Brownsville were tenements built before 1919, structures with commercial space on the first floor and apartments for often as many as five families above, or wood-frame two-family rental dwellings. As the old housing stock deteriorated, the vacant apartments became catch basins for the poor, because they were the only housing people could find. Community activists campaigned hard. "Brownsville must have public housing" was their clarion cry. The makeshift tenements were readily demolished. Between 1941 and 1955, four major public housing units were built, including the Brownsville Houses in 1948, which the *New York Times* called "terrifying new slums."

Between 1940 and 1950, the black population of Brownsville doubled. The synagogue on Riverdale Avenue near Hertzl Street became the People's Baptist Church. Integration in the projects, crime, and fear of crime spurred the departure of the remaining low-income Jews to nearby East Flatbush or Canarsie. Fires devoured the frame houses that were still standing. Weed-wild lots dotted the landscape. Some brick dwellings were constructed on side streets, but mostly the deterioration continued unabated. The 1960s brought the scourge of heroin, the living dead who scratched like chickens through the torched and abandoned private buildings around the projects. By 1970, in a community of 1.9 square miles, there were seven hundred completely deserted buildings. The city took the opportunity to load the area with clinics, halfway houses, and rehabilitation centers for the dysfunctional and the troubled.

At first the projects seemed an improvement over rural poverty and tenement life. But the new black residents of Brownsville, many of them migrants from the South, ran into an old brick wall. The March on Washington of 1963 and the Civil Rights Act of 1964 raised hopes, but governmental policy, gerrymandering, redlining by banks, and deindustrialization mocked ambitions. The winners were the property speculators, the demolition companies. Breadwinners lost their jobs. More poor people poured in. The Latino population swelled. The projects grew like mushrooms. There were uprisings, tumult in the streets. In 1968, residents of Brownsville and nearby Ocean Hill fought for community control of local schools, setting off a citywide teachers' strike. The National Welfare Rights Organization took the city to court to make the Housing Authority stop banning welfare recipients. Over thirty years, the city lost six hundred thousand industrial jobs. Designed for the working poor, the projects filled up with the unemployed. Then, in the late 1980s, crack cocaine materialized and guns poured into the neighborhood by the trunkload. Soon the poverty of Brownsville's past seemed a golden age.

Places like the Cypress Hills Houses, a vast housing project at the eastern border of East New York, and, on the other side of the stark pillars of the elevated subway tracks in Brownsville, the Unity and Brownsville Houses, are now some of the most dangerous spots on earth to live. Last year eight people were murdered in the Unity Houses alone; one building is so deadly the Housing police call it the slaughterhouse.

Murder is horror, but it is also entertainment. The first people on the scene this night look and mutter, ask stupid questions. "Is he all right?" These are just the folks who happened to be nearby when someone chased this young man from the front of the school to the back and shot him in the chest, the people out and about when he staggered down the four cement steps and collapsed, when he went from the living to the "likely."

News of the deed begins to seep through the neighborhood as the Housing cops perform the first real function of their shift, looping a yellow and black crime scene tape around the area. They complain. Housing police officers in Brownsville are often patient, sometimes valiant, but they almost always complain. This time they grumble about the size of the area designated as a crime scene. They complain about guarding the scene of a homicide so obviously off-project.

When there is a crowd, EMS removes the body with some dispatch. So it is this spring night. But not before news of the shooting spreads beyond the curious to the boy's acquaintances, and from them to his family. A girl straddles a pink bicycle thirty yards off, at the entrance to the schoolyard. She holds four spread fingers to her open mouth. "Not my brother," she whispers.

Her big brother is dead in the schoolyard, the place where fifteen years before he arrived cleaned up and crisply dressed for school, where he stood, hand in mother's hand, waiting for kindergarten to start. Maybe the schoolyard wasn't such a strange place to die. This was where hope foundered, where the child came face to face with the country that didn't need him. Perhaps the school was the right spot for this, the place where the promise was made and where it was broken.

The words reach home, words that should have been swept away by the wind. A fifty-five-year-old woman in a housedress and bare feet sprints down the sidewalk beside the twenty-foot Cyclone fence that borders the blacktop. Arms pumping and knees high, she comes in undignified haste, followed by a man with a ghastly gray face. Eyes bulging with bad health, belly swollen, he runs but a step behind his wife. The parents charge across the yard, straight at the two cops, who halfheartedly block their approach to the bus just as the body of their son is loaded up.

Electronic derision now: the belch and shriek of sirens float up, a background for the human lamentations. The mother pounds on the Irish Housing cop's chest. "I know who did it. I know who did it!" she screams.

At first there were dreams, a trip from the South to New York, better schools, escape from poverty, segregation, and that deep dust of hatred. Some grabbed the frayed rope of opportunity and hoisted themselves up and out of the neighborhood. Others snatched up city-subsidized mortgages and carved out a homestead. But for many the hope flickered. The dream faded to simple daily pleasures, pocket money, girlfriends. Youths like the one who fell tonight found fast friends, squeezed thick nuts of bills in their pockets. Trouble. The parents watched and worried. Soon the worry wasn't a sharp twinge but a dull presence, and every time this young man left home there was the possibility he would not come back. He was so alive and so close to death. He was a son of Brownsville. Then, murder most predictable.

SUMMER

DON'T GIVE UP ON YOUR DREAMS

Seventeen-year-old Sharron Corley slides center stage. It is a glove-soft evening in early summer, downtown Brooklyn. Sharron is glowing with perspiration and conviction. Danny, the character he is playing in the opening night performance of the Thomas Jefferson High School play, *Don't Give Up on Your Dreams*, has had a revelation.

In the play, Danny is a singer who lives with his single mother and sister in a barren apartment in the ghetto. He is tortured by temptation, the conflict between the street and the straight, between selling drugs and suffering until he gets his break. Through the opening scenes, he wanders on the wide stage in a trance, wrestling with his moral dilemma like Hamlet. Then his singing group, Danny and the Dream Team, is cheated out of $50,000 in prize money for a talent show they deserve to win, and Danny decides to turn to the beckoning arms of Rufus, a jewelry-bedecked drug entrepreneur. "I know what I'm gonna do," Danny says. "I'm gonna make some real money for a change. That's right. Danny is gonna get paid." Rufus is upstage, coiled like a snake, chanting, "I've got what you want. I've got what you need. I've got what you're lookin' for and more."

The play is being performed at the Paul Robeson Theater, miles away from Pennsylvania Avenue in the Brownsville/East New York neighborhood where Jefferson is located. This is the first performance in a scheduled week-long run of shows, and already the production is tight. The audience is filled with beaming parents and girlfriends, wide-eyed younger brothers and sisters. The star is Sharron. He acts. He sings. He "profiles:" At five-foot-nine, he is broad-shouldered, saluki-trim, and wickedly muscled. His split-level fade stands three inches straight up, a crisp headdress, autumnal gold on the top inch and deep walnut the rest of the way down.

All his short life, Sharron has wanted to be admired. But that is not what always happened. He was a quiet, shy child. "We used to think there might be something wrong with him," his sister, Shawanda, says. When he was fourteen years old, it came together. He grew, his shoulders stretched like wings; a modest regimen of pushups and his pectorals looked like burnished plates of armor. To his utter delight, girls started calling him "pretty boy." He could not believe his good fortune, checked himself in the mirror a score of times on the day he first heard the term. Nearly four years later, he holds still at the sight of his own reflection, unless he is in a great hurry.

Tonight Sharron does not need a mirror. At the end of the first act, as he approaches the footlights, he bursts into song. Then he strips off his jacket and casts his voice to the dusty rafters. The teenage girls in the packed house go mad. Their hands fly to their faces. They shriek and rise from their seats. How has it happened that the very sight and sound they conjured in the secret places of their hearts has come to life? Sharron sinks to the wooden floor. From a pushup position, he thrusts his hips down; his muscled stomach, chest, neck, and head follow. Undulation after undulation, faster and faster, until the rippling effect is lost in a series of rapid thrusts.

Throughout most of the second act, though, Sharron, as Danny, is depressed and worried. He is supposed to begin working for Rufus soon. In one scene he sits slumped over the kitchen table listening to the cautionary words of his mother. Then he leaps to his feet, turns his back on her, and broods in guilty silence. He fingers the flimsy curtains his mother is so proud of, and sneers. Danny craves legitimate success, wants to make his mother proud. But the path is just too difficult. Everything he sees around him is hollow and cheap. The goal of Hollywood, success in the world beyond the neighborhood, beckons, but the road? Where? How? Rufus and his ways are at hand, close at hand.

Danny steps out of the apartment onto the painted Brownsville street set, lifts his eyes to the rafters, and with a great racking shudder thunders, "Hell, no!" In a feat of rectitude, he reverses his decision to work for the drug dealer. Rufus is not pleased. He materializes on the apron of the stage, chuckling darkly, and allows his body to sag a bit to the left. With the move, Rufus's jacket swings away from his body. He glances sharply under the garment and back at Danny. Throughout the play, Rufus has habitually moved with this list, again and again looking under his coat. The body language is a reference to the weight of a big gun, the drag of a "burner." The maneuver is not wasted on Danny, who braces himself for the worst.

Rufus is lurking, scheming for just the right time and place to send a message through the neighborhood that "nobody plays me." Danny's girlfriend, Gloria, played by Nareida Torres, approaches Rufus to plead for her lover's life, but the pitiless gangster yanks his gun. *Bam bam bam;* three shots ring out, and she crumples to the stage, mortally wounded. From the fourth row of the audience, Torres's seven-year-old brother screams in horror, bolts from his seat, and runs to his fallen sister. He tries to vault onto the stage. "The black man shot her," he howls. The boy is led away, struggling. No amount of explanation will console him until after the show, when he sits in the first row of the lit theater and holds his sister's hand.

Indeed, this is just a play, adapted by the faculty director, social studies teacher Sharon King. As much as she stressed authenticity in the dialogue and realism in the professionally designed set pieces, to show the world of Brownsville, King allowed for a happy ending.

In the final scene, Sharron Corley, dressed in a tuxedo, approaches the microphone and wraps up the loose ends of the plot: "Danny and the Dream Team received the fifty-thousand-dollar prize money, and a few days later Rufus was slaughtered by his own men. Don't give up on your dreams."

As Sharron turns his profile to the audience in the rising houselights, a livid scar is visible, running like an arching fault line from an inch beyond his hairline next to his left ear to the dimple near the corner of his mouth. Far from being a tour de force by a professional makeup artist, the scar comes compliments of the Brownsville streets, delivered by a razor in a street fight on the day before last Valentine's Day.

Sharron drops his hands to his sides and bows his head to the audience. On cue, the full thirty-member cast floods the aisles of the old theater and belts out a medley of inspirational songs.

There is a flush of accomplishment on the faces of the performers as they filter from the cramped dressing quarters into the empty hall minutes later. The glow will last for hours, at least as long as it takes to ride the subway back to the neighborhood. These are just kids now. They are neither frightening nor afraid. Tonight, diminutive Sheryl, Sharron's new girlfriend in the cast, does not feel or look like one of the Gucci Girls from the Linden Houses when they eye a white girl's earrings on the A train. Sharron does not feel like a member of the LoLifes when they slip through the Fulton Mall, watching for the slow, the weak, the turned head, the unguarded rack of clothes. These are just children now, centers of attention, sources of hope.

The energy in the musty hall is mountain fresh as King assembles her cast to discuss what went right and what went wrong with the performance. They settle to immediate attention. There are no artificial constraints on speech. No threats, no pleading for silence. There are things King knows that the kids want to learn. The young teacher wears black leggings and an oversize white T-shirt; her tawny skin is damp. Her huge amber eyes scan a pad with notes about the performance — the missed entrances, the speeches that did not quite work. One girl gave a monologue during the talent show segment of the play, portraying a woman waking her sleepy young son for school. But the girl's diction was so bad the performance collapsed.

"If you don't start to enunciate the way Ms. Oldham taught you to do, we are going to have to take your speech out of the play," King warns. "It's as simple as that. You studied this voice thing for four months, and tonight you sounded like you hadn't had a voice lesson in your life." There are no tears, no tantrums. The girl takes King's words as truth.

"What do *you* say about tonight?" King asks the group. Willowy Kenya springs to her feet. Her portrayal of Rufus's atonal singer girlfriend brought the house down.

"There are some boys who are hanging around the area where we're supposed to change costumes for our song. That shit is hard enough without some peeping Toms."

Before the titters die out, a six-foot-three, squeaky-voiced bit player apologizes. "I think she's talking about me. I had no place to stand. It won't happen again."

"What happened to the breathing we taught you?" King asks. "You've *got* to breathe. All I'm hearing are lines. Remember, the script is your gun and the words are your bullets." A moment later she offers a gratuitous observation. "I have so much respect for you guys. It takes more courage to get up here on the stage than it does to pull the trigger of a nine." She is talking about a nine-millimeter semiautomatic gun, a popular weapon in Brownsville. Though King is from the Caribbean, not from the American urban or southern background of most of her students, when necessary she can switch from standard English to the most convincing black American slang.

There is a murmur of dissent from the actors. "It does," King insists, "it takes more courage to perform."

These teenagers have seen too much for such glibness. They have heard the hollow hump of the nine-millimeter and the boom of the .357, and they have watched the deadly series of moves that track to the instant of gunfire. They know all about these things, and they are not about to truck with a cliché, even from their beloved Ms. King.

It was sometime in late February when King decided that Sharron, a cinnamon-skinned ladies' man recently anointed homecoming king of Jefferson, would be the lead in the play. King invited him to the after-school drama program and auditioned him for the role of Danny. "Sharron was the only one who could sing, and that helped him. But he was also the best actor. He wrote his own monologue." When King posted the cast list and the unacademic Sharron won the lead, he snapped to attention.

The funding for *Don't Give Up on Your Dreams* came from a foundation called the Jackie Robinson Center for Physical Culture, which provides Brooklyn schools with a range of after-school enrichment activities. The foundation spent $20,000 on the production, and spent it wisely. Besides King, an actor with professional aspirations, they hired scene painters, an acting coach, and a voice teacher. The production staff held weekly meetings on Sunday at King's apartment. "We did everything right," King says.

The kids in the cast had seen the spacious old auditorium at Thomas Jefferson High School, and the ancient swimming pool, of course. But they knew that those grand features had been built for someone else, for the immigrants who had passed through Brownsville decades before. This school play was lavish and it was just for them. From the very outset, the program was a success. Sharron showed up at school every day and never missed an after-school rehearsal. For one hour after regular school ended at three o'clock, the cast attended academic classes and counseling sessions. The rest of the time, sometimes late into the night, they worked on acting technique and rehearsal. There were drills and improvisations. The young actors wrote and performed skits in which they imagined their characters in various situations. They practiced singing and dancing, and they helped King rewrite the dialogue. The superlative of the hour was not "awesome" or even "cool" but "mad," as in "mad house party." Dope dealers were "slingers." And the most important term of all, the word that explained much of the apparently irrational behavior in their world, was "props," probably derived from southern slang, "propers," meaning proper respect.

Sharron treated the play as if it were the chance of a lifetime. He bound his script elaborately to protect it from the elements, folded the pages in a way that gave him quick access to his scenes. He taped his lines on an audio cassette and lay for hours on his bed with his Walkman, listening to the words. He learned his lines before anyone else, even though he had five times as much dialogue as any other actor. In rehearsal he was all business, as if he had been an actor all his life. He set the standard for the others.

"He's a professional, for God's sake," King said. "You can ask him to do a scene a thousand different times, in a thousand different ways, and he'll do it happily. I couldn't get him out of the place at night. I couldn't get the rest of them out either."

The only problem King had with Sharron was his trademark whisper. When he came into his own with the girls, he developed a tone of voice that was too soft to be heard by anyone but a young girl who was somehow tuned to his soundwaves. Teachers, parents, even male friends, shook their heads and leaned ever closer to hear. But like a dog whistle, young Sharron's speech was meant for certain ears. "I got him to lift his voice,"

King says, "but there were still parts where he would whisper." The tough-guy segment of his performance had been fashioned in the neighborhood, where the reviews could be brutal. Sharron had always been convincing on the street — cold and heartless for the eyes of the little gangsters, sweet and wounded for the young ladies, reflective and earnest for the adults.

At the closing night party, the principal of Jefferson, Carol Beck, a brown-skinned woman in her mid-fifties with a spray of tiny moles beside her wary eyes, mingles with the guests and chats with the administrator of the Jackie Robinson Center. Nationally recognized as the savior of the high school, Beck has almost singlehandedly brought this troubled high school, rated the most dangerous in New York City just a couple of years ago, into an era when moments like this are possible. Now she stands in one spot and says little. Her presence stalks the room. When Kenya, the young actress, slips over to the tape player and switches off the bluesy voice of Sade, the conversation in the room stops. Beck lifts her eyebrows ever so slightly at Kenya, who offers a broad smile, injects her own tape, punches the play button, and puts her fingers in her ears to ward off the protests of her elders as a booming hip-hop beat fills the space. Beck's nod of acquiescence is imperceptible to all but Kenya, who charges off to recruit dancers. In a moment Ms. Sharon King, surrounded by her charges, hip-hops to the beat. "Go *Sha*ron. Go *Sha*ron." The dance is on.

In a corner, Sharron Corley's pretty thirty-five-year-old mother, Gloria, stands by, proud but shaky, not sure what to say or do. She doesn't know anyone. Wine is served, but Gloria is careful not to drink tonight. She drifts slowly into a back room, wipes her red hair out of her face with the back of her hand, and leans over a large sink to wash the dishes.

The actors who are not dancing assemble and reassemble, gossip, and nibble the hors d'oeuvres. They stand in clusters like spring flowers, drenched in promise. There is not a hint of disrespect or rowdy behavior from the kids in the room, and there are no sirens or gunshots in the night air outside the wide open windows. This is downtown, out of Brownsville. For one night, for one week, this is the way other kids grow up.

GUN COLLAR

Housing cop Eddie Hammil leans back in the driver's seat of 9717, the RMP (radio mobile patrol car) that stalls every few minutes, and handles the steering wheel with two thick fingers. Beside him is Del Migliore. The two are nearing the end of their eight-to-four shift on a sunny day in Brownsville. Both have been cops for three years. They are not regular partners, and they haven't been getting along well all day. When Hammil wants to eat, Migliore says ride. At the corner, Migliore nods to the right; Hammil makes a lazy left off Sutter Avenue onto Pennsylvania Avenue. Hammil, short and soft with an oval face, is a wise guy.

"I got passed over for the sweep team 'cause the other guy's black and I'm white," Migliore moans — the same complaint he has made all day.

Hammil slows the cruiser almost to a stop in front of Thomas Jefferson High School and peers at the square-jawed, handsome Migliore. "You're white?" he says.

The high school stands unceremoniously flush on Pennsylvania Avenue — no front walkway, no shrubbery, just two stone steps off the sidewalk to a mud-brown bank of double-locked metal doors flanked by Doric columns. The six-story red-brick and limestone building was built to last a long time.

The school is mute. It's 3:30, and the kids are gone for the day. But directly across the street is the corner of Dumont and Pennsylvania, home of the quick and the dead. Beneath a blue and red Puerto Rican flag, high and slack on a traffic light stanchion, a dozen men stand and shuffle, confer with arrivals, and

16

duck inside a building. Mickey Mundell, a thirty-two-year-old "stem," as crackheads are known, fidgets in front of the corner bodega, studying the faces of people in the distance, looking for someone he knows so he can borrow three dollars for a vial of crack. The sand-colored brick wall of the corner building, 666 Dumont Avenue, is decorated with a crimson R.I.P. in memory of Lyty, a girl recently assassinated on the sidewalk there. Another memorial is painted close by, for Na Na, and above there is a humble benediction in black spray paint, "R.I.P. Cano."

Hammil makes another left turn, pulls up to the gaping maw of 666. Everything about the building is worn and grimy but the gleaming, newly installed inside security door, replaced and reinforced regularly by the crack dealers to slow the cops on their charges upstairs to the drug stash apartments. Hammil surveys the congregation of jumpy young men in their late teens and early twenties. Teenagers are rarely crack users in Brownsville; heroin addiction among teens of this generation is unheard of. Instead, kids are found in the center of the action as lookouts and street dealers, as gun bearers, and as they grow older, as shooters. There are almost no older adults hanging around today. Wary customers head quickly in and out the front door.

A twenty-two-year-old Hispanic in baggy shorts and bright white tube socks stretched to his knees limps over to the patrol car, using a cane to support a damaged right hip. "Wha's up?"

"I saw your brother," Hammil tells the youth.

The kid's eyebrows knit. "Where at?"

"Over at Brookdale. But he's O.K. I don't know what was wrong with him, but the doctors were treating him like shit."

"He wasn't shot or nothin'?"

"No, I don't know what it was. They were dissin' him big-time, though. He was pissed." As Hammil talks, his gaze floats to the front door, where traffic has slowed for a moment with the arrival of the police car, then resumed. The kid crouches slightly, using his cane for balance, and looks inside the RMP at Migliore.

"O.K., be safe now," Hammil says. "You haven't seen anybody selling any drugs around here, have you?"

The kid swivels his head. "Nah. Not lately."

Hammil rolls ever so slowly away from the spot up to the light. He turns to Migliore, who is staring straight ahead. Right now, Migliore is thinking about how great it is to be a cop, remembering last Saturday, when he was driving on the New Jersey Turnpike to Atlantic City and his girlfriend got nauseated. When he pulled over under a NO STOPPING sign, a Jersey state trooper drove up and asked for identification. Migliore was fishing for his badge when the girl threw up on the trooper's shoes. The trooper took a look at Migliore's badge, walked over to the tall grass, wiped his shiny black shoes off, and drove away. Respect. Migliore is smiling to himself when Hammil snickers.

"The mope doesn't even have a fucking brother."

Second-year Housing cop Gary Lemite has two, an older one who was a cop in Florida and a hell-raiser of a kid brother on Long Island. All three have creamy skin that turns dusky at the first kiss of sun, a wan mustache, and gleaming black crinkled hair. After being rejected for high blood pressure on his first ten department screening physical exams, Gary finally got on a police force himself. He sailed through the academy and spent the next eight months as a probationary officer. Though his uniform cap is a bit too large for his head, his chin vague, and his smile wide and gentle, Gary has the peace of mind of a man who has found his place in the world. He was born to be a cop.

At Police Service Area (PSA) 2, the Housing police station over on Sutter Avenue, near the border of Brownsville and East New York, just two blocks from Thomas Jefferson High School, Gary Lemite is downstairs at his locker getting dressed for his four-to-midnight shift. He scoops a bag of sunflower seeds from the vending machine and settles on a metal chair in the roll call room across the hall. In a few minutes the sergeant is calling the roll, giving out the posts. He's taking care of the guys he likes, putting the heavy hitters, the cops who like to make arrests, in the cars and the lazy guys on hospital duty, where they can sleep, and sending the PCOs, the footposts, out to their places in the projects. The Housing police are a separate entity from the New York City police, responsible for public housing. In Brownsville and East New York, that includes some scatter-site housing, but mostly it means the projects — the Howard Houses, Pink, Brownsville, Unity, and Tilden, Cypress, Linden, Van Dyke, and Langston Hughes, which the cops call Langston Blues. Fifty thousand people live in these buildings.

"Lemite. Exterior security."

Gary frowns. Exterior security is a no-action, no-arrest detail. The assignment is to walk around the PSA and guard officers' cars against vandalism.

"And yeah," the sergeant adds. "Pay attention to this. You get in an accident, rack up the RMP, and you lose three days' pay, no matter whose fault the accident was. So watch where you're driving and check the sector car before you take it out so you don't suffer for somebody else's mistake. And don't bitch, 'cause you've been told. It comes from the top."

Upstairs, Gary waits in line to check out his radio from the radio room. The devices are worth $1,500 and have to be signed for. If an officer loses his radio, he forfeits about five days' pay. When Lemite checks the device, it fails to operate.

"Drop it on the street. It'll work," a veteran advises him. "Really. Drop it on the sidewalk." Gary exchanges the radio.

He makes a lap around the building, back to the schoolyard, and a trip across the street to the parking lot on Sutter. Now he is just standing, rocking back and forth, thinking. His family — his wife, Lisa, and two young children, Erica, three, and Zachary, two — has been living in the basement apartment of his mother's house in Elmont for three years, and that cannot go on. Too much pressure. The wife has been threatening for over a year to move to her sister's house and take the kids. Her married sister is childless and would like nothing better than to have Erica and Zach around the house for a while, maybe forever. What Gary needs is a house, one like the house he grew up in. That would cut down on the arguments, the tension. The kids would have the yard; Gary could cook his special buffalo chicken wings in the spacious kitchen. But it is going to take time, overtime, and that comes from arrests.

Gary is thinking that he is not going to get any overtime standing in front of the PSA when along comes this big kid. Gary watches as fifteen-year-old Michael T., all six-foot-one, 230 pounds of him, walks past. Michael is wearing an oversize white sweatshirt with blue stripes and carrying something heavy. Lemite is new on the job, but he has ten years' experience as a store detective in department stores all over Long Island and Queens. He knows when someone is carrying something under his clothes.

He falls into step about twenty feet behind as the kid makes the turn off Alabama onto busy Sutter Avenue. You cannot miss Michael T., because he is about the biggest young guy on the block. He lives nearby, at 280 Georgia Avenue, in the Unity Houses, and hangs on the corner in front of the bodega, sometimes with his boys but mostly alone. Fact is, Michael has to do something crazy every once in a while to keep his reputation intact. He believes the only thing worse than being a pussy is being a big pussy. Michael is huge, but he will never succeed as a real bad guy, a stickup kid, because the left side of his face is covered by a seared slab of skin, as if someone applied a red-hot iron to his cheek while he slept. Michael will never be able to get away with anything.

Michael T. has smoked marijuana lots of times, felt the slow dance of the reefer and the sour dry pop of a gulp from a forty-ounce bottle of Power Master when he is high. But that rush is weak stuff compared to the sensation of having a pistol in his hand or tucked in his waistband, feeling its hard advantage against his skin. The gun is the thing. With it, he no longer feels as if he's just wandering along Sutter Avenue with nothing to do. He feels as if he's in a movie.

Gary Lemite has a sixth sense about these things. Not only does Michael have a faint bulge under his sweatshirt, he holds the inside of his arm unnaturally tight to his side to pin whatever it is he's carrying, to make sure it does not fall to the sidewalk. Like a horse trainer moving around a stall, watching the thoroughbred's opposite flank for the flex that means the horse is about to shift its weight and deliver a kick, Lemite knows the subtle signs. "Hey," he shouts at Michael's back.

Michael T. may be in a conflict about letting people know he is carrying a "four-fifth" (.45) Ruger Red Hawk single-action hunting pistol, but he is not ambivalent about getting caught and spending time in the Spofford Juvenile Center in the Bronx, or upstate. Besides, he is still watching the movie with him in the starring role. What does the gangster do when a soft-looking, light-skinned Housing cop, probably some punk rookie, orders him to stop? Michael T. reaches for his four-fifth wheels, and points it straight at Lemite.

"What the *fuck* do you want?" he hisses.

Gary freezes at the sight of the gun leveled straight at him from killing distance. A moment, a long moment.

This is the first of many times he will face a gun in the year to come. He will see jolting flames from muzzles, he will dive from bullets, and he will fire back. This time he spins out of the line of fire and flattens himself against an abutment in the rough gray stone of the outer wall of the PSA.

The kid's play is bold and stupid. If Lemite had asked his question with his own gun drawn, things would have been different. "Looking back, I would draw and ask him to stop," he says. "In which case, if he turned and reached like that, I would've shot him. Send me in front of a grand jury. I'd rather be tried by twelve than carried by six."

Michael T. is not a "mad agent," Brownsville slang for a psychotic. He's not about to shoot a cop. He's buying time with the draw, and he uses the moment when Lemite dodges to turn and sprint to the corner of Williams and Sutter. Lemite is in pursuit now, yelling a breathless "10-13" (officer in trouble) into his radio. Maritza, the narrow-hipped, black-eyed proprietor of the bodega on Williams, watches the chase from the front of her store. Dave, the guy who cleans up the PSA, is sitting with a couple of his cronies across the street in front of the cops' parking lot. "Big kid. Big gun," he observes.

The PSA 2 crouches beside a six-story public housing building on Sutter. Behind the building is a narrow parking lot for patrol cars fronted by a Cyclone fence. Beyond the fence lies the wide asphalt playground of an elementary school. By the time Lemite gets to the corner, Michael T. has crashed through a pile of garbage on the sidewalk and made another turn, pushing his 230 pounds of muscle and baby fat across the schoolyard, back toward Alabama Avenue, where he hopes to dive into a building, disappear into an apartment.

Lemite has his gun drawn now, but there are kids on the sidewalk. There are kids in the schoolyard and there are kids on the street. The 10-13 has brought four cops out the back door of the PSA just ahead of Gary, only yards behind Michael T. as he rumbles down the street and heads into 580 Blake, a building near the corner. Sector cars from the nearby 75th and 73rd NYPD precincts stream to the scene. Two police cars collide with a glass-shattering crash and a whoosh of steam on the corner of Sutter and Williams. Radio in one hand and gun in the other, heaving with exhaustion, Lemite falls behind as Michael T. and the four officers trailing him plunge into the Blake Avenue address in the Unity Houses. The kid scrambles up a stairway, but the cops are right there to grab him. Captain Charles Kammerdener, the commanding officer of the PSA, is even on hand by the time Lemite comes deep-breathing to the spot where the kid is held, next to the second-floor garbage chute. Lemite nods vigorously at Michael T. and Kammerdener orders the young cop to cuff him up.

The rookie officer's hands are shaking as he does the honors on Michael. Three clicks and the silver cuffs are on. The NYPD Emergency Service Unit (ESU) arrives in moments to open the basement, where they find the six-shot hunting revolver sitting on top of the trash inside the garbage compactor. Then Lemite folds the big kid into an RMP for the short ride to the PSA.

A large American flag flaps over the front door of the PSA. Lemite opens the glass door for the handcuffed Michael T. Inside lies a wide bright room. On the right side of the room is an attached row of blue plastic chairs; beyond the chairs, the entrance to the detective squad room. Across the tiled floor to the left, a four-foot-high steel crossbar mounted on two poles keeps prisoners and complainants from approaching a high-countered partition. Lemite and his prisoner stand behind the bar as a lieutenant holds the huge pistol, turns it over in his hand, whistles, and passes the weapon over his shoulder to a cop who is a gun buff. Behind the partition two steel desks sit flush against one wall. Opposite the desks stands a huge radio receiver bedecked with flashing red lights. High behind the desks is an arrangement of framed photographs of Housing police brass and a duty chart for PSA personnel.

Lemite walks Michael T. down a short hallway to the lockup behind the desk area and guides him into the first of four holding cells. An old-timer sprawled on a chair beside another gray metal desk nods at Lemite and cocks his head at Michael T. "That's the same cell we used to lock Mike Tyson in. He used to stand on his hands with his feet against the bars and do push-ups. Nice guy, Tyson," the cop remembers, "robbery recidivist."

Michael T. is a "juvy," a juvenile, which complicates matters. He stands silently for two hours as Gary fills out the endless papers and snaps the required Polaroid of the exotic weapon. It is eight o'clock before Lemite can arrange a ride for Michael to the Spofford Juvenile Center in the Bronx.

Two months later, at his trial, Michael T., a.k.a. Miz, will plead guilty and burst out crying in front of the judge, while his lawyer importunes for a sentence that will keep the hulking fifteen-year-old out of hard-core Spofford. When he gets a sentence that sends him to an easy juvenile facility upstate, the tears stop. "You know I'm a gunman," Michael will say to the people in the hallway. "You know that, right?"

When Michael T. is gone, Lieutenant Jack Lenti, second in command to Kammerdener, joker to Charlie the K-Master's straight act, calls Lemite into his office.

"Why didn't you fire your weapon when the kid drew down on you?" he wants to know. Lemite doesn't answer. He understands that he is not here to talk, he is here to listen.

The black-haired, narrow-faced Lenti pushes himself back from his desk, puts both hands behind his head, and leans against the wall in his tiny square room. He removes his wire-rim glasses, opens his eyes wide, and squeezes them shut. He has been reading arrest reports all day. When he opens his eyes again, he studies the eager mocha-skinned cop in front of him.

"There were four rounds in the kid's gun, the . . . Ruger, whatever that big fucking thing was. Could be the kid pulled the trigger but there was no bullet in the cylinder." Lemite remains quiet. Lenti wants to make sure that he is not afraid to use his weapon. In the academy, the emphasis is on restraint. This is the street.

"Next time somebody pulls a gun on you, shoot him," Lenti says simply, and points to the door of his office.

On his way back downstairs, Gary passes a large bronze plaque on the wall of the front room, which memorializes Anthony O. McLean, a Housing cop shot dead by a drug dealer in the stairway of the Tilden Houses in 1988. An inscription beneath McLean's silver shield and bas-relief likeness reads, "Blessed are the peacemakers, for they shall be called the children of God."

ONE MALE BLACK

t is the heat that wakes Sharron, not the light. Though it is after nine on the abundantly sunny morning of the first Monday of his summer vacation, it is gloomy in his cluttered room. The view out the curtainless window is blocked by a gray cement wall ten feet away.

School is out. Usually that means there is not much for Sharron to do but stay out of trouble. But this summer it's going to be different. The man who painted the sets for *Don't Give Up on Your Dreams* has arranged a job for Sharron with Summer Youth Employment at Brooklyn Youth Outreach in downtown Brooklyn.

Sharron has no alarm clock. By the time he sits up on his dusty, sheetless day bed, it is almost nine-fifteen. Ms. King told him to be downtown by nine o'clock. No problem. There will be plenty of time to be just an hour late.

Sharron nudges the door of his room open with his foot. Sounds from the apartment drift in — the thud of a closing refrigerator, the rush of water from a flushed toilet. Sharron comes alive slowly. He stretches, rocks to his feet, and slouches to his dresser for his toothbrush and hair pick. The walls of his room are covered with curious artifacts, including no fewer than four signs that say POLO and a picture of Sharron with the caption "Sexy." On his small wooden dresser sits a trophy with a gold-painted figurine of indistinct reference. On the wall closest to the door is a two-foot-long sign that trumpets POLO in stenciled letters spaced widely apart, with the word "LoLifes" beneath. Nearby is another photo like the ones taken for a fee

in front of garish dropcloths on Forty-second Street in Times
Square. In the Polaroid, Sharron is dressed in a billowing outfit
of matching yellow and green jeans and jacket that makes him
look for all the world like a circus clown. There is a picture
next to the closet door of Sharron in a crouch, eyeing the camera; above this photo is the nickname Shalo. On the outside of
the door of the room is a sign that reads, "What are your suggestions? We'd like to know," above a photograph of Sharron
stooped over with laughter.

Beside the bed is a red folder with the numbers 2010 stenciled
on the cover. It is Sharron's imagined life story, which he wrote
as part of a school assignment early in the year. A reflection
back on his life, it is told from his perspective as if he were
thirty-seven years old.

> It often gets boring, explaining to people, mostly TV talk show
> hosts, my story. For those who don't know I'm a professional rhy-
> thm and blues recording artist. I was a late bloomer. I can't say I
> always looked as I do now. In high school I was blooming pretty
> fast and to add to that I had a smooth sensitive voice. I confess
> right now I have a strong sense of nostalgia. I graduated from Tho-
> mas Jefferson High School and went on to Howard University for a
> degree in business. During my college years I signed with Epic rec-
> ords. I have had twenty one albums. My albums hit gold sixteen
> times. My personal life isn't that special. Basically, due to my im-
> age, I keep my personal file as confidential as possible. I give to
> charity as much as I can, I also try to be a positive role model for
> the youth. I would like to say thanks to all my fans for their sup-
> port and interest in me and my music throughout my career.

Sharron crosses the hall and pads to the bathroom. Before he
turns on the water, he opens the mirrored door of the medicine
cabinet so he can watch himself shower.

Sharron Corley's building, 830 Saratoga Avenue, sits on a
small rise half a block from the bustle of Pitkin Avenue, a commercial street which, like Belmont Avenue a block away, trails
sneaker outlets and record stores down the spine of Brownsville
into East New York. When the Jews lived in this neighborhood,
Pitkin was called the Fifth Avenue of Brownsville. It stood in
regal contrast to Belmont Avenue, where fishmongers and egg
sellers hawked their wares from pushcarts. Now, just a few feet
from the public phone that Sharron considers his personal head-

quarters, an old movie theater houses a three-story furniture store selling gaudy bedroom sets on layaway. Both sides of Pitkin Avenue are lined with cheap yellow-and-red signs that advertise such appliances as refrigerators and washer-driers. Shops run by swarthy men with suspicious eyes sell clothing, jewelry, and sneakers. One store sells huge earrings shaped like Nefertiti's head for $39.99. In the window is a small old sign hawking "back-to-school gold."

This morning Sharron is delighted to be heading out of the neighborhood for the day. "It has been more than obvious for some time that there are just too many trigger fingers in the neighborhood," he wrote in another assignment for school this spring. Sharron has been in trouble himself lots of times, picked up for shoplifting and petty crime like jumping the turnstiles in the subway, and he believes he will be less likely to have such problems if he is keeping busy in another part of the city. But he is happy that he will be spending much of the summer outside Brownsville for another reason.

A few years ago, when he was about fifteen, Sharron discovered a principle familiar to those who crave celebrity. He found that the less he was seen around the neighborhood, the more he was admired. That year, through his friend Terrance, he got a job cleaning up and doing light clerical work for a small law firm on Fifty-seventh Street in Manhattan. While the job lasted for only a year or so, it gave the aspiring star money and kept him out of the daily mix. He could see a flicker in the eyes of the local cutie-pies when he reappeared after working for a weekend or a couple of afternoons in a row. The $100 a week he was carrying around gave him the means to buy some clothes — Guess jeans, Polo sweaters.

The quest for clothes took Sharron into the company of a loosely organized and far-flung group of young shoplifters who call themselves the LoLifes. At first Sharron and Terrance would head over to the Unity Houses, where a contingent of LoLifes lived, to purchase purloined Polo clothing. It was always Polo, because Polo was the trademark and inspiration for the name LoLifes.

"I don't know if the statement 'the clothes make the man' truly exists anywhere else," Sharron wrote, "but in Brooklyn it is considered a motto. With this in mind I have no problem admitting my being materialistic. I was seldom given credit for the things that I had done except for my vocal talent. When I had gotten into clothes it gave me character, so to speak."

There are straight-arrow young men in Brownsville, boys who have never had a whisper of problems, who go straight to school and home. But they remain outsiders, curiosities, sometimes targets. Sharron Corley doesn't want that profile, doesn't want to walk close to the curb and stay inside after dark. His relationship with the LoLifes is complex. A clear step in the wrong direction, it has also been a factor in his blossoming. "Sharron did not become Sharron until he got with the LoLifes," an old girlfriend attests.

Like many street gangs in Brooklyn and throughout the New York area, the LoLifes are not a gang in the traditional sense of an organization that has a set membership and turf. There was no ritual initiation for Sharron, just a casual shift from outsider to LoLife. Each member of the crew receives a street name that is a combination of the initial syllable of his first name and the suffix "lo." Sharron is Shalo; his two best friends, Frank and Terrance, didn't fare quite as poetically, as Franklo and Terrlo. But they are LoLifes, as is a slim fifteen-year-old from the Linden Houses named Ian Moore, who signs his graffiti moniker, E-lo, all over town, and the Crown Heights boosters Jaylo and Marco Polo. If a member of the group has a girlfriend who shares the Polo mania, she is a LoWife. Silly names and name-brand gear — trivial stuff in most places, but in "the Ville," mystique can be a life-and-death matter.

"If you are nobody and somebody shoots you," Sharron says, "then nobody is gonna come back for you. You just go out. Simple. But if you got props, you got respect and you got a crew. People think twice about cappin' you, 'cause then there are people who are coming back."

"What makes Polo so appealing?" Sharron wrote. "It has style, originality, uniqueness, eye snatching designs etc. To the LoLifes it is more than a piece of clothing. It is what represents us as the best dressed group of guys in our environment."

Sharron remembers fondly the first time he boosted as a LoLife. He had stolen candy bars, bubble gum, and notebooks, but this was different. He wanted the merchandise, but more important, he wanted to feel part of something. He was nervous but ready. He knew each time you boost something, the more props you get, "like stripes on a soldier."

It was a Sunday morning last fall, just before Sharron was elected homecoming king. Sharron, Terrance, and Frank had been planning their caper since Friday. On the empty #3 train to Manhattan, they put the final touches on their strategy. They planned which entrance they would take into Bloomingdale's to avoid being "sweated" by the guards, how they would quickly remove the pop-off plastic alarms and make their way out of the building.

The threesome threaded their way to the Polo department on the basement level. There were no "DTs" (store detectives) working on Sunday, something the LoLifes anticipated. Sharron was jumpy and lightheaded. His eyes swept the store. He had an almost uncontrollable urge to look over his shoulder for guards, so he locked his gaze ahead, on Frank and Terrance. Then he began to worry that his attachment to his two friends was too obvious, so he drifted behind a display of Polo sweaters and sucked deep breaths. While he was pulling himself together, his two friends, out of his sight, were "gettin' busy," stuffing shirts into the bicycle shorts they wore like girdles under their baggy jeans. Sharron emerged and began rummaging for a sweater he had seen on a previous visit. By then Frank and Terrance were clearly nervous. The look on their faces told Sharron they had seen a DT, so Sharron dropped the sweater he was fondling and the boys headed out of the building. Frank and Terrance gave Sharron a "steaming out" look just before they reached the door. Sharron couldn't figure out why, unless the guys had stashed items without popping off the alarms. As the boys blasted into a dead run, the alarms went off. But the LoLifes were already in the wind, six blocks away in just over a minute.

When Sharron found out the others had stashed, he felt a dreadful sinking sensation. He begged them to go back with him, but Frank and Terrance didn't want to risk it. Sharron felt compelled to return to the store and prove he could "catch" something, prove that he was "able to be down with this threesome, worthy of being a LoLife." So he told the others to meet him on Fifty-seventh Street, where he and Terrance worked for the law firm, then stalked back to Bloomingdale's alone. He was determined to come out of the store with a Polo sweater, no matter what. He was full of heart. "If I get caught, I just get caught," he said to himself. Nothing was going to stop "his quest."

Sharron hunkered right down to business. No lurking behind display counters this time. He grabbed the sweater he had held in his hands before, a white Polo with an American flag covering the chest and "Polo USA" stenciled under the flag. He folded it quickly into a tight ball, stuffed it up under his knapsack. As he neared the door, he knew he had not popped the alarm, so he was ready to steam out into the street. But the alarm failed to sound. Elated, Sharron loped down Lexington Avenue anyway, ducking and bobbing through the pedestrians on the sidewalk. Like a farm kid who has just caught his first fish or a suburban boy after his first home run in Little League, Sharron ran to tell.

When he arrived at the office building, the guys were in the back room, detaching the alarms from the sweaters. Sharron walked in with his head down, pretending to have failed in his mission.

"Yo, Sha, what's up, son?" Terrance asked.

"It was rough, son," Sharron returned slyly. Then he banished the hangdog look and broke into a howl. "I caught the big flag."

The boys were so happy they cavorted like fools around the supply room of the empty law office. Terrance jumped into Sharron's arms and the two swung madly. While they were twirling, Terrance cut himself on a broken light fixture on the wall. But the wound was hardly noticed in the giddy celebration. The boys were just so happy with one another. Sharron had proved to himself that he was indeed one of the group. Many times he had felt as if it were Terrance and Frank, with him as an outsider. No more. "It will always be this way," he believed, "the three of us so tight, acting the way we can only act when we are alone with each other." He stepped back and sat on a desk in the corner of the supply room. "I love these guys," he decided. At the same time, he began to see himself as the smoothest character anywhere, as if he could never do anything wrong again, ever.

Even though he came into the Summer Youth Employment Project a week late and was an hour tardy for his first day of work, it seems as if things are going to work out. Aubrey, the lanky director of the Brooklyn Youth Outreach site on East Street, is on the phone when Sharron appears in the doorway of his office.

"C'mon in." Aubrey gestures for Sharron to sit and studies his new worker while he listens to the voice on the other end of the line with mounting impatience. Then he moves the receiver away from his ear and rolls his eyes while the person continues to talk.

"I've heard a lot about you," he begins, still holding the squeaking receiver away from his ear. Aubrey, Sharron has heard, is from uptown, Harlem, and is slick and funny.

"Will do. Will do," Aubrey assures the person on the other end of the line, without returning the receiver to his ear. He hangs up the phone and addresses Sharron. "Do your job and we'll be cool. We'll be cool. I know about these things." He steps across the room and places a large bony hand on the boy's shoulder. A wave of tangy aftershave floats with him. Though Aubrey is an inch under six feet and of average build, Sharron can't believe how big he seems, standing close, how heavy his hand, how deep and comforting his voice.

"Cool," Sharron whispers.

"You aren't going to be just a worker, you're a site monitor," Aubrey says. "Which means you got responsibility for more than just yourself. After you get used to the job, you'll give orientation talks to kids and you'll break in other monitors. That's if you show you can handle yourself." Aubrey pauses, backs up a step, and studies Sharron, who makes full eye contact. Then Sharron glances quickly at a jar full of pencils on Aubrey's desk.

"Should I write stuff down?"

"Nah, not right now." Aubrey chuckles at his bright new charge. "You're gonna be all right."

Sharron's immediate job is to travel around to various youth employment sites in Brooklyn, picking up time cards and checking on site conditions. The very first afternoon, he finds himself traveling in the hot sun from the Brooklyn Navy Yard to Long Island College Hospital, over to Columbus Park on Jay Street. Everything is fine until he gets off at the wrong stop on the #2 train and finds himself beneath the crumbling St. George Hotel in Brooklyn Heights. When he steps out into the daylight, he takes a turn west and sees nothing but white faces. "Damn," he thinks as he checks the street signs. "Pineapple Street? Cranberry Street? Got to be a white folks' neighborhood."

Sharron makes a left at the corner. A woman walking her dog strains her ocular muscles to their very limits, using every single degree in her sweep of peripheral vision to watch Sharron without moving her head as he makes his way down the other side of the street. Three more blocks of cheery brownstone buildings with sparkling clean, unbarred windows at street level. No police cars in sight. No people now. Strange sights. Another two blocks, and Sharron stands frowning on the famous Brooklyn Promenade, which looks out over the harbor at the Manhattan skyline. But Sharron isn't interested in the sights or the roller skaters or the people strolling in the sun "actin' like nothing could go wrong."

"No, son. You want Carroll Gardens. Now that is a walk. But you're *young*, aren't you?" a hard-of-hearing gentleman observes after Sharron shows him the address of the old-age home he is looking for. Fifteen minutes of brisk walking and Sharron is at the site picking up the time cards, just as Jerry told him to.

Sharron is young, and $320 will come in every two weeks from his new job. He has his own modest welfare budget, but that goes to his mother, Gloria, to pay the rent and cover food and utility bills. In Sharron's view, this job is just right, because it has respect, props. It's one thing to be a senior monitor, checking on things, quite another to be packing bags in a supermarket or sweeping the back room of some business.

One rainy summer day Sharron asks Aubrey for a couple of hours off to travel with Ms. King to an open audition for young actors in Manhattan.

"All right, but I don't want to be seein' your name in lights just yet," Aubrey says. "We need you around here."

On the #3 train, a whippet-thin boy with a chevron carved in his fade widens his audience across the aisle of the half-empty car to include Sharron. Ignoring Ms. King, he continues his account to his companion of a subway mugging in which he and another kid took part. The boy is a born storyteller.

"Check this out. Dude's in the last car. Briefcase an' shit. We check him out, an' like he knew we was clockin'? So he tries to reach in his coat. I come in his face an' ask him all cold, like 'You got a weapon, sir?' Ah-ah."

Slam, he demonstrates how the man was pinned and stripped of his valuables. *Crash*, he staggers to show how somebody in the car pulled the emergency cord, jamming the train to a halt. Then the kid shows how he slithered off the train between cars and hit the tracks, how he fled down the tunnel straight into the arms of the Transit cops, who trained their big guns on him. Big fun. He leans toward Sharron for affirmation, the ritual touching of hands. But Sharron's loyalties are divided, and he is scrupulous not to disrespect Ms. King by putting his stamp of approval on such a roguish adventure. He waves a perfunctory hand in the direction of the storyteller as the boy reaches for a righteous slap from his original listener.

In the Times Square office of the casting agent, a thick orange shag carpet fails to muffle the racket of automobile horns outside the sooty second-floor windows. An assistant in a bulging striped vest and gray patent leather shoes is ill-tempered and rude.

"Are you auditioning?" he asks King.

"No, I'm with Sharron."

"I thought you were Sharon."

"I am, but this is Shar*ron*, and I'm with him. I'm his teacher." The man raises his pale eyes to the ceiling.

"Have your glossy ready," he says, referring to the photograph actors hand over at auditions. Sharron glances at King. He does not have a picture to submit.

"No picture. Ahhh." The man groans. King's eyes glint. The assistant is about to get cursed out. Sharron reaches across and lays his hand on King's arm. The assistant spins to the crowded room and raises his voice. "Absolutely no talking. Do you understand?"

People in Brownsville and East New York are much more careful about whom they disrespect, more conscious of the possible consequences of any personal interaction, than people in most other places. If you are insulted in the Ville, you can be sure that it is personal and that it is on purpose. In this white world, it seems to Sharron, slights and insults are served up carelessly. He accepts the disrespect goodnaturedly. Somehow this man does not count.

Sharron sits next to King on the cracked Naugahyde couch and looks over the pages of the script. He will read the part of Terry Malloy in *On the Waterfront*.

"Not my night? Not my night? I coulda torn Wilson apart.

But you, Charlie. You and Johnny, youse went for the price on Wilson. He gets the title shot in the Garden and what do I get? A one-way ticket to Palookaville."

Before he enters the room for the audition, which will take two minutes, Sharron turns to Ms. King and asks, "What's Palookaville?"

"GET OUT OF BROWNSVILLE"

■t is five o'clock on a Thursday in the first week of July. Ninety degrees, the first real heat of the summer. Sergeant Jimmy Priore has just changed over from two weeks of day tours to the four-to-twelve. Hammil is his driver today, and the two are headed to Brookdale Hospital, where Priore has to check the paperwork on some white kid from Brentwood, Long Island, who was shot in the head while making a cocaine deal in Unity.

The emergency entrance of the red-brick hospital opens like a wound onto busy Linden Boulevard. A two-foot loading dock sits at the head of the small parking lot so the EMS people can roll the damaged goods right into the hallway. Beside the dock is a ramp. Priore strolls up the ramp with a handful of papers and a happy smile. Hammil, less enthusiastic about the day, takes up the rear. Just inside the door to the emergency area, Priore pauses near the white kid, who lies on a gurney in an alcove, barely out of the traffic in the emergency room hallway. The young man's name is Gilmore. He has a rose tattoo on his forearm. A glowing dot hops like a mountain goat across the dark screen of a monitor above his head. He is brain-dead.

"They're gonna use him for parts," Priore says, still smiling. "The word was that a fourteen-year-old kid was the shooter. We had a tip where the kid was. We didn't know his name. We end up talking to his father. The father says, 'Yeah, my son? He's right over there,' and we arrest the kid. But before we can cuff him up, he punches his father in the face. Drops him right to the pavement." Priore mimes the punch and the falling father.

"The kid says to his father while he's on the ground, 'You gave me up, you fuck. I killed a guy.'"

As the sergeant and Hammil leave the hospital a few minutes later, there is a radio call. Priore slaps his radio to his ear. Hammil slows the car and waits.

"Shots fired, in front of 393 Dumont Avenue."

"Check the callback," says a voice from a radio car in the area, requesting verification and further information.

"We have a callback, K. One male believed shot at that location. Housing sergeant respond. K."

Priore moves the radio to his mouth. "This is the Housing sergeant, Central. We're on our way."

When Priore and his driver pull up to 393 Dumont, a cluster of blue-and-orange Housing patrol cars are arranged in a fan on the broad sidewalk in front of the twenty-one-story building. Twenty-five women and children with opaque eyes shuffle close to where a man in his mid-twenties lies, a foot from the wrought iron fence that lines the walkway. The fountain of compassion here is as dry as powder. You can see it with police officers and with the residents. This shooting is nothing special. There is no child on the pavement, clutching a teddy bear. No one has used a baby as a shield. The newspapers will not arrive.

There is a thickening puddle of blood by the victim's shoulder. He is lying on his stomach, with a dingy plaster cast on his right forearm. His brother squats on his haunches on the far side of the hip-high fence. "Breathe easy, breathe. Just breathe slow." Like a partner in a Lamaze birth, he is coaching, helping his brother stay alive until the EMS arrives.

A little boy strides up to Priore. "I'm Born Son's brother," he lies. Then the child offers some unsolicited opinions on the conflict between Born Son, a local drug dealer, and Bobby Schulman, a Housing cop who has been trying to lock Born Son up. "Schulman isn't shit," the kid pronounces. "Schulman just wants to steal Born Son's Jeep."

Priore looks at Hammil and rolls his eyes.

The cops stand by, as numb and inactive as the residents, making halfhearted attempts to keep the curious away. Only the brother acts as if there is anything more than a dying pigeon on the pavement.

"Stay down. Breathe," he repeats, holding his arms straight out with his palms down, the signal baseball players use to tell a base runner to slide. It is late afternoon and a shadow spreads over the scene as the crowd waits for the bus. The pool of blood on the pavement congeals.

"Oooo, is that liver?" a little girl wants to know.

As the bus pulls up, the brother, alone spurred to haste, vaults the fence and clears a path through the crowd, pointing to his bleeding sibling. The shooting victim is hoisted onto the tight white sheets of the gurney and rolled to the ambulance. With a whoop and a holler from its siren, the ambulance pulls off. The crowd quickly melts back to its early summer business. A boy bounces a basketball off to the right.

Back in the station house, Sergeant Priore remains in fine spirits. "Man down at 393 Dumont. Not likely," he tells the officer, a lieutenant, behind the desk.

"I hope it was Gilliam," the officer muses.

"It was," Priore is delighted to inform him. "Hey, lieutenant," he jokes. "We don't have a scrip on the shooter. It was probably *you*." He leans over the desk and performs a mock frisk on the duty officer. "Let me take a look at your gun."

A moment later the barrel-armed weight lifter Jeff Desimone walks up to the front desk with a prisoner who looks to be thirteen.

"Hey, wha's up, K.K.," a detective leaving the squad room says, greeting the kid.

"I thought you said you were never arrested before," Desimone says to the boy.

"I said I never been arrested for stealin' no *car* before."

John McMullen, a wisecracking Irishman, is standing near the glass front door in his street clothes. He is in a grand mood, about to walk out the door for a two-week vacation. But first, he has something on his mind.

"I've been meaning to ask you." He addresses Desimone, who is staring at his tiny prisoner, shaking his head.

"Yeah?"

"How big are your arms?"

Desimone twitches. It would take McMullen to ask such a question. Querying Desimone about his arms is a scary thing to do, like asking Cyrano de Bergerac about his nose. Luckily for McMullen, Desimone appears disposed to answer. He leans against the gray restraining bar and takes a long look at his right arm, where his bicep is laying siege to the fabric of his short-sleeved uniform shirt.

"Last time they were measured?"

McMullen nods. The lieutenant stops writing and listens. A hush descends on the front room of the PSA.

"Nineteen and three quarters."

Ten minutes later, after Desimone has led his young charge to the holding tank, there is another call from 393 Dumont. "Retaliation," Priore speculates.

But it isn't. The front door of an apartment on the seventh floor is smeared with blood.

"Don't touch the door, boss," an earnest-eyed uniformed cop says to Priore as the sergeant steps from the crowded elevator.

Domestic dispute. Like the residents of Brownsville themselves, the police pronounce the word "*dis*pute," with heavy emphasis on the first syllable. Hammil comments, "My wife asks me what the hell is a *dis*pute?"

Inside, there are three rooms full of police officers and family members contemplating the crime and the victim, an under-grown forty-year-old woman dressed like a teenager. Her wispy but strong body offers a contrast of weakness and strength, health and decrepitude. The woman is either a marathon runner or a substance abuser. A friend, a woman who has fled the scene, slashed her from the spot where her jawbone meets her neck to her clavicle. The wound is dangerous, but the woman is resisting aid, waging a mighty battle against the state of shock that descends on her as the EMS workers try to persuade her to ride in a wheelchair down the hall to the elevator and out to the ambulance.

"Assault one, disfigurement," Priore announces to Hammil as he documents the crime in his thick black memo book. Priore is the very picture of professionalism. There is a benign symmetry to his features. His dark hair and gleaming black mustache go perfectly with his hat, when he wears it, and with his uniform. He is a remarkable police officer, but his attempt at irony falls short. All he can manage is the tone of cheap complaint that is the one-note song of the New York City police officer. "Probably plea-bargain to disorderly," he says.

Finally the wounded woman allows herself to be rolled out.

37

She presses a piece of gauze to the wound. Between great shivers, she mutters threats: "I swear to God I'm gonna fuck her up." The woman is more worried about her role than about her wound. She refuses to see herself as a victim, refuses to be seen by others as such.

The performance doesn't work. Two women in their warm weather outfits, a white-and-red-striped sunsuit and an orange tank top over biking shorts, take a moment to observe the severity of the knife wound as the victim moves the hand with the gauze away for a moment to step up into the ambulance.

"Oooo. Somebody cut me like that, it's time to shoot to kill," the one in the sunsuit observes.

"I'm gonna get the fuck out of Brownsville this summer," says the other.

J.R. JUNIOR

The next day Gary Lemite is on his meal break, seated on one of the old couches in the officers' TV room across the hall from the locker room. No one else is in the room. The mounted television is silent. The only sound is the clink of metal on metal, somebody doing fast repetitions in the weight room next door. John Reynolds, nicknamed J.R., an ultra-savvy street cop who was one of Gary's training officers, strolls in and settles across from him.

J.R. is something else. He has a WASP name but the jet-black hair and raven mustache of a Mediterranean, the dark eyes of a Valentino. He has nine years on the job. His father was a city cop. According to the NYPD way of looking at things, Housing police is a second-class department that works in third-class neighborhoods. Appointment to the Housing police means that an officer will spend his career patrolling the projects where, according to the Housing police union, he is five times as likely to be shot at as NYPD cops throughout the city. When the city started assigning officers to the Housing police by lottery, a wave of fear went through NYPD families like J.R.'s.

J.R. had read every book there was about New York City police. He could recite the names of officers killed in the line of duty as if he were quoting Scripture. But the Housing police it was. On the first Thanksgiving after he went on the job, his old man looked down the groaning table and frowned at his son. "Pass the gravy, *Housing*," the old man snorted.

Today J.R. has something on his mind. "I just resigned from OSC," he announces to Lemite, referring to Operation Safe Community, his plainclothes unit. "Too much bullshit. I'm going back to uniform. Midnights." Midnights, haven for lost souls, promised land for the easily annoyed. "Eleven years of midnights and out," he repeats.

Lemite nods. J.R. has a glittering reputation he gained as the PCO assigned to the Howard Houses, a complex just three blocks from Sharron's Saratoga Avenue address. J.R. walked into Howard like a sheriff in a western town. He got to know the people, the old ladies trying to make it to the store for some household items, the single mothers trying to raise their kids. Then he went head-to-head with the mad agents and the slingers who were making life hell for everybody else. He simply intimidated the perps until they folded up shop and moved their business somewhere else.

"I'm gonna need a partner," J.R. adds.

Gary slows his breathing and cocks his head, trying to appear cool. He knows he is receiving a most flattering proposal.

"My last partner was the baddest guy in Brownsville. He hit a guy once, the guy's feet went six inches off the floor. My partner's fist was under his chin the whole ride up. I need somebody, above all, to watch my back. Can you fight? Have you got balls?"

"Yeah," Gary answers without hesitation.

"How do you know?"

Gary thinks for a moment and shrugs. J.R. is satisfied.

Midnights. It is 12:30 A.M., the beginning of their shift. After a few days of riding with J.R., Gary knows the routine: the rookie gets the dirty jobs. He circles the RMP, checking for dents. Then he leans in and removes the back seat. He scoops up a handful of newspapers and a soda bottle and pauses to check for any drugs and weapons that were "offed" by a prisoner during the previous shift. The drugs could get somebody in trouble. The weapon could get somebody killed. Gary replaces the seat, slides in the front, and turns the engine over. He checks the gas gauge, feeling behind the sun visor for the gas card he will need to refuel.

The radios are quiet, so the partners ride over to the Greek coffee shop on Fulton by the bus depot for a cup of coffee. When the girl at the cash register tosses her black hair and beams at Gary, J.R. issues his first directive.

"I don't care if you flirt with her for twenty years. Don't screw her. She'll end up pissed off. And I don't want anybody fucking with my coffee."

Then it is the streets for eight hours. Night after night, the midnight streets, with Reynolds teaching, Lemite listening, watching. "I foresee a plethora of good arrests," Reynolds predicts. He's right; the collars start pouring in. If Lemite has a hunch — "Hold it. J.R., back up. I think that kid is carrying something" — Reynolds respects his instinct. More often than not, Lemite is on the money. In the mornings, Lenti and Kammerdener look at the arrest reports and shake their heads.

"Somebody has got to do something about these people," Gary says, looking out over the windy dark streets of Brownsville one night a week after his partnership with J.R. has begun.

"Who are *these people*?" J.R. asks. "It doesn't work like that. Remember that it doesn't matter if a guy is an asshole. If he's not acting like an asshole *today*, he's not an asshole *today*. Tomorrow, things may be different. But today you treat him with respect. The only thing a person out in Brownsville is looking for is a fair shake. Like in a fight. You know how you ask for a fair one? That's what I give them, a fair one."

It is 3 A.M.; a call comes over about shots fired by two males in a burgundy Lincoln. J.R., driving across Sheffield at Glenmore, spots the car on Blake, and with a howl of his siren hooks a half-turn so the RMP sits headlights to headlights with the suspects' car. Gary leaps from the RMP with his gun pointed.

"Show your hands out of the car. Put them on the roof where I can see them," he commands, striding toward the vehicle.

A search of the Lincoln produces no weapons. After the men have driven off, J.R. drives around the corner and stops in the dark beyond a streetlight. He stares at Gary.

"You're embarrassing me," he growls. He reaches into his shirt pocket and lights a cigarette. "What did I do?"

Gary is quiet. But J.R. wants an answer.

"Where did I stand?"

"Behind the door of the RMP."

"Why?"

"Cover."

"Always do your talking from there." J.R. blows smoke out into the summer night. "When you approach a car from the rear, tap on the trunk to make sure it's closed. There could be a

41

shooter in there. Remember, when you're dead, I'm the one who is gonna have to knock on your door and tell your wife."

A few days later, a man slips out of Gary's grasp after a street pursuit. "Don't grab the guy by the shirt," J.R. advises with a grin. "He can run out of his shirt, but he can't run out of his hair."

The next night J.R. stands in the doorway of a kitchen, next to the refrigerator. The partners have been called to the ninth floor of a building in the Tilden Houses for a domestic dispute. A mountain of a man has violated an order of protection against his ex-wife, punched her, terrorized the kids. The man is standing, foam-flecked and ready to rumble, in the kitchen, the worst possible place to try to effect an arrest. There are all kinds of weapons within the guy's reach. J.R. nudges Gary gently out of the room and addresses the problem.

"Let me tell you how this is going to be," he begins. "I am going to place you under arrest for violating an order of protection against your wife, who called us. You punched her and you are definitely going to jail."

"Step on," the heaving bruiser challenges. Gary is behind, unsheathing his baton, ready to do his part. The wife and kids have fled to a friend's apartment. The boldest of the neighbors are craning their necks in the open front door of the apartment to see the fight.

"No, no, wait. I haven't finished," J.R. says, raising his eyebrows and waving Gary back. "As I was saying, I am going to place you under arrest. You may resist. We may fight. I have no doubt that you can kick my ass. But my partner is behind me. He will jump in. Before he does, he will radio for help. If necessary, we will bring cars from Manhattan till this room is full of cops. Make no mistake, you *will* be arrested. Now turn around and place your hands behind your back." The cuffs only close one click around the man's huge wrists. J.R. looks over his shoulder at Gary and rolls his eyes.

As the cops escort the man down the hall, J.R. puts a hand on the head of a five-year-old who stands weeping near the elevator. "Daddy's all right. Everybody's gonna be nice now," he says.

As they walk the man out the front door of the project to the patrol car, a voice taunts the arrested man with a rhyme from behind a curtain in an upper window. "See ya. Wouldn't wanna be ya."

Dealing with people in Brownsville, where nerves are frayed so fine they can be lit by a hot glance, is not a simple job. J.R. is a master, but many of the cops in the PSA don't have the easy touch.

"It's not only that they don't know anything about black people, or that they are not sensitive," a retired black Housing cop says. "It's that they have no humility. When I first walked into a family dispute and I looked at this old gentleman who was on the edge with some family problem, I said to myself, 'Who am I, a kid, to tell this man who has seen and been through so much how to deal with his problems?' I was humbled. Some of these fools walk in like they own the place and start telling people where to stand and how to talk."

After the big man is safely locked up in the back room of the PSA and the paperwork is done, J.R. and Gary ride out for a last cup of coffee. Their shift is nearly over. It is almost eight o'clock in the morning. As their sector car rolls down Sutter Avenue, dozens of junkies are showing up already for their methadone a hundred yards from a day-care center on Powell Street. On the opposite corner, Rony Shoman and his brother, Zaid, are rolling up the steel gates that blanket the windows and doors of their supermarket. Rony casts a jaundiced eye over his shoulder at the congregation of dope addicts, who will soon shift across Sutter Avenue to spend the rest of the morning in the parking lot of his store. There they will socialize and sell various forms of pills among themselves, including "spitbacks," doses of methadone that are dispensed into the mouth at the clinic and, as the name suggests, spit back into a container for sale.

Balancing a Styrofoam cup on his clipboard, J.R. lights yet another cigarette and explains his philosophy of police work to Gary as the two cruise past the supermarket back to the PSA to sign out.

"You don't look for trouble. If you can, you talk your way through. If a guy could kick your ass before you got the gun and badge, he can still kick your ass. But if a guy tries to hurt a cop, you make sure he doesn't go to the lockup. He goes to Brookdale."

Gary takes the message to heart. Just a few nights later, a 10-13 comes over from Transit. When J.R. and Gary pull up on Junius and Livonia, a handful of officers are struggling with a strapping twenty-five-year-old male who is pinned against a sagging chainlink fence. The officers cannot seem to get handcuffs on the thrashing man. The Transit cop whom the man suckerpunched, starting the incident, is stumbling around in the street, holding his head and moaning. Suddenly Gary lunges into the group and cracks the suspect across the neck and shoulders with his nightstick. Incredibly, the recipient of the blow stays on his feet, defiant. He cannot see who hit him, but he can guess. "Who was that? Transit? You punk motherfucker. Transit punk." Cuffed and in the back seat of the police van, the man is still shouting challenges as Gary and J.R. drive off.

"Hurt a cop," Gary says. J.R. nods.

It's difficult to stop a man from doing something that he thinks may save his life. The police have seen too much of the justice system to believe that it can protect them. They have seen the dozing grand juries, the incompetent, inexperienced assistant district attorneys, the sneering defense lawyers, and they have decided to protect themselves. It seems simple.

But just days later, it becomes more complicated for Gary. Early in the shift a call comes over. The dispatcher's voice is high and tense as she reads the job even before all the information is in, something done for 10-13s and other emergencies.

"10-13," Central reports — a robbery in progress. "Howard and East New York. Awaiting further. Who's going?" Central is buzzing. "Who's going," she demands again.

"73 Adam." The A sector car is going.

"73 Charlie."

A moment later Central has more information. "The perp is a male black, twenty-five years of age, green fatigue pants, white baseball cap."

Then a unit on the scene reports, "Central, be advised the perp made believe he was stranded. When the motorist attempted to assist him, he jumped him and pistol-whipped him. White Toyota Maxima. New York reg. Henry, Lincoln, Charlie three-two-one. Suspect is five-nine, one sixty-five, wearing army pants."

"10-5 the plate number, Central," J.R. asks, scribbling as Central repeats the number of the license plate and adds that the victim of the carjack was beaten and stripped of his clothes.

"Fucking carjacker," Gary mutters. "When I drive into Brownsville, like now, in the summer? I roll up my windows and keep my off-duty on the seat. Shit."

"Why the gun? Nobody wants that '72 Dodge you drive," J.R. scoffs. "Especially with blue carpet glued to the fucking dashboard. Who had that bright idea?"

"Guy I bought it from. I didn't do that."

The officers continue their patrol, tensing slightly every time they see a white car. An hour later, the radio reports that a white Toyota has sideswiped another car on Hinsdale and left the scene of the accident. "New York plate Henry, Lincoln, Charlie three-two-one."

"Take a drive by the Complex," J.R. directs. The Complex is a series of connected projects that run along Dumont and Livonia avenues and includes the Brownsville, Tilden, and Van Dyke Houses. Ten minutes later, J.R. stiffens like a hunting dog. A white Maxima is parked in front of the Brownsville Houses.

"Don't get too close. Just so I can get the plate," he says as Gary eases the sector car down the street. "That's it," J.R. snaps. "Stop."

The two Housing cops back around the corner and wait for the perp to show his face. Just ten minutes. A man in billowing camouflage pants appears, strides up to the car, and reaches for the driver's side door handle.

"Go."

Gary guns the RMP and nails a screeching stop beside the man. Doors fly open and the chase is on.

Gary is in the lead. J.R., behind, calls the pursuit over the radio. The two cops trail the man down a walkway through the deserted project grounds. The suspect is wearing sneakers. Gary and J.R., weighed down by bulletproof vests, gun belts, and radios, lose ground. The chase goes around a cluster of buildings and then around again. On the third lap, just as a 73rd sector car and then another arrive, the suspect plunges into a lobby and disappears.

J.R. and Gary pause at the base of the stairs to catch their breath. J.R. points upstairs, and four fresh-legged white NYPD cops charge up the steps. A minute and a half pass. As the rejuvenated Housing cops trot upstairs, the NYPD cops are already on their way down. One cop gives Gary a big wink and points to the roof. When Gary and J.R. reach the suspect on the pebble-strewn roof, he is semiconscious. Blood trickles from his right ear.

"Damn," J.R. says, pursing his lips with disapproval. "Get a bus."

The hospital report reads that the prisoner has a broken femur, a bruised heart, and a fractured jaw. The arrest report surmises that the injuries were received in the earlier car accident. But Gary has been on the job long enough to know that he has seen for the first time what the cops call a "freebie." When a crime involves a car accident, some police officers respond enthusiastically, at least in part because they know they can administer a beating and blame the injuries on the collision. The NYPD officers had most certainly arrived under the cover of silence, never reporting that they were responding to the call. Officially, they had not been at the scene.

Gary and J.R. have been together on the midnights for over a month. It is midsummer.

"Well, if it isn't J.R. Junior," Hammil cracks as Gary walks from his dusty blue Dodge to the PSA one night. The quick-study Lemite is not offended in the least by the nickname. Not for now. Tonight, he and J.R. ride down Dumont Avenue, past the Complex. It was here, in the Tilden Houses, that Willie Randolph, long-time second baseman for the New York Yankees, grew up, and here that Housing police officer Anthony O. McLean was gunned down in 1988 by Johnny Ray Robinson, a mid-level operative in the Baby Sam gang. The Housing police had been searching for an eight-year-old girl, missing for a day. The detectives had knocked on Gita Malave's door and questioned her daughter, Tashana, a friend of the missing child, but both Gita and Tashana shook their heads. The child had vanished. When McLean, a uniformed officer, started his vertical search of another building in the Tilden Houses, he surprised the armed Robinson in a stairway. "A freak accident," one of the locals called it. The girl was found at an aunt's house the next afternoon.

J.R. slows the car at 340 Dumont Avenue and, as he does most times he passes the spot, remembers. J.R. remembers everything. Sometimes his memory is a curse. J.R. sees a smiling

Tony McLean in his blue uniform and the dull gold inscription under his memorial plaque. The dark circles under J.R.'s eyes deepen; his face seems to sag. There is a shout, and J.R. turns to the other side of the street, his sadness swept away by a scowl. Across the street is 295 Dumont. J.R. and the "children of God" of the PSA 2 are not happy with what is going on at 295 Dumont Avenue.

At that address, at all hours of the night and day, a lookout stands like a cardboard cutout in the fifth-floor window. The figure, one of the Worthy clan, which has occupied the connected apartments 5A and 5B of the building for more than a decade, is watching for the Housing police. According to Housing cop Bobby Schulman, the family is nothing but a drug gang. There is no back entrance to the building, so the police can never enter without alerting the lookout, can never effectively raid the premises. "Like they built the place for the perps," Schulman laments.

The Worthys are working for a new gang that has taken over the crack trade in the Complex. The group is run by a personable twenty-three-year-old basketball whiz named Born Son, a kid who grew up under J.R.'s watch in Howard. The crew has been making life miserable for some people, good for others. Among the miserable are the people who live in the building. "We can't go on like this," a resident moans. Among the happy ones are some teenagers. "Born Son employs a lot of people in this project," says plainclothes cop Lonnie Hayes, who grew up in Brownsville. "When Born Son goes down, he's taking the eight-to-four shift and the four-to-twelve shift with him." So far the cops haven't been able to do anything but harass the operation.

In the middle of their shift on this starless summer night, J.R. and Gary take a walk up the five flights just for the hell of it.

The project stairways are known for sudden meetings and ricochets. These cinderblock passages are an unnerving combination of public and private places, places for a stolen kiss or a brutal robbery. Here the walls are freshly painted in Housing Authority yellow or beige but covered with boasts and warnings, territorial markings of young hands; "International Rude Gal," "The Gucci Girls in Full Effect," with a roster of members' nicknames below. Other stairways proclaim "Decepticons," "Crack Busters," "Dirty Bunch," "Wyona Dogs," and the phrase "LoLife$ Get Paid."

J.R. and Gary are ready for trouble as they crunch red-and-blue crack vials underfoot on their way upstairs. But neither has his gun drawn. And neither is the slightest bit afraid. Comradeship is an antidote for fear. Besides, they are the hunters, not the prey.

"You looking?" J.R. asks, wondering whether Gary is interested in making a collar, as they reach the third-floor landing.

"Nah," Gary says. "Got marriage counseling tomorrow."

J.R. jerks his head back. He has never seen Gary value anything above a collar before.

Before the officers reach the fifth floor, J.R. politely detains a cherubic young mother of three and her smiling blade-faced girlfriend on the staircase.

"Live in the building?" J.R. asks. The plump woman claims to be visiting a friend.

"At three o'clock in the morning?"

The questioning seems unnecessary. But the women endure the search of their pockets by the deferential J.R.

"Anything in here that's going to stick me?" J.R. asks, ever wary of the threat of the AIDS virus.

"No," the woman answers sweetly, her voice rising like the chiming of small bells.

Surely this is why the police are so disliked in the neighborhood. They don't go after the fearsome Born Son and his boys, Tai Stick, Supreme, and Bang. They harass good people trying to make a casual social visit.

J.R. rifles one pocket and then the other, sifting the contents like an archaeologist while Gary watches. The woman and her chatty friend seem to have no end to their tolerance for the policemen. As the search goes on, a teenage girl walks out of Apartment 5A. A scab on the top of her left ear marks the spot where a hot comb strayed. A skim of grease pins a tab of stiff bangs to her forehead. She has a smattering of pink scratches in the flesh over her cheekbones.

"What's up, Tanya?"

"Nothin'."

J.R. greets her casually, as if they have known each other all their lives. She is neither surprised nor upset to see the police, though she is a fugitive in some sense. Only sixteen years old, Latanya Worthy is a runaway, a dropout, and a petty thief, designated by the courts as a PIN, a person in need of supervision. Even the other Worthys describe her as uncontrollable. She skips down the stairs and out the front door.

"Ah-ha." The cheerful staircase hoppers are crack smokers. J.R. turns the cloudy crack pipe over and over in his hand. With his eyebrows raised, his lips pressed together, and his head cocked in gentle reproach, he looks like a kindly grandfather. In one woman's handbag are three Bic lighters, two green and one red. J.R. lets the women go with a warning. They appear embarrassed, but are probably disappointed at being barred from Apartment 5A at this late hour. They head downstairs, back to their own building.

As J.R. and Gary leave the building, they pass a couple of plainclothes cops. The next stairway hopeful hasn't been so lucky. He can't name anybody in the building he knows. His stretched skin and deep eye sockets mark him as a pipehead, a "stem." Neither of the plainclothes guys really wants the collar.

"Name three states and we'll let you go," the dark-haired cop offers.

"Rochester" comes the quick reply.

"Cuff him up," the second cop says, lounging against the chipped cinderblock landing.

"Rochester's a state," the man protests. "My brother lives there."

"That don't make it a state," the first cop instructs as he click, click, clicks the cuffs on.

PROPS

harron is waiting patiently in the lobby of the elevated station at Saratoga Avenue. His date is forty minutes late, but he is confident she will arrive. If she wanted to play him, why did she go to the trouble of passing her telephone number out of a moving bus on Belmont last week?

Frank witnessed the exchange. "Damn," he marveled at the time. "I didn't even know the windows of those new buses opened like that. I thought they was all air-conditioned."

Still, the new girl is nowhere in sight. The buzzer indicating another approaching Manhattan-bound train sounds its tone. Then, with a flurry, she appears, dressed in shiny black pants and a white blouse. Her shoes and fingernails are pink. Sharron slips in past the turnstile without paying as his date hands over her $1.25 for a token. It isn't that Sharron doesn't have the money. He has $40 in his sock for this movie date. It's that he does not want it to be said that he has gotten soft enough to pay his way on the train like a sucker.

In the same spirit, he refuses to scamper up the stairs, and the train pulls out of the station, leaving the two young people to face their first real conversation.

"You're crazy, Sharron," the new girl says. "I like your eyes. I'm glad you didn't wear the sunglasses."

Sharron doesn't have much to say. He lets the new girl do the talking.

"My friend seen you when we was on the street. And she said that I was scared to speak. And then the bus had came? So I just wrote the number. And gave it to you."

Soon the single headlight of the #3 train coming in from East New York appears. The platform shudders faintly as the cars slow to a halt. But Sharron and his date are at the end of the platform. This is a Saturday, and the train is short. The last car sits fifty feet away. Once more, a run is necessary. Once more, Sharron refuses to hurry. Wearing an oversize shirt draped over droopy straw-colored jeans, he walks with a dip and a slide. He glances over his shoulder to make sure that no one is watching before he deigns to trot the last few steps to where the new girl stands holding the closing door. She reaches out and yanks Sharron toward her. With an involuntary laugh, he swings into the train and into her arms and kisses her lightly on the neck.

When the gay couple turns to find seats on the all-but-empty car, Sharron is greeted by a most unpleasant sight. Seated directly across the aisle is his nominal girlfriend, Sheryl, shoulder to shoulder with a clean-cut boy who looks like some kind of college guy.

True, Sharron has not called her in over a week, has not been to visit her in the Linden Houses, to charm her mother and grandmother, since the play closed. But this is too much. He does not flinch or speak. His brown eyes lift over the offensive sight, and he leads the new girl up the train into the next car. Even when the train snakes around a bend at the Borough Hall stop twenty minutes later, he does not look back to the last car to see what is going on.

Sharron writes the romance off. It is just lucky, he thinks, that the new girl does not know Sheryl, that the scene was not witnessed by anybody from around the way who could spread the story of his being played by Sheryl.

On the way home from the movie on Forty-second Street in Manhattan, Sharron leads his date off the train at the Clark Street stop, where he got lost two weeks ago.

"Where we goin'?" she wants to know.

"Chill. I got a spot I know you're gonna like."

Sharron walks his new friend down to the promenade. The deep summer night rides over the harbor. A sailboat drifts in the distance, and the lights of the Manhattan skyscrapers flash like tiny diamonds. The girl at Sharron's side stares at the strolling people. No one on the promenade is looking over his shoulder. There is no sense of threat.

"Don't even feel like we're in Brooklyn. I feel like I'm in Hollywood," she says.

Sharron nods, and places his arm around her shoulder. She looks up at the mysterious young man at her side and wonders how he knows of such a spot, and what other wonderful places he has been in his life.

In fact, Sharron has never left New York City. He was born in Kings County Hospital. "My, that's an ugly child," Sharron's grandmother, Tina, said when she first laid eyes on the baby. "And it's no damn surprise, either, nasty-lookin' as that man is." "That man" was Sharron's twenty-three-year-old, dark-skinned, gap-toothed hustler of a father, who had already begun to melt into the maze of Brooklyn streets. To complete the cycle of foolishness, Sharron's daddy's people did not like Gloria's looks. They thought she was the ugly one.

One of Sharron's earliest memories is of a day when he was five. He was playing outside in the street when his mother called him from the window. He bolted across the street into the path of a car, which screeched to a halt. The driver emerged, looming and angry, loosening his belt to administer a whipping to the boy he had almost hit. He was a huge man, the image of a father who had not lingered long enough to dispense either love or anger. Sharron might actually have received a beating if his mother had not threatened the man from the window. But Sharron never forgot that incident. He remembered so well that another time, when he was actually hit by a car, sent tumbling through the air with his bicycle, he popped up and pedaled home on a bent wheel without looking back.

When Sharron was six, he lived on Hancock Street in Bedford-Stuyvesant, a vast black area of Brooklyn known in the seventies and eighties as a hellhole. "Bed-Stuy, do or die" was the motto of the youngbloods from Gates and Stuyvesant, from Boys and Girls High School. But Bed-Stuy, as tough as it was, never had the capacity for urban terror that Brownsville has now. The difference lies, at least in part, in the architecture. Bed-Stuy, like Harlem, was once home to the affluent and the middle class, who left their wide streets and brownstones behind. The apartment Sharron, his mother, and his sister shared on Hancock was a reminder of that earlier time; it was a comfortable five rooms.

More important, it was a haven from Gloria's overbearing mother. Ever since Gloria gave birth to Shawanda, things had not been right living with Tina, over on Herkimer Street, a few blocks away. Grandma had a good heart, all right. When Sharron got hit in the head with a metal stickball bat, she flew to St. John's Hospital with him in her arms. But after he was stitched up, when it was clear that he was going to be all right, she turned her anger on her daughter. "Where were you?" she yelled. "How come you aren't here for your children? These are your children. These are *your* children, these are not my goddamn kids. I raised my own kids."

Tina had not been ready to be a mother; now she was a grandmother, and she did not like it. "She had a terrible temper," Sharron remembers, "and she didn't like my father. Mommy and her were fighting all the time." The apartment on Hancock had changed all that. The relentless friction was gone. Now there were just money problems.

A year later the problems worsened. One day, when Sharron was seven and Shawanda was nine, they found themselves alone. Gloria was out paying some bills. All morning Shawanda tried to fix the blurry triple-vision TV set. She was aggravated, but she never stopped trying. Sharron was under the couch, where he found some matches on the floor. He took a deep breath and blew some hanging strings until they lay flat against the bottom of the couch. When he ran out of breath, they swung down again. Then he struck a match. It flashed and he threw it on the dusty floor. He struck another and fired one of the dangling strings. Shawanda spotted the flames as Sharron scrambled out from under the couch and ran into the kitchen to get a cup of water.

"The fire began to spread and spread until it was dangerous and uncontrollable for anyone but the Fire Department," Sharron recalls. "Everyone was out of the building but Shawanda. Then a man went inside and came out with Shawanda in his arms." Sharron was mightily relieved, but then Gloria arrived to watch the apartment gutted by flames. "She grabbed us, hugged us, and kissed us. Then she went into strong worry about our next stop." When Gloria found out that her son had started the fire, she couldn't even look at him. "I got beaten and punished for a long time, but that didn't make me feel as bad as knowing that Mommy's last resort was Grandma's house. Just knowing what I'd put Mommy through was taking a toll on my feelings."

As bad as things may have been for Gloria back at Tina's house, they weren't that bad for Sharron, who remembers his time there as "the days of my exceptional childhood." "I didn't have to worry about clothes or making a name for myself. All I had to worry about was having fun."

While Sharron was running around with his friends, having rock fights and climbing fences, Tina was holding little card parties and drinking hard, "to get away from her problems," she told the boy. "She would raise all kinds of hell once she got aggravated. To our family and friends she was known for her quick temper."

It seemed to Sharron that Gloria was hardly ever home. She was looking for a place to live, on a mission to get out of Tina's house. Then she found Brownsville. The four-room apartment on Saratoga was simply heaven for Gloria.

It was not long before she met John Hill, Jr., a member of a Brooklyn religious sect known as the Five Percenters, who called himself Alleke. Alleke hustled for a living, but he was a family man at heart. Every time he had even a little money in his pocket he would come to the apartment with brown bags of groceries so big he could hardly carry them. Sharron would spy him from the window in Gloria's bedroom, struggling with the bags down on Saratoga, and rush downstairs to help. Alleke would set the packages down and hand a few of the items on top to Sharron to carry. Soon he was living with Gloria and her children and Sharron was calling him Daddy.

But Alleke had a drug problem. He would stay away for several days at a time. More than once young Sharron saw his stepfather standing on the sidewalk somewhere in the neighborhood, knees bending slowly, head sinking to his chest, eyes half closed, in the throes of the telltale heroin nod. Sharron's stepfather no longer takes drugs. Nowadays Alleke dons his worn navy pea coat and a pair of Sharron's old sneakers and shambles over to a pocket park on Pitkin, where he drinks some and sits, slack-faced, with his cronies. His hustling days are over; even his days as an angry Five Percenter are gone. He just hangs. He is forty-five years old.

Sharron's relationship with Alleke is complicated. "The man took very good care of us when Mommy was spending time hanging around with the pretty boys. I give him respect in the house, but if I was to see him in the Burger King I wouldn't speak." Sharron admits that if his gaunt and shabby stepfather approached him in the street, there might be a problem. "If I was trying to talk to a girl I would react [negatively], 'cause he knows it is not about that. He knows."

"Me, myself," Sharron writes in "The Story of My Life," "I've been through a lot of incidents that weren't all that pleasant. I've always had, to put it in the least, to prove something. It could never be simple, no matter what the circumstances. Like being able to get the attention I felt I needed with peers, or girls, or being compatible with the homeboys around the way."

From a very young age, Sharron would do almost anything for adulation. He was nine years old when he tried to outdo some strong swimmers by launching a back flip from a spot too far from the edge of Betsy Head Pool, a block-size oasis of green water below the #3 train on Livonia. When he flipped over, he smashed the bridge of his nose against the metal edge of the pool. When he came up, his nose was broken and there was blood in the water. The girls were gasping and holding their hands over their mouths. "I guess it just wasn't meant for me to have it going on that day. The trick couldn't have backfired any worse than it did." The accident left a short, crooked, deep scar on the bridge of his nose, so deep that Sharron would say later that he was lucky it didn't scare the females away. It was not the last scar that he would earn, and the pool accident didn't teach him much about the perils of trying to impress people.

Sharron's urge to make an impression was not restricted to his peers. "When I was with my friends and we were doing something, I would always stop so the grownups would think I was a good kid. I always wanted to be good. I have a whole lot of uncles and stuff and most of them are in jail. I was going to be better."

It was at the age of thirteen that Sharron broke into song. A junior high school teacher, Miss Morley, noticed him hitting all the right notes when he was singing with the class and asked him to stay after school. She played the piano, hummed, and nodded to the boy. Sharron began humming along with her. Then he started to sing. But Morley's encouragement dried up one day, and she lashed out at Sharron in class. "She yelled at me, all nasty and mean, said I was taking advantage of our relationship. And then when she called my mother she told some lies. She said I had talked back to her, which I never did. So I haven't talked to her since that day."

When Sharron found he could sing, when he found he had the tools to turn the girls' heads, he went to work and never stopped. "I hadn't actually been confident in my features until guys who in my book had it going on started calling me 'pretty boy.' Sometimes they may not mean it in friendly terms. But all in all, it is being said."

There were still obstacles. "It was never easy." Sharron sighs. What he calls "the drama," danger and trouble, "started up early, and it kept going on. All day every day, twenty-four seven. Maybe I should take lessons on living a monotonous lifestyle, because I just can't seem to do it."

Sharron Corley is a son of Brownsville. In the Ville, it is almost impossible for a young man to behave in a way that will keep him untouched by trouble. It is not healthy to stay in the background and appear passive. But it is not such a good thing to stand out on merit, to excel with the girls, to dominate on the basketball court or in the classroom, either. The kind of admiration young men want most is that which is mixed with traces of fear. Sharron is doing quite well by Brownsville standards. On the street, he is known widely as a pretty boy, and not one who just runs his mouth. He is known as someone who "gets paid," who shows up with impressive stolen gear, as a result of his LoLife affiliation. Sharron's props have been further enhanced by the school play and his growing reputation as an actor and a singer.

THE SCREAM

Metal on metal. The front door of 380 Dumont Avenue in the Tilden Houses blasts open, colliding with its frame, and Powerful charges out. The two men who slipped in the back door and surprised him in the lobby are twenty feet behind, firing their guns. A white puff of cement fragment kicks up from the sidewalk beside Powerful's foot. He ducks into a crouch and flees like a crab out onto the sidewalk, waddling furiously along the low iron fence. From the first shot, Powerful and everybody else outside knows this is no joke. This is a hit, an assassination attempt.

The previous April, more than one hundred wild shots were exchanged across the street in a running gun battle between the Young Guns, from the Brownsville Houses, and Ninja, Powerful, and the boys from Tilden. But these shots are coming from behind, and the shooters are only steps away.

"You have to remember about these kids and guns," Lonnie Hayes says, "they don't really know what they're doing. They run up and *pow, pow, pow,* they run away. They use dirty bent-up bullets, anything they can find for ammunition, and they have no training. They don't know how to deal with another armed man. One time we had a guy that was actually aiming and shooting guys and then coming up and shooting them again when they were down to finish the job. I had the perps coming to me saying, 'Lonnie, you got to do something. Who the hell does this guy think he is, an Italian?'"

This time somebody knows how to shoot. Powerful is nailed in the leg. He crawls a few feet and is hit again and again. Then silence. Everyone on both sides of the street is running. It is hard to tell where the shooters are. Just eight shots and Powerful lies dying in the gutter on Dumont Avenue. The word on the streets is that Tai Stick has been trying to set Powerful up. And when the running stops, all eyes look across the street at the Worthy family.

When twenty-two-year-old Nikia Vinson, granddaughter of Kate Worthy and cousin to the brood of Worthys at 295 Dumont, captured the heart of young Bobby "Born Son" James, the charismatic basketball player from the Howard Houses, a coalition was formed. Born Son and his buddy Supreme came together with a slickster from the Brownsville Houses, Chris Muncie, nicknamed Tai Stick, and the many Worthy brothers. Born Son was the boss, Tai Stick his lieutenant. Supreme took care of security, and the Worthys peddled the drugs, much of it out of Apartment 5AB. Business got so good that the crew needed more muscle, so they recruited a slope-shouldered bad actor named Billy Odums, known in Brownsville and the Coney Island projects, where he had just beat a homicide charge, as Bang. Odums had been in a California junior college on a football scholarship. When he hurt his knee, he came back to Brooklyn to handle a burner for the gang that was now calling itself the Young Guns.

But the local dealers from Tilden, across the street — Ninja, Justice, and Powerful — were not happy over the rise of the Young Guns. At first the two groups tried negotiation. There were half-a-dozen meetings to settle on rules for sharing the crack trade in the Complex. There were beefs and counterbeefs. "Like they would make a deal at a meeting with some of the guys from Tilden or whatever," a Worthy explains, "that they wouldn't sell treys [three-dollar vials], that they would only sell nics [five-dollar vials]. And then somebody would start sellin' treys and then the shooting would start up, and once it started it wouldn't stop for a while. Then they'd have another meeting about who was gonna sell where, and the same thing would happen all over again."

Then there was a personal argument between some of the girls, a "he say, she say thing." The Worthy girls — Nikia, Renee, Omean — were not backing down. The "girl thing" got violent. It came down to Born Son and his boys against Ninja, Justice, and Powerful. The war was on.

Gary and J.R. are a block away, on Mother Gaston Avenue, when the call about the Powerful shooting comes over. J.R. yanks the RMP around the corner. Gary is stunned by what he sees.

"Be advised there are hundreds of people on the block, Central. I want a bus now," he stutters into his radio.

In moments, Gary and J.R. are standing over Powerful, who is on his back between two parked cars, gushing blood into the street. Dead silence. Gary watches as the veteran J.R. swings into action. J.R. checks out the burgeoning crowd and leaps on top of a parked car.

"You. You. You. Let's go. We need a path for the ambulance." J.R. points to the biggest bruisers, guys he calls his parolees, guys with jail muscles, to help him. The heavyweights, eager for a function, any function, jump to their task.

In Brownsville, time and time again the scene is replayed. When there is an emergency, scores of alert young black men stand idle, strong hands useless at their sides. Other men show up in big black-and-yellow rubber coats to put out the fires, in green jackets to save the sick and wounded, and in blue coats to keep the peace. The jackets change color, but the men who wear them are almost always white. They have the training, the tools, the authority, the respect. They get paid.

A passing Fire Department ladder truck pulls up and the T-shirted firemen scramble to stop Powerful's bleeding. There is blood everywhere, no rubber gloves in sight. Still the firemen work furiously, battling to keep Powerful alive. EMS workers push forward with a respirator and an inflatable orange device that looks like a raft for a back-yard swimming pool. They struggle frantically to get the thigh-length pressure pants over Powerful's legs.

Gary is still wide-eyed, not so much at the wounds or the crowd of gaping, jostling people, or even at the shoving between some arriving NYPD units and people on the outskirts of the event, as at the contradictions. He has heard on the street and in the PSA that Powerful is a ruthless killer, and the firemen and EMS workers are going to extraordinary lengths to keep him alive. Despite his wounds, Powerful is still breathing when the ambulance wails away from the crowd toward Brookdale, with J.R. and Gary and Powerful's mother trailing in the patrol car.

Inside the emergency room, the two cops stand aside, J.R. with his memo pad at the ready. If there is a lull in the activity, he will tap a doctor on the shoulder, slide next to the bed, and lean close to Powerful, hoping to get an ID on the shooter. The pressure pants are removed. Gary winces and turns away as a catheter is forced up Powerful's penis. The EMS technician who worked so feverishly to keep Powerful alive on the street goes berserk at the sight of the pressure pants on the floor.

"You stupid fuck!" he screams at the doctor. "I had him stabilized. You just killed him." And sure enough, in moments Powerful is dead.

The doctor stares straight ahead and draws a deep breath.

A sergeant from the PSA appears in the doorway of the room and asks Gary, "Did you ever hear the scream?"

"No," Gary answers.

"Follow me."

Powerful's mother and his sister are waiting forty feet away, around the corner in the hallway by the nurses' station. Just as Gary and the sergeant arrive at the spot, another doctor steps up. "We did everything we could, but we lost him," he tells the mother flatly.

Powerful's mother releases a noise that Gary will never forget, a rifle-shot scream, the unique result of the unbearable collision between two elements of the world meant to remain far apart, young life and death. Then she faints, collapsing on the floor.

The next night a pair of young boys call to Gary and J.R. as they ride slowly down Dumont Avenue. The kids point to a clump of grass near where Powerful fell. J.R. gets out of the car and spots an old .32 revolver half concealed near the metal fencepost. J.R. guesses that Powerful ran past his gun because the shooters were too close behind. Everyone on the block knows the Worthys had something to do with the shooting. But no one is saying a word.

PAYDAY

It is going to be everybody-on-everybody-else's-last-nerve hot, no-damn-sleep-at-all hot. And it is just the end of July. On Fulton Street, in the downtown mall just off Hoyt Street, a blue-suited man is preaching. The man holds a hefty Bible in his right hand, a microphone in his left. The words from the microphone, alternately husky and metallic, ring out. Each sharp sentence is punctuated by a blast of air, a pneumatic period. "Do you think it's gonna be that easy? Huh. When you get shot in the head? Huh. When you get shot in the back? Huh. Do you think it's gonna be that easy to talk to Jesus then? Huh. Satan might be leapin' and rippin' through the land, huh. But payday is comin', huh. Who knows what day the check is comin'? Huh. Payday is comin', huh, payday . . ."

Sharron ignores the preaching as he walks over to the check-cashing place on Fulton to cash his first full check from Brooklyn Youth Outreach. With the $320 in hand he hustles over to the electronics store on the same street to buy a beeper. He forks over $75 for the device, an unusual white model, along with $8 for the first month of service. On the way out of the store, he breathes a long sigh of satisfaction. He is now connected. Sharron does not have the beeper for any illicit purpose; he has it for style and function. Mrs. Dukes, the Corleys' next-door neighbor, is nice enough to take emergency calls for the family, but she is not going to stand for social messages, especially the harvest of phone calls Sharron expects to be reaping soon. The beeper, visible on the waistband of his pants, may raise some eyebrows among adults. But Sharron doesn't care. He and his friends, like many young black men, have nothing to do with drugs, yet they don't seek to dispel the impression that they do, because dealers have props, they "get paid."

The roadway narrows and traffic is restricted to city buses on Fulton Street west of Flatbush Avenue, creating the Fulton Mall. The shopping area is dominated by a large department store on one side and lined with clothing and shoe stores on the other. This Friday afternoon the mall is jammed with people from all over the borough of Brooklyn. The sharp smell of incense drifts down the street from the card table where a man in a white robe sits selling bundles of the stuff.

Sharron is looking for a summer shirt. As he strolls through a small boutique, he is tempted to lift a brown-and-mauve-swirled Hawaiian shirt off the rack and stash it in his pants. But he doesn't have his bicycle shorts on, or his backpack, and the Korean store owner, seated on a high chair by the wall, is as wary as a cat. Besides, Sharron thinks, what is $22? In two weeks there will be another check. Two weeks after that, another $320. And later more money. It's great having a job, he says to himself on the way down Fulton Street.

In fact, Sharron has never minded working. When he was fifteen, he got the "legit" job in a Manhattan law firm. "Any street attitude from this point was controllable," he wrote in his life story for school. "I began to become familiar with work-related people, how to speak with them, how to act around them. I picked up work skills, to continue to work if needed."

A woman, Mrs. Jacks, an office manager at the job, took a special interest in Sharron, always checked to see that he felt comfortable, talked to him and Terrance with respect. That is why Sharron felt so bad when Terrance got them both fired. Things had been slow at work anyway, not much filing or anything else to do. The boys were going in only once a week. But Terrance had the keys to the office on Fifty-seventh Street. Once, after Sharron and his date and Terrance and his dizzy girlfriend left the movies in Times Square, Terrance got the bright idea to head over to the office. He and Sharron could show the girls where they worked and maybe manage to get some "skins" (sex) on the carpeted office floor. Terrance took the boss's room, with its big desk and conference table. He was laughing about it all weekend, telling how his girl's skin squeaked on the shiny wood. Big fun. Sharron just listened. He didn't get any skins, just some kisses in the front office chair.

The video camera did the boys in. Mrs. Jacks called Terrance's house on Monday and told him not to come in anymore, and then she asked him to put Sharron on the phone. "She asked me why we did it, but I couldn't think of anything to say. She sounded disappointed."

After that, Sharron tried a couple of other gigs. He even worked at a supermarket, packing bags. But he was so obsessed with his image that the job went up in smoke the day a girl in his class mentioned that she'd seen him working. "Didn't I see you packing bags at the Associated?" she blurted innocently in front of a bunch of kids. The blood rushed to Sharron's face. His fear of ridicule snapped in him like a giant trap. Luckily, no one on hand picked up the hint, followed up the lead and "woofed" Sharron for being a bag packer. Before the scandal could spread, he quit his job. He didn't even call the boss, just never went back.

Shortly after that, he began writing and recording songs with his cousin Morris, a promotion manager for Warner Brothers Reprise records. The two worked together on and off for two years without a professional breakthrough.

But Sharron was achieving another kind of stardom. He was elected homecoming king at Thomas Jefferson High School in what everyone around the school thought was his junior year — quite an honor. The truth was that in three years at Jefferson he had earned just nine credits. "I loved going to school. I loved walking around and getting all the attention. I loved *beamin'*. That's all I would do. Talk to girls and profile. When I got home I wasn't even thinkin' about no homework, I was all about hittin' the street and flammin'." Deep in his heart, Sharron knew that he was a fake. Like the emperor with no clothes, he was the king with no credits. Still, he couldn't help but devour the attention at the homecoming pageant. "My mother was there, my best friend, Terrance. I rode on the float over to the football field. I have pictures. The girl who was queen, Lorna Mae Silcott? Lorna was fine."

Lorna Mae was certainly that. She barely came up to Sharron's shoulder, and her hips ran to thick. Her hair was unremarkable, medium length and drawn simply off her forehead — no billowing curls, no lustrous sheen, no locks down her back as the boys favor. But Lorna Mae had the most seemly, symmetrical features, almond eyes that caught the light and held it just so, and priceless brown skin that made people shake their heads in wonder.

Sharron struck up Thomas Jefferson High School's version of the perfect romance with his queen. "People always said we looked good together. I was goin' with her for a while." But Sharron found out that fame has its price. "I got so popular that it was hard for any girl that would go with me. The other girls would always give her some trouble. We wore like matching sweaters one time and the girls in the school always had something to say, like 'She thinks she's all that.' It was too much pressure."

There was no confrontation. The approval of their fans had brought them together, and it was their public that pulled them apart. Soon Sharron and Lorna Mae stopped speaking to each other in the hallway, just kept walking, turned to other companions and passed each other by.

By Thanksgiving, Sharron's head had already been turned by a fifteen-year-old freshman named Chantal. Chantal had a generous ponytail and fetching eyes under glistening black eyebrows. She was very pretty, but not a star at Jefferson like Lorna Mae. She didn't go to class much — not something that would ordinarily disqualify her from the upper echelon at Jeff — but she was too eager to please, too tiny and tentative. She was not in the school play, either. She was just another kid, but she rang Sharron's chimes.

"Chantal is pretty, prettier than the average girl, maybe," Sharron wrote in the diary that he had been keeping for the past year to help his song writing. "But her attire didn't match her beauty as far as style and name brands. But I sported her anyway because I knew how she would be if I had fixed her up."

Chantal was undoubtedly Sharron's type; her immaturity was actually an asset to him. It allowed him to dress her and mold her in the way that he liked. Much of Chantal's wardrobe came from Sharron in December and January, when they were an item. "She was short, very short, up to my chest, a very attractive girl," Sharron wrote with quaint and wooden passion. "She had an awesome walk. She looked like a little woman, a woman who would soon be by my side, walking down the aisle of matrimony."

But sometime in the spring, as Sharron got deeper into his role as Danny, he ran out of things to tell Chantal, ways to shape her. As the romance began to wane, she started dropping hints about pregnancy.

One day in April, after school, Sharron was reclining on a table in the fifth-floor cafeteria. Chantal was all over him, prattling about a baby. "My friends thought I was playing myself by being publicly involved with her," Sharron admits. He was still attracted to her, despite the mixed reviews she was receiving. But she was getting annoying with this pregnancy talk. Sharron came right out and asked her if she was pregnant and she answered no. Just a couple of days later, Chantal heard reliable news that Sharron was messing around with Sheryl, who was in the play. She demanded that he tell her what was going on, but he just smiled and changed the subject. "I could always get her to forget what was on her mind and make her laugh."

The next day, while Chantal was making what Sharron refers to as her little debut in the second-floor hallway by the security guards' room, jabbing her finger at Sharron and demanding to know her status, another girl happened by and asked Sharron if he wanted to hang out for a while. It was Lorna — "Yes, Lorna," Sharron recalls with guilty delight. "The whole thing was so cold." Sharron walked away after Lorna. Chantal followed for a few steps, then stopped and watched her sweetheart glide around the corner, out of sight. Her brown eyes brimmed with tears. She fled to the nearest stairway and ran out the side door. After that day, little Chantal stayed away from Thomas Jefferson High, just slipped out of Sharron's sight.

Sharron stands for moment on Fulton Street with the bag holding the Hawaiian shirt in his hand, thinking. He has plenty of money left. He decides to make one more purchase. Carefully, he studies the display window of a store near the end of the block, then steps inside to pick up two gold fronts for his teeth. After, he heads downstairs to the Hoyt Street subway stop with almost $200 left from his check. As he waits for the train to arrive, he shoots a swift look around him and deftly shifts his cash from his front pocket to his sock for the trip back to Brownsville.

The sign on the front of the arriving train says the New Lots

Avenue stop in East New York is the end of the line. It is hard to believe somebody did not plan it that way. Sharron, standing in the first car, closes one eye against the glare as the silver #3 train rises out of the Utica Avenue station into the sunlight, a resurrection attended by barbed wire. On both sides of the elevated track, razor ribbon drapes walls and rooftops. The Sutter Avenue stop arrives and the train moves above Brownsville.

Brownsville begins at Ralph Avenue and ends at the elevated L train on Van Sinderen Street. From there to Conduit Boulevard is East New York. On the far side of the Conduit are the family homes of Ozone Park, Queens. Brownsville and its sister, East New York, loll against the rump of Queens, hemmed in by a maze of parkways to the east and by the white enclave of Canarsie to the south. Most areas of Brownsville and East New York do not look forbidding. There are flimsy stores on Pitkin and Belmont and sagging one-family homes on the side streets, but for the most part the Ville is dominated by the symmetry of clean and well-ordered projects.

Sharron knows that if he passes Broadway to the north, he will be out of the Ville and into Bedford-Stuyvesant. If he crosses Linden Boulevard to the south, he will be heading out. By the time he reaches Flatlands Avenue, he will be far gone, and he had better not dally after dark. As he stares absently out the train window toward Canarsie, he isn't bothered by the fact that a real estate office that tried to rent homes to blacks in Canarsie has recently been firebombed. He isn't thinking about prejudice or even about how nice it would be to be able to spend a summer day at the Canarsie pier on Jamaica Bay, just a neighborhood away. His dreams do not include a modest home in a working-class neighborhood like Canarsie anyway. Sharron is dreaming about convertible cars and cellular phones. He plans to be a star. Besides, it is hard enough keeping his props up to par on his side of town without worrying about all that black-white stuff.

At the Saratoga stop, Sharron skips down the stairs, turns north up Saratoga Avenue, and walks past the spanking clean one-story Nehemiah Homes toward his apartment building. Two kids from the block, Fonzo and Fitty-sen, the latter so named because when he was younger he was always asking people for fifty cents, nod as he walks by. Nothing about Sharron is lost on the two boys. They spy his new white beeper and make a note to acquire one like it themselves someday. They spot the package with the shirt in it and wonder why Sharron did not boost whatever he has in there. But mostly they just admire what they see and plan for the day when they will have the same props.

"NO, ROBO, NO"

Hey, Mac," Gary calls to John McMullen as their paths cross in the PSA. "They're lightin' up your project again. Last night somebody capped your man Jo Jo."

"You sure it was Jo Jo?" McMullen asks, fresh back from vacation and eager for any information about the Complex, his post for the past several months, where he has been riding the Worthys so hard they have taken to calling him Robocop.

"Yeah, his leg was twitchin' in the ambulance. I think he was hit in the thigh. Probably late for his lookout shift so they shot him."

"Fuckin' projects. Let 'em kill themselves," an officer nearby chimes in. "Like a self-cleaning oven."

When McMullen arrives on the block for his shift, he sidles over and uses a key to scratch "Robo is back" onto the door panel of Tai Stick's new blue Honda Prelude, a message to the Worthys. Then he walks away, smiling.

It's all about reputation in the projects, and that doesn't hold only for the kids. The cops slip into the same mentality. McMullen, a rangy twenty-six-year-old with a gray rug of a crew cut, starts right where he left off before his vacation. He locks up Randolph one day for slinging, and Jimmy Worthy the next. Then it's Edward, and Jimmy again. McMullen knows he can't clean up the Brownsville Houses, but at least he isn't going to allow his reputation to suffer as the place goes to shit.

Kate Worthy stands near the corner of Dumont and Mother Gaston avenues with one of her tiny great-granddaughters in hand and watches McMullen stroll along the walkways of the

Complex. "There was a time when I went down South to Bowman, South Carolina," she says wanly. "I had a little house . . . brick. It was so nice. But Brenda, my eldest, was having all kinds of problems and I came back and I just stayed. I had ten head at that time. Edward, Noren, Randolph, Carlton, and Lennie all stayed with me, an' two of my daughters and their babies."

Kate's husband died and she was left to deal with a growing brood that had become an outlaw clan. "They became uncontrollable," she says. "I have to get out of that apartment. I'm not gonna die like this."

For Kate, her children, and her grandchildren, the police are loudmouthed, ignorant yahoos who can be relied on to bungle their job and demean and brutalize people while they are doing it. The Worthys and their cousins the Asburys are going nowhere and they know it. But this is their home, and they offer up a daily ration of abuse to the police, as occupied people do everywhere. It must be no different in Belfast or the West Bank. Domination, disrespect, gunfire, and death.

Many of the best Housing police make their reputation by setting a project straight. They get to know the people and they learn who the bad guys are. Then, just like the marshal in the cowboy movies, they clean out the town. Of course, the "good guys," as the police actually call themselves, don't always come out on top. With the Housing police of the PSA 2, it isn't usually for lack of trying. The stereotype of the cynical doughnut-eating police officer doesn't hold for them. Though there have been several corruption scandals in nearby NYPD precincts, a massive drug-stealing and drug-selling mess at the 77th precinct, and more recently, front-page exposure of a rogue cop gang in Brownsville led by an officer from the 75th precinct, the Housing cops of the PSA 2 don't have those kinds of problems. They may go to the Dunkin' Donuts over on Flatlands Avenue to grab some coffee, but they do not gorge themselves on sugar-coated doughnuts, and they hustle back to the Ville. They do not want to give up the streets to Born Son. They do not want to give up the possibility of a promotion to a specialty detail, and they definitely do not want to give up the overtime.

The next afternoon, Ninja, one of the players in the Tilden drug trade, is involved in a brawl in the lobby of 320 Dumont.

McMullen jogs across the street, strong-arms his way through the crowd, and separates the combatants.

"I don't want you anywhere near this building for the rest of the day," he tells Ninja.

Ninja, who is about five-ten and maybe 180 pounds, walks toward McMullen with his hands open in a conciliatory gesture. He steps all the way up to the six-foot-two McMullen and places his hands on the 190-pound officer's shoulders.

"Wha's up with that? For serious, Robo? I got to get in the building," he whines.

McMullen starts to raise his arms to knock Ninja's hands off his shoulders. But as he does, Ninja leans back and rocks McMullen with a stunning right-hand wallop to the side of the cop's pink face. Like a jolt of electricity, the word travels up through the building and across the street.

"Ninja's kickin' Robo's —" The kids, town criers of the neighborhood, can't even get the last word out before they run back to see. A huge crowd gathers. One of the saddest sights in Brownsville is people sprinting from all sides to get a look at a fight. A fistfight is topnotch entertainment for young and old; a local tough fighting a cop hand to hand is almost too good to be true.

The circling crowd stays well back. They know Robo has a gun; they are not sure about Ninja. Robo has been shaken by the sucker punch but manages his own roundhouse to Ninja's head. The cop leaves himself unprotected with the big swing and absorbs another straight cracking shot to the cheek. Now Robo steps in to clinch. He grabs Ninja by the shirt with his right hand; with his left, he rains on Ninja's head. Ninja hooks his finger under the neck of Robo's bulletproof vest, hangs on, and pounds Robo with his free hand. Like two hockey players, the cop and the Tilden tough guy punish each other.

The crowd is beside itself. "Oooo," it moans when one punch lands, "Aaah," when the retaliatory blow arrives.

The battle wears on. Not everybody in the neighborhood is rooting for Ninja. Upstairs, people are calling 911.

McMullen's radio has been dropped and kicked into the bushes. "10-13. 320 Dumont. Numerous calls," the portable sputters. All over Brownsville, cops hear the dispatcher say, "Officer being beaten by a man at that location."

Though McMullen doesn't know it, help is coming fast; footposts are sprinting, radio cars are wailing, mounting sidewalks to get past traffic. Still, the nearest cop is more than a block away. McMullen starts to go down, his knees wobbling. In desperation he reaches behind, unhooks the silver handcuffs from his belt, and smashes Ninja over the head with the steel restraints.

"No, Robo, no." There are people leaning out of the windows all the way up to the top floor of the seventeen-story building, and many of them do not approve of the cuff-swinging maneuver. "No, Robo, no," they howl.

The tide turns with the jolting handcuffs. Ninja sags almost to the pavement. Stooped with exhaustion, his arms slack, eyes glassy, Robo stands over the crumpled figure. Then he looks down and shudders with horror. He cannot believe what he sees as Ninja shakes his head, snorts, and starts rearing back up. The rejuvenated young man yokes the dazed McMullen in a headlock and starts pumping uppercuts. The light of the afternoon fades to dark gray for Robo; the squeals of the crowd dim to a muffled hum. Beaten, he gives up the fight.

At that moment, Robo hears a sound that brings a faint smile to his battered lips: the rasping static from the radios of the approaching police. The fair fight is over. Two guys from the 73 fly in and grab Ninja. Then the Housing cops arrive. It takes seven officers to beat Ninja down.

"When he wouldn't go down after I hit him with the cuffs, I realized he was high. Fucked up," McMullen says. "When I heard the sound of those radios, it was as good as sex."

"Look at this." Bobby Schulman calls McMullen to the door of the detective squad room an hour later. He is holding a sheet of paper with the cross statement Ninja has given describing his version of events. McMullen reads out loud.

"'I deal drugs right in front of Robo's face and he can't do shit about it. And today I kicked his fucking ass. Signed, Ninja.'" McMullen tries to laugh but coughs instead.

THE FEDS ARE CLOCKING

What the fuck is that?"
Balding, lean Bobby Schulman swivels his chair around to face the six federal drug enforcement agents in their country-boy-clean jeans and glossy shoes, behind him in the smoky alcove of the PSA 2 detective squad room. He smirks. "You mean that sound?" Schulman asks. "I'll play it back."

Schulman has been showing the agents videotapes of the drug dealing in the Complex. Ever since Kammerdener got back from FBI school, he has been talking about getting federal agencies involved in stopping the drug traffic in the projects. Schulman knew somebody in a DEA enforcement group who was looking for a case in Brooklyn. Now the DEA people are in Brownsville to consider a cooperative operation. When Schulman replays the tape, the same repetitive popping sound is heard. He pushes the stop button. "Probably a nine," he says, and lets the picture roll again. The agents glance at each other. "Sounds like it's coming from 340 Dumont — probably Ninja. Doesn't get along with the Young Guns."

In the next sequence, one of the Worthy boys is seated on a bench in front of 295, servicing a stream of crack customers. Each time a person approaches the bench, Lennie Worthy hands him a cigarette and palms a bill in return. He glances quickly at the bill as his hand slips to his jacket pocket and comes out with a pack of matches. As he lights the customer's cigarette, he passes the vials of crack, all in one motion.

"Smooth," Mathew DeJong, a pockmarked, taciturn agent, says.

"As whale shit," Schulman answers.

DeJong has spent most of his career doing water rescues and special projects for the DEA. For him and the rest of the DEA agents crowded into the room, most of whom gained their law enforcement experience as state troopers stopping cars on the interstate, the videotape of life in the Complex is amazing.

"The stuff never stops," an agent says.

"Twenty-four seven," Schulman replies, twirling the tips of his handlebar mustache. "Besides 295, Born Son and his boys are dealing out of 265 Livonia, 285 Livonia, 345 Dumont, and 312 Osborn. They have that whole side of the Complex. We're getting sometimes three thousand vials going through there on a busy weekend day." Schulman pauses for a moment. "Yeah, and they shoot people. All the time."

Half an hour later the agents flinch as they stand in the front room of the PSA, preparing to accompany Schulman on a tour of the neighborhood. It is the same hollow popping noise they heard on the tape. Only this time it is coming from somewhere above — if not from the building above the PSA, then from very close by. A couple of uniforms hustle out the front door.

"Now that *is* a nine," Schulman says over his shoulder as he confers with the duty officer at the desk, "or maybe an oowop," he adds, using the street name for an Uzi machine gun.

Several days later, the DEA agrees to assign Mathew DeJong and several backup teams of agents to an operation designed to build a case against Born Son and his Young Guns. Schulman, DeJong, and several assisting teams of federal agents will concentrate on 295 Dumont Avenue. Kammerdener wanted the feds because they have the resources, the surveillance vehicles, and the clout to score wiretaps and warrants. More important, they brandish the heavy mandated federal sentences that the K-Master hopes will strike fear into the young slingers, who have been shrugging off the modest state sentences. And Kammerdener wants to take down the slingers in the Complex because that's where Tony McLean died.

Kammerdener gives the case to Schulman. Together with DeJong, he goes about the tedious work of putting an end to Born Son's reign in the Brownsville Houses. The team moves methodically, watching and taking pictures from their unmarked van, listening to telephone conversations. Somehow word gets to the Worthys that the feds are "clocking," but the Young Guns dismiss the rumors and go blithely on with their crack-peddling business in the Complex.

Schulman and Born Son already have a history. A year ago, Schulman stopped him when he was driving a late-model BMW down Dumont Avenue. While the officer checked the papers, Born Son turned and fled into 295 Dumont Avenue. Schulman was in hot pursuit, but he tripped and stumbled onto his knees in the street, which allowed Born Son to race upstairs and hide under a bed in Apartment 5AB. The Housing cops couldn't find him for half an hour, until they brought in a dog to sniff him out. Before the cops took Born Son from the apartment, through the throngs of curious tenants, they beat him up.

"It was eerie," Lonnie Hayes remembers. "It was pitch dark in there, and all the time Born Son was gettin' his ass kicked he didn't make a single sound."

Later, in the cell area of the PSA 2, the bloody Born Son raised all kinds of hell, laughing at Schulman for tripping in the street during the chase and cursing the police.

"Callin' Schulman everything but a child of God," Born Son's mother says. "And that's why Schulman hates my son, because he was shamed when he fell and Born Son talked back like that."

In a couple of days Born Son was set free, but the threats continued from both sides. The Housing police reported telephoned death threats against Schulman. The kids around the Brownsville and Howard Houses, where Born Son grew up, swear that Schulman put the word on the street that he was going to shoot Bobby James in the back. The conflict was in part about business — the Housing cops doing the job they were paid for, Born Son trying to stay in the crack trade. But it was also personal, about reputation. Bobby "Born Son" James had the biggest props in all of Brownsville.

Born Son, the son of Margaret James, is less impressive than his name and reputation. He is an unprepossessing five-foot-nine, 165 pounds, with the bark-brown skin of his mother. He has generous lips, which he likes to keep wet with his tongue. "I didn't let him out of the house until he was eighteen years old," Margaret avows. "I kept him in, and when I heard the guns going off, it was like the wolves were howling outside." J.R. remembers Born Son around Howard as something of a mama's boy, but also as a kid who was always in trouble. "He was a punk. He used to get his ass kicked every day."

"I told him after a while," his mother says, "don't come up here with no bloody nose. All his life people have been messin' with him. The same way they mess with me."

Margaret tried to be strict. But she was working, always. First as a cashier, then as a secretary. When Bobby and his boys would cause some trouble around Howard during the day, somebody would tell the building maintenance man, Charley, and he would tell Margaret. When she got home from work there would be hell to pay. "When we saw her comin', guys would just take off," one kid remembers.

Born Son didn't spend time in the house, despite his mother's claims. And he learned things out and around Howard. The locals remember him as a kid with so much style and class that he was imitated from an early age. "You know they got that commercial about Michael Jordan, 'Be Like Mike,'" a kid from Howard says. "Well, everybody wanted to be like brother Bobby. Talk like him, stand like him. I mean, Timberland boots made *money* from people imitating Born Son. He had heart, and people fear heart."

The guys around the way describe Born Son's charisma as a mixture of intimidation and kindness. If you were his man, he would do anything for you, give you anything. Hank Walters, a coach and amateur boxer who has worked at the Youth Athletic League center in the Howard Houses for the past twenty-five years and who took Bobby under his wing as an eight-year-old, remembers that "what made people fear him later on was that terrible temper, and the fact that he always did what he said he was going to do."

Born Son was also a point guard on the basketball court, with serious "ups," or "hops," as the locals call jumping ability. "We could play him at off guard or small forward even, because of his jumping," Walters says. "But I had to sit him down many times because of his lack of control. I went up to his school when he was just a little kid and I talked to the teacher's aide. She told me, 'Someday Bobby is going to kill somebody.'"

When Bobby was just fourteen, Walters heard that he was carrying a weapon. When the kid walked into the center one night, Walters searched him and came up with a forty-five. "I told him I was going to hold it until the end of the night and give it back. Instead I gave it to his younger brother, who took it upstairs."

Hold it till the end of the night? Take it upstairs? This was not a water gun. It was a forty-five. The decision to give the gun back does not tell you as much about Walters, a reasonable man, as it does about Brownsville.

The recollection of Born Son hurts Walters. "When I was coming up, with the Tomahawks and the Jolly Stompers and whatnot, it was bad in Brownsville, but this is much worse. The kids put a dollar sign on the value of a life." Walters remembers the bell of the gym door kept ringing during pickup basketball games, and Bobby would keep running over and answering the door. Walters would catch glimpses of hard-looking guys outside. Bobby was not one to volunteer for such things, so Walters became suspicious. "I said, 'I'll answer the door next time,' but Bobby insisted." Turned out Born Son was making some kind of transactions from the gym. "I knew he had taken the other way," Walters says, "but I didn't think that he would put the other kids at the center in jeopardy like that." It costs only a dollar a year to be part of the center. Walters had pleaded with Bobby for years; after that, he had to cut him loose, for the safety of the others. He gave Bobby back his dollar and told him he was not welcome at the center anymore. Hank Walters had lost his battle for Bobby.

There are several stories about how Born Son got into the drug business. Margaret blames Nikia Vinson. But the Howard locals remember things differently. They recall that when Bobby became too old to play in the "D and D" basketball tournament, a heavy dealer around Howard nicknamed Trip, a man with drug connections all up and down the East Coast, gave him a spot in the organization. Reportedly, Bobby was part of a triumvirate that included his cousin, Knowledge, and a fellow known as Rockhead. Street history says Knowledge killed Rockhead. He was convicted and incarcerated for the deed, and Born Son found himself in charge of Howard at an early age.

Walters made one last plea. When he was sure that Bobby was in the drug business and saw that his younger brother was getting involved, he pleaded, "For God's sake, turn your brother loose." According to Walters, Bobby complied. "I do respect him for that," Walters says now. "His brother is now in school, I heard. Bobby was such a remarkable kid. He had a scholarship to Laurinburg Prep in North Carolina, but I heard that when he went down there he just started with the Brownsville mentality, threatening the coach and all that nonsense, and the coach wasn't having it."

Back in Brownsville, contracts were being put out all over the place in Howard. If Bobby was not shooting people, it was said, he was influencing his growing passel of disciples to do so. "One thing I know," a local says, "is that he could never leave Howard Houses unless he had his people with him. If Bobby went past Langston Hughes or Brownsville Houses? No questions. They would start shooting at him."

Bobby did get shot. When he recovered, he got shot again. "I used to search their room for guns, but I never found them," Margaret says unconvincingly. "He wasn't into that mess with guns and all that. Born Son just kicked ass. He kicked natural ass."

BLOODY VALENTINE

My name is Sharron. I'm your representative from the Brooklyn Youth Outreach."

Mrs. G., the Youth Employment supervisor at P.S. 32, glances up from her desk at the young man brandishing a smile in front of her. Sharron extends his hand. "Hello."

As Mrs. G. reaches toward him, Sharron seems to soften slightly. He almost blushes. His eyes hurry to the floor. His handshake is as light as silk.

"I'm kinda new at this, but . . . I'm checking to see how many kids you have, and if there are any problems. Are the kids getting along?"

The middle-aged Mrs. G. pauses for a moment to consider the new site monitor. Sharron raises his deep brown eyes and levels them at her. Can he be flirting? Mrs. G. has to smile. "Yes, as a matter of fact," she begins, "I'm delighted you came by today. I've been meaning to call. But maybe you can handle it. I've got two girls, sisters, who have the flu. I asked them to stay home, but they just keep coming in. I'm sure they want the full paycheck, and I can understand that."

In a moment Sharron is handling the problem like a veteran. After a call to Aubrey, he escorts the coughing, sneezing sisters to the Outreach all-purpose room, where they will spend the rest of the week out of the mix of children at P.S. 32.

Sharron is one of Aubrey's favorite workers now. When the director passes, he squeezes Sharron's arm supportively. Sharron has picked up the routine quickly, even designed a persona for the position. "I present myself as a young man who is mannerly and can handle all technicalities and responsibilities," he tells Ms. King on the phone.

It's too late to travel to another site today, so Sharron hangs around the basement office of the Youth Employment Project on East Street until quitting time, then strolls to the subway to go back to Brownsville. On his way to the train station, he straightens and slumps his shoulders, experimenting with first this look on his face, then that. The late July sun dances beside the landmark Long Island Railroad building on Flatbush Avenue. The big clock there reads six o'clock. As girls walk by, Sharron mumbles. One slim girl in neon green culottes and a lime green T-shirt pauses.

"What'd you say?"

Ah! This is the way it was always supposed to be, Sharron thinks. A pretty boy loose in a city with thousands and thousands of girls.

"You say something?" she repeats. Sharron sidles up the sidewalk like a cat. He hadn't said a word. Why devise some witty phrase? If the girl wants to talk to you, he reasons, she will jump at the mumble.

"I said, I like your eyes," he whispers.

"I like your beeper. I never seen a white one."

Sharron allows himself a bare moment to revel. He has learned not to lose his head; anything can happen. The girl's boyfriend could happen by. Like an experienced salesman, Sharron knows it is important to close the deal. He quickly scribbles the girl's phone number on a scrap of paper like the three or four he has in his pockets and the dozen in the drawers and on the floor of his room. He writes his beeper number down and hands it to her. As he speaks, the sun blazes on Atlantic Avenue, delivering a fierce sting down the length of the scar on the left side of his face. As the girl studies his sincere brown eyes and his handsome wounded face, he sticks the pen back in his pocket, cups his hand over the scar to shield it from the sun, and smiles so she can see the two new gold fronts on his teeth.

Sharron got the scar around Valentine's Day, just before Sharon King tapped him for the drama program last spring. His wardrobe was down then, and that meant he was low. He had gotten caught in the rain with his white Polo sweater, and it was all stretched and messed up. Worse, either Shawanda or Alleke had made off with his jeans jacket. It was out of the question to ask Gloria for money to go shopping. She was out of work, had her own problems. And Sharron had his pride.

The LoLifes were on the move, what they call a "meow," an expedition. Franklo and Beklo, the crew. This would be a rush number. Eight LoLifes charged into a leather store in the Fulton Mall; Jaylo punched out the owner, who was the only security. The crew grabbed as many coats as they could and jetted into the Saturday afternoon throng. Sharron heard later that two guys got snagged by undercover Transit. Not Shalo. He floated home in the back of a gypsy cab, tired but happy.

There were four leather bombers, two for sale, one for a girl-friend, and one to keep. On the next Monday, Sharron headed over to Jeff to try to sell the two. The price, $100 apiece. The bombers were easily worth $300. No luck at the school, so Shar-ron jumped on the bus up Pitkin Avenue and got off in front of a laundromat around the corner from his house, where he used to hang out. Being seen in the neighborhood peddling stolen merchandise was nothing to be ashamed of. Sharron and others around the way often avail themselves of $100 sneakers for $20. It is just the way things work. In fact, selling stolen merchan-dise is a way to show that you are a person of substance, not just a front; that you do "get paid."

Inside the laundromat, Sharron shopped the leathers to sev-eral neighborhood guys.

"What's up?"

"Not a damn thing."

"I got some bombers." Sharron turned to the left and right to include the half-dozen people around. One of the boys, a guy he had seen around for years, somebody he knew just well enough to greet on the street, nodded toward Sharron's knapsack, and Sharron shifted it around in front.

The boy looked at a tuft of brown leather bulging from the bag and lifted his chin.

"A buck," Sharron answered.

His strategy of staying out of the neighborhood has disadvan-tages. His alliances on the block were marginal. He checked the faces around him. The vibrations inside the laundromat were no problem. But no one wanted to spend any money, so with his two leathers crammed into his big bookbag, he walked over to his apartment on Saratoga.

As Sharron quit the laundromat, two boys, one stocky, one lanky, followed him. The heavier one he used to hang with a while back. The skinny guy he had seen around a few times.

"Yo, wait up," they called from the corner, and he stopped walking. Maybe they had changed their minds about buying a leather. The situation did not look good, but there was no running away. Here, you deal with things as they come up. Besides, just maybe, Sharron thought, his instincts were wrong.

The stocky kid approached; the other lingered several feet behind. The first youth kept walking and headed into Sharron's building, where he stood between the outside and inside doors, waiting. Any fool could see it was a trap. Sharron bought time with a front. He reached his right hand into his jacket, placed the bookbag with the leathers between his legs, faced the kid in the street, and demanded, "Wha's up?"

The boy by the curb, about Sharron's size, said nothing. Instead, he gave a quizzical look to the boy inside. Something had gone wrong with whatever plan the two had hatched in the laundromat. Sharron turned his head to check the guy inside the door, and the kid on the street lunged for the bookbag, snatched it, and backed around a car at the curb. With one hand he shook the jackets out of the bag. With the other he brandished a seven-inch knife. His head disappeared behind the car for a moment while he stooped to pick up the leathers. Then he dropped the bag in the street and shifted to the far side of Saratoga.

The inside guy popped out, emboldened. "Give it up." He pointed to the shearling Sharron wore.

"You're lucky I don't blow your fucking head off." Sharron summoned his foulest scowl — his coldest grill. That part of the front worked.

The kid's eyes widened, his jaw fell slack. "I'm not really down with this," he sputtered lamely, and scampered across the street.

Sharron climbed the yellowed marble stairs to his mother's fourth-floor apartment, thinking. The situation was not a disaster. He had not lost his own shearling. There were still two leathers left. It had been a nerve-racking experience trying to peddle the things anyway. The real damage had been done to the reputation he had worked years to construct. Robbed in front of his own house by guys he knew. Something would have to be done.

Sharron grabbed the scratched and pitted gray-handled .25 Raven he kept high in his closet and strode outside with a great display of irritation. He traveled the stretch of Pitkin Avenue to the laundromat with the small gun held at his side, walked up to the steamy window, and peered inside. No sign of the robbers. No one could say that he had been robbed like a pussy. He had looked for the thieves with his burner in full view. Done. Sharron wrote the coats off.

The next day was the day before Valentine's. Sharron was looking good. His fade had taken a while to grow into its own since the last cut. Now it was the perfect length, glittering gold on top, rich brown below. He was looking so good he could not bear to stay in the house. Outside by the pay phone, his phone, he profiled, shooting handsome looks all the way across the avenue while he waited for the girl in front of him to get off the line. He was catching all kinds of attention. He would not call Chantal; that could wait till Valentine's Day. Even when he couldn't reach the girl whose number he had written on a tattered orange bus transfer ticket, he decided to stay on the corner as long as the damp wind would allow.

"Shit." The two coat-snatchers were crossing Saratoga on the other side of Pitkin. Sharron spun on his heel and hustled upstairs for his gun. This time he charged outside, lest it be said by anyone who was watching — and it is axiomatic for Sharron that people are watching — that he abandoned his spot on the corner at the sight of the two thieves. Besides, he was angry. It was one thing to match wits with the downtown department stores, he believed, something else to rob somebody around the way who has props. This was all so complicated. So much drama. Every move had to be timed, considered, and perfected. The spirit of the players had to be robust, the reflexes wired like a race car. If Sharron did survive this life, how would he ever leave it behind? How could he sit down with a book, laugh off a social slight, focus on long-range goals?

The two Pitkin Avenue rip-off guys were heading back from the pizza shop up the street when Sharron reappeared. "Walking around like it's O.K.," Sharron thought. "Mad disrespect." They had two other guys with them now. One was a friend of Sharron's, and as the group came toward him, that kid stepped discreetly off. Sharron stood on the corner of Pitkin and Saratoga, his soft palm pressed to the chill metal of the Raven in his pocket. The moment was howling in his ear.

"It would have been so much easier to be a girl," he thought.

There were three, but Sharron had the gun in his coat. His clammy palm tightened and loosened around the handle of the baby burner.

"Whatever," Sharron said.

"Whatever," the stocky kid answered. He was the one who had stayed in the building, the punk who had fallen for the gun front. He was not going for any front this time. It was Sharron's mistake to think that the next order of business would be a knuckle-number. Things had gone too far for a fistfight.

The only plays he had were to cap somebody, shoot right away, or step off. He waited. The stocky kid flipped his slice of pizza in Sharron's face. Hot oil and cheese to the bridge of the nose, to the eyes. As Sharron reached up to brush the pizza off, the kid made an arcing move with his right hand, a glancing blow to the side of Sharron's face. Sha dipped low to punch back. Then the blood.

The kid had struck with a razor, laying Sharron's face open from ear to mouth on the left side.

Sharron glanced at the horrified eyes of an onlooker in the street and sprinted off with his hand over his face, pressing the wound. He took the stairs two at a time and burst past Gloria to the mirror. What he saw — the howling gash, suddenly bloodless white — buckled his knees. In a moment there was blood over everything.

"Jesus Christ." Gloria fought tears as she bent over Sharron where he sat glassy-eyed on the edge of the tub. She pressed a towel to the torn flesh and stroked his forehead. She raised her wet eyes to the light bulb on the ceiling. "My baby." She felt a rising sob, and canceled it with a curse. "Dammit." She had always feared losing Sharron. "When you go to college, I'm comin' too," she always told him. "It's O.K.," she said now. But she was not sure.

Four hours later, after Gloria had rushed Sharron to Brookdale Hospital, where a doctor put fifty-five stitches in his face,

Sharron sat at home, staring into the dark. The door of his room was shut tight, the window draped with a blanket. He sat motionless on his bed all that night and the next day, thinking, the left side of his face drumming with every aching pulse beat. Like a brooding monk, he mulled over sin and salvation.

One side of the ledger was the grievous attack. The kid who cut him lived in the neighborhood, was sure to be seen again. He should be shot, at least shot at. Anything less would be a serious breach of Brownsville ethics. Sharron had the loaded Raven, hidden again, high in the closet. A short walk in the street to the laundromat would do the trick. Then, come what may. On the other side of the ledger was the fact that there could be a gunfight. He could be killed. Even if he whacked the kid, everybody would know who did it. There would be big-time beef, payback. If he played that off, avoided the avengers, he would probably be jailed.

Sharron had never committed violence for its own sake, was never one to express himself through the quick punch, the knife, or the pistol. He had other resources. His violence had always been tactical, designed to win friends and ward off future attacks. He was a singer, a pretty boy, or at least he had been. Alone in his room, he was frantic with worry over what the scar would look like. "What are your suggestions? We'd like to know." The sign hanging on his door mocked him. Angry, injured, and depressed, he stayed in his room another day, and then another. Sometime in those hours, as the droning sounds of endless TV game shows drifted in from the next room, he decided not to reach for the Raven.

On the third day, Chantal came running. When Sharron had not called or arrived with a card on Valentine's Day, she had been angry. But when she heard the news she rushed to his apartment and pushed on the door to his room.

"Sha, 's me. Chantal."

No answer. In the afternoon shadows, Sharron sat up on the bed and twisted his back to Chantal, the hood of his Champion sweatshirt pulled high. He was not receiving visitors. She worked her way slowly to his side, lifted his hand, and kissed it. She slipped her hand under his white sweatshirt and let her freshly lacquered pink fingernails ride across his back. Then she lowered his hood, touched her cool cheek to the left side of his face above the bandages, and placed her petal lips on his. Sharron sank onto the bed and pulled her down.

Chantal wasn't much good at anything but making love to Sha. She held him close and kept him warm, squeezed her eyes shut and clamped her teeth tight to keep from crying out. And when it was over, Sharron collapsed in a fit of giggles.

"It was beautiful," he says now. "I always remember that, 'cause that is the moment when I got my confidence back. After that moment I was all right."

In the way of things, Sharron's scar turned out to be an asset. Nothing could give a pretty boy instant credibility on the street, a permanent membership in the hard club, better than the looping scar that ran across his sweet face. The scar was not gnarled, jagged, or lumpy. It was almost graceful. It was danger, mystery, everything a scar could be.

THE TROOPS

How 'bout some cold ones tonight? Johnny Ray Robinson got thirty-five years. *That* you got to drink to." Gary is speaking out the window of his RMP to Eddie Hammil and Jimmy Galvin, who are standing in front of the PSA. "Those bad boys are gonna taste awful good after that warm piss Maritza serves." Twenty minutes later, he tries the hard sell on a young cop who has a new live-in girlfriend. "C'mon, how many nights in a row you think you can spend with the bitch before she gets sick of your ass?"

It's a Monday night in mid-July. Gary is beginning to feel he's nearing the end of his partnership with J.R. Rumors have been floating around the PSA that Reynolds will soon be offered a detective shield. Besides, word has come that Robinson, the guy who killed Tony McLean, has just been sentenced to thirty-five to life. By midnight, Gary has recruited almost a dozen bodies for his drinking party.

The heavy wooden front door of Katie Cassidy's on Woodhaven Boulevard deadens the sound of roaring engines of cars that make the traffic light outside and squealing brakes of those that don't. It is precisely one o'clock on a Tuesday morning, a time when bartenders in most places have seen their best customers come and go. But Cassidy's is a cop bar, and the four-to-twelve tour will be along soon. It is then that most of the PSA 2 drinking will go on. The troops sometimes assemble over by "the Wall," a secluded spot along a desolate stretch of Belmont Avenue, which the K-Master declared a "cooping prone location," an unauthorized resting or socializing spot. Other nights they drink at Cheap Charlie's in Ozone Park, or here at Katie Cassidy's.

The walls of the front room of the Queens establishment are decorated with wooden plaques marked "Roscommon," "Tyrone," "Kilkenny" — the counties of Ireland. In the center of the low-ceilinged room sits a rectangular bar; beyond the bar, a room with tables and a fireplace. The regular cops, in jeans, sneakers, and black satin PSA 2 windbreakers with white skulls and crossbones stenciled on the back, arrive and congregate around the side of the bar closest to the front door. One fresh-faced cop wears a T-shirt with the words "Attitudes adjusted while you wait." Shirts like this, including one with the slogan "Boys on the Hood" over a cartoon of a black youth handcuffed over the front of a patrol car, are popular with the officers. The detectives, in discount Sy Syms suits, stand in pairs on the other side of the bar. Cops and detectives rarely socialize, but the Johnny Ray Robinson verdict brings both groups out tonight. "That motherfucker's parole officer isn't even born yet," a detective rasps across the bar.

The detectives sit on barstools and talk softly. They smoke cigarettes and finger short glasses of hard liquor. The cops stand and drink beer. Tall brown bottles of Budweiser are everywhere. The cops scrupulously buy each other rounds of Bud. Not one officer drinks another brand. If one guy slows his drinking for a moment, he becomes the focus of derision. "What? You got empties. You weak shit. Beer for the man." Not single bottles but handfuls of Buds are pushed across the bar at the slow drinker. Stacks of soggy bills cling to the bar top.

"I'm callin' for an investigation," the young cop with the new girlfriend announces. Heads turn. "I'm wearing a condom. I get finished. I look down, and the fuckin' thing has disintegrated. All I got is a rubber band around my dick. So I write a letter to the company. They write me back, 'The condom has to be donned correctly.' I write back, 'I am an experienced condom donner, and I *donned* the condom correctly.'" He finishes to a roar of laughter.

Officers congregate not only to exchange stories and to feel the camaraderie, so strong it hangs in the room like a scent, but for the practical purpose of making sure they are not out drinking alone when a stickup takes place. Stories abound of gunmen who have come down the bar searching and robbing each patron. As the thieves come toward him, an officer has to make the life-and-death decision whether to draw and shoot it out or let the perps discover his shield and gun. With an eight-beer handicap, the cop is likely to make the wrong move.

Without effort, Gary is already one of the boys, though he is the only black man in the room. He listens while one cop revises the story of the Robo-Ninja fight to the satisfaction of the audience. "The guy who kicked Robo's ass was just out of Riker's." Everybody nods knowingly. "Just out of Riker's" is a compliment; it means that the person is a muscleman.

A detective overhears and gestures with his drink as he speaks. "It's a bitch when you take somebody to trial. These guys look like skels on the street. A couple a months in jail, three meals a day, lifting weights, a clean suit, and the jury is looking at this guy and saying to themselves, 'Why would they mess with this nice-looking fella?'"

"Look at Reynolds." Hammil points to J.R., who is grinning on the fringe of the group of Housing cops. "He likes these guys. Tell 'em about your amnesties." J.R. shakes his head. Two more beers and he'll be ready to tell some truth. Now he'll let the others take the lead.

"Fuckin' J.R., when he was the PCO in Howard and he caught a guy fuckin' up on a holiday, he'd let the guy go. A lot of times. One time J.R. checks this mope's ID and finds out it's his birthday and he lets him go."

"Birthday amnesty," J.R. concedes. "But what'd I do the next time we caught the guy?"

It's Hammil's turn to concede. "You launched him down the stairs."

"*And* gave him a dis con," J.R. adds, referring to a summons for disorderly conduct.

"What about the time the lady wanted you to make her kid go to school?" another cop interjects. "J.R. slaps the kid around and sends him to school, and then later he fuckin' *calls the school* to make sure the kid is there."

"What about the lady in Cypress that's afraid of ghosts?"

J.R. can't resist this one. "Lady is all fucked up. Second time in the night she calls me and Gary, worried about ghosts coming in her apartment. So I check all the rooms. She's followin' me. I check the windows, and then I tell her to bring me a bag of flour. I sprinkle the flour in front of her front door. 'What's that for?' she wants to know. 'This way,' I tell her, 'when the ghost comes back, he'll leave a footprint. *Then* you call us, and we'll have a clue.'"

Confident in his storytelling, Gary leans into the center of the group and launches into an account of a recent experience with an emotionally disturbed person.

"I'm workin' with Paddy. We got a call in Unity, an EDP, and there was this guy on the floor by the door of the apartment. The guy has the most incredible build you have ever seen. He looks like a statue. Shoulders to here. Waist this small." Gary puts his half-empty beer on the bar to perform the identifying gestures. "This guy is lying on the floor of the apartment nude, and he has his arm around like this, and he has his thumb up his ass." Small bubbles appear at the corners of Lemite's mouth as he giggles. "No shit, he has his thumb up his ass, and I ask him what's up. He says, 'I've got it. There's a bug up my ass and I've got him.' No shit. This guy thinks there is a bug up his ass and he is holding it in with his thumb."

Gary takes a small glance over at his chuckling mentor, J.R. "So I tell the guy that his thumb and arm must be getting tired. You should have seen the size of this guy. He *musta* just got out of Riker's. I tell him that he should switch thumbs. He takes one hand out and goes to put the other thumb up his ass. I grab one hand, Paddy grabs the other, and we cuff him up. I swear."

Several hours and dozens of stories later, the party breaks up. As Gary turns the ignition and the old Dodge kicks over, he thinks to himself, *I love cops.* When he was asked on the psychological segment of the police test why he wanted to be an officer, he knew enough not to tell the truth. "I am interested in the good salary, the possibility of advancement, and the benefits," he said. He had learned from friends on the force that it would not be good to tell the examiners that he craved the action, had dreamed about being a cop since he was a kid.

Even in the middle of summer, he waits several minutes for the car to warm up. He has had eight beers. He double-checks over his shoulder before he pulls onto Woodhaven Boulevard and maneuvers carefully over the wet leaves on the dark and quiet streets of Queens toward home. A blue and white NYPD cruiser pulls alongside after Gary makes a very slow left turn. Not a flicker of concern crosses his face. It is virtually impossible for a New York City cop to get a ticket for drunk driving from another cop, unless there is an accident. This was the way he knew it would be: the respect, the adventure, the stories, the friends for life.

Gary is doing great on the job, but not so well at home. Just two days ago, on a dripping Wednesday afternoon while Gary was working a four-to-twelve, Lisa moved out. She took Erica and Zach with her to her sister's house and now refuses to come back. And there is not one person in her whole family who is sticking up for Gary, telling her that she should try to work it out. True, she is white and he is black, but color never seemed to make a difference before. Now Gary is beginning to wonder. How is it that her brother-in-law and her mother, whom he has taken to calling a "master hypocrite," can turn on him like that? It is as if they are glad to be rid of him. There have been arguments. Sure, Lisa was still mad because he stayed away the day that Zach was born after they argued over the boy's name. But you'd think that should be washed away by now. Then there was that time in the spring when he had the collar with the two teenagers he chased into an apartment. He had the perps, but no stolen property, no weapon. He called one of the kids' mother at work and she told him he could search the apartment if an adult neighbor was present. He found the stolen wallet. He found the gun. That collar was too beautiful to hand over to another cop, wedding or no wedding. But that was all in the past.

Gary parks the Dodge on the silent street and walks up the driveway to the side entrance to his empty apartment. He scoops up Erica's tricycle with one hand, unlocks the door with the other, and steps carefully down the steps in the dark.

The separation stretches from days to weeks. It's not fair. Lisa has no responsibilities at her sister's house. No wonder she likes it there. A lot of her problems have nothing to do with him, he reasons. She had a tough childhood. Gary remains supportive. Whatever she wants to do is all right. He buys a book on codependency, goes for a visit with Lisa to her grandfather's grave. What good does it do? It seems that every week they are getting further apart.

When Lisa first left, Gary sampled the single life, and didn't like what he found. There were a few halfhearted interludes, a cute Dominican woman in the Brookline Houses with a white Caddy and a big laugh. Gary is young, good-looking, a little shy. He will do all right with the girls, just as he did before. But he is a family man now. He pines for the folded clothes and the meals on the table. He wants nothing more than his wife and kids, happy and under one roof.

That will take money. Collars for dollars.

J.R. is gone too. An interview he had taken for the detective squad two years ago bears fruit, and he is off the midnights and bound for the Bronx squad. Gary calls over a couple of times and leaves a message, but gets no call back.

One afternoon at the PSA a week after J.R.'s transfer, Sergeant Priore hollers over to Gary, "Hey, you see J.R.?"

"No," Gary says.

"Yeah, he was here to pick up his check. I told him you were downstairs."

"Really. That fuckin' J.R."

EDDIE ON THE BACK

Three A.M. in an apartment on the third floor of the Van Dyke Houses. Forty-five teenagers are squeezed into a pitch-dark living room. A huge gray tape player on the floor by the open window is humping a question to a hip-hop beat by the group Naughty by Nature: "Are you down with OPP? Yeah, you know me." Over and over the song asks, "Are you down with OPP?" meaning other people's property, props, or pussy. The tile floor is slippery with spilled beer. But it's too crowded for anyone to fall down. The raw smell of reefer floats from the bathroom. Shouts and laughter almost drown out the music, which is now a speed-word rap song, "Ghetto Bastard," also by Naughty by Nature.

When the woman who rents the apartment scheduled a week-end trip to Atlantic City with a couple of her card-playing girl-friends, her sixteen-year-old daughter began some preparations of her own. A sophomore at Thomas Jefferson, she couldn't re-sist the idea of throwing herself a belated sweet sixteen party. She spread the word. Kids in the school were talking about the upcoming affair for a week. The girl is not totally irresponsible, though; she has put the gold-painted table lamps in the hall closet and slid the couch into the bedroom and turned it against the wall so nobody can sit or spill anything on it.

A jam blocks the open front door and kids trail down the hall to the elevator. People are still arriving. There's been no trouble so far. Then the stairwell door swings open and a pride of young lions step into the mix. Bashim and the Howard Raiders are in the house. These are not even the real tough guys from Howard; Born Son and his Young Guns are too old for this kind of stuff.

This is the next generation, the ones who stood by, leaning on their bicycles, watching as Born Son fought his way to the top of the Howard heap.

Bashim, a "cock diesel" or burly, streetfighter, has cooled out in the past year. Always a smart kid, he is starting to show it after six years in high school. At five-eight, 240 pounds, he has finally found something to do with his bulk besides kick ass. Last spring, Carol Beck got him to join the football team and go to class. He's not starting trouble, and he is not carrying a gun anymore. But his boys are. Of the ten who arrive, seven are "strapped."

Before Bashim and his friends can get through the front door, there is some kind of trouble. Someone has brushed against someone else.

"I didn't say you *touched* me, son. I said you *stressin'* me," one of the originals at the party growls to one of Bashim's boys, and the Howard crew backs out, nice as you please. For once, the presence of so many guns seems to have a pacifying effect on the situation. Outside, one of Bashim's group decides to try out his burner. "When you get a new bis you wanna shoot it," Bashim says. "We go on the roof, in the park, wherever."

Bam bam bam bam.

It is 3:20 A.M. Gary Lemite is with his temporary partner in the Eddie sector car, three hours into his shift, cruising Brownsville looking for a collar, when the report of "shots fired" sings over the radio. The call is redundant, because shots are blasting through the limp air above the patrol car.

Some of the officers — sons of cops, like J.R.; grandsons of cops — were born to this business. Gary feels he was called to the job. A new rule says you have to have a couple of years of college to be promoted to sergeant and lieutenant, even if you place high enough on the test. Gary is not a good student or a good test-taker. He has no "hook," or connection, in the department. The only other kind of promotion open to him is the detective path, by appointment. He has decided that he's simply going to collar up so many criminals that the brass will have to reward him. The strategy has drawbacks. This is not a professional sports league, where performance is carefully calculated and rewarded. There are racial politics and jealousy, and there are the bullets.

Beep beep beep. On the tail of the staccato radio alert, used for 10-13s and serious crimes in progress, comes the voice of the dispatcher: "Numerous males with guns. Blake and Powell, no callback. K."

Before the fluttering message has died in the sector car, a flock of preteenagers spill out of the breezeway between the project buildings and scatter across the street. They bound like young deer. Then the automatic gunfire comes again. The sound is almost festive. The scene is like a carnival. But the *hut hut hut* of the gun is too mechanical for real fun. It is the chuckle of a cruel machine, a robot's laugh.

Two cops from the 73 who pulled up on Bashim and his boys around the corner are in pursuit.

"Adam-Boy, we're behind 'em . . ." The voice of the running cop from the AB sector car comes over the radio, weak and thready, as if he's crying.

"10-5 that location, Adam-Boy," Central responds. "You're breaking up," the dispatcher warns as the cop on the street begins losing contact.

"Eddie on the back," Gary hollers into his radio as he jams the Eddie sector car to a rocking stop to back up the cops in the AB car. He rolls out the door and sprints across the sidewalk, headed toward where he thinks the shots are coming from. The canyon walls of the clustered buildings produce echoes, and he is not sure exactly where the guns are until he sees a muzzle flash. He has learned not to run with his gun drawn unless he has to. Head up, right hand at his side, pinning his holster to his leg, and left hand holding the radio ear high, he charges into the flat face of gunfire.

A number of factors contribute to the strange sight of cops running into gunfire without taking cover. There is courage, and the fact that if a cop does it several times, he begins to feel he'll never be hit. There is also the fact that the kids most often do not fire at the police. They shoot at each other. They run from the police. The rule is not iron-clad.

Lemite continues his headlong plunge through Van Dyke as the last of the shots are heard ahead. A voice drifts down from a window high above: "Fuck the police." Life is so tough in Brownsville that people don't have the luxury of prejudice. If someone can be trusted, is willing to help, that person, white or black, cop or drug dealer, is quickly known as "good people."

Nevertheless, police as a group are simply despised here. The slightest confrontation brings the mantra "*Fuck* the police, fuck the *po*lice, fuck the po*lice.*"

Gary Lemite, in search of a future for himself and the family he wants to keep, and maybe of an intoxicating rush of adrenaline, charges down the walkways in pursuit of youths unknown.

Two kids fly through the back door of a nearby building with the 73 driver right behind. "Goin' in. Blake and Powell. 85 forthwith," the driver hollers, indicating that an officer is in need of immediate assistance.

"10-5 the *address*, Adam-Boy," Central yells.

The driver's partner, Sergeant Marino, dashes around to the front of the building to head the kids off if they run out that way. At the corner of the building Gary runs into him. Marino has worked this twelve-to-eight shift for the past decade. He is the best, a legend; they call him the Ghost, because every time there is a shooting he appears.

The shooters are inside. Marino's driver is bounding up the stairs from the back entrance. With guns drawn, Lemite and the sergeant wheel and barge into the lobby of the fourteen-story building. The sergeant heads straight to the stairs. As he enters the cinderblock stairwell, there is a clatter of steel on cement. A bull-necked youth with droopy eyelids emerges from the stairway and begins to walk casually out of the lobby. Lemite connects the clatter to him and orders him against the wall.

"Got a gun," Marino yells to Gary. He has scooped up the discarded weapon, and he continues upstairs. Gary tries to cuff the mumbling youth as Marino takes the stairs two at a time. In the second-floor hallway, Marino's driver is kneeling on the back of a small-boned teenager with his gun to the back of the breathless youth's head. The driver knows there is more than one gunman around, and he hasn't heard or seen his partner in half a minute. He howls, "Raise my partner, raise my partner" into his radio, like a man searching for his wife in a shipwreck.

Downstairs, Lemite is having trouble with his prisoner. There is the smack and thud of bone on flesh, grunts. Gary's partner arrives and dives on top of him and the kid, and they wrestle on the floor. Soon reinforcements flood the lobby and the pile gets larger. In an attempt to get a shot at the kid, the cops on the outside throw stomps and wild punches. Gary and his partner get the worst of it.

Bashim and his boys gather outside to watch through the window. Their guns are safely hidden on top of car tires, where the cops don't look. Twenty black youths study the fifteen white officers and the café-au-lait Lemite.

"Those vests won't stop a .357," a kid warns a pair of cops who are just arriving.

The kids eye the heavy youth who is being dragged roughly to his feet. The second teenager is brought downstairs by Marino and his driver. Marino produces the gun, a futuristic semi-automatic .22 Intratech machine pistol with holes in the barrel, ostensibly to cool the weapon down but really, as one Housing officer puts it, "so that when the guy starts pumping it on the corner, all these sparks start coming out and he looks like a real gangster." There is also a cracked plastic banana clip with thirty rounds in it.

"You ain't had a burner," Bashim yells, hefting a forty-ounce bottle of beer in one hand and pointing with the other at the slender youth just brought down from the second floor. "Punk. Lettin' the cops think you got a gun. I'm gonna fuck you up." Bashim curls his scarred upper lip. Later he will say, "I just said that shit to throw the police off."

All eyes are on the gun now. The officers handle it, and one cop seems to adjust a broken piece on the clip. "They broke it. It's inoperative," one of the Howard boys outside announces, with the implication that the inoperability of the gun is crucial to the charges its possession will bring. "They tryin' to fix it." The onlookers are right. If the gun cannot fire a bullet, the assistant district attorney will reduce the charge from a felony to a misdemeanor.

"Why cops always want to beat people up?"

A cop near the door overhears. "We're not here to trade blows with you people."

"'Cause they can't fight" comes the answer from one of Bashim's boys.

"Cops don't fight. They kick ass," the cop replies.

A thirty-year-old woman walks through the lobby as the police prepare to remove their two young prisoners. She turns to the gathering of surly boys. "Why don't you boys go out and look for some girls? Where are the girls?" But the boys are not interested in girls just now. Their eyes are still on the gun.

Bashim, cradling his bottle of brew, pretends he cannot get over the fact that the slim kid is getting credit for being a gunman when he isn't. "You think 'cause the cops got you, everybody think you got a burner," he scoffs.

A burner, a jammie, a bis (for "biscuit"), a kron, an oowop — there are a score of ever-changing names for the gun, the most recent scourge of Brownsville and East New York, the one single element that has changed a desolate existence to a nightmare. The gun is the drug of choice for the young here now, giving them release from the shadows of doubt to the white light of power and respect or death.

The herd of big young cops in dark pants and pale blue summer shirts moves out of the lobby and through the growing crowd of teenagers and residents. The cops have a hundred feet to go before they reach their cars.

Pop. Whoosh. Pop. Bottles are flying off the rooftops of the twelve-story buildings, shattering to fine dust on the pavement. The officers break into a trot, dragging their prisoners with them. "Brownsville ticker tape," a cop mutters as he guns his patrol car away from the project.

It's four o'clock in the morning. The PSA is deserted. Behind the steel bar at the front desk, Lemite's collar is playing the hardrock, won't give his name. The desk officer puts it simply: "You act like an asshole, you spend an extra couple days in the system. Put him in as a John Doe." The officer leans closer. "Who stepped on your face?" he asks.

"The kid saw everybody run upstairs, and he rolled off the wall before I could cuff him up," Lemite says simply, and leads the kid into the cell area.

Lemite then sits and fills out the endless papers, the voucher for the gun and ammunition, the on-line booking sheet, the complaint report, and a lab analysis form, used when the gun is to be tested to see if it can fire a bullet. He is methodical. He wants to be known as a cop who can do it all, not some street cowboy who can't handle his paperwork. It's almost 6 A.M. when he stands, flexes his knees, and snaps a Polaroid of the gun and the rounds piled up on the gray desk. It has become custom at the PSA with gun collars to display pictures of the guns, especially exotic weapons like the Intratech machine pistol, in a glass-framed board on a wall in the front room.

Gary is a young man, but the signs of middle age are already there. He's not a weight lifter like his tightly wound younger brother and cops Del Migliore and Jeff Desimone, and he is no runner like Kammerdener. In a couple of years he's going to be broad in the ass and fleshy, unless he has a change of habit. Tonight he's satisfied. After securing his gun in his locker downstairs, he hitches up his gun belt and strides across the room to where the young gunman is standing in his cell. Time for fingerprinting. Like young lovers, hand in hand, Gary and his prisoner cross the room to the alcove where the printing is done. There Gary's pale hand guides the kid's dark hand, pressing each finger in turn onto the fingerprint pad.

Next comes the ride down a deserted Atlantic Avenue to Central Booking, on Gold Street, near downtown Brooklyn. The kid in the back seat says nothing. Every few minutes he winces. His cuffs are fastened behind him, and they are tight, digging into his wrists every time the car lurches over a pothole.

There are dozens of prisoners on the benches in the second-floor holding area at Central Booking. "Step along. Go to the door and stop," an officer orders a row of men who are handcuffed to a long chain. They are heading out of the building to be arraigned.

It will be afternoon before Lemite meets an assistant district attorney, who will determine the charge in the case. He knows enough to make his account short and sweet. If the kid has warrants, he will remain in the system. If he has no warrants and the ADA does not like the gun-in-the-stairwell story, he might be on the #3 train back to Brownsville by nightfall.

At 3 P.M., Gary is asleep on a sheet of newspapers on a bench in a waiting room. There is a hit on the fingerprints. An old rape warrant drops on the kid, who turns out to be seventeen years old, and the ADA decides to stick with the gun charge. Gary smiles faintly as he trudges over to the A train stop. His feet are hot and damp, his eyes dry and red. He has been awake for more than twenty-four hours, and he will have to change trains to get back to Brownsville. But he got eight hours' overtime and he caught a bad guy.

Gary is scooping up guns off the street at a rate that has some cops calling him Magnet and others Lead-ass, because they are sure he is going to get shot. But Gary is not about to make any stupid mistakes. And because they are best for overtime, he sticks with the midnight tours, when Kammerdener and Lenti are home with their families. But the numbers are speaking for themselves, and Gary is given the quarterly achievement award for excellent police work. A color photograph of him in full dress uniform hangs just inside the front door of the PSA.

OLD-TIMERS

Outside, it is breezy-warm. Inside, the Brownsville Recreation Center gym is flush-heat, full-sweat. It is late Saturday afternoon, in the third week of July. There have been five basketball games already, from the Pee Wee to the Legends Old-Timers game, and now the finale, the Pro Am, where the young stars of the neighborhood and players who have not made it to the NBA, who play in the minor league or in Europe, mix with the famous guys. Together, they strut their special moves for the hometowners.

Fly Williams threads his way down court, pounding the basketball on the golden gym floor. With a grimace, he pushes his ruined body into the air and casts an arcing jump shot toward the basket. The ball careens off the rim. As both teams charge past him toward the other basket, Fly stands rooted, glowering at the hoop of iron as if it has wronged him grievously. The packed crowd roars approval of his antics while Fly heads to the sidelines, calling for a substitute. He settles on the bench with a backhand wave to his admirers.

"He only has one lung, you know," a grandmother tells the people in her area of the bleachers. Like Rasputin, Fly is mad, connected to a higher power, and indestructible.

The game is the highlight of Old-Timers' Week in Brownsville, seven days of events that begin with a parade from the Betsy Head Pool to the storied Brownsville Recreation Center on Linden Boulevard and a "reunion night" featuring impersonations of Nat "King" Cole, Sam Cooke, and Billie Holiday. No rap songs or hip-hop. This is the generation born to the folks

100

who led the black migration to Brownsville in the fifties, the women and men who grew up in the Ville when it was a mixed neighborhood.

This basketball tournament is sponsored by Jerry "Ice" Reynolds, of the Orlando Magic. The shirts he donated for the occasion bear his name. Earlier in the day he emerged from his Lincoln Continental, a six-foot-eight prince bouncing a baby in his hands.

But if Ice is a prince, then the king, the failed and wicked genius of the basketball court and of the Ville, is Fly Williams. At his best, in his prime in the 1973–74 season, the Fly was the third leading scorer in the country, when he played for Austin Peay State University. At six-foot-five, he was quicksilver. He could rise off the ground like a fool, extend like a rubber man, and shoot the ball like a machine. He had long arms and moves unknown. But like Sharron Corley, Fly was addicted to attention. As his short professional career with the St. Louis Spirits, of the American Basketball Association, crashed, he continued to unfurl his streak of insanity like a banner.

Insanity plays differently in places like Brownsville, where the authorities are uninvolved in the commerce of daily life. When people are poor and live in close quarters, when the perks are few and the competition great, there is an undeniable advantage in being known as crazy. It grants a person space. No one wants to lock horns with a madman. There were times when Fly would drive his Rolls-Royce to the Howard Houses basketball court and leave it in the middle of the street, creating a traffic jam while he watched a game. Whether it was an act or not, the folks in the Ville appreciated the virtuosity with which Fly played the part. They simply loved him and his game. Fifteen years later they still do.

Fly is here to play, but just a little. On the bench, he is still gasping for breath after five minutes of rest. He is beloved not because he was a success, and not even because he was such a spectacular failure. Like Leonard Bernstein in a crowd of music lovers, Fly draws people to him because he was once *chosen*, once stood with the gift glowing in his hands, and everybody remembers.

It is easy to believe that Born Son and his Young Guns are devoured by the love of money. They themselves will say that cash money drove them into the street with their "eightballs," brown paper bags full of crack vials, and their semiautomatic weapons. The motto of Sharron's LoLifes, scrawled over courthouse stairwells, is "Money, ho's [women], and clothes." But it's not the truth. Ice Reynolds, still out on the Brownsville Recreation Center court running like an antelope, is a millionaire and a successful pro ball player. But he will never have the aura in the Ville that Fly has. Now, after becoming addicted and surviving a shotgun blast to his back, Fly sits on the sidelines, wizened and stooped but still deeply admired for his gift, and for the fact that he never really showed that gift to the world. He cared more to flaunt it in the Ville.

Waves of admirers flow Fly's way as the game continues, and there are a hundred small claims on him. He folds over in pantomimed collapse. "I'm takin' names," he says. "I'm not kickin' ass, but I'm takin' names."

He can talk that talk, but he cannot play that game anymore. He contents himself with shouted bons mots from the bench. A claque of spectators is more interested in his reaction to the game than the court action itself. A diesel-powered six-four forward vaults to the rim. "The parade passed you by," a fan shouts to the slouched Fly. "I seen that. I seen that," Fly assures the crowd. The move was nice, though nothing like the buccaneer game Fly used to play.

One fan, sucking on a forty-ounce beer in a wet paper bag on the far sideline, isn't having it. He strides across the court during a time-out and confronts Fly. He is angry, and it doesn't have anything to do with Fly's decrepitude. Everybody falls apart. The harder you live, the faster you crumble. Apparently, the man is upset about truth. In Brownsville the truth is important. The wider world is full of hype; people with nothing to offer get rich and famous off the lies. But Fly Williams was always the real deal. Now he isn't. He should not be playing the game.

"You're a fake," the man sputters to Fly's face, "a fucking fake."

Fly screws up his face and waves the man off. He is too old, too cool, and too tired to deal with this.

"That's an old-timer now," a fan yells in Fly's defense.

"I can't hang out," Fly announces to the crowd. "I'll leave the drivin' to y'all." With that, he retires from the court and heads out the door, followed by three or four fans, who keep a respectful distance.

The weekend is a revelation. The people in Brownsville, the folks of the previous generation, are warm and happy. There are hugs and laughs all around. "Don't be fooled by Brownsville," an old-timer warns. "If you take a fast look, all you see is bad things. You stay around a while, you'll see the good things. This is a community that comes out in shifts."

Most days Brownsville is no place for old men. Very few elderly or even middle-aged people ever walk the streets here. The ones who do shuffle with children or sit on benches. The church folks, slow-moving gents and women in exultant hats, come out on Sunday mornings, and in the summer, here at the old-timers' activities, the giddy survivors emerge for an entire week. Whenever these people gather, an observer would swear that he was in a small happy southern town where the conversation is about family and barbecues. These are people who have arrived at this time and place with epic dignity and uncommon good cheer, who know more about right and wrong than an army of police and legions of judges.

Old-Timers' Week is the time when the history of the neighborhood comes to show its face to the present, like a vigorous grandparent leaning over the bed of a dying child. A block away from the newly renovated and spanking clean Recreation Center is New Lots Avenue, one of the most lawless and dangerous places in the country. The street is an unending drug bazaar. The ramshackle subway station above, New Lots, is a study in peril. Transit police rate the station one of the very worst in the city.

Basketball player Tony Jackson, the legendary St. John's University jump shooter, knows better than to venture onto New Lots. He and a retinue of his admirers gather around a fan of cars across Linden Boulevard and hold a tailgate party. But when guys like Smiley Smith, Big John Jocko, and Leroy Wright walk over to get a six-pack at the bodega on New Lots, junkies beg them for money as if they are tourists. These rare robust middle-aged men are outsiders in their own community.

Gita Malave, a lovely forty-three-year-old redhead with lofty cheekbones, is here with a boyfriend who coaches the old-timers' basketball team. She has lived in the Ville for twenty-three years but remains aloof from the palpable good cheer. She is standing outside on the cement ramp to the gym when her sixteen-year-old son Kendall appears, his T-shirt soaked with sweat and his eyes glittering with accomplishment.

"Mom, who am I?" he demands.

"You mean, what are you?"

No, no, Kendall presses. "Check out the hat. Who am I?"

Gita eyes her son's cap, with a Chicago Bulls emblem bordered by glittering rhinestones. Kendall has fifteen or so different sports hats he has decorated.

"You're a clown?"

"Don't fool around, Ma. I'll give you a hint. I was bustin' dudes at the park. Goin' between my legs with the ball and usin' dudes." Kendall pauses and points an index finger at his chest. "The kid was just usin' 'em. Couldn't nobody hold me."

"Ahhh." Gita sighs, lighting a cigarette.

"Don't be smokin', Ma. Secondary smoke is gonna shorten my career. Who am I?"

"O.K., you're Michael Jordan, all right."

"You're close. I am Jordan, yes. But they call me *Baby Jordan*." Kendall howls and sprints off into the afternoon sun.

"How come they don't have something like this for the kids?" Gita grumbles, watching her son move off. "All this food around and they don't even have a free hot dog to give to a kid. Half these people don't even live here anymore."

Gita is not really thinking about recreation anyway. Ever since she started college, she thinks about little besides her courses in legal studies and her six children, aged thirteen to twenty-four, all of whom live at home.

There is a bittersweet taste to this week. It isn't just that these people have lost what used to be a hometown; that has happened to almost everybody. It is not even that the ones who have stayed here live under the threat of the gun. It is that the youths who are growing up, the ones who skulk around the edges of the proceedings, hanging around, who keep showing up at the Summer League games run by Jocko Jackson, looking to make their mark, trying to find a place out of the line of fire, will never have the memories that these aging men toss back and forth, that they live from. For the boys who survive, what will there be to look back on?

"They're animals," Eddie Hammil says as he drives by 295 Dumont, casting a cold eye up at the lookout in the fifth-floor window. "And the grandmother is the worst of the lot."

Kate Worthy is not at the old-timers' festivities. Instead, she is sitting on a bench in front of 295. She and her husband moved in 1951 from a small town called Walterboro, near Charleston, South Carolina. They settled in Brownsville, and when their entire street was condemned they relocated to Bed-Stuy. They headed back to Brownsville as soon as an opening came up in the projects in the late seventies.

With her pastel pants suit and sensible crepe-soled beige shoes, Kate looks like any other retiree. She is not a large woman, nor is she slight. She keeps a pack of Kools in one pocket of her pink double-knits, a supply of heart pills in another. She is quick-witted and feisty, nobody's fool. Her coppery face droops; her eyes are suspicious slits. But Kate can be charming.

The cops have another view. "She's a perp," Bobby Schulman insists. "We have her name on the registration of at least two of the vehicles the gang has, an Audi and another one."

Kate is probably not actively involved in the crack operation, as the Housing cops say, but her loyalty is to her family, hard as that may be. "I don't know what happened," she moans. "They just won't listen. They're always running in and out. I told them so many times to keep the door closed."

"Keep the door closed" — a pitiful solution, to be sure. But even the Housing police have developed a mania about the front door of Apartment 5AB. They have tried everything they can think of to slip past the lookout and burst inside to catch the Worthys with the goods. A couple of times they have been successful. A bantam rookie actually scaled the bricks in the back of the building like a rock climber, surprised the lookout, and barreled inside. He didn't find the cache of drugs he was looking for, but he was the talk of the PSA for months.

While the cops are trying to get in, Kate is trying to get out. Her application for retirement housing out of Brownsville is on file and she can hardly wait.

"It's just crazy," she says. "I went to court four times this week. Everybody's in and out of jail — Lennie, Edward, Randolph. They send me letters. When I have a little money, I send it to them for commissary. I do love to go to Atlantic City with my little money, though. I haven't been able to go for some time. Those slot machines talk to you. They do," she says with a sly smile.

Kate seems resigned, strangely removed from the collapse of her family. When did she lose control, what did she do wrong? There was a series of shockwaves. While the rest of America was living through the Vietnam War, a heroin epidemic was lashing the black ghettos. The future was written for the Worthys when Kate's daughter Brenda married a heroin user named Ray Asbury. The change from hope to daily disaster came on fast. Soon Brenda was an addict. The couple had five children: three boys and two girls, Renee and Omean, both of whom had children before they were fifteen. All those kids grew up in a festering world of syringes, dope buys, strangers, and stupefied parents. The second wave was AIDS, which killed Ray Asbury at the age of forty-two in 1988. Brenda was stricken with the disease a year later. Renee and Omean and their children were on their own. The third wave, crack, blew the doors down. Into this chaos rolled cars loaded with weapons purchased from gun stores in Virginia, brown boxes packed with guns delivered by mail order.

"I can never get a good night's sleep," Kate says now. "They come running up the stairs. There are so many faces I don't know who's who."

Kate is interrupted by one of her granddaughters, who is sitting beside her on the bench. "Tell about the time they was gonna shoot Randolph."

"Couple of guys," Kate recalls. "I never saw them before and they came upstairs and they had Randolph on the stairs, pointing one of them big guns, I call them cowboy guns, at him, talking about they were gonna kill him. I told them to get their behinds out of the building." Miraculously, the gunmen obeyed the seventy-year-old Kate.

The contradictions of living with the bitter smoke of the guns are stunning. Teenage gunmen are sent on their way by unarmed grandmothers. Even Kammerdener exploits the maternal factor. The "safe homes" antidrug program changes locks and provides some police presence in targeted buildings, but the linchpin of the initiative is the tenant representatives, most often mothers and grandmothers, who are stationed in the lobbies. Their job is to tell the drug dealers to move on. A lot of the time it works. The women have known the kids since they were little, and the natural instinct is to take the business somewhere else.

But Kate isn't even holding her own. She knows the chronology but not the reasons. "It all started with Noren and the mailbox. The drugs. The kids just got used to it."

The following Monday afternoon, DEA agent DeJong and Officer Schulman, dressed in white overalls and caps, disguised as Housing Authority painters, heave a large plastic bin on rollers up the ramp into the lobby of 340 Dumont Avenue, in the Tilden Houses. No one pays them any mind. Painters go in and out of the building regularly to work on vacated apartments. But Schulman and DeJong don't have paint supplies with them. Instead, another federal agent sits in a fetal position inside the bin. Upstairs, in an empty eighth-floor apartment, Schulman, DeJong, and the third agent set up shop. Schulman adjusts the video camera, DeJong squats on an overturned twelve-gallon drum and produces a notebook to record drug activity, and the third agent watches the door for trouble. There are no tables, couches, or mattresses in the apartment, just four walls and a window that looks directly down on 295 Dumont Avenue, across the street.

"You say you wanted to see what it's like to live in the projects?" Schulman quips to DeJong. "Now you got your chance."

For twenty hours, Schulman intermittently tapes the drug traffic at the door of 295 Dumont. But he isn't just looking for sales. He has plenty of those. He is watching for Born Son, Tai Stick, Supreme, or Bang, trying to build a case to prosecute the Young Guns as an ongoing criminal enterprise. Hour after hour, he witnesses nothing but a numbing parade of crack customers. Every six or eight hours, one of the younger Worthys shows up on a bicycle or in a gypsy cab, presumably to resupply the dealer on the bench with crack vials, delivered from the spot where the drug has been cooked and packaged.

The room where the cops wait is stifling hot. Schulman is

propped on a beach chair by the window, shirtless but wearing a sweat-dampened powder-blue bulletproof vest. "Where the fuck are they carryin' the bombs?" he wonders, using the street term for resupply packages.

Halfway through the shift, a black federal agent, who has an easier time than whites getting into the building without arousing suspicion, arrives with a bag full of Chinese food.

"You couldn't think of anything else?" Schulman asks.

"That's all they got around here. Besides," the agent says, glancing out the window, "you got to live like the people you're investigating. Look."

Outside, across the street, a Worthy is arriving with a white plastic bag with red lettering, identical to the one the agent has placed on the floor. Schulman crouches by the window and trains his binoculars.

"I think Born Son and his boys are addicted to Chinese food. That's the third time today," DeJong says.

"Yeah," the agent guarding the door adds. "They're always going in and out of the Chinese restaurant in front of the Albany Houses, too."

"Fuckin' A!" Schulman exclaims. "They're bringin' the bombs in the *Chinese food containers!*"

For their next shift, two days later, Schulman, DeJong, and the third agent slip in the back door of the project building and head upstairs. Within an hour, they get good stuff. The cops have not only been trying to connect Born Son to the sale of drugs; they want evidence to prove that he is the manager of the operation. Bobby has been smart enough to stay away from 295 Dumont, but not today.

Schulman whistles. "Born Son himself."

Just before noon, as an insistent wind tells of an approaching squall, Bobby's black Pathfinder rolls down Dumont and stops in front of 295.

"Born Son . . . and out comes Tai Stick, and . . . holy shit, Bang," Schulman reports. A blue Honda Prelude pulls up behind Born Son, and the bruiser who has been handling security for the Young Guns steps onto the pavement. DeJong scribbles names furiously in his ledger while Schulman adjusts the camera and narrates the action.

"They're having a board meeting right by the bench. This is too much."

Bobby is talking and the others are listening.

"I'll bet somebody is runnin' right now to tell Ninja and his boys. This shit here is a message," Schulman explains. "Bobby's lettin' everybody know, 'Make no mistake, I am the man.' We might see some shooting."

But there is no trouble. The only commotion is caused by the police. Five hours later, in the early evening, as DeJong, Schulman, and the third agent prepare to quit the observation post, Schulman places a call to a sector car in the area. "Eagle's nest OP requesting a car stop on Dumont."

The Housing sector cars in the area know the deal. The patrol sergeant told them at roll call that Schulman and the agents at the so-called eagle's nest observation post might call for some kind of diversionary tactic so they could get out of the building unnoticed.

"9711 on the set. We'll make that stop. ETA 17:40."

In the middle of Dumont Avenue, just a few doors down from 295, the driver of car 9711 flips on his roof light and pulls over a hapless law-abiding Transit worker. Both officers approach the car with guns drawn. They order the occupant to step out of the car and place his hands on the roof while they make a show of checking his driver's license. Folks standing in front of 340 Tilden wander over to see what's going on. A handful of children trot out of the Complex to see. Even the slinger on the bench at 295 looks up to see what kind of mischief the "Five-O's," the cops, are up to now. All eyes are on the humbled driver and the two officers in the street as Schulman and DeJong and the other agent slip out the back door of 340 Dumont.

Old-Timers' Week is over but the summer is not. There is a huge tent going up near Sutter Avenue for an outdoor revival meeting. And a week later, National Night Out, a gospel fest on the floodlit ball field at Betsy Head Park, is sponsored by the 73rd precinct. The theme of the evening is "We've come this far by faith." Two hundred people venture out. Children frolic and tumble on the illuminated grass while local choirs and a visiting contingent from out of state kick up a holy ruckus on the temporary stage. The guest choir, some forty strong, ends the night. The rich and reverent tones of the group are interrupted by individual members seized by the spirit, who bound onto the center of the stage, inspiring the chorus behind to a devoted frenzy. Soon the plywood stage under their feet is threatening to buckle. No less than a hundred police officers from the 73rd and 75th and the PSA 2 stand guard. The lights are still on when the out-of-towners' charter bus rumbles away and the police pack up and roll off. But no one lingers in the park.

"I NEVER MET THE MAN"

Gary is at roll call, chatting with Marlene Pemberton, a short black officer with her hair twisted in braids and a talent for bawdy language, which makes her popular with the troops. Marlene leans to Gary's ear.

"I heard that guy is in the Ku Klux Klan."

"Who?"

"That guy, over there, anticrime, the one with the long greasy blond hair. He's got a key chain with like a KKK emblem. No shit. Check it out."

Gary shrugs. "Really?"

"You goin' to the Guardians meeting Friday?" Marlene asks, referring to the black police association.

"Where is it?"

"It's uptown, in Manhattan. You should go," she advises. "You know we got no hook. I don't know about you, but I want somebody watchin' my back on this job."

"I'm watchin' your back, baby."

"I'm not talking about my beautiful ass, Lemite."

"When they hold the meeting in Brooklyn, I'll go," Gary promises.

The sergeant is talking. "Take the riot helmets with you to your post, have them in the RMP. No excuses. And there will be inspection tomorrow. I have said it before, and I will say it again: anybody with the Indian head missing from his hat is getting a complaint." There are snickers from the assembled officers. On the front of each officer's hat is a silver medallion with the figures of a pioneer and an Indian. In an obscure protest gesture, possibly in the spirit of ethnic solidarity, some cops have taken to decapitating the Indian.

PSA 2 is not a Fort Apache, not a crumbling antiquated wreck of a structure, staffed by cynical, burned-out, cooping racists. Instead, it is a crisp, well-lit place, which under the administration of Deputy Inspector Kammerdener is known for its cleanliness. "You can eat off the floor in the officers' lounge," a visiting captain gushes.

When Officer McLean was shot, Kammerdener knew that the brass would be arriving for the memorial. The heavy hitters would be there. So he arranged for the walls of the PSA to be paneled, but only as far back as the brass would be likely to walk. Downstairs and around the corner, where the officers' TV room and lockers are, the paneling peters out. For the memorial, Kammerdener had someone research, write, and frame short histories of the Brownsville landmarks on which the projects are built. One plaque says that the Howard Houses are built on a spot where a man named Howard ran an inn that served as a stagecoach stop in the eighteenth century. Kammerdener also made sure that the chiefs were fed. According to the grumbling rank-and-file, one of the female officers was given time on the clock to bake cupcakes. When they proved a big success, she was given a department commendation for her "police work."

The Housing police force has a history that is starkly different depending on whether it is told by a black officer or a white one. In the opinion of many of the white officers and a segment of the public, the original, almost all black Housing police were unmotivated and undisciplined. According to this way of thinking, the PCOs, or foot patrolmen, assigned to the various project complexes were ne'er-do-wells who signed in, headed over to their project area, and either read the paper for their entire shift or hung out with their girlfriend. The aim for these guys, the story goes, was to blend into the background and avoid trouble at all costs.

Larry Phillips, a retired black PCO and former community affairs officer at the PSA 2, is livid over that reputation. "What is the stereotypical black man like? Lazy and incompetent. What were the Housing patrolmen supposed to be like when the force was predominantly black? Lazy and incompetent. C'mon.

Nobody is going to buy all that. Now, when the force is more and more white, it's getting more and more competent and more dedicated. Blatant racism. Every time the white men show up, they call it a renaissance."

Phillips rankles when people talk about community patrolling. "We were out there alone in those days." The officers did not have the radio communication they have now. Even if they did, according to Phillips, they were reluctant to use it. Phillips explains that the white officers in the old days were not often PCOs. They were in the car, riding around with the sergeant. "If we called for assistance, an 85, we did it rarely, because when these guys showed up they didn't know how to treat people, and they made matters worse. We were alone, like a sheriff. We had guys who were the best. But they didn't go up the ladder because they didn't have the hooks. Same story all over. Ask people about Al Lane," Phillips says, referring to a legendary black detective. "Kammerdener was always second to Al Lane, and it still drives him crazy."

When Gary Lemite made out his wish list at the police academy, he used all his wits. He had heard that you don't usually get your first choice, so he picked a precinct that was near his Elmont home, just across the Queens border. His real desire was for the superactive PSA 2, so he put it second, and it came through, just as he thought it would. It was the first of many plans that have worked out for Lemite in his short career as a Housing cop.

The cops at the PSA are not sure how to treat the easygoing Gary. "Hey, that guy Lemite," a white sergeant wonders, "is he black or what?" Gary's mother's father was Lebanese, her grandmother half Italian, half black. Gary's father was one quarter Indian, one quarter French, and half black, looked like a Spaniard. Both his father and his mother emigrated from Haiti in their late teens.

Gary grew up in Island Park, a white community on the south shore of Long Island, just north of Long Beach, between the Oceanside dumps and Reynolds Channel. "The place is one hundred percent white," jokes Mike Scully, a real estate agent in Island Park who was one of Gary's boyhood friends. There is more than some truth to the statement. Gary, his mother, and his brother could easily be taken for Cuban or Lebanese. The Lemite family was tolerated in Island Park because they had money and they were so light-skinned. There were other reasons why the Lemites got along so well. The assertive Serge Lemite spent hours on the telephone, wrote letters, and stood up at town meetings to speak his mind with his exotic Haitian accent. "Nobody wanted to take him on," Mike Scully's father remembers.

"We never thought of Gary as black," Mike's mother insists. "We really didn't. He was just one of Mike's friends. That was it. The only comment I ever heard was when somebody said, 'Who is that beautiful black woman living over on Long Beach Road?' That was Gary's mother."

Gary's mother has the same sand-pale skin as her son. From the frozen cleanliness of her upstairs quarters, it is apparent that Mrs. Lemite is not an easygoing woman. Whenever she came down to Gary's basement apartment before Lisa left, she leveled a dangerous eye at her mischievous granddaughter, Erica. "When we were kids and me and my brothers did something bad," Gary recalls, "my mother would make us get on our knees in the bedroom and stay that way until my father came home and gave us the belt. All we could do was stare at the floor and wait."

Gary's father had a successful construction business, Lemite Building Co., with a dozen trucks. Gary remembers that his father used to carry two bundles of shingles on his back, when most roofers could only handle one. "And he always had a wad of bills that he would pull out. Just like a drug dealer." Serge was busy, but he found time to ride bicycles and play soccer with his frisky sons in the back yard.

Gary spent his summers playing at a tranquil beach a block from his home, so close he could hear his mother banging a fork against a can to call him home. He passed the days with his friends, swimming underwater from pier to pontoon, playing shark and games of tag. "I could hold my breath forever. I would just wait at the bottom at low tide, about ten feet down. Then I would just go right past. I was a fish." As he got older, Gary took to the boats. His friends worked at the marina, and he would go joy-riding with Jamey, Marty, and Mike on the customers' boats when they were not around.

Gary gets along famously in the PSA because he has been running with a bunch of guys just like the officers since he was a teen. "Nobody messed with me and my boys in Island Park 'cause we were tight. It's such a small place. We used to go over to the Nathans' on Long Beach Road and kick the shit out of the guys from Oceanside, which is much bigger. We got over 'cause they had all factions in that town. We stuck together."

Gary grew up with almost no idea of prejudice in the middle of a racially restrictive community. In fact, for Gary, racism is mainly a curiosity. The only time he felt he had been discriminated against occurred when he and a friend were drinking beer behind the city building near the railroad station. One cop said they could drink there, but another cop gave them a summons. The town held a kangaroo court. Gary was ordered to pay a $50 fine, and the other kid got community service, cleaning up the sink at the fire station.

Sometimes Gary heard door locks click down when he walked through the parking lot of the Times Square Store near his house. "But I didn't blame them. None of it bothered me."

Island Park had no blacks, many people believed, because Senator Alfonse D'Amato kept it that way. When money was first allocated to Island Park by the Department of Housing and Urban Development, it was earmarked for minorities. D'Amato turned it down. Somehow, he managed to get the housing money designated for Island Park residents only. "Of course, there were no minorities in Island Park, so the houses went to people who knew somebody," Mike Scully says. "Simple."

D'Amato and others worked hard to keep Island Park white. It was one of the things that kept the senator popular. "There used to be houses with black people in them," Scully remembers, "but Tippy — that's what we call D'Amato — got rid of them. He did all kinds of things."

Newsday reported that in 1971 D'Amato and Mike Massone, Island Park's superintendent of public works, conspired to get rid of twenty-five tenants they considered undesirable at 93 Quebec Road by using the excuse of a small fire to condemn the building. A bus was parked out front to pick up the tenants and take them to the Nassau County Department of Social Services, in Mineola. Scully recalls, "Massone ran through the building with a megaphone telling the people to get on the bus because they were going to get some kind of a payment from the county. The building was bulldozed within hours."

The people in the bullhorn eviction were not black, but the modus operandi of Tippy D'Amato was established. In 1975 twenty-one poor black families were evicted from 347 Long Beach Road after Island Park blocked the landlord's attempt to rehabilitate the property. There were more demolitions. The result was to reduce the black population in the town from 116 to 35 between 1970 and 1980, according to U.S. census figures, in a total population of 4,100. New York State Board of Regents data show that now one tenth of one percent of Island Park's school population is black: one student.

The only trouble the prosperous Lemite family ever had with the D'Amato-dominated town was when there were complaints about the Lemite Co.'s fleet of trucks being parked on the street. Serge Lemite would move the trucks into a parking lot until the pressure eased, then start leaving them on the street again. "D'Amato came to the house and my father gave him handfuls of money. That happened a number of times," Gary recalls.

Serge had a lucrative business and a summer house in Long Beach. But when he was in his early forties, things started to go terribly wrong. At first it was small things. Serge was forgetful and distracted. Then he started to hear things. He began to believe he was Jesus. There was a short stay in a hospital, and life went back to normal for a while. Then there was another episode. Serge began wandering around the neighborhood knocking on doors, praying on people's front steps. He sent telegrams to the president. The stays in the hospitals got longer, the periods of sanity shorter. Three years between breakdowns, then two years, then just months. Customers and suppliers started taking advantage of the frequent lapses, and the construction business went into debt. The business was lost. Gary's father succumbed completely and entered a home. Gary was eighteen.

Gary Lemite has the Long Island accent and body language of a white cop. His legs hyperextend when he straightens them and he fondles his small potbelly. "Gotta go on one of those Slim-fast diets," he says unconvincingly.

In this society, he is called a black man. But he doesn't see things that way. "Gary doesn't identify with his race," a sergeant at the PSA remarks. Gary wants to make it on his own because he's the best cop, not because he's a member of a minority group.

It's difficult to sort out the right and the wrong of his attitude. It is an affront to some of the black cops, especially the older ones. "I have heard about him — he's a hotshot," a retired black cop says. "I'm glad I never met him." For black people conscious of their second-class status, defections like Lemite's are simply unforgivable. They believe he is simply currying favor with those in power. Lemite, whose buddies are both black and white, insists that he is refusing handouts because of his race. More important, he feels he has talent. He is sure of his memory, his eyesight, and his judgment. "He knows a hell of a lot for a guy with as much time on the job as he has. But he doesn't know as much as he thinks he does," a supervisor says. Maybe the best way to understand Lemite's position is to imagine an art lover who finds that he has the gift of color and stroke, a connoisseur who discovers that he can create. Gary is a police buff who believes that the potential to be a great cop resides within him. How can he be faulted for dismissing group politics and special-interest considerations? Perhaps his great fault is that he has no sense of tragedy — a gift he may be better off without in Brownsville.

When Gary does attend a Guardians meeting, he sits quietly in the back row, behind Lonnie Hayes. When it is over, he walks out mumbling. "All they did was complain about 'the man.' Who the hell is this man? I never met the man."

After the meeting, he heads over for a couple of beers at Cheap Charlie's. It is three o'clock in the morning when he pulls in front of his mother's house in Elmont in his faded blue Coronet. He stoops slightly to enter the basement door. Inside, he digs his .38 service revolver from under one side of his belt and his .38 backup gun from under the other side and lays them on top of the narrow glass-doored cabinet in the living room, where Erica and Zach cannot reach them. Lisa never liked the spot. "If somebody breaks in the house when we're asleep," she always said, "he'll have the gun before you do."

Gary would like nothing more than to move his family back to Island Park. Last year Mike Scully offered a deal, $130,000 for a handyman's special. Gary could have rented out the top floor to a tenant to defray the mortgage payment. But he needed a $15,000 down payment, and he just didn't have it. Within a year he should have enough for a deal like that. It would be great there. No crime. Then Gary remembers that his wife may never come back. He sits on the side of the bed for a long time before he switches off the light and tries to sleep.

HELL NIGHT

Saturday night in late August, just before 1 A.M., and according to Vanessa's way of looking at things, the party is a drag, the boys in attendance hopelessly uninspiring. There are two parties in the neighborhood tonight; coming to this one was Vanessa's cousin's idea.

"This is corny," Vanessa complains.

"We out," her cousin replies.

The two girls prepare to leave the party and walk several blocks to the other one. But as Vanessa and her cousin step out the door, they catch sight of hazel-eyed, dreadlocked Frank, Sharron's friend and fellow LoLife, heading in. The girls reach the sidewalk and slow their step.

"Did you *see* him?" Vanessa gushes. "Girl, I ain't goin' nowhere, if it's somewhere where *he* ain't there." The pretty teenagers double over with laughter. They delay a few moments in the night air, composing themselves, disguising their eagerness, before strolling back into the house.

Vanessa has been partying seriously, making the most of the fading summer vacation. She has not been getting much sleep; "been up for about two days," she tells her cousin's friend, the hostess, as she reenters the wood-paneled basement of the house on Saratoga Avenue, just a block from Sharron's home. Though she looks fine to everyone else, Vanessa is not at her best; she is raggedy and unkempt by her own standards. Her hair is losing its signature flip, her red-on-red nail polish shows tiny chips, her glowing white Fila sneakers are imperceptibly smudged. This is a girl who likes to do things right.

Vanessa attended Catholic school for all except the past two years. Now she is a senior at Wingate High School, and a pretty fair student, with college aspirations. But she is also an associate of the LoLifes, and though never a LoWife, she was a good friend of several members of the Crown Heights contingent before she moved to Brownsville. "I do feature Polo," she concedes, "but I will wear Guess."

Vanessa slips back into the party and dips into the bathroom, where she confers urgently with a friend. Her enthusiasm for Frank has been overwhelmed by even stronger stuff. "I walk in, lookin' like this, and there is this *Sharron* standing by the wall with his shirt off." Vanessa has known Sharron from around the way for the lady's man he is. Though she once did ask a friend to deliver a message to him that she liked him, she has never spoken to him directly, and believes that she is not really interested in him. "I have like five guys. I'm like that. I *keep* a lot of guys. Forget him." Still, she cannot explain why the party, which just a half-hour before was tired, the music beat, and the presence of supervising adults upstairs stifling, has taken on such an exhilarating flavor of possibility.

Soon Vanessa is dancing in the center of the low room, just an arm's length away from where Sharron lounges on the sidelines. Sharron makes eye contact, beckons for her to come even closer. She is tempted to comply but delays the move. "He's callin' me on the down low, so nobody can see," she whispers to her cousin. Sharron's idea is to make it look as if Vanessa has approached him unsolicited. More props. He keeps beckoning and Vanessa continues to resist, though the outcome is inevitable. When Vanessa does slide over and the two start dancing together to a reggae song, Sharron moves in very close and commences to sing. He doesn't sing along with the record. Instead he sets out on his own, crooning the words to a Bell Biv Devoe hit. "Tell me when will I see you smile again," he harmonizes, the notes struck softly an inch from Vanessa's ear. "I thought it was funny," she confides to her friend later. "I think Sharron is crazy."

Crazy enough to receive her telephone number. Sharron writes the number with an eyebrow pencil on a torn piece of notebook paper. But he doesn't call for five days. When he does, his voice sounds much deeper over the phone and Vanessa is not sure who it is. To remind her, Sharron sings again.

But the romance stalls. Not because of Chantal or Sheryl. Sharron has not phoned Sheryl since just after the time on the

#3 train when he came eyebrow to raised eyebrow with her, sitting with that boy she claimed on the phone was her cousin. Sad little Chantal is long gone. Friends of friends say she moved down South. It's that Vanessa feels that Sharron isn't serious. She just likes his company. "I'm not *talkin'* to him," Vanessa explains to her mother the Friday before Labor Day, as she prepares for Sharron's first visit, "and I'm not *with* him. I know what he's about, so we're just friends."

Sharron lives only two blocks from Vanessa, but when he leaves her house an hour after midnight on Saturday morning, he takes the long way around, so he does not have to walk past the Howard Houses. The golden moon above the project rooftops is cleaved precisely in half. The night is quiet, save for the low rumble of an airliner lumbering for Kennedy Airport to the east. In a few minutes, Sharron is safely home, the dangerous summer months all but gone.

A block and half from Sharron's home, Housing cops Danny Horan and Jimmy Galvin, a couple of Gary Lemite's friends on the midnight tour, are beginning their shift, sitting in their patrol car talking. Horan is a likeable, knowledgeable officer who should have become a sergeant or a detective years ago. He has white hair, a pockmarked face, and a family.

"I've been trying to save up money for a house, and I might not make it," he tells Galvin. "I'm coming to grips with that idea, but I gotta tell my wife and I haven't done it yet. Last week she tells me we're going to spend all day on Saturday shopping for furniture for the new house that she doesn't know we don't have the money to buy. So I start to tell her and all hell breaks loose. Ah, what the hell." He sighs. "What're we gonna do for dinner? You feel like Italian?" he asks after a pause. "You want Italian — pizza?"

Galvin ponders the proposal.

Horan is hungry. "What? Hamburgers?" he presses.

Galvin continues to consider.

"Possible 30," the radio blurts. "One male black armed with a sawed-off shotgun at Wendy's, Linden Boulevard . . ." Horan shrugs. The call is too far away for a quick response, and it's off-project. "So it's pizza then," he concludes.

Horan is heading down Sutter Avenue when a group of bare-chested Hispanic youths stampede past. They are in full flight.

121

A breathless runner carrying an aluminum baseball bat in one hand points behind him and yells, "Amboy" — Amboy Street, the home of the infamous Amboy Dukes. Amboy Street was the hard cradle that rocked Mike Tyson. At 176 Amboy is the building where Tyson grew up and raised enough hell to get locked up scores of times. But Amboy Street has calmed down. A number of buildings have tenant patrols. There is even a contingent of unarmed private security guards who watch over select buildings. Tonight none of that matters. Somebody is shooting bullets on Amboy.

At the light on the corner of Sutter and Hopkinson, Horan stops just two feet behind a car. It is a mistake for a police car to get that close to the car ahead at a light; in an emergency, it will take several moves to get around the vehicle. Both Horan and Galvin breathe quickly and hunch toward the dashboard, their eyes slicing at Amboy. Neither man speaks. They hear shots. Afraid that the siren will warn the shooter, Horan flashes the roof light, but the car in front doesn't move. Seconds slip by. Whoever is pegging shots on Amboy, a hundred yards away, won't be there long. Still Horan flashes the light. Danny Horan is simply not hell-bent. He favors what the police call "controlled response." Gary Lemite and some others — Del Migliore, for one — would have jacked that RMP backward and roared down Amboy Street looking for bullets. Horan himself would have done that if the call were a 13. He has medals to prove he is a brave man and a good police officer, but he has been answering these "gun run" calls nightly for ten years, and may well answer them for another decade. He is primarily concerned with going home to his family after work.

It's five seconds before the car in front moves up and Horan sweeps down the street to the site of the shooting, where a chubby young man is sprawled on the sidewalk, a puddle of blood around his head like a dark halo. No one else is on the street. The sweet smell of burned tire rubber lingers in the air.

Soon the residents of Amboy Street slip slowly back out onto the sidewalk they quit so quickly minutes before. No one speaks to Horan or Galvin. They whisper among themselves. The children talk loudest. The story comes out.

"Just rolled up and . . . sh', I ran."

"Why they gotta shoot up the whole street?"

"Witnesses. You spray, you run 'em off."

There is a grandmother upstairs with a superficial wound and a young girl who broke her ankle with a dive into a lobby.

The EMS people arrive and roll the body over. The man is still breathing, but the crowd lets out a "whoooo" of dismay when they see that the back of his head has been blasted loose. The victim wears blue jeans but no shoes. He lies directly under a sign that reads DRESS UP YOUR NEIGHBORHOOD — CONTEST WINNER — 1985.

Several youths use the top of a car like a high table and converse across the space. "The guy with the scar flipped on him," a kid says.

A purple banner with gold letters, drooping in the still night air, is strung across from second-floor apartments on either side of the street, welcoming people to the big end-of-summer block party the next day.

"People think you're a white cop from Suffolk you don't care," Horan mutters. "You see this, you care."

Twenty-eight-year-old Euston Brown, the "vic," is carted to Brookdale. Horan and Galvin sit on the crime scene and wait for the crime detectives to arrive. It will take some time. Somebody says that there are already five shooting victims in Brookdale Hospital tonight.

"I was over at Brookdale last week," Horan begins, lighting up a Marlboro, "and I saw my doctor there. This is *my* internist, the guy who I send my family to, and here he is in this fucking zoo. Right away I get worried and I start to wonder. I thought he was a good doctor. Now I'm starting to think he's a butcher. I go up to him and ask him what the hell he is doing. And he says he only has this one patient and the guy was admitted to Brookdale, so he makes the trip. I was relieved. Did you ever see what goes on there?"

Scalia pulls up. This is a half-pint sergeant who, the story goes, turned out the lights, put his feet up, and fell asleep behind the front desk in the Coney Island station house. Scalia was sound asleep when a shooting victim, trailing blood, staggered through the PSA and collapsed in the sergeants' locker room. Scalia was transferred to PSA 2 for his lack of vigilance. But tonight he is on his toes. In fact, he is on a little rampage. He walks past Horan to Galvin.

"Did you call me a dick on the radio?" he asks. It is the same question he has been leveling at the more irreverent officers on the midnight tour all night.

"No, Sarge, I've only got three years. I don't even know about doin' shit like that," Galvin answers earnestly. Scalia listens intently. Perhaps he is listening to the timbre of the voice rather than to the content of the denial. There is a small chance he isn't as stupid as he seems.

At five o'clock in the morning, the crime scene station wagon shows up and Jacques, a towering bald detective with a deep-sea voice, steps out of the car. There are still a handful of people on the street waiting for the festivities to start. The detective stretches and burps loudly. He stretches a long hairy arm and points his index finger straight down the street toward Livonia. "First Fortunoff's, right over there on Rockaway." Then he goes about his business. "Waited for him to flat-line. The kid went DOA at four," he announces as he heads back to his vehicle to get his gear. In a few moments, he's picking a spent round out of the tire tread of a parked car.

But the shooting isn't over tonight. There is a DOA at 315 Fountain, in the Cypress Houses. And, at the first touch of dawn, a call to the Brownsville Houses. Renee Worthy is sitting on the bench in the middle of the Complex. People are lined up behind the green benches. There is no banter. James Awe, twenty-two, nicknamed Boy, has been shot dead beneath the window of his mother's third-floor apartment. Plastic yellow and black crime scene tape, the hideous funeral bunting of Brownsville, mocks the death. "He don't never bother anybody," Renee says. The victim's stately, long-necked sisters stalk the grass around the body like Furies. His mother, a great crumbling woman, is on her knees. "What's going *ooon?*" she howls.

"They killed Boy," Renee announces softly to a late arrival. "Six people got killed this summer here. Spider, Mousey, Tango — you heard about Tango. They shot him in the mouth with an AK-47, some guys from Cypress. People shot Sean, Clinton, and now Boy. Six. He don't bother nobody. All he want to do is drink beer and joke around."

"They took him to Brookdale," Renee tells a woman in a white and purple sweatsuit.

The woman frowns. "Brookdale ain't shit. You take your baby over there, you wait from 8 A.M. to 8 P.M. on a chair in emergency. Nobody helps you. By that time, the baby's all better and you go home. Fuck a Brookdale."

"He dead? Oh, no." A woman passing by at 5 A.M. flinches as if she has been backhanded. There are people here who are numb, people who pull the triggers and sleep like babies, but others, the mothers and the sisters and the brothers, the fathers and the friends, hurt again and again.

Nine young men have been shot already in Brownsville and East New York tonight. Four are dead. A sickly sun is up now. Shots pop in the distance. Nobody moves. A woman approaches half a dozen uniformed Housing officers.

"There is an apartment. And there are these crackheads in there?" The woman pauses to see if the cops are following her account. No one nods or encourages her to continue. "And they have my fifteen-year-old daughter and they want her to suck their dick. Or they won't let her leave."

The cops slouch in careless fatigue. "Call 911," an officer tells her, and yawns. "Probably they wouldn't give her any crack," the cop says as the woman walks away.

The morning air is moist and sad. Unbelievably, there are more sirens. The cops stoop and cup their ears to their radios. A shooting at 1750 Prospect Avenue.

Officer Fahey and his partner take a ride over. "I hate Prospect," mutters Fahey, a square-faced cop with a crew cut who was almost killed last year by a perp whose gun jammed. "I call it NASA 'cause they're always throwing bottles off the roof."

When the two Housing cops arrive, the bus is just loading. Two hundred people congregate on the sidewalk in clusters of ten and fifteen. It is twenty minutes after a drive-by. Automatic weapons this time. The victim is not likely, but he cannot go to Brookdale. Brookdale is now full, closed to gunshot victims. The wounded youth will take the ride to Kings County Hospital.

Fahey pushes his way through the crowd and stands by the lobby door. More people drift outside and stand in eerie silent communion. Above, black faces fill a dozen windows high over the cement approach to the building. Fahey sneers. His arm snaps outward to describe the expanse of Brownsville. "They should dynamite this fucking place." Then, looking up at the faces above, he shakes his head in a spasm of disgust. "Fucking baboons."

KIDS' STUFF

It is Labor Day in the Cypress Houses quadrangle. The September sun is flashbulb bright. The picnic on the grass at the foot of the seven-story building at 1260 Sutter Avenue is just gearing up. Thirty-seven-year-old Nettie Epps and her mother, Connie, have done most of the cooking. Two card tables sit laden with chicken and potato salad, bottles of hot sauce and mustard, collard greens, hot dog rolls, and several huge bottles of discount orange soda. Husky chest-high speakers by the side of the building kick out the beat. The young girls walk around, arching their necks and rolling their eyes at the boys, whispering to each other. Trevor Epps and his friend Marcus McClain absorb the attention and rededicate themselves to music production. This is the way things should be. Sunshine, food, and family, good times under the eye of the elders.

Grandmother Connie stands in the midst of her friends, thinking how much she is going to miss the place. But she has been having such hard times. Six months ago she lost her husband. Now Nettie's sister is getting ready to die. "Has the cancer from the AIDS," Nettie reports flatly as she fires up the barbecue grill. "Been smoking crack for eight years. She couldn't stop crying when Mama left her in the hospital. But I told her, if you stay here and you start eating and you get your weight up, Mama will take you back. You ever see *Tales from the Crypt* on HBO? That's what my sister looks like." Connie just wants to go home to South Carolina. "She's a strong woman," Nettie says, "but this is too much." Connie can't take it anymore. This is to be her last day in Brooklyn. Tomorrow she will move down South.

The smell of charcoal and barbecue sauce wafts to the upper windows, and more kids and adults float down to the picnic. "Where the hell are those police?" Nettie whispers to Connie.

Nettie Epps has two sons. Donald is eighteen years old, Trevor sixteen. These are the dangerous years. Nettie has lived in Cypress for thirty years. She was in the sprawling fifteen-building complex when there were white people here, when you could get a ticket for throwing a piece of paper on the grass or shouting out a window. She raised her family here through the late eighties, when the A Team ran Cypress, when the building at 315 Fountain Avenue belonged to the gang, not the Housing Authority. The members of the A Team would double-park half a dozen brand-new Hondas along Sutter Avenue and go about their drug-dealing business, until one day a rival dealer, Chris Moore, firebombed the row of cars. "You could see the smoke all the way to the 81st," a cop from that Bedford-Stuyvesant precinct remembers. Then someone, perhaps Chris Moore himself, offered information to the police that sent the leaders of the notorious crew either to jail or, in flight, to Pittsburgh.

Moore seems comfortably situated now as the man, the owner of a lingerie shop on Euclid and Belmont, around the corner from Cypress. He keeps his gleaming white Jeep parked there and runs drugs through the projects the same way the A Team did a few years ago. Moore makes it all look easy, but nothing is easy in Cypress. A group of young pistoleros who call themselves the New A Team, including a kid named Nephtali, has been giving Moore trouble, taking shots at his slingers. As the A Team started to disintegrate, when the big guys went to prison, they put what was left of the drug business in the hands of young bloods like Nephtali. Sergeant Priore explains, "They tell a kid with no business experience whatsoever to run a complicated cash operation. Every time the kid has a problem, he shoots somebody."

If you ask a kid in Cypress if he is afraid he will be shot, he laughs. Many of the young men here have already been shot. Nephtali, who came up as a gun bearer for the A Team, has been shot three times. "We got teenagers walking around with colostomy bags," Priore says. Sometimes the cops come across youths with leg wounds but no bullet holes in their pants. They don't have holsters, and they simply shoot themselves by mistake.

*

127

Later this afternoon the #3 is a ghost train as it squeals to a halt at Pennsylvania Avenue. The breeze wafting in the doors of the subway cars is cool. The only person on board is Nigel, nick-named Indio, a cook in a Caribbean restaurant in Manhattan who is coming home to his place near the Cypress Hills Houses after a night of partying in the Manhattan clubs. Pink-eyed and bone weary, Indio nips into the corner bodega for a moment. When he comes out, he stands beneath the elevated tracks and studies the meager traffic for a cab, any kind of cab. He's careful how he waves for a ride. With half his paycheck left in his sock, he doesn't want to attract attention.

When Indio arrives on Sutter Avenue, he can hear the music from Nettie's picnic. He's careful not to let anyone see him han-dling the change from the $20 bill he has given the driver. Indio knows all about the Cypress Houses and East New York. He even knows Yellow Man, an albino who was arrested for pop-ping off eight rounds when Mayor Dinkins appeared to talk about gun control on the grassy common of Cypress last spring. "He went out duckin' like everybody else," a resident told a reporter.

Indio, who comes from Westmoreland in Jamaica, speaks with a billowing lilt, different from the Skilsaw whine of the cops and the shock speech of the youths here. "It is ruf dung deh," he says of Jamaica. "*Reeel* ruf. Di police come and beat ya up, and ya cyan sey nuttin'." It isn't the police Indio worries about here, it's the locals. He keeps his gun in that twenty-four-hour bodega near the subway stop. Picks it up when he comes back from Manhattan. Drops it off again when he travels back into the city.

When Indio is asked if he is scared he will get shot in Cy-press, he shouts, "Mi *been* shot, don't you know? I shot in the leg, mon. Mi ride me bike an alla da leaves start shake. It neh because a de wind. A wen da bullets. Bwoy in front get sixty shot inna im." Indio nods up and down vigorously to bolster his fantastic bullet count. He says he and his friends in Jamaica have a saying: "If ya wan dead, go a Cypress."

Indio is headed upstairs to sleep, but Nettie Epps isn't tired. She's in high spirits, presiding over her glorious picnic. Sergeant Priore, just starting his four-to-twelve tour, is on his way over to provide some security. "There was a party over there on Friday night and we had a man on the roof. Everything went all right," Priore muses on the ride over. "We'll just stop by for a couple of minutes."

The Labor Day picnic has been a righteous farewell to Connie. Nettie is delighted as she starts the cleanup, wrapping a piece of tinfoil around a package of uneaten hot dogs. The good food has slowed the kids down a bit, quieted the laughter too.

Three kids from the building across the sidewalk from 1260 Sutter show up quietly and assume position on the sweet-smelling grass under the sycamore tree fifty feet from where the big speakers are doing their work. Quani, a fifteen-year-old wild child, opens fire. *Bam bam bam bam;* the shots echo off the brick walls. Trevor Epps spins away and dives through a doorway as bullets chip off pieces of the brick face of the building and punch through glass in the front windows. Mothers and grandmothers dive and crawl, roll and run. But Marcus McClain is caught in the open. He yanks his own silverplated .45 from under his oversize T-shirt, but it jams. Probably a bad bullet, one of those refilled casings he bought cheap. He doesn't know how to rack the slide on the gun to eject the defective bullet and chamber a new one, so he pulls the trigger again, and again nothing but sickening clicks. The barrage takes only seconds. Quani walks over to a spot in front of the bullet-pocked speaker and fires one shot into McClain's head. Then he runs.

In just a few minutes Priore is on the scene. The shooters are out of sight, but they are still somewhere in the projects, and Priore orders a vertical search of the nearest buildings. Cypress has fifteen buildings, five thousand residents. Fifty officers are on hand in minutes, milling about. The body has been whisked away, the building entrance draped in the familiar crime scene tape.

"Excuse me," a girl asks matter-of-factly, "can I see if that is my brother in there dead?"

"Nobody's in there, ma'am," Priore answers.

Nearby, a nine-year-old boy whispers to another, miming the action shooting.

"Goin' on? Goin' on?" A young Hispanic woman with sweeping black eyelashes snorts at a young cop. "Smoke 'em up. Shoot 'em up. Beat 'em up. That's what's goin' on."

A slate-blue Plymouth Fury rolls across the sun-dappled

grass. The DTs get out. The black detective is wearing a gray suit and a salmon tie. Cypress sits innocently under the gaze of the DTs. Then Charlie Kammerdener, recently promoted to inspector, shows up from his home in Queens, just minutes away.

The residents are veterans of this kind of thing, but today they are shaken. Some reflect on the nature of things. A bearded man is distressed enough to look to a cop for the answers. He asks in Priore's direction, "What would you do? As a Caucasian man, you would know what to do."

The bearded man's friend shakes off that kind of thinking. "All black people aren't illiterate and all white people aren't intelligent. It just looks that way. We are not animals." He points at Priore. "They the ones who cover this shit up. Housing don't care."

A bruiser approaches the yellow tape and spits. "Little punks. This shit is outta hand."

Nobody knows what to do but Kammerdener. He eyes the complex craftily and points at a building. Three uniforms hustle over to search it again.

Everybody has had enough, but Trevor Epps is the one ready to do something. He steps up to the white detective. "I know who did it. It was Quani." He coughs the name up like a piece of spoiled meat. In a moment he is in an improbable position, sitting for all to see with his grandmother in the back of Priore's sector car, on the way to the PSA to give a full statement. He doesn't speak in the car, just rocks back and forth. Connie stares at the back of Priore's neck and moves her lips silently. The police car pulls off down the walkway as the assembled residents watch and wonder if the Brownsville aphorism "Snitches get stitches" will hold.

The sergeant drops Trevor Epps off at the PSA, where he disappears into the squad room with his grandmother. The black detective pulls up and heads toward the front door to interview him. Before he enters, he pauses on the street beneath the American flag. The detective is close to retirement. He straightens his stiff tie and thinks about days on a boat on a quiet river somewhere. "Hired in my twenties. Retired in my forties. Can't touch this," reads a police union bumper sticker on his private car in the officers' parking lot. But the detective will never be able to forget, really forget, Cypress. "Society has to know about this," he says before he leans on the glass door and disappears inside.

Priore returns to Cypress. When he gets there, Charlie Kammerdener is standing stock-still, squinting at the walls of Cypress as if he has x-ray vision. *Crash;* a shirtless youth bangs open the front door of 1200 Sutter, the building Kammerdener ordered searched, and flees across the grass toward Fountain Avenue with a cadre of heavy-legged Housing cops in hot pursuit. Priore jogs to his car and roars out of the narrow walkway onto Fountain Avenue.

"One male black. Fleeing on foot," Central repeats. "Can I have a location, K?"

Scores of cars from the 75th and PSA 2 sift through the streets around Cypress, but the kid has disappeared. "Perp magic," Priore mutters. The radio leaps; the kid bounds across the street ahead. You cannot help but admire his heroic stride. He wears state-of-the-art sneakers and blue jeans.

Gone again. Priore backs his car at breakneck speed down Sutter Avenue, peering down cross streets with the radio kicking out sightings.

"Belmont and Pine."

"Belmont and Euclid."

Suddenly, a cop who must be on foot is heard. His shouts are breathless.

"You're breaking up, K," Central says. The dispatcher cannot get a location of the foot pursuit through the barrage of static. There are jumbled shouts on the radio. The dispatcher commands, *"Units stay off the air."*

The kid is possessed by speed, covering a quarter mile in less than a minute. The radio is quiet for a moment and then it spits again. "He is on Pitkin. We've got a call from a resident. He's in a lot."

Then he is out again. The cops get fleeting glimpses of him between the one-family homes along the side streets. He is in the back yards. The police cars back up and squeal down another street. And then they get him.

"One under, Central," comes a voice as calm as the sky. A car from the 75th has him, with no shots fired. He's standing with his hands on the roof of a parked car, at the entrance to an open lot. His eyes are wide, his skin polished to a high glaze. He is surrounded by twelve white cops, all in uniform. A call comes over that the boss wants the kid to be held. Twenty seconds later, an unmarked car pulls up and a stooped man with dappled skin and gray hair gets out. His neck juts forward from his shoulders instead of up. He is an NYPD captain. He walks to where the kid is held, stands inches from the youth's face, and stares as if he is examining a specimen. The white man takes off his glasses and peers again. The kid, rankling under the insult of such clinical study, pulls his head back.

"Remember me?" the old captain asks in a sick, soft voice.

The kid shakes off the dripping intimacy. "I don't know you."

"Take him," the captain says, jerking his head toward the patrol cars.

"Have a nice life," a cop yells.

It isn't Quani. Instead, the cops have come up with Eric Lema, one of the two boys who was with Quani. He sits with his hands cuffed behind him and stares straight ahead. The officer who has the collar sits next to the kid. "Good eyes, Jimmy," Priore tells the fleshy young cop. Lema just stares. Nobody pays him much attention.

That night Priore gets the word from the street that even though McClain was Chris Moore's operative, the shooting had something to do with a loaf of bread. For Nettie Epps it doesn't matter what the cause; the shooting has changed things forever.

"I'm so proud of Trevor for doing what he did," she says as she tries to squeeze an antique suitcase closed over a mound of Trevor's clothing. "But he's going to have to go with Ma when she leaves tomorrow. I had a dream somebody came out and took a shot at him when he was packing up the car."

It is after midnight. "Quani is the devil in disguise," Nettie says wearily. A couple of years ago Quani's brother was shot dead. Nettie was looking out the window and saw him fall. People said it was guys from the Pink Houses. "Quani has been running amuck ever since. He steals people's wallets and bicycles. Basically, he does whatever he wants to do. He used to just shoot people in the leg and arm. But now this. He's gone too far."

Nettie forces a puff of air past her lips. "They were thinking of bringing the white people back. But after this, I don't know. Chris Moore told everybody to get off the streets tonight because retaliation is comin' down. It's going to be World War Three out here."

Nettie wants her older brother to pick up Connie and Trevor at six the next morning for the trip down South, but her son is adamant. "I ain't scared, an' I ain't sneakin' out of here. Tell him come at eleven. I got to say goodbye an' shit."

The next morning at a few minutes past nine, Trevor carries two shopping bags and a suitcase full of clothes downstairs and arranges them in the trunk of a waiting Buick. Then he returns to kiss his mother. None of his friends or enemies are awake to see him swagger outside the second time, pause beside the idling car, and take a last look at the Cypress Houses.

FALL

JEFF

***

Shalo is back. His skin tone has been deepened half a shade by a summer in the sun, his hair is trimmed a quarter inch, his shirt and pants droop with infinite precision. He stands alone just inside the front door of Thomas Jefferson High School, deftly brushing the extended hands of acquaintances and admirers as they file past on their way to class. It's the first day of school, and the freshly waxed floors of the school are gleaming. Shouts and peals of laughter echo off the walls of the first-floor hallway, the same way they must have in 1924, when Thomas Jefferson was built as a monument to the aspirations of a generation of Jews. The new clothes, the promise, the well-lit path . . .

Thomas Jefferson was constructed as part of the presidential series of Brooklyn high schools. With its worn brick facade, mixed bag of classical design features, and lower windows framed by brown steel security mesh, it looks like any other New York City public school built before the Second World War, only bigger. Inside the front doors, a life-size statue of Thomas Jefferson, painted a dull gold, sits on a pedestal. Around a corner, across the hallway from the small, neat library, is the honor board. Framed in dark lustrous wood, the board tells a story of Brownsville. Under the heading "Alumni Notable for Distinguished Achievement" are columns of names from the 1930s and 1940s. Next to each name is an engraved reference to the alumnus's field of excellence. There are physicists, scientists, and diplomats. Dr. Frank Field, meteorologist; Shelley Winters, actress. The board boasts leaders in the fields of journalism, literature, public health, government, science, international law, and education. The list goes on. That is, until 1960, about the time that Brownsville and Jefferson became predominantly black. After 1961, there are only two names on the board, John Brockington and Jim McMillian, professional athletes of some renown.

Sharron Corley walks past the honor board without a pause. He is at Jefferson today to arrange his transfer to another high school, in what seems a strange maneuver for an eighteen-year-old who has achieved the kind of popularity at Jefferson that Sharron dreamed of as a kid. But at Jeff, Sharron is dogged by both admirers and detractors. And here, the kids who do not like you do not just scrawl bad things about you on the bathroom wall.

Two weeks ago, on a late August morning, Sharron traveled to Chambers Street in lower Manhattan with his buddy Frank to look at an alternative high school, the Satellite Academy. It was Frank who was seriously considering the school. Sharron was along for the ride, checking the facilities and prospecting for a rich new lode of girls.

There were papers to be filled out, an interview with a counselor, entry tests to be taken, and at each stage there was a room more than half full of girls. Sharron squinted his eyes slightly, adjusted his new clear glass "lo frames" by Ralph Lauren as if something were troubling him, held his head at a tilt, and avoided eye contact. He appeared worried, and impossibly shy under his war bonnet of brown and gold hair.

To his surprise, just three days after the interview, he received notification in the mail that he had been accepted at Satellite. Sharron was admitted so quickly because he was a perfect fit for the "mid-risk" student profile at Satellite Academy: a student with reasonable academic skills and less than critical personal problems who was not progressing at his own school. Frank was placed on the waiting list; a week later he was accepted as well.

Today Sharron is at Jeff to soak up some attention and collect his transfer papers. The attention will have to hold him for a while. Satellite is a quiet, low-key venue, no place for a star. The school has about two hundred students and a faculty of twenty. Sharron likes the friendly vibrations there, the way the students call the teachers by their first names. He also believes he will be permitted to participate in the school play at Jefferson. If things work out according to plan, he will have the best of both worlds.

Though it came to pass by accident, Sharron's decision to transfer is neither capricious nor unusual. Things are so wild in the Ville and East New York that more and more students opt to attend school in distant communities, even in neighborhoods that are also rough, in order to cut down their chances of catching a bullet, either as a bystander or as the object of a vendetta. Mothers play a deadly game of chess with their kids. Some, like Nettie Epps, who has just delivered Trevor to South Carolina for the school year, send their sons South. Several years ago, Margaret James sent her favorite son, Born Son, to South Carolina to get him out of harm's way, but he couldn't stand the quiet and came back to Brooklyn and the worst kind of trouble. Others, like Gita Malave, of the Tilden Houses, across the street from the spot where Born Son would take his big fall, don't have the finances or the relatives to make such tactical maneuvers. So Gita watches her teenage children and worries, heads off to work and college at night with her fingers crossed tight.

The teenagers here are undereducated in most things, but they are connoisseurs of pop culture, ready receptacles for the jingles and scattershot imagery of television. Their speech is drenched in the verbal flotsam of television shows. The police are called Five-0's, after *Hawaii Five-0*. They know the stars of the soaps and sitcoms as well as they know their neighbors. Brand names tyrannize the classrooms; prestige cars are worshiped. The world Sharron travels in is a pure consumer culture; the LoLifes are more an outlaw consumer group than a gang. With a neighborhood unemployment rate so high the methods of measuring it are no longer valid, these youths are slated by society to be nothing more than consumers, and somehow they know it.

But they are also a driving force behind pop culture throughout the world, and one of the only charismatic protest cultures left in the United States. The project kids, the so-called homeboys, have been housed far from commercial and cultural centers, away from the white and the black middle class. They have an identity separate from the white, adult-monitored mainstream. Young white kids watch with rapt attention everything they do and say. If they wear their baseball hats backward, their trousers low and loose, kids in the suburbs are quick to swivel their brims to the rear. The designers and marketing machines register the trend and spread the word. In a year, lines outside trendy clubs in Paris and Tokyo are filled with would-be homeboys in backward caps and droopy pants.

The irony is that the young white kids are not rebelling against anything, and neither are the boys in the Ville. The young black men in Brownsville indict society by their total belief in it. They trust what they have been told about image, status, competition, hierarchy, and the primacy of self-gratification. Their faith is lethal, mostly to themselves.

Chantal, Vanessa, and their friends sacrifice the chance to display their feminine charms to dress exactly like the stickup boys because they are the ones in the Ville who get the most props. The media know and respect the homeboy because they know he cannot be ignored. He is original, dangerous.

Even Gita Malave copies the manner of speech of the rough-and-ready guys who hang in the parking lot and by her elevator. "Yo, what's up?" she likes to say, just like the kids. "Don't play yourself." She is only half kidding. One of the salient features of Brownsville is the simultaneous primacy and neglect of the children, especially the boys. This is a country where children have always been abused and worshiped. In Brownsville, they rule with a murderous innocence.

Here comes Chantal Redding, down the hall past the guidance office toward Sharron. Transfer papers in hand, the young king of Thomas Jefferson lingers in the hallway opposite the entrance to the auditorium, nodding to his faithful, granting brief audiences with his courtiers. Chantal moves on tiny sneakered feet, a gamine lost in a pair of baggy Guess jeans and a double-extra-large T-shirt. This is the first time Sharron has seen her since their spat in the hallway in March. She never had much besides her undeniable cuteness. Today she has news.

"Sha, wha's up?"

"Same old. I ain't seen you in a while. Where were you?"

"Down South. You still here?"

"Nah, I'm transferrin'. Too much drama."

"Word."

As Sharron speaks with Chantal, he absorbs the waves of attention that roll toward him. Slowly, he maneuvers the conversation fifty feet down the hall to a spot in front of a display case, opposite the statue of Thomas Jefferson. The location is his favorite in the school because in the back of the display case is a full-length mirror. The soft lighting in the hallway is just right to highlight his skin and backlight his hair. As his ex-girlfriend talks, he rotates his head this way and that. Life is grand. Not only is the girl he left behind making a public attempt to get back in his favor, and not only are the new and old girls in school "sweating" him big-time from all angles, but he is now in a position not only to gather the harvest of admiration but to watch himself receiving it. It's a shame to leave all this, Sharron is thinking. But a plan is a plan, and he knows better than anyone that familiarity breeds disrespect.

Chantal is telling about her visit down South. Her voice is soft, her consonants flabby, babyish, as she describes how quiet and dark it was in Fayetteville and how there "wasn't nothin' to do but chill." Her account is notable for its gaps. There is no mention of boys, and boys are what makes Chantal's world spin around and around. The first period of the school day ends with a droning five-second tone, and the second begins. Still Sharron and Chantal stand and talk.

Sheryl happens by and shakes her head. That unfortunate encounter on the #3 in June could be forgotten, she has decided. She has been considering a reconciliation. Sheryl knows that any girlfriend of Sharron's is going to have to deal with "shade" from the other girls. He is simply what they are looking for. Sheryl is realistic. She can deal with the shards of jealousy and with the relentless hopefuls, but she is not sure she can deal with reruns like Chantal, though that is exactly the role she is contemplating for herself.

When Sheryl passes by again twenty minutes later and Sharron and Chantal are still deep in conversation, she flushes, her breath quickens. "Chantal needs her little ass kicked." But when they are still head to head an hour later, Sheryl simply writes off her own comeback.

Sometime between second and third period, Chantal reveals her reason for leaving town.

"I don't know how to . . . tell you. Sha. I had a baby. Andre. He's yours."

"Mine?" Sharron looks over both shoulders and back at Chantal.

She nods solemnly. "He's so cute. He be sayin' things already. Talkin' almost."

"You *know* he's mine."

"Yours . . . I was gonna keep it from you. I know you got a future. I didn't wanna mess it up for you. Sha?"

Ah. Those carefree moments of youth are short, when all the world is right and all the doors are open. Sharron is jarred. He catches himself frowning in the mirror, quickly recasts his features, and mouths a policy statement.

"I'll do the blood test thing. If it's me, I'll take the responsibility."

Chantal moves several inches closer. Suddenly, a less calculated reaction grips Sharron. Later he explains, "She was standin' there, and I was lookin' down at her and she was lookin' up and she was looking so good. And I remembered how we were close. And she was wearin' a yellow Champion T-shirt with red writing and dark blue jeans. I was wearing a yellow Polo sweatshirt with red writing and dark denim Guess jeans. It was incredible. I just got this feeling — that we were meant to be together, that we were made for each other."

Sharron is so impressed that he makes a spur-of-the-moment decision. He had heard that Chantal had gone down South with some guy who is back in New York with her now.

"I'll do what I gotta do with . . . for . . . Andre. But you gotta stop dealin' with this dude."

Chantal nods and presses her small face to Sharron's chest to hide the big bubble tears on her cheeks. Sharron recoils momentarily and places his left hand over his heart so the back of his hand will stop Chantal's tears from staining his sweatshirt, then crushes her to him with his right arm. For the moment, he does not care who is watching.

Upstairs in Room 544, Sharon King is introducing herself to her third-period global history class, working her mojo on the sophomores and freshmen, who have never seen anything like her. She is dressed like a lounge singer, in shiny black pumps and a black skirt that accentuates a prominent behind, which she likes to call her "African rhythm section." Glowing with good looks and zeal, she is hip, hipper than that. She "knows what time it is," the kids who know her from last year whisper. She knows how to put a lesson together, too. Some of the other teachers are envious of her relationship with the students. "Hell, I don't blame them. I'd be jealous of me too," she says.

King has arranged the seats in her room in a rectangle, allowing for a center performance space in which she can do her own special brand of motivating and instructing. The first thing veterans in a tough school tell a new teacher is "don't smile until Christmas." But King pirouettes so students on all sides can see her smile.

"I want you coming in here every day with a notebook. Not some raggedy pieces of paper you borrowed from somebody five minutes before you walked in here. And cover your textbooks. If you don't have your notebook and your cover, talkin 'bout 'I don't have the money' or some shit like that, I'm gonna *give* you the money." The class titters. "Word up. I *will* embarrass you like that."

King has stacks of printed handouts on the desk behind her. Each of her lessons will be laced with lively role-playing. The twenty-five students relax visibly. They will not be left to their own devices.

"We're gonna get busy in here. Ask Theresa." King nods at a student who has been in her class before.

"Word," Theresa testifies.

The door swings open and fifteen-year-old Khalil Sumpter appears. He waves broadly to Dupree, his best friend, and Melvin Jones, another buddy, seated in the back row. Khalil is wearing a gold jeans jacket. He is five-ten and sturdy, a bad actor. He slides into the room with much fanfare, waves and touches hands left and right. Nothing terrible in that, just the classic tone-setter for a classroom in which nothing will get done. His boys slide apart so he can sit in the middle of the back row, leader of the opposition party.

King never has trouble with a class. Her package is too potent for all but the most disturbed kid. If there is a clown or even a cadre of ne'er-do-wells, she takes it straight to them, with the rest of the class as noncombatants. No one can take sides against Ms. King.

While King attends to some opening-day paperwork, Khalil

and his friends have plenty to say behind cupped hands. Khalil is the brightest of the three. His records show that he is a very smart kid who has decided that academic achievement is counterproductive to his goal of gaining and holding props.

Something else is bothering him. A year ago, Khalil and a kid named Tyrone Sinkler were arrested for stealing a kid's hat and lunch money outside nearby George Gershwin Junior High School. Sinkler, who had prior arrests, was packed off to Spofford for almost a year for his part in the crime. Khalil was turned loose with probation. After Sinkler was sent away, word began filtering back to Khalil that Sinkler was calling him a snitch. Now, after his release, Sinkler has transferred from Westinghouse High School to Jefferson. Khalil has already seen the hulking, scowling Sinkler in the hallway, and he is bracing for trouble.

Khalil and his boys in the back row giggle and "snap" (joke) about getting skins from girls. They believe they know what will transpire in this room. The asides will always be funny, the lesson always boring and meaningless. But the likes of Sumpter, Dupree, and Jones have never met the likes of King. The contradiction in their scenario is that in their closed adolescent society, their world of bawdy one-liners and guffaws, a curvaceous female like Ms. King is never to be ignored, cannot be excluded. From the opening bell, this will be a different kind of contest. When King steps back into the center space, she has their full attention.

"What's up, gentlemen? The three new wise men of Jeff. And the man in the middle, a day late and a dollar short." She nods at Khalil's bare desk. "Where's your books?"

Khalil loves the attention. "In the library, where books belong. Aaah, snap." He turns to his laughing classmates and raises his hands in recognition of their appreciation. There will be no unbearable boredom here. He will see to that, his gesture promises. This should be a good one. The classic disrupter and the strutting master teacher. Who will win?

"But there's no *skins* in the library," King retorts, with a saucy toss of her head and a wink. "So you hustled your behind up here. Good decision."

Sharron leans into the open doorway to catch King's eye. She breaks away from her class for a moment and steps outside to confer with him.

"Boo Boo," she coos, "I can't believe you're transferring. I heard it from Sheryl."

Sharron is embarrassed. "Ms. King," he whines, curling his body around an imaginary knife in his heart, "it's somethin' I got to do. I'll still be in the play. Just too much going on here."

King has already heard something of Chantal's pregnancy. "Yeah, sweetie, I've heard."

There is a burst of laughter from inside the room. King slips back to her class. She cannot afford to leave the stage to the pretenders for too long at this time of year. Later, when she has developed personal relationships, done important favors for every one of her students, when she has her merit system in place, she will be able to do almost anything. Right now she must keep the spotlight on herself, before Khalil and his crew gather momentum.

Minutes later, Sharron is heading out the front door. Cortez Sutton is walking in. Cortez is as dark and bright as a glittering midnight sky; a razor-featured junior honor student, he is also a wit and a basketball player, a left-handed point guard. He is headed to the main office to effect his transfer from Lafayette High School, where he was given a superintendent's suspension last June for brandishing a screwdriver at two white kids who threatened him. He lives near Sheryl on Pennsylvania Avenue, on the other side of Linden Boulevard, in the Linden Houses. Jefferson is the nearest high school, so it was the natural alternative when Mrs. Sutton decided to pull her son from Lafayette. This is a chance for Cortez to put the academics and the hoops together and grab a ticket to a green-shrubbed campus and the outside world. But Cortez won't be able to play ball for Jeff in the regular-season games unless the suspension is lifted. He knows all about Jefferson. He has plenty of friends here, including his buddy Ian Moore, E-lo. Cortez is smart, too smart it seems, always the guy with the quickest woof. That is what got him in trouble at Lafayette. But he is a comer. Maybe he can keep his mouth shut over here at Jeff.

Cortez is far less besotted with clothing and girls than Sharron, who is drifting down the street away from Thomas Jefferson like a sailboat. Sharron has already recovered from the shock of having a son, believes that the inconvenience will be minimal. The young grandmothers, Chantal's thirty-year-old mom and Gloria, will take care of the child. Life will go on without a hitch. But the alarms have been going off in Cortez's head ever since he got suspended. He knows that if he is going to prevail in the world outside the neighborhood, he is going to have to make his move now, keep rocking the books, and pray that he catches a college scout's eye with his left-handed sorties to the basket.

Principal Carol Beck stands on the front steps of the school. It is five minutes before the end of the first regular school day. A recipient of a *Reader's Digest* American Heroes in Education award, Beck is riding a groundswell of acclaim and positive publicity. The idea now is to keep the ball rolling, build on the success. In recent years, Jefferson had the worst reputation of any school in Brooklyn, perhaps in the entire city, and ranked at the top in violent incidents and dropout rate. Beck has slowed the heavy wheels of decline, and she is determined not to let them roll again. But the problem came right at her at 8:40 this morning, surging down the hall: five hundred new students, freshmen, from seventeen feeder schools. They come from all kinds of educational environments, many of them exquisitely chaotic. They have no idea about the new regime at Jeff.

Beck smiles at two security guards with walkie-talkies, turns, heads inside, and takes a position near the likeness of Thomas Jefferson, studying the freshmen as they leave the building. Dressed in a blue suit, and white sneakers for speed, she knows she can't control the school from the principal's office. Twenty years in the New York City public school system have taught her exactly what has to be done. It will take savvy and inhuman endurance. Luckily, through a freak of nature, the fifty-four-year-old principal has more energy in her veins than any three children. If she did not have this job, it seems, she might have to take tranquilizers or be restrained.

Beck grew up in St. Louis. She was a musical prodigy who came to New York City after college to sing in the Metropolitan Opera. When she found herself headed for the chorus, she took a job as a music teacher for the board of education. "I come from gangsters," she says with a mysterious arch to her eyebrows. "I know their pain."

From her position in the hallway, she manages to make eye contact with each of her veterans and new recruits. When

Michael T., back in school after an abbreviated stint upstate for pulling the gun on Gary Lemite, tries to slip by, she detains him with her hand, looks into his eyes, and shoots him a smile both sweet and lethal. Bashim Inman, the Howard Raider, is next. Bashim, another rambling heavyweight, has been attending Jeff for a long time. Beck has been principal for four years, and Bashim was at Jeff before she was. He started in an honors program at Martin Luther King, Jr., High School in Manhattan. But early years in the Howard Houses did not serve him well outside Brownsville. "I was always getting beef, carrying a gun, all that, so I got transferred to Jeff."

He did not want to come. Jeff is the arena where contingents from the various projects meet. Linden and Howard, oil and water. Bashim is a hardrock, a tough guy, but when he saw "Thomas Jefferson" written on the piece of paper, he said, "No way." "It was wild then," he recalls. "I carried a .32 Luger. And then a four-fifth. I loved that gun. My baby. Big thing. Stuck right in my pants. I had it all." Big Bashim talks about his guns with the affection some kids in the suburbs have for the used cars they once owned. "It was funny with all those guns," he remembers. "Guys had to start resorting to some other way to deal with things. Like you have a beef, you try to melt the other guy with the ice grill. If that don't work, we knuckle up."

Early in her first year, word of an impending "throw-down" reached Beck, and she summoned Bashim to her office. "Bashim, you've got to get your people under control. This is just not going to happen like this."

Beck's strongest suit is that she can deliver the message that she is more committed to order than the kids are to chaos. If they are willing to fight and shoot, then she is willing to die. She makes them believe that, and it might be true. "This is a tough age," Beck states, "but we love these children. They have one dimension of experience, and we are trying to make them bicultural. They have one channel, and we are trying to give them cable." Beck believes more in education than the kids do in the status quo of beefs and counterbeefs, violence for goods and violence for status, violence for entertainment, violence out of habit.

That first year, Beck was savvy enough to put her finger on the juice behind those "little bastard Smurfs who were running amuck on the fifth floor." After Bashim's talk with her, he headed upstairs and waved a hand over the waters. "It's chill," he said with his ice grill.

The same thing had happened on almost the same spot some thirty years before, when Smiley Smith, the six-foot-five leader of the terrible Roman Lords, had stood looking down at basketball coach Sam Beckman in the first-floor hallway at Jeff, listening. "Something clicked," Smiley says about the moment that changed his life. "I don't know what it was about that little man. He was kind of mean. But something happened and I started going to class." Smith became a basketball star at Jefferson and is now a community leader in Brownsville. Beckman had something. It wasn't pity or even concern. It was respect, and a plan for something different. Mr. Beckman and Carol Beck had more than good intentions; they had the gift.

Bashim Inman is a powerful ally. Beck watches him warily. He can control the action with his size and smarts, think on his feet like a barrister. But at nineteen, he has been in high school for six years. "I'm like a chameleon," he says. "I have game for any situation. I want to be a politician." The girls do not like him much; with his round pumpkin head and knuckle-gnarled upper lip, he looks like a classic bully, and he is. Even now, he cannot resist throwing his weight around a little. On this first day of school, near the guidance office, he spots a posturing would-be gangster, Khalil Sumpter, and makes a mental note to harass him the next time their paths cross. "If I can't be bad, then can't nobody."

"COME BEHIND ME"

A week after the opening of school, Born Son cruises to a soundless stop in front of Thomas Jefferson High School. It is 2:40 P.M., dismissal time. Born Son is dressed in a green iridescent suit over a black silk T-shirt, and the smooth dark skin of his neck is festooned with chains of gold: an inch-thick rope for weight, and a finely woven strand with an anchor-shaped medallion for style. On his left hand he sports a diamond-studded ring custom-made in Manhattan. He is seated in regal solitude behind the wheel of his jet-black Jeep Pathfinder. In minutes there is a jostling throng of a hundred profoundly impressed students.

Bobby James was always just a little smarter than the fellows around the way, could talk just a little better, always knew where the parties were. Everybody wanted to hang out with brother Bobby. A security guard tries to disperse the growing crowd and inspires more curiosity. A girl trips and screams as she fights to regain her footing. More students rush up to get a look at what is really just another kid. Throughout the mini-riot, Born Son, bathed in myth, sits serenely astride his Jeep.

What does Bobby have to make him seem such a prince? It is not that he makes so much money dealing crack — perhaps a thousand a week, probably less. He has some gold jewelry, a custom-made suit. But the Jeep he drives is not a fairy-tale chariot like a Rolls-Royce, just the middle-class vehicle of commuters and spoiled suburban kids. It is the things Bobby James has in contrast to the desolate lives of the people around him that make him seem so special.

Born Son shifts his Jeep into gear, smiles, and floats down Pennsylvania Avenue on a wave of heartfelt admiration. Like Sharron Corley, he cares far more about his image than he does about money, his future, or even his safety. The Worthys, especially Nikia, are not constrained by such abstract notions. When push comes to shove, when the feds flash their badges, it will be Born Son's loyalty that will be his downfall.

Sitting in their orange and blue Chevrolet Caprice on the corner of Dumont and Pennsylvania, Hammil and his partner cannot help but curse their station in life when they see Born Son's flashy car. "I got a fucking two-year-old Escort and this fucking mopehead is drivin' a fucking Pathfinder," Hammil whines.

"And you just know he doesn't have any registration. The papers are always fugazy," his partner concurs, using a cop slang word meaning phony.

Hammil cannot touch Born Son. He is Schulman's case, the subject of a federal investigation, immune to petty harassment. But when a white Mercedes-Benz with two young men in the front seat and two in the back rolls by a few minutes later, the car stop is inevitable. Hammil flips on his red roof light.

The scene is familiar. As the boys pile out of the car, black people walking by exhibit varied emotions. The older ones avert their eyes. The youths are probably drug dealers, they think. The middle-aged folks, the ones with jobs, sometimes share the perspective of the police. How, they wonder, have they worked all their lives and failed to acquire such a machine to transport their aching bones? When the teenagers leaving the high school see the flashing red light, the luxury auto, and the splayed doors of the police cruiser, they whip off their Walkmans and edge close. With jutting chins, hands on hips, they mutter loud enough for the police to hear, "Always fucking with a brother. Can't stand to see a brother with somethin'. Ain't this a bitch. That's why they get hurt. That's why somebody always shootin' they ass."

A couple of days later, Schulman is in a slate-blue surveillance van watching Nikki. His CI, as confidential informants are known, has given him the time and place she is supposed to make a pickup.

Nikia is the smartest of the Worthys. The police know it, and her grandmother Kate knows it too. "Nikki is slick. Always has been." She was slick enough to be somewhere else when her cocaine dealer boyfriend died in a stiff breeze of bullets in the Chelsea section of Manhattan in 1988. After that, she lived in a shelter until she moved in with her cousins at 295 Dumont. It was penny ante there until she met Bobby at an after-hours place for hustlers on Pitkin Avenue.

"I knew the girl was trouble the minute I saw her," Margaret James swears. "The minute I *heard* about her."

The bootleggers of the twenties had their speakeasies; the Brooklyn crack retailers had the Limelight. Everybody was frisked at the door. "The drug dealers all went there," Bobby Schulman says, "but they left their business outside. They didn't socialize with each other, just stayed in their little groups."

A Howard Raider remembers the night Bobby and Nikia met. "Bobby used to come in the Limelight with all gold and shit. He had serious props. He tried to push up on her and she wasn't havin' it. Bobby was sweatin' Nikki, and she was playin' him."

The story goes that Bobby told his boys to rob Nikki, relieve her of her jewelry. But the robbery did not happen. Instead, Born Son was smitten. "She had heart comin' in there," one of Bobby's young followers says. "Next thing I knew, they was together."

Nikki is not a lush young woman. At twenty-four, even after three children, she looks girlish. She is wiry, tough, built for the long march. Both earlobes show scars from earrings that were torn away in anger. She talks in a combination of sharp exclamations and warp speed mumble; her vocabulary is state-of-the-art street slang. Not for effect; she does little for effect. Whatever the street recognizes as cool is Nikki. Her intelligence has never been used for anything but the street. She can take the measure of a player quickly, can tell what is going to go down long before the guns start popping. She is brave but not vainglorious. Nikki can handle drug dealers, thugs, and just plain troublemakers with ease. Cops, prosecutors, and judges are not that much harder for her. "I'm goin' out to get me some money," she likes to say. She is everything that Bobby admires.

In Scarsdale, New York, among young people Nikki and Bobby's age, it is all about what college you go to, what fraternity or sorority you join. Bobby and Nikki had other credentials. He was the main man in Howard. She had been part of a crack operation already. She knew how and where to cook it up, how to add the baking soda and bag it. She had a steel trap for a memory and a head for figures. She was rough and ready. It wasn't long before Nikia got pregnant and gave Bobby a son; they called him Little Bit. The Young Guns had become a mom-and-pop operation.

But the good times are over. Schulman and his partner from the federal task force, Mathew DeJong, have most of their case. It is time to snatch up Nikki and force her to roll over. The plan is to bring her in on a state warrant and try to scare her into providing evidence for the federal investigation. This is the day.

When Schulman, DeJong, and a handful of backup DEA agents pick up Nikki at her mother's apartment in the Albany Houses in Bedford-Stuyvesant, she is unconcerned. Back at the PSA, Schulman begins to explain the situation to her.

"We got tapes, Nikki. Matt, get the videotapes."

"I don't want to see no tapes," Nikki mumbles wearily, rolling her eyes. She tilts her head down and shines the smudge off one of the studs on the sleeve of her $1,700 leather outfit. Nikki has been in and out of police stations all her life. She won't frighten easily.

"Nikki, we got sound tapes, talkin' about you runnin' things in the Complex while Bobby was stayin' away. We got pictures of you with money. *Beaucoup* drugs. We got people to testify."

Nikki levels her eyes at Schulman. "I'll give you a powder spot an' a homicide."

"That's good, I think we can work with that. Let me make a call," Schulman says.

He takes down the information and calls Robert Fineberg, the federal attorney assigned to the case. It's bad news for Nikia.

"Thanks for the powder spot, Nikia, and the other thing. We're gonna put you back on the street for a while. But the DA says you got to give up Born Son. It's like a game. We tag you. You tag Bobby." Nikia is silent.

In the next week, the task force breaks the Young Guns' operation down, getting warrants on apartments the crew uses on high floors so they will move the operation lower in the building and consolidate. The idea is that when the final arrests are made, the lower apartments will be easier to hit and likely to yield more drugs.

A week after Nikia's first arrest, Schulman and DeJong take her down again. This time they show her the federal arrest warrant. She twitches, puckers her lips, and regains her composure. The first time Schulman brought her in, she believed she was dealing with a state bust.

Nikia's lawyer shows up at PSA 2 and confers with his client for just a few moments. "I'm going to leave the room," he tells her. "I'm sure they'll do the right thing for you," he says, nodding at Schulman and DeJong.

The usually unflappable Nikia is worried. She taps her foot, drums her fingernails on the tabletop, and stares at Schulman.

"Born Son," the cop says.

"I got to testify in front of him? I don't want to do it in front of him."

"If it goes to trial, you'll have to testify in open court. He'll be sitting right in front of you. Nikki, this is no joke. You are in deep shit. You give us Bobby, the DA writes a letter to the judge and you're out in a couple of years. Otherwise, you don't see Little Bit till he's in his thirties."

Nikia nods slowly. Her voice cracks. But she does not weep as she tags Bobby James, the father of her baby boy. "You got it," she says.

It's time to take the whole operation down. Three days after Nikia agrees to testify, the Housing cops and the DEA grab Born Son and Tai Stick in their Pine Street hideout. They snatch Supreme and Billie Odums on the street.

Through a relative, Nikia manages to deliver a terse message to Bobby. If a deal is to be made with the feds, it must be made quickly. "Come behind me," she tells her lover. But Born Son and the Young Guns are still not deeply concerned, even after they learn what the federal charges are all about.

They should know better. They had heard rumors that the feds were involved for some time but had not heeded them. The maximum they would have served in state prison for the offense they are charged with is eight and a third years. Federal time is five times that. And there are the sentencing guidelines. As part of the 1984 Sentencing Reform Act, which went into effect in 1987, judicial discretion is severely limited in drug cases. Sentences are mandated based on a chart that takes into account only drug type, quantity, prior record, and role in the criminal organization.

Schulman and DeJong mention the possibility of a deal to Born Son if he gives up his connection. "Give us Chris Moore," Schulman offers, "and we can do business."

Dan Murphy, Bobby's lawyer, leans close and whispers vehemently in his ear. He is begging him to do himself some good. But Born Son has too much heart for that kind of thing.

"I don' know nothin'," he says with a jerk of his head toward the door of the squad room. "Y'all finished?"

The Housing police breathe a sigh of satisfaction over the arrest. The Worthys are out of business, and the four Young Guns are not just going to be locked up, they are going to be locked deep. Schulman and DeJong confiscate Born Son's Jeep, and right away Schulman begins using it as a surveillance vehicle in the new Chris Moore investigation, occasionally wheeling it past 295 Dumont — "to send a message," he says.

"STRAIGHT TO THAT HOLY HOUSE"

Lieutenant McGinty is downstairs in the PSA roll call room, briefing his sweep team.

"A message, Lieutenant?" asks Gary Lemite.

"That's right. A fuckin' message. Ever since Lavin left Fiorentino, the place has gone to shit. Yesterday some fucking mutt made a threat on Mike's life."

"Yeah," a team member affirms. "We had a gun run in there last week. All kinds of mouthin' off. Fuckin' mopes in Fiorentino are out of control."

"Today we go in and snatch some bodies," McGinty orders.

Gary Lemite, recently promoted to the sweep team, which concentrates on special conditions in the projects and so-called quality-of-life infractions, shakes his head slowly back and forth. Then he looks over at Mario Palumbo, his partner for the day. Mario points straight up, and the two officers head upstairs. The calendar says the summer is over, but outside the air is damp and oven warm. Gary reaches in his shirt, hooks a thumb under his bulletproof vest, and pulls the body armor away from his chest to let some air near his skin. Despite the heat, he would not even consider removing the stifling thirty-layer "point-blank" vest.

One sweep team member has to use the bathroom, and the sergeant has some paperwork to do. Those two will be along shortly. Gary pulls the blue van around the front of the PSA to pick up Mario for the ride over to Fiorentino, and the two young cops cruise through Brownsville in thoughtful silence, staring out the open windows at rows of silent dark young men.

*

The Jews who left have fond memories, but Brownsville was always a ghetto. During the Depression no area of the city had a higher percentage of families on relief. Jacob Riis called it "that nasty little slum." In the 1940s, the police credited it with producing more gangsters than any other neighborhood in New York City. It was said to be the toughest neighborhood in the United States. Poolrooms were three times as numerous as playgrounds. You could get a pretzel and an egg cream at Midnight Rosie's on Saratoga and Livonia. Between sips, you could also arrange for Murder Inc. to reduce the number of your acquaintances by one. There were twenty murders in Brownsville in 1939. When a local softball team played a team of inmates at Sing Sing, Murder Inc., also known as the Combination, supplied the uniforms.

Some say that it was a friendly ghetto, no doubt because of its homogeneity. The construction of the ramp to the Williamsburg Bridge uprooted thousands of Lower East Side Jews, who simply rode the soon-to-be-completed subway line over the new bridge and six miles out to Brownsville. In the early part of the century, Brownsville was almost entirely Jewish and self-sufficient, with a flourishing economy complete with "rotating credit associations," entrepreneurs, numerous small businesses, and manufacturing. It was home to a paper box factory, a staple manufacturer, U Bet syrup, and Holland Steel. It had its own shopping district. Pitkin had banks and fancy clothing stores, and people lined up for two-cent movies. Belmont had the open-air market with its pushcarts and the smell of herring and pickles. Saratoga Avenue was the place for junk shops, tinsmiths, garages, and stables.

There were scattered Italians and pockets of blacks living in shacks on the eastern border, under the elevated subway. One black old-timer recalls, "Back then we were accepted, even welcome in people's homes, because there were too few of us to be a threat." The neighborhood was dense, 140 people to a square acre. This was at once the new suburbia and a traditional shtetl. Around it were sleepy fishing villages like Canarsie.

Until World War II, the Jews did not go anywhere, not even to the next town. Those who lived in "Brahnzvil," as they pronounced it with their Yiddish accents, did not wander into neighboring communities. The borders of the surrounding German and Irish working-class areas were policed by gangs of youths. But the Jews did not have to travel. Every kind of good and service was for sale in Brownsville itself. New residents could always find work in the needle trades.

Many people were poor and even hungry. When a kid went to a fresh-air camp, the success of the vacation was measured by how much weight he gained. But the Jews of Brownsville prided themselves on the fact that they were the descendants of merchants, not peasants. They believed in the future. The homes were cheaply built and cramped, so the residents put their hopes in the schools and public institutions. Brownsville was the home of what was hailed as the first free public children's library in the world, on the corner of Mother Gaston and Dumont, half a block from where the Worthys live. Records show that on January 4, 1914, 2,645 volumes were borrowed from its shelves in four hours. A photograph from the 1930s shows a block-long line of dark-haired children waiting patiently outside the two-story brick building to exchange books. All you had to do was show clean hands and you could get two books for a week, one hard and one easy.

Thirty years later, the African American residents of Brownsville also wanted the best for their children. But the fruits of even a partial victory in the bitter controversy of the late 1960s over community control of the schools were sucked away by corruption and intractable bureaucracies. The credit associations and small businesses were gone by then. All that remained of the old Brownsville was its fearsome reputation. The neighborhood was so tough that the owners of Mr. Softee–type ice cream trucks saw fit to use the name Kool Man on their vehicles in Brownsville. In the 1970s, young Riddick Bowe, from the Noble Drew Ali Houses and Thomas Jefferson High School, walked softly around his Brownsville neighborhood because he did not want to run afoul of a local tough the kids called Bummy Mike, Mike Tyson. Both later became heavyweight boxing champions of the world.

In the 1980s, the East Brooklyn churches fostered a plan for private subsidies of one-family tract housing in Brownsville. The dwellings were called the Nehemiah Homes, after the biblical prophet who supervised the rebuilding of the walls of ancient Jerusalem. The one thousand Nehemiah Homes, offered to

157

any family with a household income of $20,000, were quickly filled, mostly by city workers with good credit. The rows of private homes were an unqualified success. But the immaculate Nehemiahs, complete with driveways and back yards soon stocked with lawn furniture and barbecues, were simply too few to ease the misery of the projects, which stood above them like great poisonous trees.

Fiorentino Plaza, on Pitkin Avenue, is one of those projects. Reidus Saab, a retired female corrections matron, lives there, just biding time before she moves back to Clarendon County, South Carolina. "I'm a highland Geechee," she declares. "That's why you don't hear me talkin' all that stuff about 'Hey, mon,' like some Jamaican." Saab and the rest of the residents used to call Fiorentino PCO Brian Lavin "Sneaky," because of his stealth and persistence in apprehending drug dealers in the project. "That's my baby, Sneaky. He was a roof man," Saab explains. "Used to clock 'em good. Then he'd slide up on 'em all nice and smooth and put his hand on their shoulder."

When Officer Lavin was rewarded with a transfer to a plainclothes detail, the residents held a party in his honor. A sixteen-year-old girl wrote a rap song in praise of his work. The lines of the song, written on the cracked keys of an old-fashioned typewriter, are tacked to the glass-covered photo board near the back stairway in the PSA.

> Lavin's his name. Sneaky's his fame.
> And this cop puts old Kojak to shame.
> They run and hide when they think he's around.
> When he's gone they come right back.
> But Lavin been hidin' he don't cut no slack.
> He pops right out and puts them on the wall,
> Till they start to bawl.
> This Lavin is like no other.
> He makes the drug dealers cry to their mother.

But Lavin is gone now, and as the young poet predicted, the dealers came right back. "I live on the first floor," Saab says. "I'm tired of payin' rent and sleepin' on the floor. Have gun will travel, that's this place here. So many bullets come in you be a fool to sleep in the bed."

So this steamy fall day, Gary Lemite and Mario Palumbo are

headed over to Fiorentino to do something about the situation. Gary has taken his first small step up the career ladder already, with this promotion to the sweep team. He is still in uniform, but from now on, no more sector cars. He will be sent out in a van with a group of officers on assignment.

Mario Palumbo is on the team, but one look at him and you can tell he is a free-lancer at heart. You can tell by the way he wears his hat, the way he stands and walks, the way he does, or does not, smile. Mario is tight and loose at the same time. He has the hot-wire moves and the balls, good instincts all around, but he has made a few mistakes. He was caught off-post once or twice, and he has been in too many shootings. They were good shootings, everybody, including internal affairs, Kammerdener and Lenti, and anybody else who matters, says. Good shootings. But good or not, Mario's record, his personality, and especially the gunplay make him a perceived liability by the bosses in the department.

An officer at the PSA tells about the time he sat in a car with Mario late one night in the parking lot in Cypress. A round went off somewhere nearby. Mario raised his hand to his partner with the index finger extended, as if to say, "I have just the right thing for this." He fished under his jacket and removed his unauthorized nine-millimeter automatic so he wouldn't have to use his service revolver, slowly rolled the window down, leaned out, and fired two shots moonward. "Scuds," he explained as he replaced the weapon. In a moment there were two more reports as the original shooter answered the challenge with a couple of ballistic rooster crows of his own. On the second shot the cops spotted the muzzle flash. In five minutes Mario and his partner had the kid and the gun in hand.

Mario and Gary are in Fiorentino Plaza to give support to the handsomest cop in Brownsville. It is not going to be an easy thing to fill Sneaky Lavin's shoes in Fiorentino, but Seeger, the guy with the wavy dark hair and professional good looks, whom the other cops call Matt Houston, is going to try. A handsome face does not count for much in Brownsville and East New York. The stress is so great here that people soon find out what is inside a person. The environment of a housing project is so hypersocial that people get to know each other fast and well. There are so many chances to do good, bad, or nothing that each person writes his résumé every day right in front of his neighbors. It is no different for the police officers. Matt Houston looks like a Hollywood cop, but he doesn't have the heart and style of Lavin, and the locals jump on him quick.

Earl Frazier, a Fiorentino fixture and small-time drug dealer, knows all about the sweep team, so when he sees Gary and Mario he puts down his half-finished forty-ounce and grabs the receiver of a pay phone on the sidewalk. He stands on the corner of Pitkin and Van Siclen, behind the stairway to the A train, and pretends to listen to a voice on the other end of the line.

Gary walks up on one side. Mario approaches from the other. On another day the incident might be over before it begins — a nod, a warning. Not today.

"I showed respect. I put the bottle down. I'm talkin to my girl," Frazier explains nervously. He knows the beer in his hand gives the cops the right to search him, gives them the keys to his pockets.

"I'm not askin' you, I'm tellin' you. Get off the phone now," Lemite orders. "Put the phone down," he growls, stepping closer, now chest to chest with Frazier. Mario stands a foot behind. But Frazier does not comply. He knows he is about to go to the wall for a toss and a ticket for public drinking.

"I didn't dis you," he whines. Then he spins, pushes Mario against the wall, and bolts across Miller Avenue toward the courtyard of the project. Gary is ten feet behind, charging for a quick catch. But as Frazier reaches the far side of Miller Avenue, just before he will make the turn and fly through the walkways of the project buildings, he digs in his waistband and comes out with a seventeen-shot nine-millimeter Beretta, turns halfway toward Gary, and pops four evenly spaced shots at him. Unhit, Gary draws and fires three quick shots back. There is no fear in him, just a massive dose of adrenaline from somewhere under his rib cage and a sensation of closure, the crystallized conviction that he will never see Erica and Zach again.

Frazier quicksteps toward the end of a wall along the sidewalk and the turn into the courtyard. Gary has not moved. Instead, after a moment, he fires three more shots. Frazier's right shoulder lurches forward, and his right arm swings away from his body as he wheels out of Gary's sight and sprints through the buildings toward Bradford Avenue. The kid is hit.

Gary is running, Mario right behind. Gary is having second

thoughts about pegging more shots at Frazier. Women and children flood the courtyard from the first-floor apartments. Miraculously, the barrage of gunfire is drawing people outside. There is swirling movement to Gary's right and left as curiosity becomes madness and people run toward the action. But Gary only dimly notes these people. His vision is funneled through the mud-brown brick buildings to Frazier, who is flying out the other side of the plaza onto Bradford. Gary stops in front of a sign that reads 340 Miller Avenue to jam a speedloader into the cylinder of his gun, a tricky maneuver that has always taken a few tries in practice and now requires just one pass. The speedloader slides in like butter; the empty cartridge rattles to the cement. To Lemite's left are doorways into the Fiorentino buildings; to his right, a small sunken playground with a green cement turtle and a frolicking red dolphin.

As Lemite, winded, resumes the chase, Palumbo sprints past and tails Frazier out of the plaza to the right up Bradford. Gary, now five paces behind, is on the radio spitting out the 13, giving cross streets. He fancies himself a radio man. Accordingly, he reports the location crisply, despite the lock on his lungs. Mario hears Gary say "Bradford" on the direct, but he repeats the location to Central as "Thatford," naming a street seventeen blocks to the west. There will be no backup cars soon. Mario is not a detail man. If you want somebody to stand post, stay in one place, don't pick Mario. If you need a partner in a shootout like this, he is just right. Mario lets a round go at Frazier on Bradford, and the chase continues. Most foot pursuits last only a few moments. This is a marathon, and it is far from over.

Reidus Saab hears the shots and looks out her window, an ill-considered maneuver that she can't resist.

"All them shots are ringin' and I see this officer right there. I guess God didn't have work for him that day 'cause he wasn't hit. I knew the boy who was runnin', sure. They shoot up this place all the time. Now when they come runnin' by that day, I know where that boy was headed. Straight to that Holy House."

As Lemite pushes himself up Bradford, he feels the presence of a narrow boy running by his side. Nothing in Brownsville and East New York is done alone. The people who live there know it. They have known it since the days when the Jews crowded these streets. The great and small moments of their lives are performed in front of witnesses. They know each other, they love

161

and/or hate each other. They cannot get away from each other. The enforced intimacy is maddening. Lemite cannot guess the intentions of his frail shadow, but he doesn't have the energy to look closely or shout him off.

The chase turns onto Glenmore, again onto Miller, and back down toward Pitkin, as Frazier heads toward "that Holy House," a crack-blighted apartment building near the far corner of Pitkin and Miller. One last straightaway. Gary and Mario, thirty-year-old men on the heels of a twenty-year-old, suck in air that feels like ground glass and hang on to the kid like hounds. The streets are lined with people like the finishing stretch of a famous road race. The runners are old rivals.

Frazier tries to dive into a parked car on the corner of Pitkin and Miller, but the three men inside lock the doors. He flees around to the rear of the Holy House and disappears inside. Finally, help is here. An Emergency Service Unit truck is screeching to the curb. Cars from PSA 2 and the 75th are alighting on the street like great screaming birds.

"We'll take off every fucking door," a Housing sergeant is saying. It isn't long before a trail of blood leads to the wounded Frazier, who is found changing clothes in a second-floor closet.

Outside, Gary Lemite peels off first his shirt, then his bulletproof vest, then his gun belt, which he drapes carelessly over his shoulder. Things do not seem to matter to him. He stands blank-eyed in the street. Behind him is the Xima beauty salon. On the wall beyond the salon is a mural with a motorcycle and the words "R.I.P. Manny." Nearby is another memorial, "R.I.P. Ant," and a picture of a gravestone, "Luis, 1979–1991."

The three men in the car Frazier tried to hide in have been detained. The fact that Frazier sought their help is enough to make them suspects. In their vehicle is half a pound of cocaine and $4,000. Gary is still dazed on the street. Chips of glass from bottles broken long ago sparkle at his feet. An open fire hydrant wastes a funnel of clear water in the oily gutter. A resident bellows from a window high above, "Let my people go," as Frazier, who has been bounced off a few walls on the way downstairs, is loaded into the ambulance for the trip to Brookdale. Still Gary stands.

Plainclothes Housing cop Gus Platt sidles through the crowd with a cheap smile. "Welcome to the club," he says to Gary. He means the shooters' club, for those cops who have been in gun battles. This is the first time Gary has fired his gun at a human being.

But Gary is not listening. His mind has stalled. Too many thoughts have been stashed away in the past few minutes, too many considerations put off in the simple world of action; no more ideas can penetrate until the brain disposes of its workload. He stands with his knees locked, hips forward, staring straight ahead. Then he hears a voice.

The kid who ran beside him up Bradford and Glenmore, down Miller — guardian angel, thrill-seeker, perp, whatever — is at his ear. "The gun," the kid whispers. "Let's go get the gun."

The gun. An image leaps to Gary's mind. As Frazier turned off Bradford onto Glenmore, he heaved the gun in a lofty arc across the street into an auto lot. The Emergency Service, an elite NYPD unit, is called over to check the lot. The search is crucial, because a police officer has shot someone. Gary stands by, the kid next to him. ESU finds the Beretta.

Still Gary is unfocused. "La-la Land," he calls it later. It is Sam Tilly, a Housing cop who was shot in the arm in Harlem, who brings him back. It is not the pats on the back or the words of praise that do it, just Sam close by. For a year after his shooting, Sam was trapped in a never-ending replay of the moment. He watched the shooting in slow motion and real speed. He could even freeze the action at will, but he could not make it go away. Sam understands. One look in his eyes and Gary feels much better.

But not for long. The thing is over, but adrenaline has life of its own, and Gary can't relax, can't even sit down. He shot the kid. He is glad he hit the kid, but he is all twisted up anyway. He hit the kid.

Very few cops ever actually fire their guns, much less shoot a human being. For Gary, a veil has been lifted. What if he had been hit? What if he had killed someone? What? Then a mood swing. "I know I can shoot. If I had a chance to get ready, I would have punched his ticket," he declares.

An instructor at the academy told Gary, "Someday you will look back on what you did and you are going to freak out," and now Gary knows exactly what the man meant: pride, confusion, and a buzz that won't go away. Gary walks to a pay phone and dials Lisa at her sister's house. His voice quivers.

"Lisa?"

"Are you all right?"

"Sure," Gary says.

"Sure?"

"Yeah, I'm O.K." Gary minimizes the gunplay. He and Lisa talk for a minute about how Sam said that Gary should see the police psychologist before he goes back to work. Another half a minute. There are long silences, and Lisa begins to edge off the phone. Gary hangs up, stands for a moment, and calls again. This time Lisa hears his voice and places the receiver gently back in its cradle. This is not her world anymore. She will not be forced into the role Gary needs her to play now. She just hangs up. The buzz of the dial tone releases a flood of rage in Gary as he walks toward the corner of Pitkin and Van Siclen to the car, where Sam is waiting to drive him to the hospital.

Things are not going any better for Mario. Expecting a reward for his valiant pursuit, Mario tells the inspector who interviews him after the shooting, "I'd like NEU." As aggressive as Gary was, it was Mario who was on Frazier's trail like an Exocet missile. But the inspector tells Mario that a promotion to the city-wide plainclothes detective path unit is out of the question. The big boss lets Mario know to expect a move in the opposite direction — a transfer, at the very least. It is about numbers. Mario now has four shootings in four months. If he does something bad now, people are going to ask why the pattern was not seen, why something was not done. The brass will try to protect themselves from that kind of second-guessing now. It is unlikely that Mario will be back at PSA 2.

Frazier's arm wound is superficial and he is out of the hospital in hours. Back in the squad room, the detectives are not happy with Earl Frazier. He tried to kill a cop.

"You came in here with some information and your handsome face," a detective tells Frazier before the kid sits down to be questioned. "You're not leaving with both."

Even with that, Frazier cannot get his story straight. He tells the detectives and the circuit-riding ADA who takes preliminary statements in the local precincts that he carried the gun because some guys were looking for him. He ran because he did not want the gun charge, and as he fled, he passed two Spanish guys who were shooting at each other. One of their shots, Frazier says, hit him in the arm. His second story is that he took the gun out of his waistband as he was running and it went off.

As he thinks about the shooting in the ensuing days, Gary becomes convinced that the people who let Earl Frazier hide in their apartment should be charged. "If they didn't let him in voluntarily, as they claim, then Frazier should be charged with breaking and entering or burglary," he argues.

It seems that Gary has been making too many good moves on the street, stepping out of his place in the pecking order of the PSA. The good-natured kidding directed at him from the other officers has all but faded away, and in its place a vague wariness has arrived. Downstairs in the PSA, somebody has written "Knows it all. Does it all" on Gary's locker.

Two days after the shooting Gary still cannot sleep, cannot lasso the galloping adrenaline. At three o'clock in the morning, his eyes jammed open in the dark of his bedroom, his pulse roaring for action, he is on the phone talking with a friend about Earl Frazier, and about his wife. He has seen the police shrink, told the man he is O.K. But he still feels jumpy. Near dawn he gets some sleep, but he's gummy-eyed when he wakes. Frazier. Damn. It's not about Gary's performance on the job or his ambitions anymore; the shooting has released a swirling cloud of uncertainty. Gary has been cleared by the department doctor to come back to work later in the week. At noon, he calls the PSA to find out what his schedule will be. He discovers he will be out a day longer than he thought he would be. "They mean well," he says of the psychologists and supervisors.

As thoughts of the shooting subside, another tide of anxiety rises. Gary cannot stop thinking about how Lisa hung up on him. He has to get back to work. Every moment the telephone in his basement apartment sits mute on the wall, every silent meal he eats, makes the possibility of their reunion seem more remote.

The beat goes on. With no family to go to, no wife to call, Gary throws himself back into the streets. He is riding hard, watching every move of every kid, looking for bulges and quick step-offs. Some of the other officers have other things on their minds. One afternoon Gary spots a kid with what he is sure is a big gun. He tells the driver of the van to turn around and the cop just keeps driving down the road. Gary does not say anything at the time, but back at the PSA he vents his anger to guys he knows will tell the driver. The next day the driver of the van comes up and says to Gary, "I hear you're saying I'm the devil. Am I the devil?"

"Well, no. I wouldn't call you the devil," Gary says.

A couple of days later, Gary rocks a fresh-mouthed kid against a wall in the lobby of Seth Low Houses. It is the kind of thing that brought J.R. good reviews. But Gary is called back to the PSA within an hour of the incident. Lenti wants to know the story. The mother just called, complaining that Gary was drunk. Satisfied, Lenti sends him right back out, but it is not long before Gary learns that the mother has filed a civilian complaint over the incident.

SATELLITE

Sharron is standing slouched at the head of the small classroom, his wrists crossed in front of his genitals, hands loose, ready to move. His head is down, eyes up. He is fiercely nonchalant. Twenty students watch carefully as he speaks the body language of the street. This is a role-playing exercise. At Satellite, the school day doesn't begin with an anonymous homeroom but with a "strat," or strategy period, a counseling session designed to help students deal with personal distress. Strat can be a boring annoyance or, when a topic catches on, an opportunity to help students confront their own trauma. The man in charge of Sharron's strat is Neil, a tall, bald and bespectacled veteran instructor who is also Sharron's science teacher.

Today's exercise finds Sharron cast as a witness to a street crime. To the uninitiated, his posture indicates an insolent lack of discipline. In fact, it is both functional and articulate. The exaggerated slouch communicates to the thief that Sharron is not a regular citizen, a "vic," constrained by laws against possession of weapons. The placement of the wrists is a stylized martial arts pose, offering protection and potential for quick reaction. The tucked chin protects the vulnerable neck area.

In the scenario, an elderly woman has been robbed; the mugger bolts toward Sharron, who has an opportunity to rescue the woman's pocketbook, which holds her rent money. "Help me, help me, please," the girl portraying the victim wails. Like a matador, Sharron steps smoothly aside, and the thief is gone. His classmates nod approvingly.

"Go, *Sharron*," a girl in the back applauds. In the students' eyes, volunteer crime prevention is misguided and frightfully dangerous.

Like most adults, Neil takes a quick liking to Sharron. Things start in September on the right foot. The other students accept Sharron just as quickly. For his part, Sharron is not interested in cutting an astounding figure in this small theater. He is content to lie low. The pressure on his wardrobe will not be as intense; the clothes on his back will not be the subject of such rapt attention as they were at Jeff. Simply, there will be less drama.

Satellite Academy is housed on the drafty second floor of an old office building facing the back wall of City Hall in downtown Manhattan. The quarters are cramped and the equipment is limited. There is no gymnasium, auditorium, or library, no labs, few computers. But the classes are tiny, the teachers warm and zealous. "The students help make the decisions here," a henna-haired Hispanic girl says as she lounges by a desk in a reception area. "If you fight, you get kicked out, no matter who threw the first punch. So you don't see any fighting. And you can take a teacher to school court if the teacher gets all loud with you."

Sharron may have made the best move of his life going to school outside Brownsville. With the accelerated credit program at Satellite, he stands a chance of earning enough credits to graduate by June. When he accompanied Frank to Satellite High, he serendipitously placed himself on the cutting edge of instruction on the urban high school level. Carol Beck is a phenomenon, to be sure, and it would be difficult to conjure a teacher with more assets than Sharon King, but schools like Jefferson may well be obsolete. With eighteen hundred students, Jefferson is simply too large and impersonal for the kids it serves. When such schools were designed, centralization aimed at offering varied programs and specialized equipment that would be impractical for every small school. The large public high school could bring students together with teachers who had special expertise. It was a good idea for its time and place. Clearly, it does not work anymore.

In the future, educators and urban planners may despair that cities stuck with the megaschools as long as they did. The schools are like the projects themselves — a good solution to a bygone problem. The adolescents who go to Jeff need personal attention. The baby talk that Ms. King dispenses fills a personal and emotional void for her charges. These students fail to learn high-level reading skills not because they don't understand or can't remember — they manage to create and revise their own language every month — but because they harbor a mistrust of the words on the page and the teacher who introduces those words. What they need is an educational environment that is structured to make personal relationships between the teachers and students possible, so the kids can bond with mentors.

It will still be a tough year for Sharron. He faces courses in anatomy, ideas, interdisciplinary writing, and novels. And he will have to find a way to do some homework for the first time in his life. If he is to negotiate the land mines around him, live through the school year, and emerge with a high school diploma or on the verge of receiving one, he will have to stay out of the way of the bullets and the law. But there is more to his dilemma. Despite pledges to his mother and Ms. King, despite his words, there is something deep in Sharron that resists the passage out of Brownsville, the relinquishment of his hard-earned props.

If Sharron does graduate from high school in June, he will be the first in his family to do so. Shawanda dropped out in the eleventh grade, and Gloria stopped going in the tenth, when she had Shawanda. Even with his arrests, his shoplifting, and his fights, and despite getting left back in seventh grade, Sharron carries his mother's lofty expectations with him as surely as if he were the scion of a wealthy family.

Gary's sister-in-law, Melanie, and her husband, Bill, do their very best to make their own sunshine. They have a swimming pool with a sun deck and a hot tub and plenty of extra room in their airy childless house. Bill is a "can do" guy with a consuming desire to make his wife happy. Here, Lisa has her own room and much less responsibility than she had in the basement in Elmont. She can sit around the pool while her sister and brother-in-law fuss over the kids, even sunbathe nude on their enclosed deck.

Gary was never the ideal husband, or boyfriend, for that matter. When he first started to date the open-faced, blue-eyed Lisa, he treated her with the same cavalier approach he used with all his girlfriends. When he picked her up for a date, he would pull up in front of her house and beep his horn. Lisa's parents were irritated, but she was mad about her Haitian suitor with the body language and accent of a Queens construction worker. She would skip out to the car. But soon she had enough of Gary's self-satisfied ways and stopped seeing him. This first defection shook Gary in a way that he did not fully understand. He managed to conceal his mounting desperation and woo her back, but he never forgot the feeling.

Lisa still has a soft spot for Gary's smile. And after a couple of sea breezes at a local bar during their first attempt at reconciliation, her grievances over his mania for the job, his casual attitude toward her happiness, and the rabbit warren of a basement he calls a home lift magically away. All she can think of is lying down with him again. It has been a month since they have held each other.

When they get home, Gary undresses her in the half-light of their bedroom. She has not lost the weight she gained from carrying Zach. But that does not matter. Gary holds handfuls of her thick chestnut hair in his hands, draws them to his face, and inhales. After they make love, he reaches to the table lamp and switches on the light. Lisa is a quarter Cherokee; a red Indian head tattoo glistens on her shoulder blade, and her skin is soft and deeply, gloriously tanned.

Gary snaps his head back, drawing his chin down to his chest. "What the fuck is this?"

"What?" Lisa wants to know, her eyes round with innocence.

"You know what I'm talking about." Gary's voice quivers. "I told you about taking your clothes off. You can do whatever you want, but not with the kids around. I told you."

Lisa has been preparing for a moment just like this. "Neither you nor anybody else is going to tell me what to do. Understand that?"

The light from the small lamp beside the bed shows that Lisa's suntan is uninterrupted by spots where clothing might have been — should have been, according to Gary. The evening is ruined. After Lisa leaves, Gary sits in the kitchen with the lights off, plagued by images of her loose behavior in front of the kids, of family conspiracies against him, of Lisa's imagined infidelity. Why will no one put in a good word for him? Dammit, hasn't he helped every one of them at one time or another?

The only bright spot is the weekly Friday night visits Gary and Lisa are making to see the pastor at Lisa's church. Merle is a middle-aged midwesterner who can be very helpful when he is not rigging sides on volleyball nights or rubbing people the wrong way with his hypercompetitive play in all sports. He seems as if he really wants the couple back together, wants Lisa to think about giving the marriage another chance. The pastor advises patience and support.

Gary Lemite has jeopardized his marriage by his singular focus on his job, while at Satellite, Sharron Corley is risking his last chance at a high school diploma. He is having trouble making it to school on time. This day in October, after missing strat and his first-period class, on the brain, he strides into his interdisciplinary writing class, his face soft from sleep. Two energetic young team teachers flutter earnestly about the room, working with individual students. They accept Sharron's late entrance pleasantly, taking a moment to hand him the topic sheet for the writing assignment. After ten minutes, he has done no writing.

"Are you all right, Sharron?" one of the teachers asks.

"Yeah, cool." He smiles and adjusts the position of the assignment sheet on his desk. He stares at the paper. But his Polo frames fail to deliver a studious appearance as he yawns through the session, thinking about what kind of lunch period he and Frank will have. The two friends have taken to jumping the turnstiles, riding the train to Greenwich Village, and "taking lunch." Besides such mischief, he is bothered by an energy deficit. Even though he had endless patience for the Jefferson play, he seems now to be dragging himself through every school day. He has always gotten his spirit of perfectionism from the spotlight. But Satellite is no kind of stage, no fashion show. There isn't even a proper mirror anywhere in the joint.

At Jeff, Sharron's lateness and lethargy might be overlooked, but here at Satellite, Neil is watching. When Frank and Sharron slip up the back stairs after lunch, late for their class, the towering Neil is standing akimbo in the hallway. He does not say a word, just raises his arms over his head with his fingers spread, as if to say, "What's up? You guys are faking the whole thing here, and I know it."

Sharron slinks sheepishly off to class, but still he has other

things than school on his mind. Following his conversation
with Chantal the day he went to Jeff to get his transfer papers,
Sharron determined to meet his responsibilities as he saw them.
He hit Macy's and Bloomingdale's and began a boosting spree
for his girl. On his second trip to Manhattan, he "caught" a
brown and beige reversible goose-down vest for Chantal to wear
when the weather turns cold.

When Sharron gets home from school, before he heads upstairs, he stops at the pay phone and places a call to Chantal.
"Yeah, I miss you," he tells her. Baby Andre is babbling and
cooing in the background. "Let me speak to Andre."

Chantal is reluctant. Sharron doesn't call every day, and she
wants him to herself. "Oh, Sha, you know he can't say nothin'."

"You said he could talk."

"He *do* be talkin'. But you can't tell what he's sayin'."

"Put him on the phone."

Andre produces a variety of sputtering sounds into the phone.

"What you want? What you want? Why you spit so much?
When you comin' to see your daddy?"

In a moment Chantal is back on the line. "Sha?"

"Andre says you been smokin' cigarettes, an' you ain't been
goin' to school."

"Who says I . . . Oh Sha, stop. It's hard. How come I beep you
an' you don't call?"

"Sometimes I be in the train. Or school. Or rehearsal." Sharron has been spending time in his cousin Morris's tiny sound
studio, singing with Frank, who Sharron has discovered pos-
sesses a talent for rap, and a boy named Chris, whom Sharron
has nicknamed "the choirboy."

"We sound mad good," he tells Chantal. "I got a new song,
'Nothing Can Go Wrong.'" He begins to croon the lyrics into
the phone.

> *I've got a job to do.*
> *Let's get it done, get it on.*
> *It can only get better.*
> *'Cause nothin' can go wrong.*
> *Nothin' can go wrong.*

*

A local in Unity aims a finger at Gary Lemite one day and asks Lonnie Hayes, "Who the hell does that half-white motherfucker think he is?" Hayes just shrugs.

The bleak landscape matches Gary's mood. His heavy hands are earning him enemies on the street, but his spate of gun collars is bringing him props in the PSA. The rumor mill says he will be promoted again soon.

Today he is still on the sweep team. It is noon. Five officers approach the van. Marlene Pemberton is at the wheel, Sergeant Billy Bright in the passenger seat. John McMullen greets Jimmy Galvin as he steps up to the vehicle. Each of the two cops has recently been called a major disappointment by the sweep supervisor, Lieutenant McGinty. McMullen snaps his hand to the brim of his cap in a crisp salute.

"Good evening, Major Disappointment."

"At ease, Major Disappointment," Galvin returns.

"How was it last night?" Galvin asks Marlene as the van begins to move.

"Good to me. Better to him." Marlene turns to Galvin and McMullen behind her, doffs her hat, and wiggles her eyebrows.

"Watch the road," Sergeant Bright admonishes.

"How many rounds?" McMullen wants to know.

"The distance."

"The distance?"

"Yeah, this golden pussy probably kill one of you needledicks."

"How can you say that, after you licked my pickle last week?" McMullen protests.

"Slow down," Gary snaps from the back seat. Marlene slows the van next to a group of kids. "Nah, go ahead," Gary instructs.

"Whaa, Gary, you see a bulge? Marlene, Gary saw a bulge. You wanna go back?"

As the van rolls down Rockaway Avenue, a youth makes steady eye contact with the officers in the van. "That's that asshole that we had on the dis con. The one with the bullets, a couple of months ago," Galvin remembers.

Police officers depend on their powers of recall, shine their memories up and roll them out like fancy cars.

"Nah. It was a holster. Black holster," Gary corrects.

There are problems for Gary with the sweep team detail. The

quality-of-life assignments they are sent on are often seen as harassment by the tenants, who call them the Goon Squad, and civilian complaints pile up. The sweep team is also trouble for cops like Gary because it forces them to sink to the level of their squad. Virtually everything the group does is agreed upon in advance by all four or five cops and the supervising sergeant in the van. There is much discussion, but limited spontaneous, instinctual police work.

Now the team is waiting outside the PSA for Sergeant Bright to emerge from the bathroom.

"What the fuck is he doin', layin' cable?" McMullen gripes.

One aspect of police work that cops like is that it has room for all types. An officer can shift from one profile to another at will. There are the hotshots, like Lemite and Lavin and Schulman, and the guys who never want to make a collar, who just walk through the motions. A guy can tear up the streets for a while. Then, if he thinks he's been screwed by the job or he goes through a change of life, he can make the transition to being a cleanup man. No questions asked.

The only advantage to driving around with five guys is the jokes. "You gap-toothed Irish bastard," Galvin says to McMullen. "The reason your father put himself in a home is 'cause he didn't want to pay your dental bills."

For his part, McMullen, formerly Robocop of the Brownsville Houses, who now insists on being called McDaddy, is delighted, giddy, to be back at work after a dreadful accident some months ago. He was searching a project rooftop for a suspected robber and climbed up a ladder to a wooden water tank. As he was coming down, the ladder snapped off and he fell ten feet to the graveled roof. He shattered his pelvis and was rushed to Bellevue Hospital, where he shared space in the intensive care unit with perps of all kinds. When Jeff Desimone showed up to visit, he whispered, "Wake up, asshole." McMullen roused himself from a haze of painkillers. There were intravenous tubes in his arms and a catheter in his penis. "Get me the sex crimes unit," he quipped. "I'm being violated."

Many police officers dream of getting out on three quarters, tax-free disability. The chiefs and the superchiefs routinely come up with some "job-related" injury or heart ailment that puts them in the comfort zone of a disability pension. One

NYPD chief got out on three quarters because he said he had incurred irreplaceable hearing loss at a Rolling Stones concert at Shea Stadium. Many cops dream of shedding the "blue burden" and going on to another life, but McMullen is not one of them. He is not as collar-driven as Gary — a bachelor, he does not depend on the overtime — but like Gary he loves the job. When he recovered, he came back to work. His first day back, it was all he could do not to skip down Sutter Avenue.

High-riding October clouds sail over Pennsylvania Avenue. Across the street from Jeff, on Dumont, opposite the drug house at 666, Michael T. stands near the center of a group of boys tossing Selo, a game of dice. It is just 1 P.M. on this school day. The cubes rattle against a cement wall and tumble onto the sidewalk as the sweep van pulls slowly to the curb. Gary is on the sidewalk side of the van in the back seat. The dice game is over. The boys back off slowly, except for Michael T. "That's the cop I almost clapped," the big kid tells his cronies, forming a gun with his index finger and thumb and pointing it at Gary. "Shoulda clapped him."

"Starts talking that shit again," Gary grumbles to his partners, "I'm gonna lock him up."

IN FULL EFFECT

he first bite of autumn finds Carol Beck harried. Her lower lip is dry and cracked. She wears a blue suit with a wide white tie and her Nefertiti brooch. She is moving down the hall at the head of a platoon of security guards, looking for class-cutters, interlopers. A handful of disappointed miscreants are caught in the open, herded into an elevator, and escorted to a holding room. "Run them through the computer," Beck snaps. Within minutes, a call will be placed to each child's home — that is, if the student has a phone.

On her way back to her office, Beck is summoned to a fourth-floor window. Five girls are standing on the pavement across the street from the school. With help from a guidance counselor, Beck identifies four of them. Their names are fed to the computer, the calls made. Within ten minutes, an irate mother is on the street, jawing at her daughter.

The two toughest seasons at Thomas Jefferson are the fall and the hot days of late spring. This fall is probably more difficult because of the triumphs of last year. There was the naive feeling that the battle had been won. But in a big city high school, the battle is never won. Suddenly, Beck feels she must sit down. "We can't schedule that meeting for second period tomorrow," she tells her assistant principal, who trails her down the hall, "because we have a sweep second period. This is like a war. I won't give up the hallways. And I won't give up the street outside my school. I'll take a bullet if I have to."

Bashim remembers when Beck was a brand-new principal. "She was standing up on the stage and giving out the rules and whatnot. You know, the do's and the don'ts that she had. It was a whole list of shit. All of a sudden some guy yells, 'Fuck you!' Beck comes down off the stage and smacks the shit out of the guy right there. All the people are sayin', 'Hey, we aren't havin' this. Nobody is gonna smack me, blah blah,' and we walk out. Get this. There's all these kids standing out in front of the school and Beck comes out and says, 'Get back in the school,' and people went back in."

Another time there was a fight between a group from the Linden Houses and Bashim's Raiders from Howard. "It was wild — dudes was throwin' down right in that small space on the first floor. The security guards were like peekin' through the little windows at the end of the hall. Beck is right in the middle of it, pullin' guys off each other. There were razors flyin' through the air, whoosh, whoosh, and she was right there. Carol has heart. Everybody knows that."

Still, Beck is under siege. There are about a hundred freshmen who are not adjusting. "They are like mercury," she observes, with a look on her face as if she has seen something new. "Half a dozen come together just to rob people in the stairway, and then just like that — apart. I had to throw eight of them out this week. They were jumping my football players in the stairwells." As she arrives at the door of her first-floor office, she adds, "We have a contradiction. We have the sweetest, the smartest, and the craziest." She shakes her head slowly. "They don't believe." But Beck doesn't allow herself to sink for more than a moment. In a flash, her face breaks into a wide, disingenuous smile. She often makes exaggerated faces so she can be read by the students more easily. "They shot Wesley in the barber shop," she says solemnly, and then, clapping her hands like a little girl, "We got land from the city to make a garden."

Beck retreats into her meeting room and collapses into a hard chair, breathing deeply, resting. In front of her is a scarred wooden table large enough to accommodate a dozen people. But despite School Chancellor Fernandez's school-based management plan, designed to broaden the decision-making process, Beck is running this campaign alone. And in her own way. Behind her is a private bathroom, which she makes available to a steady stream of students, an astounding practice for a New York City principal.

A newly curvaceous sophomore enters. "I just want the transfer paper," the girl insists shyly. It seems she has had an argument with her mother, the guidance counselor has been prodding her to improve her attendance, and she wants to go to Thomas E. Dewey High School.

Beck is seductive. She stands and steps back, examines the student, and fairly blushes with admiration. Then she moves her hands in the air to describe the girl's new shape.

"You aren't a bucktoothed girl anymore. You have fashion. I see those hats you wear. You're a star, a born leader, smart and beautiful."

The girl is touched. She stares at Beck as though hypnotized.

"Thank you, Ms. Beck."

Then the principal snaps the curve ball. "But in two years you will not know a single one of these people that you are trying to impress now. It's sad but it's the truth. We're up your nose now because we care. When we stop talking to you, that's when you start to worry."

The girl decides to stay at Jeff.

When she exits, Beck remarks, "A beautiful girl, and she's just finding where her zippers are. All that attention. I have to combat that with my own brand of attention."

A few minutes later, the revitalized Beck is lecturing a dozen boys in a small room used for music instruction. Seated in the ascending seats are the survivors of the final cut for the varsity basketball team. In the front row is Cortez Sutton, the quick-witted transfer from Lafayette, whose suspension will bar him from league games; behind him is Willie Brown, a four-square junior swingman who started on last year's team. Another veteran, Musbau Ogunyemi, a knobby-boned center who calls himself Nick, is on hand, sprawling at the end of the first row near the wall. Newcomers Jude Princivil, a junior forward, and his brother, Carl, a sophomore point guard, are positioned several rows up. The coach, George Moore, a six-foot-four, thick-waisted, light-skinned man with a short scraggly beard, stands by. Moore, about forty years old, is a corrections officer who doubles as security chief at Jefferson. He has been head basketball coach here for three years.

The glory days of Jefferson basketball have been over for a while. The National Basketball Association has had a handful of Jefferson players in its ranks of millionaires, including several, such as Sidney Green, who plays for the San Antonio Spurs, who are still there. The neighborhood courts are still brimming with talented players, but life is so tough here now that the best players from the Ville either drop out or go to school outside the neighborhood. If they do stay at Jeff, they have trouble sticking on the team. Beck has made it perfectly clear that the basketball team is a sidelight to academics in her regime. She will have no truck with superstar ne'er-do-wells at Jefferson. It is part of her plan to deemphasize basketball and highlight gymnastics, fencing, tennis, and swimming to erode the stereotype of the black male. She is tough with the ballplayers.

"I will not have you play for me and play with those Gauchos or Hauchos," she begins, referring to the citywide teams sponsored by private businesses. "Those are basketball entrepreneurs. They try to buy you with a pair of underwear and a pair of sneakers. If you play for me, that's all you do. I don't know what their agenda is, but if you can be bought with a pair of sneakers, something is wrong." Nick makes eye contact over his shoulder with Jude and nods his head affirmatively. *I told you Ms. Beck knows the deal,* he seems to say.

"We are not using you as a tax write-off," Beck continues. "We are here to help you become what you want to be. There was that kid . . ." She turns to Moore. "What was his name? The kid who got shot. He went to Jefferson as a freshman."

"Lloyd Daniels," Moore says, referring to a six-foot-eight playmaking *wunderkind* who was expelled from the University of Nevada at Las Vegas after he was arrested in a crack house. The players nod knowingly. Daniels was later shot in the stomach; after he recovered, he struggled through the minor leagues and made it to the San Antonio team in the NBA.

"Lloyd Daniels couldn't even write his name," Beck continues. "I want you to be like Bill Bradley." She stops and eyes her players. This time the squad comes up blank, except for Cortez, who whispers the word "senator" over his shoulder. "I want basketball to help you be what you want to be," the principal explains. "Basketball is too short a career."

Beck notices that rangy Jude Princivil is wearing a hat. "I don't want you with the hats." Jude snatches it off. "They don't sell those hats anywhere but East New York. I don't want people to know you're from Brownsville and East New York just by looking at you. Like that little monster from 176 Amboy Street who is getting ripped off by Don King." Nobody in the room has to mention Mike Tyson's name.

"We will check your eligibility," Beck warns. "You can count on it. We will not be slippin' and slidin'. You will have your proper average, and when the scouts come, you will have your transcript in order. And if it means I have to play with less talented players, I will do it."

Little Michael Washington looks at the floor. He is undergrown, has minimal court skills, and knows he is on the team only because he has been going to class and keeping his repertoire of wisecracks under wraps. Beck knows Michael well. "We will never be embarrassed that you went to Jefferson," she says in his direction. "Nobody will have to mention your name being involved in any foolishness. You are my leaders, my *men*. If I have to take your hat, I am going to be outraged. We are not wearing hats. It makes you look like hoodlums. You are not hoodlums. You are talented stars."

Beck finishes her speech and leaves the stage to the athletic director and the coach. It was a good speech; it showed the players the tone of the program, which is not about excellent basketball but about acceptable schooling. The one thing that Carol Beck perhaps did not understand was the purpose of the hats and the hoods. Kids like Jude and Cortez, and the instigator Michael, do not wear those accessories for their style alone. They wear them for safety. It is hard enough walking home through the Linden Houses to the Boulevard Houses, or walking past Unity, without wearing a sign on your back proclaiming that you are a straight arrow, with your eye on the future. The gangster look is surely protective coloring. The hoods and the hats serve the same purpose as the ski masks and goggles that the kids in Crown Heights have taken to wearing; they give the chilling impression that you don't want to be identified. The droopy-pants look comes out of the house of detention, where belts are confiscated to prevent suicide and mayhem. This is the gear of the trouble kids, the robbers and the baby gunmen. Who can blame Nick, the lanky center, who takes a ride home every day with the basketball coach, if he does not want to make it immediately apparent that he is unarmed and not disposed to violence and cruelty, that he is much closer to being a victim than a perpetrator? It is easy for Beck to ask the kids to dress like squares and bookworms. She will not have to pay the consequences.

When Beck leaves, the boys relax, but only a bit. Coach Moore is not to be taken lightly. He steps up on the raised lecture space and begins his policy statement in a sweet baritone voice. "Plain and simple. You must have an eighty percent attendance rate. You must go to class. You must come to the study period in Room 242–244 seventh period. If you don't come to the study period, you don't practice, and if you don't practice, you damn sure don't play in the games. I don't care who you are. An example is Nicky. I love him, but if he doesn't go to class, he will not be here. And about the hats. Don't wear hats in school. Homos wear hats in school." (Homophobia is standard fare in Brownsville and East New York. There are no openly gay students in the school.)

"You must learn not to react. Most teams are hostile to Jefferson. When we showed up at Fashion Institute for a game last year, the first thing the coach told me is 'We don't want any trouble.' I am the last coach to let my players fight. Let the other team woof. We want you on the team. We have a player here, as you all know, Ronnie, who is very talented. He is a man in a boy's body."

"A boy in a man's body," Cortez corrects, from his seat.

"But he will never play on this team," Moore continues, "because he doesn't go to class.

"We are a team. When things go wrong, we are a team. The crowd is gonna be yelling and going crazy, and you look up and down the bench and all you have to rely on is your team. And stop louding [constantly criticizing] each other. Don't laugh if a guy has short socks or a funny-colored hat." Like Beck, Moore is on tough ground here. Cortez, for one, has built his entire personality around the argumentum ad hominem of the streets. Already he has taken to calling starting point guard Ed Alcy "Head." When someone asks why, Cortez points: "Look at him."

"We are going to South Carolina to play in the tournament like we did last year," Moore announces proudly. "You get all you can eat, and believe me, last year Nick ate all they could offer. And when you get down there, be ready, because those country boys really get psyched when they come against you city boys."

"They got a mall," Nick announces to his teammates.

Carl is concerned. "Them country boys can really jump, right? But they don't bounce the ball 'cause they live on dirt?"

The same afternoon, upstairs on the fifth floor, Ms. King is entertaining her global history class. The back of the neat classroom is lined with ancient steel lockers covered by dozens of coats of thick paint, the last a pale blue. The lockers, used in the past for students' books, are now empty. The floor of the room is worn wood.

"Mussolini was a *dick*" — King waits like a borscht-belt comic for the word to sink in — "*tator*." She adds the final syllables with a wink. Things are going well in the class. King, prepared as always, has piles of typed handouts, even though today's lesson is drawn from the textbook. The atmosphere in the room is cheerful, not loose; the students are upbeat, not giddy.

A hard justice is dispensed to those who teach poor black and Hispanic kids in the city. A hard-working, talented teacher is often rewarded for his or her efforts, just as a bad one is punished. The reinforcement does not come from the administration, it comes from the students. If a teacher is lazy, afraid, incompetent, the students make his life hell. Disrespect mounts to mockery and outright abuse. The teacher retreats to fearful inactivity or bitter reprisal, jawing with students in the hallway, flouncing into the office with the big complaint. Not King. She is having a ball, and so are the kids. She is teaching about nationalism, aggression, and appeasement, about the sense of impending disaster throughout Europe before World War II.

Fifteen minutes into the lesson, Khalil Sumpter and his man Dupree stride in, late as usual. This rankles King. She was on a roll. Khalil sprawls in his seat with his head tossed back and to the side, his jaw slack with mock exhaustion. King walks over and positions a textbook on the desktop in front of him. She smiles tightly. He has been coming to class every day, but that is not enough for her.

One day a few weeks ago, in late September, she called him

into the hall and stared deep into his eyes. "What am I doing wrong?" she asked him.

From the refuge of his slouching, indifferent manner, Khalil thought for a moment. His standard school affect was not really working with King. His was not a flexible stance. His strategies were not designed to deal with the golden skin and sweet scent of a Ms. King. "Nah, 's not chu," he allowed softly. He didn't want to tell King about the fights with his nemesis, Tyrone Sinkler.

"Tell me what I'm doing wrong, Khalil, because I really want to do better." King pressed her advantage.

He just shrugged.

"If it's not me, then it must be you," King said kindly. "So I'm gonna assume that since you come to school, you want to learn. That you actually want an education. So I'm gonna make sure that you have your books and you keep them open. And that you write down the things that I'm saying."

Khalil nodded.

But of course it is not that easy. Khalil is coming to class and helping himself to the little kisses that King gives out, insisting that she give him his dead on the lips. He thinks he is conning her, getting over.

According to King, Khalil Sumpter is the smartest kid in class. "One time, I thought he was copying a paper from a girl. He had the girl's paper on the desk in front of him and he was writing for half an hour. I told him, 'No, you aren't slick, Khalil, you copied the paper of a girl who hasn't been in the class in a month. Now both of you can fail.'" Amazingly, Khalil's paper, while obviously done in haste, fulfilled the requirements of the assignment and didn't contain a single phrase in common with the girl's paper. According to King, he is brilliant, one of the smartest kids in the school. But he is quite simply "acting like an asshole."

King is back in the front of the room, selling global history for all she is worth, when Khalil flips his textbook shut and releases an audible groan. The soft-sell time is over. King's system has been working like a charm. She is handing out "chill bills," tickets to be turned in for small rewards, for students who are on the ball. The class is hooked. But Khalil is a dead weight.

King jams her World War II lesson to a halt and strides over to Khalil's desk by the back wall, next to Dupree's. "Open your notebook."

Khalil snickers. He mumbles something about a bitch and sits motionless, waiting for King to give it up and move on. But he underestimates the teacher. This classroom is her life, her world. This is what she cares about, what she does best. And right now it is all about World War II. Khalil Sumpter is not getting the best of Sharon King, not this time, not any time.

King puts her hand firmly on Khalil's shoulder and he shrugs it off. She reaches down and opens his book and he snaps it shut.

"What are you gonna do? Fight me?" King wants to know.

He mumbles menacingly.

She bends over and takes off her shoes. She is not from this world; like Beck, she has never lived in a neighborhood like Brownsville or East New York. But she knows that the only way to succeed here is to accept certain interpersonal truths: if you are not willing to get down, you cannot hang in the Ville, and Ms. King is in the Ville to stay. She is not about to summon any security guards or assistant principals.

She tosses her shoes aside and gets ready to rumble in Room 544. Her loyal students, the ones who love her, stand up, edge closer, and watch, ready to make a move. It is no easy business, this. A wrong move can bring dire consequences from Khalil and his friends.

"I can't hit you. You know that," he says, "'less you hit me first."

Smack. King lashes out with a locked elbow; her open hand slaps the side of his face. "Fair now?" she asks.

The teacher has crossed the line. She was born to cross the line. That is what all the kissing is about, what she is about. The slap is a stupid move for a teacher. But King is not just a teacher. She is something else.

The students jump back and huddle against the wall nearest the door. Theresa, the girl who is taking King's class for the second time, begins to weep. Khalil is stunned. Greg Harris, a six-four, 195-pound athlete who is a King aficionado, leaps forward and holds the two apart in a meticulously nonpartisan, nonconfrontational way. Sumpter and Harris eye each other, worried boys in the bodies of soldiers, trying to understand what kind of men they will be.

At last Khalil shrugs himself free and stalks out of the room. Ms. King is unfazed. This woman has bad days, never bad dreams.

"The Italians loved Benito Mussolini," she resumes, gesturing for the students to go back to their seats. She pauses for a moment as they sit. "Because Mussolini made the trains run on time."

GOING TO REPRESENT

Crossed signals. It is 4:30 in the afternoon on the last day of October and Ms. King is standing at the front of the auditorium in I.S. 55, a junïor high school near Saratoga Avenue, some twenty blocks from Jefferson. This is the first meeting of the year of the Jefferson drama program, and understandably, King has big plans. But things are wrong from the start. For one, Sharron is not here to reclaim the spotlight. He didn't have the money to pay for his beeper charge this month, so King had to leave a message with his neighbor, Mrs. Dukes, and word never reached him.

There are worse problems. "Excuse me. I said, excuse me." There are seventy-five kids on hand, but few respond to King's request for quiet. They continue to chatter and giggle. "I'm not going to raise my voice. I don't *do* shouts," King says softly.

The fifteen veterans of last spring's play sit in the front two rows in a tight cluster, their faces raked with annoyance. They had looked forward to the start of the drama program with the enthusiasm of a gifted athlete looking forward to the sports season. They are ready for bigger and better things, ready to be stars again.

Finally, the beauteous, smoky-eyed comedienne Kenya, last spring's showstopper, who has traveled all the way from Sara J. Hale High School to be here, has had enough of the yapping. She raises herself slowly out of her seat, turns, and glowers at the witless bunch around her. "Shut up," she hollers in her stage-trained voice.

But it's no use. Almost all the other kids in the room are

junior high and elementary school students, from I.S. 55 and the surrounding neighborhood. King controls herself throughout the rest of the afternoon as the preteen rabble tries to focus on a fuzzy videotape replay of *Don't Give Up on Your Dreams* but ultimately succumbs to its members' rambunctious natures.

At six o'clock, King's outspoken regulars gather in the hall. The Jeff students have traveled to I.S. 55 by bus. Worse, they have had to come through unfamiliar neighborhoods. It is very important to these kids that they know an area. Even the most timid of them will express confidence that no one on their block or in their project will bother them because they "know everybody." It is hard enough for them to negotiate their way to and from regular school without doubling their vulnerability by having to travel to a second school for an extracurricular activity.

"I don't have car fare to be comin' over here every day," Sheryl complains.

Kenya rolls her eyes at the children scampering through the hallway. "This shit is just whack," she says.

"I don't know who was responsible for this, but we aren't going to have it," King says, and she quickly arranges for a protest meeting in Carol Beck's office the next day. She will stay out of the politics, let the students state their case and try to find out what the drama program is doing at I.S. 55.

For an educational initiative to be successful, it has to be active. The students have to have some feeling of power and be involved in problem solving. It is also crucial for the experience to have immediate application beyond the walls of the school. King's drama program last year, with its glorious week of performances in the spring, was just such an endeavor. Word got around Jefferson that the teachers in the drama program were "for real," that the school had spent serious money on the production. This was the kind of activity that could compete in the students' world with the cult of name-brand clothing and disrupt a hierarchy based on jewelry and violence. The Thomas Jefferson school play should have been used as a springboard to even bigger and better things; instead, it is headed for oblivion.

Somebody fouled up. Somehow, the Jackie Robinson Center got the impression that Carol Beck did not want its program back at Jeff. It may have been a matter of timing. A hands-on

principal, one as accessible as Carol Beck, runs the risk of allowing organizational problems to develop. Usually Beck's loyal
and fussy assistant, Ellen Greaves, rides herd on such details.
This time something went wrong.

Mr. Ozelius Clement, the director of the Jackie Robinson
Center, claims he waited as long as he could for Beck to commit. But Beck was having problems. She was juggling money
from several sources and battling the centrifugal force of her
freshmen Smurfs. The waning of the theater program, which
King and her students will soon abandon completely, is a significant mistake, the kind that principals with much less command of the situation make regularly. The Jackie Robinson Center, with its layers of supervision and checks and balances and
its emphasis on generous funding, was rated as one of the ten
best such programs in the country by a federal commission.
Nevertheless, Beck is unchastened. "I got along great before and
I'll get along great after. If I want it back, I'll get it back. I know
Jackie Robinson's widow."

"I know my son," Gloria Corley says, moving four steps through
the living room into the doorway of the cramped kitchen. Plates
of cold, half-eaten chicken sit on a counter next to the refrigerator. A plume of light backlights her carefully arranged, hennaed
hair. "He doesn't even like house parties. It's ironic. He's the
one who doesn't like them and he is the one who is going to get
hurt."

It's early November; Indian summer is gone for good. This
is clothing weather, profiling weather. Sharron is headed to
a house party, and he's not listening to warnings from either
Chantal or Gloria.

"I'm goin' to represent," he explains.

"Represent what?" Gloria scoffs as Chantal ducks her head
behind her hand and giggles. Chantal has been tucking Andre
under the goose-down vest Sharron boosted for her and carrying
him over to the Corley apartment several nights a week. When
she is not with Sharron in his room, she sits up with Gloria in
the kitchen, playing with the baby and gossiping.

"He's gonna have your eyes, Chantal," Gloria decides after
studying Andre's ruddy little face and glancing at Chantal. Gloria's full cheeks catch the light as she turns and smiles. The
features of her face seem to have been created with a soft brush.

By contrast, Chantal, seated at the table with Andre sprawled in the crook of her arm, was drawn with a sharp quick pencil. She has black chevron eyebrows and cheekbones that jut against stark pale skin.

"I dunno. All babies got squint eyes," Chantal says. "You gotta wait 'fore you could say that."

Gloria chuckles. Her head rocks slowly. "Got a point, sweetie."

Chantal turns her attention to Andre. "Say, 'Don't play me.' Like your daddy says. Go ahead. 'Dooon't play me.'"

"Don't teach him that shit. Bad enough we got one fool around here," Gloria says, nodding toward the bathroom where Sharron is preening for his party. She laughs again. She is great company until she has had two or three drinks of vodka. Then she changes from a young mother to a vamp, a transition Sharron despises. Her hand rides her hip. Her voice gets husky, and she parades in front of the mirror, adjusting her hair this way and that, talking about ways and means to party.

Chantal has already asked Sharron to stay home, playing both sides of the fence. She wants to get closer to Gloria, whom she has taken to calling Mommy. But she knows full well that Sharron's decision to attend a party in Flatbush, at which both the LoLifes and the Steam Team will be present, has not been made lightly.

Gangs of the fifties used to fight; the Brownsville Jolly Stompers and Roman Lords called it rumbling or jitterbugging when they headed over the bridge to fight the gangs from "the East," East New York. But the LoLifes and Steam Team plan to go at each other tonight with designer clothing as the weapon of choice. They will sashay through the darkened party rooms, seeking pools of light, striking poses, "representing," comparing "ITs," name-brand items. The battle will rage between the Polo fall line, favored by the LoLifes, and the season's offerings of Guess, specialty of the Steam Team. Many of the garments will have a small tear somewhere in the fabric where the plastic antitheft alarm has been ripped away. Some of the kids are even glad when the tear is visible, proof that the IT was earned, not bought.

"It's about props," Sharron tells his mother when he emerges from the bathroom.

"What're props going to get you?" Sharron does not answer

189

the question, so Gloria responds herself. "They're going to get you killed."

"Yeah, but then my son will have them," Sharron answers back.

On cue, Chantal reaches for the cooing baby and slides her tiny finger over his glistening pink lips. She is keeping her mouth shut now, but she is already a grateful beneficiary of Sharron's props. Both Chantal and Shawanda are taken more seriously in the neighborhood because Sharron has maintained their modest wardrobes and kept his reputation in order.

Sharron was the star of the play. That was a bonus, a one-time payoff. The LoLifes are a steady gig. And respect is an everyday kind of thing.

"You may have the props," Chantal explains to Gloria after Sharron has left. "But you have to work to keep them. You have to represent."

Besides, the LoLifes are not about heavy beefs. These are not the Young Guns, or even the Howard Raiders. Nonetheless, Sharron is uneasy as he waits at the Franklin Avenue station for the #2 train to Flatbush. It is true that he does not like house parties. There is too much jealousy, especially in situations involving girls. But this is an exception. He knows many of the members of the Steam Team, and the party will be safer because it is outside the Ville.

Tonight, Shalo is sporting a gold jeans suit over a brown 450 Polo turtleneck sweater with a large horse head knitted on the chest. He has on high burgundy Timberland boots and his thick gold chain bracelet, a birthday gift from his mother. He has slipped gold caps onto two of his front teeth and topped the look off with a pair of yellow-tinted Nautica sunglasses. He even has an extra shirt under his arm in case he feels the need for a fashion change in mid-party.

Sharron arrives at the small Jamaican club on Flatbush Avenue shortly after eleven. The term "house party" refers not just to parties in private homes but to any small affair that is not hosted by an official organization. The spot is nothing but a dank two-room storefront social club. But there are plenty of girls here, the music is blasting a reggae song, "Me Me Me Na Na Na Wan Go Riker's Island," and the place is dark. Sharron pays no attention to the music; the dancing will come later.

Now he shifts through the crowd in full attitude, profiling. In the back room an earphoned DJ tucked behind a large table bobs to the music. Beside the disc jockey is an exit to a small back yard where people go to get fresh air. Sharron is drawn to the outside area because in his eagerness to represent, he has worn too many clothes for the weather. His extra shirt, awkward to carry, is on under his sweater by now.

After a few minutes in the night air, he takes the plunge back inside, slapping hands at waist level over and over again as he brushes by LoLifes he knows or has seen. He pivots and assumes a spot in the half-light near the disc jockey.

"Wha's up?" he responds again and again, jiggling his head just a bit to the music. Sharron does not want to converse too long with anyone now. He is a solo act for the time being, and he doesn't want the sight lines blocked. But the heat of the crowded room drives him again toward the doorway to the back yard, for a combination of cool air and light. There is someone behind him, and as he shifts his weight, he steps on the guy's foot. The guy taps Sharron's shoulder, and Sharron turns slowly. He can barely see the kid in front of him, but the kid can see Sharron because he's standing in the light.

"Yo, watch where the hell you steppin', mon." The island voice comes from the shadows.

"Yo, couldn't you have said that better?" As Sharron speaks, his face hardens to an ice grill and his hand slides to an inside pocket for his razor-edged Exacto knife. He has every intention of pulling it out, but the kid walks away into the party and Sharron eases up on the razor. It is not so much what the boy said as how he said it. There is no such thing as a minor insult in this setting.

When the boy is a few yards away, he turns and starts ragging. "What ya got der, boy?" he sneers. Sharron steps inside. The Jamaican turns to a small group of friends and utters a sentence or two out of the side of his mouth, keeping his eye on the advancing Sharron.

Sharron can't understand what the Steam Team boys are saying, so he moves closer and assumes a stylized prefight pose, back to back, cheek to cheek with his antagonist. The tension is so thick that Sharron decides he had better get some of his people, so he steps away. Just as he gets to the entrance to the next room, someone grabs his collar. He doesn't turn around, just lunges ahead, trying to free himself. He feels the hand lift from his collar. But before he can turn around, more hands grab the back of his jacket. Sharron fights to get to his razor, but the inside pocket of his jacket is blocked by the folds of the extra shirt.

By now the girls have spotted the fight and a tumult of shrieks drowns the music. Panicked teenagers scramble through the dark for the front door. Everybody wants to be out before the bullets fly. As Sharron lies pinned to the floor, an image materializes in his mind of a silver gun suspended in the darkness. Somebody shouts, "Where is he? Just hold him," as he wriggles on the floor. There are punches to the back of his head, three. Something tells Sharron not to turn over. Then a force lifts his assailant off him and heaves Sharron out the front door into the clear fall night.

Hysterical kids are bounding in all directions. Sharron still has guns on his mind, so he dashes around a corner, rolls onto a lot with high grass, and lies very still. No one has followed, so after ten minutes he rises on all fours and prepares to stand. As he does, he feels the back of his head where he was hit. When he draws his hand back, it is covered with warm, sticky blood.

He shuffles toward a streetlight and tries to hail a cab to St. John's Hospital. But when the empty gypsy cabs catch sight of him, they hurtle past. Then a police car appears.

"Yo," Sharron yells.

The NYPD cruiser slows to a halt. The driver's side window rolls down. "Yo? Did you say yo?"

"I had a accident. I think I should go to a hospital 'cause I'm bleedin'." Sharron extends his blood-webbed fingers toward the officer, who flinches.

"Is that how you call a policeman, yo?" Sharron is silent. The officer nods at Sharron's hand. "How did that happen?"

"I cut myself on a fence."

"*What* fence?"

Sharron breathes deeply.

"If you don't tell us how that happened and who did it, we can't help you," the officer says, lighting a cigarette and blowing the smoke from his first drag out the window at the starry sky.

Sharron sucks another breath and turns away. No disappointment, or anger.

He has to call an ambulance for himself. It takes him ten minutes to find a public telephone, another twenty-five for the ambulance to arrive. He sits on the curb with his right hand pressed to the wound, then his left, shivering. All the time he imagines himself bleeding to death. At Kings County Hospital, he receives twenty-five stitches.

When he arrives home it is 6:45 A.M. and he falls right to sleep. When he awakes at noon he walks out to the kitchen, where Gloria is doing the dishes. "I got cut," he says, wheeling to show the white dressing covering the back of his head.

"Yeah?" Gloria turns and stares blankly at her son. Maybe this is how she will lose him, she thinks, not all at once to a bullet but piece by piece to the knife. For a moment she sees him as a boy, wondrously bright, bounding out the door to play, then coming home weeping, telling her everything in his heart.

"I'm sorry, Mommy," Sharron says.

APARTMENT 5AB

A visit to 295 Dumont Avenue by anyone other than a resident or a known crack customer sets off the vocal alarm. But the wily Nikia Vinson wants some publicity, so she has summoned a reporter. Recently released on bail because of her avowed willingness to testify, Nikki has refused an offer to enter the Federal Witness Protection Program. Instead, she has been promising people in the project she will double-cross Schulman on the witness stand.

It has been over a month since Born Son's federal bust. He and his boys are in the Metropolitan Correctional Center hard by the rushing traffic of FDR Drive in downtown Manhattan. Several times Nikki has bundled up Little Bit and taken him by gypsy cab to the jail, past the shotgun-toting guards stalking the sidewalk outside, to visit Bobby and assure him of her loyalty. Now she has another idea. She wants the press to know about Schulman's vendetta, and about the beating the Housing police administered to her lover a year ago, when they chased him into Apartment 5AB.

The walk up the short path to the front door of 295 is quiet. It is gray November in the projects. The last of the few leaves are gone. The only green left in the neighborhood is the surface of the all-weather basketball court, a state-of-the-art court complete with viewing stands, a block down Dumont. There is no one standing in front of the building, no one sitting on the bench there, but every step the stranger has taken has been watched from the dingy brick ramparts. The lookout on duty in the fifth-floor window picks up the intrusion. "Yo, hold up," he yells. The visitor waits. A report is made inside, the way cleared. "C'mon." The stairs to the fifth floor are still strewn with tiny red- and blue-tipped crack vials. There are no fortifications on the metal door, no double locks, no bullet holes.

Inside the apartment, the small living room is silent and hollow. Nikia and her square-faced cousin Renee sit beside each other in bright jogging suits on the edge of a damp and tattered brown couch. They are about the same age, but Nikki is in charge here. There are no curtains in the room, no lamps, no bulb in the overhead light fixture. There are no rugs, no stereos or televisions, no pictures on the wall. The apartment looks like a clubhouse inside an abandoned building, more a hideout than a home. The morning light seeps through the sooty window.

Through the hallway, past the kitchen, is another bleak living room, where two sheetless mattresses cover the floor. Between them lies a clutter of white Chinese restaurant takeout containers. In the bedroom beyond is a bunk bed sawed in half so the two pieces sit beside each other. The floor of a second bedroom is strewn with other mattresses and the overflow from the drawers of a missing dresser. A young man sits in his wheelchair in the shadows, listening to the sounds of a small radio. Renee's child toddles through the bedroom clutter, down the hall, and over to the couch. Renee keeps her eyes on her cousin as she hands the baby a box of dry cereal.

"They beat on Bobby with a radio," Nikia begins, referring to the time Schulman chased Born Son after the car stop. "He cu'n even walk. His eyes was close'. Mouth bleedin'. They still kept up tryin' to make him walk. We was asking what was the charge, and they kept sayin', 'Don't worry 'bout it. Y'all'll find out.'"

"Schulman put his gun in Grandma's face and called her a bitch," Renee adds.

In the fuzzy gloom of the apartment, Nikia continues her story. Another baby, this one in pink pajamas, waddles past as two tall, gaunt, scowling men in black full-length Los Angeles Raiders jackets enter the front door and stride through the room. These are the Worthy boys. They are in the apartment for thirty soundless seconds, then they leave. A stick-thin woman appears, picks her way through the living room, and goes back to the bedrooms at the rear of the apartment, all the while studying the floor like a nervous shorebird, muttering how pitiful it was to see the cops beat Born Son.

"They don' arrest nobody in all the projects," Nikia observes with a sweep of her arm. "They been sellin' around here for years." She squints and tosses her head toward the front door. "Still are," she says. "Schulman wanted one 'pecific person. That's who they wanted an' that's who they got, an' that's how they wanted it to be. Say Bobby came over here shootin'. Huh? How many times Born Son come over here? From Howard?"

"Once," Renee says. "That's it."

"Schulman killed a kid in Seth Low, you know?" Nikki thinks for another moment and adds, "He got 'Born Son Dies' wrote on his ammunition thing in white stuff," a reference to Schulman's speedloader. "Don't he?" Nikki looks at Renee, who nods.

Then Nikki attempts to humanize Bobby, to undo the myth that has grown too big. She starts with his name. "Born Son? His mother named him that 'cause she was in labor for a long time an' she was glad he was finally born. They say we made a *million* dollars. Say we was makin' eight hundred or nine hundred a day. Schulman watchin' too damn many movies. The person who's sellin's got to be paid. They got to be paid." She makes a gesture of disgust in the direction of the lookout on the fifth-floor landing. "We din't make nothing but seven hundred a day, all of us. You think if we was makin' crazy money Tanya'd be stealin' earrings and snatchin' dollar bills?"

Work is a funny word. Run ten miles around a track; that is play. Sell drugs morning, noon, and night, it's a crime. Federal Attorney Bob Fineberg, assigned to prosecute the Young Guns, and Bobby Schulman are certainly working hard on this case. Late at night in the basement of the federal building on Cadman Plaza, at the foot of the Brooklyn Bridge, they sit across from each other in Fineberg's tiny office and pore over the records of the case. There is a seized notebook, crack, drug paraphernalia, one gun, and jackets with "Young Guns" emblazoned on the back. There are months of surveillance records and videotapes. Much of the case, though, relies on Schulman's believability in front of a jury. Fineberg, in cowboy boots, suspenders, and a red bow tie, is behind an antique wood desk. Across the room is a cabinet holding his law books. Above the cabinet hangs a black-and-white picture of his father in an expensive suit, surrounded by distinguished-looking men. On another wall a movie poster celebrates the opening of *Die Hard*.

Fineberg is grilling the Housing cop on his testimony, checking anything a defense lawyer could shake him with: dates, angles of vision during surveillance, if and when he ever promised to get Born Son. Fineberg has a flat nasal accent, reassuring in its lack of passion.

"When I am cross-examining you, look right at me," he begins. "And don't let Bobby's lawyer make you nervous. The judge won't let him badger you." Schulman nods. He has been through this a hundred times in state court. This is Fineberg's first crack retail operation case, and it is he who is nervous. He has been shocked by the accounts of violence in Brownsville. Up until now he has prosecuted the kind of defendants who never make threats or carry them out. And he is more than a little wary of Born Son and the Young Guns. A week ago he asked Schulman for a bulletproof vest. Fineberg is also concerned that the defense will make Schulman out to be a gunslinger. The fatal shooting in the Seth Low Houses is sure to come up.

Fineberg has two identical pairs of glasses. He takes one pair off, replaces them with the other, and studies the Housing cop. Several years ago, Schulman was searching for a man wanted in a series of robberies. When he cornered the suspect in a project stairwell, the suspect pulled a replica of a gun and Schulman shot him dead. "Tell the truth about Seth Low. It's as simple as that. Don't at any point get aggressive. And don't volunteer any information. Just answer what is asked of you."

Schulman, wearing his bulletproof vest even in the stuffy office, runs his fingers along his handlebar mustache. "No problem," he assures the attorney.

Schulman's accent is pure Long Island, though he was raised in Florida and didn't move to the New York suburbs until he was fifteen. He is the real expert on this case. He has listened to hours of tapped telephone conversations. He knows which of the people he is locking up are stupid and which are deadly smart.

"I know what they're going to try to say," he continues. "I never said I was going to get Born Son. This was strictly business."

Fineberg nods his head. He is listening for the high pitch of the true believer, that plume of fanaticism that could ruin the case. But Schulman is level and straightforward. He will be just fine in front of a jury. In fact, Fineberg is starting to like Schulman quite a bit.

"Let Nikia talk all she wants," Schulman continues. "When it comes down to it, she knows she has to tell the truth on the stand or she's fucked."

When he and Fineberg finish for the night, it is after eleven. Schulman rises.

"Where to, Bob?" Fineberg wants to know.

"I gotta go back to the PSA."

"How're you getting there?"

"I'll take the A on Jay Street to Broadway Junction, switch to the L, and take that to Sutter. It's just five blocks to the PSA. I'll walk."

Fineberg, who has never been to Brownsville, is appalled. "You're not going to take the train out there this late?"

"Sure." Schulman laughs. "I have a gun and a vest and a radio. I'm set."

Still Fineberg is worried. He offers to give the cop money to take a taxi, and when Schulman refuses he hands him his home phone number. "Please call me when you get to the PSA," he insists. "I don't care how late it is."

"HE LOOKS LIKE A PERP"

A silver moon rides the barren black sky over the roof of a building in Van Dyke. Gary Lemite is looking for a body. A call came over the radio reporting that there were three young men with guns on a bench in front of a building and a shooting victim inside. The teenagers were there all right, two tall thin boys with large puppy feet and a stocky bow-legged friend, but no guns. A couple of bored 73rd guys arrived for backup and are holding the kids outside while Gary and his partner for the night, Jeff O'Donnel, search for a victim.

Of all his duties, Lemite dislikes the vertical search most. He and O'Donnel start with the roof. They play their flashlights over the graveled tarpaper in the space behind the brick elevator housing, where the pale moonlight doesn't shine. Nothing. They take a moment to lean over the railing and look down on Brownsville. Both cops are hatless in the sharp night breeze. O'Donnel rubs his eyes and gazes off toward Canarsie and Jamaica Bay, then turns toward the winking lights of the Manhattan skyline. Gary keeps his eyes on the streets and walkways. More than once he and J.R. spotted crimes from these roofs.

Then the cops turn and head for the stairway. With guns drawn, they work their way down the stairways at opposite ends of the building. On each of the sixteen floors they lean into the hall and nod to each other. Each time, Gary holds the door for a moment so it won't slam shut. On the twelfth floor, he waits a while for O'Donnel, who appears finally with a wave. On the tenth-floor landing, a cardboard box and pillow mark the spot where someone has been sleeping. Beside the makeshift bed lies a hypodermic needle. Gary steps lightly. If an officer is not looking for trouble, he bangs his stick on the cinderblock wall or turns up his radio so he won't surprise anyone. As he moves steadily down the bright yellow cinderblock stairwell, the only sound is the distant tinny notes of a stereo from somewhere above.

"You stick your head around every corner and you don't know," Gary says. "You see a little kid, a couple of teenagers making out, a mad guy, a bad guy." He keeps his finger off the trigger, straight along the barrel of the gun, to give him a fraction of a second of hesitation, so he doesn't shoot somebody if he's startled. Nothing. No victim.

As Gary and O'Donnel converge in the lobby, a handful of noisy kids are headed in. Another report comes over. Both cops freeze and tilt their heads to their radios. This time Central has the goods.

"9717," the dispatcher calls.

"17," Gary answers.

"Be advised, anonymous caller says the guns are in the mailbox."

The boys are standing thirty feet away, uncuffed, still guarded by the 73rd guys. After Gary and O'Donnel take the call, they hustle into the courtyard, but the boys have overheard the radio call on the backup cops' radios. The one named Errol stands his ground, but his two taller friends are of a different mind. They realize that the call will mean jail and simultaneously decide not to go without a chase. Like twin antelopes, they bound the two-foot fence and flee through the Van Dyke Houses. The 73rd officers stand rooted.

Officers from the 73rd and the 75th don't relish running into the project mazes, don't want to leap those fences or sprint along those walkways, where they are vulnerable from above. And God knows they want nothing to do with those stairways. Except for officers like Marino, NYPD cops give chase in the projects only if they have to.

But Lemite and O'Donnel take off after the kids, who run in different directions. O'Donnel bursts out onto Blake Avenue thirty feet behind one kid, who turns and bolts back into another cluster of buildings.

"Which way did he go?" the cop asks a handful of teenagers assembled around yet another bench.

"What I look like? A 911 tape?" comes the reply.

O'Donnel runs on, but only for a few feet. *Hut, hut, hut, hut;* it is a rounded, pneumatic sound, not as fractured as the noise of a firecracker. It is very close, probably from above.

"10-13, I'm fired on. Dumont, Gaston to Powell," O'Donnel screams into his radio as he backs out of the Complex. The kids on the bench scatter. In seconds an Emergency Service Unit truck skids up, along with three Housing sector cars, and a herd of cops charges back into the Complex with guns pointed up and eyes trained on the roofs. They scour the buildings facing the courtyard from top to bottom and find no one, no spent rounds on the roof. The two fleeing kids are gone for good. But Errol is under arrest. There are two guns in the bent and battered mailboxes, a .38 and an ancient four-fifth.

There are plenty of new TEC-9s, a weapon originally designed for South African security forces, and Berettas in the Ville. Incredibly, a good percentage of the new guns come in legally through Federal Express. But there are even more old used guns. Brownsville and East New York may be the used-gun capital of the country. Several times Mayor Dinkins has offered amnesty to the owners of illegal guns and a reward of $25, $50, or $75, depending on the type of gun surrendered. The gun has to be unloaded and wrapped in paper. But the response has been disappointing. "We got some inoperative guns, and a lot of people who we caught with guns trying to say that they were on their way to turn it in," a cop says.

As the police take Errol down the walkway toward the sector cars, a crowd gathers. Everybody is sticking up for him.

"He's a good guy, a funny guy. All he do is make jokes. When I was in jail, he was the only one who came to see me. I love Errol," a man in his twenties testifies. But somebody did not like Errol; somebody "dropped a dime," a street term that has been used since the price of a phone call was ten cents.

As Gary places his hand on top of Errol's head to guide him down and into the back seat of 9717, a stout woman on the sidewalk complains loudly. "It ain't the guy. Fuckin' cops always, always get the wrong person." Gary comments over the car to O'Donnel as he gets in the front seat, "It's the wrong guy again.

Did we ever get the right guy? These people got to decide whether they want to have guns around here or not."

"In this neighborhood, it is not aberrant behavior to have a gun for protection," Larry Phillips says. "The cops get all worked up about it, like it is a moral issue. Ask them how many guns each one of them has. We have an officer in the PSA who is in charge of keeping track of all the guns that the cops own. Some of them have ten guns. They live on Long Island and they have ten guns. Why?"

Just after 10 P.M., Gary is downstairs changing into his street clothes for the trip to Central Booking with Errol. He'll probably have to take the train home, and to avoid getting involved in an incident on the trip, he feels it is best to be out of uniform. O'Donnel is at the desk in the cell area, starting the paperwork for Gary, working slowly, doing his best not to make a mistake, when he hears that Errol's family is at the desk.

"Your mother and your sister are outside," he says over his shoulder toward the cell where Errol is standing. "Don't they have to get up early to go to work? I forgot, niggers don't work. Ha-ha." His voice is as relaxed and stress-free as if he were chatting it up at the Wall, far from Lonnie Hayes and Gary Lemite. His epithet is rare in the PSA, where blatant racial baiting is almost always replaced by code words.

"Suck my dick," Errol sputters back from his cell. These kids craft and reprise the most hilarious, embarrassing, devastating estimations of each other, but tonight Errol is frozen at the very moment he most needs his ability to hurt another with words. One cannot help but think that the same wall exists when it comes to deadly force. The kids will shoot each other with shockingly little consideration or remorse. They hesitate to shoot the white man — perhaps because killing a cop, or a reporter, will bring down more heat than they want to handle, but also because the white man is outside their system of initiatives and responses.

O'Donnel is having fun. "Let them out of the zoo, I guess," he says with a chuckle.

"Your fuckin' sister," says the voice behind the bars.

After a few minutes O'Donnel gets ready to fingerprint the kid. As he was taught in the academy, he secures his gun in a locker and calls for Gary to stand by. There must be two officers on hand, one to do the fingerprinting and one to provide security for the uncuffed prisoner. When Gary arrives, O'Donnel has nothing to say about race.

"Watch your back," O'Donnel says to an officer who has entered the room and whose gun is exposed, as he walks with Errol toward the fingerprinting area at the rear of the office.

Errol is not speaking, barely seems to breathe, his face a cloud of hate. For his part, O'Donnel appears to have forgotten his obscene words of just moments before. Maybe he believes that the shots fired in his direction were the real profanity; maybe he believes that the word "nigger" is not so bad because the black people use it themselves. Maybe he does not know about the history of that word and the dark country roads and the ropes on trees. He might not know much about history, but he does know procedure.

"Don't try to help me with the fingerprinting," he explains patiently, as if he is talking to his younger brother. "If you try to help and you move wrong, you'll smear the print."

Errol stares straight ahead as O'Donnel touches his fingers to the tray of black ink and presses his hand on the paper. In a moment, Errol, the funny guy, the kid everybody likes, is back in his cell.

"How much does a gun like that cost, Errol?" O'Donnel asks cheerily as Gary settles down at the desk to complete the forms.

At sunrise a van from the Manhattan Correctional Center transports Born Son and his boys over the Manhattan Bridge and up Tillary Street to the federal courthouse on Cadman Plaza. The shiny silver elevators are three times the size of the elevators in the Brownsville Houses. There are no bullet craters in their gleaming doors. In Judge Leo Glasser's courtroom on the fourth floor, there are no gang logos carved into the gallery benches as there are in the state courthouse on nearby Schermerhorn Street. The court officers here don't have to shout for silence. The room is as quiet as a church; the ceilings are thirty feet high, the floors spotless. The judge is far away and well elevated, high and mighty.

By afternoon Bobby is seated with his boys and their lawyers at a large glossy conference table behind the wooden barrier separating the participants from the spectators. He is well dressed in his green iridescent suit and flowered shirt, but unprepared. In the months since his arrest he has ignored entreaties from his lawyer to cooperate and restricted his strategy to trying to get Nikia to marry him from jail, presumably because he thinks she wouldn't be able to testify.

Nikki is not on hand today. Fineberg has told her that she will not have to testify until tomorrow at the earliest. Somebody has put in a call from Otisville Prison to her mother's house, threatening to have a bullet put through Nikki's head if she testifies. But Nikki is not one to be intimidated. She was raised on this kind of give-and-take. Her word to Bobby and the rest is that she will testify to avoid a long jail term that would take her away from her kids, but she will not agree to the quantity of crack the feds are insisting on. That way she will help herself by cooperating and help Born Son too, because federal sentencing guidelines are mandated by volume of drug sales. If she can shrink the weight, the sentence will go down considerably. It is a tricky plan. If she does not satisfy Fineberg, she won't get the letter of cooperation and request for a "downward departure" from him that the judge needs to sidestep the sentencing guidelines and let her off with light time.

After a droning morning of jury selection, Glasser starts the trial of Bobby James and the Young Guns. Tai Stick's mother and sister are on hand, as is Odums's father, in blue work clothes. Supreme's sister and mother sit stiffly in the back row. Born Son's mother is up front.

"Born Son James." Fineberg begins his opening statement. "This Born Son . . ." he continues in a wavering intonation thick with implication. The jury has to wonder. What kind of man is named Born Son? Neither Judge Glasser nor the jury understands the significance of the blizzard of nicknames in Brownsville, where the air is full of Boo and Smoke and Poppa. The new police computer lists thousands of nicknames, including a score of Justices, Blacks, and Kojaks.

Born Son's mother, Margaret, sitting in the third row, picks up the prejudicial drift. She is in a state of perpetual indignation. "How dare they say his baby name like it's proof that he committed crimes," she says out loud, cutting her eyes at Dan Murphy, Bobby's lawyer. "Why don't the lawyer protest?

That old drunk. How would the DA like it if we used his baby name?"

"How long have you been a police officer?" Fineberg asks Schulman, who is the first to take the stand.

"Ten years."

"And in what kind of areas have you done most of your work?"

"In public housing," Schulman says. "In the projects."

"What is life like in the projects?" Fineberg asks.

"The projects are low-income developments that house mostly people on welfare." There is a gasp and a howl of indignation from the relatives of the defendants who have taken the day off work to attend the trial.

"Objection," several of the defense lawyers interject. It is late in the afternoon. Glasser sustains the objection and adjourns the trial for the day.

The next morning, Nikia, in a burgundy and white running suit, Renee, and a full complement of shifty, slinky Worthy boys in their early teens are slouched on the polished wooden bench in the marble hallway outside the courtroom. Carlton, wearing balloon-legged jeans, scoffs at Schulman down the hall: "Tight-pants bastard." But the wisecracks are muted. The Worthys have seen plenty of rundown schools and grimy city agencies; they know all about Spofford Juvenile Center in the Bronx. But this is new. There is real money and power here. Only five miles away, but so far from Brownsville.

"I'll fight her, sure," Nikki pipes up, referring perhaps to one of Born Son's old girlfriends who is rumored to be coming to the trial.

"On federal property?" Renee wonders.

"Sure."

But there will be no fight. There won't even be a trial. Billy Odums is the one member of the group who is not intimidated by Born Son. He is simply too physically imposing, with great spreading muscles and sloping shoulders, to worry about anything. Besides, Odums came late to the group, never really had a chance to fall under Bobby's influence. Last night, spooked by Nikia's promised cooperation and offered a separate deal because he has the shortest involvement with the gang, Odums pleaded guilty. In return he got a promise of a letter of downward departure, which will probably spare him the prodigious sentences the others face. Maybe just five years, his lawyer guesses. When Odums rolls over, the remaining Young Guns plead guilty.

Only a day old, and the trial is over. Margaret James is down the hallway near those fancy elevators, smoking a cigarette during a delay in the proceedings, when Alan Polak, Chris Muncie's lawyer, steps out of the courtroom with the news. When Margaret hears the bitter words that her son has pleaded guilty, she screams, stumbles toward the courtroom, and falls. Only Bobby's lawyer, Murphy, is there to hold her off the floor. With his arms under hers, knees shaking with her two hundred pounds, he drags Margaret to where the Worthys sit, wide-eyed.

"My baby is dead," Margaret howls.

"You have two other children," Murphy manages. He may have dropped the ball for Born Son in court, but he is not about to drop Margaret James. In a state of extreme embarrassment and real fatigue, he pleads for someone to take the semiconscious woman from his arms. Nikia steps up and takes the burden. As soon as Margaret feels the whipcord arms of her son's woman, she stiffens and wipes her ink-black braids from her eyes. "Bring me Little Bit," she hisses.

Mid-November, and Gary's promotion to OSC, Operation Safe Community, has come through. Kammerdener has gone to the position he had his eye on all along, second in command at the citywide detective bureau. Jack Lenti is the new commanding officer. For him, the choice of Lemite for promotion to the OSC plainclothes detail was obvious. What could be better than a black officer, a collar machine who sweeps up guns like a magnet, one with no chip on his shoulder, who doesn't go crying to the Guardians every time he sees something he doesn't like?

Gary has been on the detail a week. He waits in line to pick up his radio in the front room of the PSA. Lonnie Hayes is twenty feet away, feet wide apart, chin on his chest, eyes alert, waiting for him. Both Hayes's and Lemite's partners are off, so the two will ride together tonight. Hayes is wearing a huge hooded parka and oversize sweatpants. There is no telling how many guns he's carrying. He smiles sweetly and strolls to the back of the room, where a young officer named Bauer is standing by himself. Bauer has been having all sorts of trouble on the street. He was hired under new department disability guidelines. His neck twitches and his eyes squeeze shut every thirty seconds. Most of the cops are avoiding him, calling him an EDP behind his back, and the locals around his solo footpost are eating him alive.

Bauer greets Hayes and launches into an account of a recent incident. Hayes nods, acting as if everything is going to be fine.

"He had like . . . four guys with him, talkin' shit. So I called the 85th," Bauer explains.

"Yeah." Hayes considers. "And they ride in and kick ass. But that doesn't do your props any good. Next time you're on solo footpost like that, you walk up to the guy in front of his friends, take out your radio, and call for a bus."

"A bus?"

"You say over the radio, 'Send me a bus, one male down,' and you give your location and a description of the guy in front of you. Look him in the eye, and you say, 'Hurry that up. He's bleeding profusely from a head wound.' Then you take out your stick."

"Really?" Bauer asks.

"Yeah. He'll walk away. He won't fuck with you anymore."

Twenty minutes later, Gary takes the wheel of the gray anti-crime car and Lonnie settles beside him, quiet, peaceful. Neither officer quite knows what to make of the other. Unlike Gary, Lonnie was raised in Brownsville under much the same conditions he polices now. He's so streetwise that the ADAs sometimes enlist him to translate the slang in taped confessions. As a cop, he had a run as a heavy hitter in the collar department. But lately he has been looking at things in a new light.

The two cops cruise past the low-rise project buildings on Williams, by the Fat Albert building, which has a huge color mural of the cartoon character on the front wall. Then onto Sutter, up over the hill, and past the supermarket. The store is draped in corrugated steel gates, but there are no gates on the roof, and the place has been burglarized repeatedly in the past several months. Gary slows the cruiser down and glances at the front door of the store. It's seven o'clock; Rony and Zaid Shoman will be doing business until after eleven.

Gary turns right at the red light on busy Rockaway Avenue and goes past the Amoco gas station, where kids from Langston Hughes High School routinely rob motorists who stop for gas. The young highwaymen have escaped via the back door of 301 Sutter Avenue in the project so many times that the Housing Authority has welded the door shut, in violation of fire and safety codes. Gary turns on Belmont and picks up speed as he drives by the pacing, laser-eyed whores outside the factory on Belmont and Williams. Soon the two cops are riding by Fiorentino Plaza. Lonnie jerks his head toward Bradford Avenue. "That's where you were dodgin' all those bullets?"

Gary nods. Something about his reluctance to talk about the incident lights Lonnie up. He wants to tell Gary things.

"When I'm in pursuit," he begins, "I don't even chase the perp into the building anymore, 'cause I know somebody, not from the PSA but from the 73rd or the 75th, is going to mistake me for a perp. I almost got shot this week. I'm bending over getting ready to cuff this guy, and I see some idiot drawin' down on me. Then I look at him, and he moves the gun and says, 'I wasn't pointing my gun at you.'"

Gary says nothing, but his respect is palpable. "I'm getting a call that a guy is in trouble," Lonnie continues, "and I'm supposed to run up ten flights and fight for this guy's life, when he thinks deep down that I'm just another nigger? Stress. I'm a burnout. When cops start their bullshit, beatin' on motherfuckers, I make a wall in the air." Lonnie raises his huge hands to show how he separates himself from the white officers. "That's them. This is me. I tell the people."

Lonnie is rolling now; his words are not for entertainment. "One time I was bending over a guy who's shot. His people was cryin' and shit. I was gonna put somethin' under his head and then I stopped. I didn't do nothin', because in the reality of it, we're not healers. We're the Gestapo."

He settles deeper into his down jacket. He is only two years older than Gary, but he seems like a concerned big brother. He doesn't do much reading, but he does a great deal of thinking and listening. And he has heard the word on the street. The locals have asked him about Gary, complaining regularly about the "half-white motherfucker" they think is too heavy-handed. Lonnie himself is no stranger to violence. The story goes that a big-mouth threatened him once. In a blink, the guy's nose was broken. No one saw Lonnie's hands move. But he has come to grips with some things.

"I used to kick ass when they called me a Tom," he tells Gary. "Now I just hit them with a shot of cold truth: 'At least I ain't robbin' no grandmother.'"

Lonnie is "no joke," they say all over Brownsville. He's the strongest man in the PSA, with a black belt in karate. He is well liked by the white guys because of his friendly nature. But he stopped socializing with cops a while ago. He used to go drinking with his fellow officers at the Wall, but after a few beers, somebody would slip and say something about niggers, and after that he could never look at the guy the same way again. He advises Gary after a silence, "Don't be a fuckin' superman. It ain't worth it."

Gary steers down Mother Gaston Boulevard, past the library near the Brownsville Houses. The library used to have long lines of eager kids waiting to get inside. Now, at six o'clock on a fall evening, ten young men stand in an arc on the corner. They look as if they are waiting for something too. But their backs are to the locked doors of the library as they stare at the unmarked police car with midnight eyes.

"Project kids are different," Lonnie says. "They crew up early. They have to. When I was a kid we used to run in packs. We'd ride the subways and kick ass. We fought so much we trained. One guy would teach some karate, and another guy would teach boxing, and we'd get an older guy to show us jailhouse fighting moves." But as he talks about his youth in Brownsville, he never mentions guns.

Gary bumps the car up a curb and guides it carefully along the footpaths of the Complex. It's dinnertime, and windows glow up and down the five-story buildings. He slows the car to a stop as a pair of schoolgirls take their time stepping off the path.

"Thank you," Lonnie says to the girls, who cannot maintain their childish scowls in the face of his good cheer. An attractive woman entering a building stops at the door, turns, and bends slightly to get a look at him. She beams a winsome smile and waves. Lonnie waves back.

"Say you're walking down this street with your woman,"

Lonnie goes on, "and some guy around your building says, 'Hey, I want your lady to suck my dick,' and you just grin." Lonnie displays a lame smile. "Then the guys get together and they start talking. You know, 'Hey, I told that guy's woman to suck my dick and he didn't do nothin'.' Then they start getting the idea that they should rob you." Lonnie acts out the robbery, with the victim raising his hand in a feeble gesture of protest. Then he assumes the role of the tough guy. "'Put your hand down. I told you not to move your fuckin' hand.' The next thing you know, they have your old lady up on the roof and they really *are* makin' her suck their dicks.

"It's the same if some guy robs your mother on the way home from the subway. You get the name and the description and you go down by the train station and, 'Sure I know who it was. It was that guy Petee and his man.' Sure enough, there's Petee standing down in front of his building with his man. Then you hear, 'Be careful, Petee's crazy and he's got a gun.' Now, you know it won't do you any good to talk to the guy. He'll probably shoot you. You have to decide what to do. If you decide to take him out, you have to do it right, because if you fuck up, he'll kill you. You come up on him real fast with your head down and your hands in your pockets. Or you get your crew. That's why you need a crew. That's how you act when you live around here, and that is why so many brothers are in jail.

"There's only one answer." Lonnie twists his mouth into an unhappy smile and looks at Gary. "Take the guns away. Nobody wants to stab somebody. They figure they'll get hurt themselves."

But some of the kids have already begun protecting themselves against gunshots. The next night Bobby Schulman and Brian Lavin are staked out near the Cypress Houses, sitting in their car. Quani, the kid who shot Marcus McClain at the picnic on Labor Day, has been sighted. The scrip is over the air. He is wearing black jeans with a white handkerchief in the back pocket. Suddenly he darts by, his white handkerchief bobbing. Schulman takes off on foot and Lavin uses the car. The chase ends on Belmont. Lavin cuts the kid off and Schulman grabs him from behind. "I can't believe I got caught by an old man," Quani says in the car. He is wearing a bulletproof vest.

*

Two days later, November 14, 9 P.M. A crooked moon sits behind a scrim of purple clouds beyond the Pink Houses on Loring Avenue. Del Migliore and a couple of other Housing cops from PSA 2 crowd onto the elevator along with detectives Deutsch and McCabe. The group is headed to Apartment 7F in search of a kid alleged to have shot a guy in the head. McCabe knocks on the door.

"Yes?" says a woman on the other side.

"Housing police," McCabe begins, flashing his white shield near the peephole. "Detective McCabe. Mrs. Charles?"

"Yes," the woman answers slowly.

"We'd like to talk to your son. Will you open the door?"

"My son isn't home right now."

"You know why we're here. And we'd rather not yell in the hall. You don't want your neighbors to know your business. Do you?"

No answer.

"We'd like to come in, just ask a few questions, get something straightened out. Will you open the door?"

"He's not home right now."

McCabe turns and rolls his eyes toward Migliore and the other officers standing behind him in the hall. "I understand that. But we'd like to come inside, Mrs. Charles. We're not going to go away."

"My son isn't home now," the woman says in the same maddening tone.

"We will be back with a warrant," McCabe snaps. "He's in there," he growls to the others, and steps across the hall. He knocks on a door and asks the tenant to use the phone. He is going to call the PSA and ask for a lieutenant. Perhaps if a boss shows up at the door, he will be able to intimidate the woman into opening up.

Two officers stand in the hallway to watch the apartment door while Migliore and Detective Deutsch head outside. Migliore goes to his car to wait for instructions, and Deutsch walks over to advise a late-arriving sector car.

"Watch the windows," he says. "These fuckin' guys'll jump from anywhere."

But inside the apartment, the kid isn't thinking about jumping. He's on the phone to an accomplice in another apartment in the building, asking for a favor. The kid wants his friend to fire out the window to draw the cops in the hall outside so he can make his escape.

Migliore is out the front door, halfway to his patrol car, when half a dozen shots ring down from a top-floor window. He crouches and draws. Another shot hits him in the foot; his leg swings out and up as he topples to the pavement. He crawls off the sidewalk to the grass, rolls over once, and returns fire. Another sniper volley of seven shots blasts through the air, and a round catches Detective Deutsch in the calf. From a prone position, Migliore empties his gun at the window. An NYPD car roars to a stop, a cop drags Migliore and Deutsch inside, and the police car careens off to Brookdale Hospital. Alone on the street, an officer returns more fire at the window he believes the shots came from.

In minutes, scores of NYPD officers surround the wrong building. Gary Lemite and a group of Housing cops charge into the correct address, but Kammerdener orders them back outside. Massive searchlights play up and down the brick walls. The cops still aren't sure where the shots came from.

The members of an Emergency Service Unit team carry metal body shields into the Loring Avenue address and use a wedge to open the door of Apartment 7F, but the suspect is nowhere to be found. The NYPD canine unit is called in, and the animal finally sniffs the kid out. He is *in* a couch, not under it. The young fugitive somehow squeezed inside the mechanism of the convertible. No guns are found in the apartment.

"Smell a perp anywhere," an NYPD guy brags. When the kid is dragged out of the couch, the boss on hand suddenly has business in the hallway, turns his back and lights a cigarette, a tacit signal that some controlled ass-kicking is all right. No flashlights or head wounds this time, just body blows.

A search of the building does not turn up the sniper. Outside, the officers rub their hands together in the chill air and mill around the crime scene till after midnight, while detectives toy with laser guns to determine the origin of the shots. At 1 A.M., Chief Keeney of the Housing police department shows up. "These officers acquitted themselves well," he pronounces.

Some off-duty guys are waiting for Migliore to get out of Brookdale so they can go for ritual beers at the Wall or on the

Canarsie pier. Both Deutsch and Migliore will be all right. All Migliore has is a swollen foot; the bullet kicked off the side of his shoe. The damage to his feeling of invincibility will be much more lasting.

Gary, finished with his shift, arrives in his claptrap Dodge to join the vigil. He has a six-pack of Budweisers on the seat beside him for the wait and the toast. "What's the shooter look like?" he asks a cop, who doesn't quite understand the question.

The officer shrugs. "Wha'? He looks like a perp."

"TRAP OFF"

Friday afternoon and a fight has broken out on the fourth floor at Thomas Jefferson High School. Gray-uniformed security guards thunder down the hallway, knocking students aside to get at the action. Walkie-talkies spit codes as students flood into the hallway to taste the chaos. Down the hall, a white male teacher and a black girl trade insults outside a classroom. The walls are free of graffiti, neatly decorated with black history displays featuring magazine photos of black heroes, but the air is crackling with trouble.

Last May, Dan Rather portrayed Jefferson on an evening news feature just the way Beck wanted. Television viewers across the country saw images from East New York that warmed the heart: gymnasts, a steel drum band, and young girls carrying five-pound "babies" made of flour as part of a program to teach them how difficult it is to be a mother. But now, six months later, things are not going well here.

On the first floor, the five members of a video team, commissioned through the board of education by Beck herself, set their equipment on the floor outside the gymnasium and rest for a few minutes before heading out to their van. They have been in the school all day, taping a promotion. They have been trying to highlight successful programs, such as the moot court team and the College Now program, in which students can earn college credits while still at Jefferson. They have not been looking for trouble, the way a regular news team might. The video is slated to be shown in East Brooklyn junior high schools so the better students will not opt to leave the area for other high schools, as they have done in the past. But the crew is shell-shocked. Given the run of the school, they have seen enough. Their words are sheer blasphemy.

"This is very rough," the director says.

"We've been to six high schools in Brooklyn already," a cameraman adds, "and this is one of the worst. The students tell us they just want to get out."

Can it be true? Are the Smurfs winning? "There's one teacher who's something to see, though," a young technician adds. "A woman, teaching global history. She's up there on the fifth floor doin' this rap lesson . . ."

Sharron is on his back in his bed on the night before Halloween, with Andre lying on his chest. The baby is fat-faced, with skin the color of rosy butterscotch, enormous black-marble eyes, and wicked little fists. Each time Sharron flexes his chest muscles, the baby bounces and squeals with pleasure. Chantal is sitting beside them, with her back against the wall and her thumb in her mouth.

"Mommy's takin' him next week so I can go to school for the new markin' period," she says absently.

"Whose mommy?"

"Mine."

"Mine's got school five days a week, Chantal."

"I know. I'm not sayin' nothin'."

Sharron places his finger in the palm of Andre's hand, and the baby squeezes tight.

"Little man's got serious grip action. Check it out. Look. Look at him tearin' it up. He's gonna be a guitar player. I'll be big-time by then. He can play backup." Sharron draws Andre closer and kisses him. "Baby got it like that."

"Where you was when I knocked two days ago, Sha? I know you was home."

"Who says?"

"Shawanda."

"I was at rehearsal."

"Yeah, right. Don't play me, Sha."

Halloween night passes, and still Sharron stays home with Chantal and Andre. It is more than a week since his tangle with the Steam Team. If it hadn't been for Little Earl, the kid who pushed him out the door, things could have been a lot worse. As it is, he has an inflamed and itchy row of stitches in the back of his head. Just as well, he thinks. There isn't a worse night for trouble than Halloween. Chantal lingers another night and then another, with the baby. Gloria is almost always happy to have visitors. She likes activity around her, and she has always liked to keep Sharron close, liked for him to do his thing with Chantal at the house. And Andre, of course, is a novelty. So quiet and good, bubbling, spitting, and waving his arms like a little fool. Chantal likes nothing better than to lie in the bedroom with Sharron while Gloria or Shawanda looks after Andre. But such an arrangement cannot go on forever. In the middle of the week, Chantal goes home and Sharron rallies himself back into the swing of things.

He calls his cousin Morris to arrange a practice session in Morris's studio. There is still a good chance that Sharron and Chris and Frank will get the opportunity to sing backup on a demo tape for a singer named Antoine. A couple of weeks ago, it seemed as if the gig was all but set. Antoine's agent said it was just a matter of scheduling. After that there was no word. When it comes to his singing, Sharron does not like to wait for opportunity to knock. So the Friday after Halloween, he calls Chris and Frank and arranges for a rehearsal at Morris's place the next morning. Morris's studio is only available until noon, and Sharron knows that neither of the others is reliable. But Sharron is all business when it comes to his performing career, so he sets himself the task of rounding up his partners.

The bright, cold November morning finds him on Chris's doorstep, staring up at the second-floor window. He has been knocking for fifteen minutes. Chris's mother, not happy with the commotion, has already waved him away from the door twice. Sharron retreats to the pavement and reaches for a handful of pebbles to toss against the window of his friend's bedroom. Then a white curtain moves and Chris's round face appears.

Frank is easier to rouse, but not easier to control at the rehearsal. He is the designated rapper of the trio.

"Frank, you gotta get into it," Sharron explains after one flat run-through of the half-rap, half-ballad he has written, "Nothing Can Go Wrong."

"I can't, Sha."

"Man, you got to ask questions about your life. You got to think about things that happened to you. This ain't just words. You can't just say the shit."

"I ain't into it," Frank insists.

Sharron looks at his watch. Morris is waiting upstairs. "Now let's do it. And don't fuck around."

Frank is not happy with Sharron's self-appointment as leader. It was easy for Sharron to direct the kids in the Jefferson school play. They were "just regular pupils," in Sharron's words. But Frank, like Sharron, has a reputation, props. His personality is wired to resist domination of any kind, even constructive leadership.

"Why you curse me, Shalo?"

"Niggers, we here to make *money*," Sharron insists. "I'll do what I got to do."

"Yeah, you better be ready to do what you got to do."

"You know, you stink, like you know . . . you smell bad?" Chris says to Frank, then falls to the floor, laughing.

"Shut the fuck up, chipmunk-eye motherfucker," Frank growls.

"That's it!" Sharron exclaims in Frank's face. "When you say the words in the song, you got to get mad like that."

Sharron manages to get an hour's good rehearsal from his undisciplined partners.

"This is business," he reminds them on the train on the way home. "Not some little-boy shit. You got to understand that."

Chris and Frank promise to concentrate better during next Saturday's rehearsal, when Antoine himself might appear. But it doesn't work that way. The next Tuesday, Morris gives Sharron the bad news. "Eddie, Antoine's manager?" he begins, as Sharron listens on the pay phone on his corner. "He's decided to go with just Chris and his brother as backup. They sing in the choir together and he likes their sound."

"Cool," Sharron answers, controlling his disappointment. He promises to call later in the week.

Life is not right. Not at all. Sharron skips school the next day and retreats to his room for the weekend.

On the following Monday, Frank and Sharron head down Saratoga Avenue to visit a friend, a fellow LoLife called Filo. Filo lives in a private home on Saratoga, past Livonia, a house covered with dozens of metal security bars painted white. The three boys share a forty of Power Master on Filo's stoop, tugging on the bottle till it's drained, looking up and down the avenue all the while for girls.

"Man, when you go to jail, you gonna feel right at home," Frank says, surveying the front of Filo's house. "You already behind bars."

"How the hell you gonna get out if there's a fire?" Sharron asks.

"We got a fuckin' fire alarm."

"You mean a smoke alarm," Frank corrects. "An' I know you disconnected that shit, 'cause your mother burns up the grits, aaah." He spots a pair of girls moving down the sidewalk and starts a low chant, matching the cadence with their steps: "She can't, she can't, she can't." As the girls pass by, he finishes with a flourish, "*Control that butt.*" The girls disappear, but Sharron is suddenly expansive.

"There was this guy in my school," he explains, jumping to his feet. "And we was fillin' applications for Job Search? And this dude writes in the spot where it says, 'Who do you contact in case of emergency,' he writes, 'The hospital.' Aaah."

Frank tumbles off the stoop with laughter, slaps Sharron's hand, and laughs some more. Then he and Sharron head back down Saratoga Avenue. They trot up the stairs to the subway platform so Frank can use the pay phone beside the token booth to call his girlfriend, Maxine. On the far side of the booth is a kid standing by himself in the grimy waiting room. Frank has seen the kid around the neighborhood. "Pussy," he says out the side of his mouth to Sharron, sliding his quarter into the phone and jerking his head toward the kid.

The young man, about Sharron's age, is wearing a burgundy wool Polo jacket with a blue crest like a police badge. It irritates Sharron to see a kid with a sucker's reputation wearing a jacket he would love to have. He himself is wearing his prize shearling on this chilly day. Frank has on a matching jacket. Both carry weapons in case someone tries to steal the coveted garments.

Sharron snorts in disgust and looks from the kid back to Frank. Frank is chatting with his girlfriend, but he's following Sharron's train of thought and nods sharply, affirmatively. A soft kid with a Polo jacket standing right in their faces: this is a call to action. Sharron's pulse lifts; his breath comes slower and deeper.

The youth is Sharron's height, maybe a bit heavier, but he is a punk, of that there is no question. There is no proud carriage to indicate that he's a martial artist, no street slouch or bulge in his clothes to signal a burner. He's just a vic, and Sharron will be damned if he's not going to take that Polo jacket for his collection. It will be just the thing to banish the blues about Antoine and put his head straight.

He walks straight across the small ticket lobby, catches the kid's eye, and speaks, not unpleasantly. "Let me try the jacket on."

The kid's hand moves to the zipper and stops. "It's kind of cold." The kid lobs the words softly, lest they offend.

Behind Sharron, Frank slaps the receiver onto its hook and skips down the stairs to the corner. This is a one-man sting. Sharron Corley, star of the school play, shining light of his family, and homecoming king of Jefferson High, fashions his features into a wicked "screw face," an ice grill, and opens his shearling to display the steel shank of the ice pick he has tucked into his waistband.

"Take the shit off," he orders.

When the kid's coat is over his arm, he twists toward the stairway, then turns back to the kid, who stands, jacketless and confused, rooted to his spot, just out of sight of the token collector.

"Are you gonna stand there?" Sharron growls. The kid takes off. Sharron hits the opposite stairway and hurries down Saratoga to his apartment building.

Done. No violence. "I wouldn't have stuck him anyway," Sharron tells himself. "Just perfect." He is delighted. He has passed the challenge, acted "on point," with courage and skill. His reward is his soaring heart, and the jacket. There is no way he would ever buy a jacket like this. No way he's going to give "them people," as he calls department stores, his money. There will be no problem with the cops, because the kid will never tell, and he is too much of a punk to grab a burner and come looking.

Sharron hangs the jacket in his closet, using the heavy wood hanger to make sure it doesn't lose its shape. He feels like a new person, and he has not even tried it on yet. "Clothes do make the man," he decides.

Gloria Corley has seen the expensive sweaters and coats. She has seen the shearling. She has warned her son about shoplifting again and again. Now she has let it drop. How can she deny her favorite child the only things he wants, things she cannot give him? Times are too hard to lose sleep over some penny-ante boosting. But the beautiful burgundy jacket in Sharron's closet has not been boosted. It has been stolen from another young man, with a weapon. There can be none of Sharron's rationalization about how it is all right to steal Polo merchandise because Ralph Lauren charges higher prices in the cities, where black folks live. This is simply the strong taking from the weak.

At 6 A.M. two days later, two Transit police detectives, Ricardo Perez and Dexter Blake, along with five members of the Transit police's warrant squad, arrive at 515 Saratoga Avenue. One officer stays outside to watch the windows in case any contraband sails out; two others head for the rear stairway. One cop positions himself on the roof. There are no battering rams, no machine guns. "We like to do these things at dawn," Perez explains about the warrants, "in the hours before the neighborhood is up, before the word can get around, before anybody is drinking."

The night before, Perez had the victim go through five hundred pictures of youthful subway robbers. "With that big scar and the high-top fade haircut, this kid Corley wasn't difficult to pick out," he says. When Sharron's picture was identified, Perez recognized it. "I had read something in the paper about this kid who lived in the area who was very talented, an actor in a play or something." There was something else distinct about Sharron Corley. "My teenage daughter still lives with her mother in the area," Perez explains, "and she told me that the kid with the fade, the one who was in the paper, had come up to her and her friend on the street around the way and had tried to pick up her friend. Nothing unusual. But it was the way he did it. He just walked up to her and started singing on the street corner."

Now Perez and Blake knock on the Corleys' door.

"Who?" Gloria wants to know.

"It's the police department."

The door swings open.

"I'm Detective Perez. This is my partner." Perez slurs the word "detective" and palms his gold shield quickly, trying to minimize his mission. "Sorry to disturb you. But we're here to talk to your son about an outstanding warrant he has for fare-beating a couple of months ago."

"*That's* what this is about?" Gloria questions, with equal measures of disgust for the police, the hour of the morning, and Sharron.

"Right."

Sharron steps into the living room, embarrassed but not worried. Jumping the turnstile is a way of life; getting a summons for it is just part of growing up, like breaking somebody's window with a baseball in suburbia.

"Nah, no handcuffs," Perez tells him cheerily. "But stay in the living room here. And don't touch anything." Perez glances at Shawanda, who had been sleeping on the couch and is now standing in the kitchen, rubbing her eyes. "Your sister?" Sharron nods. "Maybe your sister can go and get you your jacket and whatever else you need. This won't take long." Shawanda is dispatched to the bedroom to get Sharron's jacket for the trip to the Transit police headquarters. She comes out with the shearling.

"It's not that cold," Detective Blake comments, feigning concern for Sharron's comfort. Shawanda walks back to the bedroom, reaches into the closet, and grabs the burgundy Polo.

"I was looking all over the apartment for the jacket," Perez remembers. "When she came out with the burgundy, it was all we could do not to laugh."

"It won't take more than an hour," Blake tells Sharron.

Still, Sharron is not cuffed. If he were, it would not be the first time. He has been arrested half a dozen times. When he was fifteen, there was a fight between him and Frank and two neighborhood kids. A couple of plainclothes cops driving by thought it was a mugging and arrested Sharron and Frank after a scuffle. That was a misunderstanding. But there have been other arrests, one for robbery when he was sixteen, one for petty vandalism, one during rehearsals for the school play, when he was mistakenly identified for a robbery, and the turnstile-jumping thing.

As Sharron rides over to the Transit headquarters, he's convinced this is just a nuisance. The cops even stop off at "Mickey

D's" and buy him an Egg McMuffin. Nevertheless, he is frowning as he walks between the two detectives down the stairs at the Franklin Avenue subway stop and along the platform to the headquarters at the rear of the station. The frown is a choice, a selected demeanor to fit the circumstances. If the video cameras were rolling, as they almost always are in Sharron's head, this would be the right look. As he moves past the precinct cell area and into the small detective squad room, his scowl deepens.

Inside, Perez sits at his desk, leans back, and motions for Sharron to sit. The detective pats the four fingers of his right hand on the Formica top of his metal desk for a moment, then breaks the news.

"The real reason you're here is that you stole a kid's coat with an ice pick last night at the Saratoga station."

"No, I didn't," Sharron says, looking above the detective at a poster of a man wanted for homicide.

"The kid pulled your picture. He knew where you lived."

"Not me."

"Well, you can deny it, but you're gonna look pretty stupid when that kid walks in here and you're sitting there wearing his jacket."

Sharron confesses, even pens his own statement. "He was an easy kid," he writes. "When he knew we had him, he just gave it up. Me and my man, who is unimportant in this matter, saw a kid from around the way who in his point of view was a pussy. I approached him with the ice pick and willingly he came out of his coat and his beeper."

"Some of these guys stonewall the whole thing," Perez says. "He was no problem. But when we asked him why, he just sat there — no explanation whatsoever."

"The cops really played me," Sharron remembers.

The kid picks Sharron out of a lineup. All along, Sharron is worried but also offended. "You don't call the *police*. You just don't do that," he whines. It's confusing. The vic has simultaneously sunken to a new level of punkdom and shown some heart. Totally unpredictable.

The gates of Sharron's life are closing slowly. The deal is simple. Robbery two: plead guilty and get six months in Riker's Island, with five years' probation. Plead innocent and all kinds of bad things can happen. There is the matter of the ice pick, which the cops have found in Sharron's room. The charge then would be robbery one — a couple of years if he blows the trial. The kids call the choice "trap off."

The very next day, the shoe is on the other foot. Sharron finds himself in the bullpen at the Schermerhorn Street courthouse, waiting for arraignment with three guys who know each other. One of the three flashes a jailhouse burner, the sharpened end of a twist of metal spring extracted from a bed, and Sharron's beloved burgundy Timberland boots are gone. They are not worth getting cut for. Sharron just gives them up, and squeezes his lips together tightly as he laces up a pair of dirty, sweat-softened, black-and-white Nike highcuts.

With the six-months deal done, it remains only for him to return for formal sentencing. Sharron has stepped from the winding and difficult path of accomplishment onto the beaten trail that leads the boys of Brownsville to the jailhouse. He boards the blue and white corrections bus for a trip to Queens and Riker's Island. The hatless Corrections Department driver grinds the gears down, and the dirty bus rattles to a stop on the corner of Tillary and Jay streets, near the Brooklyn Bridge. Sharron watches the rough young men around him, all gaping at the girls crossing the street, heading to classes at a local college.

"Yo, yo, light-skin," they scream through the mesh-sealed windows. "You got a man. Yo, check it out, light-skin?" The boys are frantic to get a reaction. But from the outside, viewed through the mesh, they are nothing more than shadows. "Stink bitch," one boy yells.

The bus rumbles onto the Brooklyn-Queens Expressway and over the Kosciusko Bridge, high above rolling acres of grave-stones. The words of the reggae song that was playing at the Steam Team party come to Sharron as the bus picks up speed on the Grand Central Parkway and the boys around him fall quiet.

You never wan' go Riker's Island.
When de yout' first com' a New Yawk,
Da tell 'em learn a trade or go to school.
Don't skylark an' play yaself fa' a fool.

Incarceration. It is a rite in Brownsville. Sharron sighs. Shit, a lot of guys have done bids in Spofford or upstate. Most guys. Not those "pupils" maybe, the actors in King's play, the basket-ball players, but most of the LoLifes have been away, and that cock-diesel kid Bashim, who punched him in the mouth once over some "he say, she say" bullshit.

The bus shudders to a stop beside the checkpoint at the foot of the bridge to Riker's Island. There isn't a sound on the bus now.

Out of the window to Sharron's right are the runways of La Guardia Airport, jutting into the East River; ahead, the rocky shore of Riker's Island. Garbage bags, caught high in the razor-ribbon fence and weathered to a deathly gray by the wind from the river, flap like shrouds around the jail. Sharron's shoulders sag. Riker's is no place for the son of Gloria Corley, no spot for a sweet-tempered, talented kid like him. He's not hard-core. He is supposed to be going places. His mother loves him. Jail is supposed to be for the sons of mothers who do not care, kids who run the streets.

At the rear of the C-74 building, a corrections officer conducts the boys off the bus and through a reinforced steel door into the jailhouse. Sharron Corley has made it out of the Ville.

If the Housing Authority has its way, the Worthys will be leaving the Ville also. Judge Ira Harkavy is standing in his robes before the bench in his courtroom in the Housing court building at 141 Livingston Street in downtown Brooklyn. The eviction proceeding, *New York City Housing Authority* v. *Renee Asbury*, is about to begin, and the judge looks like a man who is enjoying his work.

"We've had ninety-five of the drug eviction cases so far," he reflects. "If I have the slightest inkling that those involved are users and not purveyors, I throw the case out. But we've had ninety-four evictions so far. It works."

Mike Pratt, a Legal Aid lawyer standing nearby in a blue suit and Italian tie, doesn't like Harkavy's self-satisfied tone of voice or his words. His clients, Renee and Kate, are sitting within earshot. This process is supposed to be about justice, not efficiency. What's more, Harkavy's figures are wrong. Pratt knows of at least three cases where public housing tenants turned back attempts to evict. But Pratt is upset for another reason. When the proceedings begin, he approaches the bench.

"Your Honor, we have done some background checking and we have found that the Legal Aid Society is representing someone else who may have contrary interests to the respondents here. We therefore cannot act as representatives for Renee Asbury, the legal tenant in this case. I'm sure you know that I cannot go into the details of our other representation."

Apparently Legal Aid is representing one of the Worthy boys arrested for selling drugs in the vicinity of the apartment. Just like that, Pratt is gone, and Renee and Kate don't have the slightest idea what to do. They shift on the bench in the second row of the small hearing room and look at each other. Kate snorts a puff of air through her nose and rocks her head back.

To open the hearing, the Housing Authority lawyer cites ninety-one criminal cases involving crack peddling around the premises of 295 Dumont. A building manager and half a dozen police officers testify about vials of crack dropped, bought, and sold by, and confiscated from the likes of Randolph, Lennie, Edward, Willie, and Jimmy Worthy and Blue Asbury. What they cannot do is place a single one of the sales within the apartment, or connect Renee, the lessee, with any of the sales. But the defense attorney is gone. The law says that Renee has no absolute right to a lawyer in this kind of case. There is no one to point out the weakness in the Housing Authority's case.

In a pathetic attempt to keep her apartment, Renee allows herself to be sworn in and takes the stand in front of Judge Harkavy. Without an attorney to guide her through her testimony, all she can do is mumble about how the Housing cops "beat on people."

"You are going to have to speak louder," the judge says softly.

"Tell how they busted in the door," Kate whispers from her seat.

"What?" Renee mouths the word. Kate shakes her head and draws the corners of her mouth down. She won't take the stand herself. Renee sits sullenly for a moment in the witness chair, then shrugs and joins her grandmother.

The hearing is over. The nineteen-member Worthy clan, including women, children, and the wheelchair-bound Philip, have just been evicted from their double apartment, 5AB, at 295 Dumont Avenue, under an archaic state statute known as the bawdy-house law.

"I don't know if I would call it a railroad, but it is a case of accelerated justice," a Legal Aid supervisor observes later about such evictions. The city has one judge to handle all the bawdy-house cases, and Legal Aid attorneys worry that hearing so many similar cases cuts down on Harkavy's ability to see each one on its merits. Even more dangerous, they believe, is the city's practice of building an eviction case by offering young offenders sentences of time served in exchange for guilty pleas in minor drug offenses, then using those pleas as evidence for eviction.

In the hallway, a burly white Housing police officer with a stiff brown brush cut can't suppress a snicker as Kate Worthy limps for the elevator. She hears the laugh and wheels. She spits a curse: "Motherfucker."

"At least I got somewhere to live, Kate," the cop says. He is right. When abuse fell on Robo and Schulman, it came down on a day or a night shift, on an eight-hour tour. When the bad news hits the Worthys, it is on their lives.

"IT HURTS, PRICE"

It's Tuesday, November 26, 10 A.M. The door to Carol Beck's office is shut tight. The principal is taking no calls, no visitors, "no damn messages." She's poised, hands folded, leaning, straining to catch every syllable from Dorian, Kerrol, and Taji, a matched set of handsome, soft-voiced sophomores seated at the conference table. Two worn teddy bears and a Snoopy doll cling together at the center of the table.

These three boys are neither honor students nor troublemakers. They combine just the right measures of street bravado and restraint to make them popular in the school. When they walk the halls, they slap high, low, and middle fives all around. The girls study them, write their names on notebook covers. But they are more interested in having fun with their buddies than in following up on the girls. These are close friends, with special phrases and inside jokes. When one laughs, they all laugh, even when there is nothing to laugh at. All for one and one for all.

Dorian, an ocher-skinned, clear-eyed seventeen-year-old, is describing Jermaine Bentley, sometimes known as Joker, a friend who is not present. "Jermaine was like down with us, but he wasn't really down? He was always playin' around." Dorian pauses for a moment to find the words to describe Jermaine's status. "A wannabe," he says, and looks at Kerrol and Taji, who nod.

Jermaine was nervous and touchy. His playfulness had an air of desperation. He envied Dorian, Kerrol, and Taji their easy ways, wanted to hang out. He didn't have much to recommend him, just a passion to belong. And deep in Jermaine's heart there was something even stronger — ambition.

"He was like . . . a nobody. But he wanted to be the man," Dorian explains to Beck.

Jermaine wanted to set the styles, to be admired, imitated, and feared. Ambition can be the force that builds bridges, cures diseases, gets your name painted on the hallowed Jefferson honor board. Not this time.

"Jermaine was never a good fighter," Dorian continues. "He would take somebody's hat and then he would run behind me. I get around, but not in a violent way. After a while, it was known that he was with us. He tried to make it like if he got into something I would jump in with no questions, but it wasn't like that. I mean, I was like 'I'm chill with you, but I ain't ready to die for you.'"

There was another kid on the periphery of the group. His name was Jesse. At five-seven, he was no taller or heavier than Jermaine, but his face was etched with nicks from long-forgotten street fights, and his eyes were arctic cold. Jesse was always ready to raise the stakes.

"Jesse just don't care about nothin'," Taji says. "His man is Chubby and they always tight, they the same. They got brothers in jail and they used to shit, and they don't care if they get shot, if they die."

"When you have an older brother with a big reputation," Kerrol adds, "if you don't live up to the rep, you aren't nothin'. That's some heavy shit."

Ambition collides with pathological courage in a bleak world, and the process is born.

"Jermaine started all kinds of stuff," Dorian explains, "like arguments. Like he would even try with me. Then he would say like 'I didn't like what you said, so when you come around the way you gonna get jumped.' And then I would say to my people, 'You know, I got to do something about what he said.' But with me and Taji and Kerrol, we would come back, and he says like 'I didn't really mean what I said before, I was mad,' and you know. But with Jesse, he wasn't havin' all that."

Early in September, an everyday dis from Jesse led Jermaine Bentley to make the claim that he would be coming to school the next day with a gun. When he didn't bring the gun, he became a figure of scorn.

"Jermaine thought the gun would give him amp," Kerrol says, "but everybody was laughin' instead."

It wasn't over. In Brownsville, it's never over. There is no comfort zone where a young man or woman can relax, go for a stroll with a girlfriend or boyfriend, think about nothing but the other. There are borders, vendettas, trouble from long ago. Anything can be cause for a beef: if you look at someone or you don't look at him, talk to the wrong girl, step on somebody's new sneaker, take too long on a pay phone, accomplish something, make a joke.

Yesterday, a Monday morning, Jermaine and Jesse, the two wounded personalities, came face to face on the fourth floor. Those who knew their history understood the deadly possibilities. It is a rule of human behavior that people will do what they do best. Neither Jermaine nor Jesse cared much for school. They had fought on the street more often and more intensely than they had learned in class, practiced a musical instrument, or played a sport. Even though Jermaine was not much of a fighter, there was nothing he could do better.

Just before the fistfight started, a jubilant crowd gathered. On one level, the students at Jeff are delighted that their school has started to become functional under Carol Beck, has become a place where you can actually learn something. But a good fight is a welcome relief from the droning teachers. Forty students surrounded the spot where Jesse and Jermaine performed their scene obligatoire. The standing audience was five deep. Girls in the back of the crowd leapt up to get a glimpse of the action.

Dorian shouldered his way through the throng. "You got a gun?" he asked, reaching to pat Jermaine's midsection. Jermaine jumped away.

"Nah, my little man got it," Jermaine bragged. Dorian stepped away. He knew Jermaine didn't like to carry a burner. The reference to Jermaine's "little man" was lost on him in the swelling excitement.

First Jesse popped Jermaine, a quick jab to the neck, then staggered him with a chopping overhand. Dorian grappled with Jermaine's brother, fourteen-year-old Jason, to keep him from intervening. Jesse was pouring it on, blow after blow.

"Let me go. I won't do *nothin'*," Jason pleaded.

Dorian loosened his grip just enough for Jason to break free and land a punch on the back of Jesse's neck. Dorian and another boy pulled Jason back and the fight continued, with Jesse still in control. Jason seemed to sag in Dorian's arms, as if resigned to his brother's beating. Dorian eased his hold once more. The combatants were on the floor now, Jesse squeezing Jermaine in a headlock. Jason lunged again, this time with a bottle in his hand. He clubbed Jesse. The bottle skidded to the floor and broke.

"Fuck this. Fuck this. I don't need to do this with my hands. Gimme my bookbag. Gimme my bag," Jesse demanded, still pinning Jermaine to the floor. Dorian squeezed Jason.

"I won't do nothin', I swear," Jason begged.

"You already said that two times," Dorian answered.

The spectators assumed that Jesse's demand for his bookbag was a call for a weapon, but nobody left. For almost everyone in attendance, this was great stuff. One of the byproducts of television, coupled with lack of guidance and long-term goals, is a withered attention span. In everything the kids do, they go for the quick jolt, the instant payoff. This was "slammin'" drama. Did Jesse have a burner in the bookbag?

Jesse disentangled himself and began to step back into the crowd to get the bookbag. Jason wriggled free one last time. He would now do what he had to do. He reached into his backpack.

There are no metal detectors at Thomas Jefferson High School. It is Carol Beck's passionate belief that the obvious advantages are outweighed by the message their presence sends to students and society. Metal detectors greet youngsters every morning with the unequivocal statement that they are in a violent and dangerous place, that they themselves are dangerous. Beck also believes the devices will lull society at large into a false belief that something has been done about the problem of guns. "What good are metal detectors if the kids shoot each other on the street outside the school and in the playgrounds?" she argues.

What had happened so far on the fourth floor was not unusual here. This was still just a fistfight between a fool and a tough guy, or two fools. What happened next was madness.

Jason's hand came out of his backpack with a silver gun. He held the heavy piece away from his body at shoulder level, a lost look on his face. A girl's voice rang out from behind. "Do it. You gonna shoot it?"

Jason, the little brother, scant backup in a major throwdown, waved the pistol. It presented him with some major problems. Any person, even a little brother, would be profoundly discredited if he had a burner and was afraid to light it. Jason did not aim. He was standing alone now. The appearance of the gun had sent the audience scrambling. Jesse was fifteen feet away, down the hall; Jermaine, on the floor. Now was the time. Maybe Jesse was about to come up with his own jammy, his own piece of adamancy. Jason turned his head away, held the gun with one hand, out and up, with locked elbow, and pulled the trigger three times. His arm flew up with each shot as if he were holding on to the thrashing tail of a baby alligator. *BAM . . . BAM, BAM.* There was a long hesitation between the first and the second shot. The second and third shots were close.

The sound of the gun in the crowded hall was like a cannon blast, the noise stupendous, the chaos imaginable. In a shootout in the street you can take cover, but everybody here knew that a hallway means ricochets. The girls nearest the fight, so willing to see someone else get hurt, jumped for safety. In a reversal of their usual inclination, the students fought desperately to get into a classroom, any classroom. But the teachers and kids in those rooms had heard the shots and slammed the doors, and were holding them shut. All except the shop teacher, Robert Anderson, who stepped into the hall in time to catch a bullet in the neck. His hands flew to his throat and he pitched forward.

The concussion in the enclosed area of the hall threw Dorian to the tiled floor. He landed next to Daryl Sharpe, a fellow sophomore. "You O.K.?" he asked Daryl. "You shot? Check. You shot?"

Dorian's hands ran down his own torso to his thighs and stomach. He gazed blankly at his legs and arms. They seemed to belong to someone else. He looked up to see Jesse running down the hall straight at Jason, "like he didn't care if he lived or died." But Jason fled in the chaos, sprinting down the hall to the stairway.

Dorian still was not sure whether he or anyone else had been shot.

"You got shot?" he asked Daryl again.

"I don't know." Daryl was on his back in the last moments of his life, and he did not know whether he had been hit. "Get me up," he said. "Get me up." The more he spoke, the softer his voice became. "I can't feel my body," he whispered. "I can't feel nothin'."

"Where you got shot?" Dorian asked again.

Daryl pointed to his chest, but then he saw that he had blood on his collar. A lost, sad smile stuck on his lips.

"No. No!" Dorian screamed. Hands reached under his arms and lifted him up and away from Daryl.

Officer Kevin Price, the 75th precinct cop assigned to Jeff, was on his knees hovering over the wounded boy as the shooting call went out to sector cars in the area.

"It hurts, Price," Daryl whispered. "Price, it hurts."

In a minute the halls were filled with running policemen, their guns drawn. The shooter had not been found, and nobody knew if there were more guns. Beck, in white sneakers, was running too.

"I was afraid of a Wyatt Earp thing," she said later. "That blue brain trip. I was afraid someone would trip with their gun out and . . ." But in the next few moments, she was fluttering about, congratulating the officers on their control and restraint.

"Aren't you afraid to work in this place?" a young white cop asked Price as the EMS stretcher carrying Daryl Sharpe moved toward the elevator. Price, who is very close to the Jefferson kids, did not like the question.

"To tell you the truth," he spit over his shoulder, "if I got shot in here, I'd be more surprised than anything. I'd be more pissed than shot."

Dorian wandered around the upper floors of Jefferson stiff-legged, eyes cast far ahead. "I shoulda known, 'cause Jesse had all his people there and Jermaine didn't have nobody but his little brother," he rambled on to a girl he hardly knew. "I shoulda known he had a gun, 'cause Jermaine was acting with all kinds of heart." Dorian paused by a window overlooking the school parking lot on Dumont Avenue. He noticed ambulances streaming away from Jefferson down Pennsylvania toward Livonia, on their way to Brookdale Hospital. He had seen shootings before. He had seen people recover and return to the block. But now, out on the street below, kids were moving in slow motion. Two girls clung to each other, their bodies bucking with sobs. They stumbled against a fence and almost fell, but didn't let go of each other. Dorian knew then that Daryl Sharpe was dead.

Twenty minutes after the shooting, Beck got a call from Chancellor Joseph Fernandez of the New York City Board of Education, who suggested that she keep the students in school for the rest of the day. "That's too long," Beck told her assistant principal. "But we're not going to dismiss them right away, either. We have our next class. We don't do anything with a knee jerk." Thirty minutes later, she called the eighteen hundred students to the school auditorium to tell them that their classmate and a teacher had been shot. "It's your school, your community," she advised. "You don't have to talk to the television people. You have a right to your pain and your space." Later she would say, "These are not the Cosby kids; they'd know that they had the right not to talk. But our kids don't know what they are entitled to." "Don't whore your sorrow" is the way Ms. King put it.

Beck was everywhere. On Pennsylvania Avenue, a television reporter pressed too hard for an interview and she threatened to put her foot to the woman. A black cameraman came up. "I want to shake your hand for that," the man said. "I was proud of you."

Beck had to handle the students, the media, and the staff. She called the teachers in. "One of your own was shot. Robert Anderson will live, but I don't want to minimize it. You all are under stress," she told them. Then the United Federation of Teachers union drones showed up, talking about closing the school.

The next day, Thomas Jefferson High School is again swarming with officials and reporters. Beck holds a quick news conference. "I have retired teachers and Hy Smith, a guidance counselor, coming in to help in case other teachers don't show up. And do you know that the only teachers who haven't shown up are ones that were absent yesterday and were sick? When I saw the cars pull into the parking lot, I felt like kissing them all." Then Beck closes the school to the media.

She is determined to control things. She could not stop Jason, but by God, she will have something to do with how the press portrays this event. She speaks to the students and the staff again. She arranges for therapy workshops throughout the week for faculty and students, calling in crisis intervention experts to run sessions for the children. She roams the school, making sure that everything runs right. But of course, everything is not right.

In the library, a trauma counselor helps students express their feelings.

"Are you scared?" the trim, dark-haired man asks.

"No," a six-foot, baby-faced junior answers.

"What is Jefferson?"

"A name."

"A school," says a girl with a broad forehead and gold thread woven into her towering hair.

"A second home," a boy with glasses offers, looking around to see if he has said something foolish.

"I don't want to get shot in my second home," the baby-faced junior adds.

"Do you want to leave?" the counselor presses.

"Yes."

"How often do you see something violent? Something bad?"

"Once a day."

"More than once a day."

"Every half-hour," the boy with glasses blurts.

"It's according to where you live at."

The students are asked to form human sculptures of a table, a trash can, love. Shyly at first, then with enthusiasm and much laughter, they comply.

"Can you change your environment?"

"No."

"It's not the school that's bad, it's the students."

"Are the students bad?"

No answer.

"What are you learning in school?"

"Science. History. We learn that life is gonna be hard when we get out," the girl with the gilded hair says.

"Whatever you say. Whatever they say will go in one ear and out the other," a frowning girl leaning on a bookshelf by the wall insists.

"Do the teachers come to teach?"

"Most teachers are scared of us because of the way we are. They stay away from us," the baby-faced junior explains.

Upstairs, extra chairs have been crowded into a small lounge on the third floor. This is a quiet place where the teachers re-

treat from the torrent of adolescent energy in the classrooms
and hallways. Today, ten teachers and teachers' aides are discussing the shooting.

"I think this is harder on us than it is on the students," a
plump white man begins. "They're used to this kind of thing. I
am traumatized."

Another white man is muttering and shaking his head. He
has a confession to make. "I don't know if I'm a sociopath or
what. I have seen shootings and I have seen stabbings here. I
have seen heart attacks. I saw a Spanish teacher stabbed by a
student. And when I saw this boy being taken out, all I could
think about was . . . next period. When I heard that there were
going to be memorials and grieving sessions after this shooting,
I thought, why bother, what for? Let's just go on."

There is a long silence, and heads nod.

A white woman with excessive, nasal vowels pipes a lament
that grows more frantic with each phrase. "I used to *think* I was
safe here. I don't feel that way anymore. I don't know why I felt
that way. I shouldn't feel that way. It wasn't healthy." More
nodding.

All is not well here. A rotund teachers' aide launches a complaint about a certain teacher who has been treating him with
lack of respect. It is not unusual to find an aide who would
make a much better teacher than the certified instructor he or
she assists. This aide's eyes dart accusingly. He may not have
his degree, but he knows full well that he can do a better job
than he has been witnessing at Jefferson.

The woman who used to feel safe attempts to pacify him, but
the aide is having none of it.

"I was standing in the hall when the shots went off. I saw the
fire come out of that gun. And I thought I was going to die. And
I didn't see a *single* teacher come out to see what I was screaming for or to assist in any way. If you're talking about 'being
together,' what the hell kind of thing is that?"

"It's a natural thing to stay inside when there is shooting in
the hall," a slight, middle-aged black woman offers gently. "I,
for one, was not going to come into that hall. You can understand that."

But the aide is making the most of the session, opening up
wide. "How do you tell a mother that her son is dead? How do

you form your lips to say that? How do we keep failing? Where do I turn . . . for a future?" The man stops for a moment. "I will never forget as long as I live standing there *by myself* in that hall. The boy turned and came toward me and I ran to the elevator. I was sure there were going to be more shots, and I banged on the elevator and the boy kept coming. Then those doors opened like the gates of heaven and I stepped on. And do you know that I have not gotten on that elevator since that day? And do you know why?" He waits a long moment before he gives the answer. "Because you do not ask the doors of heaven to open twice."

IF YOU MISS SCHOOL, YOU MISS OUT reads a bright red sign outside the Jefferson auditorium. Inside, both the balcony and the orchestra of the packed auditorium are bursting with anticipation. This is, several days after the shooting, a memorial for Daryl Sharpe. For the occasion, Carol Beck has invited rap singer Dougie Fresh.

The program starts on a low note. A board of education representative, a woman in a broad silk scarf and oversize tinted glasses, gives lugubrious condolences in a tone of involuntary, but nonetheless palpable, condescension: "We feel the pain, the pain of the mother who must bury her son. And just like you, we wonder what to do. But like you, we will find the strength." This lady is smart enough to know that platitudes will not suffice now. She determines that for once, she will appear without varnish. But she fails. She sounds as if she is talking to a crowd of infants. The assembled students are cold-eyed. They are uneducated in almost everything but the subject she is lecturing them about. These are graduate students of violent death.

They listen politely until a girl with a furrowed brow growls, "Fuck this," hurls down a notebook on the floor between her legs, and stomps to the back of the room. She tries to get out but is accosted by the ubiquitous Ms. King. "This is bullshit," the girl proclaims. "Ain't nobody gives a shit. Nobody cares. They just talking shit."

"Nobody?" Sharon King won't be included in the indictment. "Are you saying I don't care?"

The girl yanks King's hand off her. "Fuck this," she repeats, and pushes out the door.

Soon it is King's turn to be irate. The crowd gasps as the rap singer, Dougie Fresh, appears at the door and heads down the aisle toward the stage on a wave of energy, like a fighter heading toward the ring for a championship bout. With lustrous brown skin and even features, he has a delightful boyish glint to his eye. He wears his hair in a short fade. In the mid-eighties, he pioneered the rap genre with his music video "The Show." But he hasn't had a hit in years. In the world of rap music, he is old news. That doesn't matter to the kids now.

Fresh fondles the microphone. "Each of you has got to be strong enough to do your own thinkin'. It's got to change, and it's got to start with you." He mesmerizes the audience, but he has nothing new to say. At the end of his short, earnest presentation, he starts a gentle rap riff. The lyrics prepared for the occasion are appropriately grave, and the mood of solemnity holds for a while. But even the subdued hip-hop cadence of his words juices up the six student leaders seated behind him on the stage. One girl jumps up and snaps her skirt around her knees; several others rise and rock to the beat. Students in the audience leap to their feet, shouting and waving their arms.

Fresh ends his short song and bows. As he descends the steps at the side of the stage, the decorum breaks completely and two dozen students quit their seats and rush toward him. Nareida, the young actress who played Sharron's girlfriend in *Don't Give Up on Your Dreams*, clambers over her seat and charges down the row behind to get to his side. She tugs and pushes, turns sideways, and squeezes through the tight mass of screaming students toward the performer.

On the opposite side of the auditorium, Sharon King is horrified at this riotous development. She circles in front of the stage and does some pushing of her own till she gets close enough to grip Nareida by the shoulders and yank her back.

"What the hell are you doing? Are y'all crazy? This is a goddamn *memorial!*" she screams at the startled girl.

Despite King's protest, pandemonium breaks loose and more kids run up to Fresh. Much of the behavior of these young people is based on what they have seen on television. It's all theater, and as they mob Dougie Fresh, they are just reading from the wrong page of the script. The hysteria is macabre. Enraged, King wades into the crowd, tossing adolescents aside like sacks of flour. It's all she can do to refrain from throwing punches. It is five minutes before order is restored.

Most of it is an act anyway. Beck, King, and the counselors are trying to mark the death of Daryl Sharpe as a tragedy. But the teacher who said that the faculty was more traumatized than the students was right. The death is only shocking because it happened in the hallway of a school. These are the young of the Brownsville Houses, of Amboy Street and Cypress. They were close by when Officer McLean was killed at 340 Dumont and Tango, Boy, Powerful, and the rest lay dead in the Complex last summer. How much grieving can they do?

Later in the day, Carol Beck and a flushed Sharon King are seated in the principal's conference room. Beck is wearing a cobalt-blue blouse and her ever-present ivory Nefertiti brooch. "We are going to a new place as a school, as a community," Beck says, chortling. "They tell me not to talk to the press, but if I don't they start digging up and creating things. This way, they all get the same things and they go." She is subtly but relentlessly self-congratulatory. The effect is entirely sympathetic. She seems to be building herself up for the benefit of the school. If she is wonderful, so is Jefferson, and so are the students, even though some of them may be shooting each other. She has seen negative images followed by violent behavior all her life, and she is determined to throw sticks in the spokes of that dreadful wheel.

The woman from the board of education walks into the principal's office and slumps into a chair, tired and upset. She has gold-tipped gray hair and carries a beige Vuitton bag.

"A child that can't be buried . . ." The woman sighs dramatically. King, across the table, rolls her prodigious hazel eyes. Beck cuts her a glance, warning her not to disrespect the board's representative.

"I'm not a politician. I'm a teacher. We get paid much less," King says, and walks out.

Beck is a politician and a teacher. After the board of education lady and King have left the office, she sits alone and exhausted at the huge table. Slowly, she unties the string around a box that turns out to hold a white and pink cake, a gift from several parents. "Cheer Up," says an inscription in blue icing. Beck thumbs through a pile of mail offering sympathy and best wishes for her and the school. Among the letters is one that reads, "Do what you gotta do. Keep the faith." Enclosed is a check for $500, made out to Thomas Jefferson High School. The letter has been sent from the Manhattan Correctional Center. It is signed "John Gotti."

The next day there is another sit-down with the media, this time with two members of Geraldo Rivera's *Now It Can Be Told* television show.

A young black producer with copper-colored hair blithely sets sail into Beck's waters. "We realize your dedication —" he begins.

"And I realize your need to follow up a story to get in the headlines," Beck interrupts, firing a cannon shot across his bow. "We're not about that. We are going to transcend sensationalism here. This is a different kind of energy. We are not going backwards. We are not about raising the Neilsen ratings, or selling newspapers."

"We believe this is a microcosm," the producer's smooth-faced sidekick says.

"We know all that," Beck fires back. "I'm not paranoid. I am racially secure. We know the problem. We want solutions."

The producer is intrepid. He graduated from Syracuse University with a degree in journalism, moved to Manhattan, and sailed to the top of his field like a weather balloon. He is barely thirty years old. East New York and Brownsville are the provinces to him, places important only for the story he has come to cover; Carol Beck is an insignificant drudge who just happened to be on the watch when something remarkable happened. He does not understand that in many ways this place, this school, is the most significant place of all, the place on which the future of the country will turn. And that Carol Beck is the important person, the kind of person he is so sure he is.

"What are those solutions?" he asks, with a cockiness that reveals how many things he has not felt.

Beck is calmer now. "We are trying to come to a different emotional and psychological place. You are constrained by time on television. You cannot get into the psyche of the black and Hispanic man. As a people, we are through with the talk show. I don't care about those people on Sutton Place. They are not here. They will never be here. Now is time to do some other things. I am not sure what they are, but I know that you are not going to get at them in forty minutes."

"I can see you're trying to do this yourself. We would like to talk to the parents," the producer says.

Beck calls across the room to an assistant, "Jerry, I'm not getting through to these people." Then her voice begins to trill with anger. It is now clear that she did not come to this discussion in good faith. She is using Geraldo's people to make herself feel better. "Why would you want to talk to the parents?" she demands.

"You don't have to raise your voice," the producer protests, wishing he had not made the trip.

"You want to show a picture that says, 'This is what the mother of a child who has been killed looks like.' I ain't about this anymore. Where is the benefit, the intellectual growth, that is going to come out of that? It's a type of prostitution. I'm not telling you about my pain anymore. It's tragic, yes. But do I need to share this with the white middle class? No, I am not exposing my wounds to Sally Sue in Kansas. If it has to stop with me, maybe other blacks and Latinos will also stop."

"We are not miracle workers," the producer's slim sidekick says.

"I didn't think you were," Beck snaps.

RIKER'S ISLAND

Front-page news for two days, the shootings at Jefferson are quickly forgotten. Today, sheets of rain assail a line of friends, relatives, defendants, and victims that stretches from the Brooklyn Criminal Court down Schermerhorn Street around the corner toward the looming Brooklyn House of Detention on Atlantic Avenue. In the middle of the line, a white woman with a bloated face and three grimy children straddles a puddle of rainwater. Her baby daughter drops a pacifier into the filmy water. The mother snatches up the rubber mouthpiece and dips it into her own mouth for cleaning before she hands it back to the toddler. A platoon of teenagers cut the line and wedge their way in toward the metal detectors beyond the revolving doors. No one complains. The courthouse where Sharron will be sentenced late this afternoon is an eight-story eyesore, a dingy, grimy contrast to the bleached stone and tinted glass of the federal court on Cadman Plaza a few blocks away, where the Young Guns pleaded guilty. The Schermerhorn building houses courtrooms, probation offices, record departments, and other offices.

The cops who have to testify here shuttle back and forth to the court from a building down the street they call ECAB, the Early Case Assessment Bureau. On the seventh floor there they sleep on filthy padded blue chairs with newspapers for blankets, waiting to be called for interviews with the ADAs, who will decide what kind of a case to make out of their collar. On a wall of ECAB's waiting room some misguided soul has written "The Killing Crew," with a short list of names of Housing officers from PSA 2 who have killed perps in Brownsville and East New York over the years. The list starts with the nickname Grahambo.

The cops are not allowed to use the clean semiprivate bathroom on the floor. Somebody scrawled "ADAs blow," "[ADA] Lynn Jaffee is a lesbian," and numerous references to "niggers" on the stalls, which upset the lawyers and minority complainants. The cops have been banished to a filthy toilet on the ninth floor.

In the courthouse, from his seat in the bullpen of Part V on the fourth floor, Sharron cannot see the rows of benches in the courtroom, where Chantal sits with Andre in her lap. The busy courtroom is half full of spectators and young men, who are here for any one of a score of reasons related to a criminal case pending against them.

"Didn't your lawyer advise you how to dress and conduct yourself when you come before this court?" a judge asks a flabby youth convicted of an infraction that is not serious enough to warrant incarceration. "This is the second time you have arrived here asking for a delay in the payment of your fine. Next time you are scheduled to appear, you bring some money with you. I don't care if it's a ten-dollar bill. Or you are going to jail. Do you understand?"

It is late afternoon by the time Sharron's name is called. He slouches out to meet the judge and hear the numbers he knows already.

"No reading," a court officer shouts at a man in the back.

Chantal and Andre are in the third row. Sharron nods. Though he is not cuffed, he does not wave. Chantal holds the kicking baby up to see his handsome father's face, but only for a moment. Sharron turns to face the judge. His plea has been accepted, the deal delivered, all in record time. Six months in jail and a hefty five-year probation. It is not about graduating from high school now. It is about doing the time without getting hurt. Maybe it was about that all along.

Sharron nods to Chantal and Andre again on the way out. He does not smile; his face is a jailhouse mask already. But Sharron Corley is a lucky man, or a lucky boy, as the case may be, because the judge has decided to put him in the adolescent house, even though he is eighteen and could have been assigned to the adult wing with the heavyweights. Sharron breathes a deep sigh when he finds he is going down with the boys.

At 5:30 on Sharron's first morning in Mod Six, the "newjack" barracks in the 4 Building at Riker's Island, a bank of lights flashes a stunning wakeup call in his eyes. He sits up and blinks, looking down the narrow room filled with thirty beds. Next to each bed is a waist-high steel locker.

"*Walkin' to the mess hall*," a corrections officer's voice booms. "*On the breakfast.*"

Only four boys sit up. The rest roll over and cover their heads with blankets. Sharron does the same. Later in the morning, as he watches the boys around him dig into their stashes of cookies and potato chips from the commissary, he regrets his decision. Throughout the morning, he is alternately hungry and nauseous. The smells of disinfectant and boiled meat drift up from the mess hall and mix together in the room like a fresh insult. There is nothing to do but sit and stare until 12:30. The barracks and the TV room are filled with lean, staring boys, many of them coming through the system for the first time. Their eyes are open, their mouths closed.

"*On the lunch.*"

This time Sharron lines up for the trip to the mess hall. "*On the gate*," the corrections officer hollers and waits for each barred partition to be opened on the trip downstairs. In the bright green mess hall, the food is served through two narrow slits in an otherwise blank wall. There is a choice of halal, ritually slaughtered meat for Muslim inmates, or regular fare. Sharron's meal is three pieces of white bread, one bloated frankfurter, a fistful of cool mashed potatoes, an indistinct yellowish vegetable, and a container of milk. He gobbles the frankfurter, skirts the potatoes, which glow faintly green in the corner of his partitioned plastic plate, and swallows his milk in two gulps.

Back upstairs in the barracks, he cannot sleep anymore, so he stuffs his worn woolen blanket into his pillowcase for extra cushion, the way he has seen others do, and gazes dumbly at the low ceiling. Bursts of canned laughter drift from the television in the day room. He has heard that there is a school program; he has even been supplied with a notebook and a stubby pencil, too short to be used as a weapon. But it will take time for the school paperwork to go through. So for his first two days Sharron just sits glumly on his bed, staring across at veteran inmates talking for as long as half an hour on the telephone in the hallway. He watches the phone, but does not make his move.

There is no middle ground in the adolescent areas of Riker's Island. Either you are an exploiter or you are exploited. If you are soft and have no connections, you will be forced to "go shopping" at the commissary for the more powerful guys and you will get no time on the horn. If a guy wants to stay out of trouble at all costs, his family may not hear from him for weeks or months at a time, because the only thing that produces phone time is juice, props. And juice is acquired mostly through violence.

The Mod Six dormitory is small, now housing twenty-five inmates, observed at all times by a corrections officer from a window. But in the day room around the corner, where the television is, there is a spot visible from the CO's bubble only if the officer takes his eyes off the security televisions, takes a step to the right, and cranes his neck.

In Sharron's first week, a boy comes through Mod Six who had trouble "out in the world" with a friend of one of the Hispanic leaders of the "4 Building gangsters." Even though Mod Six is separated from the other housing areas in the 4 Building, a pecking order flows through the walls, communicated through meetings in the gym and mess hall and enforced by the "gangsters." Sharron sees the system at work one afternoon and records his observations in his notebook:

> We were all in the day room, and I felt the tension in the air, so I was on point. The next thing I know, this huge Spanish guy has the new guy in a sleeper hold and drags him to the blind spot. The new guy finally went to sleep, and the others walked out, so the corrections officer couldn't notice the event. Then, in the same order, they all came back into the day room and began carving up the guy's face something awful. Each slice sounded like a zipper being pulled up. Then they awoke him to a pool of blood.

Sharron spends the next few days in a flurry of concealment, his indolent walk, bitter eyes, and scowl-twisted face a desperate cover for his fear. In the world beyond Brownsville, his asset sheet holds his good looks, charm, sensitivity, singing talent,

Brownsville circa 1910: the corner of Thatford and Belmont avenues
(Courtesy of the Brooklyn Historical Society)

Brownsville today: on the border with East New York, overlooking the Van Dyke Houses
(Mitchell Zykofsky)

These "Rest in Peace" murals are now found throughout the Ville.
(Benny J. Stumbo)

Sharron Corley
(Charlena Berksteiner)

Sharron using "his" phone on Pitkin
Avenue *(Charlena Berksteiner)*

Sharron at age nine, with his sister,
Shawanda, eleven *(Courtesy of Sharron Cor)*

Gary at age fourteen, with his grand-mother *(Courtesy of Gary Lemite)*

Gary Lemite *(Mitchell Zykofsky)*

Gary with Lisa, Erica, and Zach *(Andrew French)*

This statue of Thomas Jefferson sits between Principal Carol Beck's office and the metal detectors at the school's entrance. *(© Eli Reed/Magnum Photos)*

Thomas Jefferson High School
(Charlena Berksteiner)

Sharon King *(Charlena Berksteiner)*

Carol Beck *(Courtesy of the Jackie Robi. Center)*

The Thomas Jefferson High School basketball team. *Left to right: front,* Willie Brown, Cortez Sutton, Carl Princivil, Marvin McLaurin; *kneeling,* Jude Princivil, Musbau (Nick) Ogunyemi; *back,* Greg Donaldson, Adrian Bradshaw, Kevin (Tumbo) John, Coach George Moore.
(Courtesy of George Moore)

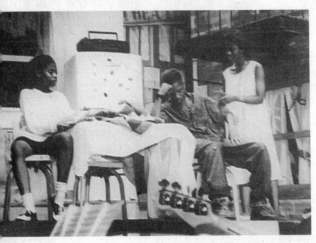

Above left: Sharron and other members of the cast of *Don't Give Up on Your Dreams* practice outside.
(Courtesy of the Jackie Robinson Center)

Above: Student leader Bashim Inman at the side door of Thomas Jefferson
(Mitchell Zykofsky)

Left: Danny, played by Sharron, is warned by his mother and sister of the dangers of life on the streets.
(Courtesy of the Jackie Robinson Center)

Left: The entrance to the PSA 2, on Sutter Avenue *(Benny J. Stumbo)*

Above: Cops on the four-to-twelve shift stand in line to pick up their radios. *(Mitchell Zykofsky)*

Left: John (J.R.) Reynolds and Gary Lemite on the job *(Mitchell Zykofsky)*

Officer Kevin Price, at left, helps carry the dying Tyrone Sinkler out the front door of Thomas Jefferson. *(Benny J. Stumbo)*

Sharon King comforts students after the second shooting at Jeff. *(© Eli Reed/Magnum Photos)*

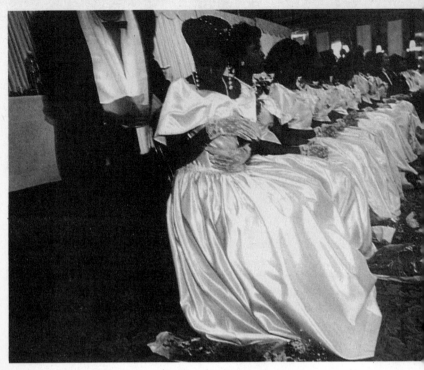

Students await the beginning of Carol Beck's cotillion. *(© Eli Reed/Magnum Photos)*

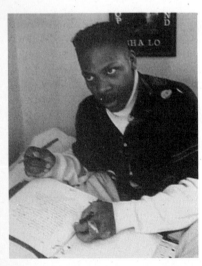

Sharron at work on homework, making his way toward completing high school
(Charlena Berksteiner)

Gary Lemite, wearing the medals that made him the most highly decorated New York Housing cop in 1992
(Andrew French)

and quick mind. On the negative page are his obsession with image and his association with the LoLifes. In Riker's, the pages are switched.

After a little more than a week, Sharron is transferred to Four Main. As he enters the cell area, the inmates stand with their faces close to a Plexiglas window near the guards' station, watching his every move. Stepping through the sliding gate into their midst, Sharron knows that even a flicker of concern on his face will identify him as "new to this," as a sucker. Accordingly, he maintains a modified ice grill as he passes the cluster of boys, a pillowcase in his hand holding his belongings and boxes of cookies he has just purchased at the commissary. At the back of the group of staring boys stands Ralphlo, a Crown Heights LoLife. Ralph has two gold chains looped around his neck. It's clear at a glance that he is a person of some stature here. Sharron suppresses his delight at finding a LoLife with props in the bowels of Four Main and mumbles, "Wha's up, Ralph," as he steps past on his way to his cell. There is no response. Maybe Ralphlo is waiting to see how Sharron handles himself, waiting to see if he is a sucker, before he acknowledges their acquaintanceship. All eyes follow Sharron's dangling pillowcase as he moves toward his cell. The boys in Four Main have not had a trip to the commissary, have not been shopping, in two weeks. There isn't a cookie to be found in the housing area at any price, and now Sharron walks in like Santa Claus.

For Sharron, there are a number of quick decisions to be made. Should he secrete the cookies in his locker or should he toss them on his bed as a challenge to those who would steal them? In the spirit of Ralphlo's flaunted chains, he throws the three boxes onto the bare mattress for all to see. Before he can look up, a voice floats from over his shoulder and to his right, "Yo, Sha, wha's up."

Sharron keeps his head down and does not answer. The voice is familiar; Sharron caught a glimpse of the guy on his way in. It's a kid from around the way. Still, he doesn't respond. There's no telling if the boy is a sucker in here. Ralphlo is afraid Sharron is a sucker. Sharron is afraid this guy is a sucker. As Sharron lifts his head, he finds another kid before him, with a shaved head. This one certainly is not any kind of sucker. He looks like trouble. So soon.

"How 'bout a cookie, man?" the boy asks. Sharron watches

the kid's hands for signs of a burner. He has heard that guys in Four Main have melted pieces of razors onto the tips of their toothbrushes. How to answer? Should he shoot the request down pointblank? Should he respond matter-of-factly, or should he hand over a cookie? The kid with the gleaming head might be waiting for just such an excuse to slice him. But if he gives up the cookie, he might look soft.

"Take one, man," Sharron says flatly, then raises his voice for all in Four Main to hear. "But I got *no fuckin' food to be givin' away.*"

After tightly tying his prized cookies in the pillowcase and putting the bundle in his locker, he flops on his bed. He considers his situation. He has met Ralphlo only once before, on a meow, a shoplifting excursion, to Union Square in Manhattan, when a crew of LoLifes rushed a sporting goods store and made off with a rack of summer shirts. For Sharron, the connection is invaluable, but the introduction has to be done just right.

A couple of hours later, he approaches Ralphlo in the day room with the deference that a recent college graduate might use to introduce himself to a distant but influential relative.

"S'up?" he ventures.

"Do I know you?" There is not the slightest trace of warmth in Ralph's voice.

"Wow. Don't do me like that," Sharron answers. Both he and Ralph know the significance of the conversation. "We was down on a meow. Like, summer 'fore last."

Ralph pages through his memory. He wants to be fair. He runs three fingers down his cheek and looks hard at Sharron, who turns his head to display his scar. Ralphlo shakes his head.

"Nah," he says.

A few minutes later, back in his cell, a rebuffed and deeply concerned Sharron is on his bed, showing his photographs. He asked Gloria to send him a packet of photos for display. He is playing all his cards to impress the gangsters. One picture is a three-by-five color school portrait of Vanessa, the girl he met at the end-of-summer party; another is of a mighty fine Chantal. The Puerto Rican dudes Sharron is so wary of are "sweatin' Chantal big-time," studying the picture for minutes at a time, because she looks like a Puerto Rican sister. Another photo is of Sharron and his man Frank wearing Polo gear.

Ralph wanders over to the periphery of the small group checking out the shots. He leans in and gets a good look at Frank and Sharron in green Polo pullovers, and his face finally brightens, a blessed moment for Sharron.

"Yeah, downtown in Ma'ha'an," Ralphlo pronounces. "Bum shop. Got paid, son."

For many Americans, connections are a way of life. When a kid from Brownsville faces an interviewer for a job, there is never a familiar figure across the table, an uncle or a friend of the family somewhere behind the scene to shuffle his résumé to the top of the pile. These kids are not able to work off the books for a cousin's cousin in the summer, loading trucks or laying concrete, like the young guys in Canarsie. The trade unions are closed up tight. The only place these kids have connections that pay off is in jail. The only time the way is smoothed for them is when they get locked up. The LoLifes are Sharron's salvation.

"In Four Main I'm a gangster now," Sharron writes to Vanessa, "'cause I have props. I am hooked with Ralphlo, I now have no problem with the horn."

But he is lonely; he has no visitors. Gloria is pissed off, swears she will not come. Chantal is under age. Vanessa is busy going to school and working. Visiting day after visiting day, Sharron waits for his name to be called.

"Goddamn," he mutters, and slumps back on his bed as the line of boys heads out to the visiting area. "Down" two weeks now, and he still hasn't gotten a visit. He doesn't have sneakers or extra underwear. The photo bit will only impress the guys for so long without some pretty girls on the set. But he doesn't want to appear too disappointed, doesn't want to look like a loser. Though Four Main is a cell area instead of an open barracks, interaction is constant. Guys have tiny metal burners, what they call "guns," glued up under their beds with toothpaste or on portions of the bedframes they have managed to magnetize. Your things can get stolen, or you can get punched out or cut while you shower or watch television. Even though Sharron has important props, the pressure is still intense. He spends all his recreation time lifting weights. By the fourth week, his pectorals and triceps are straining against his gray uniform jumpsuit.

With his prized minutes on the horn, Sharron coos to Chantal or any of several other once and future girlfriends. There is no time limit on phone conversations. Each boy stays on as long as his props permit. As Sharron speaks, his housemates float closer and closer, like wolves to a flickering campfire, and brush him, or toss something in his direction, as he sits huddled, trying to create his own world out of a cupped hand and the black phone receiver.

"Yo, why you wanna do that, mister? No man, that ain't right," he complains when harassed. This is not going to be easy.

Then there is real trouble. Sharron has been keeping things together in Four Main; he got a job on "suicide watch," making sure nobody hangs himself and earning a couple of dollars to use in the commissary. He has even bragged to Chantal that he is a gangster with "mad props." Then one night in the day room, just after recreation, a fight breaks out. Two boys, then three, five. Soon a dozen boys are warring in the walkspace between the rows of cells. The beef has nothing to do with Sharron until he is passed a three-inch, razor-sharp burner with the understanding that he will back up Ralphlo and his people. A kid is carried out, his face wrapped in gauze, on his way to the infirmary for ninety-six stitches. One of Ralphlo's boys, who started the fight, gets ninety days in the bing. Sharron is scheduled for fifteen, and is transferred to East Mod. But somehow, with the move, the corrections officers lose track of his involvement in the incident, which could cost him his early release. There is still a chance that if he can stay out of trouble, he will get out in four months instead of the scheduled six.

"All of a sudden," Sharron writes in his diary, "I'm in East Mod and I'm nothin'. I just sit here and don't do nothin'. I'm with a lot of Puerto Ricans again."

A week later: "It's getting better, like I'm in the middle now, but when I first got here I was like chill. I wanted to get on the jack so bad I was ready to flip."

Sharron just cannot get comfortable. He catches some guy trying to steal his picture of Chantal. The attempted theft is a major transgression, but with his lack of status in East Mod, he doesn't really have the props to make any kind of a move. Ralphlo is on the other side now. Worse, Sharron's ally is in the bing again, this time for thirty days. By now Sharron has his own tiny metal burner, a twist from a clotheshanger which he keeps hidden under a carefully loosened floor tile in the bathroom. Burner or not, the sorry truth is that he is back where he started, looking longingly at the telephone, minding his own business, watching his back.

In Brownsville, Rony Shoman is hard at work, but he's watching his back too. *Pop pop pop.* Rony freezes for a moment, his hand suspended over the keys of the cash register in his supermarket. With eyes as blank as stone, he looks across at his brother, at the next register, and goes back to work.

The sweep team is right outside, cruising down Sutter over the bridge separating Brownsville and East New York, when the cops hear echoing shots and charge into the Van Dyke Houses courtyard. Gary Lemite swings out of his unmarked car, right behind. But the shots are coming from an upper window of 301 Sutter, in the Langston Hughes Houses, at the corner of Sutter and Rockaway, a block away.

"*Stupid!*" a woman yells, pointing her finger at the top floor of 301 Sutter. Quick little Willie Arroyo, a new sweep team member, knows when he is hearing the truth, spins, crosses the street, and sprints along Sutter. He turns onto Rockaway, trying to make it to the cover of the canopy over the pumps at the Amoco station at the corner. Gary is a few feet behind him, running sideways, presenting as small a target as possible, hugging the wall. The shots are cracking somewhere above. Arroyo figures if he can make it to the cover, he'll have a short run to the back of 301. From there he can slip around to the front door. But as he dashes around the corner, an ancient, sinewy arm reaches from a doorway and bony fingers tighten around his blue jacket. An old man pulls him to the safety of the doorway.

"*Está ciego?*" The old man asks the young cop if he is blind. Arroyo shrugs.

"*Gracias, señor,*" he whispers, turning and preparing to sprint across the street to the canopy.

Sergeant Toney and a couple of his anticrime boys have already made it to the floor below the sniper, and they can hear the sound of the shots throbbing through the walls. Across Sutter, Sergeant Bright, McMullen, and Galvin are heading for the same cover, running with the deep conviction that no bullet is meant for them. But Del Migliore, like Arroyo newly promoted to sweep, has lost the faith, especially when it comes to snipers. He moves down Sutter in a deep crouch, with a stricken look on his strong face. He holds a fiberglass clipboard over his head as a pathetic defense against a bullet, which, ever since he was shot outside the Pink Houses, he knows can find him.

"Look out. Look out!" he shouts to Gary and the charging sweep team. "The job's not worth it!" he yells, his voice trailing off. A few minutes later, the snipers, two men in their early twenties who took time off from an apartment painting job to get drunk and try out a new gun, give up sheepishly.

That night, Gary walks into his apartment in Elmont and his family is there, the way they used to be. The way they should be. The kids are all over him before he steps down through the door, Zach hanging on one leg and Erica on the other as he places his guns high up on the living room cabinet. Then he hoists them up in the crook of each arm, their heads almost brushing the low ceiling, squeezes them together, and kisses both their laughing faces at once. Lisa stands off to the side in the doorway to the kitchen, beaming.

Gary is not surprised to find Lisa and the kids back. The Friday night counseling sessions with Merle, the pastor in Elmont, have grown less strained, the dinners and Sunday afternoon drives more and more enjoyable. In the past few weeks, when Lisa and Gary found themselves alone in the house, there was less arguing, more lovemaking. Anything Lisa wanted, she got. And Gary mapped out a plan for how long it will take him to get the family out of the basement apartment, to save the fifteen grand for the down payment on a house, including how much overtime he can expect to pull. Lisa was impressed, and she has never stopped wanting him. The kids have been missing their father too. And they have been raising too much hell at her sister's house.

Before the evening is over, Gary is dispensing discipline to Erica and trying to get little Zach to stick up for himself: "Erica, if you hit Zach again, no ice cream. Do you understand?" He tosses Zach up and down, calling him Bobo, trying to toughen him up. There is time to be made up.

The next day Gary drives Erica to her day-care center. On the steps of the school building, she points out a little boy named Paul. Later, as she says her prayers, she makes an addition. "Now I lay me down to sleep. Wish my soul for heaven to keep. I want God to bless Mommy and Daddy and Grandma . . . and Paul."

"What was that?" Gary asks.

Erica smiles mysteriously.

"Now don't forget to bless Aunt Melanie and Uncle Bill," Gary reminds.

"God bless Aunt Melanie and Uncle Bill . . . and Paul," Erica adds as she lays her head on the pillow.

Kate Worthy is thinking about lying down somewhere, anywhere. She stops at the foot of the subway steps, grips the handrail, stoops over, and breathes deeply. Her heart is acting up. "You all right, Grandma?" twelve-year-old Shantay wants to know.

"Yeah, I'm O.K. Just catchin' my breath."

Five Worthy kids between the ages of seven and thirteen shuffle and stare numbly while Kate wheezes herself into condition to mount the stairs. Just like the Housing cop said after the eviction hearing, the Worthys have nowhere to live. It is 5 P.M. and the family is at the end of a long trip on the #3 train to Abyssinian House, a Tier II shelter on 138th Street in Harlem. It took the Housing Authority over a month to evict the family from Apartment 5AB. When it did, many of the older ones found lodging in the projects in Brownsville. Renee, Wanda, and their kids found a spot with a cousin; Lennie, Randolph, and Blue, with friends. But the rest headed right to a Tier I shelter in Brooklyn, the kind of place where hundreds of cots are arranged in one large room.

After a sleepless night, Kate complained, and the Human Resources Administration assured her that if she took her passel of grandchildren and great-grandchildren up to 138th Street, they would have their own private lodgings, along with a range of social services.

It's six o'clock and dark when Kate walks into the front office of the five-floor shelter with her band of weary Brownsville refugees. When they are shown to their facilities, they are clean and indeed private. Just two people to a room, even a small kitchen.

"We don't have food, and no pots or nothin' even if we did," Kate points out to the shelter employee, an unsmiling Jamaican woman.

"Three blocks away from here we have a pantry, and we have pots and silverware."

Kate turns and smiles, touches Shantay's shoulder. A change in luck, she is thinking.

"Does Grandma got to go to the pantry? 'Cause she's tired," Shantay asks. "Can we get the food?"

"I'm sorry. There must always be an adult on hand," the attendant insists.

And that is the rub. Kate already has a small apartment in a senior citizens' building in Brooklyn. The only reason she has been trudging through the transit system, climbing those stairs, is that the kids need somebody to get them in the shelters. So Grandma Worthy and three of the kids head over to pick up some canned beans and vegetables, cereal and milk from the food outlet. For tonight, everything is all right. There is no giggling and no joking around. Everybody falls fast asleep.

But the next day finds the entire group — except for Kate, who heads to her apartment for some rest — back in Brownsville on the bench in front of 295. At dusk, Kate collects the brood and starts the trek to Abyssinian House. Evening after evening, she rides the trains with her ragamuffin band lined up on the subway seats beside and in front of her, from Brooklyn, through the throngs of well-dressed, home-bound commuters in Manhattan, up to Harlem.

In less than two weeks, all the kids are absorbed by one household or another. "Some left their clothes up there in Harlem," Kate says. "One day we just didn't go back. Left the food too, but that was free."

The sun is not up yet. Chantal is sitting in the kitchen of the Saratoga Street apartment, perfectly at home in this household, getting her hair unbraided by a neighbor in preparation to go visit Sharron at Riker's. Shawanda is busy looking for the package containing a plain pair of pants and some underwear, which her brother has been demanding for the last three weeks. Sharron has made it clear that he does not want any clothing desirable enough to be stolen.

Chantal has on a pair of black jeans and a black sweatshirt with the brand name Guess written in gold over her left breast. Her unbraided hair is oiled and pulled tightly back from her face, her ponytail cinched by a pair of red rubber bands. Shawanda, beside her, is not concerned with beautification. She is trying to gather the articles Sharron needs. Gloria is still asleep.

"I had the package. I had the thing last night."

Shawanda has a calm, authoritative air and miraculously small feet; her pink-and-white sneakers are almost as little as the shoes people hang on rearview mirrors. She has a fresh black eye, which she claims she got from her boyfriend, John, when he rolled over in his sleep. Since Sharron has been gone, Shawanda and John have taken up residence at the Saratoga apartment. They sleep in Sharron's room, in Sharron's bed.

Alleke glides into the kitchen like a dark ghost. His arms are wrapped around the package with Sharron's pants and a pair of unusual canvas sneakers, more like deck shoes, that Sharron tried to introduce as a style at Jefferson when he was riding high as the star of *Don't Give Up on Your Dreams*.

The girls leave the house at seven o'clock and join the march of working folks down Saratoga to the subway. A trip to Riker's Island is an all-day affair, a numbing exercise in shuffling, waiting, standing. On the #3 train, across the aisle from the hard-eyed day-shift people headed to Manhattan, Chantal suddenly turns to face Sharron's sister.

"Andre got ammonia," she blurts.

"What?"

"Ammonia, the doctor said it was."

"How the fuck the baby get pneumonia?" Shawanda grimaces.

"Maybe when we was at court when Sharron got sentence," Chantal answers. "That's the only time we was really out. Else maybe it was the window."

"What window?"

"The broke one in Mommy's room where Andre be sleep."

At Forty-second Street, the girls change for the #7 train to Queens. On the twenty-minute trip to the Queens Plaza stop, where they will catch the Q101 bus to Riker's Island, Shawanda recalls with some fondness how she once visited a boyfriend there.

"I'm sittin' in the place where you first come in and you get a number to go to the next room, and I see this bitch I knew he was messin' with sittin' there. I said to myself, 'Oooo, buddy, we gonna have some shit today.'" Chantal nods. This is her first such trip. But she knows that a confrontation with a rival at Riker's is not unusual for the eligible young ladies from Brownsville.

The bus from the train station heads from the commercial district of Queens through the neighborhoods of Astoria and past the neat row houses on Hazen Street, the homes of some of the New Yorkers who have jobs. The men here, washing their cars on this Saturday morning, do not look up.

Chantal and Shawanda chat about Sharron as the bus rolls over the narrow bridge spanning a stretch of oily water and shiny oozing mud. The smell of the East River at low tide is at once a salty notice that the city has been left behind and a sickening indication that a bad place lies ahead.

"Sharron called me when he was first there and he sounded all happy, like he was at a party," Chantal reports, as cheerful as a girl on her way to a dance. "And he said, 'Don't play me.' That's what Sha always says. 'Cept he says it different, like 'Dooon't play me.'"

At the reception center, the girls wait in a twisting line to sign in and receive a yellow registration card from an irritated corrections officer. He addresses the visitors as if they were second-graders. "Anyone with a Walkman or a radio of any kind, turn around and leave the island right now. *Pay attention.* I am giving you a card. Look at the sample on the wall. Put your last name first."

After they receive their cards, the girls will wait to be moved to the C-74 waiting room, another area of the reception building. After a lengthy wait there, they will ride a yellow school bus one hundred yards to a parking lot next to the C-74 building, where Sharron is housed. There they will be frisked for weapons and contraband, place their jackets, jewelry, and handbags in lockers, and wait again. When their names are called, they will be body-searched and moved upstairs to the last waiting room before they step into a visiting area the size of a basketball court.

Chantal and Shawanda sit side by side in the registration area, filling out their yellow cards and glancing up at a flickering television screen. In each waiting room along the trip to the visiting area, a television is bolted to the wall eight feet off the floor, so the army of toddlers cannot fool with the dials.

"Stop it, Reuben. I'm going to tear your butt up," a woman yells to her boy, who is running in circles like a windup toy. Shawanda and Chantal hand in their cards and return to their seats.

There are a thousand women here today, half of whom have children — kids visiting fathers who once visited *their* fathers here. In the crowd there is one flashy girl resplendent in fashionable fall plaid. But mostly this is a family affair. These are the plain girls, the ones who have a stake in their men. These are the reliables.

After Chantal and Shawanda spend thirty-five minutes in the registration area, a corrections officer arrives. "Seventy-five through one hundred," he announces. The girls step quickly down the hall to the C-74 waiting area. There, a woman with two bright-eyed children in tow squeals with delight at the sight of the rap duo Kid 'n Play prancing on the TV screen above. Information is exchanged about the state of Kid's towering fade. Kid — or is it Play? — cavorts around the stage in an imitation of the way the young men in the Ville walk and move, the way they slouch and gesture with the backs of their hands. Neither of the two performers onscreen is from Brownsville or anywhere like it. They are college kids from Queens. The homeboys from the ghetto have become big business. But the real homeboys are locked inside.

Every third or fourth woman in the waiting room has a scar on her cheek or neck. A husky-voiced Hispanic woman, Reuben's mother, has fresh marks on both sides of her neck. She holds a third child, an infant, while Reuben and Stuart, identical four-year-olds in impeccable matching winter jackets, stare at each other and wait to see if their most recent bit of mischief is enough to summon a smack. Later, during the visit, the twins will sit glumly by as their beefy, tattooed father fondles and coos with the baby and pays them little mind.

Someone knew what he was doing when he put televisions here. On weekdays, every set is tuned to the soap operas, and the seated women are mesmerized by the goings-on. An older

Hispanic woman says in a clear voice to her young friend, "The trick is to stay out of the system." The girls to her left and right don't even twitch their heads away from the televisions. There is no sense of regret in the women, no hint that they feel they have selected the wrong man to father their children. This experience, this day, is just a fact of life.

Numbers. They are calling number sixty-eight. Shawanda checks her card: ninety-four. It is almost one o'clock. A woman who has been here since eight-thirty in the morning, waiting for her son to be summoned from his housing area, starts to complain to the women around her, and then to the female corrections officer who stands surrounded by waiting women.

"Step back. Step back, *please*," the officer shouts, flashing three silver teeth. "I want you to step back. Y'all are breathing down my neck. I can feel your *breath* on me." She shudders involuntarily.

A woman on a bench in the back, with skin the color of a damp brown paper bag, the face of a pretty clown, and the body of a girl gone slack with beer, yells out, "I'm gonna come over there and breathe on you in a minute." There is a tense moment as the group separates so the two women can get a look at each other. The heckler smiles. The scar that runs like a river across her plump right cheek squeezes. The smooth flat section on the bottom folds up to kiss the lumpy top part. The corrections officer laughs and waves at the woman, a regular.

Shawanda approaches the guard. "How long you think?" she asks sweetly.

"Dunno, they could be bringin' him from commissary or mess. What's his ID number?"

Shawanda stares blankly.

"I dunno how you got this far without no ID number."

Shawanda stays while Chantal leaves the C-74 waiting area and uses a phone in an adjacent building to get the number from prison information. While she waits for the operator to retrieve the number, a satin-skinned youth about Sharron's age and size strides up to the phone beside her. The boy is handsome, with a wisp of a charcoal mustache on his finely carved upper lip. A rakish effect is supplied by two slashes shaved in his right eyebrow. When Chantal spies him, she undergoes an extraordinary transformation. Her eyes enlarge to ovals, her shoulders drop, and her coral lips part. The hand that holds the telephone receiver drops to her side as she angles herself slowly into the boy's field of vision. She is entranced, available, brazen, all in an instant. The boy is unimpressed. He conducts his business on the phone privately, cocks his head at Chantal for just a moment, and walks away. Chantal Redding, fifteen-year-old mother, Sharron's "shorty," slowly returns the phone to her ear and listens for Sharron's ID number.

The ID does no good. The girls have arrived on the wrong day. Visiting hours at Riker's Island are scheduled on rotating days. One week, inmates with last names from A through L have visits on Thursday, those with names at the end of the alphabet on Saturday. The next week the days are switched. All inmates have a contact visit on Sunday. Shawanda leaves the package with the sneakers and the pants with a guard, and the girls head home.

Sharron is beside himself. He calls Ms. King. "I can't believe Chantal isn't here. I need things. I need some clothes. I know she is wearing my clothes. I know Shawanda is in my room, in my closet, wearing my clothes." He eases off, waxes diplomatic. "That's O.K. They need the clothes. I can't worry about my clothes. They're out there, and I'm in here.

"I don't want to lift too many weights," he tells King. "If I get too big, I won't fit my clothes." He lobbies for a sweatshirt and a pair of sweatpants, plain, black or gray. He now has a small black eye, something like the one his sister sports. "I wonder whether I should have somebody tell the people in Satellite that I'm in jail. I know a lot of people are disappointed in me. I can't believe my girl isn't here. I'm fed."

On his way back to his bunk, Sharron pauses outside a circle of boys talking about misdeeds.

"Dude hands the bis to his man an' points to this other dude an' he says, 'Do 'em.' An' his man wets him up, *bam bam.* Shit was cold. Like a motherfuckin' movie."

Sharron isn't in the mood to laugh, slap hands, and marvel. Instead, he continues on to his bed and digs out his diary.

"There are the drug people," he writes.

For them, guns are a necessity. They have to feel ruthless so they can pull the trigger. Then there's guys who are just part of the swing of things around the way, like some character in a story. Some characters play good and just want a gun for protection from the trigger-happy ones, who play the bad character. I'm more the good character.

I've been the stickup kid. If I had another chance to start all over in the same neighborhood, I don't think it would be different in most of my decisions. After all I've been through I like to think of myself as a determined and motivated guy, compliments of my mother, and people who've given me a hand and helped me positively. But there's times when I've had none but my mother and I couldn't see, or wouldn't see, her hand, due to my obsession with props and image and girls. In my earlier teens, I would stay in the streets of Brownsville doing mischief, or even take a ride with a friend or two to Manhattan on the Number 3 train to continue mischievous deeds to keep from having the misfortune of long meaningless days with empty pockets and minds full of ponder. I would always imagine some big-time producer knocking on my door saying, "C'mon, there's a whole world out there waiting for your talent." I'd suddenly be famous, known over most parts of the world, pursuing a career, taking care of my family. Then I'd wake up from my daydream with a tap from my friend, getting us ready for our meow. "Yo, Sha, check it."

Sharron has requested that his mother stay away, but Chantal has been begging her to go anyway, since she needs an adult to accompany her. Finally, just before Thanksgiving, Gloria relents and takes Chantal to Riker's.

Once again Chantal is bright and jovial, despite the fact that Andre has been in Kings County Hospital for a week for treatment of his lingering pneumonia. Gloria is silent. Chantal's mindless good cheer is putting her in a truly foul mood.

"I don't know nothing about Riker's Island," she growls. "I have never been there. I have never had any *reason* to go there." Gloria would like to make it clear to Chantal and the others around her on the rattling bus that she is not accepting her son's lawlessness or this trip as a part of her life, past, present, or future. "When he was under my supervision, there was none of this shit," she says.

In fact, Gloria would like to be traveling in exactly the opposite direction this weekday morning. Still young, intelligent, and well-spoken, she would like to be on her way to a good job in Manhattan. By a directive from the welfare department, she is enrolled in a program that requires her attendance on 14th Street in Manhattan each weekday, where she learns to write a résumé and represent herself well in job interviews. She mutters to friends that her time would be much better spent in actually looking for work, and complains that the program is really a punishment for being unemployed. She is most interested in construction work, a job she once did, because it pays the best.

"How's the baby?" Gloria asks, changing the subject.

"The doctor said he's gonna be all right," Chantal reports, adjusting the angle of her ponytail by shifting the rubber bands. "Mommy, do you know that the window in the room where his crib is at has a broken window?" she asks. "My mommy called the people but they didn't call or come. She said that she is going to sue 'cause the baby got sick."

"Sue the landlord," Gloria suggests. Chantal hesitates. She does not know what the word "landlord" means.

"Where is Andre at?"

"Kings County."

"What are they givin' him?"

"They din' say. They said he turned blue for a while. Now he's gettin' better, they said."

"Blue," Gloria repeats. "Mmmmmm," she laments softly, and goes silent for a full five minutes while Chantal stares out the window.

"Sharron told me that he didn't want me to come," Gloria says finally. "He told me I should go to school. Some mothers, when their sons go to jail, it's just like a hotel. They sit up on the phone and get everything brought to them. Not me." Gloria looks over at Chantal, who is trying to catch her reflection in the bus window.

Gloria's grumpy demeanor changes later in the day, when Sharron steps through the doorway into the visiting room. She draws a long, deep breath, closes her eyes, and shakes her head. When she opens her eyes, they are glistening. She is smiling. "My baby," she says, even before Sharron is close enough to hear.

Sharron slinks across the room like a jaguar, his eyes scanning the terrain, his face twitching from the effort to control his smile. Gloria pushes her chair back and rises to embrace her son. She presses her cheek to his. Their identical cinnamon complexions blend as they hug. Sharron looks over his mother's shoulder and puckers his lips at Chantal, who jumps to kiss them but misses. In a moment he is giving her a righteous kiss as he holds his mother's hand. When the three sit down to talk, he notices a girl he knows from Brownsville eyeing him from across the room. A flutter of delight passes through him at the possibility that Chantal will see the girl's flirtation and argue with her on the way out.

Sharron leans across the small table that separates prisoners from their visitors, whispering and kissing Chantal. He turns to Gloria with feigned annoyance.

"I told you not to come," he says like a worried father. "I told you you should be goin' to school, not comin' all out here. Stay in school," he says sternly. The phrase reveals his inability to tolerate a real picture of Gloria. "Stay in school" — as if she were plugging away on a college campus like Gita Malave.

"Sha? How you got a black eye?" Chantal asks.

Sharron shrugs, squints, and squeezes Gloria's hand. There is no sense lying about how tough it is inside.

"You got to be careful, Sha, don't be fightin' over the phone. I don't care we don't speak till you get out," Chantal says wisely.

Several days later, Sharron is on the phone to Ms. King again. "Everything is smooth," he tells her. "Just got to keep it smooth for three more months. I got eight pictures of girls, only four fit on my locker, so I got the best four." He tells her about Gloria's visit. "Moms was tryin' to act all mad an' shit, but she's cool." He mentions that he has spoken to Chantal about the baby's condition. "Chantal says the doctor says that Andre got pneumonia, the worst kind. He even turned blue, but now he's gettin' better."

As Sharron talks, a harsh voice cuts through the jailhouse din. He reacts. "Hey man, why you got to curse when I'm on the phone? 'Five minutes'? Who the hell can I call in five minutes? No, sir, you don't be cursing when I'm on the phone. No, sir, you heard that."

WINTER

"HE'S GONE"

A smoky weekday November evening, and Gary Lemite is starting his tour. "Let's go look for DeeSo," he says, getting into the passenger seat of the new OSC Chevrolet Caprice. His partner nods tolerantly. Everybody on the squad says Gary has a hard-on for DeeSo.

No sooner did Gary get the assignment to the plainclothes detail than he set his sights on this reputed middle-level drug dealer, whom he and J.R. once arrested, months ago. DeeSo, who likes to write his name Dee$o, is a clean-cut twenty-four-year-old who wheels a blue Acura Legend around Tapscott Street and the Unity Houses. He is not big, maybe five-ten, with wide shoulders and narrow hips. His muscle is supplied by a roughneck from Unity named Tiz. His brother, Ra Ra, handles the business. With his casual clothing and spectacles, DeeSo looks more like a college student than a drug dealer. And he likes to be known for his good manners. When Gary and J.R. gave him a summons for public drinking, he was not guzzling a forty-ounce malt liquor; he was standing at the arched iron entrance to the Unity Houses with a bottle of Moët White Star in his hand. "Never buy champagne cold," he advised the officers. "Keep it in a refrigerator too long, stuff gets burnt out. Check it out."

DeeSo took the "toss," the arrest, with grace, even offered the cops his version of his life story, told Gary he was just out of jail for attempted murder. He did not try to hide the fact that he had taken over the crack commerce in Unity. He never said as much, but he issued no bogus denials either. "Can't talk to you now," he said at the time. "If you catch me dirty, we'll talk. But you won't catch me like that, 'cause I don't touch shit. I show respect," he told Gary. "You will find that I always show respect." Gary was not charmed.

Jack Lenti, the new commanding officer of PSA 2, is giving the troops more freedom, and they love it. There were eight arrests under Kammerdener on the last two Housing Days, targeted dates when the Housing cops sweep the projects for quality-of-life infractions. Forty-two bodies are snatched on each of the first two Housing Days under Lenti. But the people in the community may not like this style. Surely, the politicians will not be as happy as they were when Kammerdener was in charge. When City Councilwoman Priscilla Wooten wanted something done, Kammerdener jumped. If there was going to be a meeting in a project, he sent his people in days in advance to make sure there would be no unsightly drug dealing to embarrass anyone on the appointed day. Lenti is not like that. He's a cop's cop. If someone in the community has an unjustified complaint, Jack Lenti will tell them what time it is. However, he is not a stupid man. When the representative of the Guardians, the black cops' association, showed up at his office one day, demanding to be moved to NEU, a borough-wide narcotics specialty unit, Lenti threw him out for blatant influence-peddling. Somehow, he was sent to NEU anyway. Lenti claimed it was because he didn't want him in his command anymore.

But Lenti does want Lemite in his command. Gary is leading the PSA in arrests. He's leading in overtime, and he's setting records with his gun collars. Lenti has requested that he be awarded the Combat Cross for bravery in the Fiorentino shootout.

Gary makes a right turn off Sutter Avenue and wheels up Tapscott Street, looking for DeeSo. Instead he finds the drug dealer's brother. He and his partner cruise slowly up beside Ra Ra's white Infiniti, parked on a side street. In the car are four guys Gary has never seen; piles of green bills are in plain view on the dashboard. In the back seat are boxes that once contained glassine envelopes, and rubber bands, technically drug paraphernalia. On the strength of the federal "zero tolerance" law, Gary confiscates the car. He is looking for some respect of his own.

For his efforts, he garners a quick civilian complaint.

"What you got against my brother?" a young man over on Tapscott wants to know a week later.

"I don't have nothin' against him, 'cept the fact that he's a drug dealer," Gary says out the window of his unmarked car. He is loving this. He often gets out of his vehicle now, just to talk to DeeSo or his associates, harvesting the respect he earned when he snatched the Infiniti. DeeSo won't give Gary the satisfaction of getting angry about the car. He has already written it off. "Business loss, Lemite," he tells the officer one day.

But Gary is gathering more information, watching for drop-off spots and potential informants, testing the air for slingers with grudges against DeeSo. Unfortunately, he soon finds himself under investigation for the charge that he stole several thousand dollars from DeeSo on the day he took the car. But DeeSo makes a major mistake. His boys neglected to count the money before it was confiscated. The complaint alleges that $2,000 was in the car. Internal Affairs verifies that Gary vouchered $3,900. The case is closed.

It is dusk on a clean and windy fifty-degree Thanksgiving Day in Brownsville. There is an immense mauve sky with plumes of frail gray clouds. Gary is home in Elmont, getting ready to eat dinner upstairs in his mother's dining room. But second-year officers Kenneth Finn and Gene Madden are starting their shift. They are headed out, but they can hardly wait to make it back to the PSA for a meal.

"We've got fifty pounds of turkey," Finn bubbles, "a case of broccoli, mashed potatoes."

"Don't tell me any more," Madden protests. "I'm getting a hard-on."

"Peas," Finn continues.

"But I can't eat peas. I had some peas and I farted so much I had to turn off the electricity."

It will be Madden's twenty-fifth birthday tomorrow. "I just want to enjoy myself now," he muses. "In twenty years they'll be takin' my asshole out."

Somebody makes a gobble-gobble sound over the portable. A call comes over for an aided case, some sort of health condition. A woman is having trouble breathing in the relatively peaceful Kingsborough Houses. Finn and Madden drive across Brownsville and pull up in front of the project.

"Happy Thanksgiving," a woman towing a small child says as she crosses their path. But bad feelings radiate from a line of young men hanging outside the food mart on the corner. "Housing pussies," somebody yells.

"Don't be here when we come out," Finn tosses over his shoulder to the layabouts.

The retort is well-chosen, symbolic, mock confrontational, but ill-timed. Veteran cops know never to make threats on the way inside, only on the way out. A few minutes later, after the bus has arrived for the stricken woman, as Finn and Madden are exiting into the fresh night, there is a loud crash. To their left, a figure sprints down the street. Finn and Madden jolt into a run. As they charge, another youth in their path starts to run. The first kid is long gone, but the second stops after a few strides. He probably could have gotten away, but he stops, perhaps in the belief that he should not have started running in the first place. It did not take two people to shatter the driver's side window of the RMP with a rock.

Finn and Madden corner the gangly kid. They chest up to him on both sides and scream at the top of their lungs dead in his face. They want the first kid who ran.

"Where does he live? Where does he live?" they bellow. Spit from their mouths spatters the youth's cheeks. The kid is shaken. "Take us to him. Take us to him."

The "holler" method, apparently one that Finn and Madden have practiced, is working. The kid is sputtering, starting to talk. He's about to give the rock-thrower up. But windows are flying open above, and a pack of women jog through the shadows to the spot where Finn and Madden are working their shouting game. One woman is the boy's mother.

"What the hell is going on?"

The officers don't want to break the control they have over the kid. They continue to glower in his face.

"I asked you what you think you're doin'," the woman demands.

"His friend broke the patrol car window," Finn says out of the corner of his mouth.

"What do you mean, his *friend* broke the window. What are you doin' to my son? Are you people insane?"

Finn faces the woman now. "We were answering a call for a woman who's having a heart attack. That coulda been your mother."

The woman is profoundly unimpressed. She is not buying the public servant angle. She looks as if she wants to throw up. "White motherfuckers" is her answer.

An object flies out a window and lands nearby. Finn and Madden step away from the youth and walk backward for a few paces, looking up at the stone ramparts. There have been times when community reaction here has forced officers to give up their prisoners. Once during a summer riot, a crowd swelled out of the projects and surrounded a young officer and his handcuffed prisoner. The cop fled, leaving his prisoner and his cuffs behind. The boss wanted to know what happened. "I don't know, Sarge," the cop replied. "I guess you could say he called a perp 85."

When Finn and Madden get back to the patrol car, there are shards of glass over the front seat. Madden brushes off the seat with a rolled-up newspaper as Finn locks eyes with the glaring locals. The cleanup operation takes two or three minutes. When the officers finally settle into the car, Madden balls up the newspaper and hurls it out the window in a gesture of disgust with the neighborhood.

"I got to talk to Flanagan. He's the PCO here, and he let the fucking place get out of hand. I told him that he has to control his mutts," Finn complains.

"Yeah, this is the kind of shit that leads to guns and shit. I have no desire to come home with a hole in my body that the good Lord didn't put there," Madden says. "This shit would never happen if he had the place under control."

Back at the PSA on Sutter, Finn is not thinking of turkey or broccoli anymore. He buzzes around, organizing an assault team to go back to Kingsborough Houses to restore order and respect for the Housing police. Sam Tilly, Marlene Pemberton, and others on their meal hour are ready to back his play. In twenty minutes, a caravan of three RMPs, a van, and eight cops is poised on a small hill overlooking the Kingsborough Houses.

There are radio calls coming in; Central is growing impatient. "I'm holding Housing jobs," Central insists. "9717. I have an EDP armed with a stick at Mother Gaston and East New York." But Finn is adamant. He is waiting for one more car, to make a real show of force. In the back seat of his RMP he has the "daisy chain," a metal rope equipped with a string of handcuffs. His strategy is to swoop down on the food mart, snatch up everyone who is standing outside, and take them back to the PSA, where they will be given dis con summonses.

Finally, the platoon moves down toward the delinquent project. But no one is lounging by the whitewashed front wall of the food mart. "We'll be back tomorrow," Finn screams out the window to no one.

A huge red sphere rises out of the east on a December dawn. The familiar sulfur stink of the river lifts from the mudlands as the Riker's Island bus passes over the bridge to the jail. The numbing lines are already in place at 7:15 A.M. — endless mothers and children and the occasional pretty girl in a leopard-skin miniskirt, here to impress a man who was once a prize and is now a project.

Shawanda awakened in the pitch dark to ready herself for this trip to see her baby brother, her look-alike. Gloria has always declared that Shawanda has her looks and Sharron her ways, but both children look like her, and each other.

"I only met my father twice," Shawanda says from her place near the end of the line in the registration area. "He called me once when I was sixteen and said he wanted to see me. He called from the train station at Saratoga. But he never did come over. The two times I saw him was when I was a little girl. He's little and light-skinned, like me. He has bowlegs and a mole right in the middle of his face. My mother won't talk about him to me. She tells Sharron about him. But not me.

"Sharron was so shy when he was little," Shawanda remembers, "he was like a little girl. I would bring my girlfriends over and he would run into the other room. Then he would come to me later and say, 'Ooo, she's cute.' Then I would tell him to tell her, and he would get all embarrassed and say, 'Oooo, nooo.' Then all of a sudden, when he was fourteen, he started up. I would look in the room and Sharron would be singing to them." She shuffles her tiny feet, barely visible under the folds of her droopy jeans, and thinks about Sharron's present predicament. "Now, when he's goin' out and I ask him why he's doin' shit, he says for reputation. Sharron is my brother, and I'll tell anybody he is not a leader. He is a follower."

Shawanda prides herself on her good sense, her knowledge of

city geography and the transit system. Right now, she shakes her head, as if to clear her thoughts, and sets her gaze grimly ahead. It isn't the hour of the day that is bothering her, nor the place. The jailhouse is no big thing to her. She has another burden. Shawanda's mission today is to tell her brother that Andre has died of pneumonia.

The boys in Sharron's barracks have been denied access to the phone for several days as punishment for a fight, and Shawanda has determined that Sharron cannot possibly be given the message by a stranger.

"He has to be told *something*," she mutters as she fidgets in line and readies her identification papers.

There is raucous laughter from several women within earshot. A righteous woman is explaining how she will lay down the law to her man, who has been using his phone calls to pluck the strings of an old romance, using his visits for the same purpose. No one nearby can guess that Shawanda carries a message of the death of a baby boy, the child of a fifteen-year-old girl with fetching eyes and a father who believes in nothing so much as Polo by Ralph Lauren.

When Sharron arrives in the noisy green visiting room, hours later, he wears floppy white terry-cloth slippers and his gray jumpsuit with DOC, Department of Correction, stenciled on the back. His jumpsuit is open down his chest to reveal his carved pectorals. He walks with a dip and a slide, shooting glances around the room, and embraces his sister. He is unable to suppress a smile. He is bigger, much bigger than he was just weeks ago. His shoulder muscles bunch up, and the cheap cloth of his uniform grips his swollen biceps.

"I was gonna beat you up when you got home," Shawanda jokes. "But when I saw how big you got, I changed my mind."

Sharron reviews his short history in Riker's for his sister. "We got burners and bangers. Burners are for slicin' and bangers are for stickin'." He tells Shawanda the story of Ralphlo, about how he had no time on the horn, and then he did, and then he did not. About the Puerto Ricans. About Love, the new house honcho. The fact is that after almost five weeks in East Mod, Sharron is still in a transition stage. He is not in the miserable state he was in when he first arrived, but the drama is not over. There is one cock-diesel newcomer, named Jersey, who has been lurking closer and closer to Sharron, mumbling, threatening to "get in my area," Sharron reports.

As he talks he gestures with his wrists, jailhouse style. His hands seem thicker. When he is not talking, his hands hang over his knees like indolent, corrupted bullies, slow to work, quick to violence. In jail, men's hands seem to grow because of the loose way they are carried. The inmates hold their hands so as to emphasize mass. Fingers are never raised or pointed. Hands lift slowly to accompany weighty pronouncements and are never waved about indecisively or used for punctuation or other light duty. In jail, men's hands are their only allies.

After fifteen minutes, Shawanda wets her fingertips with her lips and rubs the moisture into her eyelids. She leans across the table and reaches for her brother's hands. "Did anybody tell you anything?" she asks softly.

A wave of pain crosses Sharron's face and he bows his head. The reaction is reminiscent of a moment in his portrayal of Danny in *Don't Give Up on Your Dreams*. He raises his head and speaks flatly of how he had a notion, even before Chantal gave him the news on the phone.

"Yeah, Chantal called. And she was all nice and happy. And we was talkin', and she got all quiet and she said, 'Sharron, I don't know how to tell you this.' I said, 'No, don't tell me that.'" Sharron describes how he let the phone dangle for a moment before he picked it back up and submitted to the words, "He's gone, Sha."

It has been three days since Chantal's call, four since Andre died, after a month in the pediatric intensive care unit. "Don't worry, we can make another one," Chantal had insisted on the phone.

There was something about her tone that set Sharron off. "I told Chantal that I wasn't about that. I don't know. I don't know. I told Chantal that I wasn't gonna be with her no more. She ain't actin' right. She's in Ms. King's class and I heard she ain't been goin' to school. I mean, she looks good, but she's going down the wrong path."

Sharron's disappointment over Chantal's immaturity appears more genuine than his reaction to Andre's death. When Gloria found out Andre had succumbed to pneumonia, she was beside herself. For two days her rage leaped like a hungry beast from the attending doctors to the landlord to the hospital to Chantal and her mother. Mrs. Redding, Chantal's mother, was racked by similar anguish. "You know I got a goddamn baby here with pneumonia," she blurted to a stranger on the phone a month before Andre died. When she learned he had died, she put her hand through a windowpane, an act of desperate grief.

"Chantal's mother's eyes were all red and puffed out," Shawanda tells Sharron. "But Chantal was gettin' ready to go out. And she was laughin'. And I told her, what was the deal, and she said that she deal with her pain in her own way."

"She was laughin'?" Sharron questions. "I'm gonna leave her. She's not what I thought she was. She's not actin' right."

He stays quiet for some time, then resumes the description of his discussion with Chantal the night she told him the baby was dead. "I was like ready to flip. The guys in East Mod have been thinkin' that I was gettin' ready to flip for jack time anyway. Some guys remember when I first came, before I was down with Ralphlo, how I used to just sit there and stare at the horn, and some of them think that I'm still like that. After I got off the phone, I walked over to where the sinks are at, and tears was just like comin' down." Sharron makes a motion with his hand down his face with his fingers spread. "Then Jersey came over. Cock diesel, and he's got this look on his face . . . don't *nobody* mess with him. For two weeks the man has been fuckin' with me. And like he walks over to where I'm at, and he thinks I'm messed up about the phone. For once, he come out nice and says, 'Why you don't ask Love for some time on the horn?'"

Sharron is building his story to his moment of triumph in East Mod, the moment that set him up for the rest of his bid. He knew that he was ready to explode as a result of the dreadful news he had received. But he also understood that he could use his impending loss of control to make a move that would make his days easier, and might even save his life. He explains how he turned to Jersey, the mad agent of East Mod, ready for war. "'I just got off the *fucking* phone,' I said." As he continues his story, he rises from his seat, reliving the full flush of his triumph. "I threw that shit right in his face, and Jersey just like walked away. I knew what I had to do. I was flip. Went with it. Motherfuckers all around was like 'Wow, I don't believe he did that shit.'"

Sharron sits for a moment, thinking. He reveals no more remorse over using the news of his son's death to get props in East Mod than Sir Laurence Olivier would have felt over using personal tragedy to bring a character alive.

Sharron has managed to do something to the pockets of his prison jumpsuit that makes them bulge in a way that pleases him, and he takes a moment to describe the technique to his sister. "I really miss my gray Nikes," he says wistfully. Shawanda promises that she will try to bring him the sneakers, but Sharron interrupts. "No, I want a guy to bring the sneakers." It's only right, apparently, that Frank or another LoLife show respect by bringing him his prize gear.

"Mommy went out for her thirty-sixth birthday and didn't come home till Friday," Shawanda says. "She was partyin'. Stayed at Auntie's house."

Shawanda sits for a few moments, then swings into the second phase of her agenda for this visit. The responsibility of telling Sharron about Andre was unpleasant in the extreme. The opportunity to tell on Chantal is the reward. Not only did Chantal perform badly in her reaction to the baby's death; apparently she has another boyfriend. According to Shawanda, Chantal has had another man for some time.

"When Mommy and me came up to Chantal house, Mommy wanted to know who this guy was. Chantal tried to front and say it wasn't nothin', an' this was just a friend of hers from around the way. But he was in the house by the bathroom. He was in the room, Chantal's. We went to the house twice after the baby died, 'cause Mommy was upset 'cause she wanted Andre to have a funeral, and Mrs. Redding just wanted to cremate the baby. I mean, Mommy was crying, and so was I, and even John had a tear, but not Chantal."

Out of the pile of words Shawanda tosses on the table, Sharron grabs the dope, the part about the other man; the rest is cut, filler. He snaps to attention. "Tell me that again. Run it again." Shawanda tells the story of the other man in Chantal's life in more detail. It seems as if Sharron's big sister has been doing some investigation. The guy in the house is a seventeen-year-old small-time drug slinger. Shawanda's theory is that the boy is not an interloper at all but has been Chantal's man all along.

"*He* is her man," Shawanda insists, explaining that that is why Sharron never visited Chantal's house or had a proper meeting with her mother.

Sharron shakes his head to clear his thoughts. "Again." Like a young Othello, he demands a review of the evidence.

Shawanda is worried. Perhaps she has gone too far. The stress of jail and the death of Andre, and now this. As she talks, she maneuvers the meeting with the other boyfriend out of the house onto the stoop and alters the dialogue to include some harmless neighborhood boys who "always hang on the stoop." But Sharron is not fooled. He is not prone to free-floating mistrust or anger. Now he does not wallow in regrets. He is the very picture of wounded strength. And he has a plan.

"Get my clothes." He flies through an inventory of exactly what Chantal has that belongs to him. "I want my sweaters. I want that scarf with the flag on it."

As he runs down the list, Shawanda nods. Sister is up to the task. Seemingly, she is unafraid of the mayhem the retrieval mission will surely provoke. Sharron picks up her resolve and tempers his charge.

"I don't want you to strip the clothes off her. I want you to pack the stuff up and take it out." He describes some jewelry, then goes back over the list. "She won't have no clothes," he concludes, allowing himself a moment of bitter contemplation of Chantal's sorry state once the mission has been accomplished.

Shawanda mumbles something about the hospital. Sharron is picking up all messages now. "The dude was with her when she went to the hospital? He was with her?" Shawanda backs off once again. Sharron expands his list of items to be repatriated. There is a pair of sneakers and a jacket, the goose-down vest. But mention of the vest triggers something in him, a grace. In a moment, it is clear why it is easy to love Sharron Corley, despite his unseemly craving for approval and adulation, despite his ice pick and his burner. He has a heart. He considers the Nautica vest he boosted just for Chantal. A stricken look crosses his soft face. "She won't have no coat. Don't take the goose."

"CHRISTMAS IS FOR WHITE PEOPLE"

The next day, on the fifth floor at Jefferson, Ms. King is collecting her books following her one o'clock class. Khalil Sumpter and his man Dupree are deep in conversation a few feet from her desk. After the confrontation two months ago, Khalil has been in class every day.

"I'm gonna have to ice the dude," he tells Dupree, loud enough for King to hear.

Black men threatening to harm, trying to intimidate other black men — King has had enough of that. She takes one step away from her desk and smacks Khalil with her palm, hard, on the back of his head, for his threat against a fellow man.

"Oh shit, Ms. King, you smacked the shit out of me. Oh shit, I can't believe it." Khalil is not really shocked.

"Believe it. What I can't believe is what you just said. I don't ever want to hear anything stupid like that again. Do you understand?"

Khalil backs up to the door with his hands up, giggling. "Did you see what she did?" he says to Dupree.

Two hours later, Carol Beck is downstairs in her office sorting things out, talking with her guidance counselor, Ms. Marion Brown. It is almost four o'clock, the time when most of the staff is headed home to Long Island or already there. The dedicated teachers are still here, because this is the best time to do their job, the time of day to see the kids whose lives are falling apart. There are children here in Jeff who are homeless, and after four o'clock in the afternoon they are easy to identify because they don't go home.

Over in the gymnasium, the basketball team has gotten some

bad news. They will not be going to the Christmas tournament in South Carolina after all.

"Christmas? Christmas is for white people to make money," Michael Washington says, bouncing a ball.

In previous years, Burke High School, the host of the Modie Risher Tournament in Charleston, helped defray the costs of the trip for visiting schools by feeding the players with meals cooked by their booster club. This year money is too tight, and no home-cooked food can be provided. No trip. The kids are stoic. Cortez Sutton just turns his head to the side and snorts, even though these would have been the only games he would be permitted to play all season. Once the regular season starts, his superintendent's suspension will kick in. Michael makes a crack about how those country boys are "too black to play night games anyway."

These kids insist on designer logos on their clothing as charms to ward off just such disappointment, to convince themselves and advertise to the world that they are not unconsidered, the ones left out and left behind. They dress to cover the hurt from the time their father did not show up to take them on a promised trip or their mother could not produce the present they craved for their birthday. These are not kids who break when something goes wrong. In fact, they are quietly surprised when something does not go wrong. Not one player complains when the trip is canceled, and no one on the team celebrates a week later, when it is put back on the schedule.

Several days after the cancelation, an article in the *New York Times* sports section explains that the Jefferson basketball players, rocked by a killing in their school, will have to undergo another setback by having their Christmas trip canceled. The unwelcome celebrity that Jefferson gained when Daryl Sharpe fell dead and Robert Anderson was toppled by a bullet in his neck could be used to some advantage, as Carol Beck, who has been busy seeking funding for a dormitory for Jefferson kids living in "transient and stressful" conditions, understood early on. The *Times* article solicits contributions to send the Jefferson High School basketball team to Charleston for Christmas. A Manhattan investment banker, an ex–Ivy League college basketball player, responds quickly with a check for $2,500. A Brooklyn doctor matches the sum. There are other checks. Small donations come in from as near as Canarsie, where the less affluent of the Jefferson alumni moved following the influx of blacks, and as far away as southern California.

It's the Christmas season, but Gita Malave is not thinking about the holiday. At six-thirty on a forbidding December morning, she is leaving her eighth-floor apartment carrying two heavy shoulder bags. One is her pocketbook; the other holds her schoolbooks, a thick text for the remedial math course she has to pass and a tome for her documents course in legal studies. She pushes the elevator button and checks her watch. One minute, two. Dammit. She leans forward and peers into the crack between the elevator door and the wall to see if the mechanism is moving, lays her ear against the door to listen for sliding cables. Nothing. She sucks a deep breath and starts down the staircase. The strap from the bookbag is already digging into her flesh, and she shifts the weight out on her shoulder. Gita is no stranger to this stairway. The only people out early in the morning are the crack smokers and the working people, and those pipeheads know whoever is leaving has some money, she reminds herself. As she moves past the fifth-floor landing, she tenses slightly. It is precisely at this spot she was robbed of her pocketbook three months ago.

After she makes it safely down the stairs, the rest of the trip to the Brooklyn Medical Supply Company is easy. Here Gita answers the phone for eight hours: "Medical, how do you do?" She puts buyers through to the proper department. Five calls often light up the board in front of her. "The math is kickin' my ass," she tells Marietta, the operator by her side, the woman who suggested that she start college.

"You can do it," Marietta answers. "You're the smartest person I know." There is little time to talk; the calls are jumping.

After work, Gita hustles over for a short visit with her sister, who is in Long Island College Hospital, dying of tuberculosis. Gita visits three times a week. In these times, when the fresh hell of the gun comes on after the scourge of crack, family bonds do not hold people together so much as they pull good people under. Born Son's mother is so sick at heart that she can barely make it to work anymore. Her younger son has dropped out of college and sits in her spotless, spartan apartment watching television and brooding over his brother's fate.

Gita shakes off the gloom from the hospital visit and strides through the Fulton Mall to New York City Technical College. Five minutes late for her six o'clock class, she faces the packed elevator. It doesn't matter a whit now to her that she's a grandmother and her classmates are less than half her age, or that her daughter-in-law is walking the same college hallways. "Sorry, that's the way it has to be," she says, and pushes her way onto the elevator. "Push seven for me, please."

Gita cannot afford to miss a minute of the lecture on polynomials. If she fails this course, things are going to get rough. Her state grant money for tuition is running out. Next semester a new college policy that limits the number of times a student can take a remedial course will go into effect. If she does pass, she will have just one required course left for the spring semester, and she will be the first in her family to graduate with a two-year college degree.

She powers her way through to nine o'clock, her energy fading fast as her documents class comes to an end. But she has a good memory, a feel for the law. This is the course she really likes.

She usually gets a good half-hour of studying done on the train. She shifts her bags to the seat beside her and opens her math book. But the numbers dance and blend together tonight. What Gita needs is a little rest. She lays the book on the seat and rocks her head. There is a quick pang of guilt at the missed opportunity to review the math lesson, then a flood of relaxation. This will be her half-hour, her vacation. It's 9:50 by the time she gets off the #3 at the Rockaway Avenue stop.

As she enters her building, she nods a greeting to a boy blocking the door, and he shifts to let her past. Inside, she steps past the kids hanging by the mailboxes in the lobby. Gita has made it her business to know every small-time drug dealer and mugger on her side of the Complex. She glances at the empty, stalled elevator. The corrugated metal of the half-open door is pocked with dents from forgotten gunshots. An elderly woman stands off to the side, wondering how she will get upstairs. Gita plunges up the staircase. She is in much too evil a mood to be frightened. *Just somebody fuck with me now*, she thinks, shifting her bags to keep her hands free.

Upstairs, her children have already fed themselves, but her

son Kendall has been in not one but two fights in school, and her daughter Tashana is complaining of a cold. Gita does not raise her voice as she faces Kendall in the kitchen.

"If I have to lose a day's pay to go up to that school, I am gonna be beyond upset. This is final exam time for me. Don't pick now to act like an idiot." She lays her hand on her sniffling daughter's head. "You don't have a fever. You took the Tylenol?" Tashana nods. A blood-curdling scream rises from the parking lot below. The children hustle to the window. Gita picks up her developmental math book. "As long as blood doesn't come under that door," she says, "I don't care what madness is going on outside."

Victories do not come in clusters in Brownsville. There is no clear line of progress, no inspiring line of development. Everyone, it seems, is fighting alone. Gita is going to graduate with an associate's degree in legal studies if the effort kills her. Then she will hope to find a better job. But her children are not galvanized by her feats of faith and endurance. They will not surpass her and head off to four-year colleges, to the Ivy League. The pressures are too great for that kind of momentum to build. Instead, the victories are like sparks in a meadow; they flash and burn out. Nevertheless, her family is intact, there is no gunman stalking her son, no police officers are pounding on her door. She is not complaining.

Christmas Eve. It is just after midnight at roll call at the PSA. Gary Lemite checks out his radio and wanders over to the front desk. He is ready to hit the streets. But his partner for the night, Jay Kern, is still downstairs. Off to the left, the massive-armed Jeff Desimone has run out of patience with the stooped, narrow-shouldered night tour lieutenant. The lieutenant has long greasy hair and wears his seedy trousers four inches too short, dangling over dingy white socks. He is not a leader of men. Determined not to make a mistake, he will sit mute for hours at a time, steadfastly refusing to make a decision of any kind.

Desimone is staring at the lieutenant. "Sooner or later, Lieutenant," he says, "you're gonna have to reach into your ballbag and make a decision."

"Hey, Gary," the desk sergeant calls, "what ya doin' working Christmas Eve? I thought you had connections."

"All I got is bills."

"You see that fuck we had in the squad room Sunday?"

Gary shrugs.

"Somethin' wrong with the guy's baby," the sergeant begins, determined to tell the story even without encouragement. "Can you believe we didn't know that the baby had been abused till the guy that did it had been taken to Gold Street? Didn't get the chance to tune the fuck up. I really feel bad about that."

Jim Priore, standing ten feet away, thumbing through his memo book, has more congenial things on his mind. He looks up at the scowling duty sergeant. "On this job I have been pissed off maybe two times in ten years for ten minutes at a time, that's it." He wheels and heads back down the hallway opposite the front desk into the sergeants' locker room. There he pours himself a cup of coffee and sits for a moment. The radio is quiet. It is hard to get to the bottom of Sergeant Priore's exorbitant good will.

"I don't talk to my wife about what goes on out here. When I get home, I always hope that she'll be asleep," he explains. "I got a medal last month and she didn't even know what it was for until they announced it up on the podium."

It had been a gunmetal gray winter day in East New York. Priore was assigned to a plainclothes anticrime unit cruising around the Cypress Houses. Before his partners pulled around the corner, he stepped out of the van and walked into the International Stationery Store on Sutter Avenue. The moment he was inside he knew something was wrong. Even before he saw, he heard. Silence. At the counter, Eddie Vargas, a pistolero, was scooping up handfuls of bills with his right hand. In his left hand, he jiggled a gun. Vargas bolted straight for the only door. Priore pulled his own gun. Vargas tried to throw a juke move on the cop and blast past to the street. Priore grabbed at his weapon in an attempt to jam the slide bolt and make the gun inoperable. Vargas grabbed Priore's right wrist and shook it until his police revolver fell to the linoleum floor with a thud. Priore concentrated on the slide bolt while Vargas smacked him in the face with the extra-long barrel of the weapon. "It all took so long, so long," Priore recalls. "I kept thinking, 'Where are the guys in the van?' I was sure his gun was going to go off in my face."

Vargas pried himself loose, stumbled, and fled toward Pitkin Avenue as Priore grabbed his gun off the floor and charged after him. In front of 2763 Pitkin, Priore grabbed him, spun him around, and threw him up against a parked car. In Vargas's waistband Priore found a black leather holster and a six-and-a-half-inch Tanfoglio Titan II pistol, blue metal, with a black grip.

Some officers would have given Vargas the slow ride, taken him the long way back to the station house, used the freebie to pound him to a pulp. But on the ride, Priore was experiencing an unfamiliar emotion. "I don't know what it was. I felt this release, and a wave of feeling. Then I realized it was gratitude. I turned around to the perp and said, 'Thanks for not shooting me.' He looks up and says, 'Thanks for not shooting me.'"

That night, after he had the paperwork finished, Priore went out to get some dinner for the guy. "It wasn't any takeout shit from Brownsville," the sergeant remembers. "I went over to Canarsie and bought him an Italian dinner."

Priore got the Exceptional Merit Medal for the incident, worth about one tenth of a point added to a passing score on the civil service test for lieutenant he's planning to take.

"I'll start studying eight hours a day after New Year's. I love this job," he muses. "They'll have to carry me off it." He checks his watch; he will have some serious bicycle assemblage to deal with when he gets off his tour. "This is the first Christmas I have worked in ten years," he says. "My wife was rippin'."

Outside, it is a clear, crisp twenty-nine degrees. A fat yellow moon, a hunter's moon, hangs over the gossamer cables of the Brooklyn Bridge, and the glow carries all the way out to Brownsville. Even on this holiday evening, Gary Lemite is looking for DeeSo. Kern is driving the unmarked van.

An hour into the tour, Gary thinks he spots one of DeeSo's dealers and asks Kern to follow at a distance. "Silent Night, Holy Night" wafts softly from the radio as the two plainclothes cops cruise half a block behind DeeSo's four-door sedan. There are very few cars on the street. Lee Brown, the police commissioner, begins a speech over the portable. He's talking about working on Christmas Eve. The troops are not having it.

"Asshole," a cop says, cutting through Brown's voice with a dry whisper.

"Be nice," Central says, "be nice."

"We want the Glock," another anonymous caller interjects.

The Glock is the controversial semiautomatic weapon the cops feel is their only hope against the multitude of weapons they face on the street.

Gary hasn't seen DeeSo himself, but he continues to watch the blue Legend, now parked outside a bodega on Legion and Dumont. Every inch of the windows of the store he is watching is covered with posters to deter surveillance. Around the corner is a barber shop named the Barbers of the Ville.

"Fucking Christmas Eve and the radio is going off," Kern says as more calls come over the portable. These are jobs for the uniforms. Lemite and Kern, in a specialty unit, are released from the radio, free to gather information on DeeSo's operation.

After half an hour, a man walks out of the bodega and gets into the Legend. This time it is no minion. It is DeeSo himself. He's drunk, and he knows he's being followed. He signals ostentatiously at every corner, makes expansive turns, and pulls over on Georgia Avenue. The door of his car swings open and DeeSo staggers to the pavement. Lemite and his partner watch as he hands money to several men who stand half in the shadows, their shoulders hunched against the cold. Kern rolls the Dodge slowly up the block and Lemite gets out.

"What are you doin'?" he asks DeeSo pleasantly, nodding at the handful of bills the clean-cut drug dealer holds loosely at his side. DeeSo is usually much too careful to be approached holding a fistful of money on the street by anyone, cop, perp, or citizen. But this is Christmas; the champagne has padded his reflexes, but not his mind.

DeeSo nods at his shivering slingers. "I thought they were homeless," he tells Gary. "The holidays, you know."

Gary turns back to Kern, watching from the driver's seat. "Smooth bastard," he says softly, and gets back in the car.

Christmas Eve, East Mod. Here is Gloria Corley's best boy on his bunk, staring straight up into the dark, thinking about rhymes. "New to this, due to this . . ." It has been a strange night. No horn. The CO canceled the phone after the fight on Friday. Guys have just been sitting up on each other's beds talking, arms around each other. Nostalgic. It has been so quiet, not a shout since maybe eight o'clock. Like somebody has died. Sharron is thinking, *I don't belong here. I'm not like these guys.* But what to do? Get a job packing bags? There has to be something more than scraping by in life, he thinks. People with regular jobs in Brownsville don't even know where Bloomingdale's is, he tells himself. There has to be something more. Has to be. The lottery? Sharron sees himself, a millionaire, in a billowing silk shirt in a white car. The music will do it, if he can get a break. The advertising world. Executive, creative. He will have to wear suits, but then he will be older, so the suits will be cool.

The dream fades away quickly, and he is alone on his bunk again in the gloomy barracks. A yellow glow comes from the corrections officer's window down the corridor. Something is slipping away from him, and Sharron feels big tumbling tears. Good thing it's dark. On both sides, he hears spasms, muffled sounds. All over East Mod, the trouble kids, the quick-punch, fast-feet boys with their burners tucked away in cracks between the bathroom floor tiles and behind the toilets, are crying. Sharron listens hard at the bunk directly behind, where Love "lives." Same sound. *Damn*, he marvels. *Even the meanest niggers is broke down.*

COUNTRY BOYS

t three o'clock on Christmas morning, the Thomas Jefferson basketball players begin arriving in front of the school on Pennsylvania Avenue. Brothers Jude and Carl show up with their watchful parents. Diminutive Michael Washington pulls up in a cab with his mother. The big Grenadian center, nicknamed Tumbo after the seven-foot Nigerian NBA rookie shot-blocking sensation Dikembe Mutombo, walks down from the #3 train. Cortez arrives by car service from the Linden projects, down the street. A gunshot rings out a block away.

Mickey Mundell stands in the middle of Pennsylvania Avenue, trying to figure out how to get five dollars for a vial of crack. "Anybody got a quarter, or a candy bar with teethmarks in it?" he quips to the players and parents standing next to the humming charter bus. Mickey's family moved from North Carolina when he was a baby. He was a church boy. Now he does not sleep, stands outside at all hours, a ghost of himself, with protruding cheekbones. "Smokin' lovely," they say. Somehow he stays alive as he haunts the Brownsville streets, using his skills as a mechanic to rip off a bumper or an alternator on special order here and there.

"I almost didn't make it," one player says. "I'm recovering from the flu."

"I'd a flew you," Coach Moore says.

The players are thrilled to be going, but it takes only a minute for them to start entertaining themselves by criticizing each other.

"Let's start a fund. Everybody puts in one dollar, and the guy who gets the most pussy . . ."

"I predict none for nobody," Michael Washington yells in a prescient moment.

"You ain't seen me pushin' up strong, son. I'm gonna be gettin' busy," Cortez counters. He's the best student on the team, and the slickest mouth.

"Shut up, Cortez, when they see you down South you ain't gettin' no pussy. They gonna say you're too black," Ed Alcy cracks.

Cortez loves this. "Man, look at your head. They ought to use your head instead of that ball they drop on New Year's Eve."

"Shut up, muck-mouth," Michael snaps.

On a more serious note, another player floats an attractive idea. "When they find out we're from New York, the girls're gonna be sweatin' us."

Cortez is back on his happy offensive. "Tumbo. You took the train here at three A.M.? Ain't you never heard of cars?"

"We are livin' in luxury," somebody says and sighs. Indeed, the bus is well appointed, with reclining seats and a bathroom and television monitors.

"I'm gonna sit on this side," Michael, who has driven down South before, says. "That side gonna be crazy boring. All you gonna see is cars."

"Shut up, you black beetle."

As the bus driver guns the engine and slips into gear to pull away, Mickey Mundell heads across Pennsylvania Avenue, absorbed, thinking, watching, figuring a way to make a couple of bucks to ride a wisp of white smoke. His hands are thrust deep in the ripped-out pockets of his grease-smeared ski jacket. His fingers sort through the four Zippo lighters there, and the short pipe with the tinfoil-covered bowl. For him, there is no such thing as comfort or satisfaction at a task well done, just the dizzying jump between the worlds of bare survival and chilling happiness. The big purple and white bus pulls past him down Pennsylvania Avenue, under the elevated #3 and out toward Linden Boulevard.

Throughout the trip, Coach Moore admonishes the players for calling each other names. He points out that obsessive name-calling undermines togetherness and team play. The players are happy and truly like one another. Still, they continue to relate to each other by sometimes hilarious and often hurtful name-calling.

Many of the players — Marvin, Michael, Donnel, and others — were born down South; some even spent part of their youth in North or South Carolina. They are going back to their roots, but the thought does not cross their minds. They do approach the trip with some wonder, though.

"When we cross the border, your ass is mine," Nick tells Michael.

"They got too many niggers down there."

"I'm starvin'."

Broad-shouldered, sweet-tempered Tumbo swivels to answer the latest insult directed his way.

"Just turn your ass around," Michael warns.

"When I get in the room," Tumbo promises, "I'm gonna beat your ass all night."

"Why don't you shut up, you hungry elf," Cortez says to Michael.

The bus has been on the road for only an hour, but Moore has had it. He travels the length of the aisle to put an end to the nonsense. He gives his third lecture of the trip when the bus reaches the New Jersey Turnpike. The kids just can't stay quiet.

"I feel so good I could run down South," a player says as the bus rolls on.

The driver puts a movie starring tough guy Roy Scheider on the television monitors, positioned at every third row. The players may have left East New York and Brownsville behind, but they will not be without the sound of gunfire. The film is not five minutes old before a machine gun starts its own chatter. Halfway into New Jersey, and suddenly almost everybody is asleep. From somewhere ahead a young man's voice claims, "This is the life."

The sun comes up on the bus as it rolls through the pine forests of Virginia. "We will stop," Coach Moore announces. "My first wife left me because I wouldn't stop."

The team stops for a breakfast of grits and pancakes, while the bus driver coos to a middle-aged woman in a wig and gold-rimmed glasses, who is all ears. Back on the road, a skunk smell fills the bus full of city kids.

"Tumbo, how could you?" Michael wails. "Move your African ass to another seat."

Tumbo has had it with the foolishness. He's weary of mock threats. He enjoys silence, does not crave hilarity. He did not grow up like this, insulting his friends for fun. He sits and glowers out the window, adjusts his Walkman, and stares.

The only player who pays the slightest attention to the Carolina landscape, the black creeks and the cypress swamps, the tufts of moss on bone-gray ruins of trees, is Cortez Sutton. Cortez is from the Linden Houses, near Jamaica Bay, and is an amateur naturalist, a member of the Audubon Society, a bird watcher. He bounces from one side of the bus to the other. "A falcon, you can tell by the way they circle," he tells nobody. "A great white heron," he announces. "A sparrow hawl . . . back is sky blue, face is like striped." He sees an osprey. "The only thing I haven't seen is a bald eagle," he brags. The rest of his teammates study the spitting, crackling TV monitor as yet another movie about mayhem, this time a karate movie, *Little Tokyo*, shows.

It's mid-afternoon when the bus pulls past the great old houses of Charleston, the worn Colonials and the gleaming gabled homes with sweeping porches. The kids pay no attention. They are looking for their motel.

The team is booked into an old Ramada Inn near Burke High School, a few miles out of town, with a view of a McDonald's on one side and the brown Ashley River on the other. There is no water in the perfunctory swimming pool, just some dark, damp leaves. The players are ecstatic.

The Burke High School gym is large, with sweeping bleachers, but the floor is not wood but brown pasteboard, worn pale around the three second lanes. The Burke High mascot is a bulldog, and there are blue pawprints down the middle of the court. At the shoot-around the next day, a few hours before their first game, the Jefferson team looks like a bunch of dead-end kids. They have no practice uniforms; Michael looks like a fifth-grader.

"Yo, give me your money," he says with an ice grill to a six-foot-six player from Wilmington, Delaware, who chases a ball down to the Jeff end of the court. The Jeff players stare at the team warming up at the far end of the floor, exaggerate their big-city slouches, and whisper among themselves. Ed Alcy wears his wool cap as he pops long jump shots. The team lines up for a lay-up drill. Of all the players, Jude, at six-three, with long arms, looks the most like a ballplayer and has the most potential.

When the team manager, Adrian, appears with the camcorder Moore has brought to film the games, Cortez lights up. "I got it," he shouts, scampering off the lay-up line. "Adrian, interview me."

He reclines in the first row of the wooden bleachers as Adrian turns on the machine and delivers questions from off-camera. "What does it feel like to be in Charleston, South Carolina?"

Cortez deepens his voice. "First, I'd like to say hello to my fans down here. Thank them for all the letters."

The team gathers round. There are more interviews. Moore appears, grim-faced, in the doorway of the gym. The players pop back onto the court.

Later in the afternoon, the boys file into Moore's bright motel room. Some pile onto the beds, others sit on the windowsill. Moore is wearing an orange and blue African print Kente cloth cap. He is scowling. It is not clear why he is so perturbed; there has been no real trouble from the boys.

"I'm a little pissed off," he begins. "As crazy as Ronnie was last year, he knew how to conduct himself adequately. There is just too much bickering, too much bull. I know in the neighborhood you have to wear your hats to the side so the knuckleheads won't bother you. But you're not hoodlums and you're not bums, and I don't want you to act that way." Cortez nudges a slat from the vertical blinds and takes a peek out toward the river, but quickly refocuses his attention when Moore raises his voice. "And the stuff with you, Michael, calling Cortez black. We're all black. I don't understand that. I don't care if you're light, or yellow, or Chinese, you have to treat each other with respect. I will cancel the season," he warns. "It will be my way or the highway."

What sounds like the usual empty threats by an irritated coach has special resonance. All the players have to do is look around the room at the team's personnel to know that the best ballplayers in Brownsville are not here; not even the best players in Thomas Jefferson are here. These are the kids who can play a little ball and keep their grades above a seventy average. Carol Beck was serious when she said that she was not about to make compromises to have a good basketball team. Nick, a skinny guy with a fair jump shot, has a passive, tentative game. Willie, the clean-cut captain, is a rugged six-one and has hops, but he's not the type to lead a team. Cortez is sneaky, quick, and ever eager, but for all his self-promotion, he is very inexperienced, as is Jude's brother, Carl. Michael is in way over his head. The other subs are Marvin, who is called Face because he's so handsome, Donnel, and Lashawn, just nice kids.

At the end of Moore's speech, instead of letting the words sink in and take effect, Adrian cracks wise. Observing the coach's flashy cap, he moans, "Uh-oh. Mr. Moore has the same hat he had on when we got whacked by fifty." Everybody laughs. Moore shakes his head, then he laughs too.

In their orange-and-blue uniforms, they lose the first game big. Michael complains from the bench about the "fat pork-sausage ref." Though the Jeff team does not play badly, it is sorely outmatched. Alcy is not a natural point guard. Moore rides him so hard he has lost his confidence, and the team is lucky it can get the ball over half-court much of the time. Tumbo is a fine physical specimen, but he grew up playing soccer, and it shows. He is the bowling champion of Thomas Jefferson, one of the top bowlers in Brooklyn high schools, of all things, and the captain of the handball team. Those skills are of little use here. He does not box his opponents away from the backboard, cannot put the ball on the floor to drive to the basket. Most of Jeff's baskets come on solo slashes to the basket by Willie and Jude.

After the contest, the host team, Burke, puts out a spread of deviled eggs, salad, and cold cuts on folding tables in the courtesy room. The homemade food is for the coaches and other adults. Pizza is ordered for the kids. The gray-haired, septuagenarian Modie Risher, Burke High's basketball legend and retired master coach, after whom the tournament is named, pads across the bare utility room with the unmistakable pigeon-toed walk of a former athlete. He samples the hors d'oeuvres, twirls a toothpick deftly in his fingers, and holds court. He's not talking about basketball.

The Jefferson boys are all the way down South now, but the talk is still of killing. "We've had a killing every day here in Charleston for the past fifteen days," Risher says "The record was forty-eight. We've already got fifty-two. And the year is not over. But you know, I don't like to complain. 'Cause when people see you comin', they say, 'Let me go, 'cause here comes Modie Risher.'"

The next day, Jefferson is down 18–0 near the end of the first quarter to a local public school, St. John's. The trip looks like a fiasco, the team like badly outclassed urchins from a city that does not give a damn whether its young black men live or die, flourish or waste away. They came a thousand miles to get their skinny butts whipped by the children of the very place their parents fled for a better life. It looks as if neither trip was worth the effort.

Michael, squirming on the bench, has stopped cheering his teammates and is trying somehow not to be associated with their ineptitude. Incredibly, Jeff bangs back into the game. Nick hits a few turnaround jump shots. Tumbo muscles for the ball, works inside. Michael is informed by a fan behind the bench — a man who moved to Charleston from Brooklyn and has bragged incessantly to his friends that Brooklyn basketball is state of the art — that the ref is an alumnus of St. John's. Michael tells the stocky bus driver, who launches a diatribe against the referee that is beyond the pale for the genteel Charlestonians. The ref halts the game and warns the driver to stop his cursing.

A few moments later, on a questionable call against Jeff, the driver does go crazy. "You reffed yesterday. You're not supposed to ref twice in forty-eight hours. You cheatin', blind bastard!" he howls.

The ref blows his whistle and summons a police officer from the sidelines. The driver from Brownsville is escorted from the gym, yelling insults over his shoulder. "Don't show your sorry ass in Brooklyn!"

The fan who told Michael about the ref's ties to St. John's beams to his friends. This is the spirit he has been telling them about. The crowd is too mellow to boo the driver as he lingers in the doorway, hurling still more insults.

At halftime, Moore is in an inexplicable rage. Jefferson is executing well on offense, but he thinks they are playing soft defense. "You are not in East New York, gentlemen. Nobody is going to shoot you if you put a body on him. Nobody is going to grab a gun and kill you if you knock him down. This is Charleston, South Carolina. I want to see some bodies fly."

The second half starts with a couple of quick hoops by the Jeff captain, Willie, and soon it is too late to stop the orange wave. Released from their paralyzing fear of humiliation, the Jeff players gambol about, snatching lucky long rebounds, stealing passes. Everybody on the bench begins to believe that tonight is Jeff's night. Jude gets loose on a fast break and scores. Cortez sprints into the game. His defender plays his right hand and Cortez skirts the defense to the left for a baseline lay-up. As he backpedals on defense, dreams of stardom are etched on his face. The score is 58–57 Jeff, with two seconds to go, when a player from St. John's tries a desperation three-pointer. He misses.

Cortez is a fountain of revisionism in the locker room, describing the moves he made in his limited time on the floor. "I *left* the man. I *used* him. Did you see that move? Did you see his eyes? The man was frozen. Ha-ha. Did you see the way I charged the shooter at the end, bothered the shot? Did you see it? I saved the game." Cortez is hell-bent for recognition. He has an eighty-seven average in school, a good left hand. So what if he is banned for the regular season for that incident over at Lafayette? This is his day. He is determined to be a star.

Cortez's buddy over at the Linden Houses is E-lo, Ian Moore. The two are so close that Cortez calls Moore his godbrother. Lately E-lo has been hanging around more with Tyrone Sinkler, the big kid who has the beef with Khalil Sumpter. But E-lo has listened often to Cortez's descriptions of what it will be like when he, E-lo, sees Cortez on national TV. Cortez has already figured out what reactions will be going through E-lo's mind. "At first you'll be jealous: 'I can't believe Cortez is famous.' Then you'll be happy, 'cause when I got all those props, you'll have them too. 'That's my homeboy,' you'll yell. And you'll be happy. You can come and visit me and shit."

Post-game, George Moore is the prototype of a grumpy coach. He seems no happier in victory than he was in defeat yesterday. He takes it all out on the bubbly Cortez. "I told you not to jump at the three-point shooter in that situation. You'll give the man three foul shots and we'll lose. Did you think of that? Stop trying to make yourself a hero."

Then, with exquisitely poor timing, Adrian reports, "Coach, we ran out of videotape before the game was over."

Moore looks at Cortez, back at Adrian, and mutters, "I'll bet we got plenty of interviews, though."

The next day, several players, including Nick, Michael, and Cortez, take a cab to an upscale mall. There are several blocks of expensive shops and fancy restaurants by the water. The wharf area is a tourist attraction. But there is not a brown face to be seen in the throngs of pastel-shirted yuppies. The boys stand transfixed by a white model who has been hired to pose motionless as a promotion for a new line of clothing. With features as delicate as china, the girl seems neither to move nor to breathe.

In the Polo shop, the boys check out the gear. "Did you see the guard? He was clockin' us all the time. He like jumped when we walked in the door."

"Yeah." Michael smirks. "But it looked like it was easy. I should've stashed something."

The Jefferson team does not win the tournament. The next day, they lose the third game, 63–57. After the contest, the players climb high into the stands to watch Burke High School in the championship contest. The game pits Burke against a cross-town rival. The gym is rocking with the sounds of the Geechees and their high-country neighbors. These black Charlestonians speak a creole language called Geechee or Gullah. It is based on English and influenced by several West African languages. To the untrained ear, the Geechees have the same lilting speech tones as the Caribbeans back in Brooklyn. "What're all these Jamaicans doin' here?" the Jeff players want to know.

Burke High has a real star on its team, a major college prospect, and there is no hero like a hometown hero. Melvin Watson, six-foot-two, 190 pounds, pops warm-up shots with a delicate touch. The stares of hundreds of eyes reflect off his beautiful body. He retrieves bouncing balls and generously passes them off to teammates, benchwarmers who won't see a moment of action. The fans nod and point. Melvin is "the man" in Charleston. The locals whisper his name and legend to one another, for the edification of the Jeff players. The Brooklynites are experts. They have seen the best. Maybe even Born Son James was as good a player as this Melvin Watson. They settle back to find out.

Heads turn as Modie Risher enters the gym, waves, and takes his place in the stands. In Charleston, there is history, the kind of history that has the locals talking about the games Modie Risher played and has fathers watching their sons try to match the memory of those old feats. Here, store proprietors gush when they see the high school team's big gun walk by. In Brooklyn, it does not work that way. Even the kids who are headed through schools like Jefferson to the pros don't experience this kind of enveloping warmth. They ride the subways anonymously, gangly kids with gym bags. Maybe the bad guys cut them some slack around the way because of their basketball reputation, but the status ends there. The Jefferson kids sit in the stands and watch what it would have been like if their families had stayed down South.

But before the Burke game starts, some players on the Jefferson team draw some attention of their own. Ed Alcy and handsome Marvin are seated in the first row of the stands. Ed wears his wool hat with earflaps, the kind that a mother would put on a baby on a chilly day — a style that, along with pacifiers, has become the rage in Brownsville. Both boys also sport burgundy Timberland boots and ultra-baggy jeans riding halfway down their butts. These are the New York guys, and everybody is eager to catch a whiff of the latest craze. It's a sure bet that the baby hats will make an appearance on the streets of Charleston before long. What is more, the girls are showing a lively interest, and it is not long before the ubiquitous Cortez, Donnel, and Ed are all "kickin' it" to some country girls.

Once the game begins, the gym is a caldron of noise. The Jeff players who are not engaged in flirting are transfixed by the spectacle. Jefferson plays its home games in virtual silence; almost all fans are banned from the gym because of the threat of trouble. When a white teacher, an eighteen-year veteran at Jeff, did show up at a game early in the season, he whispered behind a cupped hand to a cheering colleague, "Don't waste your breath. They don't have the intellectual ability to understand the game."

The opposing team is playing a pressure man-to-man defense against Burke, double-teaming Melvin Watson whenever he makes a move to the basket. But he turns sideways, slips through the traps, and pulls up for short, fluid jump shots or dishes off to his teammates. On one play, he sails into the air to cuff a defensive rebound and shrinks to a cannonball as he bursts by two defenders who try to pin him to the sideline. Like a running back, he dips and weaves, and finally throws a look-away pass to a Burke player, who misses the lay-up.

Even more remarkable than his high-level game is Watson's on-court personality. He is a man among boys. You can see it on his face. When Burke is ahead in the first half, he passes the ball to his teammates, blends into the fabric of the game. He works and works some more, never complains and never shows off. But his teammates are having a bad night, and Burke is down by ten points with just three minutes left in the contest. Then Melvin Watson starts to rumble. He is burdened with four personal fouls. He's dog-tired, grabbing at the hem of his shorts as he stoops over, foraging for air during time-outs and foul shots. But the handicaps just make things more exciting for the fans.

Everybody in the gym knows Melvin is coming. He pops off a pick and scores. His team is down five. He takes the ball the length of the court and scores; three. He steals the ball; one. The hometown crowd is raising thunder, stomping on the boards of the bleachers. This is going to be one of those games they talk about for years.

Ah, Melvin, handsome, strong, willing, and able. The other teams loses the ball. Melvin rockets upcourt. He spins away from one defender and then another. His body is more than the sum of its parts. No time for passing the ball to his fledgling teammates now. No time for anything but Melvin Watson and the scoreboard. The rival team is banging him. They want to stop his roll, but they can't catch up to him. In the pande-monium, no one can hear the refs' whistles anyway. With two defenders hounding him, Melvin nails the winning basket, with no time left on the clock. According to the script, the crowd pours down onto the court to pay homage. The Charleston faithful edge close to Melvin Watson as he stands under the bas-ket, holding his small son in his arms.

After the game, the Jefferson buys walk back to the motel with no fewer than five girls. As the group moves through the parking lot of the McDonald's, they pass two cars with a heavy bass beat coming from behind dark-tinted windows.

"Country boys make too much noise," somebody among the five or six Jefferson players cracks. As they reach the exit of the parking lot, one of the cars backs up and pulls past them. The driver accelerates onto the main drag, and there is a loud report. *Bang.*

Donnel takes two long strides and dives into the tall weeds. Ed pops up and dashes off like a flushed rabbit. The rest of the team scatters for cover. The girls stand there, confused. When the boys realize the sound was the backfiring exhaust of the car and not a blast from a sawed-off shotgun, Donnel crawls out, brushing marsh grass from his clothes, and the rest sidle back up to the girls without a word of explanation. All except for Ed, who doesn't stop running till he is at the motel. He takes the elevator up to his fourth-floor room and waits for news.

Cortez was meant to be happy. He cannot believe his luck. "We got four girls in our room!" he brays up and down the hall. His group is trying to make the best of the situation with the girls; others are in Tumbo's room. Tumbo has signed up for the pay-per-view pornography channel and is charging admission to watch. There is much milling in the hallway.

The next morning, spirits are high over the girls' visit, despite Michael Washington's charge that "they just ate your pizza and drank your soda and booked."

"That's 'cause you scared them away, you black elf," Cortez mocks. Rumor has it that Donnel, the benchwarmer, has managed to have some kind of sexual contact with one of the visitors. "This nigger here was gettin' busy, doin' *work*," Cortez attests, content this one time to perform the role of witness.

Coach Moore is listening and intervenes. "I don't want to hear the *n* word," he admonishes, perhaps because there are white people close by. "It is not appropriate. You are not kids anymore." The coopting of the most hurtful of racial epithets is a complicated psychological maneuver, but Moore chooses to see it as a sloppy habit. He is also concerned about his team's seemingly thoughtless attitude toward sex. He addresses Cortez. "What would you do if you played in the NBA and girls followed you around all the time?"

"Well, I'd just get busy, that's all. I'd be pushin' up strong."

"Then you'd end up like Magic Johnson," Moore counters.

"I'd rather die gettin' skins than any other way," Cortez rebuts.

Tumbo is not present at yet another "big man special" breakfast of pancakes and eggs in the motel. Cortez is ready with an imitation of the big guy's protestations about the food. "I want some yams," he mimics, opening his mouth wide for the vowels, "and some good dumplings. And I want to go home and get a purge. Ha-ha."

"Who wants to go home?" Michael says. "I don't want to go. Do you? Who wants to go home?"

Nobody.

Cortez is the self-appointed historian of the trip, hard at work on the way home, rearranging the facts of the games and the previous night to suit himself. "I was pushin' up strong on those girls at the game . . ." He knows that before long his version of events will prevail.

As the bus rumbles through Richmond, Virginia, Lashawn, the only substitute who did not play a single minute, points out the window. "My brother's locked up there," he says glumly. "He got seven years for robbery. I was supposed to go visit him. But I came on the trip instead."

Into the dusk, there is a dead-serious discussion in the shadows at the back of the bus. The team members are gathered around, listening, thinking, and asking questions. Marvin, the pretty boy of the team, is telling a story about some kind of a knuckle-up between two students at Jeff. So far on the trip he has been quiet, because he has not been in his element. Marvin is truly no ballplayer. But when the conversation turns to mayhem, it's apparent that he may be the most streetwise of all. He lowers his voice and starts to talk very quickly, his language drenched with the most current slang for trouble in all its forms. These kids are their own newspapers, their own town criers. The problem is that unlike African griots, they feature only current events. Not one of them ever mentions where he is from, or where his parents are from, or what they do now or once did. The present commands every bit of their attention.

Marvin turns a quick phrase, and the level of attentiveness rises even higher. This is not gossip. The boys on the periphery fall silent, lean toward the speaker, and cock their heads.

"The one with the brown and gold jeans jacket, in the office."

Cortez looks down for a moment, thinking. "The guy with the fronts in his mouth?"

"No," Marvin says.

Cortez reconsiders. "The guy who just got the fronts in his mouth."

Marvin reflects. "Nah. This dude always be with Dupree, with the eight-ball jacket." He means a popular style of red leather jacket with a large eight ball stitched on the back. "He's Dupree's man," he emphasizes. "Remember, we seen him outside Ms. King's class on the fifth floor. He was talkin' about 'Who want it? Who want it?'"

The group is mesmerized. There is something critical about the information they are receiving. They are gathering data, putting together a scouting report on the tendencies of a new tough guy in their school.

"I know who you mean," Cortez says finally. "I know the guy. Brown jeans jacket. He think he's bad. Front'n. He just wants props." Cortez decides that the guy who hangs with Dupree, despite his threats, is not a mad agent.

The boys will spend five minutes trying to ascertain the identity and proclivities of any character in a story about a fight or an argument in the school or neighborhood, especially one in which weapons or death threats are involved. They want to be prepared. There are so many "front artists," they want to know as much about people as they can. The conversation goes on.

"Moe? Light-skinned Moe from Amboy? Who used to play ball?"

The level of danger in the neighborhood is apparent when the players, the boys in the school kept on the team not because they are basketball stars but because they are straight arrows, discuss their own security precautions. "I had the little .25 that time," one player says. "It seems that whenever you have something, don't nothin' happen."

Jude and Nick discuss the proper way to deal with a potentially hostile crew on the street. "I just sort of drop my head a little," Nick says, "and if I know somebody I say, 'What's up?' If the dude says, 'What's up?' you're O.K. Sometimes the guy you know don't really wanna say, 'What's up?' He wanna say, 'Nothin's up,' but he can't, 'cause he *do* know you. School I used to go to, there be mad Decepticons rollin' up after school." The Decepticons are a citywide gang with a fading but fearsome reputation. "If I don't know the people, I don't say nothin'. I don't act like I'm scared, even though I am. I just dip my head."

"You can tell when somethin's up," Jude says. "Then you run. Sometime your only chance is if the gun jams."

As the bus slows to a crawl in traffic near the Maryland-Delaware border, there is talk about how the JV team was approached last year by a group of guys with guns and Michael got beat up. More talk of guns in hushed tones. "I think the four-fifth jammed," Jude says.

Later, as the charter rumbles over the Delaware River into New Jersey, Willie and Cortez are talking about girls.

"Willie, you never had your heart broken? You ain't in the club?"

"Sure. I cut her off."

"You cut her off for who?"

"I cut her off for a bitch, and then she cut me off. I was crying, cryin'. I bought her teddies. I took her to Footlocker and bought her new kicks. When I think of what I did to get her back, I could kick myself."

"Right, Jim." Cortez acknowledges Willie's mistake with the wisdom of the ages about him.

It is after midnight when the bus pulls up in front of Jefferson High School, but Jude and Carl Princivil's parents are waiting on the sidewalk, standing in the cold.

"Home sweet home," Michael says. "Back in the jungle."

Several other parents are also waiting, sitting in cars and cabs. Thomas Jefferson High looms above like a great dark castle. One by one the cars nose into traffic and slip off; the bus growls a last time and is gone. As the last of the team fades away, Carl, Jude, and their parents are still standing on Pennsylvania Avenue, looking for a gypsy cab.

"LET THE DOGS LOOSE"

Damn snitch house," Sharron writes in his diary on New Year's Eve. "Somebody told the CO about where the burners were, under the sink, and now there's no TV. Guys crying again, all over the place. Talking about their problems. Girl gone, Mom's in the hospital. Everybody been in jail two or three times before. In here, with all the talents I have and I'm not using them. Usually the lights go out at eleven, but another CO let us into the day room to watch the ball come down, controlled the TV from the bubble. It's like a party, only no music and no girls. Guys jumping around, acting all wild. Banging on the windows. Just like a party. But in jail."

To the delight of his neighbors in Howard Beach, John Gotti flouts local authorities with a lavish display of illegal fireworks every July Fourth. The same raucous spirit of celebration inspires the youngbloods from East New York and the Ville, who are getting ready to make some noise of their own. In recent years, a tradition has developed that on New Year's Eve young men come out and fire their guns off the roofs, out the windows, or even from the walkways, up to the patches of night sky between the project buildings. The impulse undoubtedly owes something to the high spirits of the holiday, but also to the fact that there is no better time to try out a new bis than when the shots are camouflaged by the heavy booms of M-80 firecrackers and the cluster pops of slightly more reasonable types of fireworks.

But this year the Housing police are going to do their best to ruin the Brownsville party. Somebody above Lenti in the hierarchy of the department has made the decision that this year Brownsville and East New York will not crackle with the reports of TEC-9s and four-fifths, jammies, burners, and all kinds of Ravens. "In the past, we used to head over near the drag strip on Fountain Avenue, have a few cold ones, and maybe pop a bottle of champagne," a Housing cop says. "After things had cooled down, we would come back out and clean up the mess. That way, everybody would get home safe. But they didn't want to do that this year." The new idea is that if it is business as usual with the local gun wielders, the full contingent of PSA 2 officers will be on hand to snatch up the collars. It is a bad idea. Scores of cops are heading out to confront hundreds of young men bent on firing their guns, and it looks as if somebody is going to get hurt.

Sam Tilly is riding with a guy named John Montemauro; Gary Lemite is driving Sergeant Billy Bright; Hammil is with O'Donnel. For Gary, this night is unusual. Most nights he spends his time watching for subtle signs — the bulge, the quickened step, the infinitesimal list from the weight of a big gun, a heavy jacket on a muggy night. This is different.

A few brave souls who will clearly fight for their right to party are standing on street corners outside the Cypress Houses. Three hopeful girls in party dresses stand on the corner of Fountain and Sutter, waiting for transportation. A cruising gypsy cab gathers them up like wildflowers.

Eddie Hammil, seated down the street in his RMP, watches Smokey Thompson, who is not so lucky. A block away, he's pacing up and down, also hoping for a cab to come by. After several minutes he goes inside and calls one. "That fucking Smokey," he mutters. Thompson is the guy who fired a volley of shots at him several months ago. There were witnesses and recovered rounds, the whole deal. There was an indictment, but the DA refused to prosecute. Hammil remains more than a little peeved. Thompson pops out the front door of 315 Fountain Avenue, then draws back in. The moment he goes inside, the cab he called pulls up in the frosty air. Hammil sees his opportunity and pulls up next to it.

"You get a call from 315 Fountain?"

"Yes, sir," the driver answers obsequiously, his eyes sliding sideways toward Hammil. Gypsy cabs are illegal, allowed to operate only because the licensed yellow cabs will not enter the neighborhood.

"The guy who called the cab canceled. You can go," Hammil says, and Smokey Thompson's ride pulls away. Hammil chuckles.

The cops are having fun. There are numerous strange sounds coming over the radio, including an underwater howl that sounds like a whale call, made by putting the radio outside the window as the car is moving. A few blocks away, over by the Pink Houses, close to where Del Migliore was shot in the foot, Montemauro and Tilly sit with their lights off. Tilly shakes his head and laughs at the antics of his fellow officers on the radio. He is the kind of young man you cannot help but like. He has a soft stutter and a sturdy body. He plays in the fife-and-drum corps for the Emerald Society, the Irish police organization, and ever since he took a bullet in the arm in Manhattan he has been wedded to the department in deep ways.

When Tilly and his partner approached a cab in Queens several years ago, they were pretty sure two robbery suspects were inside. But Tilly let his guard down for just a moment. "When I think about it, I should have shot the guy when he rolled out of the cab," he says now. But who could think that fast? Who could be ready to shoot a man before he was sure the man meant to shoot him? Tilly waited a second. That was all the time it took for the gunman to put a bullet in his arm. As Tilly went down, his partner opened up on the guys in the cab, killing one and wounding the other.

Tilly used to think about the shooting all the time. But as the years go by, the aspect of the incident that sticks in his craw, the thing he emphasizes when he talks about the morning he got shot, is the fact that his partner got the top honor of the department, the Medal of Honor, usually given posthumously, and he got the penultimate one, the Combat Cross. He implies that black officers receive favoritism in the department. "I mean, I'm the one who got shot. Isn't that fucked up? I'm white and he's black." Then the stutter: "I g-get sh-sh-shot and he gets the Medal of Honor."

Tilly is a nice man, a good cop. "I have s-s-seen a lot of things out here that I don't agree with. I have seen people do wrong on both sides. I don't understand what motivates these kids. But I also don't b-b-believe in smacking a guy around when he is in cuffs. That is something I would never do."

In the minutes before midnight, there are dozens of calls over the radio for shots fired. "A number of shots fired at that location," Central announces calmly. It's easy for the dispatcher to say. She's sitting in a booth on the ninth floor at One Police Plaza in Manhattan, not on the outskirts of Brooklyn, on the streets of the Ville on New Year's Eve.

Montemauro and Tilly take a call at 265 Livonia, Gita Malave's building. A bullet has sailed through a window on the floor below her apartment. This time no child is shot in the neck, no aspiring musician is killed, nobody's loved one is maimed. Tilly is directed to a back room, where a large poster of rapper L.L. Cool J is taped to the bedroom wall. L.L. wears a red hat and a huge gold chain. Where his gold teeth used to be, there is a fresh bullet hole.

At 12:05 Central reports, "Shots fired, *of course.*" Soon Central is holding sixty-one jobs. All over Brownsville, young lions are roaring at the sky. Tilly and Montemauro ride over to Cypress, sit and wait again. Soon they hear the snake-thin voice of a .22 close by. The officers stiffen and look over their shoulders. There is no way to ascertain where the shots are coming from. It is time to go. Another officer, somewhere else in Brownsville, has the same idea. "Let's get the fuck out of here," a voice says.

Then a 10-13 comes over the radio like a bugle call. Tilly jacks the RMP backward, stands on the accelerator, and hurtles toward Georgia Avenue. To hell with the TV commercials; Tilly is glad there are no antilock brakes on this vehicle. He plays the skids like an old song, sliding the RMP into the turn, pumping the brakes, jamming the gas before the skid is over.

Montemauro checks cross traffic. "Good on the right. Good on the right. Good. Good. Go."

"*Slow it down*, slow it down to Georgia," Central pleads, calling the 10-13 off. Tilly eases up, but just for a second. There is another 10-13. Then there are three at one time. Each time, after Tilly, Montemauro, and half a dozen other police cars charge across Brownsville and East New York, the shooters are gone. The Housing cops are getting angry.

But over in the Unity Houses, Gary has another one of his

plans. Shots were fired from a spot in front of the building. The shooters let a few rounds go and ran inside. The scheme is to hide at the side of the building in the shadows, so when the kids fire again, Gary and the rangy, quick Sergeant Bright can pounce on them. But the officers' approach to the hiding spot leaves them in the open at the stroke of midnight. First one shot rings out, then another. There are shots coming from above, and then somebody starts blasting from a nearby parking lot. Bullets are kicking up dust around them as they skip double dutch in the dark.

To some of the cops, this is just Brownsville fireworks, but Sergeant Bright is not amused. Somebody tried to "bust a cap" on him, and the red-faced cop is stomping mad. So are the rest of the troops. Somebody is going to get hurt tonight.

As Tilly and Montemauro pull up in front of the PSA, Anti-crime is taking a skinny kid out of the car. He is in cuffs. He was not arrested with a gun, just snatched up running with a shooter, who got away. The plainclothes guy walks the kid briskly to the front door of the PSA and bangs the kid's head into the glass. "Oh, sorry. I thought the door was open," he says.

As Tilly walks past, he turns and pops the kid in the side of his head with his fist, moving at half speed. "Baby punch," he whispers sweetly. The look on his face says, "I couldn't help it."

On a Tuesday morning two weeks later, eight cars and a van assemble on Belmont Avenue for the ride through Brownsville to the site where one of Gary Lemite's warrants will be executed. The team, comprised of the borough-wide NEU SWAT-style entry team and most of the special detail officers of the PSA, will raid a small drug operation in the Breukelen Houses, a relatively quiet complex of four-story buildings in Canarsie. Commanding officer Jack Lenti rides in the third car, behind the blue NEU van with the battering ram and the automatic weapons, and the car with the roof team. "One good thing about this caravan," Lenti jokes, "is that every fucking Rasta from here to Hinsdale is gonna shit in his pants when we drive by."

Lenti is full of jokes, and his troops are ready to laugh. As the caravan moves through the "lawless" area around Riverdale and New Lots, past vacant lots and hungry dogs, smoky fires in garbage cans and piles of worn tires, a handful of frisky black kids throw sticks at an open dumpster. "Practicing their spear throw- ing," Lenti cracks. His remark draws guffaws and appreciative nods from his dark-haired, blue-eyed Irish driver.

For Captain Lenti, soon to be Deputy Inspector Lenti, noth- ing is sacred. He bemoans the "curse of the Irish," which, ac- cording to legend, leaves the sons of Hibernia with small pe- nises. He labors to spread the blasphemy evenly. But such things just won't come out even.

Lenti's openness makes him wildly popular with almost all the men, and charms Gary Lemite, who readily forgives him his remarks. "He does it to everybody. I really don't think he means anything by it. Lenti will tell you to your face if you are full of shit." He can do that because Jack Lenti himself is not full of shit. He is proud of that. But he has no respect for expla- nations of crime that cite the effects of poverty, prejudice, and isolation on people of color in Brownsville. Like virtually every other cop in the PSA 2, he refuses to apply any standard but his own narrow observation and emotion-scarred afterthought to the question of the violence and debilitating anger here.

As the assault team arrives in front of the Breukelen Houses, police officers bound from the cars and sprint across the cement approach to the buildings. Women to the left and right sweep their children off their feet and flee into the lobbies to avoid the charge. A twelve-year-old girl puts both arms straight up and freezes at the sight of the rushing officers, then runs inside, with her hands still in the air.

The location is right, the timing wrong. The only occupant of the third-floor apartment, an eighteen-year-old male, is ar- rested and handcuffed near an open window in a rear bedroom. Four officers, including Gary and Sergeant Toney, search the premises. Gary starts in the back bedroom, where the CI said the drugs would be. The room is full of boxes and black plastic garbage bags stuffed with clothes. Gary feels carefully through the folds of each musty garment before tossing it onto a pile, which is soon chest high. He taps the legs of a small table, ex- amines an aerosol can. His heart is sinking. There is nothing here but a few empty crack vials on the dressertop. In the kitchen, Toney is searching the refrigerator, reaching into the recesses of the freezer. The sergeant opens the stove, squats to look inside. Lenti lounges on the landing outside the apartment.

Then there is a shout from below. A beaming cop strides up the stairs toward Lenti, holding a TEC-9 machine pistol he found in the grass outside the open window. Gary, relieved, steps from the ransacked apartment and fondles the gun.

Lenti is pleased enough. "It's a good thing they found the jammy, Lemite, 'cause you woulda been walkin' for at least a month," he deadpans.

Sharron's haircut is not crisp anymore. The brown roots have flourished; the gold tips are almost gone. "I haven't had too many visitors," he says glumly. "I was tellin' people I didn't want them to come." He keeps looking down at his right hand, swollen from a recent fight. He has been in jail for two and a half months, and his speech patterns are jailhouse jumpy, counterarticulate. He rattles on, trying to confirm with every phrase that he belongs in this noisy, nasty, indoor world.

Sharron is in another barracks-style module in the C-76 building now. "I got it comfortable. I just worry 'cause I'm short," he says, referring to the fact that he is soon to be released. "And I don't want nothin' to go wrong. Know what I'm sayin'? Know what I'm sayin'? I saw the guy that took my boots. He came through. And I got my boots back. You know what I'm sayin'? I just spoke to my man on the other side when I saw him. I got the boots. My people duffed him up. You know what I'm sayin'? Like in here you know it's all about who you with. You know what I'm sayin'? My man Ralphlo, you know what I'm sayin'? Dude who hooked me up when I first got here, ran into a shamble with this guy in the bing, and then he sent word when the guy got out that we should duff him up. You know what I'm sayin'? Get in his area."

As he talks, Sharron hums with satisfaction at his successful metamorphosis to a jail-seasoned hardrock. This is yet another triumph for the actor. He has not only survived, he is back to his old tricks, building up props, grabbing some attention.

"I got soldiers in here. You know, when you got to do something, you just let the dogs loose, and the guy gets his ass all out. This guy owed me two boxes of cookies and I told him, 'After one week it's four, and after that your ass is out.' You know what I'm sayin'?"

He breaks character for a moment and offers an aside: "Livin' with fifty niggers ain't easy. I like my personality. I like the heart I have and my sensitivity. But you can't show none of that in here. It's a different world. You know what I'm sayin'? You show that, and guys look at you like . . ." Sharron makes a twisted face indicating that the one who shows sympathy will be the next one to be exploited. "They moved me and my boys. There are eight of us from Four Main. We brought our burners and our bangers with us. I got a guy shoppin' for me. I tell him to get this and if he don't have the money I tell him to call home and get it. That's the way it is." Sharron considers the possibility that he might be considered a leader and shivers at the idea. "I ain't a leader. There ain't any leaders."

Then he looks into the future. He has heard that Shawanda and her boyfriend have moved into his room. He has been doing a lot of thinking about sex, and he is going to need his room. "I just hope . . . when I get out, I'm just gonna stay in the house for a while. All I know is that Shawanda better get out of that room 'cause I'm gonna be doin' my thing, bangin' an rockin' those walls, you know what I'm sayin'?

"When I get out, I'm not even gonna go to Chantal's house. I'm gonna meet her at the train station and take her to the crib and do my thing. You know what I'm sayin'? That's it. I got to do that." He rises half out of his seat. "Vanessa wrote me a letter sayin' she wants to give herself to me. That's who I'm gonna be with."

Sharron tilts his head toward the floor as an attractive female corrections officer, assigned to keep the time for visits, passes by and points to her watch. A couple of months ago he would have smiled; now he scowls and rubs the back of his swollen hand under his left eye, over the faint scars from the time a cousin melted a toy soldier and flipped the scalding plastic bits at him.

From 7 A.M. to 1 P.M. Sharron has been attending math and English classes in a high school program. And he has decided that he might want to get his GED (high school equivalency diploma) when he gets out, instead of spending the rest of this year and probably half of the next one earning his regular high school diploma. In a GED predictor test given in the jail, he got 240, a good score. As he dreams of what it will be like when he gets out, the images foremost in his mind are girls, a job, and finding a way to get into Ms. King's school play, if she ever has another.

The only aspect of that dream that will be easy is the girls. It will be no simple task for Sharron to find even part-time employment. In fact, he does not know many people who have a job. Neither his mother nor Alleke nor Shawanda has one. John, Shawanda's boyfriend, has a job as a security guard for a building in Queens, but he makes so little money that he and Shawanda have had to move in with Gloria.

A week later, Sharron is lying on his bed, nursing a bruised shoulder, when he gets the word that he has a visitor. Things have gotten tougher for him. He has been transferred yet again, this time to South Main, which, according to Sharron, is another snitch house, a police house. When he and his boys around the way were growing up, they played a game called knockout, in which they would sit on a bench and take turns trying to knock out with a single punch the first adult man who walked by. But the guards in South Main do not fit the victim profile. "These COs are cock diesels," Sharron moans, "too big to be hittin' on kids. They be *destroyin'* guys." Here, the COs don't write people up, they kick ass. That policy actually has some advantages for Sharron. If he can avoid being brought up on charges for an incident in the barracks, he is due for release on March 7. At this point, he would rather take a beating than a loss of good time that would delay his release. Still, the beatings are no joke.

Sharron walks with a sly roll toward Sharon King, who wears tight jeans decorated with black panels on the front and white panels on the back. Teacher and student, coach and talented performer, visionary and vision meet. Their reunion should be taking place in an airport waiting room after Sharron's first successful semester in drama school, or in a midtown Manhattan café following his debut in an off-Broadway play. These two are not supposed to meet in a jail, and King knows it more than anyone. As Sharron approaches, she jumps off her seat, takes two quick steps, reaches back, and punches him in the chest with a thud that can be heard across the noisy room. Sharron spins away, more embarrassed than hurt, watching out of the corner of his eye to see who has seen the punch, calculating his response to meet the expectations of the witnesses. Apparently, no serious reaction is mandated.

"Ms. King . . ." he whines, crumpling in mock collapse to his chair.

But King is not finished. She remains standing, her finger pointed. "You robbed another black brother. You threatened and used a weapon to rob a brother, Sharron. And I am hurt." Her anger depleted, she sits, reaches across the table with both hands, and squeezes Sharron's face for a long moment.

At the end of the visit, King tells Sharron, who is delighted at the attention the sexy teacher is drawing from inmates and guards alike, "You bring your ass on home to me. You know what I mean. I don't care whether I'm in the school or at home or whatever. You'll be all right." Later, outside the jail, she insists, "Sharron *will* be all right. He will adapt to his environment. We just have to make sure he has a good environment. Clothes? Well, when it comes to clothes you might as well say, 'He's gotta have it.' But I'm not worried about Sharron."

DISCONTENT

February in Brownsville. An icy dawn eats into the night as working people hunch against the swift wind on their way to the #3 train on Livonia. The gusts are lashing around the corners of the Unity and Tilden Houses. Miraculously, five young men are still outside in front of 312 Osborne. "Homeboy" is only half accurate. These are young men, not boys, but they do stay close to home. Maybe they will never leave. The wind howls through the bullet holes in the lobby windows behind them. They rock back and forth and hug themselves, blowing hoary puffs into the grizzled dawn. How bad must it be inside if they are out here? Some are working, slinging, waiting for customers; others are fed up, homeless, unwanted, or locked out — boyfriends or sons no longer welcome.

Sergeant Priore and his driver step carefully to avoid patches of ice as they move past the shivering sentinels into the lobby of 312 Osborne. There are no bitter words or stares. The morning says all that. Priore removes a glove and pushes the elevator button. This is a domestic dispute. The rookie who answered the job has called for a boss.

On the twelfth floor, a muscular old man is standing in the hallway in his long underwear. "I'm gonna kill him," he promises. "Today's the day."

The rookie looks at Sergeant Priore and explains, "Kid's a crackhead, boss. Been harassing his father here, and the mother." Then the young cop whispers in Priore's ear, "Mother's a soft touch, gives the kid money."

"*Today*. Goddamn him," the man blusters, jiggling the handle of an ax at his side. This seventy-year-old strongman is used to settling disputes with his hands. All his life he has battled. He marched down the years fighting thugs, robbers, and the guys who disrespected his wife. In the last year he has grappled with his youngest son, and he will soon fight him again. But the man is old. The hand that holds the weapon shakes.

"You'll need an order of protection," Priore begins.

The man snarls. He hates his son. He has had a hard life, but he has lived it decently and has made it through with his wife at his side. Now his days are haunted by the grasping fingers of a ghoul with his face and name. The man cannot sit on the bench in front of his building with old friends without the whining, threatening shadow of his last-born to block the sun. No meal at home, no afternoon or nighttime sleep, is safe from the son's hateful visage. He is sucking the blood out of his elderly parents like a vampire. As Priore talks about court orders, William T. Loomis continues to curse and shake his stick at his son, who has materialized down the hall, near the elevator. Priore asks Mr. Loomis to put away his stick, but the father is enraged.

"I'll kill him now," he swears.

The cops turn to the lynx-eyed son who stands half in the elevator, half out of it. He doesn't challenge his father physically now, though it would be an epic struggle, the longshoreman against the street bum — strength on youth, hatred on need. No blows are struck tonight.

"You'll *never* be rid of me, William T. Loomis!" the son yells as the elevator doors close behind him.

It is a day later, the heart of the midnight tour. Priore's RMP picks its way past the debris on Van Sinderen Avenue, a one-lane alley between Dumont and Sutter avenues, running below the tracks that carry the L train. This is a place where huge mounds of tires, as high as a house, appear mysteriously in the dead of night, where a five-thousand-pound, six-foot-tall safe arrives one night and is gone two days later. "Jesus, what the hell happened to that?" Priore says. "You'd need a fucking winch to move that thing."

Ahead of the car, to the left, a spitting, smoking fire in an empty oil drum keeps a semicircle of wretched men warm. Priore's car makes a right-hand turn. Three men with filth-caked clothing are headed up Blake Avenue at four o'clock in the morning, slipping and staggering under the weight of a large door.

"Fuckin' mongos," Priore's driver mutters.

The men the cops call mongos are metal strippers. Often they are covered with grime from head to toe. Some are white, others Hispanic, but the dirt renders their ethnicity obscure. To the cops and everyone else, they are all just mongos. Like vultures, they perform a function. Nothing of any value lies around in Brownsville. The mongos will snap it up. More often than not, though, they take things that are not discarded, just unattended.

Priore and his driver pull over beside Hammil and his partner, who have already spotted the men. The metal door the men are transporting is painted Housing Authority green. It comes from a project; in fact, it is a front door. The mongos claim that there was a fire and that firemen told them they could take the door — a plausible story. They look more miserable than evil. But to be a police officer is to disbelieve. The cops search the men and find the tools of their breakdown trade — hammers, picks, and screwdrivers galore. Hammil is hurt.

"Didn't I let you sleep in there when it was very cold?" he asks. "Didn't I give you a break? And then you chump me off, play me like a sucker, and come back and take the door. You *steal* the door."

A police van arrives, and the door is lashed to the roof. A rookie takes the collar. Standard Housing police wisdom says that such a collar will bring a medal; "Catch someone stealing some property and you get a commendation," the officers insist. "Actually recover some Housing Authority property and you'll probably get a medal."

A few days later, at about the same time of night, on the same spot, Sergeant Priore spots a Dickensian mongo pushing a shopping cart filled with narrow strips of copper that look as if they may have come from the flashing on the roof of a project building. He steps out of his car and gestures for the mongo to stop. He speaks softly into his radio: "9510, Housing sergeant, Central. Have 9712 85 me, nonemergency. At Blake and Williams."

Priore wants Horan and Galvin, in car 9712, to check the roofs of two nearby buildings. He waits with the man in the street as a light snow tosses a slippery skim of ice on the black pavement of Blake Avenue. Galvin and Horan take the shuddering elevator to the roof. The copper flashing is intact. The same holds for the adjacent building. Horan drives up to where the boss and the mongo are standing. Priore is smiling through the snow.

There is something amazing, even annoying, about Priore's ability to maintain his good spirits in all conditions, as if he is mocking everyone around with his easy air and jaunty walk. You might even think he is a fool. That is, until you see how he treats less-than-able cops and frightened, tear-stained complainants. He does the right thing, always.

"Nothing, Sarge," Horan reports. "No flashing missing from either building. We checked. It's all there."

The mongo has at least three layers of clothing rotting off his frame, at different states of decomposition in different areas. His knees are down to the last level. His chest and hips bear their full complement of three outfits still. He is as filthy as a chimney sweep. No one has asked for his ID. Even to the regulation-oriented Priore, a mongo's name seems beside the point.

Priore is perhaps about to ask Horan to check a third building on the block. After all, the man got the copper flashing somewhere. Before he can speak, the man interrupts. "May I go now?" The voice is smooth and cultured. Better not to have spoken at all. The words bespeak good schools, parents, a home, and a dreadful fall. Worse, the words show that the man has landed in this awful spot fully conscious. It would have been much better to believe he had come from a family of mongos, maybe even a race of mongos, who liked their wretched midnight world of scraps. Better if he had been a groveling coward, a blubbering madman. As it is, he is just a man, and the truth is disconcerting, even to the unflappable Priore.

"What's your hurry? You got an appointment?" the sergeant snaps. Then, regaining his renowned composure, he laughs, waves the matter off, and heads back to his cruiser.

Riding with the sergeant is like riding up and down the strip with your father at the wheel. You see the same things as the guys in the hot cars and the convertibles, but you know you are going to miss the fun. Some cops who drive sergeants like the regularity, the lack of surprises, the proximity to the decision-making process. If you drive Priore, you have to like the stories.

He tells about the gangster Jose, the toughest guy in Brownsville. "I get the call. I'm the first on the scene and I run into the store he owned. 'Jimmy, they shot me,' Jose says. There was a hole so big in his chest you could see his spine." Priore makes a fist to signify the size of the shotgun wound. "I put him in the car. Fuckin' guy stayed alive all the way to the hospital, walked under his own power up the ramp to the emergency room at Brookdale. 'Jose, you're my hero,' I told him just before he collapsed and died."

A week later, on a Saturday in the final week of February, Priore has rotated onto the four-to-twelve shift. Jimmy Galvin is his driver for the tour. The two cops are in East New York near Cypress in the fading daylight when a call comes over for a 75th precinct sector car.

"75 Eddie. 10-10," Central begins, using a general code. "Male standing on the corner of Belmont and Euclid, possibly with a gun. Caller says he's wanted for a homicide."

Priore's car is just a block away from the spot. Even though the location is off-project, Priore picks up the radio.

"Housing sergeant. Be advised I'm 84. I'll check and advise. No further needed at this point."

When Priore and Galvin pull up, the homicide suspect is no more than a boy. "Kid was just in a fight on Sutter. Dude who got his ass kicked probably dropped the dime," explains a man on the sidewalk in a flame-red suit, with a vest and hat to match.

A police officer needs many skills. One of the most important is the ability to tell when he is getting good information. It does not matter that this man looks as if he has been airlifted from the 1970s, that he looks like a jester; Priore knows what he says is true. Maybe it is the kid's torn trousers, or the flush of childish concern on the boy's face.

The sergeant goes through the perfunctory toss, with the kid bent over the orange and blue sector car; he reaches between the kid's legs and up and down his torso. "You had a problem?" Priore chats soothingly. "Somebody pissed at you." He feels the kid's armpits and inside the waist of his beltless pants.

Suddenly a white chariot of a Jeep appears, and Chris Moore gets out. His 180-pound body is stuffed into tight blue jeans and a white shirt. His waxy brown skin sags a bit today. He wears no jacket and sports half a dozen gold chains around his thick neck. Moore takes a few wincing steps in his pointy-toed cowboy boots and stops ten feet from Priore. Somehow, this afternoon the drug dealer appears way past his prime and at the apex of his life at the very same moment. He looks smart, evil.

Without looking up, Priore greets him as sweetly as he would greet his neighbors in Belmore, Long Island.

"How ya doin', Chris?"

"Hi, Jim. Wha's up?" Moore answers with similar equanimity.

"Nothin'." Priore won't extend himself to explain the trivial nature of the operation. Jim Priore, who likes to tell stories, has also mastered silence.

Moore made his early money selling marijuana. He survived the A Team and the police. He bought buildings and businesses like the lingerie shop on the corner. But in recent years he has ventured into the crack trade. "Too legit to quit," he likes to say.

The guy in the red costume, eager to do something to impress Moore, shuffles and reshuffles his mental deck and comes up with a stupid idea.

"You want me to call somebody? Chris?" The man reaches inside his polyester jacket and repeats the question. Moore does not react.

There is no need to call anyone, certainly no need to emphasize to the police officers that this ragamuffin in new sneakers is a Chris Moore operative, worth a phone call to a lawyer. It is time to be quiet and still. The man in red is neither. He thrusts his hand in his jacket pocket again, as if to reach for a quarter.

Galvin is a funny guy, but he is in a bad mood. He does not have Priore's appreciation of the picaresque, does not like the way the red-suited dude is digging in his jacket. *Who keeps quarters in the inside pocket of his suit jacket?* Galvin is thinking as he moves his hand slowly to his .38.

"I don't know about you, Jimmy," he says, as the cops drive off a moment later. "If anybody was going to make a call, it was going to be to the morgue, 'cause if fucking Superfly stuck his hand in his pocket one more time, I was gonna cap him." Priore chuckles.

A woman in a third-floor apartment in the Tilden Houses is not laughing. It's another midnight tour later in the week.

"This is my castle," she says to Hammil and his partner, "my welfare hotel. I want him out." The cops mill around the apartment. "He's crazy anyway. Held a gun on me. He has a fatal attraction, and I want him arrested."

The boyfriend stands in the hallway, glaring dangerously. The cops refuse to arrest him. Instead, they escort him from the building. Once again it is icy in Brownsville. Tilden, Langston Hughes, Unity, Howard, and Pink are quiet and warm. Above, some windows are open. Public housing has its nightmares, but the city sends up the heat; you can count on it, and little else. The cops watch as the expelled boyfriend stalks down the wind-swept street.

"He'll be back," Hammil's partner predicts.

It's too early in the shift for a collar like this to bring any overtime. When the man comes back later in the night, he will leave in cuffs. "Just like Paul Masson says," Hammil comments as the two move toward the warmth of their RMP, "make no arrest before its time."

But Gary is always looking for a collar. An hour later, half a mile away, he spots what looks like a mongo crouched near the rolled-down gate of Rony and Zaid Shoman's ramshackle supermarket, hard by the Van Dyke Houses.

Gary pulls over. The young man, a mongo with a green plastic bag full of garbage, is caked with grime. Gary orders him to put his hands up on a fence and dumps the contents of the bag on the street. Isn't it hard enough to be filthy and cold and homeless, with no apartment and no suitcase, without being rousted by a grumpy, collar-crazed cop?

"What's in the bag?"

"Stuff I got from the garbage."

Lo, there is a shotgun in the bag and an armful of boxes of drugstore remedies, cough suppressants and aspirin. "You *found* the shotgun in the garbage?" Gary exclaims. "You found these drugs in the garbage?" The man is silent. "Where do you live?"

"I live right up there." He points to a window high above, in the Van Dyke Houses.

Gary cuffs the man up and puts him in the car, lifting his own nose out the window into the stiff cold as the sickening pungent smell of an unwashed human being fills the car.

Back in the cell area behind the front desk, where the grimy man is locked, Gary goes about recording the inventory of the recovered goods. The medications are perishable, so they cannot be vouchered. They must be photographed and returned to the owner, so Gary arranges the boxes of cold remedies in an elaborate display before he snaps a Polaroid of them. His partner is on the phone to the Palestinian store owners.

"Mr. Shoman? This is the Housing police on Sutter Avenue. Sorry to wake you. Our records show you're the owner of the food store on Powell and Sutter. There's been a burglary, and we'd like you to come down to identify some property we believe was stolen from your place."

Sleepy-eyed and disheveled, Rony and Zaid arrive quickly from their home in nearby Bensonhurst. Rony, thirty-four, the shorter and fuller-faced of the two, is missing two teeth. Nevertheless, he sports a wry smile. He waves off questions about the shotgun.

"Yes, you keep. Just keep."

The brothers sit on the plastic chairs in the front room and wait to get a chance to talk to the burglar. They pay $3,000 a month rent for their store, which has been robbed six times in the past two months, and they are determined to get to the bottom of the break-ins.

"Three times they come in the gate. We fix. Three times they come in the roof," Rony says. "They don't have guts to come in the day."

"Their mother teach them steal," thirty-one-year-old Zaid says.

"No." Rony won't have it. He waves the comment off. Rony's life is invested in the people of Brownsville. The Shoman brothers had a store in San Francisco. Then they moved to New York and bought a store on Ralph Avenue, in Bedford-Stuyvesant. Later they expanded to the small supermarket on Powell and Sutter. Their families live together in a two-family house.

"Six years, don't buy house. Still rent," Rony says. "Work. Don't care if eight days, twelve hours a day. Month to month." He considers for a moment the people from Van Dyke who frequent his store. "If good customer's funeral? We can't go? So send flowers. Baby? Pampers? Fifteen dollars? Take it." Rony tosses his hand to emphasize that money is not the most important thing to him. "Need money, two dollars to go to work, give."

"Six, seven steal." Zaid flattens his hand out in front of him at the height of a small child.

Rony understands more. "First six months, we fight every day. They talk from far away. They will 'kill' us, 'shoot' us. If steal a bag of chips, we fight. We no afraid. We chase in apartment and fight. Karate. A big guy, he steal meat. I catch him in parking and give him karate. But now . . ." He opens both hands and spreads his arms. "We see them more than family. They *are* our family."

Business has been bad. Besides the break-ins, there is the recession and the crack epidemic. "Some week we don't take penny out of store. We used to have five or six customers, spend three or four hundred dollars a month. Now, one hundred dollars. Things change since crack."

Their store sits at the foot of the small bridge that separates Brownsville from East New York. On the other side of the bridge is a grim flight of stairs that look as if they lead to a gallows. Actually, the steps lead to a green wooden enclosure that houses the token booth for the poorly lit, ultra-dangerous Sutter Avenue stop on the L line. Next door to the supermarket is a check-cashing place and a greasy auto body shop.

Gary, preoccupied with the arrangement and inventory of the stolen property, does not notice as Rony receives a nod from an absentminded officer at the front desk and slides into the inner sanctum of the processing and holding cell area. Rony inches closer and closer to the cell where the sleeping figure of the man who robbed his store lies. He peers into the tiny cell and inspects the ragged man. His eyes glow.

"Frank, it's you," he hisses in triumph. "Frank, you bastard, you." The man stirs, blinks, looks up at Rony, but does not speak. Rony has not sneaked into the off-limits cell area just to curse the man who broke into his store. "Frank. Who took the scale?" In one recent break-in, thieves took the cash register. Now the Shoman brothers hide the remaining cash register and the meat slicer when they close the place at night. In another raid, somebody made off with the meat scale. Rony wants that scale back.

"Who took the scale, Frank?" he whispers again. "*Who* took the scale? I know your mother, Frank. I charge your mother. I don't have to charge you. I *clean* you good, Frank. I *clean* you. I fix you up. I break you hands."

Rony's strange threats hit home. Frank lifts his head and whispers, "The guy who owns the meat store on Belmont has it."

Rony snorts, steps away to think for a moment, and stalks out of the room to the bench, where he confers with Zaid over strategy to recover the scale.

The next day, Rony and Zaid are hard at work in the store. Rony banters with the customers. "Wha's happen?" He nods at a young mother holding twin five-year-old girls by the hand. The girls are gleeful on this trip to the store. They dance as much as they can, cackling about ice cream and candy. A few minutes later, as they are led from the store, they are a study in sadness. Each head droops in response to a judgment against which there is no appeal. Their mother pushes no shopping cart heaped with essentials and treats. In fact, none of the people who have been in the store this morning have walked out with large grocery bags. The rail-thin mother carries only a plastic bag, the cutout grip of which is wrapped around her wrist as she tugs her daughters home. Visible through the milky white plastic of the bag is a green pack of cigarettes and a brown forty-ounce bottle of malt liquor.

"TWO TEARS IN A BUCKET"

February 26 is a special day at Thomas Jefferson High School. There have been a lot of special days at Jeff in the last few years, since Beck took over, and nothing less than celebrity status since the Daryl Sharpe killing in November. This week, as a public relations maneuver, Mayor David Dinkins and his administration have chosen to set up shop at Borough Hall in downtown Brooklyn, and this morning the mayor is on his way down Atlantic Avenue to visit Jefferson and address the students. At 8:30 A.M. there are twenty police officers waiting for His Honor outside the school, and many more inside. Blue uniforms are everywhere. The regular unarmed Jefferson security staff has been augmented to twenty-three for the day. At the front door there is a metal detector, manned by six specially trained security guards sent over by the board of education.

Things have been looking up at Jeff in the past few weeks. Beck's relentless sweeps have been paying off. But the principal herself has been having health problems. Early in the month she felt sharp chest pains. After a stay in the hospital and innumerable tests, the doctors proclaimed her ailment harmless angina. She hurried back to East New York. She did not want to lose momentum.

Ironically, the shooting has opened up some funding sources, given Beck a pulpit from which to pitch her dream of building a dormitory for her students. She has more security now. Even on regular days there are security guards all over the school, and a bank of TV monitors in the second-floor security office covers

318

every hallway. And as a result of the shooting, Beck has been permitted by the board of education to banish even more Smurfs. She understood the posses. "Their mothers aren't glad to see them. Their teachers aren't glad they came to school. The only smile they see all day is the one they get from their gangster friends." But she also knew what she could not handle; they had to go.

Over on Sutter Avenue, Gary Lemite is sucking down a large bottle of tea-flavored Snapple, getting ready to hit the streets for an eight-to-four shift. Khalil Sumpter is already awake, donning his brown jeans jacket, when his mother comes into his room to wake him up for school. In an unprecedented display of filial concern, he prepares to walk his mother to the train station on her way to work. Tucked in the waist of his pants is a six-shot, stainless steel Smith and Wesson Model 64MP .38 revolver. The thirty-four-ounce gun has been modified to include a thumb spur for rapid firing. It is exactly like the weapon Gary has in his black holster. In fact, Gary is carrying two such guns on his waist, minus the thumb spurs, which are against police regulations. As Khalil kisses his mother on the cheek at the train station and heads up Pennsylvania Avenue, Gary finishes his drink, tosses it in the back of the unmarked gray car, and rolls onto the streets of Brownsville.

Khalil is carrying the gun, and has walked his mother to the train, because of the running feud he has been having with a couple of guys from the Linden Houses, Tyrone Sinkler and his slim buddy, LoLife Ian Moore, E-lo. Sinkler still believes that Khalil was responsible for the year he spent in Spofford. There have been threats and fights. Khalil is not as big as the 220-pound Sinkler, and has not fared well in the bouts. Two days ago somebody pegged a volley of shots at him outside the Linden Houses, and he is sure it was Sinkler and Moore. Worse, he has heard that Sinkler is threatening to shoot his mother.

Wired and worried, Khalil Sumpter, with his brown "baby fade" and matching jeans jacket, approaches Jefferson High School, checks the mob of police at the front door, and circles around to an unguarded side entrance. At 8:40 A.M. he meets his friend Dupree, climbs quickly to the second floor, and stands at the head of the stairs. Five minutes before the end of homeroom, the corridor is full of latecomers. At the opposite end of the hall are his two enemies and two of their friends. Indeed, the crew had been scouring the school for twenty minutes, looking for Khalil. The two sides eye each other, and Khalil strides forward.

Khalil Sumpter. This is the kid Marvin described in the back of the basketball team bus. *This* is "Dupree's man," the one who asked, "Who wants it?"

This time, Khalil makes no threats. He draws, fires two shots. The first blasts Tyrone Sinkler in the head, the second tears through Ian Moore's chest. Khalil pivots and bounds down the stairs. He flees the school, but two blocks away an unarmed school security guy throws him against a car. He does not fight back.

Cortez Sutton is studying a history book in an empty room on the fifth floor. He looks up to see people sprinting in the hall. Sharon King is in the guidance center on the first floor, using nail polish to fix a run in her stockings, when a student runs by screaming about shots on the second floor. She starts grabbing kids and shoving them toward the open door of the auditorium, because she thinks that whoever is shooting might be coming down to the first floor.

Gary Lemite is on Blake, just a block away, when he gets the call: "Shots fired in Thomas Jefferson High School." He sweeps around the corner, jams his Grand Fury at an angle to the curb on busy Pennsylvania Avenue, bursts in the front door, and takes the side stairs two at a time. There are two bodies on the floor. Officer Price is giving mouth-to-mouth to Sinkler. Ms. Kim Pierre, a teacher, is asking over and over again, "You need relief? You need relief?" Price, possessed, never looks up from his task. Five compressions, a breath. Five compressions, another breath.

A few feet away, a Housing detective named Romanelli is performing mouth-to-mouth resuscitation on Ian Moore. Gary Lemite, who would run at a gun spitting red flames a foot and a half out of the barrel, charge straight at bullets promising paralysis and death, stands aside. He is not called on to do anything valorous here. If he were, he would hesitate. There is blood everywhere. Gary says later, "I don't know . . . I don't think I was ready to do that mouth-to-mouth. Maybe in another environment. These are hard kids . . . you never know."

Price and the Emergency Medical Service technicians sprint out the front door beside Sinkler's stretcher. Sinkler's neck is swathed in bandages; a green bookbag is strapped across his thighs. Moore's stretcher is right behind.

Kids lean far out the windows of the upper floors as the bodies are trundled out the front door. Cortez, who stands in the crowd of students peering out the second-floor window, sees the orange jacket on the second gurney and suspects that his friend has been shot.

Mayor Dinkins goes onstage anyway. He steps up to the microphone in a windbreaker instead of a suit jacket, as if to send the message that he is a man of action. Above him, hanging on the wall of the Jefferson auditorium, is a banner bearing the likeness of Martin Luther King, Jr., and the inscription THE CHOICE TODAY IS NOT BETWEEN VIOLENCE AND NONVIOLENCE. IT IS BETWEEN VIOLENCE OR NONEXISTENCE. To Dinkins's left is a large potted plant; behind him on metal folding chairs sit School Chancellor Joseph Fernandez and Carol Beck.

"If someone steps on your foot or disrespects you in some fashion," Dinkins pleads, "and you feel compelled to show your manhood or your womanhood, think again. I don't know what anger broke out in this young person to cause him to fire pointblank at two people, knowing that it would take lives. What I do know is that there is a better way. If you don't have a gun, you're not going to use a gun." Then the mayor asks the students to do something braver than he understands. He suggests that whenever they see or hear of anyone with a gun, they turn that person in to the authorities. Before hurrying over to his temporary headquarters in Borough Hall, the well-meaning mayor delivers a line straight out of *Mad* magazine: he advises the students to try counting to 10 or 110 the next time they get angry.

"I play a high-risk game," Carol Beck is fond of saying. The task of telling an auditorium full of students that two more of their number have been shot dead is daunting. But Beck is a descendant of a line of women accustomed to facing such moments on this country's soil. When she makes the announcement, there is a whoosh of breath, a groan, and silence. Some students cry. Others appear unmoved. They have been watching bodies pile up since they were old enough to see out the windows of their homes. Seventy-five Jefferson students have died violently in the past four years. In the same period, many more have been injured on the school grounds. These are children who have grown to adolescence watching guns go off on their TV screens and in their hallways. The demented siren of the sector cars and the EMS buses has been their lullaby. Who can expect them to cry now?

The next day, Beck finds herself once again busy at damage control. Sandra Feldman, the president of the teachers' union, has been demanding that Jefferson be closed. Parents have lined up to transfer their kids. Like a weary fighter, Beck is stuck in a corner, taking punches. It seems as if she has lost the battle for Thomas Jefferson High School. Just as she feared all along, the Smurfs did her in. Jason Bentley, the shooter in the Daryl Sharpe killing, was fourteen years old. Sumpter, Moore, and Sinkler were all freshmen or sophomores.

The press outside is thirty strong, looking for sound bites. News trucks with their transmitters erect to the sky are lined up on Pennsylvania Avenue. But why put the killing in Thomas Jefferson on the front page when kids are killed every day here? Last night a fourteen-year-old was murdered in the Pink Houses by some Cypress guys, probably members of the new A Team. But the press is here to trumpet the degradation of Thomas Jefferson High School. There won't be a word written about how none of this would have happened if Ms. King had been able to send Khalil Sumpter someplace where he would have gotten help, maybe even a real future.

On the front steps of the school, Sharon King turns her back on the reporters, hugs a student, and says of Khalil, "I knew, I knew, but I just thought I had more time."

Inside, Beck is back onstage, talking to the faculty and students. She is wearing a blue suit, with a gold African Kente scarf draped over her shoulders, and her sneakers. The chest pains are gone for now. She is getting good at this kind of oratory.

"If you have heard the drums," she thunders, "I have heard the drums. They are talking of closing this school, of closing *your* school. But this school will stay open. I want to say to you that you have it in your power to stop this. Just like you can make something happen, you can make it not happen. *You* made gold earrings and gold chains happen. You did it. And now they are doing it all over the world. You can do it. We have to set the rules. Can we do it?" But the center cannot hold. Carol Beck is standing alone on the stage of the overflowing auditorium.

King, in black-and-white bell-bottom pants and a 1970s-style puffed cap, is now drifting up and down the aisles. Despite the gravity of Beck's message, the auditorium is buzzing, not with dismay or even news but with the trivialities of youth. Giggles, urgent nothings, are flung across the rows. Now Beck is trying to explain the revised schedule for the day, but she is losing her audience. The principal is under tremendous pressure. Since 7 A.M. she has been bolstering her sagging staff and cajoling parents to leave their children in Jefferson. (Ultimately, only three parents insist on the transfer.) The United Federation of Teachers is nipping at her heels; a delegation is wandering the hallways at this very moment. They are not saying as much, but the UFT representatives cannot figure Jeff out. There is no graffiti; the place does not look at all like a hellhole. But a hellhole it must be, they figure, so they keep snooping, looking for cracks.

Beck is besieged, and at this moment she is not getting what every teacher needs from her students — quiet. To speak in the students' defense, Beck has made a rare tactical error. It is unreasonable to think that anyone, even a wired Carol Beck, can hold the rapt attention of eighteen hundred teenagers with logistics, scheduling. What do they care if there is a little chaos? Beck's message simply is not urgent enough; she does not slip it in fast enough. The principal stands contemplating the disturbing haze of chatter. Then a fountain of laughter bursts from the mouth of the student body.

"I won't embarrass you. I would never embarrass you. But you are embarrassing *me*. You are embarrassing me!" Beck shouts. Like all good teachers, she rarely raises her voice. There is quiet. Then she makes another mistake. After playing her volume card to win silence, she sends a horde of young girls to their lockers, a necessary but unfortunate maneuver. More noise. More loud laughter. "We have visitors," Beck says. The students do not give a damn what the visitors see or believe. The visitors are Beck's problem.

There is a commotion down at the left. Cortez Sutton has

been reading a newspaper about the shooting of his buddy. In front of him, a guy he does not know asks to look at the paper.

"No," Cortez says flatly. He is not in the mood for the curious protocols that mark interpersonal relations among young men in Brownsville. He gives no deferential dip of the head, excuse, or softening lingo.

"Yo, money, your paper ain't all that. They gonna be readin' about you tomorrow," the other kid says, maybe looking for a little rep on this day of big reps.

Cortez has been controlling himself all term, letting all kinds of possible trouble slip by. Not today. Ian Moore was his real friend. The two teenagers lunge at each other. Across the room, Jude, slim as a bullwhip, his hood pulled up and his dark glasses clamped on, spots the action and bounds to Cortez's defense.

In a minute, a horde of security guards has broken up the fight. Order is restored. More security guards drift down the aisles, watching.

Beck goes berserk. "I am not a lion tamer," she rails. "I am an educator. Talk about *disrespect*. You don't know what disrespect is. Real disrespect is so subtle that when you see it you won't even know what it is. The people with the power will do it to you with a smile."

She is wailing for a generation of African American children whose lives are going grotesquely wrong. She knows what they know and what they do not know, how they think. Their minds are full of dreams their country has given them little chance to fulfill. Their hearts are beating for designer clothing. Their nervous systems are programmed for daily jolts of excitement and cheap respect. They are at once victims, dangerous fools, and glorious possibilities. Beck is raging for their souls.

"Power. You think a mean face brings you power? I'm black — I know all about that. That's not power. The guy who pulled the bullets, I mean the guy who pulled the trigger, that wasn't about power. The people who really have power do it with a smile." Then Beck gets personal. It is always personal with her, the students know. They have known that since the day she showed up.

"I refuse to be defined by you. I don't give you the permission to define me. I refuse to let you define our community. You haven't got the right to have rage. You haven't earned the right. All over the country, they are thinking of you as out of control."

Beck is breathing hard. The worn, venerable auditorium, with its Corinthian columns and neoclassical details, once home to Danny Kaye and Shelley Winters, is silent, save for the crackle and hiss of security walkie-talkies. A small-boned white woman teacher with black hair whispers to a colleague, "Somebody better get her off that stage before she collapses." But Beck goes on. Her children are lost, and she wants them back.

"You aren't entertainers, you are students, and you are supposed to look bright-eyed and bushy-tailed, with pens and pencils and bookbags. Education is your last hope. And whether you know it or not, this woman standing on this stage may be your last hope. When I throw up my hands and walk away, you're finished. But I am not going to do that. The teachers and community leaders and clergymen — we are not going to allow this to happen."

Beck is on the stage by herself, but she isn't playing this hand alone. She calls Bashim Inman, who strides up on the stage.

"What are you thinking?" he asks the student body. "What are you going to do? What are you going to do?" He asks over and over again, to titters and shouts. He keeps up his challenge. "What are you going to do? I'm askin' you. You know what I'm sayin', 'cause I'm scared. You know what I'm sayin'? 'Cause that could have been me on the ground on the second floor. You know what I'm sayin'? You know what I'm sayin'?"

"You know what I'm sayin'" is the mumbled catchphrase of the Ville. It is meant to indicate that the speaker is not a person who considers things carefully or takes care to explain, that he is too primed for immediate action for the intricacies of communication.

As big as a kodiak bear, Bashim is the perfect spokesman. He glows with intelligence, promise, and Brownsville rough. He never does get to the rest of his speech. He just keeps asking what the students intend to do. He leaves the stage with the words, "This, this here, has *got* to stop. You know what I'm sayin'?"

And then Sonny Carson steps up. Opportunist, activist, convicted kidnapper, and one-time gang leader, he wears a black fez with golden studs, like some kind of wizard, and carries a walking stick. Beck has taken some chances calling in both Carson and the band of bow-tied Muslims who are sitting downstage right. But Carson keeps the antiwhite rhetoric down and holds the interest of the students.

"The brothers got to stick together, 'cause you don't understand. It's all about getting rid of you." Carson calls the school's young men up on the stage. The boys flow forward and pack themselves tightly on the wide expanse. Then Carson tells the girls to applaud the boys. When the boys sit down, he refers to the people outside, the press, "who don't want us to succeed." He says all the right things this day. He calls for a "black parents' night" in support of the school. Beck quickly steps up and reminds everyone that there are Hispanic and Asian students and that the night should best be called "parents' night."

Beck is nervous. One antiwhite or anti-Semitic word and the heat will go higher than even she can stand. She is gambling, just like she did five months ago when she brought in the Reverend Al Sharpton and the Reverend Herbert Daughtry after the Sharpe shooting. She can get away with such maneuvers because both her black and her white faculty trust her deeply. But she also knows that she needs every bit of community support to turn back the efforts of the teachers' union to shut Jefferson down.

Conrad Muhammad, a Nation of Islam minister, is up next. He is flanked by meticulously attired aides, who assume their traditional secret service agent stance, staring off into space. "Salaam aleikum," he begins. The students repeat the phrase; they are getting some kind of civic education this morning. One cannot help but wonder how things would be if this level of urgency were achieved every day at school, if the people in the country, the city, cared as much and did as much for the students.

"The Honorable Louis Farrakhan greets you and sends his best wishes in this difficult time. He understands who you are, even though you don't. There are people outside," Muhammad says, referring to the press, "not the *brother* man but the *other* man. You are not naughty by nature," a play on the name of the popular rap group. "You are divine by nature. But the *other* man keeps taking away your history. You are playing into the hands of the man who would like to see every brother in this room dead. You have *no reason* to kill each other, because you are allies in the struggle."

*

Ian Moore, E-lo, is laid out in a shirt by Polo, eulogized by a community leader, the Reverend Johnny Ray Youngblood, from St. Paul Community Baptist Church in East New York. Bill Cosby comes to the funeral and embraces Carol Beck. The national spotlight plays off the brick walls of Jefferson. James Brown arrives, declaring himself the "godfather of Thomas Jefferson High School." Even the campaigning Bill Clinton appears for a photo opportunity on the front steps of Jefferson. The students are quiet and confused, their self-image flipping like the picture on an MTV video. Are they blessed or cursed, celebrities or throwaways?

"I grew up in St. Louis, and when I lived there as a young girl a long time ago I had a friend." Beck is addressing the modest turnout of seventy-five parents and visitors at Parents' Night. "When this friend saw me on the news, he thought I needed help, and so he packed his bags and headed out here to watch my back. I'd like you to meet my friend." From the rear of the auditorium, a lanky gray-haired gentleman unfolds and gestures shyly. "Everybody has got to help in this," Beck says, "because I'm tired."

There is more talk from a succession of speakers about stopping the proliferation of guns and violence. The kind of kids on hand, like Tumbo and Nick, lingering near the back door of the auditorium, don't need to hear this. Nick is on hand because he rides home with Beck and she has been here since school ended at three o'clock. Tumbo just likes to spend time around the high school.

Afterward, in the lobby, Beck is surrounded by a group of well-wishers, "My bodyguards," she gushes. The immaculate Muslims proselytize discreetly, handing out fliers in the lobby to the earnest parents, who linger with their teenagers and toddlers.

"They have to make guns unacceptable, the way they used to be," a man with a transit worker's patch argues. "They spent the last thirty years glamorizing guns, and now it's their responsibility to turn it around. You think they can't do it, but they can. The media put its mind to it and they drove cigarette smoking right out of style. If they want to, they can do the same with guns."

Soon the meeting breaks up. It is a warm night with a peaceful mist of rain. As the parents drift back to Unity, Linden, and Brownsville Houses, with their teenagers and toddlers, Gary Lemite is out on Blake Avenue again, sitting in his car while his partner, Willie Arroyo, is on the street writing a ticket for a double-parked car.

"These guys are wearing their pants so low that they actually have to hold them up. Look at that." Gary points to a fifteen-year-old with baggy trousers halfway down his plaid boxer shorts, clinging precariously to his buttocks. The boy holds his pants with his right hand and an umbrella with his left.

An exotic sports car zips by, and Gary straightens up in his seat. Then comes a red Range Rover. "You know how much that car costs? Thirty thousand." Gary pushes a puff of air through his front teeth. Arroyo, back in the vehicle now, repeats the noise. Conventional police wisdom says that many people are manipulating the system while police officers are working hard for everything they get. The officers wear American flag pins on their uniforms, but they cannot seem to make up their minds whether America is the greatest country in the world or one big rip-off.

"It isn't the first warm night like this that gets bad," Arroyo observes. "It's the second warm night. I noticed that."

The radio refutes his theory. Twenty minutes after the parents' meeting is over, someone is sporting a sawed-off shotgun on Mother Gaston Avenue.

"Can I get a scrip on that man with a shotgun, Central?" Gary asks.

"That is one male black, heavyset, about seventeen years of age, with a striped, hooded sweatshirt, in possession of a sawed-off shotgun."

Arroyo aims the car toward Mother Gaston and Blake. Gary is checking cross streets, computing routes of escape. As they pull in in front of the Unity Houses, a sector car with Madden and Finn in it noses to a stop in front of them, and the two second-year guys leap out. Standing there on the sidewalk is a stocky young man with a telltale striped, hooded sweatshirt.

The kid is guilty of at least three big mistakes, not counting carrying a shotgun with a banana clip through the projects on Gary's tour. First, he has showed the gun to somebody who just doesn't like him or made somebody angry enough to call the police. Second, when he starts to run, he heads straight across the area known as "the circle," a hundred-yard open space between the project buildings, instead of fleeing inside, where he might find an open door or what the cops call a "bad Samaritan" to let him in. Third, and probably most damning, he is obese. As every Housing cop knows, the fat guys are the ones who get caught, because they run slowly. Madden gains on the youth, with Finn right behind, and Lemite, who got a bad jump out of the van, is behind him. The speedy Arroyo had the worst start of all, but he won the medal for most athletic in his police academy graduating class, and he is coming like a shot on the left. Three of the four cops have their guns drawn. Lemite keeps his holstered. A cluster of people stand blithely on the walkway entrance as the pistols come their way.

"Get down. Get down!" Gary screams.

On the service road that leads to the circle are two rows of parked cars. A woman with a baby wrapped in blue blankets ducks low behind a car. On the grass close to the brick buildings, shadowy figures run with the officers to watch the spectacle. Above, words are flung from windows. "He dropped it. He dropped it!" The woman shouting from above is not assisting the police in their recovery of the gun. She is trying to keep them from shooting the fleeing boy.

Almost through the circle, just before the road beyond, the fat kid falls, and Madden runs up to him. Afraid that the kid is about to roll and fire the shotgun, he has his finger on his trigger. But the kid pops the gun off his hip where he carried it under his sweatshirt, lets it drop, scrambles to his feet, and lunges away, with Madden a stride behind. The kid leans too far, gets ahead of himself, and falls again, this time flat on his face a foot from the wheels of a speeding white Buick. Madden kneels on his back and cuffs him.

Twenty feet away, Finn scoops up a curved banana clip from the ground with some twenty rounds in it. A 75th car squeals to a stop, and a six-foot-four black cop leaps to the asphalt, runs up, and kicks the cuffed kid hard in the ribs. Then he promenades back to his police car with his chest puffed out, gets in, and his partner pulls away.

The small crowd on hand is incensed. A Hispanic woman who may be the boy's mother screams, "Stop! We aren't violent people. Don't hurt him."

Finn can't take the contradictions. "Not violent? What's

this?" He holds up the banana clip. "What's this?" he demands again.

"Don't hurt him," the woman wails. An ancient grandmother, her wizened face wrapped in a dark scarf, is now by the woman's side, screaming at the police. "Don't you touch him. I beg to you. Don't."

A 75 cop with an eerie golden glow to his cheeks, as if he just stepped out of a tanning salon, is also on hand, and in no mood for dialogue or community unrest. He advances with his nightstick on the growing crowd of project residents, who have seen too many ass kickings to obey the orders to disperse. The people back up slowly and curse.

"Fuck the police. You think you all the cavalry, but the Indians was right," a man says. "I'm twenty-three years old. Don't start shit. You know how *we* get."

The prisoner is cuffed and taken off to the precinct. Arroyo circles back to get the shotgun. Just in time — a neighborhood kid is bending over to pick it up when Arroyo points his pistol.

"Don't even *think* about it. Step off," he commands. The kid walks backward into the shadows, his eyes riveted on the officer's .38 as Arroyo grabs the rifle.

"I LIKE THE WAY I AM"

A guy on the other side of the 6 Building just got banged on the head by some of Sharron's boys, but Sharron is lying in his bunk reading. He is weeks from his release and he is praying not to be drawn into the action now. Ms. King brought him some books and he has read *The Autobiography of Malcolm X, Manchild in the Promised Land,* and *A Streetcar Named Desire.* It is becoming more and more evident to the others in the building that despite Sharron's ability to act like one of the guys, he is different. When he uses a term they haven't heard or a word with a couple of extra syllables, they stiffen, as if the language is a slap at them. "C'mon, Sha, why don't you say it without all that?"

Sharron feels sorry for the guys around him. Most of them quit school in the tenth grade and have been in jail most of the time since. There is one other guy, Earl, who is thoughtful, "slick on the cap." In the school sessions, as five out of the ten guys in the class lay their heads on the desk and sleep, Earl comes up with answers quicker than Sharron. The two find furtive moments to exchange thoughts that would not be appreciated by the others.

Sharron has been thinking about his future. Lying on his bunk for hours, just thinking. But his thoughts are disordered. He sees himself getting out and taking Vanessa to his bedroom. Vanessa is definitely the one. She goes to school, has a job, and she has sworn to give herself to him. Sharron is sure of nothing more than that he will do his thing on his gray day bed next to the sign saying, "What are your suggestions? We'd like to know."

Sharron still follows the exhortation "Don't give up on your dreams," but the truth is, he does not know what the dreams are anymore. And he has no real plan to make any part of his future turn out right. Instead, he muses about writing songs and singing, and doing the right thing when he gets out of jail, which means heading off to school and not being arrested. There is nothing whatsoever in his thoughts that involves giving up his minimum standards of dress to insure that he will never get in trouble again. He does not regret boosting, and believes in his heart that he will once again reap a harvest from the Manhattan department stores.

The guys in the mod are onto Sharron big-time. "You don't belong in here, Sha," they say right out. Even the cock-diesel guards know that something is up with him. They rarely see anyone reading a book or writing. Sharron has penned scores of letters to Vanessa and a handful of notes to other girls he has met in the borough of Brooklyn. He knows full well the trouble that can come from being different in jail, but he has not been able to subdue his personality. "I like the way I am," he writes to Vanessa. Of course, he has been singing. That and the picture of a bare-chested Marlon Brando on the cover of *A Streetcar Named Desire* have raised some questions among the gangsters about Sharron's masculinity. It's a good thing his time is short. Real short.

Unlike Sharron these days, Gary is not interested in blending into the crowd. He looks like exactly what he is, a plainclothes police officer. He laces up his black workboots, puts his two-inch .38 Ruger five-shot backup gun inside his waistband, and pulls on his black-and-white PSA 2 T-shirt. He tucks the badge he keeps on a chain around his neck inside his shirt, and pulls on his black hooded sweatshirt. He checks himself in the mirror. The transition to the Brownsville look would not be hard to achieve: a pair of Timberland boots instead of the glossy military looking footgear he wears and a Triple Fat Goose down coat would have worked just fine. The gaudy eight-ball jackets are already out, in favor of toggle coats, canvas car coats with corduroy collars. It would be easy to look like a local, and by extension logical to the police, a perp. By way of disguise, Gary sometimes dons a short brown jacket he borrows from his brother-in-law, a parcel post driver. But for the most part he wants to look like a cop, because despite the protestations of the police that they are the endangered and embattled minority, the cop look is one of the safest styles of all in the Ville.

"If I walk up on a set, the spot where they're sellin' crack or whatever, and I look like just another guy, who knows what could happen," Gary says. "The dealers I'm walking up on could think that I am there to rip them off, so they start shooting. Or they could be down to rip me off because they figure I'm new in the area." The police look cuts down on the element of surprise, but there are more important things, even to Gary Lemite, than the element of surprise.

Tony Logan is Gary's new partner; it is the first time Gary has had a black partner. Logan is a huge man with a big regard for himself. At six-four and 235 muscled pounds, he gets automatic props from some perps. Despite the respect he has been garnering, though, he is raw when it comes to the street. And the street is where he and Gary are headed.

It is dusk in the "lawless" section over near Riverdale and New Lots. From the Howard Houses on the western end of Brownsville to the sprawling Cypress Hills complex on the eastern border of East New York, the brick project complexes simply do not look bad. But this corner of East New York, just east of the ravine that separates Brownsville and East New York, fenced by the intersecting elevated #3 and L lines, looks exactly as bad as it is.

As the sun dips below the roofs of the Brownsville Houses in the distance, the rusting iron stanchions of the train tracks look like prison camp watchtowers, throwing melancholy shadows over the lots of garbage and bullet-scarred derelict cars. On a nearby street, a gauntlet of dreadlocked men lean toward passing cars, whispering about "blunts," joints of marijuana, and "sens," or sensamilla, the potent form of the drug. Sometimes the 75, responsible for the area, throws a couple of blank-faced rookies onto a corner in the area, and they try their best to mind their own business. But mostly NYPD stays out of here.

Gary and his hulking new partner are in the unmarked van on their way to dinner at Mr. W's, on Flatlands Avenue in Canarsie. Gary looks at the lawless area and licks his lips, but he has to stay away. This is off-project.

Just then, Logan pulls the van to a slow stop. "I think I just saw two guys with guns," he says.

Sure enough, just forty feet behind the van is an amazing sight. In a scene from the dusty streets of frontier towns 120 years ago, two armed men stand in the street ten feet apart, staring into each other's eyes. The ruby sun is almost gone for the day, but it is high noon in East New York. Each man palms his pistol in his right hand, arm straight down at his side. Incredibly, a third man has positioned himself just out of the line of fire; he appears to be a referee. At an even safer distance on the sidewalk are thirty spectators.

Logan backs the van slowly toward the men, but the high-pitched warning tone that sounds when the vehicle is rolling backward draws all eyes toward the two policemen. Gary is first out of the van as one of the men runs north, the other south. Logan is a step slower out of the driver's side. Gary gains on the guy running north. He is almost close enough to grab the fleeing youth when the stocky kid leaps onto a garbage can, steps up on a six-foot spiked wrought-iron fence, turns, and fires a shot. A tongue of orange licks from his gun, but the shot misses as Gary slams against the wall of the building. The shooter leaps down on the far side of the fence and flees along the side of the gutted brick structure. Gary hears two quick shots from behind and to his right as he scrambles to his feet and charges around the outside of the fence through a garbage-heaped lot. When he steps around the corner, the kid is on the other side of a flimsy fence, tugging on a door. The kid sees Gary and throws his gun over the fence, then continues his struggle to open the door.

"Hands up or I'll fucking shoot you." The kid's hands move slowly upward, and he leans wearily, forehead to the wall.

Doctors say an adrenaline rush dilates the pupils for better vision, widens the capillaries for strength, produces galvanic skin responses. "All I know," Gary says, "is that I had never been near that building before, and I knew exactly where to go to catch the kid — exactly." Something else was strange to him. Something new. "If he didn't put his hands up, I was going to shoot him right there. I heard it in my voice. He heard it too."

When the chase began, the guy who fled south also ran to a locked door, at basement level in a building across the street. When he jumped back out on the street, he spotted Logan behind Gary. The man squatted in a combat stance and pointed his weapon at Logan, but did not fire. Logan did, squeezing off two rounds at the guy, who quickly abandoned the shooting posture for some pure perp flight. Logan's shots popped holes in the windshield of a red Toyota abandoned on the dirt beside the building. The perp sailed around the corner and out of sight.

When Jim Priore and a score of backups arrive on the scene, Gary climbs the fence and cuffs up the kid who tried to kill him.

"Why don't you head back over to the hospital and relax?" Priore suggests.

But Gary is adamant. "I'm not going anywhere until they find that gun." As he stands in the chill dusk, he tells a Housing cop at his side, "I was shot at. It's legit, but it's gonna look fugazy if they don't find the evidence. I want that gun."

An Emergency Service Unit truck lurches into the back lot where the chase ended. Then a 73 car with a cage in the back seat arrives, and an NYPD cop unloads a German shepherd named Rambo, who hits the dirt in a full crouch and slithers over the area with his nose an inch from the ground. But the dog can't find the gun. Gary's frown deepens, but he doesn't utter a word. Lights are played off the lot and the search goes on. An hour passes. Then a 10-13 comes over the radio, and the Emergency Service Unit truck rumbles out of the lot to answer the call. In five minutes, the dog's yelp leads the cops to the spot where the vehicle was parked. Embedded in the soft dirt where one of the truck's tires was is a Chinese-made nine-millimeter semiautomatic.

Priore has had enough. Last night the detective squad received a call from a resident on Riverdale who said that someone was hiding in his basement. The squad hustled over and grabbed the guy who had pointed his gun at Logan. Half an hour later, some uniforms arrived to transport the prisoner. They gave him the long ride, and when the man arrived at the PSA he was badly beaten.

At this morning's roll call Priore tells the thirty assembled officers how things will be. "The next time somebody tunes up a perp in cuffs, that guy is going to be headed down to Gold Street in cuffs. Because I am going to write it up for IAB just the way it happened. Everybody got that?"

Priore's promise to tell the Internal Affairs Bureau the truth about the next beating has the troops muttering as they step into the Brownsville air and head to their sector cars. "Who the fuck does Priore think he is?"

But Priore does not care what the cops are saying. "When the squad got over there," he explains, "they had the guy, and he was talking, and all that good stuff. Then these knuckleheads show up and they tune the guy up good, right in front of the detectives. The detectives come to me and want to know what the fuck is going on, and I agree with them. This guy is cuffed and cooperating, and he comes in with a broken ankle. One of the guys who did it is the same guy who is on restricted duty because of a similar incident last week."

The crux of the matter is that the police believe that the criminal justice system is either unable or unwilling to mete out punishment that will deter attacks upon their persons. So they do it themselves. It is difficult to convince a person not to pursue a course of action that he thinks may save his life. J.R.'s words to Gary resonate for the grumbling rank-and-file: "If somebody tries to hurt a cop, he isn't going to the lockup. He is going to Brookdale."

HOMECOMING

arch 6. It is three o'clock in the morning of a moonless wind-lashed night. Sharron is riding on a grim blue and white bus with thick wire covering the windows, over the bridge heading out of Riker's Island. The cop at the wheel has already warned the fifty young men behind him that if they "smoke and act wild," he is going to turn the bus around and head back to the jail. Just as with a blustering elementary school teacher, it is unlikely that he will carry out his threat and redeposit his charges inside. But Sharron is not taking any chances. The last few weeks inside were excruciating for him. Now that he is on the bus, he is not going to allow any stupidity, even uncontrolled good spirits, to set him back.

This one time, Sharron becomes a leader. He stands at his seat and yells, "Chill the fuck out." A moment later he tells the kids on his right and behind him, "No reason to celebrate. We in jail till they let us out at the subway."

When the bus pulls up at the Queensborough stop, the wind is whipping hard enough to rattle the metal bus stop sign outside the Lucky Pizza Restaurant. Wearing the gold jeans and sneakers that Shawanda dropped off two weeks earlier, Sharron is without a coat in the chill. He left his recovered Timberland boots back in the mod, for his boys to wear when they pose for photographs with their girlfriends on visiting days.

Some of the releasees head into the all-night Twin Donut Shop for hamburgers; others, like Sharron, just climb up to the elevated platform to wait for the train that will take them home.

Sharron gets to 830 Saratoga Avenue at 6 A.M., just about the time the Transit detectives showed up at his house in November. It's great to be back, but already he can see problems. John and Shawanda are asleep in his room on his bed. His black jeans and shearling jacket are tossed on a chair in the living room; someone, probably Alleke, has been wearing them. A quick look in his closet tells him that his clothes, the cornerstone of his identity, are in very bad shape. "Dammit," he mutters in the morning shadows.

It takes Sharron two days to work out the logistics of getting John and Shawanda out of his room for a couple of hours and Vanessa in. The young couple make love for the first time. It is quiet and sweet. Vanessa has been a loyal friend as well as a level-headed adviser.

But as they lie on the day bed, it is not long before Sharron starts to worry. Shawanda has another black eye. "Don't be fooled by John's smooth exterior," Sharron tells Vanessa. "He's hardrock." Just days out of Riker's, and Sharron, on probation or not, is already in a situation where he might have to do something that the authorities might not understand well: he may have to get into it with John.

"You be careful, Sharron. I don't want you back in jail. That's their problem," Vanessa says.

"I worry about Shawanda," Sharron muses. "She don't have no drive to do anything for herself. She had all these applications to college, and she doesn't do anything with them. She just wants someone to take care of her. At least Mommy got her GED and is in the training school."

The next day Sharron heads over to Chantal's house with Franklo. The visit is a near disaster. Chantal is full of seductive hugs and wet kisses. But Sharron is stiff and aloof, turns his cheek to her lips. All he wants now is a sweater and the white hooded sweatshirt Shawanda failed to recover. If the two were alone in his mother's apartment on Saratoga, he would not turn down the sexual advances. But here, with Mrs. Redding on the couch in the living room and his friend waiting outside, there is no way he is going to get into it with her. Still, back in Chantal's room, a drop of sweat rolls down his spine and the skin on his chest tingles as she hangs on his neck, nibbling at him, breathing promises in his ear. But through the glossy toss of her hair, he can see cardboard-framed photographs of her with the boyfriend that Shawanda told him about. Sharron wrenches free.

"I ain't down for that. Just get me the turtleneck and the hoody, Chantal."

"Sha, c'mon."

"Tell that shit to him," Sharron snaps, his eyes flicking to the pictures on the wall.

"*Sharron.*" Chantal is angry and insistent, standing in front of the closet, blocking access to the clothes. Sharron is tempted to smack her, but he controls himself.

"What the fuck you *doin'*?" she whines. "There's no boyfriend." Sharron looks at her and scowls, summoning his ice grill.

At last Chantal steps aside and allows him to get to the clothing. "You're lucky he's not here to kick your punk ass," she warns as Sharron walks out the bedroom door with his hoody and his sweater. He freezes in the doorway, then shakes his head, deciding to say nothing in response. He lets the threat slide and heads out the door with the armful of clothes.

The principal is in the front hallway of Thomas Jefferson today, just a few feet from the new Vortex metal detectors, eye to eye with two junior varsity basketball players. Flanking her at the impromptu conference are Mr. Singler, a roly-poly teacher who also coaches the JV basketball team, and Ms. Letteri, the frowning, nitpicking athletic director. The two teachers are hardworking members of the faculty, but they are adversaries in this proceeding. Letteri wants the players kicked off the team for their actions during a showdown game yesterday with the squad from the elite Brooklyn Tech, which is leading their league.

Just one referee showed up to work at the game. The fact that the other referee was not in attendance was not surprising to the Jeff players or their coach. Since the Daryl Sharpe shooting, there has been a rash of cancellations and no-shows for Jeff games.

After a bad call, a sophomore playmaker blew up. He stared menacingly at the referee, then sprinted to the sideline where his gym bag sat. In light of recent incidents at the high school, this was interpreted by the referee and some others as a threat.

"He just wanted to get out of the gym. He was really pissed," the cherubic Singler says, standing up for his player. "He lost his temper."

The other player in trouble was in a short fight near the end of the game. Letteri's report to Beck requests that both players be suspended for the rest of the season. Another principal might listen to the charges and rule that a serious breach of discipline occurred and the miscreants must be punished. What are the junior varsity basketball careers of two kids compared with the image of Thomas Jefferson High School? But Beck listens carefully, with a million other things flying through her mind — a trip to Albany planned for tomorrow, a segment on the *Today* show scheduled to air tomorrow morning, a cover story in *Newsweek* featuring a photo of Tyrone Sinkler's body being carried out the front door of the high school.

"I am going to take your side against my own athletic director," she tells the shuffling boys. "Do you know what that means? It means that if I ever hear of you being in the slightest way disrespectful or troublesome, I will kick your ass personally. It means that you will never play for another team at this high school. Never."

It is the contention of one senior administrator for the board of education that Carol Beck's personal approach is part of the problem at Jefferson, that her family style debilitates young men and women, weakens them in the face of the demands of a world that will not lay a warm hand on their shoulders. That complaint seems far off the mark when you see Beck doing her best to save these two young men, who may be hanging on to school by the thread of the JV basketball team, the way Sharron Corley held on to the thread of the school play.

A moment later she is on the phone, assuring the newsman Gabe Pressman that she will be available to speak on his interview show. "Don't you worry. Call me at home at any hour. I am one of God's children."

Next she takes a seat in her conference room, with Ellen Greaves, her assistant in charge of administration, by her side. There is little indication in Beck's appearance of the kind of person she is; she could be a burned-out teacher of elementary students, a weary secretary counting the last few years before retirement. Today she wears a gold-plated pin showing Sojourner Truth on her lapel. "When it gets rough, I put on Sojourner, so I can remember what the mission was." She is weary, snappish. "I have to get home and get some sleep. I'm getting evil."

Beck is copying and collating copies of the ten-page itinerary for the Albany trip sent by Assemblyman Saul Weprin, a Jefferson alumnus, so the eight students accompanying her will have their own packets. Someone is banging at the side door. There stands a mother and her towering son, who have arrived for a meeting of the Future Engineers Club, a group of some of the most talented kids in the school. The petite mother looks to be of college age; her son has a blue bandanna wrapped around his head, droopy jeans, and a shimmering gold cap on his right front tooth. He looks like a gangster, a street tough. He might be a future engineer.

The faculty member in charge of the meeting has not shown up. Some teachers have assumed that such frills have been suspended during these times of trouble. The mother can't disguise her delight at the apparent cancellation. Like the youthful Gloria Corley, she has things to do, a life to live. She cannot possibly be thirty years old. She makes a move to leave. "I understand. I told him," she says, gesturing at her frowning son, "that the meeting would probably be called off."

But Beck asks the two, along with another parent and student who have arrived, to wait in the library. She will conduct the meeting herself. She makes a disapproving face at the youth's bandanna. "What is that?"

"L.A. style," he whispers.

By eight o'clock, Nick and Yolanda, one of the best girl basketball players in New York City and a B student to boot, are talking about vocabulary as they wait for Beck to drive them home.

"Extemporaneous, what does that mean?"

"I would never use a long word like that," Nick says. "Why not use a lot of short words?" His face lights with an insight. "If you have to do a two-hundred-and-fifty-word essay, you don't want to use one word when you can use a whole lot. I am good with the *the*'s and *who*'s — I can work them good."

It is after nine o'clock when Beck drags out of her office with Nick and Yolanda in tow. On the otherwise clean yellow wall opposite the office and on the window of the vestibule by the side door are chalk letters: E-lo. Beck has left the graffiti there in honor of Ian Moore, LoLife. She nods at the letters and mutters, "Shit."

*

The following afternoon, Sharon King boards the IRT for the hour-long trip to the Bronx to visit Khalil Sumpter in Spofford. She sits alone as the #4 flies out of Brooklyn and races under the East Side of Manhattan, beneath the Harlem River, and up to the Bronx. It is another disappointing March day in a moody spring. She hustles up the walk to the front door of the Spofford Juvenile Center. The outside walls are as white as bone, stained in places by streaks of rust from the roof gutters. The building brings back memories for King. When she was fifteen, she was kicked out of her home for insubordination. When her mother couldn't locate her after a month, she filed a PINS, shorthand for person in need of supervision. When Sharon was found, she was detained in this very facility for a week.

In the visiting room there are two long rows of chairs facing each other. The adolescent prisoners sit on one side and the visitors on the other. King peers up and down the rows, but she cannot make Khalil out. Nothing but a column of gray-clad manchildren facing a long line of girlfriends and mothers. An arm reaches out from the far end of the line of chairs and beckons. It is Mrs. Sumpter. King stops in her tracks. She has wondered what she will say and do at this moment. Her anger at Khalil for his stupidity, his murderous shortsightedness, gives way, and she hurries toward the mother and son.

Khalil's mother is given to tough talk and quick tears. "What are we gonna do? What are we gonna do?" she asked King earlier on the phone.

"Ms. King," she says now, standing to face the teacher. "Oh, thank you. I'm glad you could come." Khalil rises and steps forward shyly. The three wrap their arms around each other. King and Mrs. Sumpter sob softly. Khalil squeezes them tight, glancing about the room over their heads. Then he buries his head between their faces and cries along with them. The three stand huddled until a guard pries them gently apart. Khalil sits down quickly, eyes lowered to the floor.

"What do people think of me?" Khalil whispers as King takes a seat beside his mother.

"They think you're an animal," King answers, with a sidelong glance at Mrs. Sumpter.

Khalil thinks for a few moments. "I saw you on TV," he says, referring to the news pieces on the Moore funeral. Somehow, he shares the sadness of it all. But his reaction to the deaths of his schoolmates is like that of a distant relative or a close neighbor, not the murderer himself.

"What do *you* think of me?" he asks King.

"You know what I think. I'm here." She leans forward and touches the back of her hand gently to his cheek.

"Why you dress all *Soul Train*?" Khalil asks. King is wearing black ankle-high boots with heels and sleek black slacks with a cropped jacket.

"That's the style, Khalil."

In a short time the visit is over. One of the male guards whispers a comment about King as she exits. Khalil glowers. "Don't be sayin' shit about my aunt, hear that?" he warns.

"Khalil is hard-headed," King tells her class a few days later. "William Kunstler is going to be his lawyer. Khalil won't stop insisting that he just did what he had to do."

On Sunday, Vanessa's mother allows Sharron to spend the night on the living room couch. The next morning he heads off to Satellite. He has heard through Frank that the academy is ready to take him back for the semester that starts in March. Neil, his counselor, is said to be waiting for his return.

Satellite is set up for students like Sharron. The rapid credit system allows them to make the most of the time they spend in school, with the understanding that personal problems may draw them away. A New York City high school student needs forty credits to graduate. Sharron has twenty-two, after four years. The four credits that he was taking in the fall were lost when he got locked up. Now, even if he passes all his courses in the spring, he will need to take a course in summer school to have enough credits to qualify as a senior. It is tough going. If he is not careful and lucky, it won't be long before he is just another coarsened man with dreams as shapeless as clouds of sewer steam lit by neon, a strong young man at the beginning of his life and the end of his promise, with no skills but how to use a burner and a banger, how to "get paid" without working, how to hurt someone without losing sleep.

He signs up for six courses. The science mini-course about the human brain meets in the morning, right after his strat, or counseling session, for which there is no credit. Next is a class called "Novels." Neil conducts the fourth-period human science class; the topic for this marking period is the ever-popular human reproduction. In the afternoon, Sharron has a course on ideas, followed by an African American history class. He wraps up his day with a writing course. All the units are conducted in classes with no more than fifteen students. Sharron is happy to be back, glad his life is not grist for the gossip mill over at Jeff, which he now calls a "rumor school."

SPRING AND SUMMER

"I CAN'T WALK"

t is drizzling. Gary is waiting in his gray Grand Fury around
the corner from the PSA, nibbling on sunflower seeds, which
he coaxes from the plastic package just a few at a time. The
light rain picks up as Michael T. happens past.

"Yo, Michael T.," Gary says.

Michael, who goes by the street name of Miz, looks over his
shoulder with exaggerated irritation. "I told you, man, don't be
callin' me by my government name." He stands staring at Gary
for a moment. "That your car?" He gestures across the street at
the beat-up old Dodge.

Gary nods.

"What a piece of shit," Michael T. scoffs. "I bet that car
wouldn't even make it down South."

Greg Harris, the tall, good-looking boy who helped break up
Ms. King's classroom confrontation with Khalil, wanders up.

"Watch out for this jake," Michael tells him, nodding at Gary.
"He's smooth. Slide up on your ass."

Gary laughs.

"Hey, lemme sit in there." Michael nods at the empty front
seat of the police car. "It's rainin' an' shit."

Gary starts to move some papers and a clipboard off the passenger seat to make room for the kid. Over the past few months,
he and Michael T. have developed a curious relationship, waving tentatively at each other on empty streets, teasing each
other. Anytime a kid in the neighborhood, especially one as
close to the action as Michael T., is in a talkative mood, Gary
is ready to chat. Tiny pieces of seemingly useless information

are valuable as lubricants in conversations with those who have real stories to tell.

"Nah," Michael decides. "People see me, think I'm talkin' to you."

Hanging out with Michael T., Gary thinks, and chuckles as the big kid moves off.

Sharon King has a gaggle of girls in her after-school guidance cubicle on the first floor. She dominates the conversation with a mixture of shock talk about her personal life and keen analysis of the four girls.

"What's with your hair, Tanaya?" she exclaims to a large, awkward girl who stands in the doorway. "Get it done. I'll pay for it. Please, get it done." The four girls inside eye Tanaya's botched coiffeur and nod.

King turns her attention to a girl slumped on an office chair in the corner. "Roxanne is angry. She isn't a dizball. She is messing up her life on purpose, because she's mad at her mother."

Roxanne, a pretty sophomore with the classic Brooklyn look — baggy jeans, large earrings, and T-shirt — is as cool as the spring rain that's been falling for a week. She nods in agreement with King's assessment, but adds, "I don't like school. I'm a hangout girl."

"How did you fail gym?" King wants to know.

"Gym is for white girls. I get so bored sometimes, I just want to fall asleep."

King decides to place a call on a speakerphone to Milton Lowers, who was shot, along with his friend Rodney James, a week ago. They made the mistake of visiting the Linden Houses. As they left 570 Stanley Avenue with a girlfriend, they were followed and shot by a young man named Randolph, an acquaintance of Sinkler and Moore's. Randolph knows Lowers to be a friend of Dupree's, and Dupree is known as Khalil's man. That is all it took — the wrong friend, the wrong project. Lowers was hit in the left thigh, his femur shattered; James received one bullet in the stomach. A dozen more .45 shells blasted the trunk and back window of a faded green Cadillac that sat by the curb. James will recover fully. Lowers will wear a brace on his leg for a long time, maybe forever. At Jefferson, attention is paid to shooting victims the way it used to be lavished on classmates who had the measles or were getting ready to move to another town.

"You want us to bring you something?" King asks over the phone.

"No," Lowers answers.

The girls speak up. "You don't want anything?"

Lowers mumbles something.

"What? What did you say?" Tanaya raises her voice from the doorway.

"I think he said skins," Roxanne replies. "Is that what you said, Milton?"

This time the word is clear: "Skins." Followed by a nervous laugh.

"You want me to come and give you some skins?" Roxanne teases.

"Yeah." There is a flutter to Lowers's voice; he is embarrassed.

"You want me to come and give you some *infected* skins?" The girls howl at Roxanne's joke.

"When you comin' back to school?"

"I ain't comin' back."

"Why? You scared?"

"I can't walk," Lowers blurts.

Roxanne leans to the speakerphone and asks a question that lands like a blunt instrument. "You *ever* gonna be able to walk?"

There is no answer on the other end of the phone. A frowning King takes over, promises a visit, and says goodbye with a kiss. Each girl kisses the air once for Milton Lowers, who sits alone in an apartment with a flickering television, waiting for his mother to come home from work, wondering if he will walk again.

After the students have left, King talks to one of the guidance counselors. "What would I have done differently with Khalil Sumpter? If I had the money, or the situation was right, I would've turned him on to a strong black male in the school, who could take him under his wing. Humans are the most valuable resource there is. Somebody who could have showed him that there are other ways of dealing with pressure."

King insists that Khalil is no sociopath. "If I believed he was crazy, I'd throw the whole thing out now. It isn't them that are far-fetched and outrageous, it is their environment. Look what they grow up with. These kids like Khalil are good Americans. They want something, they figure out a strategy to get it. They take risks, just like they were taught to do. I just wish I was there when Khalil came in. I'd have stepped in and I wouldn't have moved out of the way. I told Khalil that, and he just shook his head, but I pressed him. 'What would you do, shoot right through me?' And then after a while he had to admit that he would not have shot me. He's not crazy."

Two Housing detectives, Gerry Fitzpatrick and his partner, Artie Norman, are following leads in the Lowers-James shooting. Tall and fair-haired, Fitzpatrick looks like a young college basketball coach. Today he wears a purple-and-black-striped sweater under his blazer. Norman's eyeglasses are tinted a sinister yellow; he looks like a bookie. The detectives are looking for a guy named Bibo, a six-foot-seven Linden local with large eyes. The word is that he is a witness to the shooting. The detectives head straight to Apartment 8D in 570 Stanley. The apartment belongs to Charles, a forty-year-old man who looks as if he is seventy.

"Charles just gave up," Fitzpatrick says. "He lets the homeboys use his place to deal drugs and have gangbangs, and he lets us in too."

Inside the dark, filthy apartment sits Mark, a fresh-faced fifteen-year-old with skin as smooth as golden glass.

"What's goin' on?" Norman wants to know.

"Nothin'," Mark returns flatly.

"Where's Charles?"

"He went out."

"Where?" Norman presses as Fitzpatrick heads into the back room.

"He went to the second floor," Mark answers, his eyes following Fitzpatrick, "and then he said he was gonna go to the store and then he was comin' back."

"Who's he visitin' on the second floor?"

"I don't know." Mark shrugs.

"What are you doin' up here?"

"Just come up to talk to Charles."

"It doesn't look like Charles does much talkin'," the detective comments, removing his glasses and rubbing the bridge of his nose.

"He talks."

"What do you do up here?"

"I watch TV."

"There is a TV on in the bedroom. Why is that?"

"Charles leaves it on."

Norman is looking for some contradiction to crystallize the absurdity of Charles's apartment, to reveal the implausibility of Mark's story. To him, it is obvious that no clean-cut fifteen-year-old boy spends his days and nights in a dank hole with a man wasting away from crack addiction, just a few feet from a pair of blood-stained pants that belonged to another young man, who was murdered in the apartment a few weeks before. Mark's story is absurd, but Arnie Norman is not succeeding in making it seem funny.

"You seen that guy we're looking for?"

"Bibo?" Mark questions.

"Yeah. I thought you said you didn't know him."

"I don't."

"Then how's you remember his name like that?"

"Easy. Bibo, bimbo. It's not hard," the young man reasons.

"Where do you go to school?"

"I go to Linden Prep for my GED downstairs."

GEDs are designed for people who dropped out of school and want to return. They are not supposed to replace the socialization process that school is meant to provide. Mark's socialization is now being taken care of in Apartment 8D.

When Charles comes back, Fitzpatrick takes him into the bedroom for a talk. Charles is emaciated; his eyes are wide with permanent surprise. His face appears frozen in the moment after a bad decision. He weighs 120 pounds. He will soon be evicted. He will soon be dead.

When Fitzpatrick and Charles return to the living room, Fitzpatrick's light touch inspires some biography from Mark. "Charles used to hang around with my father. My father's dead now. He died of HIV in '89. He gave it to my mother. She died in January. I live with my older sister." Mark has not moved an inch. His glance slides sideways and he flashes eye signals to Clarence when he thinks the detectives are not looking.

Finally, the cops realize they are not going to get the answers they are looking for today. "We'll be back, Charles," Fitzpatrick promises. "I want you to get a little more into the housework. Be careful, Mark."

"Clean-cut lookin' kid," Norman explains on the elevator, "but he's dealin'. Every time we go up there, he's inside. Would you hang out in there?"

The detectives want Bibo badly. They continue their search for hours, cruising around the Linden Houses, looking for his car. "These guys do this revenge shit not because they liked the guy who was shot, or even to protect the honor of the neighborhood. They do it because they feel like it. It's the new thing. It gives them a rush and it helps build them a reputation," Fitzpatrick remarks to his partner, who shakes his head.

They drive around and around the block, looking, checking cars, ignoring the hard stares of the young men who stand in bunches on the street corners. The officers are disliked; years of sneering guys in blue coats have guaranteed that. But the hostility is laced with some confusion. These cops are not here to stop theft from a commercial area; there is no business here to speak of, just a few understocked gunsmoke bodegas. They are not on a mission to head off an insurrection — not yet, anyway. They are sent by the city to stop the residents here from killing each other.

Fitzpatrick and Norman have no luck on this case. But a few weeks later the detectives find the alleged shooter himself, Randolph, hiding on Riker's Island. He turned himself in on an old warrant because he knew the police were looking for him in the double shooting. He is charged with gunning down Lowers and James.

"I AM THE VILLE"

There is only half a day of school today, so Frank and Sharron head back to the Ville. Frank convinces Sharron to accompany him to the cleaners while he picks up a sweater. On the way, the two decide to visit Terrance, the third of the Brownsville musketeers, who is back in Brooklyn for a visit. Terrance, a droopy-eyed LoLife, was a big part of Frank and Sharron's lives until his mother sent him to Dallas to get him away from the troubles in Brooklyn. But he found similar trouble in Texas. He heard it was worse in Houston. It is the same all over — south central Los Angeles, Detroit, Roxbury in Boston. God help a black teen in Washington, D.C., or Miami, East St. Louis, or Milwaukee. What about Flint, Michigan, or Charleston?

For families like Sharron's, there is no getting away from Brownsville unless you get rich. You could even get a little money and not escape the danger. Scratch up a down payment on a house in Canarsie or in Queens and some racist cracker might throw a Molotov cocktail in your front window. Try to live in Island Park and Al D'Amato might show up with a bulldozer.

Sharron has not seen Terrance, or Tee, since he got back, and their reunion is heartfelt.

"Yo, money, wha's up?" Sharron gushes.

"Back in the *Ville* ready to *ill*," Tee rhymes. He steps forward and stoops slightly as he and Sharron hug like brothers. Sharron holds tight, squeezes Tee for a full twenty seconds, while Frank looks on. The moment is almost perfect.

As he embraces his friend, Sharron holds back a small, painful thought. While he was in Four Main on Riker's, during one of the endless sessions in the cell corridor when the young rogues told their fantastic stories, Terrance's name came up, and Frank's. Terrance had a more extensive citywide reputation than either Frank or Sharron. But there was another side to all that. The story that someone told that night in Riker's was about how Terrance had bragged that he had gone to Sharron's house once a year earlier, when Sharron was not home, and taken two sweaters. The sweaters were described accurately. The story was not the product of somebody's imagination, not just a mean-spirited attempt to break up friends. Sharron didn't want to hear it, but it was too late. The words yanked something away forever. Just now, Sharron feels the loss again. He doesn't say anything, but the fullness of the reunion is gutted.

Sharron and Terrance and Frank, acting like everything is just the way it always was, head over to pick up Terrance's LoWife, Dada. With her in tow, the three friends walk over to the cleaners to retrieve Frank's sweater. To get there they cut through the Marcus Garvey Houses, where a contingent of LoLifes lives. Beside a bench at the foot of the main building stand Stevelo, Skilo (who was in Riker's with Sharron), Ronlo, Beklo, and another kid, who is unfamiliar to Sharron and his friends. The spot where the boys stand, backed by the stone geometry of the building, evokes a stage in ancient Greece; so does the dramatic tension, and the ritual.

Sharron approaches first and gives a chest-level high five to all except the kid he does not know.

Then Frank says "What's up" to Ronlo and Stevelo. When he gets to Beklo, Beklo smiles and tosses his head to indicate that he is disinclined to slap hands.

Skilo follows up the slight and starts woofing. He snickers to Beklo, "So what. Fuck the kid. Fuck a Frank. You ain't got to say nothin' to that nigger."

When he and his boys approached the group, Sharron noticed that Skilo and Beklo were playing in a similar manner with each other, exchanging mock disrespect. Now he studies their faces, looking for a sign that this is more such play. It is hard to tell. Sharron decides it is a joke. Frank is not so sure.

"Ain't I good for a five?" he wants to know.

Beklo sits tight, inscrutable. It is a test of nerves, one of a thousand little contests that are won or lost in a day in Brownsville.

Frank does not want to overreact. "I don't need you to be my man, son," he says.

"Son," a complex appellation, is used by the kids at different times for endearment or disrespect. Frank uses it as a subtle diminution of Beklo. The term also calls into the mix a reminder that few of these kids have fathers who stayed around long after they were born.

The air is getting hot, so Sharron steps up and slaps some more fives around. "We out," he says.

Frank backs off across the street, muttering to himself, while Tee, oblivious, is off to the side, holding a conversation with Stevelo about Texas. Sharron moves away with Frank, as a gesture of solidarity, and flashes a sign to Tee that he is going. Tee and Dada start across the plaza toward Frank and Sharron. In the stylized, courtly manner of the Ville, Tee nods to each of the seated LoLifes, offering a "chill" with each movement of his head. The group nods back, except for Beklo, who whispers a dreamy, "Bye, Dada," and turns his head away. Tee, unaware of the previous friction, misses the tone, the move, the dis. He has already pivoted and is heading blithely out of the plaza. But Sharron and Frank see the gesture clearly, and they burn. Frank is now sure that he did not overreact, and Sharron is alerted to the possibility that he was just a shade too conciliatory.

Frank talks to himself as the foursome head around the corner to the cleaners. "Bek is the last motherfucker to be playin' me like that."

It is all information stored for later. Small tests, smaller slights that indicate power shifts, the dreaded devaluation of one's reputation from respect to disdain — it can happen in a minute, and it can ruin everything. There is not much to look forward to in the narrow world of a Brownsville teenager, but to live the life of a punk, with guys laughing at you, making open plays for your woman, or disrespecting your family, is a world of hell. Even though the loss of reputation might only last for a year or two in real time, until the peer group is dispersed by jail sentences, shootings, and relocation, Sharron and his friends truly believe it is a kind of death.

*

Gary has already had a few beers. "Get yourself a pitcher," he advises a late arrival. "The food is in the back room. They got everything. And don't lose your raffle ticket, you fuckin' ball-bag." This is a 10-13 party, held by the Housing police as a benefit to raise money for the medical bills of Charlie Devine, a well-liked officer at PSA 2. Devine used to have a thick brown mustache. Now he has cancer.

The party is held at the Castle Casino in the Bronx. The name is a double flight of fancy. The place is no casino and certainly no castle. It is a hall somewhere near the foot of the Throgs Neck Bridge. The PSA 2 cops would never even think of having their party in Brownsville. There are several hundred Housing officers from all over the city here. As you look around the room, you can spot old and new faces. Platt has brought some Fire Department buddies from his Marine Corps days. Schulman is in the middle of the room in cowboy boots, trim black jeans, and a tailored shirt, sober as a judge. But Maritza, the impatient proprietor of the bodega across the street from the PSA, is already drinking hard, waiting for the music to start. Lenti is here. He can be trusted. He's getting drunk. Kammerdener, in a sharper, crisper blue suit, is on duty. He doesn't drink and leaves halfway through the affair, with a plastic smile. The word is that the K-Master will be a "full bird" (inspector) within the week. There are just half a dozen policewomen on hand, the same number of black officers. Lonnie Hayes is not in the house.

J.R. stands off to the side, smirking, talking to Sergeant Bright. J.R. has been a detective for only a few months, but he looks as if he were born to dress like one. "It's the suits. The perps see the suits and they just put out their hands to be cuffed. They don't think about fightin'. Not a day goes by where I don't miss the Ville," he admits. "In the Bronx and Queens, compared to Brownsville, the perps are soft. I mean, in the Ville you got stone-cold perps, guys whose sole purpose in life is to be perps."

There are pitchers of beer aplenty. Devine mixes in the crowd, the picture of good cheer in a gray wool suit and wrinkled white shirt. The Housing police bagpipe contingent stands by in kilts and black shirts. There are about fifteen of them, including Tilly and Finn, and one woman from another PSA.

"About ten-thirty we'll do our thing," Tilly assures Gary.

Eddie Hammil floats past, a glint in his eye that says he is determined to have a good time.

"Hey," Gary lofts in his direction. "I thought you were on Fire Island. I thought you went with Paddy." Paddy Gleason appears and scuttles toward Lemite.

"Yeah, we did go and we came back and lemme tell you why. Listen to this," Gleason chortles. "We meet two girls. One of them is all over me like I can't believe."

"Yeah, tell us how chicks dig you," Hammil scoffs.

Gleason is determined to finish his tale. Lemite leans in to catch the words. "It's only four o'clock on a Friday afternoon. I can't believe how hot she is. But her friend doesn't like Hammil. We go back to the house. There are like five girls in the place. They share it for a season. I'm in the living room and the chick is sittin' on my lap, and the other one goes upstairs and her two friends are like goin' in and out. Then this other roommate comes in and asks like, 'Where is everybody?' Hammil is sittin' there and he says, 'Your friend Carol is upstairs in the bathroom. Linda went out five minutes ago, and the blonde, I think her name was Darlene, left with a guy about six feet with black hair.' All of a sudden the chick on my lap looks up at Hammil and says, 'What, are you a cop?' Then she looks at me and 'What, are you *both* cops?' That was it. They musta had marijuana or somethin' an' everybody was whisperin' an' shit. Ruined the weekend, ruined every fuckin' thing. We left."

Hammil heads off through the crowd, Gleason dogging his footsteps, the tale of the lost weekend at the ready.

A three-year veteran cop named Magee walks up to Gary. The live band at the rear of the hall has just started to wail a Beach Boys song, "Surfin' Safari." Magee raises his voice and explains his way of looking at things. "I know there are a lot of assholes on this job. They come on with some kind of a problem. Not me. I came on when I was twenty-eight years old. I knew who I was." Gary listens and nods vigorously. It was the same with him.

"If somebody is going to threaten my safety," Magee says with a shrug, a plastic glass in one hand and a pitcher of dark beer in the other, "then I will react. I have to react. If somebody calls me a white motherfucker, I think to myself, 'O.K. I am going home to my nice apartment and my nice neighborhood,

357

where the worst possible thing that could ever happen is an argument over a parking space,' and I keep on walking. I have no problem. But sometimes they keep it up. They call you a pussy, and you get the feeling that they really believe you are a pussy." Magee reflects for a moment, watching Maritza, who dances slinkily nearby. He is thinking, trying to reconcile what he said before with what he is about to say. "They call you a pussy and sometimes you have to react, because nobody can survive being called a pussy."

Gary dips his glass into a passing pitcher of beer and toasts Devine. In January 1991, when Devine was diagnosed with lymphatic cancer, his life became a litany of treatments. But at one time he was the PCO in the Brownsville Houses. Once he pursued Randolph Worthy up the stairs and stumbled into the apartment at 5AB. Devine, an ex-Marine, doesn't enjoy speaking about the incident. In any group, there are those who dramatize and those who don't. The two types need each other. The storytellers, such as J. R. and Priore, don't make things up. They have seen so much, they don't have to. But they need guys like Devine to chasten their reenactments, just as the Devines need the storytellers to make things live again.

"It wasn't anything." Devine struggles more with the notoriety of the event than with the facts. "As I remember, I was chasing the kid, one of the young ones. We tumbled into the apartment and we were like struggling in the dark. It was a dance. That's what I always say. I was dancing in the Worthys' apartment. It was only for a minute. I wasn't attacked by anybody. Everybody was screaming. And then the troops showed up. That was about it."

When the pipers march single file to the center of the hall and issue forth their din, conversations about guns and women die out. The primitive clamor of the bagpipes and the sight of the kilts send shudders through the room. At first Gary is not impressed by the sound, as the spellbound Irishmen around him are. "I heard they don't wear drawers under those kilts. I wonder about the broad," he whispers soggily, before he too succumbs to the spectacle.

The pipes screech and howl to the ceiling and to the four walls, a relentless din, too energetic for a wail, too high-pitched for a dirge, a fantastical knell issuing forth in great spasms. The kilted cops circle in the center of the room, forming an ellipse, like a ring of Saturn. Instinct or custom draws Devine into the center of the group, where he stands with a huge furry black hat on his bald head. In his right hand he holds a dark wooden staff with a gold tip, which he bangs in ceremonial cadence on the linoleum floor. The pipe noises leap over each other like hounds on the chase. Devine pounds the floor harder and harder. The moment is steeped in measures of ancient courage and fear. The leader of the pipes, a stout Irishman, lifts the black furry cap from Devine's head, revealing the symbol of the officer's illness. He rubs the head for good luck and replaces the ceremonial hat. Then the pipers turn and file from the room.

Around the room, the troops are getting drunk, but there is not a fall-down guy in the crowd. Detective Eddie Davison, Gita Malave's favorite cop because he caught the guy who robbed her on the staircase, is very drunk. All the kids in Brownsville know him. "He never changes his clothes. He sleeps in his car," they say. "Don't let Davison get you."

"I am the Ville," the sagging Davison proclaims with reverence.

How could a white man claim to be the embodiment of Brownsville? How could he presume to represent anything but a restraining order against the lives of the people there?

"Because I love it. I love it," he says again. "The people know it. They know there are two Davisons. I got people off drugs. If somebody is right, I treat 'em right, and if they aren't, they deal with Dave. Ask around. I *know*. I go out, and I find out." Alone in the crowd and slush-eyed drunk, he is talking more about the people of Brownsville, their courage, their identity, than he is about himself. "You ask Born Son. You ask any of them. I am the Ville."

Hammil is handing out last drinks from his pitcher with the warning "I just stuck my dick in this." Nobody turns down his offer.

The party is over. No brawls. "What a nice bunch of young men," the tiny red-haired old woman in the coatroom says softly.

Spirits are soaring as the crowd spills out into the chilly spring night. There is the distinctive sound of a pistol shot, then another. Heads turn; trained eyes scan for an image from

Brownsville, black kids running. But there are no perps down the street where the shots came from, just several cops standing by a car, laughing.

Another Saturday evening. Vanessa and Sharron tramp over to the Kentucky Fried Chicken place on Belmont Avenue. The meal is to be Vanessa's treat. The little money that Sharron does have is at his apartment. He is spending a lot of time at Vanessa's house, keeping out of the Shawanda and John mess and staying off the block.

Apparently, there is something about having Vanessa control the purse strings that bothers Sharron. When the order is placed on the counter, he strides over to a booth and sits down.

"I'm payin' for the stuff," Vanessa says, raising her voice. "Least you can do is help carry it." Sharron does not budge. When Vanessa takes the food over, he will not eat.

"Pride. You can spell that with a capital P," Vanessa says. "So stupid."

By the time the two reach Vanessa's house, Sharron has returned the $95 gold neck chain Vanessa gave him.

That night, he goes back to her place to continue the argument. Vanessa produces the photo album they have started, the teddy bear, and the sweatshirt; she insists that they return the gifts they have given each other. "But the necklace is different," she says. "I want you to keep the chain." She extends her hand, the gold rope dangling. Sharron steadfastly refuses to accept.

"I want you to have it. It was a gift. Jewelry is different." The argument continues out in front of Vanessa's building. Sharron stands on the sidewalk, his arms full of tokens of his affection, Vanessa on the middle step of the entrance, fingering the graceful necklace. "Take it." She extends the piece yet again, her voice as soft as a kiss.

But Vanessa's mother has been listening from the front window. She shouts, "He does not want the chain. Why are you trying to make him take it?" Vanessa's mother did not want her usually level-headed daughter to buy the chain for Sharron in the first place. He was a nice boy, but buying gifts for him was a bad precedent, she believed, and the thing did cost $95. Now Vanessa has it back and wants to give it away again?

"I'm sorry I raised a fool. Will you let that boy leave with his things? And you keep what belongs to you. You are making me sick. You *idiot*."

"Stop!" Sharron yells at her.

"Who are you speaking to, young man? If you know what's good for your skinny behind, you'll head on down the road."

Vanessa explodes in tears. The delicate coalition between boyfriend and mother, so crucial to her happiness, has been blasted to bits. But the clash between Sharron and her mother draws her back to Sharron almost immediately. The very next day, they are cooing on the phone, estimating how long it should be before Sharron reappears. But matters get worse.

Vanessa's mother is a churchwoman. She does not force religion on her children, but the Baptist church has done wonders for her, helped her through the breakup with her hyperentrepreneurial Caribbean husband, through the raising of her three kids with the knowledge that their father was raising another family under more comfortable circumstances in East Flatbush. Her only son is a loss, God help him and those who trust him. But Vanessa is pure promise.

Vanessa has been complaining about excessively painful cramps during her period. Her mother has tried everything — painkillers, home remedies, soothing words; still Vanessa cries for the better part of a day every month. Something has to be done about it. What is the city employee health plan worth if you do not use it? So on a Tuesday, mother and daughter head downtown and sit next to each other facing a doctor.

"Are you having sex?" the physician asks early on, pencil at the ready.

Vanessa is trapped but self-possessed. "Yes," she answers bravely. The word does not sound so bad, she decides.

The news does not have a negative effect on the doctor, who crisply checks a box and looks up. But Vanessa's mother's head snaps toward her daughter. She moans, then leaps to her feet and flees from the room.

"I'm very sorry," the doctor sputters.

Mother and daughter do not speak for a month; they communicate via notes on the refrigerator. Sharron remains banished. Vanessa insists on the right to visit him at his home. But he remains persona non grata at her house for the next six weeks.

*

The students of Thomas Jefferson High School are having a ball. In satin gowns of white and ivory, the girls face a line of boys in tuxedos. The music commences. A pudgy, splay-footed boy at the end of the line embarks alone across the sixty feet of floor with a pained expression and a curious mincing gait. This step is something he has practiced for a long time, but perhaps not long enough. Left, right, hitch, shuffle, step, right, left. Parents and teachers seated at tables around the dance floor watch the performance with suspended breath. The boy's fearless aunt records the feat with a video camera; his mother grips the tablecloth. Like a tightrope walker on his way over Niagara Falls, he is halfway there, almost across, then . . . home. The clumsy boy, transformed by his accomplishment, bows rakishly to his waiting partner, gathers her in his arms to a burst of applause, and fairly sweeps across the floor to the exuberant music. The next boy follows, and the next. Soon the dance floor is filled with gliding, twirling couples.

This is not a school dance; this is Carol Beck's "cotillion." The lobby of the fancy hall in downtown Brooklyn where the event is held is decorated with gilded mirrors and a great glittering chandelier, according to Beck's "channel changer" philosophy. She does not want to hear about basketball and rap music. She wants gymnastic teams and waltzes.

"I'm not going," Nick grumbled earlier in the week. "Thirty-five dollars, for what? There ain't no pretty girls gonna be there." But there are plenty of pretty girls for this Saturday evening affair. They flutter back and forth from their parents to their friends, flouncing by the mumbling boys. Mostly they just smile. Later in the evening, each participating student bows to his or her mother or guardian in appreciation of the support and love he or she has received. The mothers, many very young, and the grandmothers beam with pride. The evening is the height of videotaped gentility. And of course Beck has invited the press. A magazine photographer trails her around the room.

But Bashim and Michael T. are not here. Neither are Sharron, Sheryl, or any of the basketball players. Nearly every one of the thirty-five students at the cotillion is of Caribbean descent, a first-generation American. The road to this kind of optimistic aspiration at Thomas Jefferson, it seems, does not run through North and South Carolina. Teenagers from those places are the most disillusioned. Or are they just forewarned? They already know about Jim Crow and de facto segregation. There is not one white child among the eighteen hundred students at Jefferson. In Brownsville, blacks don't drop out of school at appreciably higher rates than other urban ethnic groups, but they sense there is not much of an opening at the end of the academic pipeline. So, according to laws of physics that anyone can understand, they back up, collect at the source, and stagnate.

The same reluctance is evident when it comes to taking just any job. Unlike many of the Caribbean students, young men like Sharron do not see menial work as a beginning; they see it for the miserable trap it was for their ancestors. Once, as Sharron walked by a young East Indian man pumping gas in a filling station off Atlantic Avenue at midnight, he shook his head. "Times must be hard for that dude," he muttered. "I would never do that."

TWENTY-FOUR SEVEN

A Saturday afternoon in April, and Sharron is in an unusual position, sitting alone in his room looking at an anatomy book, studying for a test. A pool of afternoon sunlight rests on the dusty floor in the hall outside his room. He shuts his door to the beckoning spring day and lies back on his bed, holding the science book aloft. "Ovary: typically paired essential female reproductive organ that produces eggs in vertebrates."

Produces eggs in vertebrates? Sharron asks himself. *What are "vertebrates"?* He scrutinizes the color diagram of an ovary on the next page and sees no mention of vertebrates there, so he thumbs to the glossary. "Vertebrate," he reads. "Having a spinal column." But the spinal column is part of the skeletal system, he remembers. Damn. He hunches up against the wall and writes "Vertebrates — ovaries?" in his notebook. Then he checks the definition again, walks across the room, avoiding the mirror, and repeats the words to himself.

Music floats through the apartment, and for a moment his concentration wavers. He imagines himself and Frank and Chris onstage. Their group, Public Figure, has been getting together again; Morris has offered more studio space so they can complete their demo tape. "Ovary, female reproductive organ that produces eggs," Sharron says out loud, snapping back to his task. "That's good enough." Then he returns to his bed. "Placenta . . ."

Since his release, Sharron has spent a lot of time with Vanessa. The last several Saturday afternoons, they traveled to the Brooklyn Public Library on Eastern Parkway to study, but today he is punishing her, not answering her calls on the beeper, because she got drunk on Wednesday and smoked a cigarette. He is convinced the whole thing was really Shawanda's fault. She's the one who bought the beer. Vanessa drank one forty-ounce, then part of another. She was fine until she got upstairs. Then she threw up and passed out. Sharron took off her clothes and cleaned her up. He collected the soiled sheets and soaked them. But he was not happy about it. Sharron does not like women who drink.

Another five pages of studying, he decides, and he will go downstairs to call Vanessa back. But a loud knocking comes at the front door and he raises himself. A neighborhood kid named Fonzo stands outside, breathing hard.

"Dude be smackin' shit out Shawanda. Beat her down." As Sharron races out the door, Fonzo adds softly, "Think it's her boyfriend, Sha."

Right there by the garbage cans, a few feet from the parked cars, John is standing next to Shawanda, who is holding her hand over her right cheek and weeping. A crowd of neighborhood onlookers stands in a semicircle at a respectful distance.

"Shit's gonna stop," Sharron says.

John wheels. His forehead is wet; his eyes are filled with menace. "Or what?" he wants to know.

Sharron feigns amusement. "Or what? Or what?" He chuckles. This is a man who is sleeping in his bed while he spends nights on the couch. He could have made a big deal out of it when he got home from Riker's. He could have insisted that Shawanda and John be out by the time he got home. His mother would have taken his side. Gloria always puts him first. But Sharron did not say a word, stayed cool, let the situation slide, and now this security guard was fronting for the people in the neighborhood.

Two youngbloods, Dee Whiz and Fitty-Sen, stand in the street studying Sharron. They have been watching him for years. They know all about his Polo signature, the LoLifes, his girlfriends, and his recent bid in Riker's. They haven't been seeing him in the street much lately, and the one time they did see him, he was carrying a book. Strange. Sharron hasn't fashioned his reputation, his props, for half a decade to let himself be disrespected in front of these people by a girlfriend-beating chump. This is Shawanda's fault, he thinks. This is how people get hurt. This is how people die.

"Whatever. Step to it," he tells John.

John is not a real hardrock. But he's not a punk either. "Whatever," he says. He wheels and heads upstairs.

Dee Whiz and Fitty-Sen assume that Sharron has a burner in his waistband, hidden by the drape of his shirt. But in order to stay out of trouble, Sharron has gotten rid of the gun. He gave it away to a LoLife in East New York a week after he got out of Riker's. Everybody knows that John has an Uzi upstairs. Guns are just like money in the bank. No matter how you dress, your neighbors usually know if you have money. It is the same with a gun. With a machine gun, it is almost impossible for people not to know.

Sharron stands his ground. This is his home. This sidewalk is where he grew up. He delivers an aside to Dee Whiz and Fitty-Sen: "Dude be doin' mad foul deeds. I ain't jumpin' in no jetstream, 'cause he *owns* a oowop. See him get busy with it."

The audience is captured by Sharron's presence as he steps forward and guides Fonzo's gaping six-year-old sister away from the lobby door, out of the line of fire. The fan of spectators opens outward, creating an alley for the bullets. A streetwise driver, spotting the no man's land, slows and stops his car in the street for a moment, then presses the accelerator and drives quickly through. It is the first balmy day of the year. But the soft breeze doesn't mean peace. The pressure goes on day in and day out. Two women walking on the sidewalk feel the tension, spy the crowd of rubberneckers and the young protagonist.

"Not again," one says.

"Twenty-four seven," her friend replies.

Sharron does not fidget or pace. He rubs the back of his hand under his nose, measures a dive and a roll behind a row of garbage cans along the side of the building, and stands his ground. He waits a full five minutes before he walks over to the phone to call Vanessa. John never does come back downstairs.

"Big front," Fitty-Sen scoffs, disappointed there has been no gunplay. Dee Whiz nods. The two teens turn and stroll down Saratoga Avenue.

The fighting continues. A week after the sidewalk beef, Sharron opens up the apartment door in time to see John flatten Shawanda with a right cross on the fourth-floor landing. The truth is, this is how Shawanda relates to John. She makes him as jealous as she can, teases him and plays him to the limit, and then he explodes. Then they make up. Neither Shawanda nor John seems to care what people think.

Sharron ducks back into the apartment, reaches into the pocket of a coat, and brings a box cutter with him into the hallway. John backs into the shadows under the stairs to the fifth floor as Shawanda storms into the apartment. The two young men measure each other in the half-light. Sharron is shorter and lighter than John but quicker with his hands. John may kick his ass here on the marble floor, but he is going to get cut doing it. Hands up, John takes a step back. Sharron does not move forward.

"This mess is over. Are you hearing me, goddammit? Over." Gloria's voice from inside the apartment is shrill with anger. She is finally telling some kind of truth.

Shawanda is not having it. "Fuck all you all! Fuck all you all!" she screams. She throws some belongings into a plastic bag and bolts out of the apartment. John slides out of his corner and the two head out of the building. Sharron can hear John questioning Shawanda as they hurry downstairs.

"What you doin'?"

The following Monday, during the first class of the day for Sharron, strat, he is not there. He is late again. He does not appear for his A-slot class either, the half-credit unit on the brain. The trip from his door on Saratoga Avenue to the #3 train and from there to the Chambers Street stop near the school takes about forty minutes. Sharron shows up at nine-fifty, dressed with care in a white Polo sweatshirt with an American flag design on the front, black-and white pump Reebok sneakers, his favorite gold chain draped outside his sweatshirt, and gold-tinted Polo nonprescription glasses for effect. He carries no book into his B-slot class, which is a course in novels. The teacher does not comment on his tardiness.

The book under discussion is *Lord of the Flies*, William Golding's fable about a group of boys abandoned on an uninhabited tropical island without adult supervision. Things go terribly wrong in the children's society as sanity is overwhelmed by moral anarchy, violence, and death. The surviving children are ultimately rescued by a naval officer in a crisp white uniform.

It seems that many of the students have not read the book.

They are polite but uninspired by the lesson, which begins with students reading aloud from the text. The first excerpt is a dialogue in which one of the boys is trying to talk sense to another. The reading drones on. Sharron is asked to read. At first he demurs, then he doffs his vanity glasses and reads competently to the class.

"What about a time when *you* tried to talk sense to someone?" the teacher interjects. "Have you ever tried to change the course of events through that kind of leadership?"

The question is a good one. The students in this class have been abandoned on their own urban islands, fashioned their own tyranny, perhaps mutely witnessed the death of their fellow children. What measure of responsibility is theirs? There is no immediate response to the question.

The teacher remains unfazed. He rephrases the question. "Did you ever try to save someone from harm?"

Satellite teachers have been selected because of their easy-going ways with the students. There is absolutely no threatening or name-calling by the teachers or students in the Satellite Academy.

"Talk sense to someone? I have no sense," says a large girl with a shock of extensions twisted into her hair. There is a flutter of laughter from the class. Then she changes her tone and tells how she tries desperately to keep her wild younger brother out of trouble. "I see him gettin' into stupid shit, and I ask him why. An' he don't have an answer. It's like he's deaf. He just looks, he just keeps on. I don't want to see him get killed over some little kid shit. But tell you the truth, what I say don't make a difference."

Often the kids in Jefferson and in schools like Satellite Academy are burdened by the responsibility of caring for siblings and even parents. Sometimes, in order to succeed in school and move on to meaningful employment, they have to abandon those responsibilities — in effect, cut their loved ones loose.

Following up on the question, a lanky girl explains, "I don't say nothin' to nobody. I let them do what they want to do. You have to mind your own business around my way."

As the discussion continues, Sharron engages in a tête-à-tête with an Indian girl with long wavy black hair and an asymmetrical face. He springs to attention when the teacher calls his name. He is facile enough to perform several tasks at once.

"I care for my sister much," he begins. He knows what words to say to make him look sympathetic in the video that is running in his mind. "But my words of advice don't have much penetration. It is the same with me. My friends told me, 'Don't hang out. Don't hang out. Don't hang out.' But I used to hang out anyway." Heads nod. It's hard enough to control yourself, the class is saying, without trying to be a leader.

As the students file out, the teacher balances a paperback copy of the novel in his hand and purses his lips. There is no rescue party coming for these kids anytime soon, he may be thinking.

The next slot is the full-credit course on reproduction taught by Sharron's adviser, Neil. A sign over the door outside the classroom reads, "Showing up is ninety percent of life." Neil has the ideal temperament for a teacher. He is seasoned, compassionate, organized, and tough. He is also fascinated by the subjects he teaches. The room is darkened for a masterfully produced educational film that uses microphotography to show the path human sperm take to fertilize an egg. As the film rolls, Sharron is once again in close contact with the raven-haired Indian girl. Seated next to each other at a small desk, their shoulders and legs brush.

A voice-over explains the images that appear on the film. Bouncy traveling music plays as the sperm swim out of the testicles. A heavy drumbeat knells as a swoosh of fluid blasts out of the prostate gland, then there is a crash of symphonic exultation as the sperm are catapulted into the woman's vagina. Sharron straightens up in his seat at the sight; the Indian girl edges a few inches away. There is rapt attention throughout the room as the sperm stampede through the reproductive canal. The class erupts in laughter as the flailing, witless sperm lose their way and one tries to fertilize the first round object it encounters, a regular body cell. "Of the two hundred million sperm," the narrator announces, "only fifty reach the egg."

"The anatomy test is tomorrow," Neil reminds his students as the lights come on and they reach for their books. Later he explains, "Sharron is doing reasonably well — when he is here, which is not all the time. He will probably pass my course with a P, although he is doing the minimum it takes to get by. He is not applying himself." Neil takes out a homework worksheet with questions like "What happens in the placenta? Why is it important?" and "Why is amniotic fluid critical to the fetus's development?" Sharron's responses are perfunctory. He wrote, "It keeps the fetus from drying out."

"True, but there is so much more to it." Neil sighs and shows the papers of more motivated students, who have listed the multiple functions of the amniotic fluid.

Sharron is coming to school most days. He is carrying books. He is far more motivated than he was in the classrooms of Jeff, but he's still not convinced of the absolute necessity of education. Many of the successful African Americans he sees on television have made it without an academic education. The black teachers, lawyers, and judges he has seen represent a compromise of identity and style that is distasteful to him. As tough as things are for him, he likes himself the way he is.

But he has another problem. "There have been a couple of incidents," Neil explains with a rueful shake of his head, "where Sharron got into confrontations when he didn't have to." It seems guys arrived from another school and got into a disagreement with a girl from Satellite. "Sharron was right in front of the school, going face to face with them. Unnecessary. To some degree, he's recreating Brownsville here."

On the last Friday in April, Sharron manages to pass his anatomy test with a 75. Also, an article he has written about his time in Riker's has been published in the school newspaper. Proudly, he carries both documents to Vanessa's house.

Across Brownsville in East New York, Gary is not in nearly as good a mood. He has been looking for a collar all night. Nothing. Now his partner has some paperwork to fill out, so Gary jumps in the sweep van, just like old times.

There are a handful of young men standing outside a doorway in Cypress. "Just roll up on them, I got a feeling," Gary instructs. As the van pulls up, Nephtali steps lightly away, then grabs his side and runs. Gary is out of the vehicle with a bound, and Nephtali runs into the building, with Gary right behind. There is a clatter. Nephtali is under arrest. "He tossed the jammy in the compactor," Gary announces. Sensing trouble, he calls for a boss. Good thing — Nephtali's mother and sister are on hand in seconds, beating their chests. The mother has dark hair; the sister is fair. When the sergeant shows up, he calls for an Emergency Service Unit to come over and take off the lock to the basement door so the gun can be recovered.

"He din' haf no gun," Nephtali's mother whistles through a broken front tooth. "I was walking with him. I don' never walk with 'im if he haf a gun."

"What d'ya do, frisk him when you leave the house?" Galvin quips.

ESU has trouble with the heavy lock to the basement. When it finally pops, they head inside and sift through the compactor. There are a dozen cops on hand now, as a crowd gathers on the sidewalk and the grass beside the ramp down to the basement door. Fifteen minutes. No gun.

The cops upstairs on the steps into the lobby exchange knowing looks. *It's about time Lemite came up wrong,* some of them are thinking. They have been around too many times when the cocksure Lemite wanted to turn left on a pursuit, they wanted to go right, and he turned out to be correct — too many times when his plans and hunches came out just the way he said they would.

The ESU is finished, getting ready to call the whole thing a mistake. "Lock and door probably cost a grand to fix," a Housing cop cracks. But Gary is not finished. He reaches into the compactor with his hands. There is a half-eaten sandwich, an elementary school penmanship assignment on wrinkled composition paper, a birthday card, the stuffing of an old pillow. And there is a goddamn gun.

"Got it," he yells to the doubting officers about to head out the door. On the way back to the van, he winks at Nephtali's mother.

JUDGMENT

I t is ten o'clock on the morning of Thursday, April 30, the day after the first Rodney King verdict. Five OSC officers are lounging in the roll call room downstairs, waiting for the moody Sergeant Toney to arrive and give the assignments. There hasn't been much for Gary to do lately. He's had to lay off DeeSo because his squad has been restricted to the Complex.

"I can't fucking believe it," Gary says to the cop beside him. "I was drivin' home when I heard 'not guilty' on the radio and I was like, 'Holy shit.'" There isn't a trace of anger in his voice, just surprise, as if a benchwarmer had hit a home run to win the World Series. All over the PSA, the troops are talking about the trial in L.A.

"I tell you, the LAPD gets more respect than we do," a stick-figured cop expounds in the hallway just outside the roll call room. "They're a professional police force. Look at their uniforms. They wear black for the fear factor. We wear powder-blue shirts like a fuckin' buncha pussies. What color are our new RMPs? White, so the community won't be 'intimidated.' Don't they know that police work is about intimidation?"

Lonnie Hayes steps out of the weight room, where he has been spending a great deal of time lately. He is wearing a leather girdle over his sweatpants. He eyes the bony shoulders and scowling face of the complaining white man. "You couldn't intimidate nobody if you was wearin' . . ." His voice trails off. The TV room is open behind him. On the screen, south central Los Angeles is burning to a cinder. "Ah, fuck it," Hayes mumbles. "Just shut up, man," he says sweetly, and goes back to heaving plates of iron.

Finally Toney arrives, twirling the corners of his mustache with one hand, holding a clipboard with the other. He positions himself behind the plywood lectern with the blue Police Department crest on the front. Toney has eighteen years on the job. His mother lives in the Complex.

"It's Healy and Lemite in 9602, Omar and Seton in 9510. There's been four robberies around 265 Livonia in the last two weeks, from four in the afternoon till eight at night. Apparently, people are being watched in the check-cashing place on Rockaway and followed into the Complex. The perp is tall and thin, about twenty-five to thirty, and he keeps his hand in his pocket, simulating a gun."

Then Toney lays the clipboard down on the lectern and looks out across the room with an uncharacteristic knit to his brow.

"After L.A., Omar wants to remind Gary that we're not going to be aggressive making arrests today."

Gary flinches but remains silent. He stares straight ahead and fumes. Just weeks ago, he was riding with Omar to deliver some paperwork to another precinct when a gust of wind blew a man's coat open, revealing a gun. "He's probably on the job," Omar said as he stepped on the accelerator. "Besides, we got things to do."

As Gary and Jerry Healy approach the Complex, Gary can't contain his anger. "What's this 'Omar wants Gary to know' shit? He's a cop and I'm a cop. What right does he have to tell me what to do? We get dressed in the same locker room. That is just bullshit. I don't care what Omar thinks. If I see an arrest is justified, I am going to make an arrest."

Later in the shift, there is a disturbance in front of a bodega at Christopher and Powell. Four cars and eight cops are on hand, including Gary and Omar. A handful of drunk teenagers are mouthing off, and one spits at the officers as they walk away. Gary pivots, reaching for his cuffs, ready to bring the kid in and write him a summons for disorderly conduct, when Omar steps forward.

"It didn't happen," he says.

Gary backs off. "You're a fuckin' empty suit," he tosses at Omar.

The same afternoon, Sharron Corley is looking for a job as a busboy in a restaurant not far from his school, on Chambers

Street. There is a surreal quality to Manhattan today as rumors of an impending race riot flash across town, up and down the gleaming skyscrapers. Fear abounds. Black looters are headed out of the boroughs, bent for the stores of Manhattan; the windows of Macy's have already been smashed, the story goes. An all-news radio station declares that a city bus has already been overturned. The crush to escape Manhattan begins as frightened office workers are dismissed from their jobs in the early afternoon. Penn Station is quickly jammed with panicky white commuters, who totter at the edge of the platform and peer down the tracks for the next train to whisk them away from the revenge of the black mob.

No such attack occurs. But a platoon of angry black protesters, some thirty strong, is stomping its way up through lower Manhattan, and it passes the restaurant window where Sharron sits, filling out his job application.

"No justice, no peace," the protesters chant.

"Get away from the windows, away from the windows!" the manager of the restaurant shrieks. "Lock the front door, no more customers. We're closing. We're closed."

Sharron shifts smoothly from one seat to another, listens to the chants, and considers the prospect of black-on-white violence. A look of dismay floods his face. He is truly saddened. "That's not right. Not right," he says to himself.

At five o'clock, Sharon King is alone on the subway, headed home from her job at Jeff. There wasn't any trouble in the high school about the L.A. verdict. The kids seemed barely to notice. King was once roughed up herself in Queens for protesting police violence and nothing ever came of her civilian complaint, so the 'not guilty' decision was nothing more than a confirmation for her.

At the Junius Street stop, three rowdy boys in their early teens pile onto the subway car. Ignoring King, they open and reopen the sliding door between cars, spit, and curse through the open windows at people on the platforms. Most adults would move to the next car to avoid them. King crosses the aisle and sits next to one, a boy of fourteen.

"What if your mother heard you talking like that?" she says sternly.

"My mother don't give a fuck about me," the boy answers.

King continues to talk with the suddenly well-behaved trio until she reaches her transfer at Franklin Avenue. When she leaves the train, she waves. Timidly, the boys wave back. But King is not in good spirits today. For the first time since she was a teenager, she is feeling left out. Carol Beck, a dozen of her staff members, and 150 or so students have gone for several days on a retreat to a resort called Falls View, two hours outside New York. The money came from City Councilwoman Priscilla Wooten's office. The idea is to promote bonding, build leadership in the student body for the coming year, and give the shell-shocked students a treat. There are to be three outings in all. King has simply been passed over for the trips. Word has circulated from the retreat organizers through the faculty that she is not wanted, that she is too "frisky" with the students.

Several days later, the early May sun reflects off the front of the glass and marble federal courthouse in front of the small park in Cadman Plaza. A racially mixed group of two dozen high school students from St. Ann's, an elite private school in Brooklyn Heights, plays an earnest game of soccer on the grass-fringed dirt field. It is sentencing day for Born Son and the Young Guns. Upstairs, Dan Murphy, Born Son's lawyer, sits on a bench in the deserted fourth-floor hallway. The courtroom of Judge Leo Glasser has been the scene of jury selection in the John Gotti racketeering trial all week. For several days, headlines have flown over the proceedings like flags. The so-called Teflon Don has even broken his characteristic silence, berating the federal prosecutor for being preoccupied with him. "Guy probably turns over in bed at night and calls his wife Gotti," he quips.

To hear Margaret James tell it, Bobby Schulman was no less obsessed with Bobby James. "Bobby used to come to me and tell me how scared he was. 'Schulman is out to kill me,' he would say. There were days he wouldn't want to come out of the house." Certainly the press and the public care less about Born Son. There is a not a single news reporter on hand for the proceedings. Counselor Murphy looks damp and bloated. "I feel sorry for Bobby," he says in the hallway an hour before the sentencing. "I just feel terrible. Nikia and Edward, the Worthys, knew how to play the game. Bobby didn't."

As it is, Born Son could not be in a worse position. He is the admitted manager of the operation. Under the mandatory federal sentencing guidelines, he faces decades in prison. All the possible mitigating factors that might allow the judge to lighten the sentence have been nullified in the presentencing report.

"I feel sorry for Margaret James," Murphy continues lugubriously. "She has a son on a basketball scholarship at UNLV and a daughter who is supposedly in medical school down South. She got two out of three out. She saved two out of three." The story about the basketball scholarship is not quite accurate; neither is the one about medical school. Margaret James's other children are not in trouble, but they are not world-beaters either. "I even feel sorry for Schulman," Murphy goes on. "I saw him at the library and he was wearing a bulletproof vest. What kind of life is that? Pray for Bobby James," Murphy says as he rises from his wooden bench and heads for the courtroom with a limp.

Judge Glasser is weary. It is four-thirty. There are just ten people inside the large and stately courtroom. Five are the friends and relatives of Born Son's associates, Chris Muncie and Carlton Smith. Bobby Schulman shows up in a cotton sweater; the dour, pockmarked Mathew DeJong, in a rugby-style pullover. Schulman has been working long hours on a federal case against Chris Moore, which is about to bear fruit. But there is more to the ballfield attire of the police officers than their work schedule. They wore suits to the previous courtroom dates of Born Son's trial because they had to. Now they have the chance to show what they really think of the most important day in Born Son's life.

Margaret James shows up late, slips into a seat two rows behind Schulman, and narrows her tiny eyes to glittering pinholes.

Licking his lips, Bobby James steps into the courtroom wearing the same green pants and flowered shirt that he wore in court almost a year ago — the same iridescent outfit that a court officer handed over to his mother after he changed into his prison togs following the proceeding. But now he has no suit jacket with him. Perhaps the jacket has been forgotten; perhaps the omission is an attempt to give the impression that he did not profit as much from the proceeds of the sale of crack as federal attorney Robert Fineberg says he has.

If such is Bobby's intent, he has a point. No one has been able to account for most of the money. Schulman, Fineberg, Glasser, and DeJong, for all their surveillance and investigation, could never find the money that would have been the result of such a bustling trade in crack. "People have a way of spending money," Fineberg says carefully, perhaps in a veiled reference to drug use. Surely the Worthys did use some drugs. Bobby tested positive for cocaine when he was arrested, but no one inside the crew or the police ever claimed that he and his boys were crackheads. "They were just a bunch of stupid kids," Margaret always said. Surely money had been wasted. But where were the millions?

The Worthys' large apartment at 295 Dumont Avenue was virtually without furniture — no lamps, rugs, toys, bicycles, or stereo equipment. Born Son spent much of his last year of freedom with his mother in her spare Bedford-Stuyvesant basement apartment. "I had to give these penny-ante kids five dollars for milk and Pampers," Margaret attests. Bobby had the Jeep, but Margaret insists that it was hers, bought with money paid on an insurance policy. Chris Muncie had a Honda. But there were no bank accounts, no savings, no homes, and no businesses. Margaret James has an answer for everything. She should have been a lawyer. But she is not, she is a mother, and this is going to be the hardest day of her life.

"My wife told me," Murphy begins, "that the sad part of this whole thing is that Bobby James had a chance to get out of Brownsville. He was a gifted basketball player. He went to Laurinburg Prep School in Virginia for a month. But he came back. And when he came back, he got involved in the kind of thing that goes on in his neighborhood. He has brains and physical talent." Murphy pauses, looking up at Glasser. "I ask you to depart downward," the lawyer says, importuning for a breach of the mandatory sentencing guidelines. His voice cracks with sympathy. He ends his short plea with a request for a ten-year sentence.

"Is he crazy?" Margaret James whispers.

But Leo Glasser is not buying the Brownsville defense. "I feel sorry for you, Mr. Murphy, and I was moved by your impassioned plea for your client. But I don't accept your attempt to suggest that the neighborhood was at fault. To do that is to condemn everyone in these communities. There are thousands of young men in Bedford-Stuyvesant and East New York who don't sell drugs, who struggle to go to work every day."

Visions of the 4 A.M. A train from East New York to Manhattan and the 6 P.M. elevated #3 from Pennsylvania Avenue float through the courtroom like pale smoke. But Glasser has probably never seen those trains. If he had, he would know that though they are packed with working people, there are precious few young men like Bobby James aboard. Government labor experts report that only about 17 percent of youths in New York City between the ages of sixteen and nineteen, the age at which Born Son entered the drug business, are employed. The employment rate in Brownsville is estimated at half the citywide figure, less than 10 percent.

"Those people are working every day," Glasser continues, "while Mr. James and others like him are bursting into people's apartments, carrying guns, poisoning those communities by selling poison to the people there." He turns from Murphy to the fidgeting Born Son. "You had a mother who cared about you, and relatives — a hard-working mother. But I guess there was just too much excitement, too many guns, and too much money. You must be some kind of Jekyll and Hyde character, Mr. James. When I read the letters that were sent by your relatives, I didn't read about the Bobby James that I have come to know throughout these proceedings."

Glasser removes his glasses, rubs his eyes, and stares above the heads of Murphy and James. "Do you have anything at all to say for yourself?" he asks after a pause. "Can you give me any reason why I should not impose the guidelines for the crimes to which you have pleaded guilty?"

By all accounts, Bobby James is a gifted talker, a monologuist of the streets. He could always make the layabouts laugh with imitations of Jamaicans, jokes, cracks, woofs. He could get all kinds of respect with his words. But he knows he cannot talk to Glasser. It's not just because of his deeds. Young men like Bobby have built their own language, and they change it frantically, precisely to exclude Glasser and what he stands for, because they understand instinctively that whoever sculpts their speech will take whatever freedom they have left. Leo Glasser does not understand how far away he is from the young man in front of him. When given a chance to speak, Bobby James mumbles something about "being fair."

Born Son is not a good guy, to be sure. But what of his decisions, his life? Sheltered by a doting mother, he was out to prove something every day on the streets. He fought because he had to, then because he wanted to. He impressed the people he meant to impress. In his own way, he tried to do the right thing. But it wasn't the right thing according to the Leo Glassers of the world. They had the schools, the jobs, cars, houses, bank accounts, and clothes. And in the end, somehow they even had justice on their side.

Glasser would be the first to admit how hard life is in Brownsville and East New York. He is a fair man, and this was a fair trial. But where were the fair men when the Brownsville schools fell into disrepair and disrepute? Where were the judges when Margaret James was paid just about enough for her car fare to and from work in job after job? Where were the fair-minded men of influence when the white people ran from Brownsville and took the teachers, businesses, and means of credit with them? Where was the justice then? The only truth and justice in the Howard Houses in those days was Hank Walters and Officer J.R. Reynolds, and God knows those men had their hands full.

"Bobby James, you never did take responsibility for your actions." Glasser lays out Born Son's criminal record: an attempt to bribe a policeman, forgery, resisting arrest, criminal impersonation. "In the end, the money and the cars and the clothes were just too easy. The money was just too good," Glasser repeats lamely. His voice suddenly slips to a whisper. He says something that ends with the words "five years' supervision."

How could Glasser know what this was all about? To understand, all he had to do was think of himself. How did he become a lawyer and a judge? He did it, no doubt, by following a path he saw before him, by determining early that he wanted to be an important man, and by persevering. Born Son is not so different. It is by no means easy to do what Bobby James did. It is ambitious and dangerous beyond imagination.

It is also cruel. Young men are still dying every day on the streets that Born Son will no longer walk. People in other cultures live on next to nothing without the murderous activities found in Brownsville. But they have a system of beliefs that gives them respect and solace. The mad American marketing machine that trumpets, "Get things, get money and don't settle for second best" makes ambition a religion, while the social system denies access to the legitimate hierarchy. The result is predictable. The kids create their own shadow system and fight each other to reach the top. Born Son, standing before the judge in his green iridescent slacks, with his bulging jailhouse muscles and shaved head, is the living record of those crazed messages. They drowned out the voice of his mother. But nothing will drown out her voice now.

"What did he do? What did he give my baby?" Margaret James demands. With a heave, she is up and out of her seat. She approaches the sheepish Murphy, who has returned to his chair by the wooden railing at the front of the courtroom. "What happened?"

"Thirty years," the lawyer announces.

Margaret James shouts, "No!," takes three steps down the center aisle, and throws herself to the marble floor. "They took my baby. They killed my baby. The stupid lawyer. Those bastards. They lied. They lied. They lied."

"Baptist flop," a handsome, middle-aged court officer sneers as he and the other federal officers bend to their duty. It is difficult to lift Margaret James. Displaying little sympathy, the white men drag her along the floor and out of the courtroom. But she is far from finished.

In the hall, the surly officers cajole and threaten. "You won't be able to visit your son if you keep this up." But she continues to howl and remains flat on her back, legs splayed on the glistening floor. The men try to drag her to a bench as a young black woman protests the treatment. In the end, there is no respect for Bobby or Margaret James. Not even for motherhood. "Leave her on the floor — that way she can't fall down" is the expert advice of one of the court officers.

Margaret's face is drenched with tears. Her wails mount. "He didn't even turn around. I didn't see his beautiful face. They took my baby." She curses Schulman, who has taken the back door out of the courtroom. "He hates my baby. They lied. They lied. The racist bastards live in their mansions and they took my baby."

Back inside the courtroom, under the cloud of a mother's curses, Glasser shows good sense and postpones Chris Muncie's sentencing. Murphy, DeJong, Schulman, Glasser, and the rest are gone now, as the EMS people arrive with an oxygen mask and an arm wrap to take Margaret's blood pressure.

"I can't do anything," she cries. "I can't even raise my child."

"BIG DAYS"

On a fresh day in June, a camouflage-colored army vehicle that military people call a deuce-and-a-half sits with its engine idling in front of the PSA. The truck, on loan to the Housing police from the National Guard, takes up three parking spaces and creates a stir in the neighborhood. Boys on bicycles and curious men sidle up and squint, step closer, and run their fingers along the steel-plated doors. What is an army vehicle, an instrument of war, doing in Brownsville?

"I seen that in the movies," a boy says.

"Shit has some big-ass tires," his friend comments. "They bulletproof."

"You stupid, ain't no bulletproof tires," the first boy scoffs. Then the two fall quiet, imagining what it would be like to be a soldier.

The deuce-and-a-half is here today to be used in the execution of a warrant at 666 Dumont Avenue, the crack house across the street from Thomas Jefferson High School. An hour before the afternoon raid, twenty-five cops are downstairs in the roll call room, waiting for instructions. Gary's OSC unit is here, as is the Housing police NEU team, a SWAT-style group with ballistic shields and battering rams. Seven agents from the Bureau of Alcohol, Tobacco, and Firearms (ATF) are on hand as well, dressed in black, carrying machine guns. Ten uniformed officers will handle backup support and traffic and crowd control.

"We're gonna hit the two doors in 666 and one down the street, all simultaneously," the lieutenant begins, producing a sheet of paper. "Hammil, you're on the roof. Lemite, the third-floor search team. Hayes, exterior."

"They reinforced the front door," a scowling officer explains to an ATF agent at his side. "Every time we break it down, they put up a stronger one. Let's see what the fuck they do now."

"You know that Puerto Rican flag they got?" Eddie Hammil whispers to Gary. "We're gonna put up the American flag so high they can't take it down. I called the firehouse over on Sheffield. They're gonna come by with the ladder."

A spit-shined National Guard officer with a crew cut steps to the lectern and faces the agents and officers. His delivery is practiced. This is not the first time a military show of force has been employed in a Brooklyn project. "Listen," he instructs, "when you come out of the truck, don't try to be Rambo and jump. It's too high. Drop your butt to the floor of the truck and slide off. Every time we do this, we have a guy falling. You've got automatic weapons, and even if you don't mind breaking your leg, it's dangerous to trip and stumble all over the street. I'm saying it one more time. Don't jump."

The briefing is short. This will be a standard warrant execution, with an entry team, a roof unit, a squad to watch the windows, recording officers to inventory contraband, and backup people to escort prisoners. The difference is that this time the troops will roll through the streets, past the projects, and up to 666 Dumont in a caravan led by the lumbering deuce-and-a-half. For once, the cops are thinking, this will look like the war it really is.

As they mill around the front room of the PSA waiting to saddle up, the officers are excited at the prospect of a full-scale assault on a crack house. So are the people from the neighborhood, who continue to gape at the war wagon in the street. The only one who remains unenthusiastic about the operation is an old cop who watches the eager invasion force from his usual position, leaning on the front desk. He is big, six-foot-three, a mountain of ruined flesh, with a little head, and the slenderest of ankles visible beneath his abbreviated pants. His gun holster, shifted to the front like a codpiece, hangs loose and low. Observing the busy preparation, he grumbles, "What happened to the good old days when nobody gave a fuck?"

Outside on the sidewalk, an NEU officer is telling one of the Housing cops about a recent warrant that went wrong. "We took the door and right away my heart hits my knees. The place is immaculate. And get this, there's a college diploma on the wall. Right away we knew, wrong fucking place. You can imagine the shit that hit the fan after that. It was in the papers, for cryin' out loud."

"Wish I could be a punk when I grow up," a boy speeding by on a bicycle shouts to the crowd of officers.

"You'll never grow up," Sergeant Toney answers from the sidewalk.

The paramilitary operation is attracting attention all around the Sutter Avenue station. As the vehicles get ready to move out, a man standing near the tailgate of the deuce-and-a-half suddenly becomes excited by police work. "I sure wish I was goin' along," he says wistfully, looking as if he would vault into the personnel carrier with the slightest encouragement. Then the big green truck shudders and pulls out, preceded by a marked car and followed by five more police cars and two ambulances. The convoy proceeds slowly down Williams Avenue to Blake and over to Pennsylvania and Dumont. The commerce of daily life is suspended as folks on the sidewalk gape, then wave and cheer. Inside the vehicle, the air reeks of stale bodies. But that doesn't bother the cops, who cradle their weapons and peek out the opening at the rear of the truck, soaking up the attention as if they were General Bradley's Fourth Infantry Division riding into Paris.

The landing party arrives. With a jolt and a holler, the officers clamber out of the deuce-and-a-half and charge toward 666 Dumont. At the corner, Mickey Mundell hops quickly onto Pennsylvania Avenue and waltzes through the speeding traffic until he is safely on the other side of the street.

"On the wall!" the cops scream at the startled people standing near the entrance to 666. "Get on the wall. Feet back. *Feet back.*" One by one, the people are searched and ordered to kneel by the side of the building with their hands behind their heads.

Upstairs, Gary Lemite and a handful of other officers are ransacking the targeted apartments, searching for drugs and guns. Lonnie Hayes and his unit stand outside, watching for tossed contraband. The day is hot, and the search drags on. A gun and a small amount of drugs are found. More drugs and crack-cooking paraphernalia are discovered in an apartment around the corner. The uniformed officers cordon off a wide area with crime scene tape and warn the growing throng of curious people to stay back. Lenti and Borough Commander Kempf stand in their shirt-sleeves in the middle of the street and chat. Forty-five minutes pass, and still the detainees — fifteen men, women, and children — kneel in the sun along the Dumont Avenue side of the building, beneath the ruby-red R.I.P. mural for a girl named Lyty. Ten more minutes, and an officer appears with a handful of garbage bags so the women won't have to kneel on the dirt or the pavement. The search drags on.

Lonnie Hayes mutters, "This is fucked up. You don't leave people outside like this. You either arrest them or you don't. You go down the line and you say, 'This is a keeper, this isn't.'"

Some cops are having a good time. "I can't wait till the Fire Department gets here and we can put up the flag," Hammil says with a chortle.

A jolly crowd gathers beside the army truck parked on a side street. "Like a fuckin' Rambo movie, bro," a shirtless Hispanic man offers. "All *riiight!*" another man yells. But this movie goes on too long. The people behind the crime scene tape slowly lose their taste for the spectacle of their neighbors kneeling with their hands over their heads like prisoners of war. Gradually the cheering section grows mute, then uneasy, as symbols of national pride give way to personal truth and the thrill of watching a gung-ho invasion becomes anger at the realization that they are the enemy. A bottle sails from the crowd and crashes near Commander Kempf. The uniformed officers wade in and push the crowd back. Another bottle thuds against the side of a patrol car.

A distraught woman arrives. Her handsome young son is among the detainees. She cries and begs for his release, studying the officers with the fierce and frightened eyes of a mother who believes her child is in danger.

"He's a *niño*," she wails.

Lenti and Kempf continue to chat and watch the front door of 666. They don't want any mistakes here. Internal Affairs is on hand, stirred to vigilance by the recent highly publicized arrest of a clique of crack-selling cops, dubbed the Losers' Club, several of whom worked at the 75th precinct.

Five young women, alleged associates of the operators of the crack operation at 666, are escorted from the building in handcuffs and seated in a waiting van. Two of the women are weeping. One, a frantic blonde, babbles the names and addresses of people she insists are the real culprits, trying to convince the officers to set her free.

Finally, a decision is made to release the people kneeling by the wall. The mother charges across the street and hugs her son as if he has been rescued from Huns. "The kid is standing in front of a building where there is a homicide every week, and she's scared we're gonna hurt him?" a female Housing cop grumbles. "Denial. The whole area is in a state of denial."

Before the officers pull away with the five women in custody, Hammil walks over to the streetlight on the corner of Dumont and Pennsylvania where the Puerto Rican flag hangs limply, midway up the pole. He hoists himself up and takes the flag down. Then he climbs back up and secures an American flag to the pole.

"The Fire Department had a call; they couldn't make it," he explains as he gets in the passenger seat of an unmarked car.

When Judge Glasser reconvenes for Chris Muncie's sentencing, there are even fewer people in the courtroom than there were for Born Son. The wavy-haired court officer who directed the removal of Margaret James the previous Friday asks, "Is she here? As long as *she* isn't here." "She was upset," another officer jokes. "She lost her source of income." The court officers chuckle with the ease of people who are among their own kind, who share stores of unspoken, forbidden beliefs.

Alan Polak, Muncie's lawyer, is much more persuasive than Born Son's attorney was. He strikes to the heart of the matter, as Muncie stands at his side. There is no talk of basketball scholarships. "If this case were handled in the state courts, it would be a class B felony, with a maximum sentence of eight and a third years actual time served." Polak pauses for a long moment, gathering his thoughts. Behind him to the right, Mathew DeJong casts a smile at an attractive female assistant arriving with a sheaf of papers.

Polak moves to another point. "There is no implication that this was a bad-faith prosecution," he allows, "but there is some reason to believe that the lead investigator had a personal vendetta, an antagonism, against Mr. Muncie's codefendant and this has had a fallout effect on Mr. Muncie."

Polak then asks Glasser to consider that the harsh sentences against crack dealers are discriminatory to inner-city black youths. "Under Title 21, section 8-41, Colombian nationals who supply cocaine would have to import more than four hundred kilos, which would net them $8 million, to get the sentence that my client faces." Schulman twists a bit in his seat. Polak points out that Asian drug gangs would have to sell seventy kilos of heroin, which would bring in about the same, $8 to $8.5 million, to get the sentence mandated for Muncie by the federal sentencing guidelines. "The effect is discriminatory," he concludes, "and I posit the court never fathomed the true effect."

Glasser covers his face with his long fingers. It looks as if he is getting ready to cry. Then his hands fall away and he bellows at the lawyer, "I didn't write the guidelines. I didn't write the law, Congress did. You are asking me to give a state sentence in a federal court. You are asking me to do something lawless. Do you think this comes easy? You think this is something I enjoy?"

Schulman and DeJong exchange a quick glance. Glasser switches gears. "These young men dealt thirty-three kilograms of crack. When the police broke into their operation, there was a veritable arsenal of guns and hundreds of rounds of bullets. There were random shootings, shootings at rival drug dealers. They broke into an apartment and pistol-whipped a young woman to force her to let them use her apartment." Glasser wearily offers some advice. "March on Washington, Mr. Polak. Let them know the horrors they have created with this law." Then, in a thready voice, the judge gives Chris Muncie, who has never been arrested before, 324 months — twenty-seven years — in jail.

Muncie says something about being sorry. Then he turns to his mother and his sister, who is wearing a white turban. Both are the color of light toast, much fairer than Chris; both are crying. He points at his mother and mouths the words, "If you're all right, I'm all right." Then he blows a kiss.

Near the elevator Muncie's sister says, "This court system is not for us. Not for us at all."

It is graduation day at Jefferson. Carol Beck spins her magic to the end. Yesterday she was at the school till midnight, making preparations for the ceremony. "I'm going to get fired because of all the reports I have not done," she says, "but I have prioritized."

You can tell something important has happened here. Not by the trumpets of pink and white gladioli that flank the podium, the wreaths, or the smiling, proud faces of the 120 graduating seniors in their blue ceremonial robes draped with orange Kente scarves. You can tell by the number of dignitaries seated on the stage in front of the graduates. There are no fewer than nineteen big shots here, including H. Carl McCall, president of the board of education, and Sandra Feldman, the UFT president.

The graduates are arranged in two groups at the rear of the stage, boys on one side and girls on the other. Every time a speaker approaches the podium, the entire graduating class rises crisply to its feet. In the audience, Ms. King slouches delinquently in her seat, sucking on a dripping mango and scoffing audibly at the self-serving pronouncements of the speakers, drawn like flies to this school, which has become oddly popular since the killings in its halls. But when the elegant McCall leans toward the microphone, King is suddenly attentive. He talks of achievement in the face of tragedy and of the responsibility of adults for the state of the world.

"This year was a test of the spirit," he declares, comparing the graduates to the biblical Job. "So hold fast to your faith, and your hope. Go out and make this world a better place. Fix the things *we* have broken . . . mend the wound *we* have inflicted . . . and scale the heights *we* have not imagined. You can make it happen. My brothers and sisters, you are the finest people in our city and our nation."

King is all ears. "That is a good man. He understands. He cares," she testifies to anyone within earshot. "Let the kids speak," she shouts when McCall finishes.

Thomas Jefferson High School receives an award for excellence in education from the National Educational Honor Society. The woman who presents the award recounts the recent history of the school, reminding her listeners how in the early eighties Jefferson had the highest dropout rate of any school in New York City. Now its students are competing for Regents scholarships and Westinghouse Science Awards for the first time. "There are over *sixty* new programs," she proclaims, citing a moot court, a civil service exam preparation program, a

P.M. school, and a College Now program in which students can gain college credits. "And," she concludes triumphantly, "there are two graduates going to Vassar College."

Satellite Academy held its ceremony yesterday, but Sharron Corley was not among the graduates. He passed all his courses, even earned an A in his great ideas class. But his stint in Riker's set him back too far. He will have to go back to school in September if he wants to get a high school diploma. The prospect of attending high school at nineteen does not bother him. "I'll be back," he says with an accent like Arnold Schwarzenegger and a hearty laugh.

Gita Malave didn't make it either. The day before her final exam in the troublesome math course, her sister succumbed to tuberculosis. Gita stared blankly at the equations she had studied so hard, and failed. For the first time since she started college, her resolve faltered, and she decided to pass up summer school.

The woman from the honor society yields the stage to the salutatorian, a wisp of a girl who has managed to graduate in three years. "Don't give up. You can do anything you want to do," she exhorts, quivering on the stage like an arrow of hope. She speaks without notes; her clipped words tumble and collide as her mind races faster than her tongue. She is not just a survivor, she is a prodigy. Her parents beam, and the attending faculty members nod approvingly.

In the center of the auditorium, Hank Walters, the youth leader from the Howard Houses, takes a deep, satisfied breath and leans back in his chair. This is a proud day for him too; his daughter is at the back of the stage, draped in blue, preparing to receive her diploma. Carol Beck, seated to the side of the podium, watches with a frozen smile. She will give no speech today. "I told the graduates what they had to know yesterday, during the rehearsal," she explains later.

The valedictorian steps up next. He is a mahogany lad, of East Indian heritage, from Guyana, and who spent a year and a half on a science project that helped him win a scholarship to Brooklyn's Polytechnic University. His address begins promisingly, with "It was the best of times. It was the worst of times." But the boy is more scientist than orator, and there isn't much originality in his speech, though a touch of faith rises from his closing words. "I don't know why I came to Jefferson," he says with a shrug. "But I am glad that I did."

Then each student crosses the stage, is handed a rolled-up piece of paper by Carol Beck, and pauses to have his or her picture taken with the beloved principal. Bashim Inman, the Howard House Raider, buddy of Born Son and perhaps future community leader, receives the loudest reaction, cheers mixed with some anonymous boos and hisses.

Only Officer Kevin Price is glum. Yesterday he attended the sentencing of Jason Bentley, who shot Daryl Sharpe in November. Jason got three to nine years for manslaughter one; his case was plea-bargained down from the murder charge. The sentence is not what is bothering Price.

"There wasn't a mention of Daryl," he says as the graduates file out into the sunshine to have their pictures taken by family and friends. "It was like his fifteen years on this earth never existed. He might have been something. He was treated like he was nothing. All Jason's father wanted to know was 'Is this everything? Are you taking care of all the charges at once?' Nobody even said a word to the Sharpe family, or even made mention of them."

On the wall of Beck's office is a sign proclaiming that over $4 million has been given in scholarship money to the graduates of the class of '92. The list of colleges exhibited includes Vassar, which is credited with giving $200,000 in the form of full scholarships to two girls. Both overcame incredible odds. One spent part of her senior year with her mother and sister in a shelter for battered women.

Their teacher, Audrey Lee Jacobs, a graduate of Vassar, engineered the admissions, advising both girls to write their application essays about the Moore and Sinkler shootings. Both have very high grades but combined math and verbal SAT scores of only about 750. The Vassar standard is about 1250. The 750 score is significant. It is not just low, it is very low. It does not tarnish the achievements or the unlimited potential of the girls; it speaks of the war zone conditions they come from. The way things are now, the best and the brightest of Jefferson can barely qualify for a good private college, and will only be noticed under the glare of a nationally publicized tragedy.

The graduation was a glorious ceremony, a celebration of significant deeds in spite of community conditions that are a national disgrace. It signaled that now there is order and hope at Thomas Jefferson High School. It is a place where better things can happen, where good teachers have a chance to weave patterns, compete for space in their students' minds with television. But it is still by no means a good school.

Beck, the image-maker, knew she needed a triumph today. The school needed it. The community needed it. Each graduate is a victory, a tribute to family and teachers and fortitude. But the happy ending Beck scripted onstage was in some sense a fiction. Of the 120 "graduates," a significant number did not really graduate. As many as one third, including Bashim, who has been in the school for six years, are "candidates" for graduation; that is, they will have to go to summer school to earn several more credits in order to get their diploma. If the "candidates" had been removed from the graduating class, there would have been only about seventy-five students on the stage.

"Some parents are mumbling, 'This ain't a real graduation. They ain't gettin' no diploma,'" Beck says candidly. "But I know that those students, ninety-nine percent of them, will get their diplomas at the end of the summer. They will come to summer school right here in this building. They won't like it. But they will come. I trust them."

There is another significant truth about the graduates of Thomas Jefferson, class of '92. Beck estimates that 60 percent of the students on the stage are immigrants from Haiti, the Dominican Republic, Guyana, Jamaica, Trinidad, and Barbados. "They even like to keep their accents," she says later, "because then they let people know that they are not American blacks. I tell them, 'Keep the accent, but try to become bilingual.'" The sad fact remains that at Thomas Jefferson High School, which has a heavily African American population, there may be as few as twenty-five African American graduates.

"These are not the Cosby kids," Beck says, referring to her students. "They are darker-skinned and bolder-featured. And they intimidate people, especially when they are seen in groups." The fact may be that despite Beck's heroics, the kind of contribution that cannot be expected to continue with the next principal, these African Americans, who have been passed by immigrant group after immigrant group, are being passed again. This time they are being eclipsed by an almost invisible contingent, one that looks like them but has come from a number of very different cultures, cultures that were not exposed to such high levels of racism. "We just didn't have so many white folks around growing up," the Jamaican Sharon King says. "We made decisions on our own."

Hanging over the day is the memory of the previous graduation. Beck played that ceremony like a sweet harp as well. She had students and parents and educators eating out of her hand then too. In September, the board of education sent her five hundred freshmen, many of them from social work caseloads. "They're comin' again in September," Officer Price says, "the kids that have to be stopped."

And soon Carol Beck will no longer be at Jefferson. After the ceremony she is exhausted. She tells King, "I'm going to retire after next year. People keep saying I won't, but I want them all to get together and put up some money, 'cause I'm going to be toes up in front of the television, watching *As the World Turns*. I'm trying to wean Jeff away from me now, trying to teach people how to pull the right strings and get things done. This Jefferson thing isn't based on me. Who the hell is me?"

BROWNSVILLE

It is high summer again in Brownsville, but a gray rain has cut the heat, and it is blessedly cool in the vestibule of the Brownsville Community Baptist Church. Gary Lemite has just finished up a twelve-to-eight day tour, and he is driving over to Cheap Charlie's to grab a few beers. From where he sits at the red light on the corner of Mother Gaston Avenue, he can see the people filing into the yellow brick church. They are coming to see *Lord, Why Can't They Hear?*, a play written by Shirley Benning, a member of the congregation.

As the arrivals enter the church, they pass double glass doors to the chapel, where two wide pews covered with royal blue material sit empty before the muted brilliance of two twelve-foot stained glass windows. This Friday evening, the buzzing church members are headed downstairs to the broad basement, which the two-thousand-member congregation calls the Fellowship Hall. There are already one hundred people inside, seated around large round tables, nibbling chicken wings and homemade crabmeat salad.

Soon there is a furious tapping of microphones from behind a yellow scrim, a fussing and shuffling. Like *Don't Give Up on Your Dreams*, the play to be performed is more than mere entertainment. It is about the loss of young lives, and the actors, who range in age from six to twenty-nine, are the models for the characters they portray. Some of the youngest performers have come to this very church seeking sanctuary from the violence in the Complex across the street. "Some who show up every day have parents who have never set foot in the church," Benning says before the performance. "But they find family here."

In five lively acts, the play delivers the message that church members should stop worrying about how good they look in their newest clothes, about their own dreams, flirtations, and pride, and start reaching out to their dying community. The first act introduces a single mother with two teenage girls who are headed in different directions: one to the church, the other to crack. "Friday night?" the mother scoffs at her churchgoing daughter's invitation to a choir performance. "Friday night, girl, is *my* night."

The second act brings on the burly Mr. Wannabe, an upwardly mobile entrepreneur with a son at Harvard Medical School, who despairs at his younger son's lack of success. The second son believes he has been called to preach the word of God. But like the self-absorbed mother in act one, Mr. Wannabe mocks the idea. "All the money I spent on piano lessons! If you think pickin' up that Bible is gonna get me to spend more money on you, you better call the prayer hotline and get the saints to put in a prayer for you."

At a church business meeting in act three, Mr. Wannabe is equally unenthusiastic about the idea of reaching out to those in the community who are less fortunate. "Knock on doors? I really don't think so. I might donate money, but I don't see myself knocking on doors."

"What would we *wear* to a community self-help group?" a well-coiffed woman at the meeting wonders aloud as she examines her face in a hand mirror. But a mysterious new member, a tall, clear-eyed woman, rises slowly and addresses the gathering with a most tranquil voice and the deepest conviction. "I will knock on one thousand doors," she says, "if I can save one soul."

There are many hilarious goings-on in the fourth act — a grandmother wants the preacher to perjure himself so she can win a lawsuit for a bogus injury — and assorted jealous or libidinous members of the congregation. Mr. Wannabe's ne'er-do-well son begins to preach the word of God despite his father's discouragement. "I want to preach when they want to hear and when they don't want to hear," he announces. "I want to preach in season and out of season."

A woman in the audience rises half out of her seat in appreciation. Then, catching herself, she explains to the woman next to her, whispering, "This is good. You know, I don't come out in the street for nothin'."

The language rolls and rumbles. "Let me. Let me. Let me. Let me explain myself to you." Mr. Wannabe's son has the message, and he wants to tell it. "It's not all about 'Let me do it my way.' Because your way is not the right way. It says here in Webster's Dictionary that to hear is to comprehend by the ear. I want you to hear. I want you to form your lives around the word of God. So you can *live* right. So you can *walk* right. So you can *talk* right. So you can *be* right."

In the final act, the beautiful young crackhead is saved from suicide by the charismatic young Mr. Wannabe, the malingering granny throws away her cane and wiggles her ample behind to the howls of the audience, and the burly elder Wannabe hugs his son so hard the collision rings out like an open field tackle in a pro football game. Then the choir dances down the aisle in purple robes, their faces gleaming. The young preacher leaps in the air.

"Why can't you hear?" the choir harmonizes. They are in a basement half a block from where Officer McLean was murdered in a stairway across the street from 295 Dumont Avenue, where Born Son and his Young Guns shot it out with the Tilden boys, where Powerful was killed, and where Randolph Worthy is now building his own modest crack business. The tumult of voices rises, falls, and lifts again, like the howling bagpipes at the Housing police 10-13 party. They are meant to quicken the heart, summon the spirit to battle.

Another July. This afternoon Gary is on Loring Avenue, outside the Pink Houses, sitting behind the wheel of a late-model Thunderbird. The car is an ATF undercover surveillance vehicle, and Gary is waiting for Sergeant Bright, Tony Logan, and an ATF agent to talk to the mother of a guy wanted for conspiracy to traffic drugs. The lightly tinted windows of the car are open only a few inches, despite the heat, because a confidential informant, the man who supplied the address of the fugitive's mother, is in the back seat. Gary says little to the man, just sprawls lazily in the front seat, drawing on his bottle of Snapple.

Gary is wearing his black polo-neck shirt and his black jeans. Both his guns are on his waist, and he shifts around in his seat a bit so they don't dig into his stomach. He is going to have to lose a little weight, lay off the beer, if he's going to have a good softball season in the church league. Maybe Merle shouldn't be the coach this year, he muses. The team did better when he left town for a while last season. Imagine, a pastor who wants to hit a home run every time up instead of just going for the base hit. Gary chuckles at the thought.

"*Up!*" The shout comes from outside the car, and there is a jolt to the left side of Gary's head. A robbery? A perp? Fucking Michael T.? "*Freeze.*" The voice comes from near the driver's side window. Gary holds stock still. Out of the corner of his eye, he can see a man leveling a short gun at him through the opening in the passenger side window.

"Police officers, don't move. Show the hands. Put 'em on the dashboard." The voice shifts toward the man in the back seat. "*You,* you put both hands out the window and keep them there."

"I'm a —" Gary begins.

"Shut up. Don't say a fucking word."

Gary moves his hands up ever so slowly, evenly, and lays them palms down on the dashboard. A long moment; nothing. Gary speaks, his voice as light as air, his carefully chosen words pure police argot.

"I'm on the job. Housing. My portable's between my legs. My tin is in my front left pocket, my ID in my back left, my service and off-duty in my waist, right side." A white hand moves slowly to Gary's pants pocket and pulls the badge into sight. The hand turns the badge over, flips it onto the dashboard.

It will be over now, Gary thinks. But neither the gun at his left temple nor the one aimed at him through the passenger's side window moves or wavers. Seconds stutter by. Gary's heart lifts in his chest. *What the hell is going on!* he thinks. Silence. More time.

"That's the Anticrime van in front of us. My team is in that house." Gary nods faintly toward the row of houses on the street.

"Where's your precinct?"

"PSA 2. On Sutter."

"Who are you?" the cop closest to Gary asks the man in the back seat. "Get out of the car."

Gary can see the blue fabric now. The guns are still pointed at him. The prodding fear. This is the same thing he has done a hundred times to perps. The extra touch, the intimidation that makes the mutts remember him, makes them hesitate to point an index finger in his direction and pull an imaginary trigger when he drives by, maybe hesitate to shoot him if that time should ever come. Intimidation. These guys are doing it to him. And they know he is a cop.

"Out of the car, I said."

"No," Gary snaps. Gary Lemite may be singularly without rancor at the behavior of the white men who are aiming guns at him, but he is not about to let them blow a case, allow them to put the informant's life in danger by forcing him to show his face on Loring Avenue. "That man is a registered federal inform-ant," he says, his voice trilling with anger and fear. "I will get out and follow all directions. But he's not getting out." Slowly the guns are withdrawn, sheathed. The cops pivot and saunter back to their car.

"We had a scrip that fit you," the 75 sergeant tosses over his shoulder. That's all. They are gone.

Gary sits still for a long time in the front seat of the car. He's not scared now, not even angry, just vacant. From the back seat, the informant is gazing serenely at Gary's silver badge, which glitters foolishly on the dashboard. When Bright and Logan pile their big bodies into the car, Gary barely hears their chatter.

"What's up? You okay, Gary?" Bright is asking.

"Yeah, sure," he says. Bright and Logan are in the mood for some pizza. But Gary shakes them off.

"Drop me off at the house," he says. "Pick me up after you eat."

With his eyes locked straight ahead, he walks across the front room of the PSA. For the next few minutes he doesn't want to see another blue uniform. He has been in mortal danger a dozen times, but this emptiness is worse. At the top of the stairs, he realizes where he's headed and quickens his step. Maybe Lonnie Hayes is down in the weight room, pushing some steel. The 75 sergeant took something from Gary. Lonnie knows what it is; maybe he even knows how to replace it.

Three weeks into the summer, in the middle of July, Sharron is doing the same job he did last summer. He is downstairs at

Brooklyn Youth Outreach, ready to head out for his site visits.

"Sharron!" Aubrey yells his name. The director isn't a funny man today. He is livid. Somebody has fouled up.

The city came up with a windfall of federal money two weeks ago, and there was a mass hiring of kids, an influx of new workers in the system. Sharron's program alone hired three hundred new youth workers. Reorganization became necessary. Juanita, Sharron's immediate supervisor, told him that he would no longer be responsible for picking up time cards from the Long Island College Hospital site, but she neglected to reassign the site. The time cards were never picked up.

"I'm gonna have people coming in here lookin' for their paychecks and there won't *be* any checks," Aubrey growls. "You know what that means?" Sharron lifts his head to answer, but Aubrey cuts him off. "It means that this is a fuckin' mess. And this is what I *don't* need."

"I was reassigned. That wasn't my site no more," Sharron protests gently. For him, confrontation is something that takes place on the street, or in a holding cell, or on a stairway. When it comes to sticking up for himself in a situation like this, he is passive, fatalistic.

"There will be parents coming down here, raising all kinds of hell," Aubrey rants, "wanting to know who's responsible for this mess." He walks around his desk and faces the window, with his back to Sharron. Then he turns slowly. "It's either going to be you or Juanita," he says. "I'll talk to you in a couple of minutes. Wait outside, please."

After a short talk with Juanita, Aubrey emerges from his office with a hard smile.

"No hard feelings, Sharron," he promises. "You're terminated, but nothing negative will be put in your record."

The only consideration Sharron requests is a letter for his probation officer. As he walks away from the program headquarters, he opens the envelope and reads the letter. It states that he has been fired for "nonperformance." He hurries back to the office. The letter will stand, Aubrey explains, but the employment records upstairs will contain no reference to nonperformance.

Sharron frowns and heads back to Brownsville.

Backup. Sharron once had Gloria and Ms. King in his corner,

but he doesn't have anybody now — no incensed father to storm down to the Youth Employment Office and straighten out the bad deal he has just gotten, talk to somebody who knows somebody to put it right. He just heads back to Brownsville on the #3 and walks up Saratoga toward home.

Sharron's gold chain, bouncing in the noon sun, catches the eye of a pretty girl, who tosses her head as she passes. For once, Sharron does not turn around. He is not in the mood. He is thinking about Aubrey. *Damn. Always got along good with Aubrey. Used to slap me on the shoulder every day, almost.*

There are a couple of young guys — Dee Whiz and Fitty-Sen, the partners from around the way — on his heels as he walks into the cool shade of his building and turns up the stairs. Dee Whiz passes him. Young kid, maybe fifteen. Sharron's head is down. *Ain't this a bitch,* he thinks. *No more $320 every two weeks. No more job to go to.* On the second-floor landing, Fitty-Sen leaps up from behind, yokes Sharron, and tries to drag him to the floor. From above, Dee Whiz dives for the gold chain.

Sharron coils, flips Fitty-Sen off his neck, and elbows Dee Whiz across the bridge of his nose. Then he flies up the stairs three at a time and shoulders his way through his apartment door, which stands half open for extra breeze. "Narrow-ass punks. Little bubble-gum bastards." He sprints into his room and leans into his closet. His hand gropes the top shelf for the Raven. The gun is gone. Sharron remembers. Handing the gun away was a difficult decision. Sharron dreams of going places, but he is still in Brownsville, and without the burner he is at a fatal disadvantage.

"Nah, nah, nah," he mutters, as he throws on his jeans jacket and hurries back outside. "It ain't gonna be like that. Fucking kids? Nah, nah."

It is white-hot on the street; the sun aims like a laser at Sharron's face. His left hand moves up to shield his scar from the stinging light; his right hand slides inside his jacket and dips down toward his waist. Fronting, acting, for the people on the street, gripping a gun he no longer has, Sharron moves slowly down Saratoga, looking for the boys who tried to steal his chain.

EPILOGUE: LATER

Born Son is serving his thirty-year sentence in a federal penitentiary in Texas. Nikia is in an Indiana prison. She will be released in two years. Margaret James talks regularly to both of them and spends her time worrying and searching for a lawyer to handle her son's appeal. Randolph Worthy now runs the retail crack trade in the Complex.

Bobby Schulman was promoted to detective. He was seated at his desk in the small squad room in the Marcy Houses in Brooklyn when a teenager tossed an M-80 firecracker through the window, which blew Schulman off his seat. "The cops always mess with me, so I messed with them," the kid stated at the time of his arrest. Schulman's hearing is permanently damaged, but he is back on the job, working on the Chris Moore case.

Jim Priore, still a sergeant at PSA 2, has his eye on a position with a proposed Housing police Emergency Service Unit or a promotion to lieutenant. Danny Horan purchased a home in Suffolk County and is high on the list for promotion to sergeant. J.R. Reynolds is a detective in the borough of Queens.

Carol Beck has retired. During her last year at Thomas Jefferson, she held a second cotillion and conducted numerous retreats, which by year's end had enabled most of the student body to spend time outside Brownsville and East New York. Her dream of building a dormitory for Jeff students took shape when state funding was allocated for planning.

Sharon King still teaches social studies at Thomas Jefferson High School, and coaches the cheerleading squad. She directed another school play, which was performed in a Manhattan performance space.

Bashim Inman graduated and is a youth worker in Brownsville, waiting for his college admission to be processed.

In his senior year, Cortez Sutton starred on the Jefferson basketball team, which made the playoffs for the first time in over a decade, and was elected president of the student body. He plans to attend Savannah State College in Georgia.

Gita Malave arranged to sit in on a math class and retake the final exam she failed. But that very day, her son Kendall was shot in the stomach in a jewelry store in the Fulton Mall while shopping for rhinestones to decorate his collection of baseball caps. Kendall is expected to live. Gita is seeking trauma counseling for herself and her son when he gets out of the hospital.

Gary Lemite was promoted to the NEU, the borough-wide narcotics unit. He received two Combat Crosses at a ceremony on the steps of City Hall, prompting Mayor Dinkins to quip that if he gets any more medals, "He'll need somebody to help him carry them home." Gary is working in a group again, and his overtime is severely restricted. The last two people he spotted on the street with guns turned out to be out-of-town police officers. At a recent meeting of his unit with the chief of the Housing police, he raised his hand. "When are they going to give these people in the projects some jobs?" he demanded, to groans from his fellow officers for his heresy. He and his wife, Lisa, have had a third child, Jasmine. They still live in their basement apartment in Elmont.

Sharron Corley was arrested for shoplifting at Bloomingdale's. When no one came forward to pay his $500 bail, he served sixteen days in jail, pleaded guilty, and was sentenced to community service and time served. He went back to Satellite Academy. Since his return, he has passed all his courses and dreams of attending college. He got a job in a clothing store to earn spending money. His singing group, Public Figure, signed a management contract with Warner Brothers Reprise records. He has auditioned for several movies and worked as an extra in a video. To stay out of trouble, Sharron spends most of his time in the house with Vanessa or writing songs.

n the year following the publication of *The Ville* there were
stunning changes in the lives of Gary Lemite and Sharron
Corley.

Gary's promotion to the borough-wide narcotics unit proved
frustrating. Against all counsel, he forsook the detective career
path and requested a transfer back to his anticrime unit at PSA
2. Soon he was on the streets of Brownsville again, developing
drug cases, watching for guns, working for a down payment on
a house on Long Island. But there were only so many times Gary
could pursue armed men down half-lit streets, so many times
he could stand alone in a stone staircase, face to face with a
man with a gun, before someone would die.

The orders for Gary and his anticrime boys on New Year's
Eve were ambiguous: "Get in the bag [wear your uniforms]. Lay
low and back up patrol." The stroke of midnight brought the
traditional fusillade from rooftop, window, street, and doorway.
A building in the Tilden Houses was particularly hot. Backing
up a sector car on one of scores of calls for shots fired, some
of Gary's unit sprinted in the building and herded a group of
boisterous youths outside. As the Housing cops moved, their
backs were exposed to the back door. Alone for a moment in
the lobby, Gary instinctively flattened himself against a wall
and watched the rear entrance. Almost immediately, two men
entered. When they spotted Gary in his blue uniform, one
bolted outside and the other headed for the stairs, a black automatic in his hand. Gary could have stepped back. He was half-
concealed behind a door already. Instead, he stepped out and
gave chase. At the top of the second landing the man with the

gun wheeled, his weapon leveled at Gary a flight below. Gary fired one shot. In the stunning explosion the man turned and disappeared. Gary dashed after him, taking two stairs at a time, expecting the noise to draw his unit in support. His radio remained in his back pocket. He knew he couldn't run up stairs with both hands occupied and he chose the gun. It was five minutes after twelve and the radio was useless anyway, bursting with static and calls for shots fired.

On the third floor he turned back. A pursuit around so many blind turns was just too perilous. On each landing the man could duck into the hallway and slip back into the staircase from his rear. No backup was coming.

"I think I just shot a guy," Gary stuttered to his anticrime team whose members now filled the lobby. But they were distracted in the chaos. What did it matter if Gary "thought" he shot a guy. There were bullets blasting down from the roof and up from the street. Gary was shaken and for several moments his report was ignored. As the unit began a hasty vertical search, a man cried his name. "Lemite. My cousin's shot on the seventh floor. You gotta help me."

Gary peered through the throng of Housing cops and tenants that clogged the seventh-floor hallway. When he spotted the man on the floor he shuddered. He was about thirty years old, dark-skinned; it looked like the same guy. The beige jacket was gone. It would be retrieved a few days later from the family. But there would be no gun recovered, no bullet casings anywhere. The lab would find no fragments in the hallway or in the body of the wounded man.

"Don't worry. You can't kill these guys," Lenti assured Gary.

"The guy from the book did it," said a voice from the crowd as the body was trundled toward the elevator. Two days later the man died in Brookdale Hospital. A Manhattan resident on parole for armed robbery, he had been visiting relatives for New Year's Eve.

In the following days, rumors flew through Brownsville and the ranks of the Housing police. Gary had not reported the shooting, the story went, the shooting was "shaky." But without witnesses and ballistics only Gary's own words linked him to the dead man. Once more, Gary found himself at home, nauseated and afraid. He had Lisa with him this time, but over and over his racing thoughts met a stone wall. He had taken a life. No gun recovered. As the investigation continued, he was transferred to a PSA in Coney Island. Lenti was afraid Gary's high profile would make him a target. He wanted Gary off the streets for a while, wanted him to slow down. Ultimately, the Medical Examiner's report supported Gary's story and his account prevailed. In three months he was cleared and requested a move back to Brownsville. There were reasons—overtime, commuting expenses from his new Long Island home—but the truth was, Gary didn't want to get run out of Brownsville.

In December, on a short trip to promote *The Ville*, Sharron walked on a treadmill in a deserted hotel gym. As he padded slowly, he stared at himself in the mirrored walls. Twisting his head, he viewed himself from one angle and then another. A soft sound floated from his lips. The voice was plaintive and distant.

"Bonjour, Sha."

"Buenos días, Sha."

In Sharron's vision, he was a superstar strolling a broad avenue lined by fans desperate for his attention. "Sha," they wailed. Sharron remained aloof as he deigned to smile and wave to the fans. However outlandish, Sharron's thoroughly wrought daydream was more than a fantasy. It was destiny.

When *The Ville* was published, Sharron's picture was featured in newspapers and on the cover of *The Village Voice*, which carried an excerpt from the book. The sweeping searchlight of the national media settled on Sharron Corley's face. For a week, phone calls pursued him like hounds. One call came from a casting director for a film by Universal produced by Spike Lee and directed by a hot new filmmaker. The six-million-dollar movie, *New Jersey Drive*, was about carjacking. In his moment of fame, Sharron was neither unnerved nor intimidated. His emergence had been scripted in his mind a hundred times. Accordingly, he rose to the challenge like a veteran and in a series of auditions snatched the film's lead role. The lofty William Morris Agency caught word of his talent and won the right to represent Sharron Corley.

The following Spring, Sharron was again on the streets of Brooklyn. Once more, there were hard words, tough looks and guns pointed his way. But this time it was all make-believe. Production assistants held back the onlookers as the cameras rolled and young men paced the restraining barriers, squinting at Sharron, wondering what life would hold for them.

ABOUT THE AUTHOR

GREG DONALDSON has written for such publications as the *New York Times*, *Sports Illustrated*, *Playboy*, and *New York Newsday*. A graduate of Brown University, he holds a master's degree in urban education. He has taught throughout Brooklyn, from Bedford-Stuyvesant to the Brooklyn House of Detention; currently he is an instructor of reading at New York City Technical College.

WITHDRAWAL

About the Author

●

CAROL GOODMAN'S work has appeared in such journals as *The Greensboro Review*, *Literal Latté*, *The Midwest Quarterly*, and *Other Voices*. After graduation from Vassar College, where she majored in Latin, she taught Latin for several years in Austin, Texas. She then received an M.F.A. in fiction from the New School University. Goodman currently teaches writing and works as a writer in residence for Teachers & Writers. She lives in Long Island.

WITHDRAWAL

The
Lake of
Dead Languages

The
Lake of
Dead Languages

• • •

Carol Goodman

WHEELER
PUBLISHING, INC.
ROCKLAND, MA

★ AN AMERICAN COMPANY ★

Published in large print by arrangement with The Ballantine Publishing Group, a division of Random House, Inc., in the United States and Canada.

Wheeler Large Print Book Series.

Set in 16 pt Plantin.

Library of Congress Cataloging-in-Publication Data Available

Goodman, Carol.
   The lake of dead languages / Carol Goodman.
      p. (large print) cm.(Wheeler large print book series)
   ISBN 1-58724-244-3 (hardcover)
   1. Women teachers—Fiction. 2. Private schools—New York (State)—Fiction. 3. New York (State)—Fiction. 4. Large type books. I. Title.
II. Series.

                                      2002069158
                                           CIP

*To my mother, Margaret Goodman,
and in memory of my father,
Walter Goodman
1924-1999*

Acknowledgments

I would like to thank the early readers of this book whose support and encouragement were invaluable: Laurie Bower, Gary Feinberg, Wendy Gold Rossi, Scott Silverman, Nora Slonimsky, Mindy Siegel Ohringer, and Sondra Browning Witt.

To my teachers whose vision and advice guided me, Sheila Kohler and Richard Aellen.

For a work of fiction, I had a lot of factual questions. Thanks to Ann Guenther, Mohonk naturalist, who told me how lakes freeze, and to Joan LaChance, Marion Swindon, and Jim Clark for talking to me about ice harvesting at Mohonk. To my brother, Robert Goodman, for answering questions about the physics of freezing, and my daughter, Maggie, who invented the corniculum.

Thanks to Loretta Barrett, my agent, and her assistant, Alison Brooks, for taking a chance on me and steering the book toward its present incarnation.

For Linda Marrow—I couldn't have dreamed up a better editor.

Most of all, thanks to my husband, Lee Slonimsky, whose love and wild, improbable faith made all the difference. I wouldn't have written this book without you.

●

*T*HE LAKE IN MY DREAMS IS ALWAYS FROZEN. IT
*is never the lake in summer, its water stained
black by the shadows of pine trees, or the lake in
fall, its surface stitched into a quilt of red and gold,
or the lake on a spring night, beaded with moonlight. The lake in my dreams reflects nothing; it
is the dead white of a closed door, sealed by ice
that reaches sixty feet down to the lake's glacial
limestone cradle.*

*I skate over that reassuring depth soundlessly,
the scrape of my blades absorbed by a pillowy gray
sky. I feel the strength of the deep ice in the soles
of my feet and I skate like I've never skated in life.
No wobbly ankles or sore thighs, I skate with the
ease and freedom of flying. I skate the way skating
looks, not feels.*

*I lean into long, languid figure eights and arch
my back in the tight spins, my long hair shedding
sparks of static in the cold dry air. When I leap,
I soar high above the silver ice and land straight
and true as an arrow boring into its mark. Each
glide is long and perfect and crosses over the last,
braiding tendrils of ice and air out of the spray
which fans out in my wake.*

1

Then comes the moment when I am afraid to look down, afraid of what I'll see beneath the surface of the ice, but when I do look, the ice is as thick and opaque as good linen and my heart beats easier. I am weightless with relief. I pirouette as effortlessly as a leaf spinning in the wind, the fine lines my blades inscribe in the ice as delicate as calligraphy. It is only when I reach the shore and look back that I see I have carved a pattern in the ice, a face, familiar and long gone, which I watch, once again, sink into the black water.

PART ONE

•

Overturn

Chapter One

●

I HAVE BEEN TOLD TO MAKE THE LATIN CURRICULUM relevant to the lives of my students. I am finding, though, that my advanced girls at Heart Lake like Latin precisely because it has no relevance to their lives. They like nothing better than a new, difficult declension to memorize. They write the noun endings on their palms in blue ballpoint ink and chant the declensions, *"Puella, puellae, puellae, puellam, puella..."* like novices counting their rosaries.

When it comes time for a test they line up at the washroom to scrub down. I lean against the cool tile wall watching them as the washbasins fill with pale blue foam and the archaic words run down the drains. When they offer to show me the undersides of their wrists for traces of letters I am unsure if I should look. If I look, am I showing that I don't trust them? If I don't look, will they think I am naive? When they put their upturned hands in mine—so light-boned and delicate—it is as if a fledgling has alighted in my lap. I am afraid to move.

In class I see only the tops of their hands— the black nail polish and silver skull rings. One girl even has a tattoo on the top of her right hand—an intricate blue pattern that she tells me is a Celtic knot. Now I look at the warm, pink flesh—their fingertips are tender and whorled from immersion in water, the scent of soap rises like incense. Three of the girls have scratched the inside of their wrists with pins or razors. The lines are fainter than the lifelines that crease their palms. I want to trace their scars with my fingertips and ask them why, but instead I squeeze their hands and tell them to go on into class. *"Bona fortuna,"* I say. "Good luck on the test."

When I first came back to Heart Lake I was surprised at the new girls, but I soon realized that since my own time here the school has become a sort of last resort for a certain kind of girl. I have learned that even though the Heart Lake School for Girls still looks like a prestigious boarding school, it is not. It is really a place for girls who have already been kicked out of two or three of the really good schools. A place for girls whose parents have grown sick of drama, sick of blood on the bathroom floor, sick of the policeman at the door.

Athena (her real name is Ellen Craven, but I have come to think of the girls by the classical names they've chosen for class) is the last to finish washing. She has asked for extra credit, for more declensions and verb conjugations to learn, so she is up to her elbows in

6

blue ink. She holds out her forearms for me to see and there is no way to avoid looking at the scar on her right arm that starts at the base of her palm and snakes up to the crook of her elbow. She sees me wince.

Athena shrugs. "It was a stupid thing to do," she says. "I was all messed up over this boy last year, you know?"

I try to remember caring that much for a boy—I almost see a face—but it's like trying to remember labor pains, you remember the symptoms of pain—the blurred vision, the way your mind moves in an ever-tightening circle around a nucleus so dense gravity itself seems to bend toward it—but not the pain itself.

"That's why my aunt sent me to an all girls school," Athena continues. "So I wouldn't get so caught up with boys again. Like my mother goes to this place upstate when she needs to dry out—you know, get away from booze and pills? So, I'm here drying out from boys."

I look up from her hands to her pale face—a paleness accentuated by her hair, which is dyed a blue-black that matches the circles under her eyes. I think I hear tears in her voice, but instead she is laughing. Before I can help myself I laugh, too. Then I turn away from her and yank paper towels from the dispenser so she can dry her arms.

I let the girls out early after the test. They whoop with delight and crowd the doorway. I am not insulted. This is part of the game we play. They like it when I'm strict. Up to a point. They like that the class is hard. They like

7

me, I think. At first I flattered myself that it was because I understood them, but then one day I retrieved a note left on the floor.

"What do you think of her?" one girl had written.

"Let's go easy on her," another, later I identified the handwriting as Athena's, had answered.

I realized then that the girls' goodwill did not come from anything I had said or done. It came because they knew, with the uncanny instinct of teenagers, that I must have messed up as badly as they had to end up here.

Today they leave shaking the cramp out of their hands and comparing answers from the test. Vesta—the thin, studious one, the one who tries the hardest—holds the textbook open to read out the declension and conjugation endings. There are moans from some, little cries of triumph from others. Octavia and Flavia, the two Vietnamese sisters who are counting on classics scholarships to college, nod at each answer with the calm assurance of hard studiers. If I listened carefully I wouldn't have to mark the tests at all to know what grades to give, but I let the sounds of sorrow and glee blur together. I can hear them all the way down the hall until Myra Todd opens her door and tells them they're disturbing her biology lab.

I hear another door open and one of my girls calls out, "Hello, Miss Marshmallow." Then I hear a high nervous laugh which I recognize as that of Gwendoline Marsh, the English teacher. It won't be Gwen, though, who com-

8

plains; it's Myra I'll catch hell from later for letting them out before the bell. I don't care. It's worth it for the quiet that settles now over my empty classroom, for the minutes I'll have before my next class.

I turn my chair around so that I face the window. On the lawn in front of the mansion I see my girls collapsed in a lopsided circle. From here their dark clothing and dyed hair— Athena's blue-black, Aphrodite's bleached blond, and Vesta's lavender red, which is the same shade as the nylon hair on my daughter's Little Mermaid doll—make them look like hybrid flowers bred into unnatural shades. Black dahlias and tulips. Flowers the bruised color of dead skin.

Past where the girls sit, Heart Lake lies blue-green and still in its glacial cradle of limestone. The water on this side of the lake is so bright it hurts my eyes. I rest them on the dark eastern end of the lake, where the pine tree shadows stain the water black. Then I pick my homework folder up off my desk and add the assignments I've collected today, sorting each girl's new assignment with older work (as usual, I'm about a week behind in my grading). They're easy to sort because almost all the girls use different kinds of paper that I've come to recognize as each girl's distinctive trademark: lavender stationery for Vesta, the long yellow legal-size sheets for Aphrodite, lined paper with ragged edges which Athena tears from her black-and-white notebooks.

Sometimes the page Athena gives me has

something else written on the reverse side. A few lines at the top that look to be the end of a diary entry. I know from the scraps I've read that she sometimes writes as if addressing a letter to herself and sometimes as if the journal itself were her correspondent. "Don't forget," I read in one of these coda. "You don't need anyone but yourself." And another time: "I promise I'll write to you more often, you're all I have." Sometimes there is a drawing on the back of her assignment. Half a woman's face dissolving into a wave. A rainbow sliced in two by a winged razor blade. A heart with a dagger through its middle. Cheap teenage symbolism. They could be pictures from the book I kept when I was her age.

I recognize the paper she uses by its ragged edge where it's been pulled out of the thread-stitched notebook. If she's not careful, pages will start to come loose. I know because I used the same sort of book when I was her age, the kind with the black-and-white-marbled covers. When I look down at the page I think I've got another piece of her journal, but then I turn it over and see the other side is blank. Athena's homework is on a separate page at the bottom of the stack and I've lost track whether the page I'm holding is one that was just handed in or was already in the folder. I look back at the page I thought was her homework. There is a single line of tiny, cramped writing at the top of it. The ink is so pale that I have to move the paper into the light from the window in order to make it out.

You're the only one I can ever tell.

I stare at the words so hard that a dim halo forms around them and I have to blink to make the darkness go away. Later I'll wonder what I recognized first: the words that I wrote in my journal almost twenty years ago, or my own handwriting.

I MAKE THE STUDENTS IN MY NEXT CLASS RECITE declensions until the sound of the other words in my head is a faint whisper, but as I walk to the dining hall the words reassert themselves in my brain. *You're the only one I can ever tell.* Words any teenager might write in her diary. If I hadn't recognized my own handwriting there would be no cause for alarm. The words could refer to anything, but knowing what they do refer to I can't help but wonder how someone has gotten hold of my old journal and slipped a page of it into my homework folder. At first I had thought it must be Athena, but then I realized that any of the girls could have handed me the page when she handed in her own assignment. For that matter, since I left the homework folder on my desk overnight and the classrooms are unlocked, anyone might have slipped the page into my homework folder.

I know that that particular page is from the last journal I kept senior year, and that I lost it during the spring semester. Could it have been on the property all this time—hidden under the floorboards in my old dorm room perhaps—and Athena or one of her friends has now

11

found it? The thought of what else is in that journal floods through me and I have to actually stop at the foot of the mansion stairs and lean on the railing for a moment before I can start up the steps.

Girls in plaid skirts and white shirts coming untucked from the blue sweaters tied around their waists stream around me as I make my way up the stairs toward the massive oak doors. The doors were designed to intimidate. They are outside the human scale. The Crevecoeur family, who donated the mansion to the school, also owned the paper mill in the nearby town of Corinth. India Crevecoeur ran a tea and "improvement society" for the female mill workers. I picture those mill girls, in a tight gaggle for warmth as much as for moral support, waiting outside these doors. My own grandmother, who worked at the mill before working as a maid for the Crevecoeurs, might have been among them.

When I won the scholarship to come here I wondered what the Crevecoeurs would have thought about the granddaughter of one of their maids attending their school. I don't think they would have been amused. In the family portrait that hangs in the Music Room they look like dour, unhappy people. Their ancestors were Huguenots who fled France in the seventeenth century and eventually made their way here to this remote outpost in upstate New York. It must have been a shock to them—this wilderness, the brutal winters, the isolation. The fanlight above the door is plain glass

12

now, but when I went here it was stained glass: a red heart split in two by a green fleur-de-lis-handled dagger and the family motto in yellow: *Cor te reducit*—The heart leads you back. I've always imagined them waiting for some deliverance from this savage place, to France, or God perhaps. But since I have found myself back at Heart Lake—a place I swore I'd never return to—I've begun to think the heart in the motto is the lake itself, exerting its own gravitational pull on those who have once lived on its shores and bathed in its icy green water.

THE FACULTY DINING ROOM IS IN THE OLD MUSIC Room. When I went to Heart Lake the scholarship students worked in the kitchen and served the teachers at meals. Some years ago the practice was discontinued as it was considered demeaning to the scholarship students. I never minded though. Nancy Ames, the cook, always gave us a good meal. Roasts and potatoes, creamed vegetables and poached fish. I never ate so well in all my life. She saved us the rolls she baked fresh for every meal. She gave them to us wrapped in thick linen napkins embroidered with the Heart Lake crest, which we were to remember to return. Walking back through the cold dusk—that last year at Heart Lake resides in my memory as one endless winter dusk—I felt the warmth of them in my pocket, like a small animal burrowed for shelter against my body.

13

Now the school uses paper napkins and the teachers serve themselves from a buffet. Tuna fish salad and packaged bread. Carrot sticks and hard-boiled eggs. What hasn't changed, though, is the mandatory attendance for all faculty. It was a tenet of India Crevecoeur, Heart Lake's founder, that the teaching staff be a community. It is an admirable goal, but on days like today I'd give much to be able to take my sandwich out to a rock by the lake with no one but Ovid for company. As I enter the room I give India's image in the family portrait a resentful look, which she, snug in the bosom of her large family, disdainfully returns.

The only empty seat is next to Myra Todd. I take out a stack of quizzes to grade and hope they will keep her from commenting on third period's early dismissal. Half the teachers at the long table have a similar stack of paper-clipped pages at which they peck with their red pens in between bites of tuna fish. When I take out mine, though, I see I still have the journal page with my handwriting on the top of the stack. I hurriedly fold it and stick it into the pocket of my plaid wool skirt just as Myra leans across me for the salt shaker. I have to remind myself that she'd have no reason to think anything of those enigmatic words even if she did see them. Unless she's the one who found my old journal.

I steal a glance at her to see if she's paying undue attention to my stack of papers, but she is placidly chewing her sandwich and staring

into the middle distance. Under the smell of tuna fish and stale coffee I catch her distinctive smell—a whiff of mildew as if she were one of her own science experiments left too long in the supply closet over Christmas break. I've always wondered what peculiar health condition or faulty laundry procedure is the cause of this odor, but it's hardly the kind of thing you could ask a person as prim and proper as Myra. I try to imagine what she would do if she came upon my old journal, and I am pretty sure she'd take it straight to the dean.

I try to imagine what Dean Buehl would make of my old journal. Celeste Buehl was the science teacher when I went to Heart Lake. She was always kind to me when I was her student—and she was more than kind when she gave me this job—but I don't think that kindness would survive a reading of my senior-year journal.

When she comes in today I notice how much she's changed in the twenty years since she was my teacher. I remember her as slim and athletic, leading nature hikes through the woods and skating on the lake in winter. Now her broad shoulders are rounded and her short, cropped hair, once dark and springy, looks lifeless and dull. Myra Todd picks the moment of the dean's entrance to mention third period's early dismissal.

"Jane," she says loudly, "your third-period class disturbed my senior lab this morning. We were at a very delicate stage of dissection. Mallory Martin's hand slipped and she nicked her lab partner with a scalpel."

I know Mallory Martin by reputation. My girls call her Maleficent. I somehow doubt the incident with the scalpel was an accident.

"I'm sorry, Myra, I'll tell them to be quieter. They get so keyed up for these exams."

"The thing to do is give them extra problems when they finish their tests. That way they won't be so anxious to finish early." Simon Ross, the math teacher, volunteers this pedagogical advice and resumes scoring a pile of quizzes with a thick red marker. The tips of his fingers are stained red with the marker, and I notice the color has bled onto his sandwich.

"I let the girls write in their journals," Gwendoline Marsh offers in a small voice. "It helps them to have an outlet and it's part of their grade."

"And just how do you grade these journals?" asks Meryl North, the history teacher who already seemed as ancient as her subject when I was a student here. "Do you read their private thoughts?"

"Oh no, I only read the parts they want me to—they circle the parts I'm not supposed to read and mark them *private*."

Meryl North makes a sound between a laugh and a choke and Gwendoline's pale skin reddens. I try to catch Gwen's eye to give her a nod of encouragement—she is the closest thing to a friend I have here at Heart Lake—but she is resolutely staring down at a worn volume of Emily Dickinson.

"They do seem to be under a lot of stress,"

I say, more to cover Gwen's embarrassment than because I want to open this particular line of conversation. There were two suicide attempts last year. In response, the administration has instituted weekly faculty seminars on adolescent depression and "How to detect the ten warning signs of suicidal behavior."

"Anyone in particular?" The question comes from Dr. Candace Lockhart. Unlike the rest of us at the table she has no stacks of papers to grade or texts to study for next period. Her fingers are never stained with ink, her exquisitely tailored dove gray suits never tainted with the ugly yellow chalk dust that the rest of us wear like a wasting disease. She's the school psychologist, an office that did not exist in my day. There is an aura of secrecy surrounding her appointment here. I've heard some of the faculty complain that Dean Buehl hired her without going through the proper channels. In other words, without giving the resident faculty a chance to gossip about her credentials. There's a whiff of jealousy about the complaints, to which I am not immune. The rumor is that she is conducting research for a groundbreaking study on the psychology of adolescent girls. We all suspect that once her research is done she will leave us for private practice, a glamorous lecture circuit with appearances on "Oprah," or perhaps a tenure-track post at an Ivy League college— some existence more appropriate to her wardrobe. In the meantime, she resides among us with her pale, almost white, hair, blue

eyes and thin, ascetic figure, like a lilac point Siamese slumming with drab tabbies.

Poor Gwen, in her faded Indian print jumper and fussily old-fashioned high-necked white blouse, looks especially dowdy in comparison. Although Candace Lockhart and Gwen Marsh are both in their early thirties, the effects of teaching five classes a day, not to mention sponsoring half a dozen clubs, have left their mark on Gwen. Her complexion is muddy, her hair limp and going gray at the roots, her blue eyes washed out and bloodshot. Candace, on the other hand, clearly has time to get her hair done (that platinum blond can't be entirely natural) and *her* blue eyes are as clear and cold as lake water.

I am sufficiently unnerved by those blue eyes to make a mistake. Of course, I should say, "No. No one in particular." But instead I name a name. "Athena...I mean Ellen...Craven. I noticed today that she has an awful scar on her arm."

"Well, yes, I know about that of course. That's old news and not surprising given Ellen's history."

I should be glad for her dismissal, but something in the way Dr. Lockhart's blue eyes glaze over, already looking past me toward whatever illustrious future fate has in store for her, irks me. I am forever thinking I am past such vanities and finding that I am not.

"Some of the pictures she draws on the back of her homework assignments are...well... somewhat disturbing."

"You let your girls turn in homework with pictures on the back?" Myra Todd looks up from her stack of papers, appalled, only to meet Dr. Lockhart's cool look of disdain. Gratified to have someone else silenced by those eyes, I go on. It has occurred to me that this is exactly what I should be doing. My responsibility as Athena's teacher, as an especially trusted teacher in whom the girl confided, demands that I seek help for her emotional problems. To whom else should I refer those problems than the school psychologist?

"Disembodied eyes with tears turning into razor blades, that kind of thing. I suppose the images aren't unusual..."

I notice that the rest of the table has grown quiet, and it occurs to me that I shouldn't be talking about my student in front of the entire teaching staff. Dr. Lockhart must think so, too.

"Perhaps you should come see me in my office to talk about Athena. I'm in my office by seven. Why don't you come in before your first class?" Dr. Lockhart suggests.

She no doubt sees my reluctance to agree to this early appointment—I am thinking of the lake swim I try to take each morning before class—and so she adds this last piece of admonishment.

"It's crucial we address any preoccupation with death or suicide immediately. These things have a way of turning into trends, as I'm sure you know from your own experience here, Miss Hudson. Don't you agree, Dean Buehl?"

19

Dean Buehl sighs. "God forbid that happen again."

I feel blood rush to my cheeks as if I had been slapped. Any thoughts I had of protesting the early-morning meeting are gone now, and Dr. Lockhart seems to know that. Without waiting for my answer she rises from her chair and adjusts a pale blue shawl over her suit jacket.

"I especially want to know if that Crevecoeur sisters legend..." The rest of her words are drowned out by the bell ringing to signal the end of lunch hour and the scraping of chairs being pushed back from the table.

Dr. Lockhart, unencumbered as she is, glides out of the dining room while the rest of us gather books and shoulder heavy canvas bags. Gwen especially seems to list to one side from the weight of her book bag. I ask if she needs some help and she pulls out a thick manila envelope and hands it to me.

"Oh, thank you, Jane, I was going to ask if someone could type these student poems up for the literary magazine. I'd do it but my carpal tunnel syndrome's acting up." She lifts up her arms and I see that both forearms are wrapped in ace bandages. All I'd meant to offer was to carry something for her, but what can I say?

I transfer the heavy folder from her bag to mine. Now I'm the one listing to one side as we leave the Music Room, and Gwen, lightened of her load, hurries on ahead to class. I trail behind the rest of the teachers thinking about what the psychologist had said about pre-

occupation with death and suicidal trends. I picture my students with their skull jewelry and kohl-rimmed eyes.

The nose rings and skull jewelry and purple hair may be new, but this preoccupation with suicide is not. Like many girls' schools, Heart Lake has its own suicide legend. When I was here the story would be told, usually around the Halloween bonfire at the swimming beach, that the Crevecoeur family lost all three of their daughters in the flu epidemic of 1918. It was said that one night the three girls, all delirious with fever, went down to the lake to quench their fever and drowned there. At this point in the story, someone would point to the three rocks that rose out of the water off the swimming beach and intone solemnly, "Their bodies were never found, but on the next morning three rocks appeared mysteriously in the lake and those rocks have from that day been known as the three sisters."

One of the seniors would fill in the rest of the details as we younger girls nervously toasted our marshmallows over the bonfire. India Crevecoeur, the girls' mother, was so heartbroken she could no longer live at Heart Lake, so she turned her home into a girls' school. From the school's first year, however, there have been mysterious suicides at Heart Lake. They say that the sound of the lake lapping against the three rocks (here the speaker would pause so we could all listen to the sound of the water restlessly beating against the rocks) beckons girls to take their

lives by throwing themselves into the lake. They say that when the lake freezes over the faces of the girls can be seen peering out from beneath the ice. The ice makes a noise like moaning, and that sound, like the lapping of the water, draws girls out onto the lake's frozen surface, where the sisters wait to drag the unsuspecting skater through the cracks in the ice. And they say that whenever one girl drowns in the lake, two more inevitably follow.

If the legend is still circulating, as Dr. Lockhart fears, there are a few things I could tell my girls. I could tell them that the Crevecoeur family did lose their youngest daughter, Iris, but she didn't drown. She caught a chill from a mishap during a boating party with her two older sisters and died of the flu in her own bed. I could also tell them that nineteenth-century drawings of the lake show the three rocks, which were called, by early settlers, the three graces. But I know that the harder you try to dispel a legend the more power it gains. It's like Oedipus trying to avoid his fate and running headlong into it at the crossroads. And once I begin to talk about the legend they might ask if there were any suicides when I went to school here. Then I would either have to lie or tell them that during my senior year both my roommates drowned in the lake.

I might even find myself telling them that since then I have always felt the lake is waiting for the third girl.

Chapter Two

●

BETWEEN TEACHING AND TAKING CARE OF OLIVIA after school, the question of who has found my old notebook recedes to background noise. I can hear the question whispering at the edge of my consciousness, but I push it away until I can concentrate on it.

That night I scramble eggs for Olivia and me. After dinner we wash out the eggshells for an arts and crafts project for her nursery school. Olivia holds the shells under the running tap water and then hands them to me. I surreptitiously scoop out the transparent jelly that still clings to the hollow cups and set them into an empty egg crate. She explains to me that not just birds come from eggs. Snakes and alligators and turtles also come out of eggs. Even spiders.

"Charlotte made a sack for her eggs and Wilbur carried it home from the fair in his mouth," she tells me. I remember that her preschool teacher, Mrs. Crane, is reading *Charlotte's Web* aloud in class. They'll study spiders and eggs at the same time and visit a local farm to see pigs. It's an excellent preschool program, one of the perks of working here.

I set the crate aside on the counter to dry.

"And then Charlotte died," Olivia finishes.

"That's a sad part, isn't it?"

"Uh huh. Can I watch some TV before bed?"

"No, it's time for your shower."

Olivia complains bitterly about no TV, about the fact she has to take a shower because the cottage we've been given by the school has no bath, and, for good measure, she throws in the fact that her father isn't here to read to her. It's on the tip of my tongue to say that he hardly ever read to her anyway, that he was usually at work far past her bedtime, but of course I don't. I tell her that her father will read to her when he sees her the weekend after next, which requires a lengthy consultation with the calendar before she grasps the time frame of every other weekend visitation.

By the time her shower is finished it is past nine o'clock and my throat is raw from teaching all day and arguing with a four-year-old. Still, I can't really weasel out of reading to her after that remark about her father. I go into the spare bedroom where I've stacked the boxes of books and papers and find one of my old children's books, a collection called *Tales from the Ballet*.

Olivia is intrigued with the idea that this is a book I had as a child.

"Did your mommy give it to you?" she asks.

"No," I tell her, and wonder how I could possibly explain to her that my mother would never have spent money on anything so frivolous as books. "One of my teachers. Here, she wrote something to me."

Inside on the flyleaf my kindergarten teacher had written, "To Jane, who dances on ice."

"What's that mean? Dance on ice."

"Ice skating. Mommy used to be a pretty good ice skater. I used to skate on this very lake when it froze in the winter."

"Can I skate on the lake when it freezes?" she asks.

"Maybe," I say. "We'll see."

I flip through the pages of the book looking for a story she'll recognize—"Cinderella" or "Sleeping Beauty" perhaps—but then the book falls open to a page marked with a dried maple leaf, its once vibrant scarlet faded now to palest russet. "This one!" Olivia demands with that odd certainty of four-year-olds.

It's "Giselle." My old favorite, but not the one I would have chosen for Olivia.

"This one has some scary parts," I say.

"Good," Olivia tells me. "I like scary parts."

I figure I can edit out anything too scary. I stop to explain why Giselle's mother won't let her dance and then I have to explain what it means to have a weak heart. She likes the part about the prince disguised as a peasant— "Just like in Sleeping Beauty"—and is sad when Giselle dies. I am thinking I will just leave out the part about the Wilis—the spirits of girls disappointed in love who seduce young men and make them dance until they die—but when I turn the page to the picture of the wraithlike girls in their bridal dresses, Olivia is instantly in love with them. Just as I was at her age. This had been my favorite picture.

So I read on. Through the part where the girls dance with the gamekeeper, Hilarion, and lure him into the lake to drown, and up to where the queen of the Wilis tells Giselle she must make Albrecht, her false lover, dance to his doom.

"Will she?" Olivia asks, her face pinched with concern.

"What do you think?" I ask her.

"Well, he did make her sad," she says.

"But she loves him, let's see...."

Giselle tells Albrecht to hold fast to the cross on her tomb, but he is so entranced by her dancing that he joins her. But because of Giselle's delay, he is still alive when the church clock strikes four and the Wilis return to their graves. "And so she saves him," I tell Olivia, closing the book. All I've left out are the last two lines of the story, which read, "His life had been saved, but he has lost his heart. Giselle has danced away with it."

WHEN OLIVIA HAS FALLEN ASLEEP I TAKE OUT THE piece of paper folded in my skirt pocket. As I unfold it I am sure that I will see now that the handwriting is Athena's, or Vesta's or Aphrodite's, anyone's but my own. But as I stare at the words again there is no escaping the truth. I recognize not only my own hand-writing, but the ink—a peculiar shade of pea-cock blue that Lucy Toller gave me, along with a fountain pen in the same color, for my fif-teenth birthday.

Still holding the paper, I go into the spare bedroom to find the box marked "Heart Lake." I tear at the packing tape and rip open the box so hastily that the sharp edge of the cardboard slices into my wrist. Ignoring the pain, I pull out the stack of black-and-white notebooks inside.

There are three of them. I started them in the ninth grade when I first met Matt and Lucy Toller, and faithfully kept a new one each year through our senior year at Heart Lake.

I count them as if hoping that the fourth one will have miraculously rejoined its companions, but of course it hasn't. I haven't seen the fourth notebook since spring semester senior year, when it disappeared from my dorm room.

At the time I thought someone in the administration had confiscated the notebook. I spent that last term at Heart Lake sure that it was only a matter of time before I was called into the dean's office and confronted with the truth of everything that had happened that year, and what I had said at the inquest. But the summons never came. I attended the graduation ceremony and the reception on the lawn above the lake, standing apart from the other girls and their proud families, and afterward I took a taxi to the train station and a train to my summer job at the library at Vassar, where I had a scholarship for the fall. I decided that the notebook must have gotten lost. Sometimes I told myself that it had slipped out of my book bag and fallen

into the lake and the lake had washed away all the blue-green ink until its pages were as blank as they were on the first day of senior year.

I open the first notebook and read the opening entry.

"Lucy gave me this fountain pen and beautiful ink for my birthday and Matt gave me this notebook," I had written in a flowery script that tried to live up to the fancy pen and ink. There were blotches, though, where the pen's nib had caught the paper. It had taken a while to get used to that pen. "I'll never have any other friends like them."

I almost laugh at the words. *Other friends.* What other friends? When I first laid eyes on Matt and Lucy Toller I had no other friends.

I take out the folded paper and smooth it out next to this page. The handwriting is surer and blotch-free, but the words are written in the same beautiful shade of blue-green.

I go outside to watch the moon rise over Heart Lake. I think, not for the first time, that I must have been crazy to come back here. But then, where else had I to go?

When I told Mitch I wanted a divorce he laughed at me. "Where will you go? How will you live?" he asked. "For God's sake, Jane, you were a Latin major. If you leave this house you'll be on your own."

And I had thought of Electra's line, "How shall we be lords in our own house? We have been sold and go as wanderers." And right then

I knew I'd go to the only homeland I'd ever had: Heart Lake.

I started to work on my Latin, which I hadn't touched in years. At night I studied from my old Wheelock textbook, picking away at case endings and verb conjugations until the unintelligible jumble of words sorted itself out. Words paired up like skaters linking arms, adjectives with nouns, verbs with subjects, inscribing precise patterns in the slippery ice of archaic syntax.

And always the voices I heard reciting the declensions and conjugations were Matt's and Lucy's.

When I had reread Wheelock twice, I applied for the job at Heart Lake and learned that my old science teacher, Celeste Buehl, had become dean. "We've never really been able to replace Helen Chambers," she told me. I remembered that Miss Buehl had been good friends with my Latin teacher. No one was sadder than she when Helen Chambers had been let go. "But then we've never gotten an old girl in the position." "Old girl" was how they referred to an alumna who came back to teach at Heart Lake. Celeste Buehl was an "old girl," as were Meryl North, the history teacher, and Tacy Beade, the art teacher. "Your generation doesn't seem interested in teaching. I haven't interviewed a graduate since I became dean, but I can't think of anyone better to take the job than one of Helen Chambers's girls. Luckily my old cottage is free. It will be perfect for you and your daughter. You remember

29

it, the one above the swimming beach." I remembered it all too well.

And although the idea of living here was at first disturbing, I've come to treasure my view of the lake. It's only a few yards from my front door to the Point, the stone cliff that bisects the lake, giving it its heartlike shape. From where I stand now I can see the curve of the swimming beach, white in the moonlight, and the stones we called the three sisters rising out of the still, moonlit water.

I go inside and look at Olivia sleeping. The moonlight comes through her window and falls on her tangled hair. I smooth back her hair from her forehead and rearrange the twisted sheets so she'll be cooler. She stirs and moans softly in her sleep, but doesn't call my name as she would if she were anywhere near waking. I know she might wake up later, at two or four perhaps, but I'm almost positive she'll sleep undisturbed for the next few hours.

I go back outside and down the steep stone steps that lead from our house to the lake. Every night I do this and every night I'm amazed at myself for taking the chance. Of course I know I shouldn't be leaving Olivia alone for even these few minutes—fifteen, twenty minutes, at most, I tell myself, what could happen? Well, I know what could happen. Fire, burglars, Olivia waking up and getting frightened when I don't come to her call, wandering out into the woods...my heart pounds at the images of disasters my mind so easily conjures up. But still I walk down the steps barefoot, feeling

30

through the soles of my feet when the stone steps become damp from the mist off the lake and then slimy with the moss that grows over the stones.

At the foot of the steps the ground is hard-packed mud. I can hear the restless slap of water on the rocks. I wade through the cold water until I am standing, calf deep, next to the first of the three sister stones. I lean my shoulder against the tall rock and it feels warm. Like a person, I think, although I know it's only giving off the heat collected through the unseasonably warm day. The three stones are made of a hard, glittery basalt, different from the soft surrounding limestone. Lucy said they're like the tors in England, foreign stones carried from afar and erected in the lake, but Miss Buehl said they were probably deposited by a retreating glacier and then eroded into their present shapes. Each one has been molded differently by water and time, and the freezing and unfreezing of the lake. The first stone, which I am standing by, is a column rising six feet high above the water, the second is also a column, but it leans in the direction of the southern shore. The third stone is a rounded dome, curving gently out of the deep water.

If you look at the rocks in succession—in the right light or through a faint mist like the one that rises from the lake tonight—you can imagine that the first stone is a girl wading at the edge of the lake, the second is the same girl diving into the water, and the third is

the girl's behind rising above the water as she dolphin dives into the lake.

The lake feels deliciously cold. The weather has been unseasonably warm for early October, but I know this Indian summer can't last much longer. Any day now a cold front will move down from Canada and it will be too cold to swim. Suddenly I notice how sweaty and sticky I feel, how sore my neck and back are from standing at a blackboard all day and leaning over stacks of papers. I remember that I won't be able to take my swim in the morning and the thought is like a physical pain. I could leave my clothes on the rock and swim for just a few moments. The cold water would wash away all thought of that lost journal and what is in it.

I am about to take off my shirt when I hear a rustle in the trees behind me. Instinctively, I move into the shadow of the second stone as if I were the errant schoolgirl caught out of her dorm at night. From there I can see three white shapes pass by me and into the lake. They move smoothly into the water, like spirits, and I am reminded eerily of the Wilis in the story I had been reading to Olivia. White sheets billow up around them like the Wilis' bridal gowns, and then, like animal brides in a fairy tale discarding their skins, they emerge out of the white billows and stroke naked out to the farthest rock.

A white clump floats past me and I pick up its corner and read the laundry marking, which identifies it as the property of the Heart Lake School for Girls.

One of the girls has pulled herself onto the farthest rock. She stands stretching her arms above her head as if reaching for the moon.

"We call on the Goddess of the Lake and make offering to honor She who guards the holy water."

The two girls in the water giggle. One of them tries to heave herself onto the rock and lands on her chest with a painful-sounding thud.

"Damn, I smashed my boobs."

"Oh, like they could be any flatter."

"Thanks a lot, Melissa."

With their giggling and bickering the three girls are transformed from mysterious Wilis to three awkward adolescents: my students, Athena (Ellen Craven), Vesta (Sandy James), and Aphrodite (Melissa Randall).

"Come on," Athena says, her hands on her naked hips. "You're ruining it. How can the Lake Goddess take our offering seriously with you two messing around? I told you we shouldn't have gotten high first."

With the last comment I am transformed from innocent bystander—amused voyeur—to responsible teacher, if only in my guilty conscience, because I still don't reveal my presence. But now I've been given some information I should act on. The girls have been smoking pot. And yet, why should this alert me to my role while the sight of my students skinny-dipping at night fails to? Perhaps because skinny-dipping and making offerings to the Lake Goddess are both old Heart Lake traditions. In my day the girls routinely made sacrifices

33

to the spirit of the lake. Sometimes we called her the Lady of the Lake (that was when we were reading Tennyson), which we later translated as Domina Lacunae, and in our senior year we called her the White Goddess. Over the years we offered her half-eaten S'mores, beads from broken necklaces, and locks of hair. Lucy said that if you gave her something at the beginning of the term you wouldn't lose anything in the lake that year. Girls are always losing things in the lake. I imagine the dark floor of the lake as faintly glimmering with broken ID bracelets, tarnished hairclips, and hoop earrings.

At the thought of the lake bottom I am suddenly cold. I remember Olivia alone in the house and I wonder how much time has elapsed. I want to go back, but if I let the girls see that I have seen them, I will have to report them to Dean Buehl. I remember her expression today when Dr. Lockhart mentioned the Crevecoeur legend and know that the last thing I want to do is remind her of girls making sacrifices to the lake. Also I am afraid to leave them here. What if one of them slips on the rocks or gets a cramp swimming back? Having witnessed them I feel they are now my responsibility. So I wait while they finish their "rite." I can tell they are cold now, their skin goosefleshed in the moonlight, and impatient to be done. I can't see what they hold up in their hands as offerings, but I can hear their "prayers."

"Let me maintain a B average this term so my mom gets off my back," Vesta says.

"Keep Brian from falling in love with someone else while he's at Exeter," Aphrodite pleads.

Only Athena says her bit too quietly for me to hear, but I see that as she whispers her plea she holds up her left arm, bending the wrist back so that her empty palm is flat to the night sky and the long scar on her forearm shows up livid in the moonlight. It's as if her offering were the scar itself.

Chapter Three

●

"ANOREXIA, SELF—MUTILATION, SUICIDE...THREE sides of the same picture. Teenage pregnancy, STDs, drug abuse, you name it. It all begins when puberty strikes. Look at your ten-year-old girls—they're bright and confident. Then look at your fifteen- and sixteen-year-olds. Girls' IQs actually plummet during adolescence. And it's getting worse. Did you know that the suicide rate among girls age ten to fourteen rose seventy-five percent between 1979 and 1988?"

Dr. Lockhart leans back in her swivel chair and waits for my reaction. It is difficult to read her expression. She sits with her back to the

window so that her body is silhouetted against the silver mirror of the lake. A light rain had begun not long after I returned to my house last night and continued through the dawn, consoling me, somewhat, for the loss of my morning swim. Now the rain has stopped and the sky, though overcast, is a bright, burnished pewter, against which Dr. Lockhart is a darker, blurrier gray. Neither the swimming beach nor the two rocks closest to the shore are visible from her second-floor office in the mansion; they are obscured by the steep rock wall of the Point. I can just make out, however, the third rock where I saw Athena standing last night.

I tell her I hadn't been aware of a rising suicide rate after 1979. I don't mention that by 1979 I was immured at Vassar, poring over my Latin books in the library until midnight. Girls got drunk at the campus bar; my dorm reeked of marijuana; boys wandered in and out of the hall bathroom; girls drove each other to the clinic in Dobbs Ferry for abortions. You could get a prescription for the Pill at the school clinic and no one had heard of AIDS. I memorized Horace and struggled over Latin composition.

"Diderot said to a young girl, 'You all die at fifteen.' "

I am startled by her statement until I realize she isn't speaking literally. I am somewhat familiar with this line of thought—that girls suffer a loss of confidence with the onset of puberty. I recognize the titles of the books that

line Dr. Lockhart's shelves. *Meeting at the Crossroads, Reviving Ophelia.* I think of what I had hoped for my life at fourteen, and it isn't so much as if I had died as that I had fallen into a long sleep like a girl in a fairy tale. But I had thought of my case as unique.

"A girl like Ellen is particularly at risk," Dr. Lockhart says.

"Why a girl like Ellen?"

Dr. Lockhart wheels herself over to a gunmetal gray file cabinet and pulls a light green file folder from the middle drawer. She looks at it briefly and slips it back into place.

"The girl's parents are divorced—the father is almost entirely out of the picture and the mother's an alcoholic who spends most of her time in rehab clinics." Dr. Lockhart rattles off these facts as if she's reciting a recipe. I remember what Athena said about her mother *drying out.* "There's an aunt who's the legal guardian, but her solution has been to shuttle the girl from school to school."

"That's too bad," I say. "I knew some girls like that when I went to school here."

"Did you?" Dr. Lockhart studies me for a moment and then smiles. "Maybe you asked them home to spend the holidays with you."

I start to laugh at the idea. Those girls from Albany and Saratoga in their shetland wool sweaters and graduated pearls might have been neglected by their wealthy relatives, but I could only imagine what they would have made of my mother's Campbell's soup casseroles, the plastic covers on the one good couch, the

view of the mill from the living room window. I look at Dr. Lockhart and see she's no longer smiling. "No," I admit. "I never thought to ask them home. I guess it *was* lonely here for some of them."

"Imagine every time you got settled at one school and made some friends having to start all over again. A person would eventually give up."

The dry tone has vanished. She really does care about these girls, I realize. "Did you go to boarding school?" I ask.

"Several," she answers. "So I can guess how lonely it's been for Athena—switching schools so often. It's that loneliness that makes a girl susceptible to depression and suicidal urges. It's essential to curb any such tendencies in our girls. Once the idea of suicide breaks out..."

"You make it sound like a contagious disease."

"It is a contagious disease, Jane. I've seen it happen. One girl might be playing with the notion of suicide, or indulge in cutting herself as a way of coping with emotional pain, then one of her friends might emulate her and succeed in killing herself. The inevitable drama surrounding such tragedies exerts a morbid pull on these girls. Notice their fascination with death—skull jewelry and black clothing, the whole 'Goth' look."

"Yes, my senior Latin class looks like something out of the Middle Ages, and they almost all have scratches on their arms."

"Do you remember *The Crucible*?"

"The play by Arthur Miller? Of course, but why...?"

"Remember how the Salem girls accused their tormentors of pricking them with pins? When the judges examined the girls' bodies they indeed found scratches and cuts, bite marks, pins sticking in their flesh..."

I flinch and Dr. Lockhart pauses. "I know it's not a pleasant topic, Jane," she says, "but it has to be faced. Most of our girls engage in some form of cutting or self-mutilation. Most people don't realize how long such practices have existed."

"No," I say, "I had no idea. How did you...?"

"My thesis topic," she explains. "Self-Mutilation and Witchcraft in Puritan New England." She leans back in her chair and looks out the window at the silvery surface of the lake.

I follow her gaze and once again I think of Athena standing on the rock, holding her arm up to the moon like an offering. A sacrifice.

"Fascinating," I say.

"Oh, it is," she agrees. "The connection still exists. Often the same girls who indulge in self-mutilation practice some form of witchcraft. It's all an attempt to gain control over a world in which they have no power. Even their own emotions, their own bodies, seem out of control. Spells, rites, initiation ceremonies...these are all strategies to order the chaos of adolescence."

I think of my three students standing naked on the rock in the lake, asking for help with

boyfriends and grades. I think of the S'mores and bangles we used to offer up to the Lady of the Lake.

"Don't adolescent girls always play with this sort of thing? I mean witchcraft and spells? Ouija boards and cootie catchers."

"You're saying you practiced witchcraft with the girls you went to school with?"

"The girls I went to school with?" The question takes me by surprise. "I'm sorry," I say. "I've been thinking about Athena all morning. What does this have to do with my schoolmates?"

Dr. Lockhart wheels her chair in closer to her desk, out of the glare from the lake, and I see her blue eyes narrow on me. She touches the edge of a folder that lies on her desk as if to open it, but then she rests her long, slim fingers on its surface.

"Wasn't there a rash of suicides during your senior year?"

"I wouldn't exactly call it a *rash*," I say perhaps a little too indignantly. I feel as if she has accused *me* of having a rash. I hear the defensive note in my own voice and apparently she can, too.

"Are you uncomfortable talking about this?" she asks.

"I just don't see what it has to do with Athena," I say.

"I had hoped we could draw on your own experience with troubled, suicidal adolescents. Perhaps what you witnessed back then could throw light on your present students' troubles."

I think of what happened during my senior year and instead of light I see murk, the kind of brownish-green murk I see when I open my eyes in the lake. But perhaps Dr. Lockhart is right. Perhaps talking about what happened back then might help me to understand Athena better. And I do want to help Athena.

"There were two students who committed suicide my senior year," I say.

Dr. Lockhart shakes her head sadly. "That must have been very hard on you. What is so unfortunate in these situations is that one suicide—or suicide attempt—spurs another. As I keep trying to tell you, it becomes almost a fad. An epidemic. The girls were roommates, I believe. Weren't you all roommates?"

"We shared a suite, yes. Lucy Toller and I shared one room and Deirdre Hall had the single."

"I believe there was an unsuccessful suicide attempt first."

"Yes, Lucy slit her wrists over Christmas break. She and Deirdre were alone here on campus. It could be pretty bleak."

"The notes I have from the school nurse at the time indicate that Deirdre Hall was particularly upset by the event, especially since Miss Toller chose to slit her wrists in Deirdre's bed."

"Deirdre had the single. I guess Lucy wanted privacy. But yes, I think Deirdre was upset about that."

"Upset enough to make her own suicide attempt. Only hers was successful."

41

"Yes, she fell from the Point and broke her neck on the ice." I can't help but look up at the outcropping of stone as I speak. Dr. Lockhart follows my gaze. And there we are, both staring at the forty-foot cliff as if we expect to see Deirdre Hall appear on its height and perform her last swan dive. For a moment a picture does appear in my mind: Deirdre standing on the point, her face contorted with rage and fear. I blink away the image and turn my gaze away from the window and back to Dr. Lockhart. "Some people thought it was an accident," I say.

"According to my files her journal indicated otherwise." She flips open the folder on her desk and reads silently for a moment. A breeze from the lake stirs the pages and I can tell they are of the light onion skin we used to have in typing class, not the smooth sheets that people use nowadays in computer printers.

"And then Lucy tried again. She drowned in the lake?"

"Yes, she went through the ice...."

"That could have been an accident as well?"

"Yes, but it wasn't. I was there."

"I see. Why don't you tell me what happened."

I look out at the lake. A fog is rising from the water, whitening the surface of the lake. I can almost imagine it is winter and the lake is already frozen.

"She had a terrible fight with her brother," I say. The words come tumbling out before I can consider whether I really ought to relate

this information to Dr. Lockhart. Maybe it is because they are words I rehearsed and repeated so many times. "And then she ran onto the ice, which was breaking apart...."

"What was the fight about?" she asks.

"I only heard part of it and I didn't understand it all." I'm amazed that the well-rehearsed lines are there, tripping off my tongue as if the twenty years that have elapsed since I first delivered them had never passed. Like my Latin declensions, they'd stayed in my memory all these years. "But it had to do with a teacher here."

"Helen Chambers." I notice that Dr. Lockhart doesn't need to consult her notes to produce the name.

"Yes, Helen Chambers. She taught Latin and Greek. She was an amazing teacher. She had us all reciting Greek plays. Our senior year, she put on an aquatic version of *Iphigenia in Aulis* in the lake."

"*In* the lake?"

"Yes, in the lake."

"She sounds remarkable. But why would Lucy and her brother have been arguing about her?"

I shake my head. "I don't really know, but Lucy idealized *Domina* Chambers. We all did. It was thought that Lucy had an unhealthy obsession with her."

"*It was thought?* What do you think?"

The question is eerily like one that Helen Chambers herself would pose. If you tried to hide behind someone else's opinion—the

introduction in your Penguin edition of *Antigone*, say, or some predigested litcrit babble from Cliff Notes—she would nail you with those icy blue eyes of hers and ask you—no, demand of you—*What do you think?* And if your answer failed to measure up to her standards for original thought she would look heavenward and shrug her elegant shoulders. "Perhaps you really haven't thought at all, Miss Hudson. Come back to us when you have."

"She could be a bit harsh," I tell Dr. Lockhart.

Dr. Lockhart smiles. "Don't you ever find, Jane, that sometimes a teacher has to be a little harsh?"

"Yes, I agree," I say, but I wonder if I do. I've never been much good at the "tough love" school of teaching. "But it was thought—*I thought*—that she sometimes went too far."

"Well, then perhaps you should think of Helen Chambers when you're dealing with your students. As I'm sure you remember, she was let go."

AFTER MY MEETING WITH DR. LOCKHART I WALK to the lodge for my first-period class. The rain has cleared and the girls who run past me have tied their regulation navy school windbreakers around their waists so that they stream out behind them like shiny, rustling tail feathers. A raucous crowd of eighth graders parts to make way and then regroups behind me never losing the thread of their shouted con-

44

versation. I might be a stone parting a stream for all the notice they take of me. It makes me feel good. Like a part of the geography.

It's all I've ever wanted. To feel a part of something. I wonder if this was how Helen Chambers felt, when she came back to teach at Heart Lake. I know that to me she always seemed the defining spirit of the place.

On my way to my class I pass the art room. I stop just outside the door and watch Tacy Beade setting up for her next class. The room hasn't changed since I went here—the girls say Beady deducts points from your grade if you don't put the art supplies back in their proper places—and neither has Miss Beade. She moves around the room, arranging palettes and easels like a nun performing the stations of the cross. Is this what I want, I wonder, the comfort of teaching in the same place for forty years? To be one of the *old girls*?

My first class is Language Discovery for Sixth Graders. I trade off with the Spanish and German teachers. It's a new idea of Dean Buehl's. This way the kids will have a basis for picking which language they want in seventh grade.

"Think of it as a recruiting opportunity," Dean Buehl had told me. "Make Latin fun. Build up the Latin program and you'll have a job for life."

When I went to Heart Lake Latin was mandatory. The idea of Helen Chambers recruiting is absurd and slightly offensive. I can't imagine Helen Chambers spending two

minutes worrying about how to make Latin fun. And yet we all loved her. We would have done anything for her.

I wonder what Helen Chambers would think of how I teach this class. I use a textbook called *Ecce Romani*. Here are the Romans. The title always makes me think of a TV sitcom. Oh, those goofy lovable Romans, with their charming villa in southern Italy and their colorful, perky slaves. There's even an episode in which one of the slaves escapes. When he's caught, he's beaten with a stick *(virga)* and branded on the forehead with the letters FUG, short for *fugitivus*, runaway.

When Dean Buehl first showed me the new books my mouth went dry. All those nights studying declensions and memorizing Catullus hadn't prepared me to talk about the weather in Latin *(Quaenam est tempestas hodie? Mala est.)*

I spent hours in front of the mirror practicing conversational gambits like a nervous teenager preparing for her first date. *Salve! Quid est praenomen tibi? Quis es?*

Now, when I enter my first-period class, I am greeted by a dozen loud voices. *Salve Magistra! Quid agis?* And though I know that *quid agis* means, idiomatically, how are you, this morning, after my meeting with Dr. Lockhart, I hear instead its literal meaning: What are you doing? Why didn't you tell her about what you saw last night? And I have to stop myself from telling my cheerful, beaming,

prepubescent sixth graders, *"Nosco."* I don't know. I have no idea.

In the advanced class that day I try not to stare at Athena, Vesta, and Aphrodite, but I find myself stealing surreptitious looks while they read their translations. I think I can detect blue circles under Athena's eyes, but then I know that the girls often affect this sleepless look by smudging kohl under their eyes, which matches the shade of blue lipstick they all favor.

She fumbles, though, in her translation, which is not like her.

"How are you translating *praecipitatur* in line six?" I ask her.

"She fell under the water."

"She?"

"It's the light, not she," Vesta interrupts. "But I don't get it: The light throws down its head under the water? Doesn't *praecipito* mean, like, to fall on your head?"

Aphrodite giggles. "I think you must have fallen on your head last night, Vesta."

Vesta and Athena exchange dangerous glances with Aphrodite, and I find myself, of all things, blushing, as if it were my secret that was threatened. Maybe it is. If they knew that I was there last night what does that say about my authority as a teacher?

"Tace," I tell Aphrodite. *"Praecipitare* means to cast down headlong. In the middle sense it can mean to cast oneself down headlong. In

47

this case it means the light casts itself below the water, or, more idiomatically, the light sinks beneath the waves."

"That's a lot of English words for one Latin word," Athena points out.

"Well, Latin is an economical language, especially when it comes to destruction."

Athena gives me a smile that chills me like a rush of lake water. "That's exactly why we like it," she says.

AFTER CLASS, I WALK TO THE PRESCHOOL TO PICK up Olivia. I am early, so when I come around the corner of the building and see the children on the playground I step into the shadows of a large sycamore so Olivia won't see me yet.

I look for Olivia in the brightly colored knots of children playing together in twos and threes, running and climbing in the mottled shade of the playground. And then I see her, apart from the others, dancing and singing to herself under the pine trees.

She doesn't look unhappy, but the sight of her alone worries me. It reminds me of something I can't at first put my finger on. Maybe, I reason, it's just that she reminds me of myself at her age. Until I met Lucy Toller in the ninth grade I had no friends.

Olivia's dance is punctuated now with little swipes to the ground, as if she were picking flowers, only I can see from here that her fingers barely graze the pine needles. It's a charade of flower-picking, no doubt part of some

make-believe. She is so absorbed in her game that she is wandering farther and farther from the playground, into the deeper woods that surround the school grounds and slope down to the lake. And that's when I realize what she reminds me of: Persephone, straying from her companions to pick flowers on the shores of Lake Pergus, where she was snatched by Hades.

I step out of the shadows to call her, but just as I open my mouth I hear one of the student aides call her back to the playground. It takes a minute for the sound of her name to penetrate her daydream, but then she skips toward the older girl eagerly. I see the aide lean over to tell Olivia something and Olivia nodding. I can tell by the way Olivia's eyes slant away from the aide that she is being reprimanded for straying away. Good, I think. But I'll have to talk to her myself tonight.

I follow the children as they leave the playground. Dismissal is from inside and I'll have to wait while they sing their good-bye song and collect their artwork. I find myself wandering under the same trees Olivia had been playing near. I can see why she likes the spot. It is cool under the pines and the ground is golden with dried pine needles. I kick the needles and unearth something thin and gold and metallic.

Stooping down to pick it up, I am reminded again of Persephone picking her flowers, only it isn't a flower I retrieve from the pine needles, it is a hairpin, or, rather, several hairpins linked together. When I lift them up

into the light I recognize the pattern. Two U-shaped hairpins linked together with a bobby pin bisecting the top one. It looks like the head of a horned animal holding something in its mouth. I shiver, not because of the shade now but because I've seen this particular configuration before, but not for twenty years.

Chapter Four

●

WE CALLED THEM *CORNICULUMS*, WHICH, AS Lucy found in Cassell's *New Latin*, meant little horned ones. Deirdre used to say she had invented them when she found Helen Chambers's hairpin in the love seat in the Lake Lounge. I have always thought, though, that they were a truly cooperative endeavor, product of a tripartite genesis.

We were in the suite's one single room, Deirdre's room, studying for our Latin midterm, fall semester, junior year, drinking Deirdre's tea to stay awake. She had the single in our suite because of a note from her mother's psychiatrist saying Deirdre had boundary issues and severe migraines. Lucy used to say it was overkill, that she ought to have

stuck to one thing or the other: boundary issues or migraines.

Deirdre's habits, which Lucy viewed as affectations, could be annoying. Her parents had something to do with foreign affairs and she'd spent her childhood in various remote corners of Asia. She wore an antique kimono to the shower room instead of the frayed and stained terry robes the rest of us shuffled around in. She liked to dress in outfits composed entirely of silk scarves clinging provocatively to her well-developed figure. It used to make me nervous looking at her in class because I always thought some piece was about to slip off, but the only time they came off was on our nocturnal swims, and then our path down to the lake would be strewn with her discarded silks.

She kept two large China tea tins on her bureau, one filled with pot, the other, and this was considered odder by Heart Lake standards, filled with loose tea. She was as particular about her teas as she was about her marijuana. Sometimes, listening to her rattle on about estate provinces and curing processes, it was difficult to know which she was talking about. I suspected she mixed more than her talk about the two, and there was many a morning I spent dazed and light-headed after drinking a cup of her dark smoky tea and many a night I spent sleepless after smoking one of her exquisitely rolled joints.

On this night Deirdre's tea had a minty bite to it that set my teeth on edge and made

the objects in her room glow around the edges. In between lines of Catullus I found myself mesmerized by the texture of the hemp mats on the floor and at one point the ceremonial dancers on a Balinese tapestry seemed to take a spin around the floor.

We were translating Catullus's poem 2, the one where Catullus says he's jealous of Lesbia's pet sparrow. Deirdre claimed that the poem was really about Catullus's jealousy of Lesbia's female sexuality. Lucy, as usual, was annoyed by Deirdre's reduction of nearly everything in Latin to sex. Having failed to interest Lucy in her interpretation of Catullus, Deirdre cast about the room for something that might capture Lucy's approbation. Her eye alighted on a bit of folded paper stuck between the pages of the Tantra Asana that Deirdre kept on the night table beside her bed.

She slipped the paper, which had been folded into the shape of a flower, out of the book and held it up in front of Lucy.

"Do you know what's in this?" Deirdre asked.

"Some illegal substance, no doubt. Honest, Deirdre, you're going to be dead by twenty if you keep this up."

"Better a short life full of glory than a long inglorious one," Deirdre quoted. Deirdre was fond of quotes having to do with death. After sex, death was her favorite subject. She kept a silk-covered notebook filled with quotes from the ancients and moderns on the subject of early death. "Anyway, it's not drugs."

Deirdre tugged at one petal of the flower and the whole thing blossomed in the palm of her hand, only to reveal another packet folded in the shape of a grasshopper. Deirdre loved this sort of thing, secrets within secrets, Chinese boxes, *sanctum sanctorum*. She knew Lucy did, too. With a flick of her long lacquered fingernail, the grasshopper sprang open. In the center of the folds lay a single hairpin.

I started to giggle. The unveiling had been so theatrical; the result was anticlimactic. Lucy, I noticed, wasn't laughing.

"Where'd you find it?" she asked, touching one finger to the coppery wire.

"Behind the cushions of the love seat in the Lake Lounge. Where *she* always sits."

Lucy lifted the hairpin out of its paper grasshopper carcass and held it aloft. A single strand of gold hair clung to the metal for a moment and then slipped to the floor where it evaporated into the straw mats. We all three leaned forward at the same time to catch it, but Deirdre plucked it from the matting with a quick dart of her fingers, nimble as a child picking up onesies at jacks.

She held it up to Lucy's short hair.

"See, it's the same color."

"You can't tell from one strand," Lucy said, but I knew, with a pang, that she was pleased. That Deirdre had pleased her. To be like Helen Chambers in any small way was all any of us wanted. To find some hidden affinity, or to acquire one by emulation, we studied her more carefully than we studied our declensions

and conjugations (and we worked on those hard enough, if only to please her). If Helen Chambers left a cardigan draped over a chair back one of us was sure to read its label. If she left her teacup in the Lake Lounge after four o'clock tea, we read the tea bag she'd chosen and studied the lipstick smudge left on the rim. Later, when we were invited to her apartment in Main Hall, we memorized the book titles on her bookshelves, the album covers stacked by her phonograph, and the perfume bottles on her dresser. We amassed our common knowledge into one eclectic but (to us) cohesive portrait: She wore Shalimar and read a Dickens novel every Christmas. She had gone to Vassar and always stayed at the Vassar Club when she went into the city, which she did twice a year to see the ballet (*Giselle* was her favorite, too) and shop at Altman's for the simple but beautifully cut black jersey dresses she favored. Her favorite novel was *Persuasion* by Jane Austen and her middle name was Liddell, which, Lucy felt sure, must be her mother's maiden name. We liked to think she was related to the Liddell of Liddell & Scott's Greek Lexicon, the father of Alice Liddell—the model for Alice in Wonderland. Wouldn't it be fitting, we thought, if she were related to Alice! But the one thing we never knew was how long her hair was because she always wore it twisted into a knot at the nape of her neck.

Deirdre held the strand of hair between the thumb and forefinger of each hand. "I

already measured it," she said, "twenty-seven inches long. It must hang below her ass."

I thought Lucy would be most interested in the hair, but instead she held up the hairpin so that its prongs faced up. The metal was crimped halfway down each side.

"That's to hold the hair better," I said. "Look." I took a pin out of my own hair. I had started wearing it up that term because Lucy said it made me look more scholarly. The pin was shaped the same but was darker to match my plain brown hair. I took my pin, prongs down, and linked it with the one in Lucy's hand. It dangled there limply. Lucy took the single bobby pin she used to hold back the bangs she was growing out that year and slipped it over the prongs of the top hairpin— Helen Chambers's pin. Then she held the thing up by the end of the bobby pin.

"It looks like some kind of animal," Deirdre said. "A goat, maybe."

"It's a talisman," Lucy said. "Of the Horned One. A..." she paused, looking into the middle distance, a look she often had right before she read her Latin translation, as if a page invisible to all but her was unfurling in the air. "A corniculum. A little horned one. From now on this will be the sign we leave for each other."

"A sign of what?" Deirdre asked. "What will it mean when we find one?"

Lucy looked at both of us. I became conscious of how we were sitting, cross-legged in a tight triangle, our knees nearly touching, each of

us leaning into the middle. Out of the corner of my eye I thought I saw the tapestry dancers take another spin around the room and then Lucy's gaze brought me back, told me to pay attention, made the room still again.

"A sign that we're always here for each other," Lucy said.

I saw Deirdre smile. It was what she wanted, a sign of affirmation from Lucy (I knew that I was beside the point, but she'd take me because I came with Lucy). It's what I wanted, too, of course, but there was something in Lucy's tone that unnerved me, that made what she said less a promise of friendship than a threat of constant surveillance.

IT'S A SENSE OF BEING WATCHED THAT I HAVE NOW, holding the little hairpin totem up so it catches the light slanting down through the tall pines. I look toward the lower school, but all the children have gone inside to collect their things. I can hear, faintly, the good-bye song they sing at the end of each day.

"So long, so long, it won't be so long till we see each other again...."

Deirdre and I used to wait here to meet Lucy when she worked at the lower school as an aide. The younger girls would follow her out the door, begging for another song, or another story. I remember there was one girl in particular, a skinny girl with pale, colorless hair like dried straw, who would trail after Lucy

dejectedly until Lucy would go back and promise that she'd be back the next day.

"Do you really *promise*?" the girl, standing at the edge of the woods, would yell.

"Yes, Albie, I *promise*," Lucy would yell back, drawing out *promise* as if it were a magic word that could bind the speaker just by its utterance.

I look behind me toward the lake, which glitters between the tree trunks like slivers of a broken mirror. The water pulses so brightly that when I turn away my vision is slashed with dark jagged shards. I have a hard time spotting Olivia in the crowd of brightly dressed children coming out of the school now. For a moment my heart pounds with the fear that she's not there, that when I go up to her teacher she will look at me blankly and tell me that someone else has taken her...didn't I send a note saying it was all right? A ridiculous thought. I saw her go into the school five minutes ago.

Still, I am so panicked that the faces of the children blur into bright spots and I can't make out Olivia's face until she rushes right into me. I can barely hear what her teacher is trying to tell me, something she doesn't want Olivia to hear, I guess, from the exaggerated mouthing adults use when they're whispering secrets in front of children.

"...a bad day..." I make out. "...overwrought..." I nod and say something about Olivia not getting much sleep the night before, how we're still getting used to the new house,

excuses that come easy and are, in their way, true.

"She's probably just tired," I conclude.

"I am not," Olivia snaps, as tired children will when told they're tired.

"Okay, sweetie," I say, taking Olivia's hand. "Let's go home." I steer her away from the school. "Let's go home and have a snack. We'll make cookies..." I say before I remember I don't have the supplies for baking. In my mind we were heading home to the kitchen in our old house where the matching ceramic canisters were filled with flour and oatmeal and chocolate chips.

"I want to go down to the magic rock and look for tadpoles," she says.

"Okay," I say, glad to get out of the baking promise. Tomorrow I'll go to the store and buy flour and baking powder and cookie sheets.

"...and then the tadpoles turn into frogs," Olivia is telling me, "and Mrs. Crane says we'll have tadpoles in our class so we can watch it happen...."

Olivia drops my hand and runs ahead on the path, chattering all the while about frogs and tadpoles. I'm left alone in the woods I used to wander with Lucy and Deirdre. We often came down this path to the swimming beach, and yes, sometimes we came at night and swam out to the farthest sister stone. We made our own sacrifices to the Lake Goddess. And once Deirdre introduced us to it, we were often stoned.

Olivia disappears around a bend in the

path, but I can still hear her voice. She is singing one of her made-up songs.

When my students ask me what the school was like when I went here, I know they expect to hear that we worked harder, the rules were stricter, more was expected of us. Some of that is true. It was a given that you'd go from Heart Lake to a Seven Sister college. Our teachers even hinted to us that after our preparation at Heart Lake we'd find the work in college easy. They were right about that. No test I ever took in college was harder than *Domina* Chambers's Latin final, or Miss North's history orals, or the slide test in Tacy Beade's art class. But what the girls don't guess—and I can't tell them—is that when I went here in the seventies the rules were already changing. In some ways, things were looser. The Pill had become available, but no one had heard of AIDS yet. There was no war on drugs, because the teachers didn't even suspect we had access to them. Cigarettes were vaguely tolerated as a bad habit, like chewing your nails or wearing laddered tights. Even the school uniform had given way to a haphazardly enforced dress code that specified skirt length but neglected to make bras mandatory.

I've come to a bend in the path where the path divides in two. To the left the path goes up to our house, to the right it slopes down steeply to the lake. I stop here and realize I don't know which way Olivia has gone. She'd been talking about seeing the tadpoles, so she

probably went straight down to the lake. I stand still and listen for her voice, but the only thing I hear is the wind sifting through the dry pine needles on the forest floor.

I still the flicker of panic that licks at my brain like a small flame. Panic. I hear Helen Chambers's voice telling us the word originated from the god Pan. The Greeks thought he inspired the unreasoning fear that sneaked up on mortals in wild places.

I head down the path to the lake. The sun has gone behind the clouds again and the water looks flat and gray. If she went to the house, I figure, she'll be all right for a minute or two, but if she went to the lake...I decide not to finish that thought.

The swimming beach is empty. I look down at the sand for footprints and see some, but they're too large to be Olivia's. I realize that they're probably my own, made last night when I watched Athena, Vesta, and Aphrodite on the rocks. I am about to turn back to look for Olivia at the house when I hear a small splash. The sound seems to come from the farthest edge of the Point and when I look in that direction something white flashes briefly and then is gone. Just the sun glinting off the rock, I think, turning back toward the steps, but then I see her. Olivia is standing on the farthest rock. Her back is to me and she stands on the very edge of the far side of the rock. I start to call her name, but then think I'll startle her and she'll fall into the water. The lake, I know, is deep on the other side of that rock.

I kick off my shoes and wade into the water, moving slowly so as not to make any noise. The water is warm at the shallow edge, but as soon as I'm up to my waist I can feel the icy cold currents from the underground springs that feed the lake. I stroke out, keeping my head up, eyes on Olivia, just like Miss Pike, our gym teacher and swimming coach, taught us in Lifesaving.

I approach the rock from the shallow end because I am afraid that if Olivia sees me she might be startled and fall into the water. I am too scared to take my eyes off Olivia even for an instant to look down for a place to put my feet, so I feel the rock with my toes. My feet hit something hard and slimy that falls away when I try to put my weight down. I try again and find a flat rock where I can get enough purchase to lift myself up onto the rock, but my foot, numb from the cold, slips just as I'm pulling myself up.

I hit the rock hard with my stomach and make a sound like "ooof." Olivia hears me and turns. For a moment I see fear in her face, but then it dissolves into giggles.

"Mommy, why are you swimming in your clothes?"

I crawl over to her and pull her down to the rock before answering. "Well, Miss, I could ask you the same question." I try to make my voice sound light, a gentle reprimand for getting her good clothes wet, but when I pick up the hem of her dress I notice that her dress—and her sneakers and white ankle socks—are bone dry.

Chapter Five

After I drop Olivia off at school the next morning I go back to the swimming beach. It is getting late in the year to swim— already the water by the shore is coated with a skin of dead leaves and a cold mist, which I push away to enter the water—but I am determined to keep to my routine as long as this spell of Indian summer lasts. The lake is cold even in summer, but since I've been back I've gotten in the water as often as I can. And, I tell myself, I need to have a look at those rocks again to figure out how Olivia got to the farthest one without getting her clothes wet.

When I asked her she told me, first, that she flew. Then she told me that it was the Queen of the Wilis who came in a magical boat and carried her to the rock. Maybe Mitch was right when he said I read her too many fairy tales. When I demanded that she tell me the truth she burst into tears and said I was mean for not believing her. I told her Mommy was tired and couldn't have this argument right now. (Talking about myself in the third person is a clear sign that my patience is slipping.) She responded by throwing her chocolate milk on the floor. I screamed at her to go to her room

and she told me she couldn't because her room wasn't in this house. I pulled her up by the armpits and said, "March, young lady." She folded her arms across her chest and stamped her foot. I gave her a little push, just to get her going, and she crumpled to floor, screaming that I had shoved her.

Things went downhill from there. Afterward I thought of what she might say to her father.

When I think of how our fights might sound, or look, to an outsider I go hot with shame. The cold water of the lake is a relief, the impact of the cold draining my body of any feeling but the rush of the cold. I stroke out past the first two rocks and then to the third, measuring the distance with my eye. There is no way that anyone, let alone a four-year-old child, could jump from the second rock to the third rock. My head is dizzy with trying to solve the problem of how Olivia made it to the rock. I float on my back, arching my neck so that the lake soaks the top of my scalp, and then I turn over and strike out for the deep water.

The lake is a half mile across from the swimming beach to the south end. When Lucy and I were here it was a graduation requirement to swim back and forth twice. Now the swimming area is roped off and the girls are only permitted to do a lake swim accompanied by a lifeboat.

My girls believe that this rule is because of the three sisters and their suicidal pull on Heart Lake girls. They tell stories about the

girls who have drowned in the lake since the Crevecoeur sisters and claim that their spirits still haunt the lake. They say you can see their ghostly forms in the mist that comes off the water on an autumn morning like this. Their faces have been seen, the story goes, peering out from beneath the ice in winter.

When I look up I see I am off course. I always swim with my eyes closed because there is something about looking into that bottomless green that unnerves me. Even with my eyes shut I see it—a sunlit grass green so bright you could imagine the light came from the bottom of the lake and not the other way around.

Halfway across the lake I pause and tread water. The lake is seventy-two feet deep here and I can feel the cold of that depth pulling at my feet. When they pulled Deirdre Hall out of the lake she had only been in the water a few hours. She didn't look so bad, considering. But when Lucy and her brother Matt drowned in the lake it took longer to find their bodies. The night they drowned the temperature dropped to ten below zero and a blizzard blew down from Canada and held the school snowbound for three days. When the police could finally start looking for their bodies they had to bring an icebreaker from the river to tear up the ice before they could dredge the lake. It took five more days for them to find the bodies. They had died clinging to each other, their arms and legs wrapped around each other and then they had frozen like that.

Their mother told me later that she had to have them buried together because they would have had to break their bones to pry them apart.

This is the coldest part of the lake—Miss Buehl used to tell us there was an underground spring that fed into the Schwanenkill at the south end of the lake. In the winter it makes a thin spot in the ice and in the summer it makes a cold spot in the water. It is almost unbearable staying still in it, but I do this every morning as a kind of penance. I think of it as an appeasement to whatever local genius inhabits Heart Lake. I don't believe in the Lake Goddess we gave our S'mores and bracelets to all those years ago, but the Romans have taught me something about *lares et penates*, household gods and nature spirits, and the importance of giving them their due. Instead of offering them crumbs and bangles I offer myself—my body flayed by the cold water.

There's a spot in my left arm where my shoulder was once dislocated that begins to ache in the cold water. When I feel I have stayed long enough—when the ache in my arm feels like icy fingers pulling at my flesh—I stroke forward with my arms and kick my legs out behind me. And hit something solid in the water. I spin around and see, directly in front of me, a white forehead—hair slicked back and pale eyes—rising out of the water. An arm arcs out of the water and grabs my hair. Icy cold fingers graze my scalp with a touch I've felt in nightmares. I open my mouth to scream and

swallow water instead, the cold mineral taste flooding my brain with fear. I feel myself slipping under and grab the arm and twist it away from my hair. It's only when I see the blue spiral on the hand that I realize who it is.

"Athena," I say in the same voice I'd use if she were talking out of turn in class.

"Miss Hudson!" Her lips are at water level and she spits a little as she says my name. "Oh my God, Miss Hudson. I didn't see you. There's the fog and I was swimming with my eyes closed."

We've pulled away from each other, beating the water with our arms.

"Well, you would hardly expect to run into someone in the middle of the lake. Don't you know you're not supposed to swim alone."

I think only to admonish her, but she turns her head fractionally toward shore and I think I might hear someone else moving in the water, but the fog is so thick now that I can't be sure.

"Yes," she says, "I know. You won't tell, will you? I mean about me swimming across the lake."

I had forgotten for a moment that it was against the rules.

"Well, you know it's very dangerous to swim alone, Athena." I mean only to withhold my cooperation for a moment—just long enough to preserve my teacher's authority. I've been thinking since my talk with Dr. Lockhart that I ought to be a little stricter with the girls.

"One more infraction and I'm out of here," she says.

I notice that Athena's chin is trembling and I'm afraid she's about to cry, but then I realize that it's her teeth chattering from the cold. Her lips are bluish-purple, the color of dead skin. I know why I subject myself to this cold water every morning, but I wonder what self-punishing instinct brings Athena into the lake. Perhaps it's only a teenage dare.

"It's OK," I say. "I won't turn you in."

The blue lips press together in what might be a smile or just an attempt to keep her teeth from chattering. I feel the beginning of a cramp in my right calf muscle and it makes me wonder what I would do if Athena got a cramp out here. Would I be able to get her to shore? We took lifesaving training every year with Miss Pike, but it has been years since I practiced. I was never any good at it. Once when I was "saving" Lucy I kicked her in the side so hard she wasn't able to play field hockey for two weeks.

"We'd better swim back," I say.

Athena turns her head, not in the direction of the swimming beach but toward the opposite shore. I wonder if she is supposed to meet someone there. I remember that on the south end of the lake, just across from the swimming beach, is the Schwanenkill icehouse where Lucy and I used to go meet her brother, Matt. I wonder if there is some boy from town that Athena has arranged to meet there.

Well, whoever it is would just have to wait. I am not about to leave Athena out in the lake alone. I feel responsible for her. If I don't turn her in and she keeps swimming out here I *am* responsible for anything that might happen to her.

"Come on," I say in as stern a teacher's voice as I can muster between chattering teeth.

Swimming back I stay a little behind her. I swim with my head up so I can keep an eye on her. She is a good swimmer, but I know that is no guarantee. Good swimmers can drown, too.

When we approach the swimming beach Athena swims to the west end of the cove, to the place under the Point where there's a shallow cave in the rock. It's where I left my clothes this morning. Athena reaches behind a rock and pulls out a sweatshirt and jeans. I find my clothes behind another rock. I feel her watching me, taking in my hiding place and the secrecy it implies. I am not supposed to be here any more than she is.

I pull my sweatshirt over my wet suit and climb into my jeans without toweling off. I feel the wet seeping through the seat of my pants almost immediately. When I turn to Athena she is finger-combing her wet hair, the blue spirals on her hand weaving in and out between the wet ropes of hair. The color has returned to her lips. I have a sudden, unbidden image of Helen Chambers in her apartment in Main Hall taking down her hair and combing it while Lucy and I watched. She had handed the

brush to Lucy and asked if she wouldn't mind combing her hair out.

I remember, too, what Dr. Lockhart said at the end of our meeting the day before.

Think of Helen Chambers when you're dealing with your students.

I'M FIVE MINUTES LATE FOR MY NINE O'CLOCK class. I quickly scan the hall to see if anyone has noticed, but luckily Myra Todd is off first period and Gwen Marsh is also late—when I stick my head in her class her girls are either writing in their journals or reading. I go into my room and tell my ninth graders to translate the next lesson in *Ecce Romani*. When they finish that I let them *read—Gwen does*, I think—because I'm not up to much in the way of teaching. I can't help myself from doing what Dr. Lockhart advised—I think of Helen Chambers.

Specifically I think about how she ended her tenure at Heart Lake.

After two of her students, and the brother of one of her students, ended up dead in the lake, an inquest was held to look into Miss Chambers's professional behavior. The effects of the two dead girls were examined and students were interviewed. Deirdre Hall had kept that journal with quotes about premature death and suicide. Several of the quotes were either attributed directly to Helen Chambers or Deirdre had credited her teacher as the supplier of the quote. Lucy hadn't kept a journal

but she had written a letter to her brother the week before their deaths. In it she told Matt that *Domina* Chambers had opened her eyes to a secret that had changed everything for her, *for the both of them,* she wrote. *When I tell you what it is you'll understand why we have always felt different from everybody else. The ordinary rules of the world don't apply to us.*

The board asked Miss Chambers to explain what her student meant by this enigmatic letter. Into what secrets had Miss Chambers initiated this young girl? Miss Chambers declined to answer the board's questions. She said it was a private matter between her student and herself and she couldn't discuss it.

Miss Chambers's students and colleagues were called in for questioning. We were all called in. We waited in a row of chairs that had been placed along the wall outside the Music Room. The cold weather and storms that had delayed the dredging of the lake had broken and it was unseasonably warm. The school grounds were awash in melted snow and slush. The foyer floor was gritty with mud and broken glass (someone had broken the fanlight over the front doors) and we sweated in our Fair Isle sweaters. We were told not to speak with one another. No one was allowed to discuss the questions they had been asked in the Music Room. Whenever a girl came out of the Music Room she went out the front door without looking back at the rest of us. Wet, *lakey* air gusted into the foyer and we all

70

sniffed the breeze like dogs scenting game until the door slammed shut and we were left in the stale, overheated hallway, the boarded-up fanlight staring back at us like the blinded eye of the Cyclops.

I was the last to go because, I assumed, as the roommate of the two dead girls I would know the most. When it was my turn I went into the room and sat at the single chair that had been placed in front of the long dining room table behind which the members of the board sat. Helen Chambers was there, a little apart, in a chair in front of a window. A dark figure silhouetted in the bright glare of the melting lake ice.

It was odd seeing her sitting apart. The board was made up almost exclusively of "old girls." Truly a jury of her peers, it was a club to which she'd not only belonged, but seemed to epitomize: women of indeterminate ages, who favored frumpily elegant dresses and wore their hair in untidy buns or cut boyishly short. They'd all gone to good women's colleges after graduating from Heart Lake and gone on to get a master's degree or some apprenticeship in the arts. There was Esther Macintosh, the English teacher, who had gone to Mount Holyoke and was supposed to be working on a book about Emily Dickinson. She even dressed like Emily Dickinson, in high-necked white blouses, her lank brown hair parted severely in the middle. Tacy Beade, the art teacher, worked her way through Sarah Lawrence as an artist's model. There was a cer-

tain slide—shown only in Honors Art—of an abstract expressionist nude that was purported to be of her. Dean Gray, Celeste Buehl, Meryl North, and even Elsa Pike, the chunky gym coach, were all there in almost identical black dresses and graduated pearl necklaces. Silhouetted against the windows they looked like a row of crows perched on a telephone wire.

I fixed my eyes above their heads on the portrait of India Crevecoeur and her family, but instead of looking at India I found myself looking at Iris Crevecoeur, the little girl who'd died of the flu. She stood a few feet away from the rest of her family, small and dark where her sisters were tall and blond, fussed over by a family servant who seemed to be trying to tie the sash at her waist. She looked as miserable and as lost as I felt.

And for the first time I realized that even though Helen Chambers was one of them—one of the old girls—she also stood apart. The black dresses she wore were cut better, her pearls had a softer gleam. She was a little smarter and much more beautiful than any of them. And now they would make her pay for that. Even before the first question I knew what the board members believed. I knew what they wanted to believe.

Did Miss Chambers encourage drug use? Miss North asked.

Only for sacred, not recreational purposes, I answered.

Did Miss Chambers encourage free sex and homosexuality? Miss Beade asked.

She said the same rules didn't apply to everybody—like in *Antigone*—and, I quoted, proud to have remembered the words, "Which of us can say what the gods hold wicked?"

Had my friends been unhealthily obsessed with their teacher, Miss Chambers? Miss Macintosh asked.

I told them about the strand of hair we found. I told them about the used tea bags we stole and the lists we kept of things we knew about *Domina* Chambers.

Did Miss Chambers encourage this obsession? Miss Pike asked.

I told them about the private teas that she invited Lucy and Deirdre and me to and how she then invited just me and Lucy and, finally, just Lucy. I told them that Lucy had stopped sleeping. She seemed upset when she came home from these teas, but she wouldn't tell me why.

Miss Buehl picked up a piece of thin blue paper. I noticed that her hand was shaking. *This is what Lucy wrote to her brother the week before she died: "Domina Chambers has told me something that changes everything. When she told me, I understood why I've always felt different from everybody else. The ordinary rules of the world just don't apply." Do you know what she meant?* Miss Buehl asked.

I told them no, I didn't know. That was true enough. I didn't know what she'd meant, but I knew what it sounded like.

Is that what she was fighting about with her brother when she ran out onto the ice?

I didn't answer right away. I couldn't tell them what Lucy and Matt had argued about on the lake. So I did what was easier. I agreed with Miss Buehl. I told them they had been arguing about *Domina* Chambers, but that I hadn't really understood what it was all about.

I saw Miss North and Miss Beade exchange a knowing look. Then they told me they didn't have any other questions and that I should go and finish studying for my finals. *We see you have a scholarship for Vassar for next year*, Miss Buehl said kindly. *You're a smart girl; you shouldn't let these unfortunate events interfere with your future plans.*

I left without looking in Helen Chambers's direction. I kept my eyes on the floor as I walked past the line of chairs in the foyer even though they were now empty. I saw specks of red and blue and yellow glass glittering on the floor—tiny fragments of the stained-glass heart and the school's motto: *Cor te reducit.* Not me, I thought, I'm never coming back here.

Outside the wind was blowing off the melting ice in the lake. I never saw Helen Chambers after that day. Dean Gray announced at dinner that night that all of us at Heart Lake must put the incident behind us and never talk about it again, lest the reputation of the school be irrevocably damaged. (Of course the damage was done. Already parents were pulling their daughters out of the school, not even waiting for the end of term.) She said that Miss Chambers had been *let go.* When I heard the words

I imagined a hand releasing its grip on another hand and I felt something slip away, and that was as much as I knew about how Helen Chambers had ended up.

Athena doesn't come to class. I ask Vesta and Aphrodite if they know where she is and they both shrug. I assume they're covering up for that early morning swim Athena took. It may be my imagination, but the advanced girls seem sullen today. Perhaps it is the weather. This spell of Indian summer we have been enjoying seems to be drawing to a close. A fitful wind rattles the windows of the classroom and I can see storm clouds massing on the eastern shore of the lake. There hasn't been a glimmer of sun since yesterday afternoon. The thought jars something in my memory—a flash of white on the Point just before I saw Olivia stranded on the rock. I'd thought it was the sun glinting off the rock, but now I remember that the sky had been overcast. Could it have been a rowboat just rounding the Point? Could it have been one of my students—maybe three of my students?—who rowed Olivia out to that rock? I look at Vesta and Aphrodite, noticing the deep circles under their eyes that look real, not kohl-induced. If they're sneaking out to the rocks at night, might they also take a boat out onto the lake? They look edgy to me, but then, so do all the girls. When called on, the girls whisper their translations, which are lost under the hiss of the steam heat. When I ask them to speak up they get nervous and seem

to think they have translated their pieces wrong. They turn their sentences around and come up with unintelligible messes. When I try to unravel their syntax I can hear an irritation in my voice I hadn't even known I was feeling. I give up and tell them to read quietly until the end of the period. Several of them put their heads on their desks and fall asleep. I let them, hoping Myra Todd doesn't come by and peep through my door window.

At lunchtime I commit the unpardonable sin of dining alone. I purchase peanut butter crackers and a Coke from a vending machine in the lodge basement and go down to the swimming beach. I stare out at the three sister rocks and across the lake to the south shore, where I can just make out the shape of the icehouse. The county extension agent used to keep her boat there. During Christmas break senior year, Lucy and I took the boat out and rowed it all the way across the lake almost to the Point. I'd written the whole episode down in my journal. The journal that I'd lost.

A wind from the north is whipping the water against the three sisters. I watch a flock of Canada geese land on the lake and take off again. When I walk back to the lodge for my last class of the afternoon I think I have gotten things into perspective.

One of the girls—one of my students—has perhaps found my journal and realized that I was involved in two deaths during my senior year, three if you count Matt Toller. I have to face the fact that it might very well be Athena.

The "rite" I witnessed on the three sisters indicates an interest in the suicide legend. Although I can't figure out what she hopes to gain by bombarding me with these relics of my past—the journal entry, the corniculum—and luring my daughter out onto one of the rocks, I can only assume she has some plan to blackmail me or somehow compromise my authority as a teacher. Let's face it, my authority has already been compromised.

I think of what Dr. Lockhart said, that sometimes a teacher has to be a little harsh.

I decide to go to Dr. Lockhart and tell her everything. Then we'll go to Dean Buehl. I imagine that I will be reprimanded, but I don't think I have done anything to merit my dismissal.

With a clear plan in my head, I feel better already. When I open my classroom door, though, my calm dissolves at the sight of Dr. Lockhart seated at my desk leafing through my homework folder.

When she looks up and those cool blue eyes narrow on me I feel a chill gust of arctic air.

"Bad news," she says. "Ellen Craven has tried to kill herself. She's been taken to the hospital in Corinth."

I almost ask *who?* before realizing she's talking about Athena.

Chapter Six

●

I FIND ATHENA SHROUDED IN WHITE. SNOWY WHITE sheets are pulled up to her chin. Her arms, which lie on top of the sheets, are bandaged from the tips of her fingers to the crooks of her elbows. Both arms. She is sleeping, or at least I hope it is sleep and not a coma.

Outside the hospital window I can see that the sky above the paper mill has gone blank and white as well. Driving here in Dr. Lockhart's car, I noticed that the sky in the west was growing overcast. Now it looks like it might snow. Only this morning Athena and I swam in the lake and now the sky is threatening snow. I know from growing up here, on the edge of the Adirondacks, that such shifts of weather are possible. (The night Matt and Lucy drowned had been as warm as a spring night and the next day we got one of the worst snowstorms in the area's history.) Still, I find the change *stunning*, although perhaps not as stunning as the change in Athena—from the strong swimmer of this morning to this pale shrouded invalid.

"Is she sleeping?" I ask Dr. Lockhart, who is standing at the window looking out at the clouds gathering above the lake.

"She's not in a coma," she replies. "She

regained consciousness briefly after her stomach was pumped. She didn't take enough sleeping pills to put her in a coma."

"She took sleeping pills *and* slit her wrists?" In my mind I hear Lucy's cool, assessing voice: *overkill*.

"Yes, I find that distressing as well. Many experts believe that the more violent the means of suicide the more it's meant as a kick in the face to the survivors. 'This is how badly I hurt,' the victim is saying, 'this is how badly I want out.' "

"But she's alive," I remind Dr. Lockhart. Or perhaps I am reminding myself. Saturated in white, her skin pale as the sky outside, her lips still stained with the bluish lipstick she habitually wears, my student looks dead.

Dr. Lockhart dismisses my comment with an impatient wave of her hand. "Only because I decided to check up on her when she didn't show up at breakfast today."

For all my concern about the girls it had never occurred to me to seek them out at meals.

"You found her?"

"Yes, so I can attest to the violence of her attempt. She used a steak knife we think she stole from the kitchen when she did her clean-up shift last night. She severed both arteries. Thank goodness it happened before the weather got worse." Dr. Lockhart gestures toward the lowering sky outside the window. "I can't imagine what we would have done with her if we'd been snowbound. I've heard that happened once."

I nod. "When Lucy cut her wrists. We

couldn't get her to the hospital. Celeste Buehl herself had to suture them."

Dr. Lockhart shakes her head. "I didn't think Ellen would make it, not with all the blood she lost. They'll have to pull up the floorboards in that room to get it all out. I don't know what to do about my dress."

I give her a puzzled look and she opens the long charcoal gray coat she has been wearing since I found her in my classroom, and had kept closed during the drive here. Under it she is wearing a dress I take to be burgundy. I think it is an unusual choice of color for her until I realize it's blood.

"I haven't had a chance to change," she says, no doubt seeing the horror on my face. "I had to call her aunt, who's at a spa in California, and then I wanted to talk to you."

"Me?" I want Dr. Lockhart to close her coat, but she leaves it open.

"After our conversation about Miss Craven I thought you might be able to help me explain *this* to her aunt." She says *this* and gestures to Athena's somnolent form. "When was the last time you saw Ellen?"

"Ellen?"

Dr. Lockhart looks at me as if I've taken leave of my senses and I do just about the worst thing I could do. I laugh.

"It's just that I think of the girls by the Latin names they take. She's Athena to me."

"Hm. That's not a Latin name."

"I know, but I let them pick classical names and this year the girls all wanted goddesses."

"That's very interesting. Are they into goddess worship? Do you talk about that in class? Goddess worship? Pagan rites? Wicca covens?"

"*Wicca covens?* What would that have to do with Latin?"

Dr. Lockhart shrugs. Her coat slips off one thin shoulder and I see that the blood goes at least halfway down her sleeve. It is hard to imagine how Athena could have lost that much blood and still be alive, but then I remember another white room with blood: It was Deirdre Hall's room, where Lucy had slit her wrists on Deirdre's bed. When I first came into that room after Christmas break I thought Deirdre's mother had sent her a red bedspread for Christmas.

"You'd be surprised what some teachers—teachers I'm sure must mean well—consider relevant to the curriculum. The digressions they indulge in—"

"I haven't been preaching New Age witchcraft to my students, Dr. Lockhart."

"I'm not saying that, Jane. I know you care about the girls, but you might not realize how much influence you have over them."

"Are you saying that it was something I said to Athena that made her do this?"

"Why are you getting so defensive, Jane?"

"I'm upset," I tell her. "I can't believe Ellen would do a thing like this."

"But you know she tried to kill herself once before. And just yesterday you told me that she leaves drawings of razor blades on the homework she turns in to you. Did it ever occur to

you that she might be asking for your intervention?"

I shake my head. I had thought the pictures were left on her homework by accident, but I can see how lame that would sound now.

"Did you ever try to talk to her about the scars on her wrists?" Dr. Lockhart asks.

I remember the conversation I had with Athena before her last exam, when she saw me looking at the scar. She told me that her aunt had sent her here to *dry out from boys*. I had laughed and turned away from her. Then there was this morning's swim. I realize now that I may have been the last person to see her before she went back to her room, swallowed her roommate's sleeping pills, and took a steak knife to her arms. Was she afraid I would turn her in?

I look up at Dr. Lockhart and remember that I had been planning to tell her about seeing Athena in the lake. I will tell her now. It is not too late.

Only it is. Dr. Lockhart reaches down and touches the collar of my shirt. I flinch as if she had been about to strangle me, but when she draws her hand away I see she has, magicianlike, pulled a long green ribbon from inside my shirt collar. Only it's not a ribbon, it's a strand of grass. The kind that grows on the lake bottom.

"Interesting," Dr. Lockhart says, holding the long strand in the light from the window so that it glows like a shard of green glass. I

notice that the white sky outside has broken apart. It has begun to snow.

"We found a piece of grass just like this in Ellen's clothing. We surmised that she might have tried to drown herself in the lake first, but for some reason couldn't go through with it. I thought it was odd to be brave enough to slit your wrists but not to drown. But then, maybe someone stopped her."

She raises one eyebrow and looks at me. I feel the blood rush to my face and for a second I think how the color red must look, in this deathly white room, on her dress and in my face. The nurse comes to the door and Dean Buehl and Myra Todd are with her. I feel caught, as if the blood in my face has something to do with the blood on Dr. Lockhart's dress and the slim blade of grass she holds in her hand is the murder weapon. What can I do, confronted with such incontrovertible evidence? I tell them about meeting Athena in the lake this morning. I tell them, too, about seeing the girls on the rock two nights ago. The only thing I don't mention is the page from my old journal. Because, I tell myself, I can't see what it possibly has to do with Athena's suicide attempt.

I DRIVE BACK TO THE SCHOOL WITH DEAN BUEHL and spend the rest of the afternoon in her office. All afternoon classes are canceled so the girls can attend a "Support Meeting" in the Music Room. After I have told my story

about what I saw at the lake the night before last and my encounter with Athena in the lake this morning, Dr. Lockhart excuses herself so that she can change her dress and meet with Vesta and Aphrodite—Sandy and Melissa, I remind myself to say—Athena's roommates. Dean Buehl thanks her for "handling everything."

"If you hadn't found the girl..." Dean Buehl's voice trails off and I notice how haggard she looks.

"It's what you hired me for," Dr. Lockhart replies, "to watch after these girls."

As soon as Dr. Lockhart leaves, Dean Buehl regains her official briskness. "Of course, you should have notified me immediately when you saw the girls in the lake," she tells me. Myra Todd nods and I get a whiff of her moldy smell. It makes me think my clothes are wet, but it is only that I am sweating in the dean's overheated office and the mold reminds me of how the changing room would smell after we swam in the lake. "You say they were naked?"

"Yes," I tell her for the tenth or eleventh time. "Of course I should have told you. I was planning to tell you after my classes today. I didn't realize it was urgent."

"You say they were making some kind of sacrifice on the rocks," Myra says. She makes it sound as if the girls were beheading chickens. "Well, I think that sounds urgent."

"We all used to do it." I hate the way my voice whines. I know I shouldn't try to explain, it

just sounds like I'm trying to excuse myself, which I'm not. I've accepted the blame. "It's an old Heart Lake tradition," I appeal to Dean Buehl, who is herself an old girl, as if I were talking about founder's day or singing the school song and wearing our school colors, rose and gray. "You'd throw something in the lake for good luck. It's like..." I grope for a harmless analogy, "like tossing three pennies in the Trevi fountain."

Myra Todd snorts. "Naked? In the middle of the night?"

Dean Buehl shakes her head sadly. "It's that three sisters story that has plagued us from the beginning. Surely you, of all people, Jane, should know how dangerous the story is. But there's something that upsets me even more than your failure to report your students' nocturnal activities. Although I hope you understand now that you should have come to me immediately..."

I nod vigorously. I can hear Myra twisting in her seat impatiently. She wouldn't let me get off so easily, that's for sure, and I imagine that what she's thinking is that I'm receiving this lenient treatment because I'm an alum. I wish suddenly that I'd kept the fact that I went to school here to myself. But how could I have? Aside from Dean Buehl there are Meryl North and Tacy Beade—old girls—who remembered me. Or at least they remembered me once I had reminded them who I was.

"What I need to know, though," Dean Buehl continues, "is if you have shared what

happened in your senior year with your students?"

I look up, trying not to show my relief. "Absolutely not," I say with conviction. "I mean, I've thought about it, when I've heard the girls telling the three sisters story, just to dispel the legend. I know that only one of the Crevecoeurs' daughters died—and of the flu, not drowning—from what was said at the inquest, but I knew if I started talking about it they might ask me other questions...and so, I've avoided it because it's unhealthy, I think, for them to hear about other girls who killed themselves. I know how that kind of thing can spread."

I am breathless from this little speech and disappointed to see that Dean Buehl looks unimpressed. Unconvinced.

"Are you sure you're telling me the truth?"

I nod.

"Then can you explain this." Dean Buehl holds up a piece of lined notebook paper with a ragged edge. I can see I'm supposed to come get it from her but I suddenly feel weighted to my chair, as if my clothes were indeed drenched and they were pulling me down into deep water. Myra Todd stands up and hands the page from the dean to me.

I am surprised, first off, that although it is clearly a page torn from a bound notebook, the words on it are typewritten instead of handwritten.

"Dear *Magistra* Hudson," the note, which I understand is meant to be Athena's suicide

note, reads, "You've been a real friend. I'm sorry that you'll lose another friend in the same way you lost Lucy and Deirdre. I just want you to know that *I* don't blame you. *Bona Fortuna. Vale,* Athena." The *I*, I notice, is underlined, by hand, three times. There is a bloody fingerprint in the lower left-hand corner.

I look up from the note. "She's the one," I tell Dean Buehl. "She's the one who has my old journal."

WHEN I LEAVE DEAN BUEHL'S OFFICE I SEE VESTA and Aphrodite sitting on folding chairs in the hall outside the Music Room. I would like to stop and talk with them, but I am already late for picking up Olivia from preschool. Besides, they look so pale and nervous I figure they don't need an extra interrogation. Aphrodite looks like she's been crying. Vesta looks like she would like to throw up. I rip out a piece of paper from the back of my grade book and hand it to Vesta.

"Write down your dorm room number," I tell her. "I'd really like to talk to you both later."

Vesta nods and writes down a number on the paper and hands it back to me folded in half. "Yeah, we'd like to talk to you, too, *Magistra*. Dr. Lockhart told us you saw us the other night and didn't tell anyone."

"Well, yes, I did see you and I was wrong not to tell."

"We think it was nice of you," Aphrodite says. I think of Athena's note: *You've been a real friend.*

"I've got to go pick up my daughter now, but I'll come by the dorm later. Good luck in there." I almost say *Bona Fortuna,* but think better of it.

WHEN I GET TO THE NURSERY SCHOOL I EXPECT TO find Olivia in tears, angry that I'm late. But instead I find Mrs. Crane, alone in her room, sorting eggshells. I am out of breath from running and can barely form the words "Where's Olivia?"

She looks up at me with the blank look I have always feared. "Her father picked her up. I figured it must be all right, since you weren't here."

"Her father?" Mitchell's visitation isn't until next week. "But I wrote on her form she's never, ever, to be released to anyone but me. You know I'm divorced. He may have kidnapped her."

Mrs. Crane pulls herself up. "There is no need to yell, Miss Hudson, we're all upset today about what happened to that girl." It takes me a moment to realize she means Athena. "I thought you'd probably be at the hospital with her since she was your student and..." She stops herself from saying whatever she was going to say next. I wonder what stories are being told about my relationship with Athena. "I thought you might have called Olivia's father to come take care of her. I'm sure you'll find them at your house. Olivia said she wanted to show him her rock collection."

"Her rock collection?" Mrs. Crane shrugs and spills a carton of eggshells onto a sheet

of newspaper. She lays another sheet of newspaper on top and takes a small rubber mallet and slams it on the table. I jump.

"For our mosaic project," she explains. I think she's still talking about the rock collection, but then I realize she's talking about the eggshells. I think about how carefully Olivia and I washed out those eggshells. Then I understand about the rocks. Olivia meant the magic rocks. The three sisters. I leave without saying thank you or good-bye and I can hear Mrs. Crane muttering something to herself as she pounds away with her mallet.

THEY ARE STANDING ON THE SWIMMING BEACH and Mitch is showing Olivia how to skip rocks on the water. Olivia is more interested in catching snowflakes on her tongue.

"Do you think it will stick?" Olivia asks the minute she sees me. "Will the lake freeze? Can we go ice skating? I want to skate around the sister rocks."

When did she start calling them the sister rocks? I don't remember telling her that story, but if I did, and forgot it, maybe I also told the same story to Athena. Or could it have been the person who took her out to the rock who told her the story?

"No, honey, the ground isn't cold enough and the lake won't freeze for a while," I tell her. The temperature is dropping fast. I zip Olivia's thin sweatshirt up and huddle her against me.

"She ought to have a warmer jacket," Mitch says, turning to me at last.

"It was seventy degrees this morning. And I had planned to take her home right after school. I wasn't expecting you."

"Well, I had some business up this way and I thought I'd come check up on you. I would have taken Olivia home, but you were late picking her up, and I don't have a key to your house."

"I wanted Daddy to see the magic rocks," Olivia says. She points at the rocks. I notice that the snow is coming down so hard now that I can barely see the farthest rock. "They're supposed to be sisters," she tells Mitch. "They drowned like Hilarious and now they're together all the time."

"Hilarious?" Mitch asks me. "What kind of bedtime stories have you been reading her, Jane?"

"I think she means Hilarion. It's from Giselle. But I don't know about the sister part. You know she has a very active imagination."

"The Wili Queen told me." Olivia sounds angry, as if I had accused her of lying.

"OK, honey, we'd better go home and get you warmed up. I'll make some nice warm soup for dinner."

Olivia heads up the path and Mitch signals for me to walk a few paces behind with him. "I thought I'd take her for dinner," he says.

"Well, all right, but I wish you had told me.

This isn't the visitation schedule we talked about..."

"There are a few things we didn't talk about. We didn't talk about you leaving Olivia alone at night when you go meet your boyfriend down here at the lake."

"What in the world are you talking about?"

"I guess you still keep a diary, Jane. You ought to be more careful about who sees it. This came over my fax today."

He hands me a piece of slippery white paper. The top line is typed with the sender's phone number, which I recognize as the school's fax number. The rest of the sheet is handwritten.

"Tonight I will go down to the lake to meet him and I'll tell him everything. I know I shouldn't go, but I can't seem to stop myself. It's like the lake is calling me. Sometimes I wonder if what they say about the three sisters is true. It's like they're making me go down to the lake when I know I shouldn't."

The page is shaking in my hands and it takes me a moment to realize it's my hand and not the wind that's causing it to shake. It's as if I can feel the hatred of whoever sent this to Mitchell in the paper itself. I have to remind myself that whoever sent the message never even touched this paper. I check the time and date of transmission: 8:30 A.M., today's date. I got back from my swim a little after 8:00 this morning. Dr. Lockhart found Athena at a little before nine. But why would Athena send this and then go back to the dorm, type me a

91

note saying I've been "a real friend," and then slit her wrists? It doesn't make any sense.

I look up from the white paper to Mitchell's face. We've reached the top of the path and we have both paused to catch our breath. He's waiting for a reaction. A denial. But what should I deny? Should I tell him yes, I wrote this, but twenty years ago, and yes, I do leave Olivia alone to go down to the lake, but certainly not to meet this boy who has been dead for nearly twenty years?

I look back down over the lake, at the snow falling onto its placid gray surface, and although I know the snow must melt when it touches the water I imagine the white flakes drifting like white stars though the dark water. The only thing that is clear to me is that whoever sent this message to Mitchell wants to hurt me. And there is no better way to hurt me than to hurt Olivia. Someone—not a fairy, not the Wili Queen—took Olivia out to the farthest stone and left her there. One false step and she would have been in the water.... I have a sudden, unbidden image of Olivia's light hair fanning upward in the dark water as she sinks, her face a pale white star extinguished in the black water.

"Maybe I should take her for a while," Mitchell says.

I can tell from the combative tone in his voice that he's bluffing. He's expecting me to tell him no, call my lawyer, tell him I've done nothing to justify his taking her. But instead I say the last thing he expects me to.

"Yes, maybe that's a good idea. Maybe you should keep her for a little while." Because even though it breaks my heart to see her go, I am beginning to think that Heart Lake isn't a very safe place for little girls.

Chapter Seven

●

THE COTTAGE, WITHOUT OLIVIA, IS TOO QUIET. After dinner (I scramble eggs and throw out the eggshells) I decide to go over to the dorm to talk to Vesta and Aphrodite. Their dorm is next to the lot where my car is parked. I can see if there's anything they think Athena would like before I drive to the hospital for visiting hours. It seems like a good plan. The dorm and then the hospital. It seems like a good way to fill the evening.

I walk along the edge of the lake because, I tell myself, it's a beautiful night. Today's snow shower has left only a faint white gloss on the ground and a clear moonlit sky. It is cold, near freezing, I think. The moonlight lies on the water like a premonition of ice. It will be many weeks before the lake freezes, but tonight I sense something stirring in the lake. Matt Toller once explained to me how a lake freezes. He

said that when the surface water grows colder it also becomes denser, so it sinks to the bottom. When the warmer water rises to the top, it's chilled by the colder air temperature and sinks. The water circulates like this for weeks— a process called overturn—until the moment when the lake is all one temperature and then the surface begins to freeze. Matt said that if you could be at the lake on that night, the night of first ice, you could see ice crystals forming. I imagine the lake now like a giant mixing machine, stirring old things to the surface.

I pause on the Point. There are ledges on either side of the Point, carved out of the same soft limestone that lines the lake bottom, but the rock here on top is made of something harder—granite I think Miss Buehl told us. Its curved surface is bare except for the cracks and scorings—chattermarks, they're called—left by the last glacier ten thousand years ago. I think of how even this rock, so impermeable that it bears the scars of a ten-thousand-year-old event, was once under the surface of the earth.

Looking straight across the water I can see where the lake narrows and flows into the Schwanenkill and from there into the Hudson and the sea. Below me to the right the three sisters march into the water off the swimming beach. To my left I see the lights of the mansion and the dorm.

The journal pages, the corniculum, the three sisters story that have come to light are just floating debris, flotsam from a wreck

that happened twenty years ago. But now the wreckage itself seems to be surfacing. Events that happened twenty years ago are happening again.

During our senior year Lucy Toller was sent to the infirmary with two slit wrists. A few weeks later our roommate Deirdre Hall was found in the lake, her neck broken. It was determined at the inquest that she jumped from the Point, landed on the ice, and then slipped into the water. A month after that I watched as Lucy, followed by her brother, Matt, walked out onto the thawing lake and vanished beneath the ice.

Could it be that there is something about this place that makes these events recur? Are all the deaths, from Iris Crevecoeur's to Deirdre's and Lucy's and Matt's, written on the landscape of Heart Lake like the glacier scores left on the rocks? Or is somebody re-creating the events, following a script written twenty years ago?

IT'S ONLY WHEN I AM IN THE DORM STANDING IN front of the security desk that I realize I don't know what room Vesta and Aphrodite are in. I dig in my pocket and find the piece of paper Vesta gave me. I show it to the matron at the desk without looking at it and she tells me the room is up the stairs, second door on the left. And so I find myself standing in front of my old dorm room, the one I shared for three years with Deirdre Hall and Lucy Toller.

I knock and a voice from inside calls, "It's open." My students, Vesta and Aphrodite (or Sandy and Melissa as I try to think of them now), are sitting cross-legged on the same bed facing each other. I smell cigarette smoke and feel a cold draft. The bed is under the window. If I checked the sill beneath the window blind I am sure I would find an ashtray, but I don't.

"*Magistra* Hudson," Vesta says. "*Salve.* What a surprise." There isn't a trace of surprise in her voice. I realize that I am probably one of a long line of adult visitors the girls have entertained tonight. I imagine the grilling they must have received this afternoon in the Music Room and the well-meaning sympathy calls from teachers.

I notice a book of poems by Emily Dickinson on the bed and detect a faint whiff of mold in the air. Gwendoline Marsh and Myra Todd must have preceded me.

"May I sit down?"

Aphrodite shrugs, but Vesta at least has the good grace to gesture to one of the two desk chairs. I sit in the maple Windsor chair and wonder if it's the same one I sat in twenty years ago. The desks look the same: soft, dark wood scored by generations of Heart Lake girls' initials. If I looked hard enough I might find mine. Instead I look down and notice the dark stain on the floor.

"I think we should put something over it, but Sandy says that'll only make it worse." It's the first time Aphrodite has spoken since I came

in and I can hear from the hoarseness in her voice that she has been crying. I look at her and take in the dark smudges under her eyes, darker than the ones she used to draw with kohl.

"I'm sure if you asked the dean would let you switch rooms. No one would expect you to stay in here with...that."

"Yeah, Dean Buehl said we could move and Miss Marsh says we ought to move to another room. She said it would be like living with a ghost staying here and we shouldn't have to..." Aphrodite's voice trails off and she looks, I think, as white as a ghost herself. I'm sure Gwen meant well, but the ghost image certainly wasn't well thought out.

"But Dr. Lockhart says we should stay and face our fears. She says that it's not good to bury the past," Vesta says. "I think she's right. What do we have to be afraid of? That we're going to suddenly decide to off ourselves just because Ellen went round the bend? I don't think so."

"Yeah," Aphrodite nods eagerly. "It's not like we believe in that three sisters story."

"Who told you that story?" I ask.

The girls look at each other. Vesta is scowling at Aphrodite, as if she is mad at her for bringing it up.

"Everyone knows that story. It's one of our great Heart Lake traditions like tea in the Lake Lounge and ringing the bell on top of the mansion so you don't die a virgin."

I laugh before I can stop myself. "You all still do that?"

Vesta and Aphrodite smile, relieved, I think, that they've gotten me to laugh. "Yeah, although it's not such a big issue with some girls," Vesta says. Aphrodite slaps her playfully on the arm and steals a look at me to see how I'm taking it. I smile at her. I remember what she asked the Lake Goddess—to keep her boyfriend at Exeter faithful.

"Did Athena have a boyfriend?" I ask. "She told me that she was upset last year when her boyfriend broke up with her. Did something like that happen this time?"

The girls go quiet. I can feel them shrinking away from me.

"How could she have a boyfriend here?" Vesta asks. "There are no boys here."

"Sometimes girls meet boys from town. When I was here..."

I see the sudden interest in their faces and stop.

"What? What did you do when you were here? Did you meet boys out in the woods when you were here?" Aphrodite asks. "Maybe on the swimming beach? You know, you can't see the swimming beach from the mansion."

I feel suddenly hot and I notice that the high-intensity desk lamp is beating down on my shoulders. I remember what I came for—to find out if Athena had my journal and, if she had it, do Vesta and Aphrodite have it now. I look around the room. If I had left it hidden in this room twenty years ago they could have found it. I would like to look in my old hiding place—under a loose floorboard behind this

desk, but then I had looked there twenty years ago. It had occurred to me at the time that Lucy might have hidden my journal, on that last night before she followed me to the lake, and Lucy was awfully good at hiding things.

Ignoring Aphrodite's question with the smile I give my students when they ask something too personal, I stretch my leg and touch my toe to the edge of the bloodstain. I notice a gouge in the wood that has been worn smooth by time.

"I wonder if they'll tear up these floorboards," I say. "They're old and loose as it is. I'll tell you something we used to do when I was here. We used to hide things under the floorboards."

I look up to see their reaction, but I can't read their expressions. They look like they're hiding something, but they've looked like that since I came in. It is a not uncommon look for a seventeen-year-old. At any rate, they've got nothing to say to my question.

"I bet you could find stuff that girls hid over the years," I say, deciding to take a more direct route. "Have you ever? Found anything?"

The girls do not look at each other, but I have the feeling they are not looking at each other *on purpose*.

"No," Vesta says evenly. "Did you lose something?"

I swivel the chair toward the desk, away from Vesta's gaze. Does she know this was my old room? Suddenly I feel like I'm the one who's

being interrogated and I start to sweat under the heat of the desk lamp. I push it away from me, knocking over an empty teacup.

"We should get rid of that," Aphrodite says. "You're the second one who's knocked it over tonight. At least now it's empty."

I right the teacup and set it next to a history textbook. I idly flip open to the first page and read "Property of Heart Lake School for Girls" printed on the inside cover. Under the school's seal are places for students to put their names and the year. The names go back to the mid-seventies and I look to see if there's anyone I knew, but I don't recognize any of the names. I was never much good at remembering my classmates' names, mostly because I hadn't bothered to get to know anyone that well except for Lucy and Deirdre. On the bottom line is Ellen Craven's name.

"Is this Athena's desk?" I ask.

"Yes," one of the girls answers; I don't notice which one.

I am looking for a black-and-white notebook; I don't know which notebook I'm looking for, hers or mine.

"I'm going into town to see Athena now. I was wondering if she'd want any of her books."

"Like her Latin books?" The note of sarcasm in Vesta's voice sounds vicious, but when I turn around her face is bland and innocent.

"No. I don't expect her to do her Latin work right now. I thought something more personal. Her journal, maybe. She did keep a

journal, didn't she? I remember seeing a black-and-white notebook."

"Yeah, she had a bunch of those," Aphrodite says.

"But you're too late," Vesta adds. "Dr. Lockhart came and took them all away."

ON MY WAY TO THE PARKING LOT I NEARLY SLIP ON the icy path twice. I keep my eyes on the ground to avoid the icy patches, but the moonlight coming through the pine branches strews the path with black-and-white blotches that dazzle my eyes. The pattern of moonlight and shadows begins to look like the black-and-white cover of my old notebook—of Athena's journals, too—so that I feel as if I were skating over the slippery cover of a book.

A bunch of those, Aphrodite said. If Athena had my old journal then it's possible Dr. Lockhart has it now. I have to find out from Athena if she had it, but will she even be conscious?

When I get to the hospital, I am relieved to find that Athena is awake, but disappointed to see that she is not alone. Dr. Lockhart is sitting in a chair by the window with an open book in her lap. The room is dark except for the small book light attached to her book. When she sees me come in, she closes the book and rises. The book light moves with her and throws lurching shadows across the room. Athena turns her head on the pillow and smiles when she sees me.

101

"*Magistra* Hudson," she says in a painfully raspy voice that makes me think of razor blades. "We were just talking about you."

"You look like you're going to sleep," I say. "I can come back in the morning."

"Oh no, I was just telling Dr. Lockhart that I wanted to talk to you."

"Yes, Ellen says that Latin's her favorite subject. I was just keeping her company until she fell asleep, but now that you're here, I'll go."

Dr. Lockhart comes around the bed and motions me to come with her. "I just want to have a word with Miss Hudson, Ellen, then I'll leave her to you."

Athena turns over on her side to watch us move into the hallway. I can see her bandaged arms in the moonlight from the window. They remind me of a horse's legs taped for a race.

Dr. Lockhart takes me by the elbow and steers me down the hall. "I wanted you to know that she's in a denial stage," she whispers. "Don't take anything she says about the suicide attempt too seriously. It would be better if you didn't ask her too many questions about what happened."

"I won't," I tell her. "There's just one thing I wanted to ask you."

Dr. Lockhart lifts one eyebrow and crosses her arms over her chest. The book light shines up onto her face ghoulishly the way the seniors used to shine a flashlight on their faces when they told us the three sisters story at the Halloween bonfire.

"Athena's roommates told me you took some journals from her desk, I wondered if..."

"If any of them were yours?"

I nod.

"No, I checked carefully. If she is the one who has your notebook, she's hidden it well. Maybe someone else has found it." She pats my arm reassuringly, making the light wobble over the dimly lit hall. The effect is like water reflected on the walls of an underwater cavern. "Don't worry, Jane," she says, "surely there's nothing so bad in your teenage diaries." She turns and walks down the hall, the light attached to her book wobbling weakly beside her like Tinker Bell in *Peter Pan*.

Athena's eyes are closed when I enter her room, but when I sit on the edge of her bed she opens them.

"Oh, *Magistra* Hudson," she says, "I've been wanting to talk to you all day. You're the only one I can tell."

The words sound familiar and I realize they are the ones I found on the journal page left for me two days ago.

"What do you want to tell me?" I take Athena's bandaged hand and try not to hold it too tight.

"I didn't do it," she says.

I think for a second she's trying to deny taking my journal, but then I realize I haven't accused her of that.

"Do what?" I ask.

"Slit my wrists. I didn't try to kill myself. Someone tried to kill me."

Chapter Eight

•

"PARANOID DELUSION BROUGHT ON BY DRUG overdose," Dr. Lockhart says when I tell her about Athena's claim that someone tried to kill her. "It's what I was afraid of."

We are back in her office with its panoramic view of Heart Lake. Although it's only been days, it seems like months since I sat here thinking longingly of a swim in the lake. Since yesterday's first snow the temperature has dropped into the twenties.

"Denial of a suicide attempt is common," Dr. Lockhart tells me. "In fact, I wrote a monograph on that very subject when I was doing my residency." She glides backward in her desk chair and reaches for a file drawer behind her. I notice her chair's sleek ergo-dynamic design as she arches back in it and how well its charcoal gray velour upholstery complements her clothes. I wonder how she got the school to order her such an expensive chair while the rest of us make do with creaky, straight-backed desk chairs.

She hands me a slim sheaf of paper that I expect is her monograph. I am about to utter some polite assurance that I'll read it as soon as I catch up on my grading, when I notice it's not a monograph at all. It is a letter, handwrit-

ten on pale blue stationery, from Lucy Toller dated February 28, 1977. The letter is to her brother, who had been sent, that last year of high school, to a military school in the Hudson Valley. True to her fashion she starts out with a quote, one I recognize from Euripides' *Iphigenia in Tauris*: "A greeting comes from one you think is dead." She then goes on to assure her brother that the official report of her suicide attempt over Christmas break was false. "I can't explain now, Mattie, but please believe that I'd never willingly take my own life. You see, *Domina* Chambers has told me something that changes everything. When she told me I understood why I've always felt different from everybody else. The ordinary rules of the world just don't apply. 'Which of us can say what the gods hold wicked.' " I remember that it was this passage that had been so damning to *Domina* Chambers at the inquest.

At the very bottom of the page she had copied a line from a poem, "And sin no more, as we have done, by staying, but, my Matthew, come let's go a-Maying." I remember the Robert Herrick poem from Miss Macintosh's English class.

I read the letter twice and lift it to see what the rest of the papers are, but Dr. Lockhart reaches across the desk and pulls the sheaf of papers out of my hands.

"As you see, even your friend Lucy denied that she tried to kill herself, and if the dean's notes are to be believed, the blood from her slit wrists soaked through two mattresses."

At her words my vision is flooded with red. I see the blood-soaked bed, the tangle of crimson sheets.

"And we know that suicide attempt was real. After all, she eventually succeeded. She walked out onto the ice and deliberately drowned herself. You saw it yourself, right?"

I nod, but realize from Dr. Lockhart's continued silence that she expects more of an answer. "Yes," I tell her, "she deliberately drowned herself."

"She didn't try to hang on to the ice? You couldn't help her?"

"She didn't want my help," I say, "she practically dived under the water. She wanted to die."

"And she didn't call for you to help her?"

"No," I say, trying unsuccessfully to keep the irritation out of my voice. "As I said she went right under. She couldn't very well call for help from under the water."

"So we can assume that first attempt was real as well. Besides it would be too awful if your friend Lucy hadn't meant to kill herself that first time."

"Why?"

"Because it was the precipitating factor in your other roommate's suicide. Deirdre Hall?"

Dr. Lockhart extracts another sheet from the stack of papers on her desk. This one is a Xerox of a lined, handwritten page.

"Whatever happens now, it's all because of what Lucy did at Christmas," I read aloud. The last lines on the page were cut and pasted

from a mimeographed handout. I read them to myself: "I will arise and go now, for always night and day / I hear lake water lapping with low sounds by the shore; / While I stand on the roadway, or on the pavements gray / I hear it in the deep heart's core." Yet another of Miss Macintosh's favorites: Yeats's "The Lake Isle of Innisfree."

"Deirdre Hall's last journal entry before she drowned herself in the lake," Dr. Lockhart says. "No, Jane, I don't think we should believe that Ellen didn't try to kill herself. I think we should watch her very closely. And her roommates, Sandy and Melissa. I consider all three girls at grave risk."

FOR THE NEXT FEW WEEKS I DO LITTLE BUT WATCH my girls. I tell myself that I am watching them for signs of depression and suicidal tendencies, but truthfully I am also watching them for hints that they have my old journal. They seem, though, if anything, less troubled. Perhaps it's only the change of wardrobe brought on by colder weather. By the time Athena returns to class all my girls are huddled in layers of sweaters, scarves, and flannel shirts. The sweaters hide the bandages on Athena's arms and scratch marks on the other girls' wrists. The girls look more normal, less sepulchral, in their bright red plaids and fuzzy angoras. It's hard to look like a Goth lumberjack.

The snows begin in earnest early, even for

the Adirondacks. By Halloween the ground is covered, by Thanksgiving the mounds on the sides of the paths are knee-high. The campus takes on that enclosed feeling it gets in winter. I know that by January the feeling may be claustrophobic, but for now it feels cozy.

I speak to Olivia each night on the phone and visit her every other weekend. As long as I don't say anything about her coming back to live with me, Mitchell says nothing about seeking permanent custody. I think it is better to leave things be for the time being.

I receive no more notes from my past. When I look at the lake I can tell it will freeze soon and I find myself looking forward to it, as if the past could be sealed under ice as well.

I go down to the lake every night, hoping to be there for the first ice. One night I find Athena, Vesta, and Aphrodite there and I almost turn back on the path, but then I see that Gwendoline Marsh and Myra Todd are with them along with a few other girls. They have blankets and thermoses of hot chocolate.

"*Magistra,*" my girls call when they see me. "Join us. We're waiting for the lake to freeze. Miss Todd says if there's a moon when it happens we'll see the crystals forming."

They call it the first ice club.

"It's a Heart Lake tradition," Vesta says, handing me a mug of hot chocolate.

I nod and burn my tongue on the hot liquid. Myra Todd gives a lecture on the physics of lake freezing and Gwen reads the Emily Dickinson poem that begins, "After great pain a

formal feeling comes..." I wonder why until she comes to that last stanza, "This is the Hour of Lead— / Remembered, if outlived / As freezing persons, recollect the Snow— / First—Chill—then Stupor—then the letting go."

It's as good a description of freezing as any I've ever heard and it's not Gwen's fault if it makes me think of Matt and Lucy's last moments. *First—Chill—then Stupor—then the letting go.* Only they didn't let go. They had each other to hold on to.

I WONDER IF THEY ASKED THE DEAN'S PERMISSION to meet. I wonder if Dr. Lockhart knows about the club. I find I can no longer judge the difference between a club meeting and a pagan rite.

When the girls start stomping their feet in the cold and the hot chocolate runs out we all leave. Gwendoline Marsh and Vesta sing "Silent Night" on the walk back. *Club meeting,* I think, definitely *club meeting.*

In the second week of December I notice a change come over Aphrodite. She arrives in class late without her translation done. She's no good at sight reading, so she can't fake it. Vesta and Athena try to cover for her. I can tell they are giving her their translations because they are too alike. If I stop Aphrodite to ask her how she got a particular translation or to identify a case ending, she flounders aimlessly amid the syntax. Out of six possible cases she

makes four wrong guesses. It's painful to watch, so I stop calling on her, but still the littlest thing makes her burst into tears: Catullus's poem about his girlfriend's infidelity, Book Four of the *Aeneid*, the definition of the verb *prodere*.

"What's wrong with Aphrodite?" I ask Athena after class.

"She's getting notes from Exeter about her boyfriend, Brian. You know, like that he's cheating on her and badmouthing her. She's on the phone with him every night and he swears none of it's true."

"She seems to be taking it pretty hard."

"Well, yeah, they've been going together since the ninth grade. She says they're going to go to college together. Only the way she's going, she's never going to make it to college."

"You mean you think she might kill herself?"

Athena stares at me.

"No. I mean her grades really suck. Haven't you noticed?"

I DECIDE I'D BETTER TALK TO DR. LOCKHART ABOUT Aphrodite. She listens to my story quietly.

"Of course I'll have a word with her," she says when I have finished, "but I doubt if it's anything serious. The important thing is not to plant the idea into anyone's head that her sadness might be suicidal. Whatever you do, don't discuss it with any other student."

I remember my conversation with Athena and the way she stared at me when I asked if

she thought Aphrodite might kill herself. I thank Dr. Lockhart for her time and leave quickly.

That night when I call Olivia she tells me all about her new baby-sitter who watches her after school, about how pretty she is and how they bake cookies together. I think that being jealous of the baby-sitter is the worst I'll have to suffer tonight until she asks me when she can come back to live with me.

"Soon," I tell her.

I get off the phone and go into her room and lie down in her bed. On her night table is the *Tales from the Ballet*. I remember the part of the story when the mother warns Giselle not to dance because of her weak heart. Even with the best intentions, it's impossible to always protect your child. I'm not sure my intentions have been the best. Did I really consider her welfare when I left Mitchell? I thought I took the job at Heart Lake because it would be a good place for her to go to school, but was I really thinking of her? Or was I following my own desire to return here? I think of the lines I read in Deirdre's last journal entry: "*I will arise and go now, for always night and day I hear water lapping with low sounds by the shore; While I stand on the roadway, or on the pavements gray I hear it in the deep heart's core.*" The last lines make me think not of a human heart but of the lake and what lies at its core.

I'm no longer sure if I even trust myself with Olivia. Am I any good to any of these girls, I wonder, let alone my own daughter? Am I, as

111

Domina Chambers was accused of being, a *corrupting influence*?

I go out of the house and listen for a moment to the lake. *For always night and day I hear water lapping.* The sound tonight is maddening. When, I wonder, will the damn thing freeze?

Instead of taking the path down to the lake I walk out onto the Point. Ice has formed in the glacial cracks. One wrong step and a person could slide off the smooth, curved surface of the rock and into the lake below. When Deirdre Hall fell to her death here some people, her parents, for instance, thought it was an accident. But then the administration confiscated her journal. Deirdre liked to collect quotes about death. She was also fascinated by the three sisters legend, especially after her roommate's suicide attempt. The last quote in her journal, the one from the Yeats poem, seemed to suggest that she felt drawn to the lake in the same way the three sisters legend suggested that Heart Lake girls were drawn to suicide.

I hear a sound to my left and turn a little too quickly. My heel catches in one of the icy cracks and for a moment I lose my balance, but then I feel a gloved hand catch my arm and right me. It's Athena. She must have been on the ledge below the Point and that's why I didn't see her. Behind her, walking up from the ledge, I see Gwendoline Marsh and Myra Todd with my other students, Vesta and Aphrodite. The first ice club.

"*Magistra*," Athena gasps in the cold air. "What are you doing up here? It's dangerous."

"Yeah," Vesta says. "We saw someone up here from the beach and we thought it might be a jumper."

Athena rolls her eyes. "We did not. We just wanted to...you know...make sure."

Aphrodite has come forward, stepping gingerly over the icy rock. She peers over the dome of the rock into the darkness. "Wasn't there a girl who killed herself by jumping from here?"

Gwen Marsh puts her hand on Aphrodite's arm to pull her back. "No dear, that's just another silly legend," she reassures her. But Aphrodite is still looking at me for an answer and I can't seem to think of one.

I FIND MYSELF THINKING THAT IF WE CAN JUST make it through the rest of December to Christmas everything will be all right. Athena is going to stay with her aunt and there's a possibility her mother might even be out of rehab for the holidays. Vesta is planning to read *Bleak House* by the pool at her grandparents' condominium in Miami. Aphrodite will see Brian and realize that those letters have all been lies. After all, I tell her, you can't believe everything you read.

And I will spend the vacation with Olivia. I've rented a room at the Westchester Aquadome for two whole weeks. It's all the salary I've saved so far, but it will be worth it.

113

We'll swim in the hotel pool and I'll take her into the city to see the Rockettes and *The Nutcracker*. We'll go skating at Rockefeller Center. Far better than skating on the lake, I tell her, which at any rate remains stubbornly unfrozen.

Gwendoline Marsh tells me at the faculty Christmas party that the first ice club has been disbanded. Gwen looks almost pretty tonight. She's got on her usual high-necked white blouse, but tonight she's wearing it with a long brown velvet skirt that makes her waist look tiny. Instead of ace bandages, her wrists are encircled by broad Victorian cuff bracelets. She's even teased out a few tendrils from her usually severe bun and curled them into ringlets that tremble as she shakes her head over the lake's unwillingness to cooperate and freeze. Myra Todd overhears our conversation and comes over to commiserate.

"I blame global warming," she says. "The lake was always frozen by mid-December."

Simon Ross, the math teacher, volunteers that the lake was only good for skating four days the previous year.

"It might not freeze at all."

I turn around to see who has uttered this pessimistic prediction and see that it is Dr. Lockhart. She is wearing a silver dress that shimmers in the Christmas lights strung around the Music Room.

"It'll freeze when we're all away on holiday," I tell her. "When we come back, everything will look different. The school always does,

114

after break." It may be the two glasses of champagne I've drunk, but I find myself oddly cheerful.

"Well, it'll do us all good to get away," Gwen Marsh says. "Imagine staying here through the whole break. I hear they used to let the scholarship girls do that to earn extra money."

"How inhuman," Dr. Lockhart says, taking a sip of her drink. "Imagine how depressing that must have been for those girls. Did you ever do that, Jane? Stay here during break?"

I notice that everyone is looking at me. I'm an old girl and so an authority on old Heart Lake customs, but no one has ever publicly mentioned before that I was a scholarship student. I wonder how Dr. Lockhart knows, but then I remember those files.

"In tenth and eleventh grade," I answer. "It wasn't so bad. My roommates were scholarships, too, so we all stayed. Our Latin teacher, Helen Chambers, stayed on campus and so did Miss Buehl." I say the last bit loudly enough for Dean Buehl to hear and she comes over, one eyebrow raised inquiringly. "I was just saying that you were always here over Christmas break. We helped you collect ice samples."

Dean Buehl nods. "Some of the younger girls even stayed with me at my cottage."

"How kind of you, Dean Buehl," Gwen Marsh says. "I wonder if any girls would want to stay here with me over break?"

It occurs to me that I haven't asked Gwen what her plans are for the break. What if

115

she's stuck here all by herself? I know she has an apartment in town, but I certainly hope she isn't spending her Christmas alone.

"Oh, I never minded," Dean Buehl is saying to Gwen. "It was company and I took the girls skating with me. I always wanted to have an old-fashioned ice harvest," she says, "like the Crevecoeurs had."

Everyone is immediately fascinated with the idea of an ice harvest. Meryl North describes the icehouse on the other side of the lake at the mouth of the Schwanenkill and explains how even in summer there would still be blocks of ice packed in sawdust. Tacy Beade remembers that when she was a student here they used the ice to make ice sculptures. I notice that as soon as the older teachers come over Dr. Lockhart slips away from the group. I've seen her avoid them before and I can't say I blame her as they both have a habit of droning on endlessly. When Myra Todd starts corralling people into an ice harvest committee (Gwen, I notice, immediately volunteers to do most of the work), I follow Candace Lockhart over to the drinks table that has been laid out under the Crevecoeur family portrait. She is standing with her back to the room, seemingly absorbed in the photograph of India Crevecoeur and her daughters, posing in ice skating costumes on the frozen lake.

"You'd think after the failure of their first ice club they wouldn't be so gung-ho about an ice harvest," she says as I help myself to some lukewarm Chardonnay.

"Well, it's tricky catching the first ice. We always tried..."

"Did you ever see it?"

"I was actually at the lake the night the ice formed my junior year," I tell her, "but, if you can believe this, I fell asleep."

"So you missed it," she says smiling into her drink, something clear and fizzy with ice. "Like you missed that last Christmas break."

"Excuse me?"

She shakes the ice in her empty glass. "You said you spent the break here tenth and eleventh grade, but not in twelfth. And that's when your roommate, Lucy Toller, first tried to kill herself. That's what started it all, wasn't it? You must have wondered at times if things would have been different if you'd been here." She turns away from me to refill her glass with club soda. I hear something crack and think it must be the glass in my hand, but it's only the ice in Dr. Lockhart's drink, settling in the warm liquid.

"I was in Albany," I tell her, "with my mother, who was dying of stomach cancer. In fact, she died the day before New Year's."

"Oh, Jane," she says, "I didn't mean to imply it was your fault what happened. Only that you might feel that way. What is it that the poet says about remorse...?"

I look at Dr. Lockhart blankly, unable to think of any appropriate line, but of course it's Gwen who thinks of one. " 'Remorse,' as Emily Dickinson says, '—is Memory—awake.' "

ON THE MONDAY BEFORE BREAK APHRODITE DOESN'T come to class. I ask Athena and Vesta where she is and they tell me that she went out early that morning to take a walk around the lake and they haven't seen her since.

After class I go straight to Dean Buehl and report Aphrodite's absence.

"We'll go to her room right now," Dean Buehl tells me.

I am not wild about being in my old dorm room with Dean Buehl, but what choice do I have? Walking from the mansion to the dorm I find myself looking at the Point, which blocks our view of the northeast cove and the swimming beach. I pull my collar up around my neck and start to shake.

"This morning's weather forecast says the temperature will be in the single digits by nightfall. If we can't find her by dusk we'll have to call the State Police and organize a search party. She'll never make it through the night in that kind of cold." Dean Buehl and I look at each other and I think we are remembering the same thing—a cold night twenty years ago when I showed up at the door of her cottage. Dean Buehl blushes and looks away first as if she were the one who was embarrassed at the memory.

At the dorm we find Athena and Vesta sitting at their desks with their books open. There is something wrong about the picture,

I think. Something stagy about the way their books are laid out and how intently they lean over them. I sniff the air for cigarette smoke and smell, instead, gingerbread. The smell, with its connotations of holiday baking, confuses me. There are no ovens in the dorm. Then I realize what it is: air freshener. The girls were expecting us.

Dean Buehl sits on one of the beds and I stand because the other bed is covered with dirty laundry and it feels strange to sit on the same bed with the dean.

Dean Buehl asks the girls if Melissa seemed upset when she left this morning. The girls exchange guilty glances.

"Um, well, actually we're not even sure she was here this morning. When we woke up she wasn't in the single. There's something on her bed, but it's not a note or anything—it's just some dumb poem."

Dean Buehl and I both look at the door of the single, which is still closed. She nods to me and I open the door and look inside. The bed is neatly made. On its pillow lies a sheet of paper with blue printing. Perhaps it is the blue writing that makes me realize what it is. Who uses mimeographs anymore? Dean Buehl passes me in the doorway and without removing the page from the bed, reads the first two lines: "I will arise and go now, for always night and day / I hear lake water lapping with low sound by the shore..." and I finish the poem aloud: "While I stand on the roadway, or on the pavements gray / I hear it in the deep heart's core."

Chapter Nine

●

"HOW'D YOU KNOW THAT?" ATHENA ASKS. "Melissa's been repeating that poem for days. Are you the one who gave it to her?"

Dean Buehl, still standing above the single bed, looks my way.

"No," I say. "It's just something I remember. We read it when I was in school."

Athena and Vesta shake their heads as if to say *Teachers! Who knows what junk they carry around in their heads!*

"Girls," Dean Buehl says, "run down to the matron and ask for a plastic bag, then come right back up. Don't talk to anyone."

The girls scurry out of the room, glad, I think, to be away from us. Dean Buehl moves as if to sit on the edge of Melissa's bed and then thinks better of it and sits on the window ledge. When she looks up at me I think she'll ask the same question Athena asked. *How did you know that poem?* But she doesn't. Maybe she assumes her old girls ought to know their Yeats.

"I'm going to my office to call the police," she says. "You're to follow with Athena and Vesta, but give me half an hour to make the call—no, make it an hour. I don't want them to overhear what I have to say to the police."

"What do you think has happened to her?"

Dean Buehl shakes her head. "I just don't know…it's all so odd…that poem—it's the same one that girl left in her journal twenty years ago…that Hall girl."

"Deirdre."

"Yes, Deirdre Hall. Right before she jumped off the Point. My God. This was her room, wasn't it?" She looks around her and then she looks at me standing in the doorway, noticing for the first time, I think, my reluctance to step over the threshold into the small room. She shakes her head. "What the hell is going on here?"

It is only 3:30 when Athena, Vesta, and I reach Dean Buehl's office, but already the sun is low behind the mansion, its last rays skating across the lake and filling the room with their deep golden light. The State Police officer, in a chair facing Dean Buehl's desk, has to shield his eyes from the glare. All I can make out of him is the copper glow of his hair in the sunlight. I usher the two girls in ahead of me and Gwen Marsh, who is sitting on a couch to the side of the desk, gestures for them to sit on either side of her. She slips an arm around each girl even though both of Gwen's arms are wrapped in ace bandages. Dr. Lockhart, who is standing with her back to the room, looks at the girls, then at me, and then turns back to the window.

"This is the teacher I was telling you about. Jane Hudson," Dean Buehl says to the police officer.

The officer rises slowly to his feet and turns toward me. "Yes," he says, "Miss Hudson and I have met before."

For a moment the air around me seems to shimmer, as if the light the lake throws into the room was lapping up against me. It's that feeling I've had that the lake, as it moves towards freezing, is churning up the past, casting its secrets into the light of day. And now look whom it's cast up—Matt.

But then he takes a step toward me, out of the glare, and the copper hair fades to dark brown streaked with gray, the golden skin ages and sallows. Not Matt. Maybe what Matt would have looked like if he'd lived many years past his eighteenth birthday.

"It's Roy Corey, isn't it?" I ask, reaching out my hand. He takes my hand and holds it for a moment, really holds it instead of shaking it, and I'm surprised and gladdened by the warmth. "Of course I remember you. You're Matt and Lucy's cousin. We met once."

He drops my hand rather suddenly and that warmth is replaced by a sudden chill in the air. The sun has gone down behind Main Hall and the gold glow goes out of the lake like a light that's been switched off. I feel inexplicably that I've disappointed this man, yet, I think I'm doing pretty well to have remembered as much as I have. After all it's been twenty years and we only met that once.

He turns his back to me and sits down. Dean Buehl gestures for me to sit in the other chair in front of her desk. "Detective Corey

was just saying we ought to check the Schwanenkill icehouse," Dean Buehl tells me.

"I believe your Heart Lake girls have made a habit over the years of meeting town boys down there."

I find myself blushing. I'm sure he's said this to embarrass me—he knows as well as I do what used to go on in that icehouse.

"This Melissa Randall, did she have a boyfriend?" he asks.

Dean Buehl tells him that she did, but that he's at Exeter.

"Anybody call to see if he's still there?"

Dean Buehl places the call and speaks to the headmaster. Twenty minutes later he rings back and puts Brian Worthington on the line. At a signal from Corey, Dean Buehl hits the speakerphone so we all can hear Brian Worthington swear he hasn't been out of New Hampshire since Thanksgiving break.

"When was the last time you heard from Melissa?" the dean asks him.

"Night before last," he answers. "I knew something was up when she didn't call last night. She calls every night." I can hear the weariness in his voice and I'm not sure whom to feel sorrier for, him or Melissa. "She hasn't done anything stupid, has she?"

Dean Buehl explains that Melissa is missing. She asks Brian to please let the authorities know if Melissa should show up at Exeter and promises to call as soon as she knows anything. When she gets off the phone, Athena raises her hand as if she were in class.

"Yes, Ellen?"

"Melissa said she was going to the hall phone to call Brian at around ten last night. We heard her talking to someone on the phone."

"Did she say she had reached him when she came back?"

Athena and Vesta shake their heads. "She didn't say and we didn't ask. She'd been crying, but that wasn't unusual."

"And did she go out after that?"

"We don't really know," Vesta answers. "She went into her room and closed the door. We just thought she wanted to be alone to... you know...cry and stuff."

"We went to sleep around eleven," Athena continues. "I noticed when we turned out our lights that her light was off. But I don't know if she was there or not. Her room has a separate entrance."

"So we really don't know how long the girl's been missing," Corey sums up. He slaps his hands on the arms of the Morris chair he's in and then shifts his weight forward as if to get up, but pauses there on the edge of the chair. I revise my opinion about him. Matt wouldn't have looked like this. He'd never have become this...solid.

"We'll start the search on the south end of the lake and split into two parties to cover the east and west sides," he says.

"Of course we'll want to be part of the search effort," Dean Buehl says.

"That's up to you, of course, all volun-

teers are welcome, but I'd appreciate it if you could keep track of your girls. Last thing we need is someone else getting lost." He lays his hands on the arms of the chair and heaves himself up. "Ask me," he says, "the best thing would be if your teachers kept the girls calm and in their rooms."

"We're perfectly capable of keeping the girls calm, Officer," Dr. Lockhart replies.

When Corey is gone, Dr. Lockhart sighs and looks out the window. It is dark outside now, too dark for her to see anything but her own reflection in the glass.

"Thank goodness we're in capable hands," she says.

"I'm sure the police will do their best," Gwen Marsh says. It's the first time she's said anything since I've come in. "I agree with that nice Officer Corey—the girls should stay in their dorms. They've been through enough already."

"That's not fair," Athena blurts out, shrugging herself out from under Gwen's arm. "She's our friend. We want to help."

"A very natural response," Dr. Lockhart says moving from the window and sitting on the edge of the couch next to Athena. "The last thing we want to encourage in the girls right now is a feeling of helplessness." She looks directly at Gwen and I have the feeling that this has been a bone of contention between Lockhart and Marsh before. What surprises me is how warmly Athena and Vesta respond to Dr. Lockhart's suggestion.

"We could organize a search team with teachers and students and work in shifts," Athena says.

I see Dean Buehl considering. "Very well, as long as there's a teacher in every squad."

"Well, of course if that's what you think is best, I'll get working on a schedule right away, but I'll need a secretary," Gwen says, holding up one of her bandaged arms. "Perhaps Sandy will help me."

I see Vesta exchange a desperate look with Dr. Lockhart, but Dr. Lockhart only shrugs and moves back to the window. Gwen has already commandeered a pad from Dean Buehl's desk and put Vesta to work.

THAT NIGHT I WATCH THE SEARCHERS' LIGHTS moving through the woods across the lake.

The shift I am assigned doesn't start until four A.M. I am touched that Vesta and Athena ask to be on my search squad. I know I ought to sleep until then, but I also know that sleep is impossible. I wonder if Athena and Vesta are asleep in their dorm room. I doubt it.

From their window, I know, they, too, can see across the lake to the south shore.

The lights moving through the woods remind me of Wilis, seeking vengeance for earthly betrayal.

At a quarter to four I put on long underwear, jeans and a sweater, gloves and a wool hat and take a flashlight. It is still dark when I walk outside, the moon having set, the woods lit only

by faint starlight reflected on the snow. I pause on the Point and look at the lake, which is so still that its surface looks like black marble. It is one of those calm cold nights that don't, at first, feel as cold as they are because there is no wind. But in a few minutes, despite the layers I am wearing, I feel the cold bearing down on me. I shine my flashlight on the scratches on the rock and imagine the mile-high glacier that made them.

I consider taking a shortcut through the woods to the dorm, but already the snow beyond the paths is too deep. Soon the paths will narrow between two walls of packed snow and daily walks from dorm to dining hall to class-room will follow the same ever-tightening pattern.

"Like rats in a maze," Lucy would say.

In our senior year she began at the first snowfall carving out her own paths, narrow deer tracks that meandered aimlessly through the woods.

At the dorm I find Athena and Vesta waiting for me on the steps. They are blowing into their mittened hands to warm their faces. "Miss Marsh was just here," they tell me, "and she says we're supposed to look down at the swimming beach—in case Melissa took out a boat or something."

"When I was a student here," I say slowly and carefully, "I once took a boat out on the lake and rowed to the stones." I am thinking not just of Aphrodite's fate right now, but of that afternoon I found a dry Olivia on the far-

thest rock and the flash of white I saw vanishing around the curve of the Point.

"Yeah, that's nice, *Magistra*," Vesta says impatiently, "but the boats are all locked up for the winter. If a person wanted a boat they'd have to go down to the icehouse. I think I heard Miss Todd say once that the county extension agent keeps a boat down there to take water samples. At least, that's what I heard."

I remember suddenly the day I met Athena swimming across the lake and the impression I had that she was meeting someone on the other side.

"Well, then, why don't we go there instead," I say.

"You mean deviate from Miss Marsh's carefully choreographed schedule?" Vesta asks, lifting both eyebrows at me.

"Yes," I tell her. "Let's use some initiative. We can walk around the west side of the lake, check the icehouse, and then continue around the east side to the swimming beach. That should warm us up. But remember what Detective Corey said about staying together— I can't afford to lose one of you."

At the mention of Detective Corey's name the girls exchange meaningful glances.

"What?" I ask, feeling suddenly like another teenager, the one not in on the joke.

"Oh, nothing, *Magistra*," Athena says. "It's just that we thought you and Detective Corey would...you know, make a cute couple. What do you think?"

I click my tongue and motion for the girls to start down the path, which is too narrow for three to walk abreast. I want to walk behind the girls so I can keep an eye on them. It helps, too, that they can't see me smiling at their matchmaking attempt. It's ridiculous—me and the stocky police officer who clearly seemed not to like me—but it touches me that they're concerned about my personal life.

We call Melissa's name as we go and, at Athena's suggestion, vary our calls of *Melissa* with *Aphrodite*.

"She really liked her Latin class name," Athena tells me. "She said in her old school her Latin teacher assigned names and she got Apia, because *Melissa* means honey and bees make honey and Apia means..."

"Bees," I finish for her.

"Only the other girls called her Ape and she was... I mean she *is*...really sensitive about her weight."

"Kids can be so mean," I say. I am thinking about that *was* and wondering if my students are telling me everything they know about their roommate's disappearance. "When I was here one of my roommates threatened to get my other roommate, my best friend, in trouble by telling a secret they shared. She teased her all the time about it, until my roommate, the one who was my friend, was nearly going crazy."

"That's pretty lousy," Athena says. "I mean, no one likes a tattletale."

Tattletale. The word is so childlike that instantly I am ashamed of myself for suspecting these girls of any wrongdoing, but then Vesta says, "Yeah, that must have gotten on your friend's nerves. You could really get annoyed at someone like that."

"It must have been annoying," I say, "to hear Aphrodite crying all the time. I could tell her boyfriend, Brian, sounded worn-out."

Vesta sighs. "God, it's all we've heard all semester. Brian this and Brian that. He's just this little pimply-faced nerd with a trust fund. Girls makes such fools of themselves over guys."

"She should have just trusted him or decided he wasn't worth it. That's what I told her. I mean, a guy's just not worth all that heartache."

"Certainly not," Vesta murmurs. "You know what they say, 'A woman without a man is like a fish without a bicycle.' " I laugh at the old aphorism. At Vassar we had T-shirts made up with that slogan.

"Hey look, we've come to another path. I wonder where that leads," Athena says.

"It follows the Schwanenkill into town," I tell them. "The icehouse should be just past here on the other side of the stream."

I had forgotten that we would have to ford the stream to continue our walk around the lake. Fortunately, the Schwanenkill is mostly frozen.

"There's a place that's narrower, just off the path," I tell the girls. "We just have to go a little into the woods..."

"Good," Vesta says. "I have to take a leak

130

anyway. I'll be right back. Can I borrow that flashlight, *Magistra*?"

Vesta takes the flashlight out of my hands before I can think to object and then disappears into the shadows of the pine trees. Athena and I stand at the place where the two paths cross and wait for her. It occurs to me that this might be a good opportunity to talk to Athena without Vesta's restraining presence.

"Vesta sounded pretty annoyed with Aphrodite," I say.

"She just couldn't understand the attraction," Athena says in a normal tone of voice, then she leans closer to me and whispers into my ear, "You know, it's just not her thing."

When she leans away I can feel the warm breath she left on my cheek crystallizing in the cold air. It's not until I watch Vesta walking back toward us through the woods, zipping her fly, that I realize that she's trying to tell me that Vesta's a lesbian.

"Oh," I say, to no one really, because the two girls are walking on ahead of me. What impresses me about Athena's revelation is the lack of malice or censure. When I went to school here girls were teased and called "lezzie," but it wasn't something you could talk openly about. For all our drug use and talk of sexual revolution, we really were still naive. And the suggestion at her inquest that Helen Chambers was a lesbian practically sealed her dismissal.

"I see where we can cross," Vesta calls back to me.

I follow them into the woods, keeping my eyes on the beam from the flashlight which Vesta still holds until I'm forced to watch my footing instead. Off the path the snow is calf deep. I feel the cold and wet seeping into my cheap boots. Each step requires effort and concentration. I watch my feet disappear into the snow and look for places where the snow isn't so deep. There are places where the snow has drifted up against a tree and my legs sink in to my knees. I slip into one particularly deep spot and find, for a moment, that I can't pull out. My hands flutter over the surface of the snow seeking for purchase but finding none. I realize how silly I must look, floundering in the snow, and look up, expecting to find the girls laughing at my predicament, but instead I see nothing but snow and pine trees stretching out around me.

For a moment I do nothing but listen to the silence. And then I panic. It's what they tell you not to do when you're drowning. Miss Pike said if you try to save someone from drowning and they panic, the best thing to do is sock 'em in the jaw and carry them back to shore unconscious. "Never risk your own life," she'd tell us. "That's the first rule of lifesaving."

When all my thrashing has done nothing but sink me deeper into the snow I stop and listen once again to the silence. The night is so eerily calm that not even a breeze moves through the pines. Then I hear, from behind me, the crunch of snow.

I try to turn around but that only makes me sink deeper.

I can hear it clearly now. Footsteps moving through the deep snow toward me. I can do nothing but wait. I imagine a blow to the head and then sinking, drowning, my mouth and lungs filling with ice.

Then I see the lights. Moving through the woods in front of me, they seem to dance among the pines. *Wilis,* I think, they've come to dance me to my death and drown me in the lake just like Hilarious. It's the last thought I have before losing consciousness and it makes me happy. Well, at least it makes me laugh.

Chapter Ten

●

"WHAT'S HILARIOUS?" SOMEONE IS ASKING ME. "For God's sake, what's so hilarious?"

The whole thing, I want to say, but my mouth is full of ice.

I open my eyes and see why I'm so cold. I'm in the icehouse. A face leans over me and I realize why I'm so happy. I am in the icehouse with Matt Toller.

"Magistra," another voice says. "We're so sorry we left you all alone."

It must be Lucy, I think, only why would she call me *Magistra*? I'm glad, though, that she has finally apologized after all these years. How could they go and leave me alone. It's all right now though, we're together again.

"Miss Hudson, please try to drink some of this." A strong arm holds me up and I sip from the thermos cup. Matt always remembered to bring the hot chocolate when we went skating.

I take a sip and the bitter, black coffee burns my tongue. I look at the man holding the cup and the wave of sadness that moves through my body is so strong I start to shake all over. I remember that when I gave birth to Olivia I shook like this. *It's because your body has lost all that mass,* the nurse told me, *it makes your body temperature drop.* Yes, I remember thinking, this is what missing someone feels like, like part of your flesh has been torn away. Looking now at the man who is not Matt Toller, who is only his cousin, Detective Roy Corey, I feel that same precipitous drop all over again.

I lean into Corey's arm and immediately he moves it away as if he just noticed he had it around me. No, I think, the girls are wrong. This man can't even stand to touch me.

I take another sip of the bitter coffee and look at Vesta and Athena.

"Your girls led me to you," Corey tells me. "I met up with them here and they were surprised you weren't right behind them."

"I got stuck in the snow," I say.

"You passed out," he tells me. "I was afraid

134

you had hypothermia, but I think it was just fear. How do you feel now?"

"Fine," I tell him. I look around the icehouse. "What are you doing here? I thought you were going to check out the icehouse first thing last night."

"I did, but then all I was looking for was a lost girl. I wasn't noticing what wasn't here."

I sit up and swing my legs over the edge of the wooden ledge. I am sitting, I see, on one of the wide shelves where they used to store the slabs of ice harvested from the lake.

"The boat," I say. "There's no boat."

Corey nods his head and twists his mouth around like a man who's made a big mistake and hates to admit it. I notice that he has the same full lips that Matt Toller had.

"I should have thought of it directly," he says. "But I'd forgotten the county extension agent used the icehouse to store her dinghy."

"You think Aphrodite…Melissa took it?"

Instead of answering, Corey looks at the girls.

"We found it at the beginning of the year and took it out once or twice. I guess Melissa could have taken it," Athena says.

"Could she have gotten it down to the water by herself?" I ask.

In answer, Corey swings open the double doors at one end of the wooden hut. At first all I see is blackness, but then I realize that what I'm looking at isn't the blackness of night, but a wide expanse of water—so still it might be air instead of water—spreading out from the edge of the icehouse.

WHEN I HAVE ASSURED COREY AND THE GIRLS that I haven't suffered any ill effects from my faint in the woods, we walk back along the east side of the lake toward the swimming beach.

We are walking two abreast on the path with the girls in front of us. Corey slows his pace a bit and signals for me to do the same. I realize he wants to leave some space between us and the girls. "We found a boat drifting off the swimming beach, caught between two of the rocks," he says in a voice so low I have to move closer to hear him, "but I wanted to see where the boat came from since the school's boathouse was still padlocked. That's when I remembered about the boat in the ice-house."

"But shouldn't you be looking for Melissa in the water?" Roy pats the air with his hand, meaning for me to keep my voice down. I hadn't realized how loud I'd spoken, or how frightened my voice would sound. It's that image of the empty boat, drifting between the rocks.

"We've called the divers in, but they can't start until sunrise. The girl's parents are flying in from California. I'd like you to get those girls back to their rooms before then. I don't think they need to see this."

"I understand," I tell him. "I'd like to come back. If you don't mind."

He looks at me. "You were there when they took Matt and Lucy out of the lake, weren't you?"

"Yes," I say. "Sometimes I wish I hadn't been."

"Really? I've always wished I had been here. You know, Matt was staying with us the weekend he took off and hitched back here." I nod, remembering that the military school Matt had been sent to senior year was near his aunt and uncle's house. "I knew he was doing it. He told me he had to see his sister. That was the last time I ever saw him alive."

So someone else has been carrying the weight of Matt Toller's death all these years. For a moment it makes me feel lighter, and then heavier. This is why Roy Corey is so standoffish with me. He blames me for what happened to Matt and Lucy.

"You shouldn't blame yourself," I say, but what I'm really saying is *please don't blame me.* "You were just a kid."

"That's no excuse," he tells me. "I've thought about this a lot since then. You can't duck responsibility because you're young. You have to take accountability."

"Is that why you became a cop? To hold people accountable for their mistakes? To unmask the villains?"

He stops on the path and looks at me as if I'd slapped him. I hadn't meant to sound so angry, but I'm tired of being blamed.

"Look," I say, laying my hand on his arm. I want to explain to him how I feel, but he moves

137

away from me and walks up the path so quickly I can hardly keep up with him.

AFTER I DROP OFF ATHENA AND VESTA AT THE dorm I walk back to the swimming beach. The sun hasn't risen yet, but I can see a lightening in the sky across the lake and know that it soon will. I was upset at first after my talk with Corey, but once I got over the fact that he obviously holds me responsible for what happened to Matt and Lucy, I realized how lucky I am to have found him.

Roy Corey saw Matt Toller just before he came back here to Heart Lake that last time. Maybe Matt talked to him about me and, if he did, I might find out what Matt was thinking about me at the end. For the past twenty years I'd felt like I'd been talking to someone on the phone when the lines went down. Right in the middle of the most important conversation of my life. Roy Corey might be able to fill in some of the lost pieces.

When I round the Point and see the police cars and ambulance parked on the road above the swimming beach I feel ashamed of myself for worrying at a time like this about Matt's opinion of me. Vesta is right, we girls make such fools of ourselves over men.

I can imagine what must have happened to Aphrodite. Frantic over Brian's purported faithlessness and feeling powerless hundreds of miles away from him she resorted to a childish witchcraft. What was that Dr. Lock-

hart said? *It's all an attempt to gain control over a world in which they have no power.* She wanted to go to the farthest three sisters rock and make an offering to the Lake Goddess. Only it was too cold to swim there, so she got the boat from the icehouse and rowed across the lake. It was probably when she was trying to get from the boat onto the rock that she slipped and fell into the water. The cold of the water must have shocked her...or maybe she hit her head...

From what Vesta and Athena have said, I know that Aphrodite could have gotten the idea to take the boat from their previous exploits. But something else bothers me. Lucy Toller and I once took the rowboat from the icehouse and I wrote about it in my senior-year journal. What if Aphrodite got the idea from my journal? Then I have an awful thought. I think: Maybe Aphrodite had my journal with her when she fell into the lake. If so, maybe my old dream of the lake washing clean those pages has finally come true. It's an awful thought because for a moment it has made me glad.

I walk down the steps to the swimming beach and stop midway. Roy Corey is there, so is Dean Buehl and a middle-aged couple in matching Burberry trench coats. Melissa's parents, no doubt. I find that I don't want to join the group on the beach, so I sit down on the cold stone, about halfway down the steps, and wrap my arms around my knees, trying to make myself small and compact against the relentless cold.

Three men in oily black rubber suits are talking to Corey. They all look at the eastern shore where the sun has just appeared through the pine trees. I can imagine what they are saying. That it's probably better to wait until the sun is higher, shining through the water. But then they look back at the parents. The first morning light hits the woman's face and it's like a blade cracking her open. I imagine this woman looked ten years younger just twelve hours ago.

The divers walk into the water. When they are chest deep they spread their arms over the surface of the water and then they dive. On the beach there is nothing to do but wait. No one talks.

The sun rises above the tips of the pines on the eastern shore and bathes the farthest of the three sisters rocks in light. I notice, for the first time, that the rocks are perfectly aligned with the angle of the rising sun. As the sun rises, the light touches each rock in turn, like a child jumping across stepping-stones. The sunlight glazes the beach and the step I am sitting on, but there's no warmth in it. Instead, I feel as if I, and all the other figures on the beach, have been sealed in ice. The lake is so still that I find it hard to believe that divers are moving below the surface, but then I see a black head surface in the middle of the cove. I see a hand rise out of the water, and Roy Corey, who is watching the diver through binoculars, waves back.

I see Mrs. Randall turn to Corey as if to ask

a question, but then she turns back to her husband and kind of leans in on him, like a tree tilting in the wind.

Out in the lake the head is gone. The surface of the water is still again.

We are all still looking toward the center of the cove so we don't notice the diver surface to the left of the swimming beach. He is shoulder deep in the water and his arms, instead of spreading across the water, are below the surface and look as if they are being pulled down as he walks slowly through the water toward the beach.

He's carrying Melissa Randall.

As soon as he lays her down on the beach the paramedics snap into life and try to resuscitate what even I, from this distance, can see is a corpse. The group on the beach contracts into a tight fist around the drowned girl. I am probably the only one who notices the second diver surfacing a little to the left of the three sisters. He is carrying something, too, but something smaller and lighter.

Roy Corey notices and breaks away from the group. He meets the diver at the edge of the water and reaches for the rusty tin box. I am up and moving across the beach, although I don't know what I think I can do about it. Roy Corey is moving his hand over the domed surface of the box, which is a little larger than a shoe box. A webbed belt is fastened around the box. I see him unfasten the brass buckle and the belt falls away, rotting, to the ground. He wipes away the layer of green

slime that covers the tin, revealing an improbable landscape of gold mountains that glints in the morning sun. He flicks back a little gold latch and opens the lid.

Inside is a heavy white cloth embroidered with a heart and words I can't make out from where I am. But I don't have to. I know them by heart. *Cor te reducit.* The heart leads you back. Roy Corey lifts the cloth, delicately, with a little flourish even, like a magician culminating his final trick. But there's no flutter of white wings; instead, nestled in a circle of greenish-gray stones, are the perfectly preserved bones of a tiny human being.

I look away from the small skeleton toward the lake and notice that something is happening. I remember again how the nurse said that after birth the mother's body temperature drops precipitously. It is as if now that the lake has given up these two bodies its own temperature has achieved an equilibrium of cold. It's as if that flutter of white handkerchief has produced magic after all because shooting out in all directions at once, brilliant in the morning sun, ice crystals explode across the still surface of the lake. It's what we've all been waiting for: first ice.

PART TWO

•

First Ice

Chapter Eleven

●

WHEN I FIRST MET MATTHEW AND LUCY Toller I thought they were twins. Not that they looked all that much alike. He had the sandy red hair, blunt jaw, and stolid build of the Tollers, while she was fair and lithe and sharp-featured like one of the water nymphs in my copy of *Tales from the Ballet*. It was in their gestures and the way they moved their bodies—like one person in two sets of limbs— that they so deeply resembled each other.

I first noticed them the summer before ninth grade. My mother, having decided I ought to meet some West Corinth kids before being thrown in with them at Corinth High School, had gotten me a job as a counselor at the swim club. How she thought spending a summer wading calf-deep in the tepid, citrinous water of the kiddie pool would gain me entrée into the world of doctors' and lawyers' children, I do not know. What it did gain me was a view, through the bitter-smelling box hedge, of the deep end and the high dive

145

where I could watch Matt and Lucy Toller practice their dives and race freestyle in the lap lane. No one ever seemed to win those races; they were more like synchronized swim events. They swam, shoulder to shoulder, their bodies tilting for breath at the same angle like two planets pulled by the same moon, their white elbows cresting the water like the two wings of one enormous swan.

WHEN I GOT TO HIGH SCHOOL I FOUND OUT TWO things about the Tollers. One was that they were not twins; Matt was thirteen months younger than Lucy. He had been allowed to start kindergarten early because, Lucy told me, he had pitched such a fit when she started school without him. Hannah Toller had gone to the principal and told him she'd either have to keep Lucy back a year or let Matt start early. So Matthew started kindergarten six months shy of his fifth birthday.

The second thing I found out about the Tollers was that although Matt and Lucy lived on the west side of the river (in Corinth it's the river and not the train tracks that divide the haves from the have-nots), they fit in with the West Corinth kids no more than I did. Their father, Cliff Toller, was a paper salesman at the lumber mill—a job only a few rungs above my father's job as factory foreman. Still, the Tollers seemed to live a little better than other salesmen's families. They had a small but picturesque house on River Street

where the doctors and lawyers lived. They belonged to the swim club and Matt and Lucy took piano lessons with the music teacher at Heart Lake. My mother assumed that Cliff Toller must do well on commission and she chastised my father for not having the where-withal to move into a sales job. When Lucy Toller befriended me on that first day of ninth grade my mother was pleased. Perhaps not as pleased as if one of the doctors' or lawyers' children had invited me home to their River Street mansion, but it was a start.

As for me, I was so relieved when Lucy asked me to bring my tray to their table I had to blink away tears before I could say yes. I was standing at the end of the check-out line, balancing a tray heavy with sloppy joes and canned fruit and two waxy milk cartons ("You get two on the lunch program, honey," the cafeteria lady had loudly informed me, "you might as well take them.") The smell of the sweet, orangy meat was making me feel dizzy while kids streamed around me to their places, as sure of where they were going as water knows to flow to the ocean. I saw where I belonged. There was the table with the East Corinth kids: the boys in flannel shirts and jeans cuffed at the bottom for extra wear, the girls in plaid skirts a little too short or a little too long and Peter Pan blouses with darning stitches at the collar. I knew them and I knew they'd make a place for me—not with the enthusiastic hugs and smiles with which the West Corinth kids greeted one another after

147

summers apart at tennis camp, but with the resigned shift of kids from big families making room for one more.

Those afternoons I had spent at the West Corinth Swim Club were shimmering and fading like heat haze just as I felt a cool hand slip under my elbow and pull me out of the current.

"Don't I know you from the pool?" she said, in a small, clear voice I had to lean toward to make out.

I nodded at her, afraid if I talked I might start to cry. I noticed that her pale hair was tinged green from her summer spent swimming in the chlorinated water and her eyelashes and brows were bleached white from the sun.

"Do you want to come sit with us? I think we've got our next class together. Did you sign up for Latin? There's only eleven of us and the rest are all that crowd'll be taking it for their SAT scores and to get into law school." She spoke in a rush I could barely understand.

I followed her to a table in a far corner beneath the cafeteria's only window. Her brother Matt actually half rose from his seat to greet me. They both had brought their lunches—identical brown paper packets of cheese and apples and thermoses of hot cocoa.

"You were right, Mattie," Lucy said, polishing her apple on her sweater sleeve. "She's in Latin."

I couldn't remember telling her, but of course she had known all along.

Matt gave me a long appraising look. "So why did you sign on?" he asked.

He made it sound like I'd joined the foreign legion. The truth was that signing up for Latin, instead of the usual French or Spanish, had been, like most of what I did, my mother's idea. She'd heard that the lawyers and doctors urged their kids into Latin to boost their SAT scores.

"French and Spanish are common," my mother told me. "You'll meet more interesting children in Latin." My mother's ambitions for me were a puzzle, because they didn't seem to come from any belief in my ability. I often felt like a piece in a game that she was moving around on a board. When I achieved some goal she'd set out for me—the best reading scores in sixth grade, a part in the school play—she seemed mistrustful of the success.

"She wants those things for you because her mother wouldn't let her try for anything," my father once explained to me. "Your mother could have gotten a scholarship to Heart Lake, but her mother made her give it up. I hate to speak badly of your grandma, Janie, especially as you're named for her, but Jane Poole was an awful cold woman. She hated the Crevecoeurs after she was let go. Your mother wants more for you, but when you look like you're going to get it, I think she must hear old Jane's voice telling her it'll come to no good."

Of course I couldn't tell Matt and Lucy any of this.

I searched my head for anything I knew

about Latin. They spoke it in church, I knew, but we were Presbyterians, not Catholics. There were those movies with chariot races and gladiator fights where the actors' words didn't quite match the movement of their lips, but somehow I didn't think Matt and Lucy spent their Saturdays eating Captain Crunch in front of the TV. They probably went on nature hikes and read books with nice leather bindings instead of the tattered paperbacks mended with yellow tape I borrowed from the town library.

I remembered then that one of those books I had borrowed that summer had been a collection of Greek and Roman myths. I hadn't thought it was as good as my beloved *Tales from the Ballet*, but I had liked some of the stories.

"I like mythology," I said. "The gods and all and those stories of people turning into something else...like the one about the girl who turns into a spider... ," I blathered on, mashing my fork into my sloppy joe, turning the meat and bread into an even more unappetizing mess.

"Arachne," Matt said.

"Ovid," Lucy said, even more mysteriously.

"*Metamorphoses,*" they both said at the same time.

"That's good." Matt held his apple up between us and closed one eye as if I were a far away object and he was taking my perspective. "Of course we won't get to it first year."

"Oh no, it'll be all grunt work with declen-

sion endings and conjugations, but *Domina* Chambers says if we study hard she'll let us read extra bits. I want to do Catullus and Matt's keen on Caesar—just like a boy, right? And she'll help us study for the Iris Scholarship for Heart Lake—only Matt's not eligible because he's a boy. But she says there's no harm in him studying with me as he'll be a help. Perhaps you'll want to join us?"

I felt I was already listening to a foreign language more arcane than Greek or Latin. I hadn't understood half of what she'd said— I had never heard of Ovid or Catullus or *Domina* Chambers—but it was a little like listening to opera on public radio. I didn't always understand the story, but I liked how listening to it made me feel. I liked how the weak sunshine that came through the dirty cafeteria window made Matt's sandy brown hair turn a fiery red and Lucy's pale, greenish hair glow like burnished gold. I liked being with them.

I think that if they had been asking me to join the foreign legion instead of only inviting me to study Latin with them, I would have followed them into the desert willingly.

151

Chapter Twelve

●

THE IRIS SCHOLARSHIP—NAMED AFTER THE CREVE-coeur daughter who died in the influenza epidemic of 1918—was awarded to the freshman girl from the town of Corinth who scored the highest on her Latin exam. It was a sop, my mother told me when I came home that first day of ninth grade, to the town's resentment of the school. When, in the early seventies, the Corinth Public School Board threatened to cancel the Latin program due to low enrollment and a scarcity of qualified teachers, Helen Chambers, a Heart Lake alum and newly appointed classics teacher there, volunteered to teach the Latin class at Corinth High.

We were her first public school class, she told us that first day, and as such responsible for whatever impression of public education she would take away with her. We also turned out to be her last public school class, so I assume the impression she took away with her was not favorable.

Helen Chambers was unlike any teacher I had ever seen before. The teachers we got in Corinth generally fell into one of two categories. There were the plump, motherly women in shapeless Dacron dresses and cardigans embroi-

dered with ABCs and apples (or whatever was in season: pumpkins at Halloween, candy canes at Christmas) who showed lots of film strips and drew happy faces on returned papers. Then there were the sternish old maids in Orlon sweater vests, scratchy wool skirts, and support hose pooling around their thin ankles who lectured in monotones and gave detention for falling asleep in class. Occasionally, some young woman just out of the State Teacher's College came to Corinth for a few years. Such was Miss Venezia, my kindergarten teacher, who looked like Snow White and gave me *Tales from the Ballet*. But if they were any good they went on, as Miss Venezia did, to better jobs in Albany or Rochester.

Helen Chambers was neither young nor middle-aged. Instead she resided in a suspended state between the two. She was tall and fair, with the sort of blond hair that turns silver instead of gray and which she swept up in an elegant twist like an actress in a French movie. She wore, invariably, black— a color ill-suited for days spent in front of a chalkboard, but then I can't recall ever seeing her use the chalkboard.

She conducted her classes, I realized later, like college seminars. That first day she had the eleven of us pull our desks into a circle, which she joined. She gave us each a plain gray cloth-bound book and told us to turn to chapter one to review the first declension. She timed us on the watch brooch pinned, like

a nurse's, above her heart. When five minutes had elapsed she told us to close our books and recite the declension of *puella, puellae,* one at a time, around the circle. She ticked off points in a small leather notebook for each mistake we made. Lucy and Matt were the only ones who got it right.

Afterward she read us a poem by Catullus about a girl who keeps a sparrow in her lap, which makes her boyfriend jealous. Ward Castle made a rude gesture at Lucy and was told he could sit in the hall for the rest of the class. She told us to memorize the first declension and the present indicative active of *laudo, laudare* for tomorrow and dismissed us by saying *"Valete discipuli."*

Lucy and Matt responded by chanting *"Vale, Domina"* and the rest of us muttered some approximation without having the slightest idea what we were saying.

The next day our class size had dwindled to nine, by the end of the week: seven. Aside from Matt and Lucy and me, the rest were the children of doctors and lawyers whose parents had told them they had to stay in Latin to get into law or medical school.

After two weeks I had memorized the first declension, but I hadn't the slightest idea of what a declension was. But I was happy chanting the words with Matt and Lucy walking down River Street after school.

I was happy, truth be told, to be walking in the opposite direction from my own home. I wouldn't have to pass the mill with its sick-

ening smell of fresh-cut lumber and its yellow pall of smoke. My house was down the hill from the mill and every day of my life I had woken up to that oversweet smell and the yellow smoke staining the sky outside my bedroom window. The lumber trucks went past my house, rattling the windowpanes and making the vases of artificial flowers on the coffee table tremble. My mother waged an everlasting war against the sawdust that my father brought home on his boots and work clothes. She made him take off his clothes in the mudroom and wash his head under the garden hose even when it was so cold that the water froze in his hair and beard. Still the sawdust crept in, forming tiny drifts in the corners and speckling the china bric-a-brac and tickling the back of your throat. At night I could hear my father, who breathed that dust all day, coughing so hard that the iron day bed he slept on in the sewing room rattled. When I came home in the afternoons my mother would be dusting and railing against the sawdust and the mud and my father's salary and the cold.

"This is the last place on earth I thought I'd end up," she told me again and again. Since it was the place where she started out, I never understood her surprise over finding herself here.

When I told her I'd be going home with Lucy Toller that Friday I saw her take in the name and roll it around in her mind, measuring its worth like a pound of sugar.

"She's a bastard, you know."

I don't think I had ever heard my mother use a word like that. She always said cursing was common.

"Illegitimate, I mean," she said, seeing I didn't understand. "Cliff Toller's not her daddy. I knew her mother, Hannah Corey, in school. A smart girl. Maybe too smart for her own good. She got the Iris Scholarship." Maybe that was why she didn't like Hannah Corey. "She even got into one of those fancy women's colleges, but she came back after a year with a baby and wouldn't say boo to anyone about whose it was. Cliff Toller married her all the same and gave her a nice little house on River Street. I wouldn't have picked her daughter as first choice for a friend, but you might meet some of her friends on River Street."

I didn't tell my mother that Lucy and Matt didn't seem to have any other friends.

"She'll probably win the Iris this year and then you'd know someone at Heart Lake."

"Lucy says I could have a shot at the Iris," I told my mother. "She says we'll study together."

My mother gave me a long look so that now I felt like the pound of sugar. I couldn't tell if she had never thought of me having a chance for the Iris Scholarship until now, or if she'd been planning for me to go after it all along. After all, I was a good student, although more out of a slavish need to please my teachers than from any innate talent.

"The Iris Scholarship," she said. Like all her

goals for me she looked at it with both desire and mistrust.

"Well," she said, "that would be something. But I wouldn't set my heart on it."

From the start, though, I think I did just that: set my heart on the Iris Scholarship. I'd never seen the school even though I'd grown up only a mile from its gates. I'd seen, though, the Heart Lake girls come into town to browse the drugstore for magazines and try on lipsticks at the makeup counter. They'd try on half a dozen shades and then wipe their mouths clean before going back to the school. I thought there must be a rule against makeup, but then I noticed how resolutely plain they were in their dress. Even when the school abandoned their uniform, the girls seemed to be wearing one. Plaid kilts and pastel sweaters. Down vests in the winter, like loggers. Scuffed penny loafers worn down at the heel. My mother always said you could tell a lady by the heels of their shoes, but there was something about these girls—maybe the perfectly straight teeth, the way their hair gleamed, the discrete flash of gold on earlobes and throat, and, most of all, a carelessness combined with confidence—that told me that the backs of their shoes might be worn to the nub but they'd never be, what my mother called, "down at the heels."

It didn't seem such a far leap—from my actual poverty to their assumed negligence.

"You're a cinch for the scholarship," Matt told me walking back to their home that

Friday. "The only other one eligible financially is Lucy."

"Well, then Lucy will get it," I said.

"Lucy's lazy," Matt said, loudly enough for Lucy, who was walking up ahead, to hear. I thought she'd get mad, but instead she plucked a scarlet maple leaf from an overhanging branch and, looking coyly over her shoulder, bit down on its stem like a flamenco dancer holding a rose between her teeth. Matt skipped up to her and, clasping her into tango position, spun her around the lawn of one of the big mansions. They waltzed through the neat leaf piles the gardeners had raked together, kicking up red and gold maelstroms, until Matt dipped her low over a bed of yellow leaves and let her drop there in a graceful swoon.

"See," Matt said, turning back to me. I had stayed on the edge of the sidewalk, standing still under the gold waterfall of leaves. "She needs some competition."

Then he grabbed me, one arm firm around my waist, the other holding my hand straight out in front of us, his cheek, cool in the crisp fall air, against my cheek. As he spun me around, the red and gold leaves blurred together like the wings of the Firebird in my ballet book. His breath, against my cheek, smelled like apples.

"Now, repeat after me," he said in rhythm to our dancing, *"Puella, puellae, puellae...."*

I repeated dutifully, shouting the declension as we spun around the lawn. When we came

158

to a standstill, Lucy was on her feet, watching us, red and gold leaves sticking out of her hair like a chaplet of beaten gold. Everything else seemed to keep spinning except for her steady little figure.

"See," she said, "you've got it memorized."

"But I don't know what it's for."

Lucy and Matt exchanged a look and then he plucked one of the leaves from her hair and, with an elaborate sweep of his arm, presented the leaf to me.

"Puer puellae rosam dat," Lucy said.

"What?" I asked.

"The boy gives the girl a rose," Matt translated.

"Boy—*puer*—is in the nominative case, so it's the subject, he's the one doing the giving," Lucy said.

"Girl—*puellae*—is in the dative, so she's the indirect object of the verb—the one who receives the action of the verb. The rose," Matt twirled the scarlet maple leaf between his fingertips so that for a moment I thought I was looking at a rose, *"Rosam* is accusative. It's the direct object of the verb—the thing that's being given."

"See, you can mix it all up," Lucy said.

Matt jumped around me and stood on my right side and held the rose, the leaf, out to his right. Lucy pointed. *"Puellae puer rosam dat.* It still means...?"

"The boy gives the girl a rose," I replied.

Matt transferred the leaf into his left hand and held it between us.

"Puellae rosam puer dat?" Lucy asked.

"The boy gives the girl a rose," I answered.

Matt held the leaf over his head. "Get it?"

I nodded. For the first time I actually did understand.

Matt bowed to me and handed me the maple leaf, which I slipped carefully into my pocket.

"Good girl," he said. "Now, let's get home. It's getting dark." Matt linked his left arm in mine and Lucy linked her right arm in mine and we walked the rest of the way up River Street, chanting the first declension into the cool, blue evening air.

Chapter Thirteen

●

THE HOUSE AT THE END OF RIVER STREET WAS NOT a mansion, but rather the sort of cottage you'd expect the seven dwarfs to live in. It had originally been the gatehouse for the Crevecoeur Mansion. When the estate became a girls' school, the gatehouse was sold separately to the school's first headmistress. How it passed into the Toller family I never knew.

The downstairs rooms were always a disappointment to me. They were furnished in

the same overstuffed and overpolished colonial style as my own house. But whereas my mother regarded each chair and end table as a prized possession, there was an air of disregard and neglect in Hannah Toller's decorating. It looked as if the furniture had been picked off the showroom floor with no regard for what my mother called "color coordination." Ugly brown plaids vied with blue and red chintzes. The curtains were a particularly horrible shade of mustard. While neat, the place looked unloved.

From that first day we spent as little time as possible downstairs. I was introduced to their parents and allowed to exchange strained conversation with them for the length of time it took Lucy to heat up some hot cocoa and Matt to raid the cupboards for cookies. I saw immediately why no one could forget that Lucy was not Cliff Toller's daughter. In fact, it was hard to imagine Lucy issuing from either of the Tollers. Cliff Toller was large and red-haired; his hands, especially, seemed huge to me. Hannah Toller was small, like Lucy, but looked so dull, with mousy brown hair and unmemorable features, that one could only think of her as a genetic neutral that would require some divine visitation in order to have produced Lucy. I remembered my mother had told me that she'd conceived Lucy in that one year she had gone to Vassar and I imagined some blond scion encountered at a Yale/Vassar mixer.

When Lucy and Matt introduced me, Mrs.

161

Toller's dull brown eyes lit up for a moment. "Jane Hudson," she said my name slowly, much as my mother had pronounced Lucy's name. "Margaret Poole's girl?" I nodded.

"I went to school with your mother," she told me. "Everyone thought she'd be the one to win the Iris Scholarship, but on the day of the exam she didn't come to school."

I shrugged. "Maybe she was sick," I said, but I knew that probably wasn't what happened. My father had told me that my grandmother didn't want her to go to Heart Lake, but I hadn't known until now that she must have kept her home the day of the exam. I tried to imagine what my mother must have felt that day, after studying for the exam, to be kept from what must have seemed her only chance to get out of Corinth and a life of dreary millwork.

"And what do you think of your teacher? *Domina* Chambers?" Hannah Toller asked me.

"Oh, she seems wonderful," I gushed. "So elegant and…" I struggled for the right word, "…and refined."

"Refined? Yes, I guess you could call her that." And she went back to stirring some pungent-smelling stew on the stove.

"Mother went to school with Helen Chambers," Lucy explained as we trooped up the steep stairs. "First at Heart Lake, and then for one year at Vassar."

"Oh?" I said. I couldn't think of anything else to say and I was glad that Lucy and Matt were ahead of me on the steps or they would

have seen me blushing and known I'd heard the whole story about Lucy's birth.

"Yeah, she got the Iris Scholarship when she was our age," Matt said.

"I guess that's why she wants Lucy to have it," I said.

I saw Lucy and Matt turn to each other at the top of the steps. Matt whispered something and Lucy shook her head as if she were angry at what he had said. I was glad to be able to change the subject by exclaiming over their rooms.

"You guys are so lucky," I said a little too loudly. "It's like your own private hideaway. It's like the attic in *The Little Princess*."

"Yeah, Lucy's the princess and I'm the little serving girl she lets clean up after her."

Lucy scooped up a pile of dirty laundry on the landing and tossed it at Matt. "As if you picked up anything ever."

The rooms *were* messy. Lucy's room, on the right side of the stairs, was tiny, with hardly enough room for a single bed and a small bureau. This was why, she claimed, she'd encroached into Matt's room on the other side of the stairs. You'd have thought from the freefall of clothes and books and swimming goggles and ice skates and loose paper and teacups and half-eaten apples that they shared his room.

Lucy had even pushed her desk over to Matt's side so that they could study better. The desks faced each other on either side of the window— "so we both get a view," Lucy told

me. "We fought terribly over it." That first day they found an old table for me and placed it between their desks facing the window.

"She'll get distracted looking out the window," Lucy said.

"She won't," Matt countered. "Will you, Jane?"

They both turned to me and I looked out the window from which I could see the river running between tall white birches, their yellow leaves catching the last light, like a band of sapphires set in gold.

I looked back at their eager faces. "No," I told them, truthfully. "I won't be distracted."

I STUDIED WITH THEM EVERY DAY AFTER SCHOOL throughout the fall term and sometimes on Saturdays until Christmas break. I had been afraid that without the excuse of studying together Matt and Lucy would disappear from view over the long vacation. My relief at their invitation to go skating was tempered only by having to admit to them I didn't have skates. I'd always relied on the rented ones at the public rink.

"You can have my old ones," Lucy told me. "Your feet are smaller than my mine." Surprisingly, she was right. Although she was tiny everywhere else, Lucy had unusually long feet. I tried on her skates and found that with an extra pair of socks they fit perfectly.

"Do you think it'll be thick enough?" Lucy asked Matt as we followed a little stream

called the Schwanenkill west into the woods, our skates slung over our shoulders. Although we hadn't gotten much snow yet, the temperature had been below freezing since Halloween. The Schwanenkill was frozen except for a small rivulet down the middle that scalloped the edges of ice on either side. The ground felt hard to me as I struggled to keep up with them. The stream bank was icy and twice I slipped and broke through the thin ice and felt the cold water seep through my thin-soled sneakers.

Matt and Lucy wore the rubber-soled boots they'd gotten from L.L. Bean for Christmas, so they could crash through the ice and water heedlessly. I think that if they had noticed I was wearing Keds, they wouldn't have taken me into the woods that day, but they could be unobservant that way. She was careless about how she dressed, more often than not wearing one of Matt's soft corduroy shirts with her faded blue jeans. It didn't matter, though, because she looked good in whatever she wore.

After we had walked about a quarter of a mile we came to a small wooden hut on the southern end of Heart Lake. When I realized where we were I grew nervous.

"Isn't this private property?" I asked.

Lucy opened the door of the hut while Matt eased himself down the steep bank to test the ice.

"I suppose so," Lucy answered with a yawn. I followed her into the hut. It was too dark at first to make out much, but then she opened

the two double doors at the opposite end and the small space was filled with the late afternoon sun reflecting off the icy surface of the lake, which came up to the very edge of the building. I noticed that the sun was only a little above the line of hills behind the Crevecoeur mansion on the west side of the lake. It would be dark soon. The walls on either side were lined with deep shelves. Lucy stretched herself out on one of the shelves as if she had come for a nap instead of a skate.

"But no one's ever caught us," she said. "And it's the best place to skate. We even have our own skating lodge." She twirled her hand around in the mote-filled air, indicating the little hut.

"What is this place?" I asked.

"It's the old Schwanenkill icehouse," Matt said, coming into the hut and swinging his skates onto the end of the shelf where Lucy was lying. "The Crevecoeurs used it for storing ice harvested from the lake." He swept a handful of sawdust from the shelf and sifted it through his gloved fingers. "They packed the ice in sawdust and it lasted till summer." He pointed to a rotting wooden ramp that led from the double doors down to the ice. "They used that ramp to haul up the ice they cut from the lake. Our father used to help with the ice harvest."

"You're a fund of historical information, Mattie. How's the ice today?" Lucy asked without opening her eyes.

"It's a bit choppy at the mouth of the

Schwanenkill. I think there's a spring there that feeds into the stream and it keeps the ice from forming solidly above it. But if we skirt around that we should be all right."

He was already pulling his boots off as he spoke and Lucy, although still supine, brought one heavily booted foot up to her opposite knee and began lazily pulling at her laces.

I looked out at the surface of the lake, which was turning a pale Creamsicle color in the setting sun. It was hard to see well with the glare, but I thought I saw dark patches, like bruises on an apple, which could have been soft spots or just shadows on the ice.

"I hear the lake is really deep," I said conversationally. I'd kicked off my Keds but I was still twisting the skate laces through my fingers.

"Seventy-two feet in the middle," Matt answered proudly, as if he had made the lake, "but this side's pretty shallow near the shore. You stay right behind me, Jane, and if there's a thin spot I'll let you know by going through first." He grinned at me with the utter, unthinking confidence of a fourteen-year-old boy. "You'd pull me out, wouldn't you, Jane?"

I nodded earnestly, not sure if he were kidding or not.

"Good, because I'm not sure about this one." He jerked his thumb over his shoulder at Lucy. "It would probably be too much trouble for her. She probably wouldn't want to get her feet wet."

Lucy swiped at Matt's shin with the tip of her skate blade. He jumped off the bench and lunged out of the icehouse with Lucy right behind him. When they reached the ice their jerky movements suddenly smoothed and lengthened. I saw Lucy catch up with him and grab his parka hood so roughly I thought they'd both plummet headlong through the ice, but instead he turned around, caught her hands and spun her into a graceful pirouette.

I was tempted to stay in the icehouse. Even if I hadn't been worried about the ice I knew I would never be able to keep up with them. But then I remembered Matt's trusting smile. *You'd pull me out, wouldn't you, Jane?* Of course, he'd been kidding, but I realized at that moment, as I tightened my laces until they hurt, that if Matt and Lucy were in danger there was no point at all to me being safe on the shore.

There's always that first step in skating, from dry ground to slick ice, when it just seems impossible. Impossible that two thin blades of metal will support you, impossible that because its molecules have begun to dance a little slower water will hold you up. There was no railing here, as at the rink, to bridge that gap between solid and liquid, only the imperceptible giving way of earthbound gravity to free fall.

I took a few tentative strokes out onto the ice and then remembered what Matt had said about staying away from the Schwanenkill. I looked for them and saw that they were skating

along the lake edge toward the northeast cove, probably to avoid being seen from the mansion on the west side of the lake. I would have liked to get a closer look at the mansion, which I had never seen before, but with the sun setting behind it I could make out little except a low, dark bulk squatting on its rise above the lake. When I looked away there were dark spots burned into my vision, and it took a moment to locate Matt and Lucy under a pine tree that spread its boughs above the lake. Lucy waved at me, but Matt, standing behind her, reached up over Lucy's head and pulled a branch, releasing a shower of snow down the back of her neck. Lucy shrieked and spun around to grab him, but he was already gone, skimming the edge of the lake with a swift hockey player's glide.

Lucy knelt on the ice and gathered together a snowball. When she got to her feet she must have realized she'd never catch up with him. He was already on the western edge of the cove where three rocks broke through the ice. She must have decided that the only way she'd catch up to him would be to cut directly across the cove.

She was halfway across the cove when one of the shadows I'd noticed before darkened and opened beneath her. Matt, on the other side of the lake, was turned the other way. I don't remember deciding to move forward, but I found myself a few feet away from the ice hole.

She was in it up to her waist, her elbows

propped on the edge of the ice to hold herself up. I slid one heavy skate toward her and a crack like forked lightning spread between us. Behind her, Matt turned and saw us. He started to skate, not directly toward us, but back along the shore, the long way.

I crouched to my knees and then lay myself down flat on the ice. I moved slowly, but still the ice hit my chest like a wall and sucked all the breath out of my lungs. I reached my arm out but I was still a foot short of her hand. Her fingertips, which had been straining toward mine, relaxed and she shook her head at me. Then one elbow cracked through the ice and her left shoulder slipped under the water. She made a sound like a wounded bird and I thought I heard its echo until I realized it had come from Matt, who was behind me now. I slithered forward, scraping my chin on the rough ice, and caught her right hand. She grabbed my wrist with more strength than I would have imagined existed in those tiny hands.

Behind me I heard Matt's hoarse whisper telling me—*her? us?*—to hold on and then I felt a tug at my feet. As he pulled, she got her left arm onto the ice and I grabbed that one, too, only she had no grip in that hand so I grabbed her wrist. Her wrist felt so cold and brittle I thought it might break, but I held on even after her legs cleared the ice and her body was out of the water.

Matt dragged us like that, both of us flat on the ice, back to the shore. When we were

both on dry ground he told me I could let go, but he had to pry my fingers away from her wrist and her fingers away from mine. When she let go I realized I had no feeling in my left arm. I couldn't even lift it to help hold her up on the walk home so Matt picked her up and carried her the quarter mile back.

It was only after Dr. Bard (who lived two houses down from the Tollers) had examined Lucy and given her an injection of penicillin to ward off pneumonia that he happened to notice how I was holding my arm. When he took my jacket off he saw I had dislocated my shoulder—the bone had been pulled clean out of its socket.

Chapter Fourteen

ONCE SET, MY SHOULDER HEALED RAPIDLY, AND even though it still hurt, my mother didn't see any reason for me to miss school. It was too bad, she said, that I had always written with my left hand, so this was a good opportunity for me to learn to use my right hand better. I told her I would try, but when I was in school I switched back to writing with my left hand even though the act of writing sent

shooting pains through my arm. That arm never felt quite the same.

Lucy was worse off. Despite the penicillin injection, she developed pneumonia from her fall in the lake and was out of school for the whole month of January and some of February. Matt was out of school a lot, too, although I don't think he was sick. I just don't think he could bear to leave Lucy alone all day.

I went to the Tollers' house after school every day to drop off Lucy's homework until *Domina* Chambers told me that she would drop the work off herself on her way back to Heart Lake. I grew shy, then, of visiting even though Matt and Lucy had always acted happy to see me. I thought they had forgotten all about me when, on my fifteenth birthday, *Domina* Chambers gave me a package wrapped in plain brown paper. I waited until my study hall and then sneaked away to an unused corridor where I'd found a window seat looking out over the school's unused courtyard—an air well really—a place I could be alone if I didn't mind burning my bottom on a hot radiator and freezing my arms against the cold windowpane.

There were two packages inside, one contained a beautiful fountain pen and a bottle of peacock blue ink. These were from Lucy. I put those aside and ripped open the second package. It was a notebook, the black-and-white kind you could buy in the drugstore for a quarter. I opened it and read Matt's note on the inside cover, written on the lines pro-

vided for a classroom schedule: "To Jane. Still waters run deep. From, Matt." He'd said that to me once when I told him I'd like to be a writer but I worried about not having enough to say. "You're quiet, but you're observant," he'd said. "Still waters run deep."

I filled the pen with ink and wrote on the first page, "Lucy gave me this fountain pen and beautiful ink..." The nib of the pen caught on the page and ink splattered on the paper and my blouse. The effort to write made my whole arm ache and I wondered if Lucy realized it would be so hard for me to use it.

"...and Matt gave me this notebook." I looked at the notebook and tried to think of something poetic I could say about it. It was a cheap exercise book, a brand the town sold because it was made by the paper company that owned the mill. The black-and-white pattern on the cover was supposed to look like marble, but to me it looked like ice on the river in spring, when the ice began to break up and the broken shards traveled downstream to the mill. In the summer the river was choked with logs heading toward the mill to be made into paper—maybe the very paper between these covers and the cover itself—so that holding this book was like holding a piece of the river, and the forests up north, and the ice formed in the high peaks.

I looked out the window at the bleak abandoned courtyard. It was full of the things that kids threw from classroom windows, discarded mimeos and thick felt erasers that

had split in the middle and curled up on themselves like small dead animals.

"I'll never have any other friends like them," I wrote. I waited for the ink to dry and then ran my fingers down the page. That's when I noticed the ragged edge along the inside seam of the book. A page had been torn out. I wondered what Matt had written that he had decided to rip out.

I DECIDED TO VISIT THE TOLLERS' HOUSE THAT day to thank Matt and Lucy for their presents. When I got there I found *Domina* Chambers having tea in the kitchen with Hannah Toller. I shouldn't have been surprised to see her there; I knew she was *dropping* off Lucy's work, but I had imagined her literally dropping Lucy's assignments on the Tollers' front stoop and hastening on her way up Lake Drive to the school. I hadn't pictured her having tea with Hannah Toller. They looked so odd together: Helen Chambers like a Nordic ice queen and Hannah Toller in her housedress like a drab peasant. But there they were, not only sharing tea but apparently sharing intimate conversation. Their heads were nearly touching as they leaned over some large book of photographs.

"Ah, Clementia, we were just talking about you. Come sit down with us." I winced at the sound of my Latin name, which I hated. We didn't get to pick our own Latin names in *Domina* Chambers's class. Rather they were

doled out to us according to a strict system. *Domina* Chambers told us what our names meant (I never saw her consult a baby name book; she seemed to know the meaning of all names) and then gave us a Latin name which had an equivalent meaning.

Lucy was easy because it meant, like her own name Helen, light, and so Lucy would use the same Latin name Helen had at school: Lucia.

Jane, she told me, came from the Hebrew for merciful, which was Clementia in Latin. Floyd Miller and Ward Castle spent the rest of the year calling me Clementine.

I sat next to Mrs. Toller and looked down at the table. The book resting between them was a yearbook and it was open to a picture of two young girls with their arms around each other's waists. The girls wore strapless evening gowns and little fur stoles. Off to the side a young man in a tuxedo smiled at the girls. He was blond and handsome and looked, I noticed with a little shock, a lot like Lucy.

"Our freshman winter formal," *Domina* Chambers said, closing the heavy book. I saw the year 1963 printed on the cover. "You knew that Hannah and I were at Vassar together, didn't you?" *Domina* Chambers lit a cigarette and leaned back in her chair. "Only Hannah wasn't so happy there, were you, dear?"

"College is not for everyone," Mrs. Toller said quietly.

"No, of course it isn't. What do you think, Clementia, is college for you? Or should I

say: Are you for college? Perhaps the state teachers college in New Paltz? You'd make a very competent teacher, I think, and we always need good Latin teachers."

I nodded. What she described was the pinnacle of my career ambitions, but on Helen Chambers's lips it suddenly sounded dreary and ordinary.

"Now our Lucia on the other hand... I see her as a Vassar girl, and then she'll go to the city and work in some arts-related field— publishing, I think, with her preciseness and gift for language. If we can only get her into Heart Lake, she'll be a sure thing for Vassar."

"It's a ways away," Mrs. Toller said.

"Nonsense! Three hours on the train. She can come home on the weekends—when she's not too busy studying or going to football games and mixers at Yale or taking in the museums in the city. We were always encouraged in Art History 105 to spend as much time as we could at the museums."

"Mattie'll half die missing her," Hannah said with an edge in her voice I hadn't heard before. "Have you thought of that, Helen?"

"Well, Mattie will just have to get used to doing without her. He'll get plenty of practice when she comes to Heart Lake next year. Now the thing to do is make sure she's ready for the exam. You're here to study with her, aren't you, Jane?"

I nodded and smiled, glad to be called by my real name for once. "Oh yes, after all, I'm taking the exam, too."

Domina Chambers reached across the table and patted my hand. "Of course you are, dear, and I'm sure you'll do very nicely on it."

I DID DO VERY NICELY ON THE EXAM. IN FACT, I ACED it. Looking back, I think I set out to do just that—ace the exam—that day sitting at the Tollers' kitchen table with Helen Chambers, if only to prove to her that I was better than she thought I was—better than someone who does *nicely* and goes to teachers college. I wrote in my journal that same night, "Teachers college is OK, but what I'd really like is to go someplace like Vassar. And to do that I have to get the scholarship to Heart Lake. I don't think Lucy would really mind—after all, she's the one who's believed in me all along."

I outlined a study schedule on the back cover of my notebook. I gave myself six weeks to memorize all of Wheelock's Latin. After my parents would go to bed I got up and sat by my bedroom window studying by flashlight. My mother turned the heat down at night so it was cold in my room. When I looked out the window I couldn't see the mill past the ice crystals spreading across the black panes. When the lumber trucks passed on the road in front of our house the glass shook and the ice patterns spread like a flower opening. Sometimes when I looked up from Wheelock and saw the ice crystals on the windowpane I imagined the picture I'd seen in the Vassar yearbook, only instead of Helen Chambers and

Hannah Toller I pictured Lucy and me, our arms wrapped around each other, smiling into the camera. And off to the side, handsome in dark evening clothes, Matt looked on. Of course, he'd come visit on weekends from wherever he went to college—Yale, maybe, or Dartmouth because, he said, he liked the idea of going to a college founded by an Indian, and he'd heard they had a big Winter Festival.

Each night I ticked off the declensions and conjugations and *sententiae antiquae* I'd committed to memory in my black-and-white notebook. My fingers turned peacock blue with the ink from Lucy's pen—the same color as the rings under my eyes.

I thought I'd be nervous for the exam, but instead I felt eerily calm and detached—as if I were recalling something I had done a long time ago.

I was frightened, though, when the results were announced, at what Lucy's reaction would be. When Helen Chambers made the announcement at school assembly and the whole school applauded I looked down, as if I were modest, but really it was because I was afraid to look at Lucy or Matt who were sitting on either side of me. But then I felt a small hand creep into mine and squeeze. I looked up at Lucy and saw that she was smiling at me with what I can only describe as a look of euphoria. She was genuinely thrilled for me.

It was then that I started to cry, not, as

everyone assumed, out of happiness at winning the scholarship, but because I knew how much *better* she was. Test or no test, she was the one who deserved to go on to Heart Lake and Vassar, not me. I would tell them all that she should have the scholarship. I would tell them all that I had cheated. Hadn't I? If not on the test, then on Lucy?

But then Helen Chambers raised her hand for silence.

"Since the days when India Crevecoeur invited millworkers into her home for educational symposiums, the Heart Lake School has always tried to preserve a friendly relationship between town and gown." There was a smattering of polite applause, which I waited through impatiently. I was wondering if I had the courage to turn down the award in front of the assembly or if I should do it quietly after the ceremony.

"But never has their generosity so overwhelmed me as it has tonight." There was a hush in the audience as we all wondered what she meant. "I've been informed by the Board of Trustees that because of the outstanding performance of another student, this year the Iris Scholarship will be awarded, for the first time since its inception, to two students: Miss Jane Hudson *and* Miss Lucy Toller."

I turned to Lucy and threw my arms around her. Mixed with my genuine joy that we would be at Heart Lake together was craven relief. I wouldn't have to turn down the scholarship. I'd been taken off the hook. Pressing my

cheek to hers I could feel that she, too, had begun to cry.

Chapter Fifteen

●

LUCY AND I WERE ASSIGNED TO A THREE-PERSON suite, called a "trip" by the Heart Lake girls. All the dorm rooms at Heart Lake were triples. My mother had always warned me to watch out for threesomes. "One always gets left out," she told me in a way that made me understand that the *one* was likely to be me. India Crevecoeur, the school's founder, thought differently. She believed that pairing girls off in twos encouraged "exclusionary friendships inconducive to the goals of community and cooperation."

"They're afraid we'll turn lezzie," our new suite-mate, Deirdre Hall, told us. "Apparently India Crevecoeur never heard of a ménage à trois."

Deirdre Hall came as a surprise to me. She didn't look anything like the Heart Lake girls I'd admired trying on lipsticks at the Corinth drugstore. She arrived in torn, bell-bottomed jeans and a sheer gauzy top through which I could see her nipples.

"They've stuck the scholarship students together," Lucy explained to me. "Although I can't imagine what she won a scholarship for— unless it was for being fast."

"You mean like in track," I asked.

"No, I mean like in bed. Can't you see the girl's a slut?"

Most of what we heard from Deirdre Hall had something to do with sex. She pulled from her army green duffel bag a veritable library of sex tomes: the Tantra Asana, *The Sensuous Woman* by J., *The Joy of Sex*, *Fear of Flying* by Erica Jong, even a huge tattered copy of the Kinsey Report appeared Mary Poppins–like from the inexhaustible duffel. She decorated the walls *and ceiling* of the single with Balinese tapestries depicting enormously endowed men performing acrobatic sex with pointy-breasted, jewel-encrusted women. Even her seemingly innocent collection of oriental tea tins proved sexual in nature.

"This tea is an aphrodisiac," she informed a horrified Lucy. "Of course the real aphrodisiac is in here." She opened up a large cask-shaped tin that was decorated with a landscape of golden mountains. Inside was a pungent-smelling brownish herb. "Does pot make you horny, too?" she asked us.

Lucy wasn't the only one offended by Deirdre's sexual references. She drove Helen Chambers to distraction by finding sexual references in every other Latin word.

"Domina?" she said on the first day of class. "As in dominatrix?"

181

When *Domina* Chambers told her that the translation of *praeda* was booty, Deirdre asked, "Booty? As in ass?"

"No," *Domina* Chambers replied, "as in loot from a conquest."

I am sure that Helen Chambers regretted that the second-year Latin curriculum devoted so much attention to the poet Catullus.

"His girlfriend's name was Lesbia?" Deirdre asked incredulously. "As in..."

"No," *Domina* Chambers interrupted, "as in the island of Lesbos, home of the Greek poetess Sappho. Catullus was acknowledging his literary debt to the Greek lyric poets."

"Yeah, but wasn't Sappho like a famous dyke?"

"Sappho did write some beautiful love poems to women. We don't know that her sentiments were expressed...er...physically."

I had never seen Miss Chambers so rattled.

"I bet she's one," Deirdre told us when we were translating our Latin together that night.

"One what?" Lucy asked.

"A lezzie." Deirdre held up her right hand and wriggled it like a fish. She was wearing a silk hand-painted kimono that her parents had sent her from Kyoto. It was patterned in pale blue and turquoise waves through which swam beautiful red and gold carp. There were slits under the wide sleeves through which I could see Deirdre's bare breasts, like two fish escaped from the kimono's pattern.

"*Domina* Chambers is not a lesbian," Lucy

had responded coldly, looking away from Deirdre's exposed breasts. "My mother went to school with her and she says that Helen Chambers was one of the most popular girls at Vassar. She spent almost every weekend at Yale."

"So why didn't she marry one of those Yalies?" Deirdre asked. I could tell that Lucy had piqued her interest. We could all picture, I think, Helen Chambers, in a sweater set and pearls, riding the train to New Haven. A boy in a tweed jacket—or maybe a letter sweater—would meet her at the station.

"She devoted herself to scholarship," Lucy answered, "to the classics."

"Then why isn't she a professor at some college? Or an archaeologist digging up Etruscan artifacts? I mean teaching high school Latin is hardly an exciting career."

I could tell that Lucy was troubled by this question. There *was* something about Helen Chambers that didn't quite add up. Even though there was a tradition of alumnae returning to Heart Lake to teach, Helen Chambers stood out just a little from the other old girls. From Lucy's mother, we knew that after Vassar Helen Chambers had gone to Oxford. She had lived in Rome for several years at the American Academy on the Janiculum Hill and published articles in learned philological journals on Etruscan vases and lacunae in ancient texts. Then she'd come back to New York to complete her doctorate at Barnard. Unlike our other teachers, Helen

Chambers was embarked on an illustrious career, but just when it seemed that she had broken free of whatever gravitational pull the school exerted on its alumnae, she had abandoned the doctorate and taken the job at Heart Lake.

"Maybe she was broke," Deirdre said.

"No." Lucy shook her head and wrinkled up her nose. The idea of Helen Chambers's life being determined by base financial considerations was distasteful to her. "I think it had something to do with a failed love affair. I think she was in love with a married man and in order to break it off she had to leave the city."

I remembered the yearbook picture I had seen on the kitchen table. The handsome blond man smiling at Helen Chambers and Hannah Toller. The man who looked like Lucy. It occurred to me that the story Lucy was telling might be Hannah Toller's story. Perhaps she was the girl who left her married lover, bore Lucy in secrecy and shame, and came home to Heart Lake.

"Yeah," Deirdre said. I could tell she liked Lucy's story. She was beginning to be won over by the mystique of Helen Chambers. "Maybe they still meet when she goes into the city. She can't spend all her time shopping and going to the ballet."

Lucy considered. "Perhaps they meet, just once a year, for drinks at the Lotus Club."

"For old time's sake," Deirdre said.

Lucy smiled at her. After weeks of her offending Lucy, I was alarmed to see that

Deirdre Hall might also be capable of charming Lucy. But then, as usual, Deirdre went a bit too far (*overkill*, Lucy would say).

"Yeah," Deirdre said, "and then, for old time's sake, they go upstairs and get laid."

THROUGHOUT THE FALL SEMESTER OF THAT SOPHO-more year Lucy and Deirdre vied with each other like dancers pulling back and forth in some elaborate tango. Although they seemed to hate each other, they couldn't stay away from each other. I understood how Deirdre might be won over by Lucy. Everybody was. At the lower school, where Lucy worked as an aide, the younger girls all adored her. When we met her there after our last class, the children followed Lucy out the door, begging for another story, a song, a hug. One girl, a pathetic-looking creature with pinched features and hair as colorless as dried straw and with the sadly apt name of Albie, used to follow us back to the dorm. It was unnerving the way she'd materialize in the woods. Deirdre would yell at her and stamp her foot the way you would to scare away a stray dog, but Albie wouldn't even flinch. Only when Lucy would go up to her and whisper something in her ear would she leave, vanishing behind the pine trees as quickly and silently as a cat.

"Poor kid," I said one day, more because I saw that Lucy had been gentle to her than because I really felt sorry for her. "What an awful name."

"Thanks," said Lucy, laughing, "I gave it to her. I told her it would be her Latin name when she started Latin next year, so now she insists everyone call her that. She just needs a little attention. Her dad died when she was little and Albie says her mother's nervous, which I think means she's in and out of mental hospitals. Every time Albie's not doing well her mother thinks it's the school's fault and she switches her to another school. She's only ten and this is her fourth school."

"Please, I'm gonna bawl," Deirdre said, lighting a cigarette. "The kid is creepy and she's getting in our way. It's like she's spying on us."

This was a concern because we had begun to roam the woods when we were supposed to be in evening study hall. Our first forays into the woods were Deirdre's idea. She wanted to find a place to smoke, cigarettes at first, and then pot. I was surprised that Lucy went along with these expeditions—Lucy refused to even try a cigarette or a joint—but I soon realized that Lucy felt confined by the regimentation of Heart Lake. She had grown up wandering the woods with Matt, eating when she wanted, sleeping late and missing school if she wished to. She hated, she told me, having to be around people all the time. She hated *the goals of community and cooperation.*

Deirdre, an old veteran of boarding schools, proved to be an expert at subverting and eluding the rules. "Sign into study hall and then excuse yourself to go to the head. We'll meet in the bathroom next to the Music Room and

slip out the back door. They'll never miss us."

It seemed to me that we could have done that without Deirdre, but if we were caught, Deirdre always came up with a quick and reasonable cover.

"Jane just got her period, Miss Pike," she explained to the swimming coach one night when we were discovered in the woods behind the mansion. "We're going back to the dorm for a sanitary napkin."

"We're looking for tadpoles, Miss Buehl," she told the science teacher when she found us sneaking down to the swimming beach. "Your lecture on metamorphosis was *so* inspiring."

She had a flair for the dramatic. After we heard the story about the three sisters at the Fall Bonfire she immediately said we had to get out to the farthest rock at midnight under a full moon and say a prayer to the Lake Goddess so we would be spared from the Crevecoeur curse.

"How can we?" I asked. "You can't get there by jumping from the other rocks. Can't we make our sacrifice from the first rock?"

"No, it has to be the third one," Deirdre said.

Lucy agreed. "*Domina* Chambers says that three is an enchanted number. And that the hero must always undergo a series of difficult tests, like the labors of Hercules, to prove himself."

"We'll swim to the rock," Deirdre said. "We do it all the time in swim class."

"But at night? We don't even have suits." We were issued swim suits for class, thick cotton one-pieces that billowed in the water and made all but the slimmest girls look hideous.

Lucy laughed. "Who needs suits? Gosh, Jane, you're so *conventional* sometimes." I saw Deirdre smile. I remembered what my mother always said: "In a threesome one always gets left out."

"If you're scared you can stay in the room," Lucy said.

I was scared, but I wasn't going to stay in the room. For this expedition we needed more time than study hall allowed. Deirdre planned it all. After lights out we would each, one by one, go down the hall in our nightgowns to the bathroom and then we'd leave by the bathroom window, which was at the back of the dorm, facing away from the lake. We'd cut through the woods behind the lower school, and then climb over the rocks on the Point to avoid being seen by Miss Buehl, who lived in the cottage at the top of the steps leading down to the swimming beach.

"But then how will we get down to the swimming beach?" I asked. "The entrance to the stairs is right across from her front door."

"There's a way to climb from the Point down to the swimming beach," Lucy said. "Matt and I did it a couple of years ago when we sneaked onto the campus to go swimming."

"Why doesn't he sneak onto the campus now and join us?" Deirdre asked. "I mean, you miss him so much and all."

"That's not a bad idea," Lucy said. "Maybe another time."

That first night we went out to the rock was unseasonably warm and curiously still for mid-October. I was sure we'd still be cold, so I wore my heaviest flannel nightgown. Deirdre wore the hand-painted kimono, which shimmered like water in the moonlight. The red and gold carp seemed to swim under the tall pines. Lucy wore a plain white T-shirt that came down below her knees and probably had belonged to Matt originally. The two of them, walking ahead of me on the path, looked like figures on a vase. I felt absurd in my stiff flannel gown with its print of teddy bears and hearts.

We stopped in the woods and Deirdre lit a joint. She handed it to Lucy who, much to my surprise, took a long, deep drag on it. She handed it to me and, still holding the smoke in, said in a tight voice, "Remember what *Domina* said about the Delphic oracle?" I remembered Helen Chambers's lecture on the ancients' use of hallucinogenic herbs. *So you condone drug use, Domina,* Deirdre had asked. *The ancients used it for sacred, not recreational, purposes,* our teacher had answered.

I took the joint and placed it, gingerly, to my lips. I wondered if I could just pretend to smoke it, but both Deirdre and Lucy were waiting to see the tip of the joint flame red. I inhaled and held the smoke in my lungs, the

way Deirdre said you had to. I also remembered that she said most people didn't get high their first time.

We smoked that joint until it was a tiny, burning nub, which Deirdre held delicately between her long fingernails. When I was sure it was all smoked down, Deirdre turned the roach around so that the lit side was in her mouth, and motioned for Lucy to come closer. Lucy, who was quite a bit shorter than Deirdre, tilted her face up to Deirdre's, so close it seemed they might kiss, and Deirdre blew a long stream of smoke into Lucy's open mouth. I was amazed at how well they did it. And then I realized it couldn't have been the first time.

I didn't think I was high, but the rest of the walk seemed bathed in a different light. The forest floor, covered with pine needles, glowed golden and seemed to roll up to meet my bare feet. The white trunks of the birch trees flicked by me like the blades of a fan slicing the shadows, spilling splashes of white into the darkness of the woods. It was as if a white figure flitted in between the trees beyond the path, but when I stopped to look for it there was nothing in the dark and silent woods.

When we came to the Point, the domed rock we clambered over glittered as if studded with diamonds. I found myself lost in its rough, crystally texture as we climbed down to the limestone ledge and from there to the swimming beach. It was better than looking over the edge at the sheer drop down to the water.

It took me longer than the others to make the climb down. By the time I was on the beach they were already in the water. Deirdre's pale silk kimono was draped over a rock and Lucy's T-shirt lay crumpled at the edge of the water. I pulled the heavy flannel nightgown over my head and stood for a moment, shivering on the shore.

I could see them, a little ways out in the water, gold and white like the beautiful carp in Deirdre's kimono. They had reached the third rock, which was the only one flat enough to climb up on, and Deirdre was pulling herself up, clumsily flopping on the rock. Lucy turned toward the shore and treaded water. When she saw me she raised her hand to wave and I saw her sink a little, her lips just touching the black surface of the lake. I remembered a line of poetry Miss Macintosh had read to us. *They're not waving*, it went, *they're drowning.* There was something in me that made me want to stand there and see how long Lucy would wave. How far she would sink.

But then I shook myself, dispersing the chill, and walked into the water. I plunged in to get the worst of the shock over with, and swam fast to warm up. I was a good swimmer. One of the strongest in the class, Miss Pike said, although, she would inevitably add, my form could use work.

I swam a little past the rock, showing off a bit. When I approached the far side of the rock, though, I found that the rock was sheer at this end, the water too deep to touch bottom.

Lucy and Deirdre had to each take a hand to haul me up.

"Good work, Jane," Lucy said.

"Yeah, Jane, you're braver than I thought," Deirdre said.

We sat on the rock for a few minutes looking out over the still, moonlit lake. I didn't feel cold anymore. The climb and the swim had warmed me up. What surprised me was that I didn't feel afraid either. The third rock was past the Point, and so we could have been seen from the windows of the mansion, but I imagined that if someone, say Helen Chambers who had an apartment on the top floor of the mansion, had looked out her window and seen us, three naked girls on a rock in the middle of the lake, she would have thought it was a vision. I imagined that we looked like the three graces in the painting by Botticelli Miss Beade had shown us.

As if responding to a prearranged signal, we all stood up. Lucy slid her arm over my shoulder and Deirdre, on my other side, slipped her arm over Lucy's. I pulled my arms up to clasp theirs, but instead I kept lifting them—they felt weightless, as if pulled by the moon—until my hands were suspended over their heads. We hadn't talked about what form our "prayer" to the Lake Goddess would take. "We'll let the spirit of the moment move us," Lucy had said. I had imagined it would be Lucy or Deirdre who would think of what to say. They were both better at that sort of thing. But now, with Lucy and Deirdre at

my side, I felt stronger than I ever had before. My mother was wrong. Three was a magic number.

"Spirit of the Lake," I said. "We come here in the spirit of friendship. We don't ask for special protection."

I saw Lucy nod. It was what *Domina* Chambers always told us. *The ancients believed they must first humble themselves before the gods. The greatest sin was hubris.*

I knew then what form the prayer should take. "All we ask," I said in a high, ringing voice that seemed to echo off the stone face of the Point, which towered above us, "is that whatever happens to one of us, let happen to all of us."

Chapter Sixteen

●

"WE NEED A STAG-KING." DEIRDRE HELD the hairpin figurine we had recently dubbed a corniculum in her fingers and wriggled it in the light from the window. A minute before she had been dancing around the room to the Allman Brothers singing "Ramblin' Man" on the radio, but then "Seasons in the Sun" came on and she switched it off.

Lucy looked up from Graves's *The White God-*

dess and nodded. "Like Cernunnos," she said. "The horned one, the antlered king."

"Like Actaeon," Deirdre said.

"Actaeon was slaughtered by his own hounds," I said. It was junior year. Deirdre had read an article in *Ms.* magazine about matriarchal cultures and goddess worship. She spent most of Latin class pestering *Domina* Chambers about "the patriarchal canon" she adhered to. "At the very least," she told our teacher, "we should be doing Ovid's *Art of Love* instead of boring old *Metamorphoses.*"

I picked up my translation for the next day's class and read aloud: " 'Now they are all around him, tearing deep their master's flesh.' His dogs ate him alive."

Deirdre shrugged. "*Domina* Chambers said he got what he deserved for spying on Diana in her bath."

"But it was an accident," I told her. "Look, even Ovid says so, 'The fault was fortune's and no guilt that day, for what guilt can it be to lose one's way.' "

Lucy sighed. "Don't be so literal, Jane. We're not going to hunt some poor boy down and eat him." Deirdre giggled and Lucy gave her a look that silenced her.

"It's a symbolic rite of renewal. The goddess joins with the stag-king and the community is granted fertility and good fortune."

"Yeah, the goddess and the stag-king get it on."

"Well, are we going to take that part *literally?*"

"I certainly hope so," Deirdre said.

"Then who gets to be the goddess?" I asked.

Deirdre jingled the hairpins so that they sparkled in the sun and she wiggled her hips like one of the Balinese dancers on the tapestries that decorated her room. "Who do you think? Who around here *looks* like a fertility goddess?"

"The goddess is the lake," Lucy said reprovingly. "The stag-king will swim in the lake, like a baptism, and that will appease the Lake Goddess."

"Oh." Deirdre looked disappointed. She tapped the hairpin that dangled from the "mouth" of the top hairpin so that it swung in a wide arc. "Is our stag-king also going to be symbolic or do we at least get a real boy?"

I saw Lucy considering. We both knew which boy Deirdre had in mind. Although Lucy and Deirdre had been friends, more or less, since that night sophomore year when we all swam in the lake, Lucy still hadn't let Deirdre spend any time with Matt. She had met him the couple of times Matt had come to Friday tea and the Founder's Day picnic, but Lucy had always been careful to keep Deirdre from spending too much time with her brother.

"He's adorable," Deirdre had confided to me. "I see why you like him. Have you ever... you know...done anything with him?"

"He's just a friend," I said, "and my best friend's brother. I don't think of him that way."

Deirdre eyed me skeptically. Just as she had a way of finding sexual meaning in the most innocuous Latin phrase, so she could inject sexual context into the most innocent friendship. Over the year and a half we had all been at Heart Lake she had posited illicit liaisons between the groundskeeper and Miss Buehl, Miss Buehl and Miss Pike, Miss Macintosh and Miss Pike, Miss Beade and three of the senior girls, and the class president and the captain of the swim team. She had taken it for granted from the beginning that I *had a thing* for Matt.

I suppose she was right. Pressed between the pages of my *Tales from the Ballet* I kept the red maple leaf he had given me on that first walk home. It wasn't a rose, but he had *pretended* it was when he gave it to me, so wasn't it almost as if it were a rose? I'd saved other things, too. The pebbles he gave me when he was teaching me to skip stones on the lake, notes he'd written me in Latin class when we were still at Corinth High, and a skate key he'd dropped in the icehouse and thought was lost. I kept them with my journals under a loose board beneath my desk. Not even Lucy knew about my hiding place or the things I wrote in my journal about Matt.

"I think Lucy misses him," I wrote in my journal. I'd used up the first notebook he'd given me and bought a new one that was just the same. I had sat a long time with the fountain pen poised over the lined paper before adding, "I miss him, too."

Since we'd been at Heart Lake we'd seen less

of him. I knew Lucy missed him terribly. For the whole first year she had slept in one of his old hockey jerseys, and sometimes at night, after she thought I was asleep, I heard her crying. If she hadn't been afraid of Deirdre going after him I think she would have thought of some way of seeing him more. After all, he lived less than half a mile from the school—only a quarter mile from the far end of the lake—and he knew every inch of the woods surrounding Heart Lake.

"I bet Matt would be interested in the Cernunnos legend," I said.

Both girls looked at me as if they had never heard of a boy named Matt. I half expected Deirdre to say, "Matt who?"

Lucy sighed. "Actually, Mattie's more interested in chemistry and physics these days."

After Lucy and I had gotten the Iris Scholarship, Helen Chambers had given up on her experiment with public education, and Corinth High School had, in turn, given up on its Latin program. Matt seemed forlorn without Latin until he discovered physics.

"All he talks about these days is the temperature/density relationship in water and the molecular structure of ice. He's keen on seeing the lake freeze."

"Well," Deirdre said, "he can watch for the lake to freeze and we can reenact the rite of the horned god. Hey, do you think that's how we got the expression *horny*?"

"We can't make Matt swim in the lake," Lucy said. "It's already too cold."

"They do it in Russia," Deirdre said. "But yeah, it's even getting too cold to hang out outside. If only we had some kind of shelter. The changing room at the swimming beach would be perfect, but they lock it up over the winter."

"There's the icehouse," I said. "We could meet there."

Lucy's head jerked up. Belatedly I remembered that Matt and Lucy had made me promise not to tell anyone that they used the icehouse.

"What icehouse?" Deirdre asked. "It doesn't sound too appealing."

"It's not," Lucy said flatly. "It's just a little hut on the other end of the lake where the Crevecoeurs used to store ice harvested from the lake. It's a good twenty-minute walk away."

"Is there anything in it?"

I shook my head no, but Lucy was nodding. "The county extension agent keeps her rowboat there, but she only comes once a week, on Tuesdays, to take water samples."

I looked at Lucy in surprise. I hadn't been to the icehouse since we had all gone skating last winter. Apparently she and Matt had been there without me.

"A boat?" Deirdre said. "Cool. We could have our stag-king rite on the water. When can your brother meet us there?"

I DON'T KNOW HOW MUCH LUCY TOLD MATT about the horned god, but he was excited

about what he called the first ice club. We met at the icehouse the last weekend in November.

Matt brought a thermos of hot chocolate. Deirdre brought a joint. Lucy brought blankets. We sat in the hull of the extension agent's rowboat using her life jackets for pillows. We'd decided it was too dangerous to take the boat out; someone might see us. Matt insisted that we keep the doors at the end of the hut open so we could look at the lake, even though it made the hut unbearably cold. It was beautiful though. Lying in the hull of the boat, looking out the doors, it seemed as if we were on the water. Across the lake we could see the stone wall of the Point jutting into the lake like the prow of a gigantic ocean liner bearing down on us. After a few hits, I felt as if we were gliding toward it.

"The lake has already begun the process of freezing," Matt told us. "This first stage is called overturn. As water gets colder it gets denser, so it sinks and the warm water rises to the top." Matt made circles in the air with his hands. "But—and this is the part that's really amazing—if water continued getting denser as it froze the lake would freeze from the bottom up."

"It doesn't?" Deirdre asked.

Lucy gave her a scornful look, but Matt continued his explanation patiently.

"If it did that all the fish and other creatures would die. But what happens is that at four degrees Celsius water becomes less dense.

That means that ice is actually less dense than water."

"I may be too dense to get this," Deirdre said, passing Matt the joint. "Science was never my thing."

I was surprised at Deirdre putting herself down like this in front of Matt. I thought she would want to impress him. It was weird, too, because Deirdre wasn't dense about stuff like this. She was actually pretty good at science. If she hadn't spent most of her time getting stoned and thinking about boys, she would have gotten all A's. As it was, she did almost no work and still got B's.

Matt took a hit off the joint and passed it to Lucy, then he reached across me and took Deirdre's hands in both of his.

"It's like this." He turned her right hand so that its back lay against the palm of her left. I saw Deirdre wince, but she didn't complain and I don't think Matt noticed he was hurting her.

"This is what a water molecule is like above four degrees Celsius. The two hydrogen atoms fit together like two spoons lying in the same direction. When people lie like that they call it spooning."

I imagined lying next to Matt like that. I imagined what it would feel like to lie against his back, against his broad swimmer's shoulders, and bend my knees to fit into the space where his knees bent. I wondered if Deirdre was imagining the same thing. Why hadn't he used my hands for his demonstration? Why hadn't I said I was dense?

"The oxygen atom lies alongside the two hydrogen atoms," he added, balling his hand like a fist against the palm of Deirdre's right hand. "But at four degrees Celsius the hydrogen atoms flip around." Matt turned Deirdre's right hand over so that her palms were facing each other as if in prayer. "See that space between your hands," he tickled the inside of her palms and she giggled. "There's a little pocket between the atoms now. That's why ice is lighter than water."

"I still don't get it," I said.

Matt dropped Deirdre's hands. I was hoping he would take mine, but instead he made two peace signs with his fingers and held them up.

"Tricky Dick," Deirdre said. She had a cartoon tacked to her wall of Nixon holding his fingers up in two V's.

He lowered his fingers so they were pointing out, into the center of the circle we made inside the boat. "You can also think of it like this. Each water molecule is made up of three atoms—two hydrogen, one oxygen—so it's like a triangle. When water is liquid, the molecules just lie on top of each other like this. He lay one peace sign over another. "But at four degrees Celsius, the hydrogen molecules flip around because they want to touch."

"Oooh," Deirdre cooed. "Lezzie molecules."

"Jesus, Deir," Lucy said, "only you could make hydrogen bonding sexy."

"Well, it is kind of sexy," Matt admitted. "I mean it has to do with attraction. In a water

molecule, the positively charged nuclei of these three atoms are stuck together by negatively charged electrons. But the oxygen atom is so greedy for the attention of electrons that it strips the two hydrogen atoms of their negative charge. That makes the hydrogen atoms attracted to other electrons, like the oxygen atom in another water molecule. That's why water is liquid. When water freezes, the hydrogen bonds hold each molecule apart."

Matt reached out both his arms and took my hand and Lucy's. "You guys hold hands, too," he said.

I saw Lucy reluctantly take Deirdre's hand and Deirdre took my hand.

"Now hold your arms out straight."

We had to shuffle around in the boat a little to make space so we could all hold our arms out straight. The boat rocked on the wooden floor of the icehouse. It was a good thing, I thought, that we weren't doing this on the water.

"See how we take up more space now," Matt said. "We're ice."

"My ass is ice," Deirdre said. She released Lucy's and my hands and stood up. The boat lurched toward her and then, when she stepped out of it, careened away from her. Lucy and I both fell against Matt. I felt Matt's arm around me, steadying me.

"Hey, you broke the molecular bond," Matt said.

"I always was a great ice breaker," Deirdre said, shimmying her shoulders and hips. Even

under a sweater and down jacket you could see her breasts swaying. I realized she hadn't worn a bra. I looked at Matt and it seemed his gaze also rested on Deirdre at about chest level.

"I think that concludes the science portion of the evening," Deirdre said. "And now for the sacred rite of the horned god. Got your antlers ready, Matt?"

Matt held up his fingers in V's again, but this time he held them over Lucy's head. "I always thought Lucy would make a good deer," he said. "She's about as brave as one."

Lucy shook his hands away and got up out of the boat. She stood at the doorway of the hut and stretched her arms over her head. She was wearing a pale blue ski parka that glimmered against the cold black water. She was like a deer, I thought, leggy and lithe. I thought of a line from Book Four of the *Aeneid*. It's when Dido realizes that Aeneas doesn't love her anymore and he's going to leave her. *"Qualis coniecta cerva sagitta,"* I recited, impressed at myself for remembering the Latin.

With her back to us, Lucy took up the passage, reciting it to the lake. As she spoke Deirdre moved next to her and held her arms up, too. I stayed in the boat with Matt. He had put his arm back around my shoulder.

"Quam procul incautam nemora inter Cresia fixit pastor agens telis liquitque volatile ferrum nescius: illa fuga silvas saltusque peragrat Dictaeos; haeret lateri letalis harundo," Lucy recited.

"Wow," I said. "How'd you remember all that?"

203

Lucy shrugged. "It's my favorite part."

"Might an ordinary mortal ask for a translation?" Matt asked.

"Just as when a deer pierced by an arrow from some shepherd, who unknowing leaves in her the flying iron, wanders the woods and mountain glades with the deadly shaft still clinging to her flesh," I told him. I had left out a bunch of words, but that was the gist of it. "It's like, even though she runs away the thing that's going to kill her stays with her. She can't escape her fate." I was surprised to hear my own voice quiver. It had always gotten to me, the way Dido was doomed to kill herself from the moment she set eyes on Aeneas.

Matt squeezed my shoulder and I felt his lips brush the side of my face. "You're a sweet kid, Jane," he whispered in my ear, "but I think these two might rip me to shreds, so I better hightail it."

He was gone before I knew it; only the sway of the empty boat and a damp spot on my cheek where his lips had brushed told me he'd been there a minute ago. Deirdre and Lucy ran after him. I could hear them, laughing and shrieking through the woods. I could have caught up with them, but instead I lay back in the boat and watched the moon move from behind a cloud. The rocky prow of the Point, as if awakened by the cascade of white light, seemed to glide toward me, silent as an iceberg in a still, black sea.

Chapter Seventeen

•

ON THE NIGHT BEFORE CHRISTMAS BREAK I came back to our room from dinner and found a corniculum tacked to the door. I was surprised because it was so cold, but Lucy said we couldn't miss the solstice because it would be a propitious night for the first ice to form. It was a windless night and the full moon seemed unusually close and bright.

"It's going down below zero tonight," Deirdre said. "We could get frostbite. And besides, I feel awful." Deirdre sneezed and blew her nose. She had gone to the infirmary that day and the nurse had excused her from her last final and said she should stay in bed until it was time to catch her train home.

"You don't have to go if you don't want to," Lucy said. "How about it, Jane? Are you afraid of the cold?"

Truthfully, I didn't relish the idea of going out in the cold. I felt like I was coming down with whatever Deirdre had. We'd stayed up late studying for finals all week. Deirdre had produced a white powder that she said was crystal methedrine. She showed Lucy and me how to snort it through a straw. It burned my nostrils and made me feel cold and brittle.

"I wouldn't want to disappoint Matt," I

said. "I guess I'll go. I'll just put on some long underwear."

Lucy turned to Deirdre, who was boiling water on her hot plate. When the water came to a boil she poured a little into a willow-patterned teapot and swished it around. Then she dumped the water out onto the window ledge. Because she had been doing this all winter unusual ice structures had formed.

"Oh well, we wouldn't want to disappoint Mattie." Deirdre knew Lucy hated it when she called him Mattie. "But I suggest we all have some tea before we go." Deirdre opened several of her tins and put a pinch from each one into the teapot.

"Someday she's going to poison us," Lucy said to me.

"Or herself," I suggested.

Deirdre smiled and filled the teapot with steaming water. "Only if I meant to," she said. She tapped the lid of a small, red lacquer box. "I have some stuff that would put a person to sleep for a long winter's nap."

Deirdre poured out the tea into three china cups. She handed one to me and one to Lucy.

"But I would never do that to you guys," she said. "I mean, you guys are the best friends I've ever had. One for all and all for one, right? *E Pluribus unum.*"

Deirdre held up her steaming teacup and we all clinked cups together.

The tea actually made me feel better. It coursed through my veins like the warm currents that you sometimes swam through in the

lake. I could imagine the glow in my blood staving off the winter chill. We waited that night until after the last bed check and then pulled jeans and sweaters over our long underwear. The hard part was holding on to the drainpipe when we climbed out the bathroom window. I had to take off my mittens to get a good grip and the metal was so cold that my clammy hands nearly stuck to it. Even after I put my mittens back on my skin felt raw. And not just the skin on my hands. The fire Deirdre's tea had lit in my blood had turned into an icy trickle. My whole body felt flayed by the cold.

We followed the path around the west side of the lake. A few inches of new snow had fallen that evening so the path looked clean and bright in the moonlight; I felt like I could see each individual crystal. The path had narrowed between two low walls of snow so we couldn't walk three abreast. Sometimes I walked behind Lucy and Deirdre and sometimes Deirdre would run forward on the path and Lucy and I were next to each other. I thought to myself that my mother really was wrong about threesomes, that the balance between us was always shifting, not set in stone. Sometimes, though, I missed how it was when it was still Lucy and Matt and I.

Just before we reached the end of the lake I heard a movement in the woods. I stopped to peer into the maze of pine trunks and the long shadows they cast on the white snow. I watched the shadow of a branch swaying in the wind and then realized that there was no

wind. The branched shape suddenly detached itself from the shadows and moved away from me, flitting over the white surface of the snow.

I turned back to the path to find Deirdre and Lucy but they had walked on without me. They must have rounded the end of the lake because they were nowhere in sight along the path. When I turned back to the woods the branched shape had vanished. I figured it must have been a deer. Nothing else could move so swiftly and silently.

Or else Deirdre really had added something to the tea and I was hallucinating.

The thought was terrifying. Had Deirdre drugged me and then somehow gotten Lucy to go along with abandoning me in the woods? What might I see next? I turned around quickly and my eyes caught a movement in the trees— a glitter like fireflies drifting through the pine needles. Only it was the dead of winter; there were no fireflies.

When I rounded the end of the lake I thought that must be it—I was hallucinating—because standing on the path with Deirdre and Lucy were three hooded figures.

Deirdre detached herself from the group and came skipping toward me. She grabbed my hand and pulled me over to one of the hooded figures. She was babbling something in my ear that I found difficult to make out. There were too many things wrong here for me to sort out: too many people and it should have been Lucy, not Deirdre, taking my hand and making sure I was included.

One of the hooded boys—they were just boys, I realized now, all three of them wearing hooded sweatshirts beneath their down parkas—nodded gruffly to me and I realized I had missed hearing his name. I noticed, though, that he had the same square jaw and ruddy complexion as Matt, even the same height and build, and it occurred to me that he must be the cousin from downstate I was always hearing about. I understood then why Deirdre was so anxious to pair me up with him. Deirdre the matchmaker. He wouldn't do for Lucy because he was Lucy's cousin.

I turned to the other three on the path: Lucy, Matt, and Ward Castle. Jesus, I thought, whatever possessed Matt to bring Ward Castle? Lucy had barely endured his insults throughout ninth-grade Latin. His favorite epithet for her was "Loose Toe-Hair." She called him "Wart."

"Hey, hey, hey, my darling Clementine," he warbled to me. "How's it hanging?"

Behind Ward I saw Matt wince. "You remember Ward Castle," Matt said to me. "Ward's my lab partner this year. He said he wanted to see the lake freeze."

"Yeah, I'm here for the chemistry lesson," Ward said.

Had Matt really believed Ward was interested in seeing the lake freeze? For the first time it occurred to me that Matt could be too trusting.

"Oh, we'll be experimenting with an assortment of chemicals." Deirdre had somehow

worked her way around Matt's cousin and Ward and repositioned herself next to Matt. She lit a joint and passed it to Matt. "Shall we start with some cannabis before the sacred rites begin?"

"Sacred rites?" Ward asked. "Like sacrificing a virgin?" Ward put his arm around Lucy and pulled her to him. The night was so still I could hear the rustle their down coats made rubbing against each other. Lucy's head barely reached his armpit. She smiled up at him sweetly.

"Yes," she said, "we're going to sacrifice a virgin. A boy virgin. Any volunteers?"

I could see in the bright moonlight Ward turn as white as the snow.

"Hey, it's a little cold out here for that stuff," he said. "I thought you said you had a place."

Matt jerked his chin in the direction the path led. "Yeah, it's up here. We just have to cross the stream." He turned and we followed.

We walked in twos now: Matt and Deirdre, Lucy and Ward, me and the nameless cousin, who seemed mute as well as nameless. He's probably mortified to be paired with me, I thought. No doubt he had been taken with Deirdre before I showed up on the path. That was why Deirdre had been so anxious to pair us off, because if she got stuck with the cousin, I'd get Matt. And I knew that was the last thing she wanted.

The Schwanenkill was nearly frozen, but when I was halfway across it my foot broke

through the ice. I would have fallen if the cousin hadn't grabbed my elbow and steadied me. It was tricky, too, getting up the opposite side. He scrambled up the bank deftly, with more grace than you'd expect from a boy his size.

He's probably terrified of ending up alone with me, I thought, as I struggled up the slippery bank. I'd taken my mittens off so I could grab tree branches to pull myself up, but my hands were still sore from climbing down the drainpipe and I couldn't get a grip. My throat felt raw, whether from cold or holding back tears I wasn't sure. I looked up, expecting the cousin to be well on his way to the icehouse, but instead he was standing at the top of the bank, his feet angled into the snowy slope for purchase, his arm stretched out toward me. I took his hand and was surprised to feel warm skin. He'd even taken his glove off to grip my hand better.

"Thanks," I said when he'd pulled me to the top of the bank.

He shrugged and mumbled something. God, he was even clumsier and shier than I, I thought, but before he let go of my hand I felt his broad thumb stroke the inside of my wrist and the movement sent a warm electrical current through the core of my body, reigniting the warmth that had started that night in Deirdre's tea.

We got to the icehouse, but the door was shut. I reached for the handle, but he stopped me.

"Uh, maybe they want some privacy," he said.

"The four of them?" I asked incredulously.

He turned his head up the path and I saw two figures just disappearing over a rise. From the disparity in their heights I guessed it was Lucy and Ward. That left Matt and Deirdre in the icehouse. And it left me and the cousin out here in the cold.

"Where do you think they're going?" I asked.

"Lucy said something earlier about sneaking back into the dorm. You two share a room?"

I nodded. I couldn't imagine Lucy and Ward together, but then a lot of things had happened this night that I hadn't been able to imagine. The cousin rubbed his hands together and blew into them to warm his face.

"I guess you'd like to get inside," I said. "There's a supply shed on the lower school playground..."

"You know, I'd like to see if Mattie's right about the ice. I've lived near frozen ponds all my life, but I can't say I've ever been there when the ice formed."

I looked at the lake. It was black and still, but as far as I could tell, unfrozen.

"We could go to the swimming beach," I said. "The boathouse is locked, but there's a place in the rocks that's almost like a little cave. At least it would be sheltered, and we can see the lake from there."

"Sounds good," he said.

We walked the rest of the way in silence, but it didn't feel like an uncomfortable silence now. Once I thought I saw something moving in the

woods and I was glad I wasn't alone. I was glad, too, when we got to the top of the swimming beach steps that I didn't have to warn him to be quiet so Miss Buehl wouldn't hear us from her house. I led the way down the steps and showed him the hollow in the cliff wall behind the second sister stone. Part of the cave was under water, but there was a raised ledge along the cliff wall you could follow to get inside and then there was a flat rock above the water where two people could sit. It was out of the wind, but as soon as we sat down I started to shiver.

"Do you think we could make a little fire without attracting attention?" he asked.

"We can't be seen from the mansion or the dorms here," I told him. "And Miss Buehl is probably fast asleep."

We gathered some branches and pinecones from the beach and banked them against the cliff wall. He took out a wooden match and lit it by striking his fingernail against its sulfur tip. Then we sat with our backs against the cliff and watched the lake. When he saw I was still shivering he put his arm around me and I put my head against his chest and closed my eyes.

I must have fallen asleep because when I opened my eyes the fire was out. I looked at the boy next to me and in the shadow of the cliff it could have been Matt. I slipped my hand out of my mitten and with the backs of my fingers I stroked the side of his face, along the jawbone, just under his ear. He stirred at my

touch and moved into the light that angled into the cave. In the dim gray light of dawn I saw that this wasn't Matt, and wouldn't ever be.

I became aware of a numbness spreading through my legs and I got up to get my blood moving. From the east, where the sun was rising, a flock of Canada geese were moving through the sky. I watched them land on the lake and, instead of skidding into the water, stand on its surface. I moved closer to the edge of the cave and saw that a thin layer of ice covered the water. I hugged myself against the cold and against the sense that I had missed something.

Chapter Eighteen

●

AFTER CHRISTMAS BREAK MATT AND LUCY'S cousin went back home. The three of them had come looking for me on New Year's Day to take me skating, but my mother had turned them away at the door, saying I had chores to attend to, so I never did see the cousin again. I was disappointed, at first, that I didn't get a chance to say good-bye to him, but then, remembering that moment at dawn when I'd touched his face, I was relieved. I knew

I'd be embarassed every time I saw him, even if he had been asleep.

By the time school started again the lake ice measured a good three inches. By all rights, we should have disbanded the first ice club. But we didn't. When the ice was thick enough Matt suggested we turn the first ice club into a skating club. Deirdre was none too happy about this development because she didn't know how to skate.

"You don't have to come," I told her, sharpening my blades. I still had the skates Lucy had given me. I'd changed from thick socks to thin in order to get into them this year. I hoped that my feet had stopped growing.

"Oh, is that right, Clementine? You'd like that, wouldn't you?"

I'd noticed that Deirdre was a little on edge since Christmas break. She'd spent it with an aunt in Philadelphia because her parents hadn't been able to leave their new post in Kuala Lumpur. Her aunt had told her, though, that she'd have to spend spring break on campus and she'd been enrolled in a boarding school in Massachusetts for the summer. I think that the sense of being shuttled between institutions and apathetic relatives was beginning to get to her. The only person she seemed sympathetic to those days was, oddly, "Lucy's little shadow" as she called Albie, the lower school girl who still dogged our steps around the campus.

"I thought she gave you the creeps," I whispered to Deirdre one day when I came back

to our room and found her helping Albie with her Latin homework. I didn't think she could hear me—the girl was in Deirdre's single; Deirdre had come out to borrow Lucy's Latin dictionary—but she looked up at the two of us and I realized it probably was obvious that we were talking about her.

"Hey, Albie," I called. "So, you're in Latin now. *Salve!*" The girl looked at me for a long moment and then looked down at her book without answering. There was something about her appearance that struck me as strange, stranger even than usual, and then I realized what it was: She was dressed all in white, a white blouse and a white pleated tennis skirt.

"Why is she wearing all white?" I scribbled on a page in my journal, which I showed to Deirdre.

"It's Miss Macintosh's influence," Deirdre wrote back. "She told the girls about Emily Dickinson always wearing white."

"Don't you think that's weird?" I wrote.

Deirdre shrugged and went back to Albie, shutting the door of the single behind her. Later, Deirdre complained to Lucy that I'd made Albie feel uncomfortable.

"Uncomfortable? How do you think she makes me feel—she looks like a ghost and won't even talk to me?"

"I wish you girls would quit bitching at each other," Lucy snapped. Deirdre and I both looked up in surprise, more at Lucy's choice of words than her tone.

"Lucy, dear," Deirdre cooed, "what have

you been picking up from Ward Castle? Nothing contagious, I hope."

Lucy flung her skate down on the floor. The serrated tip of the blade gouged a deep scratch into the wood floor.

"We don't all give out on the first date, Deir." Lucy grabbed her parka and stormed out of the room. I grabbed mine and followed her without looking back at Deirdre.

I found her on the path in front of the dorm, stalled in the crossroads between three paths. There was the path that led to the lower school, the one that led to the mansion, and the one that led to the lake. They had each grown a good foot narrower since Christmas break. It was hard now to walk even two abreast.

Lucy kicked at the thigh-high wall of snow. I put my hand on her arm, but she shook it off and suddenly, like a deer bolting from cover, she vaulted the snow mound into the woods. Half her leg disappeared into the snow but, miraculously, she kept on moving, surging out of each deep hole like a swimmer doing the butterfly stroke.

I clambered over the snow wall and tried to follow her, staying in her deep footsteps. I couldn't keep up with her though. By the time her trail led me to the lake she was gone—I couldn't tell which way. I looked out over the lake, looking for breaks in the ice, but there were none. I stood at the shore, listening to the sounds the ice made. The new ice made a skittering noise, as if a thou-

sand mice were scurrying just below its surface. It made me nervous. I felt like something was crawling up my legs. I spun around and caught a glimpse of the girl Albie just ducking behind a tree.

"Hey," I called, "have you seen Lucy out here?"

I saw half a face appear from behind a pine tree. One icy blue eye stared at me.

I took a step toward her, slowly, the way you'd approach a wild animal.

"Hey," I said again. It was the way I'd talk to a scared animal. "You know me; I'm Lucy's roommate. I'm looking for her."

The girl didn't move, but I had the sense she'd spring away if I moved an inch closer.

"You like Lucy, don't you?" I said. "I like her, too. I'm just trying to help her."

The blue eye narrowed, the way a cat's eye half closes when it's about to pounce.

"No, you're not." Her voice was surprisingly clear and strident in the cold air. It sounded like the scratching sounds on the ice behind me. "You just like her brother."

"I think you're confusing me with our other roommate, Deirdre."

Albie smiled. "Yes, she likes him, too."

"You certainly notice a lot." I thought about what Deirdre had said about her, how she'd grown up in boarding schools and had no real family. Although I had a family it didn't always feel that way. Since I'd come to Heart Lake my parents had seemed like distant strangers. My father, I think, was shy of

the manners and clothes I'd acquired here; my mother, who I'd thought would be pleased that I was moving up in society, seemed disappointed I hadn't made any friends other than Lucy and Deirdre. It occurred to me that Albie and I had something in common. She was the kind of girl I should be reaching out to, the way that Lucy had reached out to me back in ninth grade.

"I bet you know a lot of stuff about the girls here," I said. I only meant to draw her out, but I saw right away that she'd taken it the wrong way.

"Yes," she said, "but I'm not telling *you*." She practically spat the last word.

"Hey." I moved a step forward, "I didn't mean..."

I heard a crack behind me and turned back to the lake. For a moment I thought I saw a hole in the ice, but then the clouds moved and I saw it was only a shadow. When I looked back Albie was gone. She'd disappeared as quickly as the shadow that I had seen on the night of the solstice, and I wondered if it could have been Albie then. But the girl was only eleven or twelve. Surely she wasn't running around the campus alone at night.

I made my way back to the dorm, sticking to the paths this time. When I got back to the room I found Deirdre and Lucy sharing a pot of tea and trying on skates.

"Hey, Jane," Lucy said as I came in. "What do you know, my old skates fit Deirdre, too."

As the ice thickened the sounds it made changed, from a nervous skittering to a low-pitched moan I could hear even in my room. I listened to it, alone, on the nights Deirdre and Matt and Lucy and Ward went skating on the lake. It sounded to me like a woman keening and for some reason it made me think of India Crevecoeur and the daughter she had lost. I knew by then that it had been only the one daughter—Iris, for whom my scholarship had been named—who died in the influenza epidemic, but still the groans and wails the lake made could have been the sound of a legion of mothers grieving for a legion of daughters.

Deirdre was only interested in using the skates at night, so I was free to take them during the day. I felt squeamish sliding my feet into them, the way I felt putting on bowling shoes or stepping into the thick cotton swimsuits issued by the school. I'd never minded when I knew Lucy had worn them first. Now, though, I could feel how Deirdre's wide ankles had stretched out the uppers and I imagined the rough leather liner was darker with her sweat. I wore heavy socks again and pulled the laces so tight I broke two pairs and had to knot them together again.

The whole school, practically, was on the ice in the afternoon after classes. We were only allowed to skate in the shallow cove below the

mansion lawn. Miss Pike set up orange cones to mark off the safe area. She wore heavy black hockey skates and moved like a polar bear across the ice. Some of the teachers, like Miss Macintosh and Miss North, teetered nervously around the marked-off circle and then quickly found their way to the log benches on the shore and the iron cauldron of apple cider set on a small bonfire. Others were surprisingly graceful. Miss Buehl, for instance, performed daring pirouettes and traced figure eights around the cones with her arms clasped behind her back. Her short, dark hair crinkled in the dry air with electricity. Once, when she passed me, I felt a spray of ice hit my face and I could see a glittering trail of ice crystals following her like the tail of a comet.

Domina Chambers had a more modest style, but was equally proficient on the ice. She was certainly the most stylish of the skaters. She wore a sky blue Nordic sweater that brought out the blue in her eyes and trim black ski pants. Her skates were gleaming white with alpine flowers stitched into the leather. I'd never seen skates like them and once I overhead her tell Miss Buehl that they had been a gift from a family whose son she'd tutored in Geneva. She and Miss Buehl often skated together, their arms crossed and linked. They took turns teaching the younger girls and I noticed that Miss Chambers made a special effort with Albie. I thought at first that Albie was an odd choice for *Domina* Chambers to

choose as a favorite, but then I learned that Lucy and Deirdre's tutoring had paid off.

"Albie is our star Latin scholar," I overheard *Domina* Chambers telling Miss Buehl as she helped the girl to her feet after yet another fall. When she got to her feet the poor girl wobbled pathetically at first, her ankles caving painfully in, but by the end of that winter she could make it around the skating circle with a serviceable choppy stroke that made up in speed what it lacked in grace.

Domina Chambers asked me, almost every day, why Lucy wasn't skating with me and every day I gave her the same answer.

"She sleeps after class because she's up so late studying."

It wasn't difficult to believe. *Domina* Chambers surely noticed the dark rings under Lucy's eyes and her tendency to drop off in class.

"She's so very dedicated." *Domina* Chambers made a clucking noise. "Tell her she mustn't work so hard." She said it as if it were my fault. I noticed Albie, behind her, listening.

"Oh you know Lucy," I said, "she wants to do well. All your students do, *Domina*." I could see a little smile on Albie's face. Did she know, as I did, that Lucy spent her nights in the woods and on the lake?

"But she's not like you, Jane. Let's face it, you'll have to slave to achieve even a tenth of what Lucy's capable of." With that remark, my teacher spun on the ice and stroked away, the spray from her skates shimmering in the still, cold air.

Albie stood on the ice looking up at me, a small feline smile stealing over her usually dull features.

"You'd better get in, Jane," she said. It was the first time I'd ever heard her use my name. "I think you've got windburn. Your face is all red."

ONE NIGHT IN FEBRUARY I RETURNED TO OUR room after working in the dining room and found a corniculum tacked to the door. I knew it was a sign from Lucy to Deirdre that the boys would meet them at the lake. I knew the sign wasn't for me, but I decided to treat it as if it were. I decided to follow them. I pretended to be asleep when Deirdre and Lucy left the room. I waited until after the last bed check and then went to the window and listened for them climbing down the drainpipe. I put on long underwear and my heaviest jeans—the only ones without holes in their knees—and two sweaters, an old turtleneck and a blue Fair Isle cardigan *Domina* Chambers had given Lucy for Christmas.

I went around the east side of the lake so I wouldn't meet them on the trail. It meant climbing over the rocks on the Point to avoid Miss Buehl's house. Ice had filled the glacial cracks in the rock, making the footing precarious. It would be easy, I thought, for a person to fall to her death here.

I made it down to the swimming beach and looked across the lake to where the icehouse

would be on the other side. I thought I saw a glimmer of light coming from the opposite shore. Maybe they had made a bonfire. I imagined Deirdre, Lucy, Matt, and Ward toasting marshmallows over a small fire and drinking hot cocoa. I amended the picture to beer and joints. Still, it was a homey scene in my mind. Why couldn't I be a part of it? If I cut across the ice I'd be there in minutes. But then, I thought it might be dangerous to cross the whole lake.

I followed the path around the east side of the lake. As I walked I became warm under the two sweaters and parka. I took off the cardigan and wrapped it around my waist, but then I felt hot and itchy. I decided to leave the sweater on the side of the path and get it on my way back. I realized the temperature must be rising. I looked out over the lake and noticed that a white fog was hovering above the ice. I was glad I hadn't tried to cross it.

By the time I reached the icehouse the fog from the ice had crept into the woods and I had trouble seeing the path ahead of me. Twice I walked right into an overhanging branch and scratched my face. The second time something metal brushed against my face. I reached up and retrieved from the tree branch a bundle of hairpins—a corniculum. From the palm of my hand the horned face seemed to leer up at me. I stopped to get my bearings and listen for my friends' voices.

I heard voices, then, coming from the lake. It was a boy and girl, but I couldn't tell if it

were Deirdre and Matt, or Ward and Lucy. I could hear the scrape of ice skates on the ice and someone laughing. I stepped off the path into the deep snow to get closer to the lake. The snow gave way slushily under my feet and soaked my jeans. I couldn't tell, in the fog, when the snow gave way to ice, but suddenly my feet slid out from under me and I skidded out onto the lake.

I tried to get up but slipped again. The ice felt greasy under my gloves. I crouched there and looked around me.

The ice fog had grown so thick I couldn't even make out the bank, which I knew must be only a few feet behind me. But which direction was that? I'd lost my bearings when I fell and couldn't be sure which direction was the bank and which led out farther onto the lake. What was clear to me, though, was that the ice was beginning to melt.

I listened again for the voices of the skaters, but heard instead a low moan. I felt the sweat under my long underwear turn icy. The sound seemed to be coming from everywhere at once, but mostly from beneath me. From under the ice. I thought of the stories the senior girls told at the bonfires. That the faces of the Crevecoeur sisters had been seen peering up from beneath the lake ice.

I looked down half expecting to see the upturned face of a long dead girl trapped beneath the ice, but all I could see was a white void of fog. I heard, though, another moan accompanied by a rhythmic thumping that

seemed to reverberate deep inside my body. This time, though, I was almost sure it came from a spot ahead of me on the ice.

I crawled toward it. As I moved through the fog on my hands and knees I imagined what was out there. I imagined wraithlike shapes emerging from under the ice to pull me down— girls with jagged icicles hanging from their tangled hair and malice in their drowned eyes. Once I heard something on the ice behind me and when I turned thought I saw a shape, a thickening in the white fog like a clot in cream, moving away from me, but then it was gone and the only sounds on the lake came from the opposite direction. I turned and crawled toward the sounds and bumped into something wooden.

It was the icehouse door, hanging partially open over the ice. I'd made it back to the shore. The moans had led me back.

I pulled myself up, using the door for balance, and looked into the icehouse.

The only light came from a candle on one of the ledges. It cast into shadow on the opposite wall the hull of the boat rocking rhythmically as if buffeted by an invisible current.

I couldn't make out the shape of the girl lying in the hull of the boat. The boy above her was clearly outlined in the shadow on the wall, but I couldn't tell who he was either. He wore something over his head and shoulders, a hood or mask that fell in shapeless folds. The shapes springing from his head were clear. They were horns, stiff and branching like a stag's.

Chapter Nineteen

●

"WE OUGHT TO DO SOMETHING FOR MAY Day," Deirdre said.

She was sitting on the windowsill blowing smoke rings out the open window. It was raining hard and each time the wind blew a spray of rain sifted across the room over Lucy, who lay on the floor reading *The Crystal Cave*, and over the desk where I sat. The pages of my journal were damp and smeared. "April is the cruelest month," I wrote in peacock-blue ink that bled through the paper and stained the scratched, wooden desk. The glue in the binding of my Wheelock's Latin Grammar had melted in the damp and the pages had all sprung free.

After the night I had gone out onto the lake the spring rains had begun, pitting the ice and turning the paths into small rivers of snowmelt. The skating season was over.

Now it was April, but the only sign of spring was the mud that seeped into everything.

Lucy rolled over onto her back and stretched her legs up, pointing and flexing her bare toes. "There's the Founder's Day picnic," she said, yawning lazily. "And the Maypole dance."

India Crevecoeur's birthday fell on May

4, but Founder's Day was always celebrated on May Day. This year India Crevecoeur herself was coming to celebrate her ninetieth birthday and the school's fiftieth anniversary. To celebrate there would be a traditional Maypole dance. In the Music Room, next to the family portrait of the Crevecoeurs, there hung a sepia-toned picture of girls in starched, high-necked white dresses standing in two neat circles around a Maypole. They each held the end of a ribbon attached to the top of the Maypole. The girls in the outer circle faced one way, the girls in the inner circle faced the opposite way. There was a girl in the right corner of the picture whose dress hem was blurred, as if she were swaying, impatient for the dance to begin. Otherwise, it was hard to imagine these girls frolicking around the Maypole. The picture looked more like a military procession.

"They'll sanitize the whole damned thing," Deirdre said, tossing her cigarette carelessly out the window.

"Hey, someone might see that," I complained.

Deirdre rolled her eyes and hopped off the window ledge. "There's a foot of mud under our window, Janie. You'd have to be an archaeologist to excavate that cigarette butt."

"What do you mean *sanitized*?" Lucy asked, her brow wrinkled.

"A May Day dance should be performed at dawn. Naked. Or at least in flimsy nightgowns. It's a pagan fertility rite," Deirdre explained.

"Everything's a pagan fertility rite with

you...," I began, but Lucy shushed me, so I wrote in my journal, "Deirdre is such a slut."

"We should go out at dawn in white robes and bare feet," Deirdre said, "and wash our faces in the dew. It's said if you wash your face in the dew at dawn on May Day you'll be granted eternal beauty. Think about it, Jane, it's cheaper than Clearasil."

I felt my skin go itchy where scabs had formed over old blemishes. My skin had erupted in the fetid spring air.

"They also say that if a girl goes out on May Day dawn to gather flowers, the first boy she meets on the way back to the village will be her heart's true love."

It was on the tip of my tongue to ask who "they" were, but I didn't. I liked this story. It had a nice element of chance to it. Who was to say I wouldn't run into Matt first?

"We'd need a Maypole," Lucy said.

"There's one in the drama department closet," Deirdre said. "They used it last year for *The Maypole of Merry Mount*."

"And a May Queen," Lucy said.

"I think it should be Lucy," I said, anxious to be included in this outing.

"Of course we still need a stag-king," Deirdre said, nudging Lucy's leg with her foot. "He was part of the May Day rite."

"We'll let the boys decide who it'll be. He'll be masked, so no one will know," Lucy said. Then she turned to me. "We'll have three to choose from because our cousin'll be in town that weekend."

IN THE END ALL THREE BOYS AGREED TO WEAR THE stag mask. Deirdre made the extra masks in art class. When Miss Beade complimented Deirdre on her stitching (Deirdre was good at precise things like sewing and rolling joints), Deirdre told her the masks were for an extra credit assignment in Latin class. That was how *Domina* Chambers got word of our plans.

She asked us to her rooms in the mansion for tea. We'd been there before, but usually with several other girls from the class. This was the first time we'd been singled out as a group. We spent a lot of time discussing what we should wear. Lucy insisted that Deirdre wear a bra and she told me to wear my hair up. She herself wore an old plaid skirt, which I think had belonged to her mother, and a pale yellow cashmere sweater that I had never seen before.

When we got to *Domina* Chambers's room I was glad we had spruced up a bit. *Domina* Chambers had put out her good china tea set (Deirdre reported later that the pattern was "Marlow" by Minton—she'd turned her teacup over when *Domina* Chambers wasn't looking) and Mrs. Ames had sent up a tray of tea sandwiches and freshly baked scones. When we'd come with the other girls it had been paper plates and store-bought cookies.

"I got into the habit of afternoon tea when I was at Oxford," *Domina* Chambers said when we'd all been poured a cup of tea. "The

habits we form when young may last a lifetime. You girls have a good start studying Latin. Learning one form of discipline teaches one to be disciplined in other areas of life. Like diet for instance..." *Domina* Chambers glanced at Deirdre who was heaping clotted cream on her second scone. "And telling the truth."

Lucy took a sip of tea and set her teacup in its saucer, which she balanced on her knee. "Miss Beade told you about the masks," she said.

"Yes. I was rather surprised to hear about an extra credit assignment, seeing as I don't believe in extra credit."

Deirdre opened her mouth to say something, but *Domina* Chambers was looking at Lucy now and I think we all realized that she was waiting for her to explain. I was sorry it had fallen to her and amazed at how calm she seemed.

"We're planning a May Day rite," Lucy told our teacher. "For dawn. Of course, we're not allowed out of our dorm rooms at dawn, so we had to keep it a secret."

"A May Day rite?" *Domina* Chambers took a sip of tea and smiled. "How lovely. We did the same thing in our time. In fact, your mother and I used to slip out of the dorm in nothing but our nighties and swim across the lake on May Day morning."

"You must have frozen your asses..."

I kicked Deirdre so hard she spilled her tea on her blouse. Thank goodness Lucy had talked her into that bra.

"Yes, it was most bracing," *Domina* Chambers said, still addressing Lucy as if she were the only one in the room. "Do you have a Maypole?"

"We do. We…borrowed it from the drama department."

"That gaudy thing? I would have thought a freshly cut birch sapling would have been more suitable, but I suppose it will do." *Domina* Chambers sighed and for a moment I thought she was planning to actually join us for our May Day festivities. I wondered what she would make of our stag-king.

"Ah, to be young again," she said. "Well, I understand now why you had to tell a fib to Miss Beade. Of course, she would never understand."

"So you're not going to turn us in?" Deirdre asked.

Domina Chambers turned to Deirdre, looking surprised that she was still in the room.

"I mean it is against the rules," Deirdre said.

"Weren't you paying attention when we read *Antigone*, Miss Hall? The same rules do not apply to everyone. When Antigone performed the burial rite for her brother, even though she was breaking Creon's decree, was she wrong?"

"No," Lucy answered, "because she owed that to her brother."

"Exactly. *Which of us can say what the gods hold wicked?* The true tragic heroine is above the commonplace laws of the masses."

"I always figured Antigone didn't have a chance," Deirdre said. I could tell she was anxious to show *Domina* Chambers that she had gotten something from the play. "I mean, what with her mother being her grandmother and her father being her half-brother..."

Domina Chambers waved her hand dismissively. "There's far too much attention paid nowadays to the incest theme in the plays. The Greeks weren't as squeamish about such matters as we are. After all, Antigone is betrothed to her first cousin, Haemon, and no one mentions that."

"Yeah, but Oedipus did put his eyes out when he realized he'd married his own mother."

"And killed his own father. The Greeks were very clear on what a child owed a parent. But incest...well, Zeus and Hera are, after all, brother and sister. And Sir James Frazer tells us in *The Golden Bough* that in countries where the royal blood was traced through women, the prince often married his sister to keep the crown from going to an outsider. Of course, when wrongful incest did occur it was sometimes necessary to sacrifice to the goddess Diana."

"Why Diana?" Lucy asked.

"Because incest is supposed to cause a dearth...droughts and famine...so it makes sense to make atonement to the goddess of fertility."

"But I thought Diana was a virgin," Deirdre interrupted. "How can a virgin be a goddess of fertility?"

Domina Chambers waved her hand again as if Deirdre were an annoying insect. "You persist in thinking in black-and-white terms, Miss Hall. It's a very simplistic way of seeing things. Diana is a goddess of nature, and hence, fertility. It was believed she shared the grove of Nemi with Virbius, the King of the Wood. Their sacred nuptials were celebrated each year to promote the fruitfulness of the earth. There's your May Day rite. Not some silly circle dance around a gilded pole."

"So this King of the Wood," Deirdre asked, "is he kind of like the stag-king? I mean, he wore horns?"

"Yes," *Domina* Chambers answered. "Diana Nemesis is associated with the deer. It's likely that the stag-mummers of medieval May Day rites derived from this tradition."

I saw Deirdre and Lucy exchange a knowing look. *Domina* Chambers had just confirmed the way they had chosen to celebrate May Day. I wondered what our teacher would think if she knew just how literally her students were taking her lesson. But then, I wasn't sure anymore if what Deirdre and Matt, and Lucy and Ward, had been doing in the icehouse and planned to do in the woods on May Day dawn would shock *Domina* Chambers. *Which of us can say what the gods hold wicked?* I had a pretty good idea of the things *Domina* Chambers would disapprove of: sloppy Latin translations, Lipton tea, synthetic fabrics. But sex with a masked stranger in the woods? I couldn't tell.

We finished our tea and sandwiches and

scones. *Domina* Chambers played for us a recording of Stravinski's *Rite of Spring* to get us in the mood, she said, for our May Day rite. She promised she wouldn't breathe a word to anyone of our plans.

"But if you're caught," she told us at the door as we were going, "you're on your own. You must always accept responsibility for your actions, girls."

We all laughed and said we were ready to do just that.

It was only fifty-five degrees at dawn on May Day (according to the thermometer nailed to a tree outside Miss Buehl's cottage), but at least the rain had stopped. The ground was still muddy, though, and the woods were damp and misty, so we decided that the best place to set up the Maypole was the swimming beach.

"Otherwise it'll be more like mud wrestling than Maypole dancing," Deirdre said. "Not that I'm adverse to a little rolling in the mud."

"You're welcome to it," Lucy told her. "We'll have to split up after the Maypole dance."

The plan was for the three of us to carry the Maypole down to the swimming beach and perform the ceremonial circle dance around the Maypole in the middle of which we would be "surprised" by the three boys dressed as stag-mummers. We would then flee, being careful to go in three different directions. Since the boys would be masked, we decided it was

only fair that we be disguised as well, so Deirdre attached hoods to the simple white shifts she had sewn for us.

"Of course it will be obvious which one is Lucy," Deirdre said, holding up the shift she had sewn for her. "She's so small. Ward'll pick her out in a minute, which is a good thing. We wouldn't want Lucy ending up with her cousin after all."

"It's a symbolic rite, Deir. You don't have to really do anything. You're scaring Jane."

Deirdre smiled at me. "Oh, I don't think Jane's scared. After all, since she and I are the same height, she might end up with Matt and I'll end up with the cousin..."

"He has a name—Roy."

"Roy," Deirdre repeated. "Roy from Troy."

"Cold Spring," Lucy corrected. "Our aunt Doris lives in Cold Spring."

"Whatever. He looked pretty cute, the little I saw of him. But maybe Jane has her eye on him after the night they spent together...."

"I told you: We just sat on the beach and watched the sun rise. Actually, I watched the sun rise. He slept."

"Wore him out, eh, Janie?"

I blushed. Not because of Deirdre's teasing, something I was well used to by then, but because I was remembering stroking the boy's cheek...pretending he was Matt.

It wasn't easy carrying the maypole down the steps to the swimming beach. Deirdre went

236

first, then Lucy, and I brought up the rear, which meant I had the part of the pole decorated with flowers. They were cheap plastic flowers, spray-painted silver and gold by the drama department, and they scratched against my bare arms and blocked my view of the steps.

"Take it easy," I heard Deirdre hiss from below. "You're going to skewer me with this damned pole and that's not how I planned to spend the morning."

It was hard to believe it would be morning soon. We'd left the dorm at 4:30 so it must have been close to 5:00, but the sky was still pitch dark. Below us I could hear water lapping against the rocks, but not even a glint gave the lake away. Deirdre had looked up the phase of the moon and found it was a new moon.

"I think that's supposed to be bad luck," she said, "but who knows?"

I only knew I had reached the beach when moss-covered rock gave way to wet sand, and even then my bare feet were so numb I could hardly tell the difference.

"Heave ho!" Deirdre called. "Raise high the roof beam, carpenter!"

I heard Lucy's small voice inquire if that were from Sappho while I pushed the pole into an upright position and felt it sink into the sand. Deirdre pushed it deeper into the sand and Lucy knelt at the base and mounded more sand around the pole.

"We don't want it to fall over," Lucy said.

"No, a wilting Maypole would definitely be

unpropitious," Deirdre agreed. "Plague and barrenness would certainly follow."

"Why do we want fertility anyway?" I asked. "I mean, it's not like any of us want to get pregnant."

"Well, I'm on the Pill so it's not bloody likely," Deirdre said.

"Really?" I asked. I wondered where Deirdre had managed to get a prescription for birth control pills.

"She forgets to take them half the time," Lucy said. "So she's just messing up her hormones for nothing."

Usually I would have been more disconcerted to realize that Lucy and Deirdre had such a store of confidences than at the news that Deirdre had access to birth control. But the subject had been bothering me lately.

"I guess it's not likely you'd get pregnant the first time..."

"Jesus, Janie, I don't think you'll have to worry about it. Look at you, you're shaking like a leaf. Here, take a swig of this."

Deirdre had brought a wine flask made out of goatskin that she had bought at the army/navy store in Corinth.

"What's in it?" I asked, eyeing the greasy-looking sack suspiciously.

"I pinched some cooking sherry from Mrs. Ames and added a few herbs."

I put my mouth around the grooved metal screwtop and tasted, first, copper, then sweet almond–flavored wine, and finally, as an

aftertaste at the back of my throat, something bitter and grassy.

"As Horace says: *Nunc est bibendum,*" Deirdre said, passing the flask to Lucy. "Now is the time for drinking."

Lucy tilted her head back and took a long, deep swallow. Her hood fell back and in the dim light I could just make out her pale forehead and see that she had painted some kind of design there. But then her hood fell forward as she lowered the flask and the design was hidden in shadow before I could make it out.

"*Nunc pede libero pulsando tellus,*" Lucy said in a husky voice I barely recognized. "Now is the time to beat the earth with a liberal foot."

"In other words: Now is the time for dancing."

Deirdre released the crepe paper ribbons that had been wrapped around the pole. They hung limply in the still, damp air. Although the sun still hadn't appeared across the lake, the darkness had paled to a pearly gray. Looking out over the lake I still couldn't tell where water and air met.

Deirdre held up a limp ribbon and stomped the ground with one foot.

"*Nunc pede libero pulsando tellus!*" she commanded, and Lucy, stomping her feet, took up the chant. We hadn't rehearsed what to say as we danced around the Maypole. I also searched my head for some appropriate Latin and came up with nothing but the first declension.

"*Puella, puellae, puellae,*" I shouted. I thought

239

Lucy and Deirdre would make fun of my choice, but they took up the declension with me.

"*Puellam, puella, puella.*"

It sounded oddly right. *Girl, girl, girl,* we chanted as we half-skipped, half-danced around the pole, *girl* in all its grammatical permutations.

Then, suddenly, Deirdre skidded to a stop, spraying sand up my legs. She held her hand up for silence. I listened, and heard, above the thud of my heart and the lap of the lake water, footsteps on the rocks. I thought they came from the steps, but when I peered into the gray mist in that direction I heard another sound behind me; again, footsteps on the rocks, but this time they came from the lake. Someone was on one of the sister rocks.

Deirdre passed the flask around and we each took a long drink. I tasted, this time, the bitter grassy taste first and then the sweet and then the metal.

Deirdre tossed the flask into the darkness outside our circle. "*Puer, pueri, puero,*" she whispered.

"*Puerum, puero, puer,*" Lucy chanted.

Boy, boy, boy.

We began to dance again, but in the opposite direction, so that the ribbons we had wrapped around the pole now came undone. The damp crepe paper clung to my arms and brushed against my face, clammy as seaweed. Pieces came off and clung to my shift. I felt the wet strands tangling between my legs and

240

when I tried to kick them away I lost my balance and fell.

When I got to my hands and knees I was looking toward the lake. I saw, through the lightening mist, a figure balanced on the second stone. A figure with the head of a stag. I took a deep breath and told myself it was just a boy in a deer mask, but then the figure leaped off the rock and with one bound landed in the shallow water and I saw that he wasn't wearing the brown felt mask Deirdre had sewn in art class. He was wearing the bleached skull of a ten-point buck.

I screamed and somehow scrambled to my feet.

I heard Deirdre and Lucy scream, but their screams were theatrical.

"Aiaiai," Deirdre keened somewhere off to my left. To my right, Lucy made a whooping sound like a crane calling to its mate. I felt sure they hadn't seen the boy with the skull. Still, that was all he was, surely, a boy with a skull mask. I was running up the steps, though, away from him. Only when I reached the top did I look back to see if he was still following me.

He was four steps below me, his head bent down, watching his footing on the slippery rock. I saw that beneath the white skull he wore the brown felt mask, but at the nape of his neck I could see his hair: sandy brown hair that just then turned fiery red in a ray of light that skidded across the lake from the eastern shore. I noticed, too, his shirt, a hockey jersey with the name "Corinth Lions" emblazoned on

the back. Matt's team. Behind him I saw Deirdre run left into the woods, pursued by one of the masked boys. Lucy stood facing her masked partner and then she turned and walked into the water and started swimming. I didn't stay to watch if Ward would swim after her. It was hard to imagine him braving that cold water, but maybe that was what she was counting on. By taking to the water, she'd issued him a challenge.

I turned and ran across the path and into the woods. I skirted behind the lower school and the dorm and then headed west. I knew that once I got past the road there was a large tract of pathless woods, an old grove of giant hemlocks that Matt had once told me was one of the few patches of virgin forest in the area. I felt sure he would know I was heading there and that he'd know why. It was one of the few places where we were sure to be alone and, I knew, one of his favorite places. I wanted him to know that I knew it was him under the deer skull.

The sun was up now, streaming through the morning mist from behind me. I saw the first young hemlocks appear. As I ran, the hemlocks grew taller and the under-growth thinned. The trees were spread out and evenly spaced like a colonnade. I was run-ning through a wide avenue between the towering trees and their shadows, stretched out in front of me like a black pattern laid out on the gold forest floor. Echoing my own footsteps and the sound of my heart were

the footsteps and ragged breath of the boy following me.

I came to a clearing and slipped on the hemlock needles. I lay on my stomach panting until I felt a hand on my shoulder turning me over.

We were both breathing so hard neither of us could talk. The deer skull mask was gone, but he still wore the brown felt mask Deirdre had made. My hood had fallen back.

He stroked my arm and took my hand as if to pull me up, but I pulled him down. He half fell on me, but he moved one leg in between mine to keep his full weight off me. I moved underneath him and felt the heat of his skin beneath his clothes. I touched, with the back of my fingers, a strip of bare skin above the waistband of his jeans, stroking the red-gold hairs, and he moaned. He lowered himself on me and I moved down so that my shift bunched up underneath the small of my back. I could feel the small, flat needles against my bare skin and see the slanting sun streaming over his back as he came inside me.

When we were done the sun was just above his shoulder and shining in my eyes, blinding me. I burrowed my face into his collarbone and felt the damp felt of the mask brush against my cheek. I could see the green thread Deirdre had used to stitch the seam and the small green heart she'd embroidered at the edge of the fabric. She'd used a different color for each mask. "So you'll know your heart's true love," she had said. I was just about to ask him to take

off his mask when I heard voices. I felt him stiffen. He got to his knees and snapped his jeans closed. I pulled my shift down and raised myself on my elbows to listen.

"As you can see the undergrowth has become progressively thinner. This is because the fallen needles of the hemlock make a thick, acid mulch in which the seeds of most plants cannot germinate."

"Miss Buehl," I whispered. "You have to get out of here." He got to his feet and held his hand out for me, but I waved him away. "Go!" I hissed. "I'll distract them."

He seemed confused, for a second, about which way to go. The voices were approaching us from the north. I pointed south and said, "You can get back to the icehouse that way. Just make sure you make it off campus before they catch you."

Again he seemed to hesitate. It occurred to me he didn't like leaving me so abruptly after what we had just done.

"It's all right, Matt," I said, "we'll talk later."

He must have been reassured, because he turned and left instantly. I watched him running through the woods and then lost sight of him behind one of the hemlock trunks just as a troop of lower school girls burst into the clearing. As soon as they saw me the girls began screaming. Miss Buehl rushed to my side and knelt down beside me.

"My God, who did this to you? You've been butchered."

For a minute she really frightened me. What I had done with Matt had been painful and I knew there might be blood, but when I looked down at my shift I was shocked to see that it was bright red. My hands and arms, too, were stained and lurid in the morning sun. I felt faint and for a moment I think I did lose consciousness, but then I heard a familiar voice.

"Die," she said. I looked up and standing over me was Albie. She was holding a long strand of red crepe paper that she rubbed between her thumb and forefinger. "Look," she said holding a crimson hand up in the sunlight, "Dye. It's just dye."

Chapter Twenty

●

MATT WAS CAUGHT JUST OUTSIDE THE ICE-house by the extension agent who had come to use her boat. So, Lucy explained to me, it wasn't really my fault because even if Miss Buehl hadn't come upon us in the hemlock grove he still might have run into the extension agent on his way home.

It was kind of her to try to make me feel better, but we both knew she was lying. That

first sight of me, in my torn and "bloody" shift, had sparked a hysteria not easily quelled even when the "blood" turned out to be crepe paper dye. Three of the lower school girls on Miss Buehl's nature walk were so traumatized at the sight of me they had to be sent home. Not Albie though, because she had no home to go to. She sturdily related the whole story to anyone who would listen. To give her credit, she always ended by explaining I hadn't been covered by blood after all, but somehow, the way she told it, the fact that I was covered with red dye came to sound even more *lurid*.

It didn't help, either, that Miss Pike found Deirdre's wine flask on the swimming beach and correctly assessed the contents as a mixture of cooking sherry and opium.

Still the scandal might have remained localized if it hadn't been for the Founder's Day picnic. I imagine that the dean and her staff debated long and hard that morning over whether to cancel the picnic or not. The problem was that this year India Crevecoeur had been invited to the Maypole dance. How to explain to our ninety-year-old founder that because a boy had been caught wandering the campus in a deer mask and bloodied shirt (the crepe paper dye again), and several girls were found half-naked and reeking of alcohol and opium, Heart Lake's traditional Maypole dance might suddenly look like a pagan rite? By noon that day there was already talk in town that there was a campus cult that lured innocent boys into drugged sex orgies.

Deirdre laughed when she heard the rumor. "Oh, like they need to be lured into *that*." We were sitting outside the Music Room, waiting to be called in to see the dean. Hurriedly we had agreed to say there'd only been Lucy's brother (since Ward and Roy had gotten away unseen) and we'd asked him to play a part in a May Day pageant that we planned to perform later at the Founder's Day picnic.

"What about the wine flask?" Deirdre hissed as Miss North came out of the Music Room and signaled for Deirdre to come in alone.

"Just say you bought it used and it must have had the opium in it already," Lucy told her. "I mean, how much trouble can you get in for stealing some cooking sherry?"

Lucy shook her head as Deirdre followed Miss Buehl into the Music Room. "God knows what she'll say."

A few minutes after Deirdre went in, the door to the Music Room opened and Albie came out. She must have been called in to relate her story about finding me covered with dye again. She came over to us and I actually thought she might be about to apologize for causing such a stir. Instead she spoke to Lucy.

"You won't get kicked out, will you?"

"Nah, I don't think so. Besides, I live just down the road. Even if they kicked me out of the school I could come back to visit."

Albie shook her head. "You wouldn't though. Girls always say they'll stay in touch when they switch schools, but they don't."

"Yeah, but this school's different. It's in our motto."

Albie looked confused. I didn't blame her; I didn't know what Lucy was talking about either and I wondered if she was still high from the opium. But Lucy got to her feet quite steadily and led Albie to the front door. She pointed to the fanlight above the door where the morning sun was shining through the colored glass. The words of the motto glowed like molten gold, but you couldn't read them of course—they were backwards from this side of the door.

"You know what that says?" Lucy asked.

Albie shook her head.

"*Cor te reducit,*" Lucy said. "It means 'The heart leads you back.' It means no matter where you go after you leave this place your heart will always bring you back here. It means there's always a place for you here. And it means I'll always be here for you, too—me and Deirdre and *Domina* Chambers and Jane..."

I saw Albie frown and look over her shoulder at the mention of my name. I tried to smile encouragingly. Truthfully, Lucy's speech had touched me, too.

"Go on now," Lucy said, pulling open the heavy door and holding it for Albie. "Go back to your room and don't worry. And don't ever forget what I told you."

The girl nodded and left. Lucy came back to the bench and slumped down beside me. I could tell her little speech had worn her

out. I noticed that her hair was still damp from her morning swim in the lake. We'd been allowed to change our clothes, but there hadn't been time to shower. Lucy had told me to wear my nicest outfit and when she wasn't happy with what I'd picked gave me something of hers to wear. The plaid skirt she'd given me was a little too short and I kept pulling on its hem to cover more of my bare legs, which still had streaks of red dye from the crepe paper streamers. Lucy, in a dark blue jumper and turtleneck looked proper as always, except for a piece of grass caught in her damp hair. I picked it out of her hair and noticed that there was a light film of sawdust on the back of her neck.

When the front door opened I sniffed at the spring air like a prisoner who may only have a few hours of sunlight left to her. What I smelled, though, was something like talcum powder and moth balls—a distinctly old-ladyish smell. Outlined against the bright gleam of lake, a small, bent figure stood in the doorway making little clucking sounds with her tongue. As she moved into the foyer her pale blue eyes wandered over the pictures on the wall above our heads and then settled on me and Lucy. As old as the woman was there was something unnervingly steady in her gaze. I had been scared about being questioned by the dean, but suddenly I wished it were my turn to go into the Music Room.

The front door opened again and Miss Macintosh and Miss Beade rushed in—I'd

never seen either teacher move so fast. Miss Macintosh's hair was coming undone from its chignon and Miss Beade's face was bright pink.

"Mrs. Crevecoeur," they both exclaimed. "We thought you were waiting for us to escort you to tea."

"This was my home for forty years. What makes you think I'd need escorting," the old woman answered without turning to look at the two flustered teachers. "Who are these girls and why aren't they in the Maypole dance?" She waved her cane at us and came closer. "In trouble, are you?"

Lucy and I looked at each other and then at our teachers who hovered behind India Crevecoeur.

"Actually," Miss Macintosh said, moving to Lucy's side, "these girls are our two Iris Scholarship recipients. They expressed a desire to meet you and um..." I could see Miss Macintosh, who had begun so well and so boldly, was running out of innovations. Luckily Lucy, always cool in awkward social circumstances, came to her rescue.

"To thank you for the great privilege of attending Heart Lake," she said, rising to her feet. For a second I thought she might even curtsy, but she merely held out her small hand, which Mrs. Crevecoeur, switching her cane to her left hand, took briefly and then let drop.

"This is Lucy Toller," Miss Beade said, coming to Lucy's other side and standing

almost directly in front of me. "One of our finest students. Miss Chambers says she's the best Latin student she's ever had."

"Toller, eh? Your mother's Hannah Corey, isn't she?"

Lucy nodded.

"The Coreys are cousins of the Crevecoeurs, if you go back far enough. You've got the same blue eyes my girls Rose and Lily had."

I couldn't see Lucy's expression, but I imagined she was smiling modestly. I was hoping no one would notice the bits of sawdust that clung to the backs of her bare legs. I was too busy staring at Lucy's legs to notice that Mrs. Crevecoeur's attention had swerved in my direction.

"And who's this girl lurking in the shadows here? Didn't anyone ever teach you to stand in the presence of your elders, girl?"

Blushing, I got up and squeezed myself in between Miss Macintosh and Miss Beade to hold out my hand to the old woman. As I stood I saw the old woman's pale blue eyes widen, the pupils enlarge and darken. For a second I was afraid I'd missed a button on my blouse or she'd noticed the red streaks on my leg. She looked at me in a way that made me feel naked.

"Who are you?"

"Another Iris recipient, Mrs. Crevecoeur," Miss Macintosh patiently explained, clearly thinking the old woman had forgotten what she'd been told five minutes earlier.

"Remember, there were two of them last year..."

"I'm not senile," she snapped. "What's your name, girl?"

"Jane Hudson," I answered.

The washed-out blue eyes narrowed. "Who was your mother?"

"Margaret Hudson."

"Her maiden name, child," she said impatiently.

"Oh," I said, "Poole."

For a moment a film seemed to lift from the eyes. I could see how blue her eyes must have been.

"Your grandmother worked for me," she said, "as my maid. I never thought I'd see her granddaughter here at Heart Lake."

"Oh." I didn't know what else to say. I felt like I'd been caught impersonating my betters—a serving girl found trying on her mistress's fine shawl. I guess it was a shock for the old lady to find her maid's granddaughter attending her school. But wasn't that what the Iris Scholarship was supposed to do? Give us poor town girls a chance? I looked up at Mrs. Crevecoeur, prepared to offer some explanation, an apology even, but her eyes had drifted to a spot two inches above my head where, no doubt, she'd been accustomed to focus her gaze when talking to servants such as my grandmother.

I must have been overtired, because what I said wasn't very polite. "Well, here I am. Better late than never."

That wrenched her eyes down to meet mine.

She gave me a curt nod and a tight smile. "Yes," she agreed, as Miss Macintosh and Miss Beade each took a thin arm—suddenly she looked frail and very tired—and herded her off toward the Lake Lounge. I heard her as she left muttering to herself, "Better late than never. Ha!"

The door to the Music Room opened; Deirdre came out and, without looking at me or Lucy, hurried out the front door. Miss North came out of the Music Room and told Lucy that it was her turn to come in. Left by myself, I got up and paced the hall. I tried to distract myself by looking at the old photographs on the wall, but there was little in the dour faces of the Crevecoeur ancestors to hold my attention. At least not until I came to the picture directly above the chair where I had been sitting. There was India Crevecoeur again, in a smaller copy of the family portrait that hung in the Music Room. Yes, I could see the resemblance, the square jaw and haughty tilt of her chin. Both her older girls had it, too, only the youngest, Iris, skulked in the shadows. I moved closer and looked at the servant who hovered over Iris fixing her bow and for the first time recognized her. It was my grandmother, Jane Poole. That's what old Mrs. Crevecoeur had been looking at over my head—her old servant who'd unexpectedly spawned an interloper to her precious school. "Well," I thought, settling back in my chair to await my summons to the Music Room. "I might not be here long."

NONE OF US WERE EXPELLED THOUGH. THE HARSHEST punishment for the May Day affair, as we later referred to it, fell on Matt. What Lucy hadn't figured on when she'd tried to persuade her to take the blame for the wine flask, was Deirdre's history of boarding school expulsions. Heart Lake was her third boarding school in six years. Each successive school had been a little less prestigious, a little shabbier, than the last. Heart Lake was, at least, still a reputable school, but Deirdre knew that if she admitted that the flask was hers she would be kicked out of Heart Lake. What kind of school, on what frozen outpost, she might go to next Deirdre had no desire to discover. She might even end up on the Canadian border at St. Eustace's—or St. Useless, as the girls called it—known as the school of last resort—where they sent you when no other school would have you.

She told the dean the flask belonged to Matt.

"After all," Deirdre explained later to an enraged Lucy, "he doesn't go here. What can they do to him?"

Heart Lake, of course, couldn't do anything to Matt Toller, but *Domina* Chambers, as his mother's old friend, could. True to her word, *Domina* Chambers had let us take the consequences of our actions without intervention from her. But when she heard that

Lucy's brother had brought drugs onto the campus, she stepped in. She went to Hannah Toller and told her, in no uncertain terms, that Matt mustn't be allowed to compromise Lucy's chances of making something of herself. Obviously, Heart Lake wasn't far enough away to protect Lucy from her brother's bad influence. And since Lucy couldn't be sent farther away, there was only one solution. Matt must be sent away.

When Lucy told me what she had overheard in her house, I reassured her that nothing would happen right away. After all, there were only six weeks left to the school year. Surely they wouldn't send Matt away until the fall. And by then the whole incident would have died down and the Tollers might relent.

But *Domina* Chambers was adamant. On May 4, Matt took the train south along the Hudson to Cold Spring, where he was to attend the Manlius Military Academy for Boys. I didn't even get to see him before he left.

As miserable as I was at Matt's expulsion from Corinth, Lucy was inconsolable. In fact, the aftermath of May Day seemed to leave her physically sick. She lost her appetite entirely and grew thin. Mrs. Ames, frantic to "put some meat on those twigs of bone" as she put it, stuffed Lucy's book bag with freshly baked biscuits, which Lucy promptly tossed into the lake.

"An offering to the Lake Goddess?" I asked her one afternoon when I found her standing on the Point lobbing biscuits into the water.

She turned to me and I saw that besides how thin she had grown, there were dark blue circles under her eyes and her skin had a greenish, sickly pallor. Her hair, once bright and shiny, hung lank and tangled around her face. She looked like someone three feet underwater, like a drowned person.

"Don't you think we're getting a little old for that stuff, Jane?" she asked me. Then she turned and walked into the woods.

Even though she said she no longer believed in the Lake Goddess, I heard her praying to someone in the night. The first time it happened I thought I was dreaming. I awoke to an incessant whispering and when I opened my eyes I saw something crouched at the foot of Lucy's bed. The figure was so small and compact I imagined for a minute it was a succubus, like the demon in Fuselli's "Nightmare," which Miss Beade had shown us in art class. No wonder, I thought groggily, Lucy has looked so worn out: that thing is sucking the life blood out of her.

That thing, though, *was* Lucy. With her knees drawn up to her chest and Matt's old hockey jersey pulled down to her ankles, she was rocking back and forth, muttering something I couldn't make out.

I wondered if I should go to her, but there was something so private, so naked, about her grief, I felt I would be intruding.

I didn't know whom to go to.

Deirdre and Lucy weren't on speaking terms since the wine flask incident. Nor did

Deirdre seem upset by what had happened on May Day. She ate heartily and had put on weight in the last few weeks. She'd thrown herself into her schoolwork, anxious to redeem herself after the threat of getting thrown out. When I tried to talk to her about Lucy she answered brusquely, "Miss prima donna should get over it. She's just pissed I took her boyfriend on May Day."

"What do you mean?"

"Didn't you know? I was with Ward, which means she ended up with Roy. I'll tell you this: Ward wasn't sorry. He told me Miss Ice Princess—that's what he called her—would hardly let him touch her all those nights we were taking turns in the icehouse."

I thought about the scene I had witnessed in the icehouse. I'd always hoped the masked boy had been Ward. I told myself that it didn't matter. What mattered was that Matt and I had been together on May Day.

I even tried talking to my mother about Lucy when I went home for Memorial Day weekend.

"If I were you I'd quit worrying about that Toller girl," she told me. "She'll land on her feet. You ought to be thinking of how you can help out around here. Charity begins at home."

I expected the lecture to go on, but it ended abruptly with a coughing fit. My mother had been running the carpet sweeper over the threadbare living room rug while we talked. She kicked at its unraveling hem and muttered through her coughing, "Damned sawdust."

I looked at the rug. I couldn't see any sawdust, but my mother's hand on the sweeper's handle did look yellow. I looked at her and noticed for the first time how sallow and worn-out she looked, as if after a lifetime of living in the paper mill's shadow the sawdust had crept under her skin.

"Are you feeling all right, Mom?"

She put her hand on the back of her hip and leaned back. "I could use a little help around here."

My mother had told me what to do my whole life, but this was the first time I'd ever heard her asking for help.

"School will be over in two weeks," I said. "I'll be able to help out then."

I waited to see if she'd mention any summer job. For the last three years she'd gotten me a baby-sitting job with one of the West Corinth families.

"I think your father could use you around the house this summer," she said, and then resumed sweeping up the invisible sawdust.

I FINALLY WENT TO THE ONE PERSON WHO, I WAS sure, would share my concern over Lucy— *Domina* Chambers.

I waited for her after her last class and walked back with her to the mansion.

"Yes, I've noticed she's lost weight fretting over Matthew. She's got a sensitive nature, not unlike myself. I can never eat in times of sorrow. Not like your other roommate, eh?

Nothing seems to interfere with Miss Hall's appetite."

I smiled nervously, unsure of how I was supposed to respond to comments about a fellow student's eating habits. It seemed, somehow, inappropriate. I steered the conversation back to Lucy.

"She doesn't sleep either. I'm worried about her."

"Yes, I am, too. I have a plan, though. Don't worry, Clementia, I'll take care of Lucy."

We'd gotten to the mansion steps. Sitting on the bottom step, hugging her books to her chest, was Albie.

"Ah, Alba, I'd nearly forgotten it was your tutoring day."

Albie glared at me as if *Domina* Chambers's forgetfulness was my fault. *Domina* Chambers turned back to me. "Is there anything else you wanted to tell me about Miss Toller?"

I saw Albie curl her lip back and I realized it sounded as if I had been telling on Lucy. I blushed, not only because I looked like a snitch, but because I had a sudden, unbidden image of all that there was to tell: Specifically, the picture that came to mind was of the masked and horned figure in the icehouse.

I shook the picture away. Why had I thought of it? But then I realized what had reminded me of that night. It was Albie's sweater, a blue Fair Isle cardigan several sizes too big for her. It looked just like the one I'd borrowed from Lucy; the one I'd left hanging from a branch on the side of the path.

"Miss Hudson?" *Domina* Chambers repeated my name. "Are you satisfied?"

I tried to think of something to say that would make it clear to Albie that I was only looking out for Lucy. "Well, school's almost over and Matt will be home for the summer," I said. "I'm sure she'll feel better then."

"Oh, no." *Domina* Chambers shook her head so hard some strands of silver hair came loose from her chignon. "The military academy has had such an excellent effect on Matthew his parents have enrolled him for the summer program. As for Lucy, I have other plans for her summer."

It turned out that *Domina* chambers's plans for Lucy involved taking her to Italy for the entire summer break, where she had a grant to study at the American Academy in Rome. Lucy would accompany her and have the opportunity to see the art and architecture of ancient Rome firsthand.

"She says it will be excellent for my classical studies when I go on to college. Of course, I'll major in classics. I'm also supposed to study Italian. On the weekends we're going to Florence and I'm supposed to memorize like every painting in the Uffizi." Lucy was packing her suitcase. I was sitting on her bed looking out the window at the lake. We'd started swimming classes these last few weeks of school and I'd thought about coming back out to the lake over the summer and swimming,

but now I wondered if I would do it alone, without Matt or Lucy.

"Do you have to go?" I asked. "I mean, wouldn't your parents let you stay if you asked to?"

Lucy shrugged. "What difference does it make? Matt's not here anyway."

I'm still here, I thought, but I didn't say it. Lucy did rouse herself enough to realize she might have hurt my feelings.

"And you're always so busy over the summer anyway, Jane. Hasn't your mother hired you out as an indentured servant?"

I shook my head. "No. She seems to want me to stick around this summer."

"Gee, that's a change. Well, think of it this way, at least you're not being shipped off to some other boarding school, like Deirdre or Albie. Your summer can't possibly be as bad as theirs is going to be."

But Lucy was wrong. When I came home after the last day of school I found my father home from work in the middle of the day. He sat me down in the living room and told me that my mother had been diagnosed with stomach cancer and had six to eight months to live.

Chapter Twenty-one

●

OVER THE SUMMER I WATCHED AS MY MOTHER lost thirty pounds and most of her strength. By August she was barely able to get out of bed to use the bathroom. She lay, sunken and yellow, waiting for me to bring her meals she couldn't eat and complaining about the way I prepared them or how long it took me to bring them. She never complained about the cancer or the pain, which I knew about from the way she sometimes drew her lips back from her teeth, but if I had hoped that sickness would put an end to my mother's endless complaining about me, I would have been sorely disappointed.

She complained about the way I dressed and the way I wore my hair. "You look like a deranged old maid," she told me one day. My hair was pulled back in a sloppy bun, which was as close an imitation of *Domina* Chambers's chignon as I could manage, and I was wearing a plaid gym kilt and a salmon-colored button-down shirt that Matt had given to Lucy and Lucy had given to me. "Is this why I sent you to that fancy private school, so you can look like a freak?"

I could have pointed out that she hadn't *sent* me anywhere; I had earned the scholarship for

Heart Lake on my own. But then I looked at her. She had lost most of her hair to chemo by then and her arms had grown so thin that they fell back from her shoulder bones and disappeared under the covers, making her look like a double amputee. Her legs, on the other hand, had swollen to twice their normal size. Ballooning under the covers they looked like one bloated appendage. A mermaid's tail. That's what she looked like: a bald, yellow, armless mermaid. This was the person calling me a freak.

So I told her that this was the way the girls dressed at Heart Lake and, Lucy had told me, at college. I tried to distract her by reading to her my college application essays. I showed her my SAT scores and explained how good they were. I told her that Miss Buehl thought I had a very good chance of getting a scholarship to Vassar.

"Another scholarship," she said, looking out at me through her yellowing eyes. "That's all they'll see you as: the charity student. It'll never make any difference. You'll always be the housekeeper's granddaughter. Mill folk. That's what my mother tried to explain to me, but I wouldn't listen. Now look at me, I can't even die without the sound of that infernal mill pounding in my ears."

The sound of the logs being processed into lumber and paper had always been a low hum in the background of our lives that I'd long ago stopped hearing. I tried to close the windows so she wouldn't hear it, but it made the house

insufferably hot, and the hum of the mill seemed to vibrate though the windows. Each time a lumber truck passed our house it made her old iron bed shake and she would wince in pain from the motion. Sometimes, when I heard the sound of gears shifting on the hill beneath our house, I would try to hold the headboard to keep it from shaking, but then she accused me of shaking the bed myself.

My father found me one day sitting on the floor outside her room.

"Try not to mind the things she says," he told me. "It's the cancer talking, not her."

I tried not to listen to her, but by the end of the summer I felt as if everything in my world had shrunken and wasted away.

So accustomed was I to the look of sickness that it was something of a shock, then, to see Lucy on the first day of school. Apparently *Domina* Chambers had been right about the salutary effects of Italy: Lucy had bloomed over the summer. She'd put on weight, especially in the hips and chest, her skin was golden and her hair, pulled back in a new elegant twist, shone like the Mediterranean sun.

"All that pasta and olive oil," she said unpacking silk shirts from Bellagio and sweaters from Harrods (they'd stopped in England for two weeks on the way back) and beautiful leather shoes.

"My God, you've got tits," Deirdre announced the minute she saw her. "Why does everything *I* eat go to my ass?"

I expected Lucy to make a snide comment—

Deirdre had gained even more weight over the summer—but instead she smiled benignly and said, "Helen says if we all ate like the Mediterraneans we'd be much healthier. She's going to start a Mediterranean cooking club. Do you want to join with me, Deirdre?"

And so, along with all the other surprises, I found that Lucy had apparently forgiven Deirdre over the summer and wanted to be friends again.

"Matt's doing fine at military school," Lucy told us. "He spends the weekends at Aunt Doris's house. He says Roy asks about you, Jane."

"Oh?" I said, feigning nonchalance. I would have been happier to hear that Matt himself was asking for me, but perhaps this was just his oblique way of communicating.

"He'll be back for Christmas break," she said. And that was all. As if seeing her brother twice a year was suddenly just fine with her. "Oh, and he says he was sorry to hear about your mom," she added. "We both are."

"Yeah," Deirdre chimed in, "tough break." And then they were back to making plans for the year. Cooking class and a cross-country ski club—"Helen says it's chicer than down-hill skiing"—and a play.

"Helen says that when she was here they did Aristophanes's *The Frogs* in the lake," Lucy told us.

"*In* the lake?" Deirdre asked. "What a hoot! We've got to do it."

Lucy and Deirdre kept busy that fall, pur-suing extracurricular activities with a near

frenetic zeal. I couldn't participate in most of the activities because I was expected to spend my afternoons and weekends at home. I was most disappointed about not being in the class play. They'd decided, instead of *The Frogs*, to do their own version of *Iphigenia* based on Euripides's two plays, *Iphigenia in Aulis* and *Iphigenia in Tauris*. They called it *Iphigenia on the Beach*.

It came about because when our Greek tragedy class, which *Domina* Chambers and Miss Macintosh taught together, read *Iphigenia in Aulis*, Deirdre was furious that the play ended with the girl's death.

"It just sucks," Deirdre blurted out, "It's so...so patriarchal. They kill this innocent girl so these men can go off and fight their stupid war, which they're fighting all because some impotent jerk couldn't satisfy his wife in the first place."

"Well, you'll be happy to know, Miss Hall, that Euripides apparently agreed with you. Although I doubt he would have phrased it in quite the same words." The class giggled and I noticed Miss Macintosh furiously scribbling notes in her lesson plan book. Someone wondered aloud what the Greek for "sucks" was. I'd noticed that even *Domina* Chambers seemed more tolerant of Deirdre since Lucy had warmed to her.

"How do we know that Euripides felt that way, Miss Chambers?" Miss Macintosh asked. I noticed that Miss Macintosh eschewed the title *Domina*.

"Euripides wrote a second play called *Iphigenia in Tauris* in which Iphigenia reappears and tells us that just before the priest would have slit her throat she was spirited away by Artemis to the island of Tauris and a deer was sacrificed in her place."

"Cool," said Deirdre.

"Why don't we read that one next?" asked Lucy.

I saw Miss Macintosh stabbing her finger at her carefully prepared syllabus (I believe we were scheduled to read *Medea* next), but *Domina* Chambers answered without a glance in her direction.

"Excellent idea, Miss Toller. We shall."

And so we read *Iphigenia in Tauris*. Deirdre was disappointed that Iphigenia's stay in Tauris wasn't the goddess/commune she'd thought it would be. Instead, Iphigenia, as a priestess of Artemis, is forced to sacrifice any shipwrecked sailors who are unlucky enough to wash up on the Taurian shore. But Lucy loved the play. Iphigenia's brother, Orestes, and his friend Pylades, come to the island, but because Iphigenia doesn't recognize him she prepares to sacrifice him at the altar of Artemis. Lucy loved the scene where Iphigenia and Orestes talk about how they've lost, respectively, a brother and a sister without knowing that they've already found each other.

"A perfect example of dramatic irony, wouldn't you say, Esther?" *Domina* Chambers asked Miss Macintosh, who sullenly agreed.

Since having her syllabus preempted she'd retreated into an incommunicative funk at the back of the room where she kept copious notes in her lesson plan book. I knew, too, that she hated when *Domina* Chambers ignored school protocol and referred to her colleagues by their first names in the presence of students.

"I know it's corny, but it gives me the chills," Lucy said. "She almost kills her own brother."

Their identities are revealed only when Iphigenia recites a letter for Pylades to bring home to Greece. "A greeting comes from one you think is dead. Your sister is not dead at Aulis." Lucy begged *Domina* Chamber to let the class do the play.

"We can do it on the swimming beach," she said. "We can use one of the rocks as the altar at Aulis and Artemis can appear on a boat to take her to Tauris. One of the rocks can be Tauris..."

I noticed Miss Macintosh lift her head from her lesson plan book and raise her hand to object. "We couldn't possibly. Think of the insurance problems. Girls falling in the lake..." As she spoke I imagined it: stola-clad girls getting tangled in their sheets and sinking to the bottom of the lake. But *Domina* Chambers was not one to be swayed by conventional concerns. She waved a hand in Miss Macintosh's direction as if she were batting away an annoying insect. I noticed Miss Macintosh turn pink above her white high-necked collar. *Domina* Chambers admitted that the plays

were not her favorites (she concurred with one critic's assessment of *Iphigenia at Aulis* as a "woeful falling off from the sterner standards of Greek tragedy") and she thought the addition of a happy ending for Iphigenia was pure soap opera melodrama; however, she thought the material lent itself to reinterpretation.

"We should always recall," she lectured, "that the Greek playwrights felt free to bend the mythic material to their purposes—as Shakespeare did—" here she shot a meaningful look at Miss Macintosh. "And so, why shouldn't we?"

Of course, Lucy was chosen to play Iphigenia. Deirdre played Orestes. They wanted me for Pylades, but I couldn't make enough rehearsals, so they got another girl. All the speaking parts were taken by seniors. The swim team played the chorus. They stood in a lifeboat, led by Miss Pike, who looked splendid in a Greek stola. She insisted on holding a lifesaving float in case any of the girls went overboard, but she managed to hold it in such a way that it looked like some kind of heraldic icon.

We all wanted *Domina* Chambers to play Artemis. She demurred at first, recommending Miss Macintosh, as a sop, I think, to her wounded feelings, but when Miss Macintosh stoutly refused, she agreed.

Although I couldn't be in the play I helped Deirdre with the costumes. We made a gold helmet embossed with an owl for Miss North, who'd agreed to play Athena, and a silver helmet with a moon and deer etched in tin foil

for *Domina* Chambers. We already had a deer mask for the deer who takes Iphigenia's place at the altar. We used one from May Day. I noticed it was the one with the green heart embroidered on it.

The problem, as I heard Deirdre and Lucy discuss day after day, was how to make the switch—the deer for Iphigenia—dramatically. Deirdre suggested the priest could fling a sheet over Lucy and then she could slip under it and get in the boat with *Domina* Chambers.

"But everyone will see me wading up to the boat. It ruins the effect. And where's the deer going to be before she slips under the sheet? There's no backstage, you know."

"Hey, you're the one who was so hot to do it on the swimming beach!"

I had to admit I almost enjoyed hearing them bicker. But then Deirdre came up with a brilliant solution.

"If we use the second stone as the altar the deer can wait in the cave behind it. When I throw up the sheet you can slip in the water and swim underwater to the boat. The deer can swim underwater to the rock and pop up under the sheet."

Lucy liked it. The only problem was getting someone small and agile enough to play the deer. Someone who was also a good swimmer and wouldn't mind sitting still in the cave throughout the whole play.

"I know just the right girl," Deirdre woke us both in the middle of the night to announce.

"Albie. She's small and she can move without making a sound. And she'd do anything for Lucy."

On the day of the performance my father agreed to come home early from work to take over watching my mother. The play was timed to end at sunset and so I found myself sitting by my mother's sickbed anxiously watching the sun sink over the lumber mill smoke-stacks.

"You think by staring at it you'll stop the sun in the sky," I heard my mother's voice from the bed behind me. I had thought she was asleep.

"They're doing a play on the swimming beach," I told her.

"On the beach? What nonsense. It was no lucky day you won that scholarship. You should be learning practical things not wasting your time with rich girls. You'll never be more than a servant to them, that's what my mother always told me..."

"Lucy's not rich." I was only able to inter-rupt my mother's tirade because she had run out of breath. She started to wheeze now, impatient to answer me. I helped her sit up and gave her a drink through a straw.

"You wait," she said when she'd regained her breath. "Lucy'll come into her share of wealth some day and then see how much you're worth to her."

I'd have asked her where Lucy was going to get this money, but my father came home and I could tell by the angle of the sun that

I'd already missed most of the play. I ran all the way up River Street and then cut behind the Tollers' house and followed the Schwanenkill to the south end of the lake. I could see when I got to the icehouse that the play was still going on. I started out along the eastern side of the lake, but I realized I would miss the whole thing by the time I got to the swimming beach. I knew where there was a rock on the east shore where I could sit and watch at least the end of the play. I wanted to see how they managed that last scene.

As it turned out, I had a perfect view of the stones. I could see, as I settled myself on the rock, that the second sister stone was covered with a white sheet that glowed a fiery red in the light of the setting sun. It looked exactly like the bloodred altar it was supposed to represent.

From where I sat I could see things the audience was not supposed to see. It didn't ruin the effect, though, when a hand reached out from the cave and tugged the sheet away, revealing the prone shape of a naked girl tied to the rock. I could hear, over the still water, the gasp of the audience on the swimming beach.

"Jesus," I thought, "*Domina* Chambers really is fearless!" But then I realized, as the rest of the audience must have soon discovered, that Lucy was wearing a pale pink swimsuit that clung to her newly ample figure like a second skin.

The chorus's dinghy swayed erratically as

a figure in a robe with a gold foil mask dis-embarked and waded through the thigh-deep water over to the rock. The players had been lucky that the warm weather had lasted this long, but still I didn't envy the actress playing the priestess who had to stand in this water. I stretched out on my rock and dangled my hand in the water. It felt icy.

The robed figure lifted a dagger and held it above Lucy's white arched throat. Just as the blade came down toward her throat, the priestess lifted her left arm and her long trailing sleeve hid the victim from the audi-ence. There was a scream that echoed off the wall of the Point and rippled over the still water and a bright spray of blood splashed the priestess's robe. Even from where I sat it looked so real that I stood up and tried to see Lucy sneaking into the cave behind the stone. But the setting sun was in my eyes, turning the water such a lurid red I could almost believe it was Lucy's blood flowing into the lake. Barely a minute passed, but it felt like an eternity. I looked toward the beach and could see that many in the audience had also gotten to their feet and were craning to see what was behind the priestess's robe. And then the priestess swept away her arm again and we saw, in Lucy's place, a slaughtered deer, blood dripping from its torn neck. At almost the same moment a small boat rounded the Point and we saw Lucy at the prow, swathed in scarves the color of the sunset. Behind her stood Artemis holding a chaplet of gold above

Lucy's head. The boat was rowed by Miss Buehl in a short toga.

Just then there was a loud crack. I was so taken up in the play that for a moment I thought it was a sound effect, but then I looked behind me and saw the eastern sky split by a lightning bolt. On the lake, the masked figure of Artemis held her hands up to the sky and in a voice magisterial enough to carry across the water to my rock proclaimed, "So speaks Zeus! Instead of taking this girl to Tauris I will take her to Olympus where she will live among the gods."

At a nod from Artemis, Miss Buehl turned the boat around and headed back around the Point. I was marveling at *Domina* Chamber's adept improvisation when I realized that the rest of the actors were not coping quite so well with this unplanned finale. Rain came down like a curtain falling over the last act. The audience fled shrieking up the steps of the swimming beach while the chorus beached their dingy and took shelter in the boathouse. Only the priestess remained standing in the water next to the slain deer. Under the priestess's soaked robe I could see the outline of two familiar breasts. It was Deirdre. She started wading toward the beach.

She was halfway to the beach, her back to the stone, when the figure in the deer costume sat up and started struggling with the ropes that tied her to the rock. I could see her mouth was open, but her cries were drowned out by the roar of the rain. Through the cur-

tain of rain I thought I saw her looking toward me. She lifted an arm as if to signal me, but it only made her lose her balance. The top half of her body slipped off the rock and into the water. I stood for what must have been only seconds knowing the fastest way to reach her would be through the water, but I remembered how cold the water was. I turned, instead, into the woods and ran along the trail to the beach. It took longer than I thought it would because of the rain and the mud. I was sure that when I got there I'd find the girl drowned.

I ran down the steps so quickly I slipped and missed the last five or six steps. I landed flat on my stomach on the beach, my face ground into the wet sand. When I got up I saw Lucy and Deirdre dragging a wet brown figure out of the water.

They dropped her next to me and I reached out and took off the mask. "You," Albie spat at me. "You ran away into the woods to let me drown."

Lucy and Deirdre both looked from Albie to me. I tried to explain what happened, but my mouth was full of sand.

Lucy put her arm around Albie. "Jane would never run away from someone who needed help," she told Albie as she helped her to her feet. I was grateful for Lucy's defense of me, but as Albie slumped against Lucy and let herself be led from the beach, she gave me a look over her shoulder that I understood to mean she didn't believe a word of it.

Chapter Twenty-two

●

THE STORM THAT CLOSED THE FINAL ACT OF *Iphigenia on the Beach* also brought an end to the warm weather. Lucy's good mood vanished with the advent of the Canadian cold fronts and the first snows. The first thing I noticed was that she stopped wearing the beautiful clothes *Domina* Chambers had bought for her in Europe. She wore, instead, an oversized sweatsuit Matt had sent her from military school.

"It keeps me warm," she told me.

Another piece of odd behavior was that when the heavy snows began in November she refused to stay on the paths.

"I feel like a rat in a maze," she said. "I'm going to make my own tracks." And she'd leap over the banked snow at the woods' edge and take off, leaving me and Deirdre on the path.

"What we need," Deirdre said one night as we were working on our Tacitus translations, "are cross-country skis. Then we could go anywhere."

Lucy looked up from her Tacitus. I saw Deirdre's face light up at even the prospect that she had recaptured Lucy's attention. "She's even more desperate for her friendship than

I am," I wrote in my journal. "I feel sorry for her."

"Yeah, but where will we get the skis?" I asked.

"We'll have a bake sale," Deirdre said, "and raise money for a cross-country ski club."

The bake sale was a financial success but it failed to revive Lucy's flagging spirits. Where before she had given up food and sleep when she was depressed, now she did little except eat and sleep.

When the cross-country skis were delivered, she mustered some interest, but instead of practicing with the club, she took off through the woods by herself.

"What do you think is wrong with her?" I asked Deirdre one day in early December. We were skiing through the woods on the west side of the lake. Miss Buehl and *Domina* Chambers were leading the group. As soon as the teachers were out of sight, Lucy had taken off south without a word to me or Deirdre. Deirdre and I had paused on top of a rise and watched her go.

"Didn't you know?" Deirdre said. "Matt's not coming home for Christmas."

"You mean their parents won't even let him come home for Christmas?"

Deirdre shook her head impatiently. "He's going on a skiing trip with his cousin. I think Lucy's really hurt that he's *chosen* not to come home. It's like he's avoiding her."

Or me, I thought. Wasn't it more likely

that it was me he was avoiding? We were skiing through a part of the woods with little underbrush. I looked up at the sky, which was white and swollen with impending snow, through a green feathering of branches. We were in the hemlock grove through which Matt had chased me on May Day. I looked ahead and saw that the narrow grooves the skiers had made before us led to the clearing where Matt and I had made love. *Made love?* Could I really go on calling it that? He hadn't even bothered to call or write me or get a single word through to me since May Day. For all he knew, I could have gotten pregnant that morning.

"She's so upset about it she says she's going to spend the break here on campus."

"Alone?" I asked.

"I said I'd stay with her."

"Oh," I said. I couldn't think of anything else to say. My eyes were stinging and I suddenly felt unbearably cold. I dug my poles into the snow and swung my left ski out at a forty-five-degree angle to the tracks. Deirdre moved out of my way.

"What are you doing?" she asked.

"I'm going back," I told her. "My feet are cold." She didn't say a word as I stomped out a semicircle in the snow. When I'd repositioned my skis in the tracks I pushed off down the hill, my skis moving easily in the tracks we'd already laid.

I WAS HURT THAT LUCY HADN'T ASKED ME TO STAY on campus that Christmas. We'd stayed on campus Christmas break sophomore and junior year earning extra money by helping Mrs. Ames clean the dorms. But Lucy hadn't said anything to me about staying this year. As it turned out, I wouldn't have been able to stay even if she had asked. The day before Christmas break my mother was admitted to a hospital in Albany and my father picked me up after my last final to drive down there. He'd been to the dorm already and gotten my suitcase.

"Your friend said to wish you a Merry Christmas," he said. "If you want, I can wait while you go say good-bye." I shook my head no. I didn't even ask which *friend* he meant.

It was snowing hard on the Northway and my father responded to my questions about my mother with monosyllabic grunts. I finally gave up and let him concentrate on the slippery road. When we pulled into his sister's house on the outskirts of Albany he turned to me. I thought that now he would tell me how long—how little—my mother had to live, but instead he said, "You mustn't mind the things she says to you. It's the cancer talking."

He'd said this before and I knew he meant it to be a comfort, but I just couldn't believe it anymore.

"But she's always said these things to me," I complained, ashamed at how whiny my

voice sounded. "Why does she hate me so much?"

My father looked away from me. "If it seems like she's never gone out of her way to make you feel wanted, it's because she's always wanted you to get out. Not end up like she did—trapped."

"Then why didn't she ever leave?"

"She tried. She tried all her life. When she was in high school she studied for that scholarship that you got, but then her mother wouldn't let her take it."

"Why not?"

My father sighed. "When they turned the old Crevecoeur place into a school your grandma lost her job there. She must've parted on bad terms with the people up at Heart Lake, because she'd never have mention of them, or the school, in her house. Your mother still managed to get a scholarship for the state teacher's college, but by then your grandmother was sick and she had to stay and take care of her. Then she met me...and we had you..."

As my father's voice trailed off I realized for the first time that I was the reason my mother had gotten trapped in the little mill town she hated so much.

"I know it's hard for you, the way she talks to you, Janie. But you gotta try not to take it to heart. It's the way her mother talked to her. You just try not to listen. I mean, listen with your ears, but don't take it in here." He tapped my sternum with his blunt, stubby

finger. "And remember that underneath it all your mother's always wanted the best for you, she just doesn't know how to go about getting it for you."

I tried in the next days, while I sat in a chair by my mother's bed, lulled to sleepiness by the watery gurgle of the pump that drained her lungs, to feel some sense of gratitude toward her. But all I could think was that I would have traded everything—Matt and Lucy and Heart Lake and Vassar and whatever shimmering mirage of a future I'd imagined—for one good word from her. "Dear God," I wrote in my journal, "I'll give up everything for one good word from her. I'll drop out of Heart Lake and go back to Corinth High. I'll enroll in community college and take a secretarial course. I'll get a job in the mill and maybe, if I'm lucky, marry someone like Ward Castle." I reread what I'd written and then crossed out "someone like" and promised God I'd marry Ward Castle himself.

But although my mother remained lucid and conscious to the end she said nothing to me. Finally, on the day before New Year's, she took her last breath and closed her eyes on me forever.

Because the ground was frozen, my mother's remains would be stored until spring when she could be buried. There was a short memorial service held on New Year's day at the Presbyterian church my aunt's family attended. Afterward we went back to my aunt's house and I nodded politely while my father told rel-

atives I didn't recognize how proud my mother had been of me.

Later that night he took me aside and told me that he'd be staying at his sister's house for a while. He might even look into a job at the glove factory where my uncle worked. If I didn't mind that. I could still come down to Albany on weekends if I liked.

"To tell you the truth, Janie, I'm sick to death of that sawdust. I thought gloves might make a nice change."

I told him I thought it was a fine idea, and not to worry about how I spent my weekends. I'd be busy studying for finals and college entrance exams. In fact, I was a little anxious to get back.

"Of course you are," he said with such obvious relief that I had to remind myself he was only happy I had something to take my mind off my mother's death. It wasn't as if he were trying to get rid of me. "You can go back tomorrow. If you're not afraid of taking the train back yourself," he told me. It occurred to me that with all the stress he had been under my father probably didn't remember that it was still Christmas break, school didn't start until the second week in January. It seemed unlikely to me that he would have so blithely sent me back to a deserted campus.

I didn't tell him his mistake. I took the fifty-dollar bill he removed from the pocket of his ill-fitting dark suit and told him I wasn't afraid at all. After all, it was the same train I'd be taking to college next year.

I thought of that, the next day, riding the train north along the Hudson, the river a dark gray ribbon rimmed with pale green ice under a pearly sky. Because we shared the same name I'd always thought of the river as a blood relative, and it seemed right, somehow, that my future lay along its banks. Matt's school was just an hour or so south. In a matter of months I'd follow the river to Vassar and then, who knew? Perhaps I'd follow the river farther south to New York City. There my imagination reached its limit; I'd never been to New York City. But as I watched the chunks of pale green ice float downriver, even as the train took me in the opposite direction, I thought of a description from a fairy tale I'd read once of a palace formed of the drifting snow, its windows and doors cut by the wind, its hundred halls all blown together by the snow. The Snow Queen's palace with a frozen lake at its center. And even though I was moving in the opposite direction, I felt like I was traveling toward my future.

When I reached Corinth I took a taxi to the school. The taxi driver said there was a Nor'easter on the way that was expected to drop several feet of snow on the southern Adirondacks. He jabbed his finger at the windshield, at a bank of clouds massing in the north. The sky had an ominous green tinge to it. When we got to the school he helped me get my suitcases into the lobby of the dorm but he didn't ask if I wanted help getting them

upstairs. He must have had a moment's compunction about leaving me, though.

"Are you sure you're all right here?" he asked me, eyeing the empty desk where the dorm matron usually sat. "Is there anyone here?"

"Oh, my friends are here. They'll help me with my bags once I let them know I'm back," I told him. I'd pictured myself lugging my suitcases up the two flights of stairs, but suddenly I knew I was far too anxious for that. A great sense of urgency had overtaken me. Maybe it was just the weather: the drop in air pressure, those strange green clouds, that expectant sense of snow coming. I left my suitcases in the lobby and ran up the stairs.

On the second landing I paused and listened. I had thought I heard someone crying. But when I listened, all I heard was the hiss of the steam radiators. I remembered then that the maintenance crew always turned the heat on full blast over vacation to keep the pipes from freezing. Last year, Deirdre had left three pillar candles in her room and they had all melted. The funny thing had been that they had all melted differently. The red one had sunken into itself so that it looked like a Hershey's kiss. The purple one had keeled over sideways like the leaning tower of Pisa. The blue one looked at first like nothing had happened to it at all, but then we realized that while the outside shape had stayed the same, the wax had dripped out from the inside and pooled on the floor, leaving behind a hollow column.

As I walked along our hall I stripped off my coat and scarf. How had Deirdre and Lucy been able to stand it? It was like a sauna in here. When I put my hand on our doorknob it was warm to the touch.

I heard, again, the sound of crying as I opened the door. On the bed under the window—Lucy's bed—someone was lying under the covers with her back to the door. I thought it was Lucy and that she must have been the one who was crying, but as I crossed the room I heard the sound again, and another sound, like metal scraping metal. I turned in that direction just as the door to the single opened and saw in the doorway, not Deirdre as I expected, but Lucy.

She was wearing a red flannel shirt—Matt's, I thought—that was so big on her that when she held up her arms and put a hand on either side of the doorjamb, the shirt covered the whole doorway. If she hadn't been so short she would have blocked my view of the single. I could see, though, over her head, but I couldn't see why she was trying to block my view. Then we both took a step forward at the same time and nearly collided.

"Jane," she said, "what are you doing back?"

"My mother died," I said, as if that explained everything. I was looking at Deirdre's single, trying to figure out what was different about it, but the only thing I could see that was different was that she had gotten a new bedspread. A red bedspread. I didn't even notice that Lucy wasn't saying the things she should

have been saying, like "I'm so sorry" or "How terrible." I took another step toward the room so that I was on the threshold and realized that what I was looking at wasn't a red bedspread. It was a sheet soaked in blood.

I looked at Lucy and then at the body under the covers on Lucy's bed.

"She's asleep," Lucy whispered. She took my hand in her small hand and pulled me into the single. She had to pull quite hard because I didn't want to go in there. I'd forgotten what a strong grip she had.

She closed the door behind us.

I stood over the bed and noticed that the blood had soaked through the mattress.

"She tried to kill herself?" I asked.

Lucy looked up at me for a moment and then shook her head. "Yes, it's Deirdre's blood," she said, "but she didn't try to kill herself. She was pregnant. She had a baby."

"Deirdre was pregnant? How could that be?"

"You remember last year, the nights we spent out at the lake, and May Day. I think it was May Day because she didn't go out all those weeks it rained and I think the baby was early, it was so small..."

I grabbed her arm and shook it. I noticed how thin her arm felt under the big shirt. "She had the baby *here*?" I said, her words finally sinking in. *"Alone?"*

Lucy looked offended. "I was here," she said, "I stayed with her all night."

"Why didn't you go to the infirmary?"

"She begged me not to. She said they would definitely throw her out and put her in a reform school this time. What could I do, Jane? And then it came so quick. I think because it was so small..."

It was the second time she had mentioned the baby's size, but small or not it surely wasn't invisible.

"Where...?"

Lucy looked over at Deirdre's bureau and I followed her gaze to the large metal tea tin, the one decorated with golden mountains that Deirdre used to store her pot.

"It wasn't breathing," she said. "It was born dead."

My knees felt suddenly watery as if the tendons holding them together had just melted. I brushed my hand against my face and it came back wet. The one window in the single was opaque with water condensation. I walked over to the window and wrenched it open. I leaned out the window and threw up onto the ledge.

Lucy came up behind me and put a cool hand on my forehead. She held my hair back until I had finished throwing up and then sat me down on the inside ledge. She held me by the shoulders until I stopped shaking.

"Fuck, Lucy, we've got to tell someone."

She shook her head. "They'll throw her out for sure. What good will it do?"

"But what if she's still bleeding." I looked at Deirdre's bed. Could a person lose that much blood and be all right?

"I gave her a sanitary napkin and it seemed like most of the bleeding stopped an hour ago. I think she'll be all right."

"But what are we going to do about that?" I pointed at the tea tin. "We can't just leave it there."

"Of course not," Lucy said reasonably. "I've been thinking about it all morning. The ground's too frozen to bury it..." For some reason I thought of my mother's body lying in a funeral home's refrigerator in Albany, waiting for the spring thaw. I tasted bile in my throat and would have thrown up again if Lucy hadn't placed two cool hands on either side of my face. Looking into those blue eyes of hers I suddenly felt calmer.

"You understand why we have to take care of this, Jane? It's not just for Deirdre, it's for Matt, too."

"But he wasn't with her on May Day," I said.

"He was the only one caught that morning and Deirdre will say it was him. Remember how she caved in on the wine flask. It will ruin Matt's life forever."

"But if the ground's frozen..."

"But the lake's not," she said, "we can sink it in the lake."

Chapter Twenty-three

●

"We'll have to take the boat," Lucy said as we were leaving the dorm. "It's the only way we can be sure it sinks deep enough."

"It" was the way Lucy referred to the thing in the tea tin. She had placed the tin in her gym bag and carried it, not by the handles, but cradled upright in her arms—the way a person would carry a cake in a box.

Before we left the room I checked on Deirdre. She was sleeping soundly, her lips moist and parted, her cheeks pink in the overheated room. She didn't look like a person bleeding to death, but like someone drugged.

"I gave her some of that tea she's always saying is such a good sleep potion," Lucy told me. I noticed the red lacquer box lying empty beside the bed. "She'll be OK."

When we left the dorm I turned onto the path but Lucy steered me into the woods. "We can't risk taking the path," she said. "We might run into someone."

The campus felt deserted. I knew that some teachers stayed on over break. Miss Buehl, for instance, tended her lab experiments and followed animal tracks in the snowy woods. There was a groundskeeper and Mrs. Ames,

but I imagined that the workers from the town, like my taxi driver, would have gone home by now rather than risk getting caught out here in the storm.

Lucy's footpath through the woods was so narrow we had to walk single file. At first I kept my eyes on her back, on her pale blue snow parka, but my gaze kept drifting to the navy blue gym bag that she cradled over her right hip. Although I couldn't see it in the bag I kept picturing the tin. The gold mountains under a blue sky. A green lake in the foreground.

I turned my eyes to the path. It had been trod into the snow over many weeks and then frozen into a knee-deep crevasse—a miniature of the ones in the film strip on glaciers Miss Buehl showed us. I thought of the weeks it took Lucy to make the path and wondered if it would be filled in by the approaching storm.

We came out at the south tip of lake, not far from the Schwanenkill. When I looked up I noticed for the first time that there was a thin sheet of ice covering the lake.

"Damn, it must have frozen just last night," Lucy said, more to herself than to me. She shifted the gym bag to her left hip and eased herself down the bank. She swayed in the deep, untrodden snow and I thought that I should offer to hold the gym bag, but I didn't.

Lucy stretched one leg down to the lake's surface and tapped it with her booted toe. A splintering sound echoed across the lake.

"How thick is it?" I called and heard my words echo hollowly. I looked up at the sky

and saw that the ominous green clouds hung low over the lake like a shallow dome. I felt as if Lucy and I were being pressed between the sky and snow-covered ground, like autumn leaves ironed between two sheets of waxed paper.

"Not very," Lucy said coming back up the bank. "It's thinnest where the Schwanenkill flows out of the lake. I think we can break the ice with the boat oars."

First we had to cross the stream, which was only partially frozen. Lucy, usually so surefooted, seemed unbalanced by the weight she was carrying on her hip. I pictured her falling and dropping the bag and the tin snapping open.

"Here," I said, crossing the stream ahead of her, "take my hand." I planted one foot in the middle of the stream and felt the icy water creeping through the soles of my boots. I noticed when I took her hand that Lucy was shaking.

We made it to the icehouse only to find that the door was locked.

"The extension agent must have locked it after she saw Matt here on May Day," Lucy said. We hadn't used the icehouse this winter. "But I doubt she could have locked the doors on the lake side because they don't close completely. We'll have to go around."

I looked at Lucy and noticed how pale she was; her skin had a greenish cast to it, as green as the snow-laden sky. After all, she had been up all night with Deirdre and the shock of witnessing that birth—a stillbirth, no less—

was no doubt beginning to tell on her. I was suddenly filled with hatred for Deirdre. Why should we have to clean up her mess? But then I remembered that we were doing it for Matt, too.

"I'll go," I said. "You stay here and rest on this rock."

Lucy nodded and sat down on a large flat rock. She hugged the gym bag to her chest and closed her eyes.

I went down to the edge of the lake and studied the narrow ledge of mud and ice that ran in back of the icehouse. I noticed that one of the doors was wedged partially open—just as it had been on the night I'd approached it from the ice.

I came back around and called to Lucy. "This door is open." I heard "open" echo across the lake. "But the front door is probably padlocked so I'll have to get the boat out onto the water and bring it to shore."

I half expected Lucy to object. I wasn't really sure I'd be able to get the boat out by myself. But she only nodded and lay back on the rock, one hand resting on the gym bag by her side.

I made my way along the icy edge of the lake, one hand on the wall of the icehouse. Both my feet were soaked by the time I reached the open door and pulled myself into the small hut. I was relieved to see that the rowboat was still there, with both its oars lying in the shallow hull. The prow of the boat was facing the lake.

I opened both doors and then went to the rear of the boat, took a deep breath, and pushed. At first nothing happened, but then I heard a scraping noise as the boat inched forward on the wooden floor. I crouched down and put my shoulder to the stern and pushed again. The scraping sound changed to a crash that was so loud in the echoing silence of the lake that I was sure someone from the school must have heard it. I looked across the lake toward the cliff wall of the Point and for a moment thought I saw a figure standing on the rock. I thought of Miss Buehl in her cottage just beyond the Point. But then the figure vanished and I couldn't be sure if I'd imagined it or not.

I looked down and saw that the boat was drifting out into the lake.

I lunged after it, caught the rear, and pulled it back to the shore. My jeans were now soaked up to my knees, so I figured I might as well wade through the water, guiding the boat with me until I'd gotten it past the icehouse. By the time I'd pulled it halfway up onto the shore I couldn't feel my toes anymore. I trudged up the bank, the wet sucking sound my boots made somehow familiar. I paused and saw in my mind my mother's hospital room and heard the wet gurgle of the pump that cleared her lungs of fluid. I felt suddenly, of all things, immeasurably sleepy and I think that if I had been alone I would have lain down in the soft snow and taken a nap under that pillowy green-gray sky.

But from where I was I could see Lucy lying on the rock and the navy blue gym bag lying beside her. I shook myself awake and approached her. She didn't move at my approach even though the sound my boots made scraping through the crusted snow seemed unbearably loud to me. I looked down at her and saw that she had fallen asleep. Again I was startled by how pale she looked, her eyelids and lips blue in the cold, shimmering air. I shook her arm and her eyes snapped open.

"I've got the boat," I said.

She looked at me as if she didn't know what I was talking about, but then she noticed the gym bag and nodded her head. She got up slowly, swayed unsteadily, and sat back on the rock.

"We need some rocks," she said.

It was my turn to look at her uncomprehendingly.

"To weigh it down," she explained, gesturing toward the bag.

I looked around but of course any rocks that might have been there were two feet under the snow.

"In the stream," she said. "There are always rocks at the bottom of the Schwanenkill."

I turned back to the stream, expecting her to follow me, but she stayed seated on the rock. At the stream's edge I knelt in the snow and took my gloves off. I reached into the middle of the stream, I was into it up to my elbow before my fingers grazed the bottom. I felt frozen mud and something hard and round.

I pulled up a smooth, round rock about the size of my fist and laid it on the stream bank. When I'd found about a dozen rocks I stuffed them into my pockets and went back to Lucy.

I emptied the rocks onto the flat rock next to where she sat and she nodded.

"That'll do it," she said. Then she slid the tea tin out of the gym bag and opened the lid.

Inside there was a tiny white baby about the size of a small cat. Its skin was nearly translucent, gleaming blue and pink like an opal. Its eyelashes and the light hair on its scalp were sandy red. Lucy picked up a rock and wiped the mud off on her jeans. Clean and dry the rocks were a beautiful greenish bluish gray— the color hazel eyes were sometimes. Lucy arranged them around the baby as if she were packing eggshells in tissue paper. Then she took out a white cloth from her pocket, shook it out, and smoothed it over the baby. It was one of the linen napkins from the dining room, stitched with a heart and the school's motto: *Cor te reducit.* The heart takes you back. Not a bad requiem for the little thing about to be buried in the lake. Then she closed the lid and fastened the metal catch.

"We ought to wrap something around it to make sure it doesn't open. Do you have any string?"

I shook my head. String? What the hell was she thinking? She opened her coat and felt the top of her jeans. "I'm not wearing a belt," she said. "Are you?"

I opened my coat and unthreaded my belt

through the belt loops of my jeans. It was made of thick, webbed cotton—I'd bought it at the army/navy store in town—with an adjustable brass buckle.

"Perfect," Lucy said, tightening the belt around the tin and fastening the buckle. "That should hold. Let's go."

I had to help Lucy into the boat while she held the tin. This time I did offer to take it from her but she shook her head and held on to it more tightly.

I pushed the boat into the water and then hopped in and grabbed the oars. I turned the boat around so the prow faced the lake and I faced the shore rowing. Lucy sat behind me. When the boat grazed thicker ice she directed me.

"There's a path of thinner ice that goes all the way through the lake," she told me, "it must follow the underground spring." I remembered the day we had skated here and she had gone through the ice. The place she had gone in must have been over the spring.

Twice we had to stop and I had to pass her one of the oars to chop the ice. I was afraid, each time, that she'd drop the oar into the lake and we'd be stranded out here.

"It must be deep enough here," I said after we were stopped by the ice for the third time, but she shook her head and battered the ice with the oar. The chopping sounds reverberated against the layer of heavy clouds and the rock wall of the Point. The jutting prow of the Point seemed close now and I could see,

a little to the east, one of the three sister stones emerging from the ice, standing like a silent witness to our deed.

"We're more than halfway across the lake," I said. "We're getting too close to the other shore."

Lucy stopped hammering with the oar and looked behind her. Her hair was so damp with sweat that it had frozen together in clumps and when she swung her head back to face me I could hear the sound her frozen hair made brushing against her nylon parka.

"OK," she said, "here."

We both looked down at the tea tin sitting in the bottom of the boat. The blue sky over golden mountains looked to me like a dream of summer during winter. I looked up at the lowering black-green sky above us and tried to remember what such a sky looked like. Lucy knelt down in the bottom of the boat and picked up the tin. She tried to hold it in one hand while using one hand to brace herself against the rim of the boat to get up. The boat careened toward the east shore and then swung back to the west, sluicing us with icy water.

"Jesus," I said taking the tin from her, "let me have that." I heard the stones knock together inside the tin. The whole thing felt lighter than I expected and I wondered if it would really sink to the bottom. "Let's get this over with," I said. I balanced the tin on the edge of the boat and looked at her. She nodded.

I leaned over, holding the tin parallel to the water's surface in a patch Lucy had cleared of ice. I didn't like to think of it flipping over and sinking to the bottom upside down. When it was a few inches from the surface I let it go. I watched it sink below the water and saw the blue sky and gold mountains turn pale green and then vanish into the green-black depths of the lake. I stared for a moment at the shards of white ice floating on the black water until I noticed that white crystals were beginning to fill in the black spaces. I thought the water was freezing again in front of my eyes and I was afraid that when I looked back at how we had come the path across the lake would be sealed with ice. But when I looked up I saw that the path back to the icehouse hadn't closed. It was the green sky above that had opened up to disgorge its burden of snow, a stream of snow so thick it felt as if the sky were falling down upon us.

PART THREE

●

The Ice Harvest

Chapter Twenty-four

●

EVEN THE AIR HERE IS TAINTED, DYED A CITRINOUS green that shimmers under the frosted dome like green Jell-O. We spend the day splashing in murky water the same color and temperature as the air. Or Olivia swims and I lie in a plastic lawn chair staring up at the pale green bubble of sky. We play putt-putt on spiky green plastic grass. We eat our meals at a restaurant next to the pool and so even our food tastes like chlorine. Our room's only window looks onto the interior dome. By the third day I've lost all sense of night and day; it seems like we've been here for years, not days. When I turn out the light for bedtime, the green light from the dome seeps through the cracks in the curtains. Even Olivia is restless and spends the night clinging to me in the over-sized bed. I awake, tangled in her damp hair, breathing in its comforting smell of bleach and salt.

I thought it made sense to stay in a hotel with an indoor pool, so I spent the last of my sav-

ings on two weeks at the Westchester Aquadome. When I gave Dean Buehl the phone number she asked how long I planned to stay and I realized that I might not have a job anymore. When I told her I didn't know she said to call her in two weeks and we'd talk it over.

"Take some time to think about what you really want to do, Jane." The words sounded familiar and I realized it was the same thing she had said to me the day I graduated from Heart Lake. She'd come down to the train station to see some of the younger girls off. She did this every year and usually she was a cheerful sight, calling a hearty "see you next year" and waving her handkerchief at the departing trains. But that year a lot of girls wouldn't be coming back. Two students and a town boy had drowned in the lake and a teacher had been let go because she had somehow been involved. Parents reacted by pulling out their children and their money. I saw Miss Buehl first on the opposite side of the tracks, the northbound side, fussing nervously over Albie, trying, unsuccessfully, to slick back her pale wisps of hair into a large bow pinned to the back of her head. When she saw me she hurried over the bridge leaving Albie looking small and lost beside a tower of matching monogrammed suitcases.

"I wanted to wish you luck at Vassar, Jane," Miss Buehl said when she had crossed to the southbound side. "You don't know how lucky you are to be getting out now."

"Have that many girls been pulled out?" I asked.

"About half," she said, lowering her voice. "Of course, we'll get more girls, but not of the same sort."

"Albie's been pulled out?" I asked in a low voice even though the girl couldn't possibly hear us from across the track.

"I'm afraid Albie's been kicked out," Miss Buehl said in a quaking whisper, leaning her head close to mine. I thought I smelled liquor on her breath and I noticed for the first time how haggard she looked. "We discovered it was she who broke the fanlight over the doors to the mansion. She threw half a dozen rocks through it."

"Really? Albie did that?" It was hard for me to imagine frail little Albie having the strength to throw even one rock that high.

"Yes, I tried to argue in her behalf, but then there were other infractions, curfew breaking, erratic behavior..."

"Where is she going?" I asked, trying to keep from stealing a look across the tracks. I felt sure she was watching us and that she guessed she was the topic of our whispered conversation.

"St. Eustace," Miss Buehl answered.

"Oh." *St. Useless*. The school Deirdre'd been so afraid she'd end up at. I did look at Albie then, but she had turned away from us and set her small, pinched face into an expression of bland indifference, as if she were on her way to a tedious but necessary luncheon,

and not to the Siberia of girls' boarding schools. Then the northbound train pulled in and blocked my view of her.

"So you see how lucky you are, Jane," Miss Buehl had said to me. "You can put this whole thing behind you and take some time to think about what you really want to do. You've got your whole life ahead of you." She said it like she almost envied me. That she wished she were getting out, too. But then I might have imagined that. After all, Heart Lake was her whole life.

THIS TIME SHE DIDN'T TELL ME I HAD MY WHOLE life ahead of me. We both knew my options were limited, they had narrowed to...what? Did I even have more than one option? "Maybe it's not too late to work things out with your husband," she had added instead.

I suppose she would feel better firing me if she knew I had somewhere to go.

The idea of working things out with Mitch was the furthest thing from my mind when I came here, but he has been unexpectedly kind.

He joins us for dinner almost every night and has even offered to pay part of my hotel bill. When I told him, on the first day while we both watched Olivia swimming in the pool, about what the police had found in the lake along with Aphrodite's body, he thought I meant, at first, that the baby in the tea tin had been Aphrodite's. I had to explain, for what seemed

304

like the hundredth time since the diver had emerged from the lake with that tin, that the baby belonged to my old roommate Deirdre Hall. I told him, as I told the police and Dean Buehl, that Lucy and I had helped her by sinking the tin in the lake.

"Are they charging you with anything?" he asked.

"Not that I know of."

"Good," he said. "You were a minor and you were only an accomplice in disposing of the body. The baby was dead at birth, right?"

I nodded. "That's what Lucy told me."

He paused for a moment, perhaps seeing my uncertainty. Even as I assured him, I realized I was no longer so sure. Maybe it's being in this place—the warm humid air and the way voices echo under the dome. Since I've been here I've remembered standing in that damp, overheated dorm corridor listening to a thin wail of crying. "Well, if it was a lie, it was Lucy's lie. You should be OK. I'll call Herb Stanley in the morning." Herb Stanley was Mitch's lawyer. He'd drawn up our separation agreement. "Don't talk to anyone without consulting him first. You say you knew this police officer back in school?"

"He was Matt and Lucy's cousin. I met him once or twice."

Mitchell smiled at me. "An old boyfriend?"

I was surprised to detect a note of jealousy in his tone.

I shrugged my shoulders. I remembered holding hands with Roy Corey on the swim-

ming beach, stroking my hand along his face. "Not exactly," I said.

"Not exactly no either. Maybe he still likes you." I thought of the way Roy Corey flinched when I touched his arm. No, I didn't think he liked me, but I wasn't obliged to tell Mitchell that.

"You're looking good by the way. That north country air must agree with you."

I saw his eyes moving up and down my body and I felt, suddenly, self-conscious in my bathing suit. It was true I had lost weight over the fall semester, finally shedding the pounds I'd gained having Olivia. I knew Mitch had minded how I'd changed after Olivia was born. And I had minded how he minded.

"I'm sure Roy Corey is busy with his job right now. Aphrodite's...I mean Melissa's death will probably be declared a suicide, but now he's got this other body..."

I stopped myself, appalled at how the word "body" echoed in the watery air. I lowered my voice and went on. "They're going to exhume Deirdre Hall's body—she was buried in Philadelphia—and Matt Toller's body."

I stopped again, remembering the day they found Matt and Lucy. Although it had felt like spring the night I went to meet Matt at the icehouse, it had been a false spring. One of those premature February thaws we get in the Adirondacks. Overnight the temperature had plunged and the lake froze over again. They tried sawing holes in the ice the way they used to for the ice harvest. It turned out that

the extension agent had all the equipment and had been thinking of doing an ice harvest for a history demonstration. When they couldn't find the bodies, though, they brought in a small ice cutter from the Hudson and tore the whole lake apart.

I was in the woods behind the icehouse on the day they found them. The divers carried the bodies into the icehouse while they sent for the family to identify them. It must have been hard on the divers, pulling that tangle of limbs up from the lake bottom. They stood on the shore afterward, smoking cigarettes, their backs to the icehouse. One skipped a stone over the water, but stopped because there was too much broken ice. They didn't notice me when I came down from the woods and stood in the doorway.

They had laid the bodies on one of the ledges where they used to store the slabs of ice. At first I thought they'd only found Matt, but then I saw, tangled in his hair, the small hand and, nestled below his ribs on the side farthest from me, in the shadow of the ledge, her face, pressed against his chest.

They had been bleached clean by the lake, their flesh the same marble white. It was hard to tell where his body stopped and hers began.

"I THOUGHT YOU SAID IT COULDN'T BE MATT'S baby." Mitchell's voice broke into the memory of those twisted limbs.

I took a deep breath of the warm chlorinated air.

"I may have gotten it wrong," I told Mitchell. "Roy Corey seems to have some other idea."

When I told Roy Corey what had happened—from the day I came back to the school early to the last argument between Matt and Lucy—he didn't seem completely surprised. "I thought something was wrong that night Matt left to hitch back to Corinth. He said he'd gotten a letter from Lucy and he was afraid he'd 'really messed something up.' He wouldn't tell me what. I was afraid...well, never mind what I was afraid of. We'll have our answers in two weeks."

That's how long it would take to get the results of the DNA tests. They'd found an aunt of Deirdre's who agreed to the exhumation. As for Matt, Cliff and Hannah Toller had both died in a car accident four years after their children's deaths. Ironically, Matt's next of kin was now Roy Corey. I asked if he'd call me when he got the results.

"Oh, you'll be hearing from me, Jane," he said.

"At least he didn't tell you to stay in Corinth," Mitchell said. "That's a good sign."

"Yeah, but he told me not to leave this hotel without telling him where I could be reached."

Mitchell nodded. "Why don't you call and say you're staying at the house."

I thought I had misheard him in the weird acoustics of the Aquadome, but when I looked

at him I thought I saw tears in his eyes. But then it might have been the way the air here stings your eyes.

"What are you saying, Mitch?"

He shrugged. "I never understood what went wrong, Janie. I never understood why you left. Was it that bad...living with me? I know I could be preoccupied."

I looked down at Olivia paddling in the pale green water. With her purple and pink bathing suit and orange water wings she looks like one of those paper flowers they float in exotic cocktails. The truth was I didn't understand completely why I left either.

"It wasn't your fault, Mitch," I said. Yes, he had been preoccupied, but hadn't that been what I was looking for—someone who wouldn't pay too much attention, someone who wouldn't look at me too closely?

"Maybe it's not too late for us." He reached out across the space between us and laid a damp hand on my bare knee.

I felt an odd mixture of hope and nausea. I hoped that any look of queasiness was covered by the green tint that lay on everything around us, because it had occurred to me that I shouldn't be too quick to turn down Mitch's offer.

"I have to think it over, Mitch."

"Of course, Janie, take all the time you need."

TIME IS SOMETHING I HAVE AN ABUNDANCE OF here at the Aquadome, but when I try to attend to the question at hand my thoughts slither around like slippery fish in the green air. I try to go back, in my mind, to when I met Mitch and decided to marry him. I think that if I can remember loving him I can salvage some of that feeling now and it will be enough to build a new future on, the way a seed crystal teaches the other molecules to make ice. All I need is a seed, but I can't really remember ever *deciding* anything. When I met Mitchell, a few years out of college working in the city, I was nearly drowning.

Take some time to think about what you really want to do. That's what Miss Buehl had told me that day at the train station. But I didn't have to think about it. My path had already been laid out for me the day I listened to Helen Chambers's plan for Lucy. *I see her as a Vassar girl and then she'll go to the city and work in some arts-related field—publishing, I think.* I had rejected, that day, Helen Chambers's plan for me to go to the State Teacher's College and teach Latin, and decided instead to do what she meant for Lucy.

I worked hard at Vassar and got reasonably good grades. My Latin professor urged me to apply to graduate school, but I was tired of treading the same pattern of paths that meandered around the pretty campus. Wouldn't

graduate school just be another set of paths around another campus? I felt something like Lucy's impatience with the snowbound paths of Heart Lake and decided to do what I thought she would have done.

After graduation I moved to New York City and got a job as an editorial assistant at a publishing house. I shared an apartment with two other girls—both from good colleges—who worked at the same company. I wore the same kind of clothes as they did: short black skirts and silk blouses, a simple strand of graduated pearls. So what if my blouses were polyester instead of silk, my pearls paste instead of real? I stayed up late reading the manuscripts the company asked us to read on our own time. I packed my own lunch and walked to work because it was hard to make my share of the rent on the little money I made.

I turned down invitations to drinks and dinners after work because I couldn't pay my way. Besides, I told myself, it was better to spend the evenings reading manuscripts while my roommates went out. Sometimes one of the boys—they still seemed like boys to me, in their sloppily ironed Oxford shirts and slim khaki pants—would ask me out, but I always declined. I told myself it was better not to get involved with anyone just yet. But really, it was the way they all reminded me of Matt, of what Matt might have become. I'd look at one of these nice, clean-cut boys in his prep-school tie and button-down shirt and

think: Matt would be his age now, twenty-two, twenty-three, twenty-four.

One day, when I was twenty-five, I was sitting in an editorial board meeting looking at a young man who worked in copy editing and always passed my desk on his way to the Xerox machine even though it wasn't really on his way. As I looked at him a shaft of weak sunlight came in through the dirty, sixteenth-floor windows and touched his mousy brown hair, turning it a bright and shining red. I felt a chill move through me as if I had just swum through a cold current and the air around me seemed to shimmer. I was seized with an unreasoning panic that the next breath I took would choke me. I left the meeting and told my boss that I'd suddenly felt ill.

"A late night?" she asked, nodding with complicity. She, I knew, stayed out to all hours in the clubs and spent the morning hours nursing hangovers with V-8 juice and Tylenol. I hated to think she attributed my illness to the same cause, but it was easier to nod and agree to her sympathetic smile.

When it happened again, that same rush of cold followed by a fear that I couldn't breathe— this time in a conference with an author and his agent, she was less sympathetic. When I emerged from the ladies' room, still trembling and sweating, she asked if there was anything I wanted to tell her. What could I tell her? That I had begun to be afraid of drowning on dry land? That I could no longer go to movie theaters, supermarkets, subway stations, or any

other place where I had once had that sensation of drowning for fear of it happening there again?

I quit the job. I took another job as a secretary at a temp agency. That way, I reasoned, if I had an attack in a particular setting I wouldn't have to go back. My roommates had decided to move to a bigger apartment in Brooklyn. Since the subway was on my list of places I couldn't go anymore, I moved into a women's hotel near Gramercy Park. I could walk to most of the places the temp agency sent me. It was on one of these jobs, filling in for the receptionist at a building contractor's office, that I met Mitchell. He was older than I, his hair already thinning, his build a little thicker than a boy's. When he asked me to lunch, I accepted. When I told him I liked to take the stairs instead of the elevator for the exercise he not only believed me, but he approved. He told me he admired what good shape I was in. It was true that I had gotten very thin, mostly because I had so little money to spend on food and I walked everywhere.

He was impressed that I had gone to a private girls' school and Vassar, but he didn't ask me many questions about either place. We mostly talked, on our dates, about his job and his plans for the future. He wanted to go out on his own—build houses in the suburbs. He said the city wasn't a good place to raise children. He seemed to me, above all else, cautious and polite. When he asked me to marry him I didn't ask myself if I loved him. I had

assumed that my chances of loving anyone had vanished into the black water of Heart Lake the night Matt and Lucy drowned below the ice.

Those first years of my marriage to Mitchell were peaceful. He built us a house north of the city and I helped out in the office. Mitch did seem disappointed that I didn't get pregnant right away, but when I did conceive I thought everything would be all right.

What I hadn't counted on was how much I would love Olivia. When I first saw her, her body glistening with blood, I was overcome by violent shivering. The labor nurse explained that the convulsions were caused by my body's inability to adjust to the change in mass. But to me it felt like something was breaking up inside of me, setting something free that had been frozen all these years. I wanted to hold her, but Mitch said I was shaking too hard to be trusted with her.

In an unguarded moment I had told Mitchell about my panic attacks. He had seemed, at first, unconcerned, but after Olivia was born he wanted me to see a psychiatrist to make sure I wouldn't have an attack while I was watching Olivia. "You might drop her," he said, "or hurt her during an episode." He spoke as if I had epilepsy. The psychiatrist prescribed an antianxiety drug that made my mouth dry and prevented me from breast-feeding Olivia. Still, Mitchell worried. He made me promise not to drive with Olivia. Our new house was in a housing development far from anything.

I spent my days wheeling Olivia in her carriage around the winding streets that always seemed to dead-end in a cul-de-sac.

I thought, because he was so worried about me watching Olivia, he would come home right after work, but instead he stayed at the office later and later. After I got Olivia fed and bathed and put to bed I would go through my old books, which were stored in boxes in the basement. One night I took out my Wheelock's Latin grammar and started at the beginning, memorizing the declensions and conjugations all over again. I was reciting the third declension to Olivia in her high chair one night when Mitchell came home unexpectedly early.

"What the hell are you teaching her, Jane, that mumbo-jumbo witchcraft you practiced in high school?"

I stared at him, pureed yellow squash dripping from the spoon I held out to Olivia. My journals, all of them except the fourth one which had disappeared, were in the same box in which I had found my Wheelock. I'd left the box, opened, in the basement.

Olivia, impatient for the proffered spoon, slammed her small fist on the high-chair tray. Startled, I dropped the spoon and Olivia began to cry.

Mitchell pulled her out of the high chair. "That's OK, Livvie, Daddy'll take care of you."

I knew that in five minutes Mitchell would give her back to me to do the bath and bed-

time, but in that instant I felt, as he intended, his power to take her from me. There were things in those journals that made me sound like an unfit mother. There were things in the psychiatrist's files that made me sound insane. I didn't know when Mitchell had started to hate me, but I suspected it was when he discovered I had never loved him. And in a way, I couldn't blame him. I had thought it was all right to marry someone I didn't love, but what I hadn't counted on was how it felt to share someone I loved with someone I didn't.

And so I decided to make the first move. For the next few weeks, while I wheeled Olivia around the endless maze of suburban streets, my mind moved around in the same dead-end circles, trying to find a way out. When I told Mitch I wanted a divorce he laughed at me. "Where will you go? How will you live? When I met you, you couldn't even hold a secretarial job for more than a week."

I knew he had me. If I went to work in the city I'd have to put Olivia in day care ten hours a day. A lot of Mitch's business was off the books, which meant the child support he'd be obliged to pay me wouldn't amount to more than a few hundred dollars a month. I had no family or friends to turn to. I read ads for jobs I could do from home, but anyone could see that I'd never make enough to support myself, let alone Olivia. I had no skills to speak of.

"For God's sake, Jane, you majored in Latin," Mitch was fond of saying to me. "How impractical can you get?"

One day, though, I read in the newspaper that Latin was making a comeback. I knew that Mitch would never pay for the classes I'd need to get certified to teach in the public schools, but maybe I could get a job in a private school. I'd already started relearning my Latin. Now I set myself a passage of Latin to memorize each night. I found it oddly soothing. As I picked away at case endings and declensions, alone at the kitchen table, the tangled words unraveled into flowing strands of lucid meaning.

When I had memorized most of Catullus and Ovid, I called Heart Lake and asked to whom should I write about a teaching position. The secretary told me that all hiring decisions were made by the dean, Celeste Buehl. I hung up the phone. I realized then that I had been lying to myself. I didn't want a Latin teaching job at some private school. I wanted to go back to Heart Lake. But how could I ask for a job from Celeste Buehl, who knew everything.

It wasn't until Olivia was three and a half and I overheard Mitchell telling her, along with her bedtime story, that she should tell Daddy if Mommy ever acted funny, that I called Heart Lake again. I asked to speak to Dean Buehl. When the secretary asked who was calling I gave my maiden name, Jane Hudson, but I didn't say I was an alumna.

"Jane Hudson, class of seventy-seven!" Dean Buehl sounded as if she were greeting a celebrity.

"Yes, Miss Buehl, I mean Dean Buehl, I didn't know if you'd remember me."

"Of course I remember you, Jane. Tell me what you've been doing with yourself."

When I told her that I was looking for a job teaching Latin the line went quiet and I steeled myself for the inevitable disappointment.

"You know we've never really been able to replace Helen Chambers."

My heart sank. I hadn't thought that by applying for the Latin position I was trying to take Helen Chambers's place. How could I ever?

"But then," she went on, "we've never gotten an old girl in the position." It had taken me a moment to realize that by "old girl" she meant me. I vaguely heard her bemoaning my generation's lack of interest in teaching. My attention came back when I heard her say that she couldn't think of anyone better to take the place than one of Helen Chambers's girls.

When I finally got off the phone, having arranged to come up to see the new preschool and the cottage where Olivia and I would live ("It's the one I lived in when I taught science. It's not much, but, as you might recall, it has a lovely view of the lake"), I felt so warm I felt my forehead to see if I had a fever. It wasn't, I realized as that warm feeling stayed with me instead of fading over the next difficult months of arguing with Mitchell, just that I had been offered a job. It was what Dean Buehl had called me. *One of Helen Chambers's girls.* That was what my problem had been all these years. I had forgotten who I was. I had forgotten where I belonged.

★   ★   ★

NOW I WONDER, AS I JOIN OLIVIA IN THE WARM green pool, how I could ever have thought that that was what I wanted. *One of Helen Chambers's girls.* I had been lured by that old attraction, the old game that we had played—Lucy and Deirdre and me—to be like her. Look what had become of them. Deirdre and Lucy were dead. And me? I had taken Helen Chambers's place at Heart Lake and one of my own students had died just as hers had. I have nothing to offer those girls. My place is here with Olivia. So what if I'm not in love with my husband? How many wives are?

I swim several laps with Olivia paddling behind me. I do dolphin dives under her and spring up in unexpected places making her squeal with delight. Her screams echo off the opaque surface of the dome. I dive deep, all the way to the bottom, and as I begin to come up for air I see, on the other side of the water, a familiar face. The green water seems, suddenly, thick and heavy, pressing me down to the bottom of the pool. I can feel its weight pressing against my mouth, waiting to fill my lungs. I struggle to the top, but even when I break the surface I'm afraid to take a breath. Afraid that breathing in this shimmering air will drown me.

The man at the edge of the pool reaches out his hand for me and helps me up the ladder. It's only Roy Corey. I take a breath, gasping

in the chlorinated air. I'm so relieved it's him that for a second I don't even question what he's doing here—two hundred miles from his police district—but then he tells me.

"I went to talk to my old forensics professor at John Jay," he says, "and now I'm heading up to Cold Spring to visit my mother. You were on the way, so...here," he says handing me a towel, "you look cold. And pale. Don't tell me you've been in this fish bowl for the whole two weeks."

"Has it really been two weeks already?" I ask, toweling myself down and then wrapping the towel around my waist.

"Yeah. Time flies. Isn't there a saying in Latin for that?"

"*Tempus fugit,*" I say.

"Yeah, that's it. Mattie used to say that." He motions for me to sit down on one of the plastic picnic chairs that surround a glass table. I have the feeling as he settles himself down on the creaking, insubstantial plastic that what he has to tell me about the DNA results requires sitting.

"The baby was Matt's." I say it so he won't have to.

He nods. "Yeah, it was Matt's all right." He's looking at me to see how I'm taking the news.

"I guess I knew all along," I tell him. He looks so pained to be giving me this information that I find myself wanting to reassure him. "That's what they argued about the night they drowned. Matt kept asking Lucy whose baby it was. He must have realized it was his." Roy Corey

puffs up his cheeks and blows air out. He reminds me of those drawings of the wind. "But it was Deirdre he should have been mad at," I add.

Roy shakes his head. I notice the way the flesh around his mouth shakes a little. Matt would never have turned out like this, I think.

"No, Deirdre had nothing to do with it."

I feel myself smiling a tight, polite smile that makes my skin, dry from so much chlorine, crease. "What do you mean?" I ask.

"Deirdre Hall wasn't the baby's mother," he says. "The baby was Matt and Lucy's."

Chapter Twenty-five

●

"But how?"

Roy Corey holds up one hand, palm out like a traffic cop. It reminds me that he is a cop and I had promised Mitchell not to talk to him without consulting a lawyer first.

"I gotta tell you something before you say anything else," he says.

I think he is going to read me my Miranda rights, but instead he tells me that he's read my journal.

"You did what?" My voice is so loud that

everyone under the Aquadome—Olivia in the pool, a family playing putt-putt, the waiters in the poolside restaurant—stop what they are doing to look at us.

"I'm sorry, Jane, I didn't mean to invade your privacy, but it's evidence. We found it with Melissa Randall's effects."

"So she's the one who had it."

Corey nods. "Dean Buehl and Dr. Lockhart agree that she must have found the journal hidden in your old room, under the floorboards, maybe?"

I nod to indicate that this is not outside the realm of possibility. Lucy must have hidden it that night she followed me to the icehouse. Maybe she was afraid that something in it would reveal that the baby was hers. But what? If I hadn't guessed her secret, how could my journal reveal it? Could I have written something that revealed the truth without even knowing the truth? The idea that my journal contains secrets even I do not know makes the fact that it has been in the possession of one of my students even more alarming. Even if the student is dead.

"...and in acting out her paranoid fantasies of persecution..." I catch a shred of what Roy Corey is saying, mostly because the language he is using no longer sounds like his own.

"Dr. Lockhart's diagnosis?" I ask

He nods and grins. "Yeah. Basically she thinks Melissa decided to reenact the events of your senior year and torture you along the way."

"But what about Ellen's suicide attempt?"

"Melissa had a prescription for Demerol—for cramps, her mother said, can you believe that, letting your daughter take a jar full of Demerol away to school—which she could have used to drug Ellen and then cut her wrists."

I wince. "Then Athena was telling the truth. She didn't try to kill herself."

"It was a fake suicide attempt—just like Lucy's was a fake."

"But then why take her own life? Shouldn't Vesta have been the next target?"

"Dr. Lockhart says the guilt was probably too much for her. I think she was afraid of being caught. Same difference, I guess. I've seen guilt and fear unhinge tougher characters than that poor kid."

I look up and see that he is looking at me hard. I feel, like I did with Mitchell, an awareness of being exposed, only I know that Roy Corey is not scanning my body the way Mitch had. He leans closer to me, his hands on his broad thighs, and I can hear the plastic chair creak under his weight.

"You've had a lot to carry all these years," he says. His voice is husky. When I answer my own throat feels tight.

"I guess I should have told someone about the baby."

"Yeah, you should've. But then, who did you have to tell?"

I think that this is an unconventional line for a policeman to take, especially this

policeman who had lectured me about personal accountability, but then I remember that he has read my journal. He knows just how alone I was.

I pull myself up and adjust the towel around my legs. "Am I being charged with anything?" I ask. "Because if I am—"

"You'll want to call your lawyer? What would we be charging you with, Jane? Keeping a journal? Trying to help your best friend? *Believing* your best friend? I know it's embarrassing for you that I read your diary, but the one thing it does is establish your innocence. You had no idea what was really going on."

I almost laugh at the bluntness of his last comment, but instead the sound that comes out is more like a sob. I think of the night Matt and Lucy drowned, of those last moments on the ice when he kept asking her whose baby it was. He wasn't asking if it was his; he was asking if it was hers. *Matt and Lucy were lovers.* How many other things had I missed? Roy Corey is right. I had no idea what had really been going on.

Corey moves his hand as if he's going to pat me on the knee, but then thinks better of it. He is so scrupulous in avoiding physical contact with me that I wonder if he has attended some workshop on how to avoid a sexual harassment suit. "Don't feel bad. No one knew the full story. I suspected there was something *different* about Matt and Lucy..."

"But my God...it was incest."

Roy puffs up his cheeks and blows out air again, but now he looks less like a jovial wind cloud than a very tired middle-aged man. "Well, that's the other thing. When we got the DNA results we noticed that Matt's and Lucy's were entirely different...."

"They didn't have the same father," I say. "Everybody knew that."

"Yeah, everybody knew Cliff Toller wasn't Lucy's father. But what no one knew was that Hannah Toller wasn't Lucy's mother. Matt and Lucy weren't brother and sister. Apparently, they weren't related at all."

THE DAY AFTER ROY COREY'S VISIT I DECIDE TO GO back to Heart Lake. I tell Mitchell that I owe it to Dean Buehl, who has generously forgiven me all my lapses of judgment, to finish out the year. We arrange that I will come to visit Olivia every other weekend and I will stay, whether at his house or the Aquadome we don't say, for spring break. Mitchell says he is disappointed, but I think I see some relief as well. I'm not sure how that makes me feel. I have been trying, these last two weeks, to understand my marriage by reviewing the past, but now I see that I have to go back even farther. I don't think that I can come to any decision without understanding what happened at Heart Lake all those years ago.

Olivia cries when I tell her I am going. I tell her I will see her every other weekend and talk to her every night but she keeps shaking her

head at whatever I say. I say, "Don't you believe that Mommy will come see you?" and she answers, "But what if the Wilis don't let you?"

"Oh honey," I say, "no Wili will ever keep me away from you. I promise."

"But what if they drag you down into the lake and hold you under the water until your face turns blue and the fish come and eat out your eyes?"

It is such a horrible, vivid image that I am sure it comes from someone else. "Olivia, the day I found you on the sister rock and you told me the Wili lady took you there, did she tell you that would happen to you?"

Olivia shakes her head. I am relieved, but then she says, "No, she said that's what would happen to you if I told anyone about her."

DRIVING NORTH ON THE TACONIC PARKWAY I try to sort out all the new information I've received. My parting with Olivia is uppermost in mind for the first part of the drive. I am horrified by the idea that she has been living with that threat against me all these months. It's the sort of thing that a child molester would say to intimidate his victim. Not *his*, I correct myself, *her*. Child molesters can be female, too. I have to wonder now if anything else happened to Olivia out on that rock. When I asked Olivia to describe the Wili all she would tell me was that she was a "white lady." But I couldn't get out of her

whether she was referring to race, hair color, or clothing. Melissa Randall's hair had been bleached. Can I assume that since it was Melissa who had my journal, Melissa who staged Athena's suicide, and Melissa who fell from the rowboat at the sisters rock, that Melissa was the Wili? I'm not sure if I can assume it, but I do hope it. Then, at least, the whole thing would be over.

Still, when I try to imagine Melissa Randall threatening Olivia, or drugging Athena and cutting her wrists, my imagination balks. She simply didn't seem the type to do such awful things. But then, how good have I been at judging types? I bring to mind another young, blond girl: Lucy Toller, my best friend. I replay in my mind that whole last year. The way Lucy looked when she came back from Italy, rounder and curvier, but also happy and *smug*. Had she known she was pregnant? With her own brother's child? Did she know he wasn't her brother? And did that make any difference? After all they had grown up together as brother and sister.

I remember the morning I came back from Albany, how Lucy met me at the door to the single while Deirdre slept. How fast she had thought it through! Deirdre was asleep, so she could tell whatever story she wanted. How had she made Deirdre agree to the deception? But I also remember how Deirdre had adored Lucy, how anxious she had been to please her. She had been almost as devoted to Lucy as I had been. I remember all the times I blamed

Deirdre for being ungrateful. *We cleaned up her mess*, I said, again and again, to Lucy. How cool Lucy had been! And that whole trip to the lake and back. She had just given birth. All that blood on the bed—it was hers.

When I think of the blood on the bed I nearly swerve off the curving road and I see that I am clutching the steering wheel so tightly my knuckles are white. I get off at the next exit and pull to the side of the road. When I pry my hands off the steering wheel they are cold and damp and I feel nauseous. I open the car door and throw up on the grassy verge. All that blood. I don't know why it is worse that it was Lucy's not Deirdre's. I guess it's something like the difference between seeing someone else's blood and seeing your own. It explains, I realize, how weak she had been when we'd walked back from the lake.

By the time we got back to the dorm it was snowing so hard we could barely see two feet ahead of us. I begged Lucy to take the path—what would it matter, now, if we met someone?—and she agreed placidly. Halfway back she took my arm and leaned her whole weight on it so I had to struggle to keep us both upright in the driving snow. I didn't know how I'd get her up the stairs to our room, but she held on to the banister and hauled herself up the two flights of stairs.

When I opened the door to our room Deirdre was sitting up on the edge of Lucy's bed facing the door.

328

"You got rid of it?" she asked.

"Yes," Lucy answered.

"What are you going to do about that?" Deirdre pointed toward the single and the bloody bed. I was amazed at Deirdre's tone—as if we were her servants and this was our problem instead of hers. But Lucy seemed unfazed.

"I've got an idea about that." Lucy went over to Deirdre and sat next to her on the bed. They both looked at me and I think that Deirdre finally took in that I was back.

"She knows?" Deirdre asked Lucy.

Lucy took Deirdre's hand. "She won't tell anyone," she said to Deirdre, and then to me, "Jane, your suitcases are still in the lobby. Someone might notice and come up here. Could you bring them up please?" Lucy seemed calm and steady now, and in control. As I turned to leave the room I saw Lucy and Deirdre leaning their heads together, whispering.

I walked back downstairs. Five steps from the bottom I lost my footing and fell the rest of the way down, landing painfully on the base of my spine. I clutched the newel post at the foot of the stairs, leaned my head against the soft wood, and wept noisily for I don't know how long. I kept thinking someone would come—a cleaning lady, the night watchman, Miss Buehl—and I'd have to tell them everything. From my mother dying to the thing we'd put in the lake. I'd tell them everything. It was ridiculous, I realized now, to have gone along with Lucy's plan. We would never be able to explain all that blood. Deirdre would just have to fend for herself. What did I care what happened

to her? I'd tell everyone I had been with Matt so the baby couldn't be his. I'd sacrifice my name for him.

When I finally realized that no one was going to come I pulled myself up and lugged my suitcases back upstairs. The room was empty and the door to the single was closed. Putting my suitcases down next to my bed, I went to the door and put my hand on the knob. Like the outside knob when I first came back, it was warm to the touch. I turned it but something was blocking it.

"Who is it?" Deirdre's voice came to me from behind the closed door. From the direction it came I guessed she was sitting on the floor, her back against the door.

"It's Jane," I called. "Let me in."

I heard something shift along the floor and the door opened as if of its own volition. Deirdre was sitting on the floor, facing the bloody bed. Lucy wasn't in the room. Then I heard her voice behind me.

"OK," she said, brushing past me. Something silver glinted in her hands. "I know what to do, but you both have to promise me not to freak out. Jane'll take me to the infirmary and Deirdre should stay behind and bundle the sheets up. They won't be able to tell exactly how much blood there was."

I looked at Deirdre to see if she understood what Lucy was talking about, but for once she was as much in the dark as I was.

Then we both looked up just as Lucy, sitting in the middle of the bloodied sheets, took a razor to her left wrist and slashed her wrist.

WHEN I HAVE STOPPED SHAKING I DRINK A LITTLE water from the bottle I bought at the last rest stop. I look at the road I have pulled off of and notice a green-and-white sign with a stylized drawing of a figure in a cap and gown. It points to a local college, and even without reading the words beneath the generic picture I realize that I've gotten off at the Poughkeepsie exit and the sign is pointing to Vassar. It's funny, I think, that the sign shows a male figure for what has been, for most of its history, a women's college. Then I think of another picture: the yearbook picture of Hannah Toller and Helen Chambers at the Freshman Formal with the mysterious man off to the side. Hannah Toller had come back from her freshman year at Vassar with a baby. Although she would never tell who the father was, everyone assumed she was the mother. But if she wasn't the mother, who was?

I have been thinking, on the road to Heart Lake, that the answers lie there, because that is where my story began. But now it occurs to me that the story started elsewhere.

I pull onto the road and drive, not back toward the Taconic, but west, toward the river and Vassar.

THE CAMPUS, AS I PASS THROUGH THE ARCHED gateway and drive toward Main Hall, looks even

prettier than I remember it. There is a light dusting of snow on the ground and icicles hang from the row of pines flanking the drive. The winter sun warms the bricks of Main and sets fire to the green patina of the mansard roof. There is a certain clarity of light here that I instantly remember even though it has been over fifteen years since I saw the campus. I have not been back since I graduated, not for my fifth reunion, not for my tenth or fifteenth. It had always seemed pointless; I had made no friends at Vassar. And when I thought of the questions people asked at reunions, I knew I did not have the kind of life that would translate easily into polite cocktail banter at the reunion banquet.

I park my car in front of Main and get out. I notice instantly how still and quiet everything is—it is still winter break here. I am glad, as I walk toward the library, that I am unlikely to meet any of my old teachers. It occurs to me, though, that for the first time since I graduated it might not be so hard to answer the inevitable questions. True, teaching Latin at a private girls' school is no one's pinnacle of success and Heart Lake isn't exactly Exeter or Choate, still, it used to be considered rather good, and not everyone would know of its slow slide into second-rate.

I pass under the giant London plane tree that spreads its dappled boughs before the library's gothic facade. I remember the feeling of peace I had, each evening after dinner, walking beneath the ancient tree and through the

arched doorway of the library. After the tumult of high school, the years I spent behind these gray stone walls, toiling away at Latin translations like some medieval monk, had seemed like a cool balm applied to a feverish forehead.

The girl behind the main desk is young, probably a financial aid student working over the break to make her tuition. It's what I used to do. I almost think to tell her that, but I am enjoying the silence of the library too much. I ask her, briefly, where I can find the old yearbooks and she directs me to a room that contains not only yearbooks but the college's archives.

I take down the 1963 yearbook and slowly leaf through the pages. I look for Helen Chambers's picture in the seniors' photographs, but I can't find it. It seems unlike *Domina* Chambers, with her love of tradition and adherence to form, not to have posed for her yearbook picture. I have to go through the book twice to find the picture of the Freshman Formal. Then I find it toward the end of the book, between the lacrosse team and a candid picture of the bridge club. "Freshman Formal," the caption reads, "Helen Liddell Chambers '63 and Hannah Corey Toller." There is no year following Hannah Toller's name. In this book where every name is followed by those two digits, the final mark of belonging, their absence seems like a brand. The girl who dropped out after freshman year because she had a baby out of wedlock. That's how her

classmates would have remembered her. But that wasn't what happened. She had taken the blame for someone else.

I look closely at the picture. I remember thinking that the handsome blond boy on the edge of the picture smiling at the girls—why had I thought he was smiling at Hannah?—looked like Lucy. How blind had I been not to notice the resemblance? It's Helen Chambers, young, her pale swept-up hair shining like a swan's wing, who looks like Lucy. Like mother like daughter, I think. Just as Lucy pretended that Deirdre had been the one to give birth to that baby, so Helen Chambers had let her friend assume the shame of an out-of-wedlock baby. It explains, of course, all the extra attention Helen Chambers had lavished on Lucy. No wonder *Domina* Chambers had been so horrified the night Lucy cut her wrists.

I PRACTICALLY HAD TO CARRY LUCY TO THE INFIRmary. Even though Deirdre had wrapped her wrist in a thick linen napkin, blood splattered the snow at our feet. When I looked behind us, though, I saw that the drops of blood were already covered by the fast-falling snow.

When we reached the infirmary we found the door locked and a 3 x 5 card taped to the window. "HOLIDAY HOURS: 9 A.M. TO 4 P.M. FOR EMERGENCY CALL THE CORINTH FIRE DEPARTMENT."

Lucy was leaning against the wall of the building while I read the card to her. When I fin-

ished she slid down the wall and wrapped her arms around her knees. Her jeans were already damp from the snow, but I thought I saw a new stain spread over her left knee where her wrist lay against the cloth.

"We'll have to go back and call an ambulance," I told her.

"I can't walk anymore," she said. "I'm too tired. You go back and call. I'll wait here."

"I can't leave you here, Lucy, you'll freeze to death."

She didn't answer me. Her eyes were closed and she seemed to have fallen asleep. I looked out into the snow, spinning in a cone of light from the porch lamp. At least Lucy was out of the snow here. Maybe I should go back to the dorm and call from there.

I took off my coat and laid it over Lucy. When I stepped off the covered porch and out of the lamplight I was immediately enveloped in a world of spinning snow. I could barely make out where the path split off to go back to the dorm. I couldn't even tell if I was on a path, let alone if I was on the right one. I walked for several minutes when I realized I was no longer walking on a dirt path covered by snow, but over rocks sheeted with ice. I stopped and slowly turned in a circle and realized I had lost all sense of direction. I must have missed the path leading back to the dorm, but then where was I? Under the sounds of wind and snow falling I heard another sound—a creaking noise, like a door opening. I moved toward it and lost my footing on the ice.

When I stopped sliding headlong down the

curved surface of the rock I was looking down into a void of swirling snow. The creaking sound was directly below me now, but still far away. I stared into the glittering whirlpool below me and it was like looking into deep water when you opened your eyes and looked into the deepest part of the lake and saw the drifting silt lit up by the sun shining through the water. I was on the Point hanging over the edge of the cliff. The creaking sound I'd heard was new ice cracking in the wind.

I tried crawling backwards from the edge but when I lifted myself to my knees I slid forward a few more inches. I took off my mittens and felt around me for the deep cracks in the rock I knew were there. Chattermarks, Miss Buehl had called them, left by a retreating glacier. When I found one deep enough I dug my fingers into it and pulled myself around so I was facing away from the lake. I only moved forward when I found a crack deep enough to use as a handhold. By the time I'd worked my way up to level rock, my fingernails were broken and bloody and I'd realized I'd left my mittens behind. I crawled over the rock face, not daring to stand until I'd gotten to the woods.

I stood up and realized that I still had no idea how to get back to the dorm or how long it had been since I'd left Lucy. She could have bled to death by now. Even if I found the dorm it would take too long for an ambulance to get here. I stood in the falling snow and thought about the icy plunge from the Point to the lake.

Then I noticed a light shining through the woods. At first I thought it was the infirmary porch

light and I was amazed at how little distance I had traveled, but then I remembered the nights we had sneaked over the Point to avoid Miss Buehl's cottage. Could it be Miss Buehl's light? And was it possible she was in her cottage? I knew she stayed for part of the break. Also, I remembered that before she'd become a science teacher she'd been a nurse. She helped out, sometimes, when the infirmary was understaffed. She'd know what to do for Lucy.

I headed straight for the light even though it meant walking through the deeper snow in the woods. I didn't take my eyes off the light until I reached the cottage and started beating the door with my frozen, bloody hands. When the door opened I couldn't see who opened it because burning spots blurred my vision.

Someone pulled me inside and rubbed my hands. I was pushed into a chair and wrapped in a blanket. I closed my eyes and tried to get rid of the light spots dancing in front of my eyes. I was sure the afterimage of Miss Buehl's porch light would be seared into my retinas forever.

When I opened my eyes, though, I could see perfectly. Miss Buehl was holding a towel around my hands and behind her Domina Chambers was offering me a steaming tea cup.

"Drink this before you try to talk," Miss Buehl said, taking the cup from Domina Chambers.

I looked around the room and took in the cozy scene I'd stumbled upon. A fire in the fireplace, a teapot and cups on a low table, classical music on the radio. Both women in sturdy corduroys and ski sweaters.

"It's no night to be out, Jane," Miss Buehl said in the same scolding tone she used when we played around with her Bunsen burners. "Miss Chambers has been over all day working on the advanced placement curriculum and we were waiting for the storm to pass so she could go back..."

"Lucy," I said, interrupting Miss Buehl.

"What about Lucy?" Domina Chambers knelt down next to me and hot tea from her teacup splashed my already soaked jeans.

"She's at the infirmary. Bleeding." For a moment I couldn't remember the story we'd concocted. I was confused by the other blood I'd seen that day. Birth blood.

"She slit her wrists," I finally said.

"Lucy? No, I don't believe it." Domina Chambers gave me the very same look she gave me when I mistranslated my Latin homework, but Miss Buehl took me at my word. She was already pulling on boots and a coat.

"I've got the key to the infirmary in my book bag, Helen, would you get it for me?"

"But this is absurd, Celeste," Domina Chambers said, rising to her feet, "this child is hysterical."

"Hysterical or not, something is obviously wrong and if Lucy Toller is out in this storm— bleeding or not—we'd better find her."

Domina Chambers opened her mouth as if to argue, but at another look from Miss Buehl she clamped her mouth into a tight line and turned on her heel. I heard her rummaging around in the other room muttering under her breath. I'd never seen Domina Chambers so cowed by anyone.

I thought I'd had enough surprises for one night, but then a small figure appeared in the doorway of the room Domina Chambers had gone into.

"Oh, Albie," Miss Buehl said, "I'd forgotten all about you. You'll have to come, too. Go get dressed in your warmest things." She turned to me. "Albie's grandmother dropped her off a little early from break," she said, and then, lowering her voice, "She must have gotten the dates mixed up."

I thought to tell Albie that my father made the same mistake, that we had that in common, but she'd already gone back in the other room, slamming the door behind her.

BEFORE I LEAVE, I ASK THE GIRL BEHIND THE DESK— she's yawning over a copy of Dante's *Purgatorio*—if the library has a copy of the Vassar alumnae directory. She puts down her copy without bothering to save her place and slips out from behind the desk. Following her, I notice she's wearing sandals and thick white gym socks. The socks have holes at the heels. I can see her bare, unshaven calves between the hem of her skirt and the tops of her socks. I imagine how cold she'll be walking home tonight. It makes me think of my students, Athena especially, and I am, for the first time, really anxious to be back at Heart Lake.

She asks what year I'm looking for and when I tell her 1963 she gives me a scrutinizing look.

"You don't look that old," she says.

I laugh. "I certainly hope not. I was class of '81." I realize as I say it how glad I am to have those digits to name. Unlike Hannah Toller. "No, I'm looking for a friend...for a friend's mother."

"Oh," she says without interest. She pads back to her desk and picks up Dante at any old place and yawns into the book.

I run my finger down the list of names. Most of the names, I see, are in bold type followed by another name in lighter typeface. The names in bold are maiden names, the ones following are married names.

When I get to Helen Chambers's I see it, too, is in bold. So Helen Chambers got married after she left Heart Lake. I'm surprised but also somehow relieved. *Watch out you don't turn out like Helen Chambers,* Dr. Lockhart had said to me. Well, maybe she didn't turn out so bad after all. Maybe there was a life for her after Heart Lake.

But then I see that the record keepers have made a mistake. The name following Chambers in light typeface is Liddell. Someone must have mistaken her middle name for a married name. I pull my finger across the page to locate her address, but instead my finger comes to rest on a single word: deceased. It is followed by the date May 1, 1981. She died only four years after leaving Heart Lake. Dr. Lockhart was right after all. Helen Chambers had ended badly.

Chapter Twenty-six

●

WHILE WALKING TO MY CAR I NOTICE THE GIRL from the library leaving the building. She is wearing a light denim jacket and carrying a heavy backpack. I offer her a lift back to her dorm and she tells me she lives in the student housing across Raymond Avenue. I remember the complex is a good mile's walk from campus and again I urge her to take a lift from me. I see her assess me and decide I'm probably not dangerous—after all, I'm Jane Hudson '81. She is quiet, though, in the car. I ask who she's reading the Dante for and she names a medieval history professor I had junior year.

"When you do your term paper include a map of Dante's underworld and compare it to a map of Virgil's underworld," I tell her. "He loves that kind of thing—the geography of imaginary places—I think there's even some name for it..."

"Really? Thanks, I'll remember that."

Then she gets out of the car and runs quickly up the steps of the dilapidated housing complex. I remember that these units had been built as temporary housing five years before I came here. They were already falling apart then. I

341

wait until she's inside and I see the lights go on, and then I drive back to the main road and, from there, to the Taconic.

I am sorry, after a few miles, that I didn't take the better lit and straighter Thruway. The road is icy, especially on the curves. Each time the back of my car fishtails on the slippery road my stomach lurches. I keep thinking about the astounding coincidence of Helen Chambers and Lucy Toller both pretending their babies belonged to someone else. Is it just coincidence though? I think of the two of them. Both beautiful with the kind of rarefied beauty of a fairy-tale princess. It was more than their beauty though; it was a certain look they each had of possessing some secret charm. They inspired, in others, not only admiration but the desire to please and emulate. I'll never know what Lucy said to Deirdre to convince her to let me think the baby was hers, but I can imagine the way Lucy looked when she asked. And I realize that if Lucy had asked me to say the baby was mine I would have. And it wasn't just me and Deirdre who idealized Lucy. There was that younger girl, Albie. I remember how mad she was at me when we went back to the infirmary and found Lucy nearly half dead on the steps.

WE FOUND LUCY CURLED IN A BALL ON THE INFIRmary doorstep, like a cat locked out in the cold. It broke my heart to think how long it had taken me to bring her help.

"I'm sorry I was so long," I told her, but she didn't wake up.

"How could you leave her here?" The voice at my ear was so low I thought it was my own conscience, but it wasn't, it was Albie.

"I had to go find help," I tried to explain, but Albie shook her head.

"You left her to die," she hissed at me, leaning close so Miss Buehl and Domina Chambers couldn't hear, so close that I felt her hot spit prick my skin.

I watched in silence as Domina Chambers picked her up while Miss Buehl unlocked the door. What could I say? Maybe Albie was right. I should have stopped Lucy from cutting herself. I should have come back sooner. I should never have left.

Inside the infirmary, Albie switched on the light and ran to get the things Miss Buehl asked for. She seemed to know her way around. Everyone seemed to have something to do but me, so I sat down on the extra bed across from where they put Lucy and watched. They went to work quickly, peeling away the cotton cloth from Lucy's wrists, getting her out of her wet clothes, taking her blood pressure.

"She's stopped bleeding," Miss Buehl reported. "Thank God she didn't sever the arteries."

"But doesn't she need stitches?" Domina Chambers asked.

"Yes, but I can do that. Don't worry, Helen, I've done it before. What I'm worried about is her blood pressure. It's quite low. Do you have any idea how much blood she lost, Jane? Had she been bleeding long when you found her?"

343

I shook my head. I thought of the blood on the sheets, but remembered that wasn't Lucy's blood.

"We found her right away," I said, trying to remember the story we'd agreed upon. "She went into Deirdre's single and we heard her crying so we went in." I had heard crying, I remembered, but when Lucy had opened the door her eyes had been dry.

"We?" Miss Buehl asked.

I pushed away the memory of what really happened and concentrated on what we'd agreed upon. "Yes, me and Deirdre Hall."

"Well, then, where is Miss Hall?" Domina Chambers asked.

"She stayed in the dorm." I realized now that this was a weak spot in our story. Why had Deirdre remained behind? I knew the real reason— to dispose of the bloody sheets—but what reason had we agreed upon?

"Um, she was so upset and the blood was on her bed, so she stayed behind to clean it up."

Domina *Chambers clicked her tongue and shook her head. "Imagine thinking about such a thing while your roommate is bleeding to death. There's something very off about that girl. At least you had more sense, Jane."*

I smiled at the rare compliment even though I knew it wasn't fair to Deirdre, and caught Albie glaring at me again. It was almost as if she knew that Lucy had told Deirdre to stay behind to get rid of the sheets.

"So there must have been quite a bit of blood," Miss Buehl said. She was bending over Lucy, peeling back her eyelids and listening to the pulse

at her throat. "I wish we could get her to the hospital for a transfusion but I'm afraid that will be impossible in this storm. The phone lines have been down and the roads closed for hours."

"Is there anything else we can do, Celeste?" Domina Chambers asked. I noticed she was shaking and thought it was probably from the cold, and yet the room felt quite hot to me. "Will she be all right?"

"I'll give her a saline drip to get some fluids in her. That should help her blood pressure. Otherwise, we'll just have to wait. I'd feel better if she regained consciousness." Miss Buehl shook Lucy's shoulder and called her name. "Maybe you should try, Jane, you're her best friend."

I got up off the bed and walked across the room. It seemed like a long way. I noticed that the floor was slanting. I knelt down by Lucy and called her name. Amazingly, she opened her eyes.

"Jane," she said.

"It's OK. Lucy, we're in the infirmary."

"You'll stay here?" she whispered to me. "Don't go back to the dorm."

I was so touched that she wanted me to stay that my eyes filled with tears and the room went all blurry. Then it went black.

I'D BEEN TOUCHED WHEN LUCY HAD ASKED ME TO stay at the infirmary, but of course the real reason, I realize now, is that she didn't want me to talk to Deirdre. She had to make sure Deirdre went along with the plan to pretend that the baby was really hers.

It is one thing, though, to assume the parentage of a baby lost in childbirth, and another to drop out of college and raise someone else's baby. As I make the trip from Vassar to Corinth, less than 150 miles but worlds apart, the person I think more about is Hannah Corey Toller, class of —. Class of Nothing. Why had she agreed to take Helen's baby, return in shame to her hometown and raise a child not her own?

It's this question that plagues me as I drive slowly down River Street looking at the big Victorian houses set back on their snow-covered lawns. Most still have their Christmas lights up and the colored bulbs spill jewel-like pools onto the sparkling snow crust. At the end of the street I pull up opposite the gatehouse on the intersection of Lake Drive and River Street and turn off the car so as not to draw attention to myself. Really, though, I needn't be so cautious; it doesn't look as if anyone is in the old Toller house. Not only are there no Christmas lights, but there are no other lights on in the house. The house has a general air of neglect—the driveway hasn't been plowed since the last snow and one of the shutters has come loose from its hinges and hangs from the window askew. I remember that I used to think the house looked like Snow White's cottage, but now I think it looks more like the witch's house in "Hansel and Gretel."

I wonder if anyone has lived in it since Cliff and Hannah Toller died in that car accident. It happened my last year in college and

I read about it in an Albany newspaper. They had been driving back from Plattsburgh when a freakish May snowstorm swept across the Adirondacks. Their car was found at the bottom of a deep ravine. The newspaper made a big deal out of the fact that, like their children, the Tollers had died together. DOUBLE DISASTER STRIKES TWICE FOR ADIRONDACK COUPLE, the headline read.

I remember feeling unsurprised at the Tollers' fate. It was harder to imagine the two of them going on after losing both their children.

But only one of them was their child.

I wonder if at the end they thought of Lucy as an interloper—the changeling who dragged their own child to his death.

Just as I put my hand on the ignition key I see a light come on in the house and a figure pass behind a curtained window. It comes so hard upon my thinking of Lucy as some fiendish demon that the sight strikes me as a reproach—and indeed, there is something in the profile silhouetted in the top floor window that reminds me of Lucy. I feel that rush of cold and inability to breathe that marked the panic attacks I experienced in my twenties. I turn on the car and put the heater on high, but the cold persists and now I am sweating as well. I'm too afraid to drive like this. I look at the house again to reassure myself that the figure in the window is not Lucy, but the window is dark again. Instead, a rectangle of light appears in the doorway and a woman steps out into the

deep, unshoveled snow and walks straight for my car. She taps on my window before I fully take in that it's Dr. Lockhart.

"So you decided to come back," she says when I lower the window. "Better to face your demons, eh?"

I wonder what demons she is referring to, but I am determined, for once, not to let her control the direction of the conversation.

"What are you doing in the Toller house?" I ask.

Dr. Lockhart smiles. "It's not the Toller house anymore, Jane. This is where I live."

"You live here? But..."

"Where did you think I lived, Jane? In one of those cozy little apartments in the mansion? I don't think so. In my profession it's very important to maintain a distance. And I like my privacy. These boarding schools can be such fishbowls. Fascinating to study as cultural microcosms, but such parochial bores to live in twenty-four hours a day. Doesn't it get to you sometimes, being *watched* all the time?"

I hadn't thought of myself as so visible, but when I think of the events of the last semester I realize that I have felt *observed*.

"From whom did you buy the house?" I ask, if only to steer the conversation away from last semester. She straightens up and glances back at the house. I can tell she is surprised by the question.

"From the estate. The house was empty for many years..." She trails off and I decide

to pursue the subject if only because I've never seen her look this uncomfortable.

"Since the Tollers died? Maybe people thought it was an unlucky house, everyone who lived there is dead now."

"I'm not superstitious, Jane. People make their own fates. Believing this house is unlucky is like...like believing in the three sisters legend. It's the superstition that causes the problem. If Melissa Randall hadn't read about the three sisters legend in your journal she might still be alive today."

There is a note of triumph in her last comment. Finally, she has brought our conversation to where she wants it. I can't avoid talking about the events of last semester now.

"I told you and Dean Buehl that someone had my journal. What else was I supposed to do?" I ask.

"You should have told us what was in your journal: sex with masked strangers, sacrificial rites, a dead baby in a tea tin..."

"I take your point, Dr. Lockhart. Yes, I should have told someone, but it was a rather unusual circumstance. What would you think if pieces from your old journal started appearing on your desk?"

"I wouldn't know because I've never kept a journal. I would never be so foolish to commit such incriminating evidence, if I had ever done such things, to writing." I can believe it. She doesn't look like she'd give anything away.

"Well, I'll certainly be more careful in the

future. Now I'd better get back to campus. I want to see if Athena and Vesta are back yet."

"If you mean Ellen and Sandy, they're both back. Perhaps you ought to consider dropping the goddess names. Didn't your old Latin teacher use Roman names like Lucia and Clementia?"

Is it just coincidence she picked my old Latin name and Lucy's? Is it something else she gleaned from my old journal?

"Yes, but I can't see what harm there is in the girls keeping their names. Doesn't it just make a bigger thing out of it?"

"Miss Hudson, one of our students is dead. How much bigger do you want it to be?"

"All right. I'll suggest they take other names. Look, can I give you a lift back to campus?" I try to make my voice conciliatory. The last thing I want is this woman for an enemy.

"No thanks, I'm going skating." She turns her right side to me so I can see a pair of worn ice skates with decorative stitching hanging over her shoulder. "There's a shortcut through the woods behind my house. I can skate straight across the lake to the school."

"Be careful," I tell her. "There's a weak spot in the ice near the mouth of the Schwanenkill."

"Don't worry, Jane," she says, smiling, "I know where all the weak spots are."

I TAKE LAKE DRIVE AROUND THE EAST SIDE OF THE lake. Through the pines lining the drive I

350

catch glimpses of the frozen lake, shimmering under a full moon. Dr. Lockhart has picked a beautiful night to skate. I believe her when she says she is not superstitious. It's hard to imagine, otherwise, how she could bear to be alone on that ice at night. I don't think it's something I could do.

I turn off Lake Drive and park in the faculty parking lot. I'll have to haul my suitcase up the long path to my house without a light—of course I hadn't thought to leave any light on in the house when I left. Two weeks ago I hadn't even been sure I'd be coming back. It occurs to me it might be better to go up to the house first and turn on some lights before trying to navigate the path with a heavy suitcase.

I look in my glove compartment and find a flashlight, but the batteries are burned out. I resign myself to finding my way in the dark, the moon is full so it shouldn't be too bad, but when I get out of my car I notice the path on the opposite end of the parking lot, the one to the dorm, is ablaze with light. Dean Buehl must have had extra lighting installed after Melissa Randall's death to reassure worried parents—although how extra lighting is supposed to prevent girls from taking their own lives, I do not know.

I decide I'll go to the dorm first. It'll give me a chance to visit with Athena and Vesta before it gets too late. Maybe the dorm matron will have an extra flashlight to lend me. As I walk up the well-shoveled (Dean Buehl must

have had to call in a plow to clear the paths enough to install the lights) and well-lit path I realize that all my prevarication about going up the unlit path to the cottage amounts to one thing: I'm not ready to be alone in that house yet.

The dorm matron has a plentiful supply of flashlights and she is happy to give me one as long as I sign it out. She also has me "sign in" to the dorm and leave a photo ID. I notice, as I walk up to the second floor, hand-lettered signs posted exhorting students to travel in pairs and flyers for community counseling groups. I think I recognize Gwen Marsh's hand-writing. The thought that poor Gwen has spent her Christmas holiday making up flyers, with carpal tunnel syndrome no less, and planning how to help the girls cope with returning after the trauma of Melissa Randall's death, suddenly makes me feel guilty and self-absorbed. It makes my two weeks at the Aquadome seem like a luxury vacation by comparison.

The second floor is quiet except for the hissing of the steam radiators. One of the flyers advertises a "Welcome Back Sing" for tonight and I'm afraid that Athena and Vesta will be there, but when I knock on their door I hear the familiar shuffle and window shut-ting that tells me they are in, and they haven't given up smoking over the break.

Vesta unlocks and opens the door, but only a few inches. When she sees it's me she scrunches her eyebrows together suspiciously

and reluctantly opens the door the rest of the way.

"Sandy," I say, determined to avoid the girls' classical names as per Dr. Lockhart's suggestion, "nice to see you. How was your break?"

Vesta shrugs and sits down on the bed underneath the window. Athena turns around in her chair and smiles at me. I notice right away that her face looks less drawn and, somehow, more open. I can't quite put my finger on it, but she looks healthier. The two weeks away from Heart Lake have done her good.

"*Salve, Magistra,*" she says, "*quid agis?*"

"*Bene,*" I say, "*et tu,* Ellen?"

"Ellen? Why aren't you calling me Athena?"

I shift uncomfortably from foot to foot. The room is hot and damp.

"Here," Athena says, getting up from her chair and seating herself cross-legged on the floor, "take off your coat and sit down. They keep it like a sauna in here."

I sit down at my old desk. Now that Athena is sitting beneath me I can see one thing that's different about her. She's let the dye grow out of her hair. I can see several inches of her natural color—a light mousy brown—showing at the roots. I scan her books and realize that I'm still looking for the black-and-white notebook. I see instead Wheelock's Latin grammar and a paperback copy of *Franny and Zooey*. "I read this when I was your age," I say.

"You didn't answer the question," Vesta says.

"Why have you dropped our Latin class names?"

"Dr. Lockhart thinks the goddess names might not be appropriate..."

Vesta snorts. "The names are the best part," she says. "I always hated *Sandy*. My real name is Alexandria, which is even worse. If you stop calling me Vesta, I'll drop Latin."

"Yeah," Athena chimes in, "I've always hated 'Ellen.' "

"OK, *Athena*," I say, "and *Vesta*, I can't have you all dropping out of Latin."

Immediately I notice a change come over the girls. They seem more serious and somehow embarrassed.

"A bunch of girls have," Athena says. "Some of the parents didn't want their kids in the class after what happened to Melissa."

"Yeah, there's this rumor we were sacrificing babies and stuff."

I look at Vesta when she says "babies" but she doesn't seem to attach any significance to the example she's chosen. Dean Buehl said that no one was told what was found in the tea tin. But then if Melissa had my journal, she might have shared its contents with her roommates.

"It's our fault," Athena says. "If we hadn't started that stuff with the three sisters and making offerings to the Lake Goddess none of it would have happened."

"Who thought of that?" I ask. "Going out to the rocks and offering prayers to the Lake Goddess?"

Athena and Vesta look at each other and

shrug. "I don't know. We all kind of did. I guess Melissa got into it the most because she was worried about Brian." I remember the night I watched the three girls at the stones. Melissa had asked for loyalty from her boyfriend, Vesta for good grades, but I hadn't been able to hear what Athena asked for. I find myself wondering now what it was she asked for and whether she has gotten what she wished for.

"Did you notice that Melissa had a black-and-white notebook?" I ask.

"Like this?" Athena opens a desk drawer by my feet and takes out a marbled notebook. I see that the name written on the white box on the cover is "Ellen (Athena) Craven."

"Yes," I say, "something like that."

Athena shakes her head, but Vesta is looking at me strangely.

"Why do you want to know?"

I see that I have wound myself into a trap with my own questions. If the girls really don't know that Melissa had my old journal (and Athena, at least, seems innocent) I certainly don't want to tell them.

"I just thought that if she kept a journal," I say with feigned casualness, "we'd understand more about what happened to Melissa."

Vesta looks unconvinced. "You think she wrote down why she drugged Athena and slit her wrists?" Vesta points at Athena's wrists and Athena tugs at the cuffs of her sweater even though they already reach down to her knuckles. I notice that the cuffs are frayed and unraveling, as if they'd been plucked at again and

again. "Jesus," Vesta says, "who would be stupid enough to write down all that stuff?"

I MAKE AN EXCUSE TO LEAVE BEFORE VESTA CAN ASK me any more questions about the journal. I realize as I leave their room that I've made a tactical error visiting the girls before talking to Dean Buehl and finding out what exactly they were told about Melissa's death. I promise myself that I'll call Dean Buehl as soon as I get into the cottage, but I see that I won't have to. Dean Buehl is waiting for me at the matron's desk.

"Ah, Jane, I saw your name in the sign-in book and thought I'd wait for you."

The matron hands me back my driver's license without looking up at me. I wonder if she called the dean to tell her I was here in the dorm. I wonder if she had been instructed to do so.

"Did you see the note I left on your door?" Dean Buehl asks. "Asking you to call as soon as you got in?"

"I haven't been back to my house yet," I tell her. "I came here first to get a flashlight." I hold up the flashlight as corroborating evidence.

"Ah," Dean Buehl says, nodding. "I remember the path up to that cottage could be tricky. Of course I've walked all these paths so many times I think I could find my way around the campus blindfolded. Let me walk you back to the parking lot and help you with your luggage. We can talk along the way."

356

IN ADDITION TO MY SUITCASES I'VE BROUGHT BACK some boxes of books from the house in Westchester. Although I tell her they can wait until the morning, Dean Buehl cheerfully hoists up two and takes off down the darkened path so quickly I am hard put keeping up with her with my one box. I am reminded of the nature hikes she used to take us on when she was the science teacher—the way she strode through the woods, leaving her students scrambling over rocks and puddles, desperately trying to stay close enough to hear her lecture. We'd be tested on every rock and flower identification, we knew, and inability to keep up was no excuse. "The race goes to the swiftest," was one of her favorite sayings and in her class it was literally true.

Twenty years haven't slowed her down a bit. When I do finally catch up with her I have to stay behind her because this path hasn't been plowed. Fresh snow covers the narrow track that had been shoveled before Christmas break and the sound of our boots crunching in it makes it doubly hard to hear what Dean Buehl is saying. She is talking over her shoulder to me as if I had been right behind her all along and I realize I've already missed half of her "getting me up to date on the Melissa Randall affair" as she calls it. She is tossing out autopsy and DNA findings the way she used to rattle off the names of trees and wildflowers. I gather,

though, that there's nothing I haven't learned already from Roy Corey. Then I hear her refer to "that journal you kept senior year" and I interrupt to ask how many people know about it. "Well, Dr. Lockhart was there when we found it," she tells me. We have reached the door of the cottage, so this I get to hear clearly, "but the only people who have read it are me and that nice young detective. Of course, I told Dr. Lockhart a little about the contents so she could assess their influence on Melissa. It should make an interesting chapter in the book she is writing on teenage suicide."

I am somewhat unnerved by the idea of my journal figuring in Dr. Lockhart's research, but I smile at Dean Buehl in a way that I hope is ingratiating. "Thanks for helping with my stuff. I'll make us some coffee, we can sit and talk..." I gesture toward the old Morris chair by the fireplace, the armrest of which still holds the teacup I drank from the night before I left. I see her follow the sweep of my hand and take in the little living room, the battered, old floral love seat under the window, the coffee table stacked with Latin books and Land's End catalogs and piles of ungraded blue books. The lines of her face, which had looked firm and rosy from the cold air and exertion of our walk, seem to settle downward and her skin pales. I think it is my untidiness, but then I remember that this was once her home. The furniture was here when I moved in and, now that I think of it, is arranged just

as it was that night I stumbled out of the snowstorm and into this room. Only then there was a fire in the fireplace and classical music on the radio and the room shone with a kind of brightness that has now dulled with dust and the usage of uncaring tenants.

She walks out my door and heads in the opposite direction from the parking lot.

"Beautiful night..." I hear her say as she disappears down the path to the Point. "Better to talk out of doors."

I follow her to the Point where she has taken a stance—legs spread apart and arms clasped behind her back, like a general surveying her troops—on the curving rock above the frozen lake.

"Always find this a good place to think," she says as I come up beside her.

"Yes," I say, "the view is beautiful."

She shakes her head impatiently and scuffs at the snow with the heel of her heavy hiking boot like a horse pawing the ground. "Not the view," she says with the weary patience of a teacher used to hearing the wrong answer, "the rock. Right where we're standing was a mile-high glacier. This rock here is so hard it's barely eroded in ten thousand years, but the marks the glacier left are still here. Puts things in perspective."

"Yes," I say, although I am not exactly sure what the perspective is. Is it that human suffering is insignificant in the face of the majesty of nature, or that the scars of the past are still with us and always will be?

"You're embarrassed," she says. Actually, I'm more perplexed at the moment but I nod.

"Because I've read your old journal." Dean Buehl sighs and relaxes her stance a bit so I can see, suddenly, the slight curve in her shoulders and the droop in her once taut figure. "Don't be, it was a great relief to me."

I can no longer pretend to understand what she's talking about. "My journal was a relief to you?" As the words come out I realize I can no longer hide my anger either. First the outpourings of my foolish young heart are appropriated by a hysterical teenage girl, then they are co-opted as a research tool for an ambitious psychologist, and now they are balm to my former teacher and present boss?

"Yes," she says, ignoring the outrage in my voice. She looks down at the rock where she's kicked away the snow. "All these years I've felt it was my fault what happened to Helen. I thought if only I had spoken up at the hearing she might not have been fired and if she hadn't been fired she wouldn't have killed herself..."

"Killed herself? *Domina* Chambers killed herself?" I picture my old Latin teacher—her proud and haughty profile, the way she lifted one eyebrow when a student mistranslated a line of Latin. She is the last person I can imagine taking her own life.

"Yes." Dean Buehl looks away from the rock as if the perspective the rock has offered has vanished and the scars of that distant calamity are fresh again. "Four years after she

was let go. It was a terrible blow for her. For me, too." When she doesn't go on I turn to look at her. The lines in her face stand out starkly in the moonlight, like fault lines that have deepened after a quake and then I realize that the trembling that passes over her face is her trying to keep from crying.

"I even tried to get her a teaching position at a Catholic school up north," she says when she has regained control of her voice. Up north from here? That could only mean St. Eustace. I couldn't blame *Domina* Chambers for turning that down. "Some of the girls from here had gone there after...after the scandal...and I thought she might take an interest in keeping up with them, but she didn't. Instead she went down to Albany and got work as a substitute."

"Really? A substitute? *Domina* Chambers?" This surprises me more than the idea of her killing herself, even as it goes some way to making that idea more plausible.

"You can imagine what she thought of that." Dean Buehl tries to smile, but the effort seems to release that trembling again and she gives it up.

I remember how we treated substitute teachers at Corinth High. I have a sudden picture of *Domina* Chambers standing at a blackboard (she would have been reduced to writing on the board if only to write her name), her elegant black dress besmirched with yellow chalk, the silver hair coming undone from its intricate twist.

"When I heard she had killed herself I thought it was because of how she had come down in the world and perhaps I could have made a difference. And then, our relationship didn't help at the hearing..."

Dean Buehl's voice hoarsens and trails off. There's a final shudder and then her face gleams in the moonlight, her emotions so naked and exposed that I have to make an effort not to look away. "You mean you and Miss Chambers..." My words sound childish and prurient even to myself. I remember Deirdre Hall's salacious conjectures about Miss Buehl and *Domina* Chambers. I remember again the cottage the night of the snowstorm, the fire and the teapot and the classical music.... What was it she had said? That they had been working on some curriculum project together?

"*Domina* Chambers was staying at your cottage," I say.

Dean Buehl nods. "She spent every break at the cottage. It was the only time we really had to ourselves, but then that girl showed up and we had to pretend that Helen had come by to work on the AP curriculum. We had to make up a story. Do you know what it felt like? Having to pretend—like schoolgirls caught breaking curfew?"

I remember the tangle of lies I'd been caught in and nod—yes, I know what she means—but she doesn't notice; she's lost in the past.

"We had to pretend even when we knew they all knew. We knew what you girls whispered about us behind our backs and the stories

362

our so-called colleagues carried back to the board. I knew that was why they were so hard on her at the inquest, but I was afraid that if I spoke in her defense I would be fired, too. I've been so ashamed...all these years...not for what we were but that I denied it. And it wasn't just Helen who was hurt. The girls who had to leave the school because of the scandal... I felt such a responsibility for them. It's why I took the dean's job even though it was like taking over a sinking ship...." She breaks off and I look away while she struggles to get her voice under control. On the lake I see a black speck circling on the white ice. I think it's a bird but then realize it's a skater. Dr. Lockhart, no doubt.

"It wouldn't have made a difference," I say, "even if you had spoken at the hearing..."

Dean Buehl waves her hand at me impatiently. "It's not just that," she says. "You see, it was my fault Lucy found out that Helen was her mother, and I always thought that must have been what Matt and Lucy were fighting about when they went through the ice."

I look away from the skater and back at Dean Buehl. "You knew that Lucy was Helen's daughter?"

She smiles at me. Finally, I am the student with the right answer. "You guessed, too. You always were smarter than people gave you credit for, Jane."

I wonder what people.

"Of course Helen told me. We told each other everything. And it explained so much. The way

Helen missed her freshman spring semester at Vassar...oh, I was at Smith," she fills in hurriedly when she sees my perplexed look, "but I wrote to Helen often. I remember her writing that she had to go nurse a sick relative. It sounded very odd at the time. Of course I realized later she must have had the baby then and given it to Hannah...."

"Why did Hannah Toller go along with it?" I ask.

Dean Buehl stares at me as if I had interrupted her lecture on cell division to ask a question about thermodynamics.

"Well, Hannah adored her of course. From the ninth grade on. The only reason Hannah even went to Vassar was to be near Helen...." I detect a note of jealousy in her voice that she shakes off like a dog shaking off cold water. "Helen said she had first planned to give the baby up for adoption and it was Hannah's idea to say the baby was hers. She wasn't really cut out for college life, and there was a boy from back home who would marry her in a heartbeat. It made so much more sense for Hannah to give up college than for Helen, who had such promise...."

"Then why did she come back here?"

Dean Buehl looks down at the rock as if the answer were in the glacial inscriptions.

"She missed the girl. She wanted to be closer to her. I told her she might as well tell the girl she was her mother."

"When did she tell her?"

"In February. A week before she died."

I remember the day Lucy came back from tea with *Domina* Chambers and wrote Matt that letter. She told Matt that Helen had told her something that changed everything.

"That's why she wrote Matt and asked him to come," I said. "She was going to tell him they weren't brother and sister." *Only she had never gotten the chance.*

"Of course I had no idea what disgusting things they had been up to. All of you cavorting around the campus like a pack of wild dogs and right on my doorstep." Dean Buehl flings a hand in the direction of the cottage so abruptly she nearly hits me. I step back and, for a moment, lose my balance on the snow-covered rock. She grabs me by the arm before I can fall. We're quite a way from the edge, but still I feel that queasy sensation of vertigo, like when you stand on the beach and feel the tide sucking the sand out from under your feet. Dean Buehl must also be aware of the precipitous drop not so far away, because she does not release her grip on my arm right away. I can feel her strong fingers digging painfully into my forearm. I look at her face and see that the tears are gone and that look of naked grief I'd glimpsed a moment earlier has hardened into something else, something I find harder to read.

"But when I read your journal, Jane, I realized it wasn't all my fault. I may have been responsible for Lucy learning who her mother was, but you must have let on to Matt about the baby, didn't you? That's what happened out there on the ice, isn't it?"

I nod, amazed she has put together so much from that last journal entry. I had written, "Tonight I will go down to the lake to meet him and I'll tell him everything." I think of what I had written next and blush to think of Dean Buehl reading that very last line.

"I didn't tell him the baby was Lucy's and his. I didn't know that."

"But you told him enough so he guessed."

"Yes," I agree limply. If not for Dean Buehl's grip on my arm I might sink down to the cold rock.

"It was my fault," I say. *Mea culpa,* I say to myself, *mea culpa.* This is what Roy Corey had been talking about. Taking responsibility for the sins of the past.

"And that's what they were arguing about when Lucy ran out onto the ice." I nod weakly. "At the inquest you said they were arguing about Helen, but that wasn't it? Unless Lucy told Matt what Helen had told her...that she and Matt weren't brother and sister..."

"No," I say, "she never got the chance."

"So you lied at the inquest." I expect now that she will shake me, even hurl me from her, but instead she relaxes her grip on my arm and smiles at me. I've told her what she wanted to hear. I've cleansed her of sin. I can see the weight of it, lifting from her, the burden of all the guilt and shame she's carried with her all these years. She's shed it like the layer of dust the sculptor's chisel leaves and now her face is as smooth and firm and pale as marble in the moonlight. "Well, dear, don't be too hard

on yourself. The thing to do now is put the past behind you. That's what I'm going to do. I've made what amends I could and now I'm going to put the whole thing behind me. Can you do that, Jane?"

I almost laugh. Now that she's shifted the blame from herself to me she tells me to forget. But I nod to let her know I'll try.

Then she turns on her heel and leaves abruptly, that fast stride taking her into the woods and out of sight before I realize that she is leaving.

I stand for a few moments trying to collect my thoughts, but all I hear is Dean Buehl's advice to me. Forget the past, forget the past. For the moment the words seem to block out any thought, but can I really do it? Can I forget the past? Do I even want to?

I look at the skater on the lake. It must be Dr. Lockhart, but it's hard to connect the stiff and forbidding psychologist with this ethereal figure dancing on the ice. She skates over the ice like a black swan on white water. So effortless do her movements seem I am reminded of those magnetized skaters on the ornamental ponds that decorate shop windows at Christmas time. The ones with little plastic figures that turn in the same magnetized grooves over and over again. It seems that the loops Dr. Lockhart inscribes on the lake follow some pattern, too, so that if I could see the lines her skates cut in the ice some intricate mandala would be revealed.

It reminds me of a dream I've been having

lately. In the dream I am skating on the lake, as beautifully and skillfully as Dr. Lockhart is now skating. I feel, in the dream, finally free of the past, but when I look back from the shore I see I've cut a pattern in the ice and the pattern is Matt Toller's face. As I watch his face sink into the black water I can clearly read his expression. He is disappointed in me. I can't hear the words his lips are forming, but I know what he is saying. *You'd pull me out, wouldn't you, Jane?*

I suppose this is the sort of thing Dean Buehl would say is best left forgotten. Yet as painful as it is to see that look in Matt's face every night in my dreams, it's far more unbearable to think of never seeing his face again at all.

Chapter Twenty-seven

I FIND, IN THE NEXT FEW WEEKS, THAT IT IS EASIER to follow Dean Buehl's injunction to forget the past than I would have imagined. My own unpreparedness comes, blessedly, to the rescue. Since I hadn't quite believed I'd be back at Heart Lake, I didn't spend my break getting ready for the next semester. It was a sort of hedge, I realize now, against the possi-

bility of being fired. It makes me realize how much I was afraid of being *let go* (my predecessor's fate) and how glad, after all is said and done, I am to be back, even though I miss Olivia so much I feel physically ill. Again, it's a blessing of sorts to be so busy. And when I make the drive down to Westchester she seems happy enough. Happy with her father, happy with the young college girl who watches her during the week, happy to see me when I come down every other weekend. It's only when Sunday comes and I have to say good-bye that she seems to fall apart a little. When I get back to the campus on those Sunday nights I throw myself into translating to catch up on the time I've lost.

Because even though my classes are smaller, I have to scramble to prepare translations. Often I am only one step ahead of my students in the reading and occasionally I have to sight read second year's Catullus and third year's Ovid. I can't take that chance with fourth year's Virgil, though. For one thing the class is now so small (besides Athena and Vesta it's just Octavia and Flavia, who are too worried about their classics scholarships to quit the class) that I have to shoulder at least an equal load of translating or we'll never get Rome founded before the end of the year. For another thing, the Latin has gotten harder. As we approach Book Six of the *Aeneid*, I find myself dreading the visit to the underworld. I remember that even *Domina* Chambers admitted that certain passages were almost untranslatable. It was as if,

she told us, the syntax becomes as twisting as the minotaur's maze that is carved on the Sibyl's gates through which Aeneas must pass before his visit to the underworld.

I tell my advanced girls they won't be tested on the really hard parts.

"Why did he make it so hard?" Vesta asks. "I mean, didn't he want people to be able to read his stuff?" There's a note of irritation in her voice that goes beyond annoyance with Virgil. It feels to me as if she's asking why I'm making it so hard *on her* and I begin to suspect we're not just talking about Latin. I think she holds me at least partly responsible for what happened to Melissa, and therefore it's my fault they have to go to all these counseling sessions and communal sings.

I tell the girls *Domina* Chambers's theory about the language being a maze. "After all, he's about to take us into the underworld..." I notice that the girls always perk up when I mention the underworld, the way a toddler might at the promise of a trip to Disneyland. "...and that's not supposed to be easy. It's like a secret he's not supposed to reveal, so he has to disguise the instructions."

"Like they use five-five-five phone numbers on television," Athena suggests.

"Exactly." Excited, I write a passage on the board and have them take turns linking up the adjectives and nouns, the nouns and verbs, the relative clauses with their antecedents. When we are done the lines we have drawn between the words do look like a maze.

"A maze with no exit," Vesta points out. "Where's Ariadne with her thread when you need her?"

"The thread is the way the words link up," Athena says, raising her hand in her excitement even though I have long dispensed with such formalities in this little class. "When you see which words go together you solve the puzzle."

I look at her with amazement. Not only because of how she has caught on, but because of how suddenly beautiful she looks. The light coming in the classroom window touches her straggly, multicolored hair, and where the light brown is showing through the dye I see flashes of red. Her green eyes shine back at me with the pleasure of getting it right and for a moment it's as if we were alone in the classroom, teacher and student sharing that rare flash of illumination that comes after slogging through the muck. But then she notices how in raising her hand her sweater sleeve has slipped down her arm, revealing the tangle of scarred flesh. She sees Octavia staring at her wrist and whispering something to Flavia. She looks away from me and tugs the unraveling cuff down over her knuckles.

The next day Octavia is absent and Flavia explains to me, apologetically, that her sister is dropping the class because every time she looks at Ellen Craven she thinks about the suicide legend. "Our grandmother says that the ghost of a murderer is never at rest."

I ask Flavia if she shares her sister's super-

stitions. "Nah. Besides, Octavia has a good shot at a tennis scholarship, but my backhand sucks."

I am so concerned with preparing the girls for Book Six that I forget how Book Five ends. It's only while Athena is reading aloud the part where Aeneas's boat is approaching Italy that I remember this is where Palinurus, the helmsman, drowns.

As she reads I tell myself that it's not going to be so bad. After all, we can't ignore every reference to drowning just because Melissa Randall drowned. This is about the helmsman of a boat, not a seventeen-year-old girl. But there's something in the way the god of sleep tricks Palinurus into falling in the water that makes me uneasy. I look around my dwindling class and see it's making everyone uneasy.

"*Datur hora quieti,*" Athena reads. "The time for rest has come?"

I nod. "Yes, you got the gerundive. *Bene.*"

"*Pone caput fessoque oculos furare labori*— put your head down and rest your eyes?"

"Basically," I say.

"Sounds like a good idea," Flavia says, putting her head down on her desk and closing her eyes. Athena reads on, alternating between Latin and English, her words barely audible above the hiss of the steam heat and the gurgling of the radiators. I can tell from Flavia's breathing that she is asleep. I'm certainly not supposed to let the girls fall asleep in class, but I don't have the heart to wake her. Before class she told me she hasn't been sleeping because of bad dreams.

"I keep thinking about Melissa Randall in the lake," she said. "I know they found her body, but I keep thinking she's still there. Octavia says she can hear her voice coming from the lake."

"It's just the ice buckling," I told her, but I know what she means. The noise has been keeping me up, too.

"Mene huic confidere monstro?" Athena reads. "Would you have me put faith in such a demon?"

The noise the ice makes sounds like a monster trapped under the ice.

*"Ecce deus ramum Lethaeo rore madentum vique soporatum Stygia super utraque quassat tempora...*but suddenly the god took a branch, dripping with Lethe's dew and drowsy from the force of death's river..."

I can tell she's stolen most of her translation from the same Penguin edition we used as a pony, but I say nothing. The God of Sleep coaxes Palinurus into forgetfulness as the drip of the radiators lulls my students into a drugged stupor. Forget the past, Dean Buehl said, drink deep of Lethe's water and forget.

Palinurus falls headlong (*praecipitem,* my favorite Latin verb) into the Mediterranean Sea and Aeneas sails on to Italy, narrowly avoiding the Sirens' rocks, "...which once were hard to pass and whitened by the bones of many men," Athena translates. "Far out we heard the growl and roar of the stones where the salt surf beats unceasingly."

Even my eighth graders have noticed the sounds coming from the lake. "They come from where the rocks are and isn't that where that senior fell in?" one of them blurted out in the middle of a lesson on the passive periphrastic today.

Athena finishes her translation and there is a moment of silence when we all listen to the sound of the steam hissing in the pipes and the incessant crackling that comes from the lake.

"I think it sucks that Aeneas went on without Palinurus," Vesta says. Vesta hasn't liked Aeneas since he ditched Dido in Book Four.

"Yeah, but what else was he supposed to do? Stop the boat and go back? I mean, he had to get past those Sirens and found Italy. Right, *Magistra*? It was his duty. Like you gotta go on."

I am so grateful for this reading of the *Aeneid* that it is all I can do to stop myself from hugging Athena. We've navigated another minefield, gotten through another day of Latin. Aeneas is within sight of the Italian shore. Outside the lake has quieted down. But then Vesta pipes up, "Yeah, but Palinurus's death comes back to bite him on the ass."

"Vesta!" Athena says so loudly that Flavia wakes up. They look at me to see if I'll reprimand Vesta for inappropriate language, but instead I commend her for reading ahead.

"That's right, Palinurus meets Aeneas in the underworld and tells him the truth about his death and begs him to give him a proper burial."

"The dead sure are a whiny lot," Vesta says just as the bell rings. There's not much I can do but nod my agreement, but I notice Flavia turns pale at such a cavalier dismissal of the demands the dead make upon the living, and the next day I learn that she has dropped out of the class.

Now it's only Athena and Vesta and me. I have the feeling, when the three of us convene in the drafty classroom overlooking the lake, that we are the last survivors of some monstrous ice age. Each night it snows, and although Dean Buehl has asked the board for extra money for plowing, the footpaths grow narrower and narrower between the rising walls of snow that guard the edges of the woods.

One Friday afternoon the snow accumulates so fast I'm unable to get my car out of the faculty lot and I have to call Olivia and tell her I'll be late for our weekend together. She seems unconcerned enough at first—wrapped up in some television show she's watching with Mitchell, but when I call her Saturday morning to tell her I still can't get my car out she cries. Mitchell complains that he'll have to pay the baby-sitter overtime because he has plans for the evening. I try not to wonder what plans. We haven't talked since Christmas break about the possibility of getting back together and I sense that particular window of opportunity has closed.

All weekend the snow falls and I shovel my car out only to watch the snow fill in the space I've cleared. I feel like one of those

tortured souls in Hades condemned to perform some meaningless task over and over again. Beneath the soft snow the wipers are frozen onto the windshield. I spray chemical de-icer on the windshield and then reach inside to turn on the wipers. They quiver under the snow, like small animals trying to break free, and then, when they do break free, they sweep a handful of slush and de-icer into my face. The chemical burns my eyes and I have to scoop up handfuls of fresh snow to flush the de-icer out of my eyes. My vision remains blurred for the rest of the weekend, making it impossible to drive to Westchester even if the roads were cleared. When I call, Olivia is calm and tells me she understands in a voice so uncannily grown-up I am simultaneously proud and grief-stricken.

I stay in bed that Sunday and have to cancel my classes on Monday. Gwen Marsh stops by to check on me and bring me some soup and a stack of papers she's collected from my students. I'm touched by the soup, but wish she hadn't bothered with the papers. My eyes hurt too much to read or grade papers, so instead I watch the snow mounting in the window frames, depositing layer upon layer of white and gray sediment like the cross sections of mountain ranges Miss Buehl used to show us. Above these miniature ridges, large lofty flakes cling in clumps that look like cumulus clouds—a dioramic landscape to make up for the fact I can't see the real world behind the falling snow. It's the same sense

of enclosure I had the January of my senior year that I spent in the infirmary.

LUCY NEEDN'T HAVE BEEN CONCERNED THAT I'D stay in the infirmary. As it turned out, I stayed longer than she did. When Miss Buehl and Domina Chambers picked me up off the floor after I lost consciousness they discovered I was burning up with fever. I guess all those hours roaming around the campus in wet clothes had done their trick. They kept me in the same room with Lucy because, Miss Buehl later informed me, Lucy insisted I stay with her.

"She wouldn't let you out of her sight," she told me.

I remembered sometimes waking up and seeing Lucy in the bed across from me, lying on her side facing me. I tried once to talk to her about what had happened. I wanted to know if they had believed our story—if Deirdre had gotten rid of the bloody sheets, if anything had been discovered in the lake. But each time I tried to talk about it, Lucy shushed me. I heard her tell the nurse once not to bother me or try asking me questions.

"You should leave the poor kid alone," I over-heard her say once to Miss Buehl. "After all, her mother just died." It seemed as if Lucy was the only one who remembered that. Even my father, who came to visit me only once, spoke about his new job at the glove factory with such enthu-siasm that I thought I had dreamt up the hospital room in Albany and the funeral afterward. And if I had imagined that, maybe I had imagined every-

thing that followed, the overheated dorm room, the baby in the tea tin...

But then I woke up one day to find Deirdre standing next to Lucy's bed. They seemed to be arguing about something in angry whispers and I knew then I hadn't imagined any of it.

Domina *Chambers came often and I heard her questioning Lucy about what had happened, about why she had tried to take her own life.*

"I don't think I really meant it," she told Domina *Chambers. "I think I knew Jane would find me and save me."*

I was touched by the story even though I knew it was a lie.

Then one day I woke up and found the bed next to me empty. I was so alarmed I managed to get out of bed and walk out into the hall where I found the nurse. "Where's Lucy?" I asked as I was led back to bed.

"She's been discharged, honey," the nurse told me, "and if you want to be you'd better stay in bed."

Lucy visited me that day. She brought me my Latin homework. I was amazed to think that classes had started. I'd had a feeling, in the white-washed infirmary room, its windows filled with snow, of suspended time, like in a fairy tale when the whole world goes to sleep with the heroine. But then if anyone were the heroine, I thought, it was Lucy, and she looked as if she had rejoined the world of the living. Her cheeks were pink, her hair shiny, and she was wearing one of the nice outfits she had gotten in Italy. She hadn't looked this good since October.

"I'm trying to impress them that I've regained my mental health," she said when I complimented her appearance, and then, leaning closer to whisper, "If I'd had any idea what a bother this suicide thing was going to turn out to be, I think I'd have done it for real!" She giggled. "But I don't think I hate it nearly as much as Deirdre."

"Deirdre? But she didn't try to kill herself."

"No, but they've called in this psychologist from Albany who says that suicide is contagious. And since Deirdre's my roommate and they think she acted funny about the sheets they're giving her the third degree. They'll probably start bugging you once you're well enough."

"Well it serves her right," I said. "If she'd just told someone she was pregnant in the first place..."

Lucy frowned. "I guess she was too scared," she said. "Anyhow, it's over now."

"I hope she doesn't tell anyone," I said, "I mean with all this psychiatric interrogation. Then it might come out that you and I got rid of...the thing."

Lucy turned pale and I was immediately sorry I'd reminded her of what we'd done. "She'd better not tell," Lucy said. "Get better soon, Jane, I might need your help with her."

I wasn't released until the next week. I still felt wobbly but I convinced the nurse that I was all right and pleaded that I was afraid of falling too far behind if I didn't go back to class. I walked back to the dorm on a bright, sunny day, half-blinded by the glare of the sun glancing off the frozen lake. Girls passed me on the path and greeted me, but I felt like they were all moving at

a sped-up rate and I became conscious of how slowly I was walking. It made me feel apart to see them all, with their shiny hair swinging against their down vests, their pastel shetland sweaters bright in the sun. These were the girls I had admired in the town drugstore; they were the reason I had wanted to come here, but I was no closer to them—no more like them—now than I had been when I was still a townie. I hadn't made any friends at Heart Lake. I hadn't tried to. Lucy had always been enough.

When I got back to the dorm I ran into Deirdre in the hall just outside our room. "Oh good," she said when she saw me. "Maybe the shrinks can spend some time picking your brains. I'm tired of explaining that I'm not suicidal."

Lucy was coming out of the single when I came in the suite. "Did you just run into Deirdre?" she asked me. "I thought I heard you talking in the hall. What was she saying to you?"

I told her what Deirdre had said. I was a little disappointed in Lucy's greeting, but then I guessed she was preoccupied.

"She'd better hope the shrinks don't get a hold of this," Lucy said, holding up a notebook covered in red Chinese embroidered silk.

"Is that Deirdre's journal?" I asked, a little surprised that Lucy would be snooping.

"I don't think you could call it a journal," she said, "more like a book of the dead. She keeps quotes about death in it. Listen to this, 'He who saves a man against his will as good as murders him.'"

"Horace," I said. "Didn't Domina Chambers give us that quote?"

"Yes, half the quotes in here come from Helen. Honestly, I don't think it would look good for her if Deirdre did kill herself. I'll have to talk to her at dinner tonight."

I must have looked baffled. "Oh yes, since my so-called suicide attempt Helen has insisted I eat with her every night. Frankly, it's driving me batty. She keeps asking me questions about my 'outlook,' as she calls it, and giving me mimeos of poems that are supposed to cheer me up. Only they're pretty morbid, too. Here." Lucy put down Deirdre's journal and picked up a folded sheet of paper with blue printing on it. She read aloud. It was Yeats's poem "The Lake Isle of Innisfree." We'd had it in Miss Macintosh's class last term. What struck me now were the last lines: "I will arise and go now, for always night and day / I hear water lapping with low sounds by the shore; / While I stand on the roadway, or on the pavements gray, / I hear it in the deep heart's core."

"You know," I said, "those last lines remind me of the three sisters story. The way the girls are supposed to be lured to the lake to kill themselves by the sound of the water lapping against the rocks."

"How clever of you, Jane. I thought exactly the same thing." Lucy folded the sheet in two and laid it on her bed next to Deirdre's journal.

"Aren't you going to put that back?" I asked.

"Oh, I guess," Lucy said, yawning. "Would you do it for me? It was in her bureau in the top drawer. I'd better go now. Helen hates it when I'm late."

When Lucy left I went into Deirdre's single and

replaced the journal in the top drawer of her bureau. I felt nervous and, I realized, not just because I was afraid of Deirdre catching me with her journal. It was the bed. I was afraid to look at it, afraid that when I looked at it the blood would somehow still be there. But when I did force myself to look at it I saw only rumpled sheets— Deirdre almost never made her bed—and a blue and gold Indian bedspread that used to hang on the ceiling over the bed. The Balinese dancers were still dancing on their tapestries as if nothing unusual had ever happened in that bed. I thought I saw a splotch of red over one of their breasts, but when I looked closer I saw it might be part of the pattern.

I went back into the room I shared with Lucy and noticed that my suitcase had been stored underneath my bed. I pulled it out and opened it. It was empty. I opened my bureau drawers and found my clothes neatly folded (more neatly than I remembered packing them that last morning in Albany) and put away. Under one stack of clothes I found my journal. I leafed through it, wondering if Lucy had read my journal, too, and what she'd have made of what I'd written. There was nothing bad about her in it, but there were embarrassing things, like how jealous I'd felt of Deirdre and Lucy's friendship and how much I missed Matt. As I read through it I was startled by how much of what I had written could be misinterpreted. So many of the things I had written could mean so many different things, depending on who the reader was. I read through parts pretending I was Lucy or Deirdre or Domina Chambers or Miss Buehl—

or even myself when older—and with each new "reader" what I had written shifted in meaning as if it had been translated into another language.

I'd better put it back under the floorboards, I thought. But first I wrote about what happened the night I came back from Albany. It felt risky committing to paper that awful moment when I watched the tea tin sink into the lake, but there was something in me that needed to get it out, if only to my journal. "You're the only one I can ever tell," I wrote. And then I hid the journal under the loose floorboards beneath my desk.

I tried to do a little Latin translation, but the words swam in front of my eyes and I started seeing spots. At first they were only small glints of light, like gnats flying in front of my eyes, and then they merged into one large sun spot that spread across my vision like a hole burning through a home movie. I closed my eyes and lay down on my bed, but I could still see the burning spot on the inside of my eyelids. Even when I fell asleep I saw the light. I dreamed it was Miss Buehl's porch light and I was crossing the woods to reach it, only I went the wrong way and ended up back at the Point. I slipped on the icy rock and fell into black space flecked with white sparks. Snow, I thought in my dream, but then the darkness turned green and the flecks of light were golden silt drifting down to the bottom of the lake. I looked up at a pattern of white shards on black; I was under the broken ice, which, even as I watched, knit back together, sealing me beneath it. Drifting down beside me was a tea tin painted with golden mountains and blue skies.

It turned as it sank, spinning like a leaf, and then, when it reached the bottom, its lid slowly opened.

IT'S THAT SAME FEELING—OF LYING AT THE BOTTOM of the lake looking up at the underside of the ice—I have lying in my room, my vision blurred, the snowscapes on the window screens like distant mountains. I think of Deirdre, of how the ice must have looked to her as she sank into the lake. In my dreams I try to tell her that I know now that the baby wasn't hers, but when I reach for her she turns away from me, just as Dido turns away from Aeneas when he meets her in the underworld. *The dead sure are a whiny lot,* Vesta had said. But she was wrong. The dead are silent.

When my vision clears, I feel curiously energized. I decide to go skating. I had been afraid that part of Dean Buehl's "forget the past" campaign might include banishing ice skating, but I had forgotten how much she liked to skate.

"Best thing for these girls," she says on an unusually mild day in late January. "Exercise. Fresh air. And just look at this ice! Best ice we've had in twenty years."

"Coldest January in twenty years," Simon Ross, the math teacher, says gliding by on hockey skates, "until today, that is. A few days like this and that'll be it for the skating season."

"It's supposed to get cold again tonight," Gwen Marsh says, backskating a circle around me.

384

"But first we're going to get some sleet and icy rain," Meryl North, who is skating with Tacy Beade, says. "We might have a real ice storm on our hands."

I turn to say something else to Gwen, but she's gone. I wonder if I've offended her in some way. Since I've been back she's been distant. I had thought at the beginning of the school year that we might be friends, but I realize now that I've done very little to build on the promise of that friendship. As I watch my fellow teachers skating together in pairs and small groups I realize how little I've connected to anyone here at Heart Lake. It's the same feeling I had walking back from the infirmary senior year, that I hadn't bothered making other friends because Lucy had always been enough. And, in a way, she's kept me from making friends all these years. At first, I told myself, because I was afraid of being hurt again. But later it was because when I did come close to someone I would hear Lucy's cool assessing voice, criticizing something about my new acquaintance. This one was too fat, that one was too earnest, this one a little loud, that one just plain dumb.

I tried to ignore the voice, but it put a distance between me and the girls I might have befriended. Who might have befriended me. It wasn't as if there were that many candidates.

I make an effort today to talk to everyone. I skate with Myra Todd and listen to a long drawn-out tirade against animal rights activists. I discuss a plan for a reenactment of an old-

fashioned ice harvest with Dean Buehl. I catch up to Gwen, who's skating now with Dr. Lockhart, and offer to help with the literary magazine. I join Tacy Beade and Meryl North and ask Miss Beade if she'd come give a lecture on classical art to my juniors. She says she's busy right now with plans for ice sculptures to accompany the ice harvest, but will be happy to come later in the year.

"It's time to turn back, Tacy," Meryl North says. "See, we're at the Point."

"Oh," my old art teacher says, "yes, of course." That's when I realize, watching Meryl North steer Tacy Beade along the ice, that Beady can hardly see. I remember watching her set up her art room, everything in its place, and wonder how long she's been losing her sight and how long she would keep her job if the board knew. Meryl North must realize I suspect something because, as we skate back toward the mansion, she chatters enthusiastically about the coming ice harvest. I notice, though, that she keeps confusing the dates and at one point I realize she thinks it's 1977 and I'm still a student here. When Dr. Lockhart and Gwen Marsh skate by, Meryl North says, "There goes your little friend." It's sad, I think, that my two old teachers have lost the aptitudes most important to their fields: the art teacher, her sight; the history teacher, her sense of time.

My ankles have begun to hurt, but when I see Athena and Vesta I skate toward them. Vesta is wearing a fleece headband that makes her

lavender-red Little Mermaid hair stick up in spiky points. Athena is wearing a Yale sweatshirt over red plaid pajama pants. Her mottled hair, which is now about half brown and half black, makes her look like an Australian sheep dog. I realize, skating toward them, that I'd far rather talk to them than to any of my colleagues.

As I skate closer, I notice someone else approaching the two girls and it gives me pause. I try to slow my forward progress by digging the serrated tips of my skate blades into the ice, but instead of slowing down I trip and sail headlong into Roy Corey, who has reached the girls just as I do. I slam hard into his chest and I'm sure we're both going down, but instead I feel his arm curve around my waist as we spin across the ice.

"All right, *Magistra*!" I hear the girls cheering me on, as if I had just completed a double axle instead of nearly crashing to the ice. And I do feel suddenly graceful, with Roy's arm around my waist, but then he takes away his arm and crosses his arms behind his back. We skate side by side, but not touching, around the western edge of the lake. I'm impressed with how well he skates and then I remember him telling me, all those years ago, that he'd grown up skating on these ponds. Just like Matt. At the thought of Matt I catch the tip of my blade on the ice and pitch forward. I see the hard white ice speeding up to my face but he catches me just in time.

"Whoa," he says, "are you OK?"

"Sorry," I say, "my eyes still aren't so good. I had a little accident with some de-icer."

"Yeah, Dean Buehl told me. I called last week to ask you a few questions." I remember suddenly that he is a police officer and that he probably isn't here just for the ice skating.

"A few questions?" I ask. "What about?"

Before answering I see him look quickly around us. We've stopped just where the Point juts into the lake, not far from where the third sister rock curves out of the ice like the back of a whale arrested mid-dive. The rest of the skaters are in the west cove. They're too far away to overhear us, but I see he still looks nervous.

"Wasn't there a cave around here," he asks, turning to face me. "You took me to a cave that morning."

It's the first reference he's made to that night we spent together and it makes me blush. But why? Nothing happened. He was asleep when I touched his face. I notice that he's blushing, too. Was he asleep?

"There are a bunch of caves in the Point," I say, "but I think the one you're talking about is over here."

I lead him to a shallow opening in the cliff wall just where the ice meets the shore. It's not even really a cave, just an indentation in the rock covered by an overhanging ledge and partially blocked by the second sister stone.

He wedges himself into the tight space and pats the rock by his side. Embarrassed, I squeeze in next to him. He takes up quite a

lot more space than he did when he was boy. But then, so do I. Only the view from the cave hasn't changed. I can see the tall stone casting a long shadow on the ice, which the setting sun has turned a creamy orange. The cave itself is full of this orange light, reflecting off the ice and onto the limestone walls.

Roy is also looking at the view from the cave. When he looks back at me I guess I'm not the only one who's been thinking about the last time we were here.

"So what did you want to ask me?" I ask. I wonder if I should have asked to have a lawyer present. I almost laugh out loud imagining a lawyer crammed into this narrow space.

"What?"

"Nothing. I was just thinking this isn't your typical interrogation room. Can I assume this won't be a typical interrogation?"

He doesn't smile, neither does he confirm or deny what I've said. "I'm just trying to get a few things straight in my head," he says, "about Deirdre Hall's death."

"Oh," I say.

"I've been going over your journal…"

"I thought you said there was nothing to incriminate me in there. I believe your exact words were 'You had no idea what was really going on.' "

"Well, maybe I didn't give you enough credit. I read over the part about Deirdre's death and I think there was something you felt uncomfortable about. I wanted you to tell me what happened that night."

"But why? What's the point? Are you investigating Deirdre Hall's death now?"

He shrugs. "Humor me, Jane." He grins at me then with the kind of boyish grin that Matt might have given me to coax me into another fifteen minutes of Latin study. So I do what he wants. I tell him everything I remember about that night.

I HAD BEEN ASLEEP, DREAMING THAT AWFUL dream about sinking under the ice, the tea tin drifting down through the water beside me, when their voices woke me. They were in the single, arguing.

"I'm going to tell."

"You can't."

"There's nothing you can do to stop me. I've had enough."

Someone rushed through the room I was in. The door to the hall opened, letting in a slice of light, and then slammed shut. Someone else followed from the single and opened the door. I could see in the light that it was Lucy and I called to her.

Lucy spun around and then closed the door. She came over and sat on the bed next to me. "I didn't know you were awake," she said. There was a little light coming from the single, but I couldn't make out Lucy's face in the shadows. "Did you hear?"

"I heard you arguing with Deirdre. Where's she gone?"

"She's going to Miss Buehl. To tell."

"Tell what?"

Lucy paused before she answered. "About the baby," she said.

"Why would she tell Miss Buehl she had a baby?"

Lucy sighed. "I guess she wants to get it off her chest," she said. "Confession's good for the soul, and all that junk." I thought about my journal writing guiltily, but at least that wouldn't get anyone in trouble.

"But then everybody will know we helped get rid of it."

Lucy nodded. "She doesn't care," Lucy said. "She doesn't care about anyone but herself."

I sat up in bed. "Can we stop her?" I asked.

Lucy took my hand and squeezed it. "Good old Jane," she said, "that's an excellent idea. Come on. Maybe we can catch up with her."

We didn't bother going down the drainpipe. The dorm matron was asleep at her desk, so we just tiptoed by. Once outside I started running down the path, but Lucy stopped me. "I've got a shortcut through the woods," she said. "We might be able to catch up with her before she gets to Miss Buehl."

We followed the narrow trail that Lucy had carved out of the snow. I noticed that it was freshly trodden and was surprised that she had obviously used her trails after the last snow. The trail led directly to the Point. When I saw where we were I stopped at the edge of the woods, thinking of my dream. I didn't want to go out onto the rock.

"I think I see her," Lucy hissed, "get back."

Lucy motioned me back until we were hidden by the shadows. Only when Deirdre was directly

in front of us on the path did Lucy step out from the shadows, blocking her way. Deirdre was startled when she saw Lucy and moved toward the trees, but then she must have seen me, because she moved off the path in the other direction, toward the Point. When she was on the rock Lucy started walking toward her, but not on the curved surface on top of the Point. She took a step down to the ledge on the east side of the Point and approached Deirdre slowly but steadily.

"I think we should talk this over, Deir," I heard Lucy say. Her voice sounded calm and reasonable.

"I don't want to talk about it, Lucy, just get away from me." I heard the fear in Deirdre's voice and it surprised me; Lucy was so much smaller than Deirdre. What did Deirdre have to be afraid of? It made me, suddenly, angry. I stepped out of the woods and walked carefully onto the icy rock. My anger quickly turned to fear, though, when I saw how close Deirdre and Lucy had gotten to the edge.

"Hey," I called. My voice sounded feeble. "Let's go back to the dorm and talk this over."

Deirdre snorted. "Yes, Jane, let's have a nice long talk. There's a lot you might be interested to learn."

Lucy turned toward me and in turning lost her balance. Her arms flailed wide and beat the air like the wings of some large, awkward bird. I tried to grab her, but she was too far away, below me on the ledge, and I stumbled before I could reach her. Just before I landed on the rock I saw Deirdre reach for Lucy's arm and then I heard someone scream and the sound of something cracking. I

*looked up and saw one figure crouched on the rock.
I crept toward her and found it was Lucy. She was
looking over the edge of the cliff at the frozen lake
below where a long black gash had opened in the
ice.*

"You say Lucy was below you on the ledge and
that when you stepped forward Deirdre stepped
back?"

I nod. He seems lost in thought for a
moment. "What?" I ask.

"Nothing," he says, "at least, I have to take
a look at the Point again to tell if it's anything.
Go on, tell me what you did after Deirdre went
through the ice. Did you go down and try to
help her?"

"There was nothing we could do."

He looks at me without saying anything. I
remember that he's read my journal. "Whose
decision was it to leave without trying to help
her?"

"Mine," I say, and when he still stares at me,
I add, "Well, first it was Lucy's and then it was
mine."

*I tried to pull Lucy away from the edge but
it was as if she were stuck there, transfixed by that
long dark opening in the ice.*

*"We have to go down and see if we can help her,"
I said.*

*Lucy looked at me, her eyes wide. "I saw her
when she hit the ice," she said. "Trust me, she was*

393

dead before she went into the water." I saw the horror in Lucy's eyes and it frightened me.

"We can't just leave her. We have to be sure."

Lucy nodded. She let me lead the way down to the beach. When we got to the edge of the ice I stopped but Lucy walked right out onto the ice, to the edge of the hole where Deirdre had fallen through. I caught up to her and grabbed her arm and she wheeled around on me so suddenly that I almost lost my balance and fell in.

"You said you wanted to be sure," Lucy said. "One of us has to go in. Obviously it should be me. It was my fault she fell." She spoke softly but her words chilled me. She had that look she got when she was determined to have her way. I didn't doubt that she'd be willing to plunge into the icy water to find Deirdre's body. I had the feeling she wouldn't stop until she found her, not even if it meant following Deirdre to the bottom of the lake. I realized I might lose her, too.

I stared into the black water. Already I could see a thin film of ice forming on the top. How many minutes had passed since Deirdre fell? Even if she had survived the fall wouldn't she have drowned by now? Why should Lucy risk her life if Deirdre were already dead?

I put my other hand on her arm and turned her to face me. "I don't want you to do it," I said. "It's bad enough Deirdre's gone. I don't want to lose you, too." Her eyes regarded me as if I were far away, as if that thin film of ice that was forming over the black water had gotten in between us. I couldn't tell if she even understood what I was saying and then she looked back at the water

and I saw such a look of longing on her face that I immediately started pulling her back to the shore.

"But we have to tell someone," she said.

"Of course, you were right in the first place. We'll go back to Miss Buehl's cottage..."

"But what if she's gone out? No. It's safer to go back to the dorm and wake up the matron."

Lucy led the way because she knew a shortcut following one of her narrow footpaths. We went single file, Lucy walking so fast I could barely keep up with her. I was glad she had shaken off the trancelike lethargy that had come over her at the lake, but I was surprised that when we got to the dorm Lucy climbed up the drainpipe to the second-story bathroom. When I caught up with her inside I asked her what she was doing. "Why are we sneaking in? We've got to wake the dorm matron anyway."

"I need to check something first," she said. "Deirdre was writing in her journal before she ran out. What if she wrote about what we did, Jane? Do you want people to know you drowned a baby in the lake?"

"Drowned?"

"Not so loud." Lucy put a finger to my lips. Her hands were ice cold.

"The baby was dead," I said.

"It's our word against hers. What if she wrote it was born alive and you and I killed it? Do you want people thinking that about you? Do you think you'll get that scholarship to Vassar if that gets around?"

I shook my head and Lucy opened the bathroom

door, poked her head out and then gave the all-clear sign. It wasn't until I was following her down the hall that I wondered how she knew about the scholarship. I hadn't told anyone but Miss Buehl and Miss North, who had written my recommendation letters. It didn't seem the right time to ask, though, so I followed Lucy in silence.

We crept down the hall and Lucy opened our door slowly so it wouldn't creak. We'd done the same thing countless times, but always with Deirdre. I kept looking behind me expecting to see her and then I would think of her in the lake, below the ice. I remembered my dream and hoped, for Deirdre's sake, that Lucy was right about the fall killing her.

Lucy went straight into Deirdre's single and I heard a drawer opening. When she came out she was holding Deirdre's journal. She sat down at her desk, turned on the lamp, and opened the notebook to the last written page. I stood behind her and read over her shoulder. Under the Horace quote, which had been the last thing in the journal when I'd seen it this afternoon, Deirdre had written another line: "Whatever happens now, it's all because of what Lucy did at Christmas." There was nothing about the baby being alive at birth.

"What does she mean?" I asked. "She makes it sound like it's all your fault. That's not fair."

Lucy looked up at me. "She blamed me for hiding the truth. She said it would have been better if it had all come out into the open."

"But you were only trying to help." I was getting angry at Deirdre, forgetting that she wasn't around to be angry at.

Lucy shrugged. "Apparently she didn't see it the same way."

"Well, we can't let anyone see this," I said. "We'll hide it. We'll dump it in the lake. I'll never tell."

Lucy smiled. "You're a good friend, Jane, but I don't think that will be necessary. Listen." She read the line out loud. "'Whatever happens now it's all because of what Lucy did at Christmas.' It's perfect! All that shrink from Albany has been going on about is how one suicide attempt leads to another. Like it's catching. They expected Deirdre to do this. Especially since I had the bad manners to cut my wrists in her bed. They'll probably pat each other on the backs for seeing it coming."

"But she didn't kill herself," I said. "It was an accident. We'll just explain..."

"Don't be silly, Jane. It looks like a suicide. It even fits the three sisters legend because she landed right in between the second and third sister. It's what they'll want to believe. They'll lap it up like cream."

"Maybe it was a suicide," I said. "I mean, think how bad Deirdre must have felt about the baby..." I thought Lucy would be glad of my theory, but instead she seemed distracted. She looked around the room as if she had lost something.

"There's just one more thing needed to make it perfect." She popped up from her desk and crossed to the bed. I was a little startled at her energy. She snatched a piece of white paper from her bed and flourished it above her head.

"Voila!" she said, sitting back down at the desk.

397

"Ecce testimonium." It was the mimeograph of Yeats's poem "The Lake Isle of Innisfree." "I think just the last stanza will do." Lucy cut out the last stanza of the poem, being careful to cut evenly. Then she taped it into Deirdre's journal, again taking time to line it up perfectly.

"Even if it was her suicide note," Lucy said, "Deirdre was so fucking precise."

"SO YOU TWO MADE IT LOOK LIKE A SUICIDE. YOU changed her journal and then took it to the dorm matron."

"Yes. We said that I'd woken up and saw Deirdre's door open, her bed empty, and her journal lying open on the bed. I know it sounds bad, but I thought she really might have killed herself, that she felt so bad about the baby..."

"But it wasn't her baby."

"No."

"And what was it Deirdre said just before she fell?"

" 'Yes, Jane, let's have a nice long talk. There's a lot you might be interested to learn.' "

Roy watches me, waiting for me to take the next step.

"She would have told me it wasn't her baby, that it was Lucy's baby..."

"And you say Lucy flailed her arms just before Deirdre fell?"

"Yes, because she lost her balance..."

"But you say she was on the east ledge. You can't fall from there because there's a rock

blocking the edge of the Point. But it is close enough to the edge of the Point to reach out and push someone..."

"I didn't see that." I've raised one hand to my mouth and I feel the wool of my mittens dampen with my breath. Roy reaches over and pulls my hand away from my face.

"Because you were trying to reach Lucy and fell. You wouldn't have seen anything."

I snatch my hand away from Roy and press both hands over my eyes as if to blot out the picture Roy is drawing. I grind the heels of my hands into my eyes until bright sunbursts bleed into the blackness, sunspots that turn into the glitter of rock and ice, a miniature landscape of glaciers from which I look up and see, against a moonlit sky, like actors performing in front of a silver scrim, Lucy's small pale hand reaching up and pulling Deirdre's foot. A swift hard yank the strength of which must have surprised Deirdre because I see her mouth form a little O before she falls back.

Roy pulls my hands away from my eyes and when I open them I am looking directly into his eyes and I read there the hope that I have remembered something.

"What does it matter?" I say, too angry at being forced to relive that night to give him the satisfaction that he's right, that maybe I did see something more. "It happened twenty years ago. Both Lucy and Deirdre are dead. So is Melissa Randall. Whatever she read in my journal, whatever it made her do, it's all over now."

"Is it?" Roy asks. "First there's a fake sui-

cide attempt—that's like what Lucy did at Christmas—and then a girl drowns in the same spot Deirdre drowned. Two of the events from your senior year have recurred, but what about the last act? What about what happened to Matt and Lucy? We've been assuming that Melissa Randall did it all, but why? Because we found your journal with her things. But isn't that also like what happened twenty years ago? You and Lucy tampered with Deirdre's journal so everyone thought it was a suicide. What if someone planted your journal in Melissa's things?"

I stare at him now not so much with anger as with horror. What he is suggesting is my worst fear, that the events set in motion twenty years ago would never really be over until they have swept over me, counting me a victim: the third girl. And really, why should I have been spared?

I close my eyes and see once again, sharper now, Lucy reaching up to grab Deirdre's leg and know the memory's always been there. I open my eyes again and nod. "Deirdre's death wasn't an accident," I say. "You were right. It doesn't matter that we were young; I'm responsible for what happened back then. For Deirdre's death, too..."

Roy puts his hand over mine. I notice the fine red hairs that catch the light reflected from the ice at the opening to the cave. "Jane," he says, "that's not what I meant..." I look up at him, into the green eyes that look so familiar, and then I notice the light is gone.

400

I turn toward the narrow entrance to the cave just in time to see the long shadow cast by the sister stone split in two and half of the broken shadow move away. It's as if the stone's shadow had come to life and skated away across the ice, but Roy disabuses me of this notion. Getting to his feet, he skates out of the cave and I stumble along clumsily behind him. I catch up to him on the other side of the Point where he stands watching the skaters in the west cove. There's Dean Buehl, Tacy Beade, Meryl North, Gwendoline Marsh, Simon Ross, Myra Todd, Dr. Lockhart, Athena, Vesta, and a dozen more teachers and students. It's impossible to say, though, which one had been listening to our conversation inside the cave.

Chapter Twenty-eight

●

I HAVE THE SKATING DREAM AGAIN THAT NIGHT, only in this dream I can hear the ice cracking beneath me, fissures erupting in the wake of my blades. I keep skating, though, around and around, in an ever-tightening circle, as if following a magnetic track laid below the ice. Whereas in the dreams I had before there

was a feeling of lightness, now there is weight, a heaviness that pulls my blades deep into the ice. When I look behind me I see the fissure open into a crevasse: a pale green tunnel descending for miles beneath my feet. It occurs to me that I am no longer skating on the lake, but on Miss Buehl's glacier. I stare into the pale green crevasse. Its walls are bubbled, like old glass, only the bubbles are moving. I look closer and see, miles beneath me yet impossibly clear, figures suspended in the ice. Matt and Lucy and Deirdre and Aphrodite, even Iris Crevecoeur, small and brown like a sepia photograph come to life, are all there, streams of bubbles spewing from their mouths.

There's another figure in the ice, but when I move closer to see I slip into the crevasse and as I slide down, deep into the pale green ice, I can hear the ice cracking closed above me.

I awake to the sound of something cracking above my head. My room is filled with an eerie green light. The light, I realize after a moment, comes from the luminescent dial on my alarm clock, which reads 3:33. As I stare at it something crashes on the roof above my head and skitters down the walls of my house. It sounds as if the house were bursting at its seams. I swing my legs out of the bed, half expecting to feel the floor trembling beneath my feet. I am thinking earthquake, tornado, another ice age, glaciers already on the march. But the floor, though icy cold, is reassuringly solid.

I get up and shove my bare feet into felt-lined boots and pull my down parka on over my nightgown. In the living room the crashing is louder. It sounds as if an army of raccoons were bivouacking on my roof. Raccoons? Hell, it could be bears. Wishing I had a rifle, I fling open the front door and switch on the porch lamp, hoping that any nocturnal intruder will be startled by the light just long enough for me to slam the door and call Animal Control.

Instead I see, in the nimbus of light from my porch lamp, a world made out of glass, a crystal world, like the inside of a candy Easter egg. Every branch and pine needle in the woods is glazed in ice. As I step out into the clearing in front of the house I can feel a light, needle-sharp sleet falling. Tree branches, weighed down by the ice, crack and crash to the forest floor. I should go back inside but I'm enchanted. I haven't seen an ice storm like this since I was little. I know how dangerous they can be, dragging down power lines and taking down trees, but for the moment I'm enthralled by the precision of it. The way the ice turns each blade of grass and dead leaf into an artifact.

Between my house and the Point there's a giant white pine. Each feathery needle is encased in ice. I can hear, above me, the rustle of them, rubbing against each other in the wind, a sound like muted chimes or bells tolling underwater. In the light from my porch they glitter like the eyes of some woodland animal, and then I think I can actually see a

face of some sort of animal in the pine needles, watching. I move closer and see that the needles have twisted themselves into an animal face—a horned animal with its bloody prey dripping from its mouth. I reach out and pull the face from the tree and feel, under the thin ice casing, metal. I am holding three interlinked hairpins: a corniculum.

IN THE MORNING I GO OUT TO THE POINT. I SCRAPE the ice on the ground with my boots and shake the branches, but find not one hairpin. There's just the three in my pocket. I walk onto the Point and look out at the lake. The storm has passed, leaving clear skies. The rising sun sets the lake on fire. I look down at the three sister stones and see that they, too, have gained a mantle of ice during the night. The third stone looks like an opal set in gold, the middle stone casts a long shadow like a crooked finger pointing toward the cave where Roy Corey and I sat yesterday. I remember how we saw that shadow, pointing in the opposite direction in the setting sun, split in two.

I look down at the three hairpins in my hand. Miss Macintosh once said that the question the reader should ask the narrator of any book is, "Why are you telling me this *now*?"

I've been back at Heart Lake for four weeks and it has been, above all else, quiet. No messages from the past, no torn journal pages or totem hairpins or dead girls. I'd assumed

it was over, that the messages had stopped because Aphrodite was dead. But apparently I had assumed wrong. Someone had been keeping quiet. So why send me this message now? A sign that would appear innocent to anyone else—what could I say: that someone was threatening me with hairpins?—but which is full of menace to me.

It *is* menace I feel, and that I have felt since yesterday when I saw the shadow split away from the stone. Someone listened to the conversation between me and Roy. Something in that conversation has awakened an avenging spirit. But what? I go over in my mind what we talked about and instantly I remember the image of Lucy toppling Deirdre into the lake. I'm standing now at just the place where I stood the night Deirdre fell. To my left is the ledge where Lucy stood. I step down to that level—it's only about three feet below the top part, and work my way to the edge of the Point. The rock is flatter here and it almost reaches to the edge, but then there's an outcropping of stone and a stunted pine tree that blocks the edge of the cliff. Was that why Lucy stepped down here? Because the footing was better than the curved surface at the edge of the Point? She'd have known this from the nights we climbed down from here to the swimming beach. From where I'm standing I could reach up and touch someone standing at the edge of the Point. Or reach up and trip someone standing there. Once again I see the scene as I saw it yesterday in the cave.

I climb back up to the curved stone of the Point and, staying on my hands and knees, inch myself as close the edge of the cliff as I can before vertigo forces me to creep back.

I look down at the rock and see that I've dug my nails into the narrow crevices as if I were a rock climber ascending a vertical wall. The glacial chattermarks remind me of my dream—the pale green crevasse opening in the glacier.

Whoever listened to our conversation yesterday heard what I said about Lucy and me covering up Deirdre's death. They also heard Roy say that he didn't believe Melissa Randall killed herself, that whoever "faked" Athena's suicide attempt and killed Melissa Randall might still be alive. If he's right, if that person were still alive and listening, it would have sounded like a challenge. And the corniculum is an answer to that challenge.

THROUGHOUT MY CLASSES I AM SO DISTRACTED by this question that I can hardly follow the easy faked Latin in the *Ecce Romani* textbook (today we follow our Roman family to an inn on the Via Appia) let alone the advanced girls' translations of Virgil. We have followed Aeneas into the underworld where he encounters his spurned lover Dido and tries to apologize for abandoning her in Carthage. Dido, however, will have none of it.

"She turned away," Vesta translates, "eyes to the ground, her face no more moved by his

speech than if she stood as stubborn flint of Marpessan crag."

I remember the dream I had of Deirdre turning away from me.

"I'm glad Dido doesn't talk to Aeneas," Vesta, never a fan of the Roman founder, says.

"She should have done more than just give him the cold shoulder," Athena says, tugging her unraveling cuffs over her wrists. "People...people who hurt other people..."

Vesta starts to hum the Barbra Streisand song, "People, people who need people..."

"Can it, Vesta," Athena screams, clutching her *Aeneid* as if she were going to hurl it at her classmate.

"*Puellae!*" I say rising to my feet and clapping my hands. "*Tacete!*"

Both my students glare at me.

"What's up with you girls?"

"We're just tired and we've got a big chemistry exam with Moldy Todd next period."

I can't help but laugh at the sobriquet, even though I know it's the height of unprofessionalism. At least it gains me a smile from Vesta, but Athena glares all the harder at our shared mirth.

"Vesta," I say, "why don't you go out in the hall? I'll give you both some extra time to study; I just want to have a word with Athena."

Athena rolls her eyes—overdoing, I think, the role of student asked to stay after class.

"Hey," I say when Vesta is gone, "I thought we were friends. What's bothering you?"

"People..." remembering Vesta's jibe she amends, "some of the girls are making fun of me because of this." She holds up her arm and shakes her wrist so that the loose sweater cuff falls down to her elbow. "And it's not fair. I haven't cut myself since last year. Someone else did this."

"You mean Melissa?"

Athena shrugs and wipes her eyes with the back of her hand, giving me an even better view of the savaged skin. "Well, Dr. Lockhart keeps telling me it was Melissa, but I still find it hard to believe. I mean, we were friends..."

"Keeps telling?" I ask. "How often do you see Dr. Lockhart?"

"Twice a week, which, like, really sucks. She keeps asking me how it made me feel to have my roommate kill herself. Like what am I going to say? It makes me feel good? It makes me feel like shit—sorry—but it doesn't make me want to off myself. She acts like killing yourself is a kind of germ and maybe I've got it. The other girls act that way, too, like I've got cooties or something."

I almost laugh at the childish term, something Olivia would say, but stop myself.

"I know what you mean. When one of my roommates killed herself my other roommate and I had to go to counseling."

"Did it bother you?"

"Well, I didn't love it, but it really drove my other roommate crazy."

"Yeah, it would." Athena gives me a small,

tentative smile. "People thinking you're crazy could make you go crazy."

The smile encourages me to reach out and rub her arm. "Well, you'll just have to prove them wrong." The advice comes out a little forced, a little too cheerleaderish, but Athena nods and dries her eyes and tries another smile.

"Thanks, *Magistra*," she says gathering her books to go, "that's the best argument I've heard for not plunging through the ice and drowning myself."

DURING LUNCH I KEEP REPLAYING ATHENA'S LAST words, trying to convince myself that it's a coincidence that the method of suicide she chose to cite was the way Matt and Lucy died. What I can't help thinking, though, is that if someone were playing out the events from twenty years ago, that would be the next method of death. I'm roused from these morose musings by a harsh, jangling sound in my ears. I look up and see Dr. Lockhart standing by the empty seat next to me, dangling a silver key chain in her right hand and absentmindedly shaking it while she answers a question from Gwen Marsh.

"No, Gwen, I don't think we should cancel midterms because the girls are having a tough semester," she says. When she sits down she lays the keys next to her plate. Not only doesn't this woman carry a tote bag bursting with books or papers like the rest of us, she doesn't even feel the need of a purse or

pockets. No doubt the clutter would disrupt the line of her tailored suits.

I reach into the pocket of my baggy cardigan and find a pen, chalk stubs, and a note I confiscated from one of my sixth graders. I take the wadded paper out of my pocket and see that it's a "cootie catcher"—a fortune-telling device popular with prepubescent girls. There are colored dots on the outside folds and numbers on the inside, which you pick to find out which flaps to open.

Gwen Marsh reaches over and takes the cootie catcher from my hands. "Ooh, I loved those when I was a girl. Let me tell you your fortune." She slips her fingers into the folds. "Pick a color."

"Green," I tell her.

"G-r-e-e-n." Gwen opens and shuts the paper mouth for each letter. When she's done she asks me to pick a number.

"Three."

"One, two, three, open the door to your destiny."

I reach to open the flap but Gwen's already folded it back, " 'You are such a fake, go drown in the lake.' Oh my," she says. "We had stuff like, 'You will marry a millionaire.' You see, Candace, what I meant about the girls being under so much pressure. How can we give the midterms..."

"If you go easy on them, they'll take advantage of you," Dr. Lockhart says, rising from the table even though she has barely touched her lunch.

"I don't think my girls take advantage of me," Gwen says. "They mean everything to me...this school...it means everything...." Her voice wobbling between tears and anger trails after Dr. Lockhart. I wonder if she'll turn back, but it's Dean Buehl who calls her back to the table. "Candace, you've left your keys again, here." Dean Buehl scoops the keys up and tosses them to her. She catches them neatly in one hand and turns to go without a thank-you to Dean Buehl or a word or apology to Gwen.

Gwen sniffs noisily. "Well, I'm still going to bring up the issue at today's faculty meeting."

"We have a faculty meeting today?" I ask.

I hear Myra Todd click her tongue at my forgetfulness and what she no doubt believes to be my reluctance to attend. But she's wrong. Although I usually hate faculty meetings, it's given me an idea. I've finally hit on what's been bothering me about my talk with Athena this morning. It wasn't just the comment about plunging through the ice. When I told Athena that my high school roommate killed herself she wasn't surprised. It's something she could only know if she had read my old journal. It makes me wonder what's been going on at those twice weekly sessions with Dr. Lockhart. I remember a pale green folder with Athena's name on it in Dr. Lockhart's file cabinet and I'm quite sure that the key to that file cabinet, and to her office door, will be lying on the table at tonight's meeting.

I ARRIVE EARLY TO THE MEETING, BUT THEN LOITER at the door to the Music Room, pretending to read the notices on the bulletin board. Along with the usual chess club and suicide intervention group notices there's a new flyer with a black-and-white photocopy of an old Currier and Ives print. The print is of a frozen pond. A horse stands in the middle of the pond, harnessed to a wagon filled with what look like giant sugar cubes. In the right foreground stooped figures stand around a hole in the ice. One of the figures holds a long, spear-tipped rod which he uses to prod a square of ice. In the left foreground a slant-roofed shed, which looks exactly like the Schwanenkill icehouse, stands at the edge of the ice. In the background, tiny figures skate on the ice.

"ICE HARVEST MEETING TONIGHT," it says under the picture. "8:00 P.M. IN THE MUSIC ROOM. SLIDE SHOW AND LECTURE BY MAIA THORNBURY, COUNTY EXTENSION AGENT." Under the typed print someone has hand-drawn, in jagged print intended to look like icicles, but which look more like daggers, a promise of ice pops for refreshments. The notice is dated yesterday. It's just the type of thing I should be attending to get back in Dean Buehl's good graces.

"Jane," I hear from behind me, "are you interested in the ice harvest?"

I turn to Dean Buehl. "Yes," I say, "I'm sorry

I missed this, I was busy sewing stolas for our Lupercalia Festival." The lie comes so easily to me that I blush with shame at myself.

"Well, then you're in luck," Myra Todd, coming up behind Dean Buehl, informs me. "The meeting was postponed till tonight right after the faculty meeting. I could use some help bringing the ice pops up from the basement freezer."

Before I can think up an excuse, some classical garment I need to sew, like Penelope's shroud perhaps, Myra Todd passes me and goes into the Music Room. I can see the table is filling up. If Dr. Lockhart doesn't get here soon I won't get a seat next to her.

I see her then, descending the main stairs unhurriedly, the silver key chain dangling from her right forefinger. I try not to look at the keys as she comes up to me in the doorway.

"Dr. Lockhart!" I say cheerily. "Are you going to the Ice Harvest meeting later?"

She looks at me as if I've taken leave of my senses, but at least it makes her slow her pace enough so we walk into the room together. "I think it's appalling," she says, as she makes for a solitary seat at the near end of the table. "It'll ruin the lake for skating."

"Why, you're right," I say, enthusiastically grabbing her elbow and steering her toward two seats at the far end of the table. "I hadn't thought of that. Let's sit together and oppose the project." I feel her arm flinch away from my touch, but she allows herself to be herded into the chair next to mine. I watch to see if

413

she'll lay the key chain on the table, but instead she folds her hands in her lap, keeping the key chain between them. At lunch she needed her hands to eat, but here she could keep her hands in her lap the whole time.

Dean Buehl is calling the meeting to order. I notice that most of my colleagues have produced paper and pens for note taking. I scramble in my tote bag and find a Xeroxed handout I'd prepared for the senior class. It's a maze I drew of Aeneas's route to the underworld that can only be solved by following a word trail. You have to connect an adjective to the noun it modifies and then find a verb to match the noun, and so on and so on. I am quite proud of it and I admire it for a moment before turning it over and scribbling the date and "faculty meeting" on the reverse side. Dr. Lockhart apparently feels no compulsion to take notes.

The first order of business is reviewing the costs of snowplowing the main paths and installing the new lighting system.

Myra Todd, who serves as secretary to the Board of Trustees, reports that the costs were approved by the board, but that the board expressed concern over any further expenditure, "especially considering that the school's lease is coming up this spring."

I scribble "What lease?" on the back of my handout and slide the paper over to Dr. Lockhart's place at the table. She scowls at me and waves her right hand, which, I notice, no longer holds the keys, dismissively.

414

When the financial business is concluded, Dean Buehl asks Dr. Lockhart to report on the status of the suicide intervention program.

"We haven't lost any more students, have we?" Simon Ross says loudly. "So I guess it's going pretty well."

Dr. Lockhart gives Ross a withering look as she rises from the table. I notice that, in rising, Dr. Lockhart has placed the key chain on the table.

"I've had three girls come to me complaining of nightmares about Melissa Randall's death. Curiously, the common thread in these nightmares seems to be a conviction that somehow Melissa is still in the lake, below the ice."

I think of my dream of the figures trapped in the crevasse. I feel suddenly cold. I reach into my bag for my sweater, but instead of pulling it out I haul the bag onto the table with a loud thump. Myra Todd purses her lips at me and makes a shushing sound. I smile apologetically.

"Several girls have also reported that the noises from the lake keep them up at night. They think that the noises are the moans of the dead girl." Dr. Lockhart raises her voice to be heard over the commotion I am making with my tote bag, but otherwise she doesn't in any way acknowledge the disruption I'm causing during her speech. In pulling out my sweater, my Cassell's *Latin-English Dictionary* and *Oxford History of the Classical World* thud noisily to the table and slide onto the floor.

"Such ignorance!" Myra Todd exclaims.

I lift my head, thinking she's talking about my behavior, but I see that even my rudeness at a faculty meeting can't compete with attributing superstitious beliefs to a natural phenomenon.

"I've explained again and again," Myra says, thumping her hand on the table with each "again," "about contraction and expansion of the ice, but they just don't get it!"

"You're the one who doesn't get it."

Everyone at the table stares at Gwen Marsh. Two red spots have appeared on her face. I've never seen her this angry. I'm so taken aback that I forget my plans to get the key for a moment.

"Don't you see what a shock Melissa Randall's death has been to them? They haven't just lost a friend, they've lost their faith in Heart Lake. It's supposed to be a haven for them, a safe place to come back to, a place where everybody knows them..."

Someone, I can't tell who, starts humming the theme song to "Cheers."

"You can mock if you like, but unless we go easier on them there will be another death."

"If we go easier on them," Dr. Lockhart says in slow, measured tones, "we're enabling their helplessness."

"I am not an enabler!" she says so shrilly that I wonder if she's been accused of this before. I reach over to touch her arm and she shrieks.

"That's my bad arm, Jane. You know that."

She stands up and leaves the room. Everyone watches her go. Except me. I use the moment to sweep my books, along with Dr. Lockhart's keys, into my tote bag. As soon as I've got them, I rise from my seat.

"I'll go after her," I say, and I'm out the door before anyone else can offer to help.

I sprint up the main stairs to the second floor and head, not to the Lake Lounge, but to Dr. Lockhart's office. At the door to her office I have to dig in my bag to find the keys, and when I do find them the metal slips greasily through my sweaty fingers. The first key I try doesn't fit. The second does, but it won't turn. I remember that in my old dorm room you had to pull the door toward you to make the key turn. I pull the knob toward me and the door bangs against its frame so loudly the sound echoes down the hallway. I stop to look down toward the stairs, but then feel the key turn and the door, taken by a draft in the hall, pulls me into the dark office.

I have to push the door against the draft to close it and again the sound it makes is horribly loud. I'm afraid to risk turning on the light, but fortunately, Dr. Lockhart has left her drapes open and the moon reflecting off the lake fills the room with silvery light. The varnished wood of her desk, which is empty except for some stone paperweights, gleams in the moonlight like a pool of still water. The round stones cast elliptical shadows on the smooth surface. I pick up one and immediately feel that I've disrupted

some pattern that Dr. Lockhart will notice has been disturbed.

I place the stone back again, aligning it with the other two in what I hope is the same spot, and cross to the file cabinet. The middle drawer, I remember. The little key opens the drawer, which slides silently forward on its metal casters. I walk my fingers along the tops of the files, which are neatly labeled in an elegant, sloping script. They're arranged alphabetically within class years, so I find "Craven, Ellen" about two thirds through the drawer. I pull out the pale green folder and move into the moonlight to read its contents.

The first few pages are the standard forms everyone at the school fills out. I notice that Athena's parents are divorced and that the emergency contact number is an aunt in Connecticut. I flip through the pink insurance forms and Athena's transcripts from previous schools. She started at Dalton, transferred to Miss Trimingham's in Connecticut, and then went to some place called the Village School in southern Vermont. Her grades had gone from A's and B's at the good schools to C's and D's at the worse schools. While she worked her way up the northern seaboard, she'd been steadily sliding down the academic scale.

Until this semester at Heart Lake. In the first quarter she'd still gotten mostly C's except for the B I'd given her in Latin. In the second quarter she'd gotten an A in Latin and Bs in the rest of her subjects. It looked like she was trying to turn herself around. So why

did she seem so out of sorts? And why was she seeing Dr. Lockhart twice a week?

I turn next to a sheaf of handwritten notes on unlined paper. The date of each session is entered in a beautiful flowing script in the right-hand margin. The notes are in the same precise and elegant hand, written apparently with a fountain pen. I've never seen notes taken from a psychiatric session, but I would have imagined that there would be cross-outs, abbreviations, additions in the margins. There are none. Dr. Lockhart wrote from one margin to the other in a steady, slanting script. The sentences could have been exercises from a calligraphy workbook.

The story they tell flows smoothly from one session to the next. If not for the dates in the margins I would think I was reading from a novel. What stands out the most, though, is the compassion Dr. Lockhart feels for her patient.

"Ellen has been shuttled from one institution to the next with little concern for her emotional well-being," I read. "Such displacement readily explains her tendencies toward depression and self-loathing. No wonder she inflicts harm on herself when the adults closest to her take so little responsibility for her."

Farther down the same page I read, "Ellen claims to have made several friends here at Heart Lake. It is obvious, though, that she has become emotionally dependent on these girls to an unhealthy degree. She would do anything to keep their friendship. Clearly she is using

these friendships as a replacement for the affection she's failed to receive from her mother." This interpretation has never occurred to me and I'm ashamed at myself for having had so little insight into my student—a student whom I thought I was close to. It's even more chastening to see here Dr. Lockhart's empathy for Athena's situation. In fact her notes read not so much like a transcription from oral conversation as a direct channeling from Athena's mind onto the page—as if Dr. Lockhart had access not only to her mind but to her heart and soul.

I notice, too, that as I page through the stack of notes, the handwriting changes. It becomes not exactly messier so much as tighter, as if Dr. Lockhart were trying to cram more into each line, as if the story she were getting from Athena threatened to swell beyond the confines of the written words. I have to move closer to the window to make it out.

"While it is probably true that the suicide attempt in October was faked, it is unlikely that Ellen had no complicity in it. It is more likely that she agreed to fake the suicide attempt to assist her friends in their persecution of Jane Hudson. Clearly their attempt is to discredit their teacher and get her fired."

I am so startled by the appearance of my name that for a moment the words in front of me blur. Has Athena truly revealed some calculated plot to torture me? Or is this Dr. Lockhart's interpretation? The notes are maddeningly obtuse, and now, nearly illegible. I take another step

closer to the window and realize, finally, that the reason I can't see is that the moonlight is gone.

I look up at the window, expecting, I think, to find it blocked by some hovering figure outside the glass. But that's ridiculous. Dr. Lockhart's office is on the second floor. It's only a cloud passing over the moon that has blocked the light. As I watch, the moon reemerges and its white light pours down on the curved rock face of the Point so that I can see, directly across from me at roughly the same level as this second-floor window, a figure standing close to the edge of the cliff. The figure lifts its arm to its forehead so that for a moment I have the absurd notion it's waving at me. But then I see a glint of moonlight on glass and realize it's worse; the figure on the Point—whoever it is—is watching me through binoculars.

Chapter Twenty-nine

●

I LOWER THE FOLDER TO THE DESK AND THE FIGURE on the Point eerily mirrors the motion by lowering its own arm. For a moment I feel as if I'm looking into a mirror and I briefly wonder which would be worse, for the figure on the

Point to be a figment of my imagination or a real observer who's caught me ransacking school property? But then the figure turns and disappears into the woods. A moment later it reappears on the path leading toward the mansion.

"OK," I whisper under my breath, "better it's real and I'm not going crazy, but still, that's a real person heading this way."

I know I should leave right away, but I'm compelled to read to the end of Athena's file. I scan through the remaining pages looking for my name, searching for some explanation of why my students would want to persecute me. Instead I find something finally in Athena's own words.

"When asked how she feels about her teachers, Ellen replied, 'Miss Hudson acts like she really cares.' I asked her why she used the word 'acts.' Did she think Miss Hudson was faking her concern? She said that she'd had a lot of teachers who had seemed to care about her, but in the end they'd never go out of their way to help her. In the end they were too wrapped up in their own problems. 'It's not like I'm her kid or anything,' Ellen told me. 'She has a daughter.' I asked if she felt jealous of Miss Hudson's daughter and she claimed she did not, but..."

Here the handwriting becomes so cramped I can't make it out. I flip to the last entry. It's dated today. I read the last line and then hurriedly reorder the papers and place them back in the green folder. I check the path again before

putting the folder back in the file drawer. Both the path and the Point are empty.

I lock the file cabinet and let myself out of the office, holding the door carefully so it won't bang again in its frame. As I head down the stairs I find myself repeating the last lines of Dr. Lockhart's notes on Athena.

"A person who has been shut out from love her whole life may form unhealthily close attachments. When someone (a teacher or an older girl) finally seems to care about her she may become obsessed with that person. If that person fails her, betrayal may be shattering. There's no telling what the betrayed one might do."

DOWNSTAIRS I FIND THAT THE FACULTY MEETING has broken up and students are filing in for the Ice Harvest slide show. There are quite a few students. Either they are really bored or some teacher has offered extra credit for attendance.

Myra Todd, who is rearranging chairs for the slide show, scowls when she sees me. "There you are. Did you find Gwendoline?"

"No," I say. "I looked all over the building for her, but she must have gone outside."

"That's just great. She was supposed to get the ice pops and run the slide projector. How am I supposed to get this meeting started on my own?"

"Where are Dean Buehl and Dr. Lockhart?"

"Dr. Lockhart misplaced her keys, so she went to her car for her extra set. Dean Buehl and the extension agent went out to look at the lake and decide where to cut the ice."

"I see. Well, I guess I can get the ice pops."

"Do you know where the freezer is in the basement?"

"Sure, the cook used to send us down for stuff all the time."

"Well, it would be a help...," Myra says, "but you won't be able to carry them all—I've had my girls making them for a week now."

"I'll take a student," I suggest. I notice Athena and Vesta milling around the front of the room near the slide carousel. Octavia and Flavia are skulking at the back of the room, embarrassed, I think, to be seen by me after defecting from the class. Several of my eighth graders are clustered at the door, their heads bent together over something. As I approach them I see one girl is holding another cootie catcher. Her fingers open and close the folded paper so quickly it's like watching a speeded up film of a flower opening and closing. When the girls see me approaching they whisper to the girl holding the cootie catcher and the white flower disappears in a blur into a pocket.

I change my mind and head over to Athena and Vesta. "Would one of you like to help me bring up ice pops from the basement?"

Vesta stares at me blankly as if I were speaking a foreign language.

"I'll do it, *Magistra*," Athena says, rolling her eyes at Vesta. "Miss Pruneface is in a

bad mood. She failed her chemistry exam and had to show up here for the extra credit."

"Shut up, *Ellen*. I wouldn't have failed the exam if you hadn't kept me up half the night with your light on. Baby's afraid of the dark," Vesta says sneeringly to me. "She's afraid the lake monster's gonna get her. Afraid the curse of the Crevecoeurs is gonna make her off herself."

I see Athena's already pale skin go a shade paler. "Cunt-sucking dyke," she says very quietly, and then turns on her heel and heads out the door. I follow her.

I catch up to Athena on the stairs leading down to the basement. "Why are you and Vesta fighting?"

"She's such a bitch, *Magistra* Hudson. She's acting like I really tried to kill myself in October. She says she doesn't believe it was Melissa who cut my wrists..." Athena's voice cracks and trails off. She turns from me and puts her head against the wall at the bottom of the stairs. The only light down here is a naked bulb hanging from a wire at the foot of the stairs. The walls of the basement are bare, damp, moss-covered rock that swallow up the faint light and smell like dead fish. The Crevecoeur family carved the cellar out of the living rock and used the natural springs to keep their food cold down here. I shiver and wonder what the hell they needed to cut up ice from the lake for. It's cold as the grave down here.

"There's nothing to be ashamed about," I tell Athena. I'm thinking about Dr. Lock-

hart's notes. What she said about Athena being in on the faked suicide. I touch her arm and she turns on me. I see such fury in her eyes that I instinctively step away from her and back up against the cold stone wall.

"You don't believe me either," she says. "I thought you were different."

When someone finally seems to care about her she may become obsessed with that person.

"Athena, I do want to help you, but I can't do that unless I understand what's been going on." Because of the cold my voice shakes and it makes my words sound to my own ears nervous and false. Athena wraps her arms around her chest and glares at me. The lightbulb hanging above us makes her eyes glitter feverishly. The shadows make her multicolored, jaggedly cut hair look even wilder than usual.

But if that person fails her, the betrayal may be shattering.

Athena looks like someone who has been shattered. In fact, Athena looks like the madwoman in the attic from *Jane Eyre*. Only we're in the basement not the attic. I can feel icy water dripping down between my shoulder blades. I would far prefer an attic to this basement.

"You know what's going on," she says. I start to shake my head, but I see she's not looking at me any more. "It's the Crevecoeur curse," she says.

"Athena, that's just a story..."

"It's what made those girls drown themselves in the lake. You should know—it happened to your friends and now it's happening to us. It's

because you came back. The lake wants the third girl. That's what the motto means: *Cor te reducit*. The heart—meaning Heart Lake—pulls you in."

I am about to correct her translation, but then I realize she's right. Leads back, pulls in, both are acceptable translations for *reducit*.

"How do you know about my friends?"

Athena shrugs and wipes her eyes. The gesture makes her look like a tired child. It reminds me of Olivia. I want to tell her that—that she reminds me of my own daughter—but I remember what Athena said to Dr. Lockhart. *It's not like I'm her kid or anything.* I picture Olivia standing on the rock. Could it have been Athena who lured her there? Out of some obsessive jealousy?

Athena sees, I think, the look of suspicion on my face.

"Someone told me," she says. "I don't remember who. I bet you've felt bad about it all this time—about your friends dying."

How can I deny it? I nod.

"It feels pretty shitty when you let someone down, doesn't it?"

I nod again. *There's no telling what the betrayed one might do.*

"Don't worry," Athena says, almost kindly. "It's not half as bad as being the person who's let down."

BY THE TIME WE GET UPSTAIRS WITH THE ICE POPS, the lecture is already in progress. There aren't

427

two seats together, so Athena takes a seat at the end of a middle row. A few rows behind her, Octavia and Flavia reluctantly make room for me to sit between them. I look around for Vesta, but don't see her. Dr. Lockhart is sitting in the first row. If it's possible for good posture to convey disapproval her ramrod-straight spine is speaking volumes of contempt for the proceedings.

I notice that Gwen is back and that she's manning the slide projector. I try to catch her eye, but she stares resolutely ahead at the screen.

Meryl North presents a short lecture on the history of ice harvesting in the Northeast. She tells us that giant ice blocks could be preserved in sawdust so well that blocks were shipped as far as India. Tacy Beade presents her idea for using the harvested ice for ice sculptures. She shows some slides of Michelangelo's series of unfinished statues called "The Captives." "Michelangelo believed the figures were in the stone waiting for the sculptor to free them," she concludes. "Who knows what figures we'll find hiding in the ice."

There's a smattering of embarrassed applause as Miss Beade goes back to her seat. "Figures hiding in the ice," I hear Simon Ross whisper. "Where has she been all year? Does she even know there's been a death on campus?"

Maia Thornbury takes the floor to present a history of ice harvesting on the Crevecoeur estate. She is a small, middle-aged gnome with a cap of graying hair cut in a style that

I think used to be called a Prince Valiant. Her round eyeglasses reflect the mote-filled light from the slide projector and make her face appear even rounder. After all these years hearing about the county extension agent this is the first time I've actually seen her. I remember how we worried she would catch us using the boat and that she was the one who found Matt on May Day. I had always pictured her as some imposing, Girl Scout Valkyrie. She is all of four feet five. More wood sprite than Valkyrie.

"The Crevecoeur family were descended from the Huguenots who fled religious persecution in their native France in the seventeenth century," she lectures. I can hear several girls yawning. They must really want those popsicles or else they really need that extra credit. "Unlike most of the Huguenots, who settled in communities farther south along the Hudson or in New York City, the Crevecoeurs preferred solitude and self-sufficiency."

The screen darkens and then resolves into muted tones of brown and white. A row of men with old-fashioned sideburns and tall, sturdy women with strong, square jaws stand in front of a small slant-roofed hut. The women are carrying tin milk pails.

"Like most Frenchmen, the Crevecoeurs loved their homemade cheeses and butter, but they needed ice to keep them fresh in the humid Adirondack summers."

The sideburned men and square-jawed women fade and a family portrait of the Creve-

coeurs, in full skating regalia posed on the ice, appears. I've seen the picture before—it's the same one that hangs in this room right behind where the slide projector screen hangs now—so I recognize India Crevecoeur as the stately matron in the foreground, her head tilted coquettishly under a fur cloche. Although it is hard to connect the woman in the picture to the desiccated old woman who accosted me on May Day junior year, I do recognize the arrogant glint in her eyes that I saw in the old woman when she realized that her former maid's granddaughter was attending her school. I remember that the way she looked at me made me feel like an impostor, and that's just how I feel now. The caring teacher. *One of Helen Chambers's girls.*

The two blond amazons on either side of India must be her older daughters, Rose and Lily. A little to the right, a smaller girl stands unsteadily on the ice, her arms held akimbo for balance. I recognize the plain sepia face from my dream of the night before; it's Iris Crevecoeur, who died in the flu epidemic of 1918. I wonder if Maia Thornbury will mention her, maybe this would be a good opportunity to point out that one girl died, not three, and so dispel the legend. Looking at the skinny, sallow girl next to her fair, hearty sisters it's not surprising that she was the one to fall victim to illness. The way the servant hovers anxiously over her—my grandmother—also says something about her frailty. But Maia Thornbury doesn't bring up Iris

430

Crevecoeur's fate; she has another ax to grind.

"India Crevecoeur and her daughters loved to skate on the lake, but their favorite activity was attending the annual ice harvest."

If Dr. Lockhart's spine could get any straighter it does so now. I've always wondered why she seems to dislike me and now I think I know. Twice a week she listens to Athena talk about me, about how I pretend to care but really don't. No wonder she seems to see right through me.

The next slide shows the icehouse from the lake. A long narrow channel has been cut out of the ice leading to the open doors. On one side of the channel a muffled figure leans over the ice with what looks like a large saw. Another figure holds a long pole up toward the camera. He looks like an angry Eskimo shaking his spear at an intruder.

"After the snow was scraped off the ice, saws were used to cut out a 'header'—a channel through which the ice could be moved through the water to the icehouse. Then a plow marked out cakes of ice. Pike poles were used to push the cakes of ice down the channel and onto a conveyer belt into the icehouse. Would someone turn on the lights for a moment?"

I close my eyes against the sudden light and when I open them I see Maia Thornbury wielding a spear-tipped pole nearly twice her height. She shakes the pole with both hands. Perhaps my original idea of her as Valkyrie wasn't so far off.

"This is one of the original poles used on the Crevecoeur estate for ice harvesting. It's eight feet long."

"Oooh," someone coos, "what a long pole you have there."

The girls giggle while the teachers make shushing noises.

"Is that point sharp?" someone else asks.

"Oh yes," Maia Thornbury says, hefting the pole up and angling it so we can all see the six-inch-long steel tip. "It had to be to grip the ice. Would you like to touch it?"

More hysterical giggling as the girl who spoke rises from her chair. I'm surprised to see it's Athena. I wouldn't have expected her to express such an interest in ice harvesting after our scene in the basement, but here she is, walking up to the front of the room where the extension agent holds the pole parallel to the floor. As Athena walks toward the spear I have the disturbing thought that this is how Roman senators killed themselves: by falling on their own swords. I am poised to rush toward Athena, but she only lifts her arm and touches the point of the spear with the tip of her index finger.

"Sharp, isn't it?" Maia Thornbury asks like a magician testing the veracity of some trick with a volunteer from the audience.

Athena nods without taking her eyes off the spear point. Then she turns and walks back to her seat. Before the lights go out I see her look down at her finger, to a drop of blood poised there. Then she puts the finger in her mouth and sucks.

"To celebrate the ice harvest, the villagers carved decorative statues out of the ice," Maia Thornbury says as the lights go out. I am still looking at Athena when the next slide appears, so when I hear the rest of the audience gasp I have the awful thought that there's been some accident with the ice pole. But when I look up I see it's the slide that has made everyone gasp. This picture is in color. It shows a girl, nearly naked except for some flimsy white drapery, stretched out on the second sister stone. The girl and stone are so pale they could be almost mistaken for some particularly skillful ice sculpture. Except for the gash of bright red blood across her throat. I immediately recognize the girl as Lucy, but it takes me a few moments to recollect where the picture is from. As the lights go on and Dean Buehl tries to calm the now hysterical girls I try in vain to explain to someone that what the picture portrays isn't real. It's just Lucy Toller playing Agamemnon's daughter in our senior year production of *Iphigenia on the Beach*.

BY THE TIME I MAKE MY WAY TO THE FRONT OF THE room I can see that my explanation won't help. Dr. Lockhart is arguing with Myra Todd about the wisdom of going on with the ice harvest given the inevitable connotations the girls will now have. Maia Thornbury is going over her numbered slides with Dean Buehl to prove to her that the picture of the slaughtered

433

girl was not part of her original demonstration. The slide itself has been passed from Maia Thornbury to Meryl North to Gwen Marsh to Dr. Lockhart to Myra Todd, and, finally, to Dean Buehl, so any fingerprints that might have been found on it are probably now obscured. I surprise myself by thinking of fingerprints. Could I, perhaps, take this slide to Roy Corey and ask for it to be fingerprinted? Maybe, but now it's too late. I promise myself, though, that if any other relic from my past shows up I'm taking it straight to him. I pick up the slide now and look at it. Lucy as Iphigenia. I remember watching the play from the eastern shore of the lake. This picture shows the reflection of the setting sun on the side of the rock nearest to the camera, so it must have been taken from the opposite side.

Someone plucks the slide from my fingers. "Like a scene from a Greek tragedy, don't you think, Miss Hudson?" Dr. Lockhart smiles at me as she slips the slide into a plastic bag. I'm not sure if she means the slide itself, or the furor its appearance has caused.

"I was thinking we could have it finger-printed," I say, even though I had already rejected that idea.

"How convenient then that there will be an explanation for your prints on it," Dr. Lock-hart replies as she hands the bag to Dean Buehl.

"I guess the same goes for you," I say. "Since you handled the slide as well." I hadn't really planned to insinuate that Dr. Lock-

hart could have been responsible for planting the slide, but as I see her already pale skin go a shade paler it occurs to me that it could have been her as well as anyone else. I wonder, though, how she could have come by it in the first place.

IT'S AFTER ELEVEN BY THE TIME I LEAVE THE MANsion and walk back to my cottage. I take the same path that the person I saw on the Point would have taken. I look at the packed snow underfoot for some clue, but dozens of people have traversed the path since the last snow. I pause on the Point and look back toward the mansion. I can see Dr. Lockhart's window. Although the office is unlit I can see now how the light from the hall filters in and makes the interior room faintly visible. A person standing in there would only appear as a vague outline, though, like the shadowy shape her desk and filing cabinet make now. I turn from the Point and follow the path to my cottage, which is less trodden than the path from the Point to the mansion. Still I can tell that someone else has been walking there since the last snow.

When I get to my house I see that the porch light has burned out again. It takes me a moment to fit the key in the lock, and when I do my hand is trembling so hard I can't make the lock turn. And why shouldn't I be afraid? I ask myself. Someone obviously bears me some grudge.

"Then why not just come out and knock me over the head or something," I say aloud to my own door. "Get it over with. Why so coy?" My voice, I notice, sounds more angry than afraid. Good, I think. I'm tired of this game of signs.

As I enter the house I feel sure that someone has been there in my absence. I am not afraid, though, that the intruder is still there. Whoever it was would have gone back to the slide show. Why miss out on the fun? I go through the rooms, flicking on the lights, scanning the walls and tabletops for something missing, or something new. I'm expecting, I don't know what. Some bloody scrawl on the walls? For the first time it occurs to me that whoever is sending these signs is as frightened of me as I am of her. Whoever she is, and I'm certain it is a she, was silent until I talked to Roy Corey in the cave. Then she sent the corniculum. Tonight, when she saw me in Dr. Lockhart's office, she retaliated by dropping that slide in Maia Thornbury's carousel. It's as if we are playing tug-of-war with the past, you look into my past, she is telling me, then I'll fling your past back at you.

"Well, what have you got for me tonight," I call into the empty rooms. When I get to my bedroom and see the lump under the bedclothes and what's seeping from that lump my bravado fades.

"Oh, fuck," I cry as I fling the blankets off the bloody deer's head. "Fuck, fuck, fuck," I say maybe a dozen times over until I realize

it's only a felt mask of a deer's head, with red paint dripping from its felt neck.

Chapter Thirty

●

"DO YOU RECOGNIZE THIS?" I ASK, FLINGING THE mask on Roy Corey's desk. It nearly topples a Styrofoam cup half-filled with grayish coffee, but I am not sorry. I have been wanting, since eleven o'clock last night, to fling the mask at *someone*. After a sleepless night I called Dean Buehl to cancel my classes.

"I was up all night with a toothache," I lied, "I've got to go into town and have this thing out."

She seemed neither suspicious nor interested in my excuse. "I'll have your girls help Maia Thornbury with the ice harvest," she told me.

"It's still on?" I asked.

"I will not let some saboteur change my plans," Dean Buehl replied. "That would be like giving in to the demands of terrorists."

Apparently I was not the only one tired of this game of cat and mouse.

"Hey watch...," Roy Corey says looking up from the mask to me, but when he sees my

expression he stops the complaint he'd been forming. He looks back down at the mask, picks it up, sniffs at the dried red paint and inspects the stitching along its seams.

"Look familiar?" I ask.

To my surprise, Roy Corey turns white.

"It's not real blood," I say, my anger deflected by his reaction.

"Why don't you have a seat, Jane?"

"You recognize it, don't you?"

Roy picks away some of the red paint, revealing a green embroidered heart. "Where did you find it?"

"In my bed, a là *The Godfather*," I tell him. "Did you hear about the little surprise at our slide show?"

Roy nods. "Your dean called me last night. I went out there and took the carousel and slide. We're having both dusted for prints, but both were handled by so many people we don't expect much. This happened afterward?"

"When I went home. Which was around eleven."

"Must've given you quite a start."

I shrug. "I'm getting used to it." I tell him about the corniculum in the tree the night of the ice storm. "It was right after our conversation in the cave. Someone overheard us and then the signs started again."

He nods. "I thought they might."

"You bastard! You knew someone would eavesdrop on us in the cave."

"I couldn't be sure, but what with the whole school there on the ice, I thought it was pos-

sible someone might take advantage of the situation."

"You took advantage of me," I say rising to my feet. I wish I still had something to throw at him, but then I see the effect my words have had on him. It's as if I have thrown something at him. He's looking down at the mask, still fingering that green heart, as if he can't bear to look me in the eyes.

"It was only a matter of time before this person surfaced again. We're talking about a murderer—someone who drowned one teen-aged girl and drugged another and slit her wrists with a steak knife."

"Unless it was Athena who slit her own wrists."

"You mean a real suicide attempt?"

"I mean she faked her own 'suicide' and then killed Melissa." I tell Roy about the conversation I had with Athena in the basement. I don't tell him about Dr. Lockhart's file because I'd rather not admit to breaking and entering, but I manage to filter some of the information I gleaned there into my observations. "I hate to think Athena's the one," I conclude, "I've always liked her and I thought she liked me, but now she feels I've let her down and she's gotten it into her head that I've started the whole Crevecoeur curse again since it was my roommates who died."

"How does she know about that?"

"I don't know. She'd know from the journal..." I pause, remembering something Athena said to me in the basement. "She said

439

she knew I felt responsible for my friends' deaths. That's what I said to you in the cave, that I knew Deirdre's death wasn't an accident. So it might have been her listening to us in the cave." I sink back into my chair, exhausted and disheartened. I hadn't realized how much I'd wanted not to believe it was Athena who was trying to hurt me. I look at Roy, hoping he'll contradict my theory. He's still peeling the red paint away from the mask and smoothing the brown felt.

"Did she say anything else?"

"She said it felt pretty shitty to know you had let someone down, but worse to be the one who's let down."

Roy looks up from the mask. "I don't know about that," he says. "I think it's a draw. I think the guilt of hurting someone you care about can last a long time, maybe even longer than the love itself."

He whisks the red paint flakes off his desk with the side of his hand and crumples the mask in a ball.

"You mean Matt, don't you? You think he'd still be alive if you hadn't let him come back to Heart Lake that night?"

He nods. I try to think of something I could say to relieve his burden, one I understand only too well, but anything I say would only mean taking more of the burden on myself, and I don't feel up to that. Instead I throw him a crumb, a relic of the person we both miss. "You know," I say, "that's the mask Matt wore that morning. His was the one embroidered

with the green heart. He must have dropped it in the woods and someone found it."

Roy looks at me through narrow, tired eyes and sighs. He gets up and passes behind me to close the office door. When he comes back he doesn't sit down behind his desk, but instead sits on its edge, so close to me the stiff cloth of his uniform brushes my leg and I can see the fine red hairs on his arms where he's rolled up his sleeves. He's still holding the mask. His thumb brushes the last of the red paint off the green embroidered heart. *By this sign you'll know your heart's true love,* Deirdre had said, embroidering a different color heart, green, blue and yellow, on each mask.

"You're right that it was dropped in the woods, Jane. And I suppose someone must have found it there. But this isn't the mask Matt wore, Jane."

"But I saw that green heart..." I stop and look up at him, into familiar green eyes.

"This is the mask I wore."

I AM STILL LIGHT-HEADED DRIVING BACK TO HEART Lake. Exhaustion, I tell myself, fear and aggravation and frustration. All natural emotions considering what I've been through. But I know it's something else. Since that moment in Roy Corey's office when I realized who it was I was with that May Day morning all those years ago I have felt something vibrating through my core, like a hot wire snaking up from the base of my spine. When

441

I touch the cold metal handle of my car door I'm surprised I don't set off sparks in the dry air. I feel electric.

"So what," I had said over and over again to the hard glitter coming off the Hudson, "So what. So what." I had parked my car across from the old Toller house, facing the river, and waited for the hot, wobbly feeling to go away. "So it was Roy Corey I had sex with on May Day morning and not Matt Toller. What earthly difference does it make?"

By this sign you'll know your heart's true love.

Crap. It was just a stupid superstition Deirdre'd made up. Only I had believed it and believed, for all these years, that my heart's true love had drowned in the lake under the ice.

"Crap," I told myself, pulling into the faculty parking lot at Heart Lake. "Stupider than believing in the three sisters story and the curse of the Crevecoeurs. And it doesn't solve anything. Doesn't tell you who's sending these signs from the past or who killed Melissa Randall."

In the end Roy was unconvinced that it was Athena. But maybe that was because I didn't really want to convince him because I don't want to believe it's Athena either.

He thought it had to be someone connected with what happened to Matt and Lucy and Deirdre twenty years ago. Who else would know so much about what happened then? Who else could have found that mask, which Roy said he abandoned somewhere in the woods

that morning. Helen Chambers was dead. Dean Buehl had been there, but why would she deliberately wreak havoc on her own school now? Didn't she have more to lose? I told Roy my suspicions about Dr. Lockhart— "She certainly wants to stop the ice harvest"— but neither of us could come up with a motive for the other events. What could she possibly have to do with what happened twenty years ago?

"Whoever it is obviously has some grudge against you, Jane. I'm not sure it's safe for you to stay in that isolated cottage all by yourself."

"Where do you suggest I stay?" I asked, half-shocking myself with the provocative tone of my own voice. I hadn't meant it to sound like that, had I? But I was disappointed when he only shrugged and suggested I stay in the mansion.

I shuddered, thinking about what Dr. Lockhart said about living in a fishbowl.

"The dorm then?"

I thought of the hothouse atmosphere of the dorm, the hissing steam radiators, all those girls in flannel nightgowns damp from just-washed hair. The rancid smell of burnt popcorn and face creams.

"No," I told Roy. "Like Dean Buehl says, that's like giving into the demands of terrorists. I'll be OK."

He'd looked at me in silence for a few moments and then leaned down to search for something in his drawer. A lock of hair fell over his forehead and, catching the light from the

grimy window, briefly flamed red. When he lifted his head, his hair fell back, extinguishing the bright color so that I could see the ashy gray at his temples. "Here," he said, holding out something in a clear plastic bag. "I've been meaning to give this back to you. We don't need it for evidence anymore."

I look through the thick plastic and recognize my old journal. "Thanks," I say, trying not to sound too disappointed. I'd thought he was going to give me his phone number.

I GET OUT OF MY CAR AND WALK TOWARD MY house, but halfway there I hear shouts coming from the lake, so I cut through the woods and head out onto the Point. At first, when I see the black gash in the ice and the figures with poles I think the worst: Someone has fallen through a crack in the ice and they're trying to save her with long, lifesaving poles. I look for someone thrashing in the icy water, but instead I see a neat rectangle of ice floating down the dark channel toward the icehouse and I realize it's only the Ice Harvest.

They've made remarkable progress in such little time. Or else I've been gone longer than I realized. I look at my watch and see it's already four o'clock. I hadn't realized I'd spent so long in Roy's office—or sitting in my car looking at the river. While I've been gone, Maia Thornbury and the girls have cut out a long narrow channel, perhaps four feet across, from the icehouse at the southern tip of the

lake to halfway to the Point. Some of the girls are wearing skates and others, under Gwen Marsh's direction, are wielding the long ice poles, pushing cakes of ice up onto a ramp into the icehouse. The scene is as cheerful and bucolic as the Currier and Ives print I'd seen on the flyer last night. In fact, it seems more populous than I would have thought possible. Everyone must be out.

Then I look again and see that some of the figures on the ice aren't people.

What I'd taken for stationary children dressed in white are actually statues carved out of ice. As I watch I see two girls carry a cake of ice from the icehouse and stack it on top of three or four more. Other girls are chipping away at stacks of ice to form rudimentary bodies. Tacy Beade is using a pick and hammer to shave the ice away. Even from here I can hear the steady thwack of metal hitting metal with a force that's alarming considering Beady's half blind. Chips of ice fly under her hands like sparks from a forge. The shape emerging, though crude, already has the feel and motion of the human form, something trying to break free of the encasing ice.

There are about a dozen of these figures standing on the lake. I can see now that they are half-formed and incomplete, but as the last rays of the sun catch each one they seem to gain a spark of life. I look directly below the Point and for an instant the whole lake seems to spin before my eyes. The sky on the eastern shore is black with storm cloud, so that the ice,

445

lit by the low-lying sun, burns with a fierce, white light. Beside each of the sister stones stands an ice statue. Or rather the first one, the one closest to shore, stands. The second kneels, and the last one lies, supine on the white ice, only half of its body visible above the surface, so it's as if the girl is half in, half out of the lake, one arm lifted and crooked as if suspended in midstroke. But what really unnerves me is the impression made by the dark backdrop of storm cloud. It's as if the black water is rising from the ice and the pale figures are shapes seen underwater.

What I feel is a kind of seasickness. A vertigo of reversal. I tilt my chin up and focus on the horizon, a trick to avert motion sickness Miss Pike taught us when we went canoeing. At the horizon line of deep green pines I see a figure standing still as the trees. At first I think it's another ice statue, she's standing so still, but then I realize it's Dr. Lockhart. She's wearing her skates, but she isn't moving. When she sees me looking at her, though, she lifts out her arms and flexes her wrists, like a ballerina getting ready for a pirouette, and begins to spin, effortlessly, on her skates. She spins in a small tight circle, her skates sending up sprays of ice into the darkening air, like a whirlpool spiraling through dark water.

I GO BACK TO MY HOUSE AND EAT ALONE. I TELL myself I don't want to get caught out in the approaching storm, but it's a weak excuse.

446

Although the clouds in the east appear menacing and a wind has come up since the sun set, there's no snow in the forecast. Just wind and cold. On the television I tune into an Albany station just long enough to hear that electrical storms, rare for this time of year, have been reported in the southern Adirondacks, and then the broadcaster's face dissolves in a blizzard of static. I turn on the radio, but I can't even get the country-western station in Corinth.

The truth is that I don't want to talk to anyone. I can't imagine what Dean Buehl was thinking by going ahead with the Ice Harvest. And old Beady really must be senile as well as blind to have the girls make those macabre statues. I know it's all anyone will be talking about in the dining hall and I can't bear right now to field innocent questions about the three sisters legend. Even my cold, rattling cottage—shack, I think to myself tonight, it's really a shack—is more appealing than that.

So I turn up the heat as high as it goes and fry eggs over a gas burner that spits blue flames at the frying pan. Outside the wind seems to be moving in circles around the house, like an animal trying to get in. I put on wool socks and pad around on the worn rag rugs, pulling curtains shut and double-checking window locks. Twice I check the phone to make sure I've got a dial tone. The third time I pick up the phone I get such an electric shock I drop the heavy old-fashioned receiver on my toe. All that padding around in wool socks, I

tell myself. Still, it keeps me away from the phone for the rest of the night, even though I'd been planning to call Olivia to remind her I'm coming this weekend. "I'll see her tomorrow," I tell myself, but I have to admit that part of the reason I don't call is that I've begun to detect a distance in her voice, a guardedness that I might cancel on her again.

I get in bed early. My old journal, that Roy gave me today, sits on my nightstand. I flip through it, not really reading, and notice that the pages flop loosely between their covers, like a person who's lost weight wearing old baggy pants. I remember that pages have been ripped out. I flip to the end and see that the very last page is missing. Yet that's not one of the pages that was sent to me.

I put the journal back on my nightstand and decide to read *The Aeneid*. Nothing like a little classical literature to calm the nerves, I think. Unfortunately, I'm at the part in Book Seven where Juno sends a fury to goad the Trojans and Latins into war. The description of the fury is so gruesome—*a monster, hated even by her father, Pluto, and by her Tartarean sisters, so many are the shapes that she takes on, so fierce her forms, so thick her snakes that swarm in blackness*—that I'm unable to read on. I remember that Helen Chambers told us that the Furies were sent out to avenge unavenged deaths. Curses personified, she said, the flip side of the three graces so beloved of Renaissance painters. I turn out the lights and burrow deep under the heavy wool blankets,

covering my ears so that I won't hear the wind and imagine some grotesque avenging monster hovering above Heart Lake, sowing dissent and suspicion among us.

But I can't drown out the sound of the wind. And under the high-pitched keening of the wind I hear a lower sound, a deep basso profundo moan that makes my hair stand on end. I slowly lift the blankets away from me and a shower of sparks cascades through the charged air. As I get out of bed, my hair lifts off my back like a fan. I walk to the front door and open it. Outside the trees are thrashing and fine ice particles spiral up from the ground like miniature tornadoes. I listen to all the tumult of the wind, but deep and steady, under the fitful tossing of the wind I can hear the moan, like a background theme that's always there beneath the flightier variations.

I know it's got to be the lake, the ice contracting and expanding, a natural process that I've heard described a dozen times by Dean Buehl and Myra Todd. But I've got to see for myself. I walk into the woods in my thick socks and flannel nightgown and I hardly feel the cold at all. It's as if all the electricity I've stored during the day is burning inside me now, keeping me warm. The lake is shrieking like a creature that's been ripped in half and of course it has, hacked down the middle with saws and poked at with steel-tipped spears. I feel now it's calling me and who can resist the call of something so wounded?

449

It's only when I reach the Point that I see the danger. The wind is all around me, pushing like a hand at my back, tugging at my nightgown with tiny icy fingers. It lifts my hair and nightgown up and I feel myself being borne light and charged as ionized electrons toward the brink. Then I feel another grip, hard and warm, and something pulls me back into the sheltering woods.

"Jane, are you crazy? What are you doing out in this?"

It's Roy Corey who's pulling me out of the wind and holding me by both arms, my back brushing against the rough bark of a white pine. My flannel nightgown rubs against his flannel shirt and the little shocks of electricity bring me back to my senses.

"I could ask you the same thing," I say, surprised at the calmness of my voice.

"There was something I wanted to see." He points to the ledge on the west side of the Point. "I wanted to see if someone could hide there. You didn't see me when you came out onto the Point, did you?" I shake my head. His hand is still on my arm and it feels warm. The wind is kicking the hem of my nightgown up, baring my legs.

"But I saw you. I saw you moving toward the Point just as you did that night Deirdre died. If someone was hiding on the west ledge that night she would have seen you come out of the woods and approach the Point. She would have seen Deirdre back away and fall. What she wouldn't have seen is Lucy on the

east ledge reaching up to grab Deirdre's ankle."

"So it would have looked like it was my fault?"

He nods. Suddenly I feel the cold and I start to shiver. Roy takes off his jacket and wraps it around my shoulders. He has to pull me away from the tree to get it around me and as he does my flannel nightgown catches a charge from his shirt and clings to him.

"So you decided to conduct this experiment in the middle of an electrical storm?" I ask through chattering teeth. He releases his grip on my arms, but I don't move away. I can't move back, anyway, because of the tree.

"I also wanted to keep an eye on your house," he tells me. "I didn't feel you were safe."

I lay my palm flat on his chest, expecting another shock, but instead his shirt feels damp and warm and I can feel his heart beating wildly. "Maybe you ought to come inside then."

He nods, but neither of us move. I hear the moan again, only now I realize it's not coming from the lake. It's in my throat and his. I lightly touch the back of my hand to his face and he slides his fingers under the collar of my nightgown and strokes my collarbone. I feel the cold air brush against my breasts and I start to shake. He moves up against me so that I'm wedged between his body and the tree and I can feel he's shaking, too. When he ducks his head to my throat my head arches

451

back and I can see the pine boughs above us, moving like bodies in a dance, moving the way we start to move. I lead him back to my house. We get under the blankets and, wordlessly, he makes love to me, slowly, never taking his eyes away from my eyes. I understand. This is not a fluke, he's telling me, we know each other this time.

When I have breath enough to speak I turn to him and say, "How you must have hated me."

He touches my forehead, strokes the damp hair back. "I didn't hate you, Jane. I hated myself for not telling you there and then who I was."

"We had Miss Buehl and her Girl Scouts shrieking and pointing at us. Hardly the moment to unmask."

He lifts himself on one elbow and runs the back of his hand down the length of my arm. I feel his breath cooling the sweat in the hollow of my collarbone. "But that's not why I didn't show you who I was. I didn't want to see the look of disappointment when you saw I wasn't Matt."

I look at him hard so that I don't, by looking away, admit the truth of what he's saying. I want to tell him he's wrong, but I can't. I would have been disappointed—more than disappointed, *crushed*—to have seen any face but Matt's beneath that mask. And for a moment, I do see Matt's face, rising in Roy's features, as if the seventeen-year-old boy is looking out of his cousin's eyes. I see him so clearly I feel as if every minutest hair on my body were sheathed in ice.

And then he's gone. Matt's face fades from Roy's, just as in my dream it sinks into the black water, only I suspect that this is the last time I will see that face.

I can't lie to Roy, so I tell him the next best thing. "I'm glad it's you. Here. Now."

Chapter Thirty-one

●

IT'S STILL DARK WHEN THE PHONE WAKES US. I SEE from the glowing green numbers on the digital alarm clock that it's 5:33. The phone is on Roy's side of the bed and he answers it by saying his name. I'm surprised by how unsurprised I am at this. As if I'd been with him for years and known how a cop always knows the call in the middle of the night is for him.

He listens without saying anything and then says, "I'll be right there." He swings his legs over his side of the bed and finds his jeans and shirt on the floor. When he stands up he sees me propped on one elbow, watching him, and he sinks back onto the bed and cups my face with his hand.

"I'm afraid this time it's worse than getting interrupted by the Girl Scouts."

ROY DOESN'T HAVE FAR TO GO. I FOLLOW HIM down the steps to the swimming beach where a little group is huddled in a circle of flashlights. I recognize three seniors, none of whom take Latin. The only one whose name I know is Mallory Martin, the girl whom my girls call Maleficent. She doesn't look too maleficent right now, crying and shaking under a trooper's heavy leather coat.

"We came out to watch the sun rise," she's telling someone. I get the feeling she no longer needs an audience to tell this story. She'll be telling it for the rest of her life. "We thought it would look cool—with all the statues? A bunch of girls talked about doing it yesterday at the Ice Harvest. At first we thought it *was* a statue." She points a wobbly finger in the direction of the stones. On the lake, police officers bundled in heavy coats are moving slow-footed over the ice, their arms held out to their sides for balance. Their posture reminds me of something—it's how Miss Pike told us to move through water looking for drowning victims, toes feeling the bottom, arms held out to feel for dead limbs. It reminds me of the morning they found Melissa Randall's body.

I walk past Mallory Martin and her circle. I'm going to follow Roy onto the ice, but at the edge of the lake a police officer holds up his hand to stop me.

"I'm sorry, miss, we don't want any civilians on the ice."

Roy turns and sees the look on my face.

"It's OK, Lloyd, she's with me."

I don't even think about the slipperiness of the ice, but stride out to where Roy is. We pass the first stone and the ice statue standing next to it. I look at its face and am startled to see the detail there. Someone went to a lot of trouble. The surface of the ice is smooth and glowing, as if the wind last night had polished it.

At the second stone the kneeling ice figure has been whittled down by the wind, so that it looks more like a lump on the ice than a statue. I look from it to where the third statue should lie, but although the first light has reached that part of the lake there is nothing there. It's as if the supine figure had sunk beneath the ice.

I turn to Roy to ask if this is what all the fuss is about and see the fourth statue. It's stretched out on the second stone, a girl's smooth marble-white body arched up as if in some terrible throes of pain or pleasure to meet the eight-foot ice pole thrust through its middle. It's only when the light creeps over her and touches her mermaid-red hair that I recognize Vesta.

"She said she couldn't sleep and was going to go skating on the lake," Athena is telling us for perhaps the third time. "She thought it would be cool to skate around the statues. Some

other girls had talked about doing it at the Ice Harvest. I offered to go with her but she was still mad at me about keeping the light on. She said if I was going to go she'd just as soon stay and turn out the light."

Athena looks up from the low chair in front of Dean Buehl's desk and we can all see the deep shadows under her eyes. A lock of stringy, multicolored hair falls over her left eye and the hand she lifts to push it back is trembling so hard she quickly returns it to her lap and clasps both hands together. I can see from my seat on the couch along the side wall that her cuticles are ragged and bloody. She squints in the glare from the early morning light on the ice outside Dean Buehl's window. I look away from her to the frozen lake. Mercifully, the view of the east cove is blocked by the Point. I wonder if they have removed Vesta by now or will they still be taking pictures of the body? I notice two police officers standing on the Point looking down into the east cove. One has set up a tripod and is taking aerial shots of the crime scene.

"And *you* heard nothing, Jane?"

I flinch at the sound of my name and look up at Dean Buehl, but it's Dr. Lockhart, who is standing at the large plate-glass window behind Dean Buehl's desk, who has asked the question. For a moment I don't understand what she thinks I would have heard, then I remember the shrieks and moans coming from the ice last night. Could they have been Vesta's cries for help and not the ice?

456

"There was a storm," I say. "I heard wind and the ice buckling."

"The ice buckling?" Dr. Lockhart repeats. I look up at her, but the glare from the lake ice surrounds her like a harsh aura and I have to shade my eyes to look in her direction. Even so, I can't read her expression.

"Yes," I say, "cracks and pops and..."

"Moans?" she asks. "Shrieks? That's what the ice sounds like. Did you go out and look?"

"I did go out," I say, "I went to the Point, but I never looked over."

Even Athena swivels her head and stares at me.

"I ran into Officer Corey—he was...um... patrolling the area."

There's a moment of silence during which I vividly remember what happened on the Point after I ran into Roy Corey. I look down at my hands and see they are bright pink and for a moment I'm sure I must be blushing, but then I realize it's only the morning light from the window.

"So did you both look over the Point to see where the sounds were coming from?" Dean Buehl finally asks. I think we're both surprised that Dr. Lockhart isn't the one to ask, but she has turned back to the window, her attention drawn to the two men taking pictures on the Point.

"I was going to, but Officer Corey led me back from the Point—I guess he was afraid it was too dangerous out there..." I'm mercifully interrupted by a soft knock on the door, which

457

opens to admit Roy Corey. For a moment I'm so happy just to see his face that I don't think about the fact he's a police officer.

"What's going on here? Why is this student here?" he directs the question to Dean Buehl, but it's Dr. Lockhart who answers.

"It's her roommate you've been peeling off the rocks out there. We thought she might know something about it."

At the word "peeling" I see Athena's face crumple. She turns to look at me. "What does she mean? I thought she was stabbed to death."

"Why did you think that, Ellen?" Dr. Lockhart steps away from the window, walks around Dean Buehl's desk and perches on its edge. She crosses one long, gray-stockinged leg over another and waits for Athena to answer. I notice there's a small pull in her pantyhose, just where her skirt rides up, and for some reason it makes me absurdly happy to see some tiny flaw in Dr. Lockhart's usually perfect ensemble. Otherwise, she is as calm and cool as ever. I wish I could say the same for Athena.

"S-s-someone told me," Athena says. I remember that's what she said to me when I asked her how she knew about my roommates' deaths twenty years ago. I've never heard her lisp before. "Didn't someone say she was stabbed? I mean, I thought with all those big ice poles lying all over the place..."

"Which you took such an interest in during the slide show..."

"Dr. Lockhart, if you have some theory to share with the police, perhaps you'd like to come down to the station..."

"Yes, I'd like that, Officer Corey. I'd like to know why a police officer was on the Point last night, preventing one of our teachers from looking over to see where all those awful sounds were coming from?"

Roy looks at me.

"I didn't say he prevented me...," I start to explain, but then I think about what happened on the Point last night and it occurs to me that, effectively, that's what he did. I falter and look up at Roy and he sees my hesitation.

"It was windy and the rocks were icy," he offers the explanation to me instead of Dr. Lockhart, but it's she who replies.

"So did you look over the Point to see where those noises were coming from?"

"I assumed it was the ice," Roy answers.

"Then you're either even stupider than the average cop or you're trying to cover up something you did see," she says calmly.

I can see a muscle in Roy's jaw flinch, but it's Athena who loses her composure. She springs out of her chair so abruptly it topples, hitting Roy in the kneecap and forcing him to step back.

"Why are you so mean?" she screams, lunging at Dr. Lockhart. The impact of Athena's collision with Dr. Lockhart knocks the desk back a good six inches, sending Dean Buehl's swivel chair careening backward into

459

the window. I hear glass shatter, and for a sickening moment I imagine Dean Buehl propelled out into the air, but it's Athena I'm moving toward. I throw my arm over her head in a shoulder hold that I learned from Miss Pike's lifesaving class and pull her back, her arms flailing as though she really were a drowning victim. Apparently she's a victim who doesn't want to be saved, because as soon as she gets her balance she sinks, sidesteps, and drives her elbow into my solar plexus. While I crumple over in pain, she runs from the room. When I can lift my head, I look for Dean Buehl, afraid of what I'll see, but she's all right, visibly shaken but untouched by the glass of the shattered window behind her, every inch of which is veined by an intricate maze, somehow magically suspended, as if held in place by the bright morning sun streaming in now through the cracks.

Roy helps me to a seat on the couch. Dean Buehl moves gingerly away from the shattered window and sits down next to me on my other side.

"Are you all right, Jane?" Dean Buehl asks. "I had no idea that girl was capable of such violence."

"I'm fine," I say. "It wasn't Athena's fault. She was..." I falter, unable to come up with a plausible explanation for my student's behavior. The word "provoked" comes to mind. "Upset," I say instead, which sounds

weak in view of the destruction left in Athena's wake. "I should go talk to her."

"I think it's better if I go," Dr. Lockhart says. "I've been working with her. I think I understand her issues."

"She seemed pretty angry with you," Roy says.

"That's all part of the therapeutic process," Dr. Lockhart says, putting on her coat. I look to Dean Buehl and she nods to me.

"Candace is right, she should go."

Dr. Lockhart smiles at me like a child who's won at some squabble mediated by grown-ups. When she's gone Dean Buehl adds, "Candace has a special empathy with these girls—she had the same sort of upbringing. Over the years I've seen so many girls like Ellen and Candace, girls whose parents have too little time for them and leave their care to us."

"Abandon them to you," Roy says.

"Don't be too harsh, Detective Corey. It's what they know; it's how they were brought up. I'm sure they think they're doing what's best for their children. Maybe it's the best they can do for them."

I have a sudden vision of Olivia, left with Mitch for safekeeping, that reawakens the pain in my stomach where Athena jabbed me with her elbow. I'm supposed to go see her this weekend.

As if reading my intention, Roy stands up, reassuming an official air. He addresses Dean Buehl, but I understand the message is for me. "You understand that now that this is an offi-

cial murder investigation no one should leave the campus." Dean Buehl nods and, when he looks in my direction, so do I.

I CAN TELL ROY WANTS TO COME WITH ME WHEN I leave Dean Buehl's office, but there's the phone call to be made to Vesta's parents and Dean Buehl asks him to stay. I stand in front of the mansion for a moment wondering where Athena and Dr. Lockhart have gone, but there's no sign of them. I'm stalled here trying to think of the words I'll use to explain to Olivia that I have to cancel again. I canceled the last weekend I was supposed to visit because of the snow. How can I disappoint her again?

I head back to my cottage to pick up my purse and the overnight bag I'd packed yesterday with clothes and papers to grade. I cut through the woods to avoid the police officers on the Point. I find, to my surprise, a narrow trail carved through the snow that leads me right back to my house. I find another one that gets me to the faculty parking lot. Someone's grown tired of staying on the regular footpaths and made their own, just as Lucy used to.

It's only when I'm in the car, waiting for my windows to defrost (I still have the chemical de-icer in my glove compartment, but I've avoided using it since almost blinding myself with it) and the heat to thaw my hands so I can drive, that I realize the seriousness of what I'm doing. It will look as though I'm fleeing a crime scene. But Roy will know I couldn't have

anything to do with Vesta's death. He was with me after all.

But can I say the same about him? Do I really know what he was doing up on the Point? I think about what he said. Whoever was behind these events had something to do with what happened twenty years ago. Matt was Roy's cousin. For twenty years he's felt responsible for his death. What if he suddenly had someone else to blame for it? The thought is so monstrous that all I want to do is get away from Heart Lake. And even though I still can't see through my rearview window, I back up blindly and drive as fast as I can to the Northway.

Chapter Thirty-two

South of Albany I get off the Thruway to take the Taconic the rest of the way south. Driving south on the Taconic I watch the Hudson Valley unscrolling toward the Catskill Mountains. It's a familiar, gentle landscape and for a while it takes my mind off Athena and Roy Corey and Heart Lake. I think instead of how so much of my life has been played out along this corridor. I remember taking the train

from Albany to Corinth after my mother died, of how I felt I was moving into my future even as I was traveling back to Heart Lake. Now, even as I'm fleeing Heart Lake as fast as I can, I feel as though I'm traveling into my past.

I think about Matt and Lucy. I've shied away from thinking about them since I learned the baby was theirs, but now I force myself to imagine them together. It would have been May Day. The same morning I was with Roy Corey. I remember how Lucy and the masked boy faced each other on the beach and how Lucy calmly walked into the water, daring the boy to follow. When I'd thought it was Ward Castle, I thought he wouldn't brave the cold water. I didn't have time to wait and see; I thought it was Matt, below me on the steps, waiting for me to flee so he could follow.

Now I imagine what happened after I turned my back on them. Lucy slipped into the mist rising from the water and started swimming for the icehouse and Matt followed her. He would have had to take off his mask. They were strong swimmers, used to swimming side by side in the lap lanes at the local pool. I picture them, cleaving the lake, their arms curving over the green water like two wings of the same bird. They would have been cold by the time they got to the icehouse. I picture Lucy, her lips blue and trembling, and Matt wrapping his arms around her to keep her warm. Maybe it wasn't the first time. I remember the way they danced through the falling leaves on the first day I walked home with them, and how

Matt spun Lucy on the ice when we skated on the lake. Maybe it was the first time.

I imagine they told each other it wouldn't ever happen again. But then Lucy found out from Helen Chambers that Matt wasn't really her brother. She thought that changed everything. People still might have talked—after all, they grew up *like* brother and sister—but Lucy wouldn't have cared and she could always talk Matt into doing what she wanted. It might have worked out for them, if I hadn't let slip to Matt about the baby.

I think about the night they died. Matt would have hitchhiked up this same road to get to Heart Lake after he got the letter from Lucy. He probably didn't know what to make of it. Neither had I, when I read it.

IT WAS AN AFTERNOON AT THE END OF FEBRUARY. She had just come back from dinner with Domina Chambers. *She said she'd learned some things that were going to change her life and she had to write and tell Matt. I assumed that* Domina Chambers *had outlined some plan for where Lucy would go to college and what she would do afterward.*

"Also, I want to make sure he's not worried about me with all this nonsense about my so-called suicide attempt," she told me. "D'you want me to put in a message from you?" she asked. "Like...oh, I don't know... Come, my Matthew, come, let's go a-Maying?"

I stared at her but she kept on writing with her head resolutely bent over the pale blue stationery

that Domina *Chambers had given her. After May Day I had copied over Robert Herrick's poem "Corinna's Maying" into my journal. In the last line I had substituted Matthew's name for Corinna's. Had Lucy read my journal? Or had she just made up the line herself? After all, we had both read it in English last year. Either way, I was surprised at her for referring to what happened on May Day so casually.*

She must have finally noticed me staring at her, because she looked up at me. "Jane, you're blushing. I'll just write the line at the end of the letter without mentioning your name. He'll know what it means, right?" She winked at me and bent back over the page. "How do the lines go again? 'And sin no more, as we have done, by staying, but, my Matthew, come, let's go a-Maying?'"

"Those come earlier in the poem," I said.

"Doesn't matter," she said, happily folding the letter and stuffing it in an envelope. "One more thing, have you got any more hairpins?"

I had a broken teacup on my desk in which I kept paper clips and hairpins. I handed it to her. She took out two U-shaped hairpins and one bobby pin. I watched as she fashioned a corniculum and put it in the envelope, carefully slipping it between the folds of her letter.

"Why are you sending him that?" I asked.

"So he'll meet me at the icehouse."

"But he's away at school," I said. "How can he meet you anywhere?"

Lucy smiled. "I have a feeling that once he gets this letter he'll find a way to come."

I PASS A SIGN FOR BEACON AND REALIZE I'M NOT FAR from the military school Matt had gone to. It's been more than two hours since I left Heart Lake. I wonder how long it took Matt to make the trip. He must have come as soon as he got the letter. It was only a few days after she'd written that I came back to the room after dinner and found, thumbtacked to our door, a corniculum.

LUCY WAS AT DINNER WITH DOMINA CHAMBERS AND the only other person who knew about the corniculum was Deirdre. I shivered for a moment, imagining it was somehow a sign from her, but then chided myself for being so melodramatic. Obviously it was from Matt. He must have sneaked up to the room and left it as a message for Lucy to meet him at the icehouse. She'd be so happy when she saw it.

I left it on the door and went into the room. I tried to start my Latin translation for the next day, but I couldn't concentrate. It was lonely doing the work by myself. I had always studied in a group, first with Matt and Lucy, and then with Deirdre and Lucy. I remembered that first day, in ninth grade, walking home with Matt and Lucy chanting declensions and how Matt had taught me what they meant, and how he had presented me with a red maple leaf. I still had the leaf, pressed in my Tales from the Ballet. *I took the book down from the shelf above my desk and turned to where the*

red leaf lay, pressed in between the pages of
Giselle.

And then something occurred to me. What if the
corniculum wasn't a sign for Lucy, but was,
instead, meant for me? After all, Lucy had put
that line about going a-Maying at the end of
her letter. Wouldn't Matt know it had come from
me?

I got up and opened the window. A gust of
wet air blew into the room, but it wasn't cold. It
wasn't exactly warm either, but there was something in it—the smell of snowmelt maybe—that
made me think of spring. I stuck my head out the
window and took deep breaths. A fine white mist
rose from the melting snow as if all the snow that
had fallen that winter was rising back to the
sky. I could hear water dripping from my window
ledge and from the pine trees and, farther away,
the sound of water moving in the lake where the
ice had broken.

I felt, suddenly, as if something were breaking
up inside of me. When I closed the window I felt
restless. I took out my journal and wrote, "Tonight
I will go down to the lake to meet him and I'll tell
him everything," before I knew that was what I
meant to do. I paused with the peacock blue pen
hovering over the page, waiting to see what I'd
write next. I wrote, "I know I shouldn't go, but
I can't seem to stop myself." Was that true?
Could I stop myself? Would I even try? I wrote,
"It's like the lake is calling me," and I thought,
yes, that's what it is, that restless sound of water
moving through the night, not just in the lake, but
rising from the snow and dripping from the trees,

a whole watery world out there calling to me. I wrote, "Sometimes I wonder if what they say about the three sisters is true. It's like they're making me go down to the lake when I know I shouldn't." I'd come to the end of a page. I turned it and saw I'd come to the last page of the notebook. I wrote one more line and then closed the book and went out.

THAT'S HOW DESPERATE I'D BEEN TO SEE MATT; I blamed my going on the three sisters legend. It's almost funny. I notice, though, that I'm not laughing. I'm crying so hard it's difficult to see the road. It doesn't help that the sky has darkened and a sharp wind is buffeting the car. I take a curve too fast and feel my tires skitter on the gravel on the shoulder. Shaken, I pull into a scenic overview and stare at rain clouds massing over the Catskills while waiting for my crying jag to stop.

What had Matt thought of the May Day reference in Lucy's letter? Did he suspect that Lucy had gotten pregnant on May Day? Is that why he rushed up to Heart Lake? I shake my head. How will I ever know? Matt's dead. Lucy's dead. Everyone who could tell me is gone.

I stare at the soft folds of the Hudson Valley as if the landscape could answer my questions, but even this familiar vista fails me as the clouds from the west move across the valley, darkening the land and obscuring my view. But not everybody from back then is dead. Roy's

alive. He was with Matt when Matt got Lucy's letter, with him at his parents' house in Cold Spring when he decided to leave for Heart Lake. Hadn't Roy said, when he met me at the Aquadome, that he'd just been visiting his mother in Cold Spring? (*Our aunt Doris in Cold Spring,* I hear Lucy's voice, as if she were there beside me in the car, whispering in my ear.)

I wipe my eyes and look at the car clock. It's only one o'clock in the afternoon. Olivia will still be at school. I have time, I think, to make one quick stop.

As I pull back on the road I know I'm being foolish. What can I possibly expect to find in Roy's mother's house? If Matt hadn't told Roy why he was he leaving for Heart Lake, he certainly wouldn't have told his aunt. But even as I tell myself all the reasons I shouldn't be going I'm getting off the exit for Cold Spring and looking for a gas station so I can look up the address. If it's not listed, I tell myself, I'll take it as a sign that I'm on a fool's errand and drive straight to Mitchell's house.

Not only is Doris Corey listed, she lives right on the main street of town. The road into town slopes steeply down toward the river. I can see, on a bluff overlooking the river, a low dark building with crenellated towers. The Manlius Military Academy for Boys. Matt's old school. I look away from it and concentrate on looking for the Coreys' house. It's almost the last house on the street, a small yellow Vic-

torian just before the train tracks and a stone's throw from the river.

The woman who answers the door looks so much like Hannah Toller that for a moment I think the report that I'd heard all those years ago of her death in a car accident must have been a mistake. When she smiles at me, though, me a stranger standing at her doorstep in the pouring rain, I see she's softer than Hannah Toller ever was. I realize how guarded and strained Lucy and Matt's mother had always been—bowed down, no doubt, by all the secrets she had borne.

This woman, Doris Corey, has me into her house before I can even explain that I live in Corinth and know her son. "Is it Roy?" she asks, her hands arrested in reaching to help me off with my down parka. "Are you with the police, dear? Have you come to tell me something's happened to Roy?"

For all the panic in her eyes she's still polite. If I were to tell her that something had happened to Roy she wouldn't scream and make a scene; she'd know I was only the blameless messenger of bad news. I think of all the sadness she's lived through. Her niece and nephew drowning in a lake, her sister and brother-in-law dying in a car accident. She holds herself like someone braced for tragedy.

"Oh no, Mrs. Corey. Roy's fine. You see..." I try to think how to explain to her why I'm here and can think of nothing better than to tell her my name.

"Jane Hudson," the hand that was tugging

at my wet coat comes to rest on my forearm and squeezes, "weren't you Mattie's girl?"

The noise I make must sound as if I'm choking. *Mattie's girl.* It's all I ever wanted to be. But I can't lie to this woman. "I was a friend of Lucy and Matt's, Mrs. Corey, but that's all."

She waves a dismissive hand at my disclaimer.

"Oh, he talked about you all the time, dear. He told me about the time Lucy fell through the ice and you pulled her out. He said you were the bravest person he knew."

You'd pull me out, wouldn't you, Jane?

My tears are falling again, mixing with the rainwater dripping from my hair, before I can do anything to stop them. Mrs. Corey makes a soft sound at the back of her throat, something between a tisk and an ahh, and pulls me down next to her on the couch. She pulls a brightly colored afghan from the back of the couch and tucks it around my shoulders, but the scratchy wool only sets me to shivering.

"I know, I know," she says, over and over. "It still comes to me some days, the thought of those two drowning. I confess it's Mattie I think of most often. I guess because we'd come to feel he was like our own all those weekends he stayed here. Lucy...well, she was always a quiet one—not one to let you get too close. Even when she was a baby she'd struggle in your arms..."

"Did you know she wasn't Hannah's?"

Mrs. Corey sighs and smoothes the afghan over my shoulders. "Hannah was my little sister," she says. "When she came home with

that baby everyone else believed her when she said it was hers, but I could tell. She didn't nurse her—when Mattie was born she nursed him. It's not that she didn't treat Lucy good—she took extra pains with her. She seemed...I don't know...almost in awe of her. And then she didn't look a bit like her or any of us..."

"Did you confront her?"

"Only once. When she let Matt and Lucy start school together. I asked her if she thought it a good idea, encouraging the two of them to be so close. She asked me what I meant, weren't they brother and sister? When I didn't say anything to that she looked away and told me to mind my own business. We never spoke of it again, but when she asked me to keep Mattie here...well...she said she was sorry she hadn't listened to me before."

She sits back and folds her hands in her lap. She looks away from me to the mantel. I follow her gaze and see there the picture of Matt. It's a posed portrait with a flag in the background. His school picture for his senior year at Manlius. His hair looks darker than I remember it and longer, the seventies haircut looks dated. I look away from the picture to Mrs. Corey. I want to ask her what else Matt said about me. What else did he say to give the impression that I was his girlfriend. But I realize suddenly how little it matters anymore.

"Did you know who Lucy's real mother was?" I ask instead.

"I guessed it was that friend of hers, Helen Chambers. That's who the girl looked like, after all. And then after Hannah died I found out that Helen Chambers had owned the house on River Street. She'd left it to Cliff and Hannah when she...when she passed on." She unfolds her hands and plucks on the tufts on the upholstery. She doesn't want to say "killed herself." I look down at the worn chintz pattern on the couch and realize I've seen it before.

"And then you inherited the house from Hannah."

"I was the only one left," she says, "but I couldn't hardly bear to be in that house for five minutes. Roy helped me move some of the furniture—Hannah'd always had better than what we could afford—but neither of us could bear to clear out the attic rooms. We figured whoever bought the house would clear it away, but then the house never would sell. People must've thought it was unlucky."

I remember that it's what I suggested to Dr. Lockhart, but then, how had she come to live there?

"But you sold it eventually?" I ask.

"Only last year. I'd been renting it out summers, and then I got this letter from someone at Heart Lake..."

"From someone at Heart Lake?"

Doris Corey frowns. "I don't remember. Let me see, I think I still have the letter. It had something nice in it about Lucy, so I saved it." Doris Corey gets up and pushes open the top of a rolltop desk—a desk I suddenly remember

474

as standing in the Tollers' front hall. I look around me and recognize other pieces of furniture from the Toller household—a highboy carved of some dark wood, a wingback chair, a grandfather clock. They crowd around the couch, these relics from the past, like the dead heroes clamored around Aeneas in the underworld.

"Something nice about Lucy?" I repeat. "But how..."

Doris Corey comes back to the couch and hands me a letter written on pale gray stationery in blue-green ink. "Dear Mrs. Corey," I read. "I'd like to inquire about purchasing the house on River Street. I know it's been vacant for many years and I understand how you might be reluctant to part with your sister's old house."

Doris Corey points to the first paragraph. "I thought this girl must be either very naive or very rich. Or both. Imagine keeping a piece of real estate for sentimental value!"

I continue reading.

"I'd like to assure you that the house would be in very good hands. You see, I, too, have sentimental reasons for wanting to live in the house on River Street. I attended Heart Lake for three years in the late seventies (because of circumstances outside my control I had to leave) and that was how I came to know your niece, Lucy. Although she was several classes ahead of me, she was kind enough to take an interest in me. I had a very lonely childhood and I've never forgotten the kindness she

showed me, almost as if she were an older sister. When she died I felt as if I had lost a part of my family, almost, indeed, a part of myself. Now that I've returned to Heart Lake (I often think that my decision to work with troubled adolescent girls is a way of repaying my debt to Lucy) I would cherish the opportunity to live in her old house."

There followed a generous cash offer for the house.

"Can I use your phone?" I ask, handing the letter back to Doris Corey.

I dial Dean Buehl's office. She answers on the first ring and at the sound of my voice nearly shouts at me. "My God, Jane, we've been looking everywhere for you. Where are you? Are Athena and Dr. Lockhart there with you?"

Doris Corey must see how pale I get because she wraps the afghan around my shoulders.

"No. How long have they been missing?"

"Since Athena stormed out of my office this morning. We're afraid she's done something to Dr. Lockhart—"

"Dean Buehl," I interrupt. "Was Dr. Lockhart a student at Heart Lake?"

"Well, yes, for a few years, but she didn't like people to know because she was expelled. But you know all about that, Jane, I told you..."

I remember standing at the train station looking across the tracks at the small girl posed rigidly beside her luggage, her face set in a frozen glare, while Miss Buehl told me that she had been expelled for breaking the fanlight above the front door of Main.

"She's Albie. You hired Albie, didn't you? You felt sorry for her and you hired her."

"Well, yes. That poor girl had been through so much. All she wanted was to come back to Heart Lake. But I didn't lie, she wasn't an old girl because she didn't graduate..."

"But you should have told me."

"But Jane, I thought you knew. After all it's what her name means in Latin: white. That's why she was called Albie."

Candace. It means fire-white. That's what I feel now—a mix of fire and ice that tingles in my veins and gets me to my feet, Doris Corey's afghan falling to the floor like a pile of brightly colored leaves.

"Listen," I say to Dean Buehl, "explain all of this to Roy Corey. Tell him that Dr. Lockhart is Albie and tell him I'm on my way back."

BEFORE I GET BACK ON THE TACONIC I STOP AT A pay phone and make another call. I could have used Doris Corey's phone but I'd been ashamed to make this call in front of anybody. I'm out of change so I call collect.

Mitch accepts the charges and without a word to me hands the receiver over to Olivia.

"Mommy? Are you almost here? I'm waiting up for you so you can read me my bedtime story."

"Honey," I say, and then pause, letting my head rest on the cold, grimy metal pay phone booth, "Mommy's going to be a little late, but I'll try to be there when you get up."

There's a silence so long that I think the connection's been broken, then I hear a small voice, which sounds in the rushing static as though it were underwater. "But you promised."

There's just nothing I can say to that. I tell her I'm sorry and that I'll try to make it up to her and I get off the phone before she can ask me just how I think I'm going to do that. Then I get in the car and drive north and try not to think about Olivia. I think, instead, about another little girl: Albie.

I try to remember what Deirdre and Lucy told me about her, but the truth is I was never that interested. She was a homely little kid who tagged along following us all over campus. Lucy seemed to accept her adulation as her due. Deirdre felt sorry for her, because, like herself, she was shuttled from school to school, unwanted. Even *Domina* Chambers had taken an interest in her. I had tried to talk to her once or twice, but she never seemed to like me. Maybe she saw me as a rival to Lucy's affections.

As I drive farther north, the rain turns into icy sleet. My windows frost up and my car slithers and fishtails on the upgrades. I drive fast, though, wiping the frost away from the windshield with the heel of my hand like a child pushes tears away.

Or was it the other way around? Had I seen her as a rival? After all, how many poor scraggly "orphan" girls could Lucy befriend? I think of all the times I caught her spying on us in the woods. How many times had she

watched us without me knowing? I remember the figure I thought I saw on the Point when Lucy and I sank the tin in the lake, the sense I had of being watched the night Deirdre died.... What was it Roy had said? If someone was hiding on the west ledge it would have looked like I was the one who made Deirdre fall to her death.

When I reach the Northway I expect better road conditions, but instead I hit fog. The sleet, which I expected to turn to snow as I got farther north, turns back to rain. Most of the traffic stays in the right lane and crawls slowly through the dense white shroud. I get in the left lane and do eighty.

And that last night...the night I'd gone down to the icehouse to meet Matt. I had that same sense of being followed through the woods. What would she have made of that final scene on the ice? I close my eyes against the picture and nearly run into the guardrail. She would blame me for Lucy's death. Had I even thought, twenty years ago, of looking for her after Lucy died? To comfort her? No, I was too busy with my own grief. The next thing I knew about her was that she'd been expelled for smashing the stained-glass fanlight. The one inscribed with the school's motto. I remember the day Lucy explained to Albie what the motto meant. "It means there's always a place for you here. And it means I will always be here for you, too..."

But Lucy hadn't been able to keep that promise. In her rage, Albie had thrown rocks

through the window—through the broken promise of those words. Then she had been sent to St. Eustace. *St. Useless.* Where they sent you when you were no use to anyone.

I spot the Corinth exit with barely enough time to cut across two lanes of slow-moving traffic and skid onto the exit ramp. The fog is even worse now that I'm off the highway. I can barely see the side of the road. I roll my windows down and fix on the little reflective bumps that mark the median to gauge the two-lane road that climbs up to Corinth. About halfway, I come up against a slow-moving lumber truck that is crawling up to the mill. There's no way to pass it, so I put my car in low gear and tail so close behind that I can smell the sickly sweet smell of fresh-cut pine.

I can tell I've reached town by the yellow tinge to the fog as I pass the mill. I sniff at the familiar scent of pulp. I used to think when I was little that the yellow smoke that rose from the mill was the ghosts of trees, and the white paper the mill produced their earthly remains—the bleached white bones of northern forests.

Finally, the truck pulls off and I accelerate through the rest of the village, crossing the bridge so fast my teeth vibrate. I'm on River Road, passing the old Victorians, which loom out of the fog like prehistoric monsters. At the end of the road, just before the turn off to Heart Lake, is the little house that always seemed to me like something out of a fairy tale. The only thing I hadn't realized was that as far as

the woman living in it is concerned, I'm the bad witch. I made Deirdre fall off the Point. I let Lucy drown under the ice. I lied at the inquest and got her favorite teacher fired. I sent her into Siberian exile.

I turn the engine off, wishing I'd thought to park farther down the road or at least turned my headlights off. When I do that now I see that the house is not completely dark. Like the first night I found Dr. Lockhart here, there's a light in the attic.

What I should do is find a phone and call the police—see if they can reach Roy. What I do instead is reach deep into my book bag until my fingers graze cold metal. Dr. Lockhart's keys. I still have them. That I should use them seems the next logical step. I open my glove compartment and look for something I can use as a weapon. There's the flashlight, but its batteries are still dead and it's made of cheap, light plastic. The only other thing in the glove compartment is the small aerosol can of de-icer. I slip it into my pocket, figuring I can use it like mace. Then I get out of the car as quietly as I can and walk through the unshoveled snow to the front door. By the time I make it there my jeans are soaked to the knees and I'm sweating under my down parka. The snow, I notice, is slushy and steaming, exuding a thick white fog like some pestilential vapor. When I touch the doorknob I find it's warm.

There are only three keys on the chain and I already know that two of them are for Dr. Lockhart's office and filing cabinet. I put the

third key in the lock and it turns easily. I push open the door into a darkness that feels smoky, as if the fog from the melting snow had somehow gotten inside and turned black. I look around the living room, trying to make out the shape of furniture, but after a moment I realize that the room is completely empty. There isn't a single stick of furniture on the first floor.

But the light I saw was coming from the attic. As I go up the stairs the darkness pales and turns pink. When I get to the head of the stairs I see why. There's a night-light in the shape of a pink poodle plugged into an outlet. The only other source of light comes from the room on the left. Matt's room. I go in and see that the light comes from a green-shaded banker's lamp on one of the desks by the window.

Lucy's desk. There's no other word for it. Even before I walk across the room and reach it I know it will be exactly as I saw it the last time I was in this room twenty years ago. The same lumpy pottery cup that Matt made for her in second grade holding the same collection of peacock-blue fountain pens. A brass eternal calendar in the shape of a globe, the day marked February 28, 1977. There's a blue Fair Isle cardigan hung across the back of the chair, which, when I lift, holds the shape of the chair in its shoulders. I see by its faded label it's from Harrods. It's the sweater I borrowed from Lucy and left in the woods.

When I drop the sweater back to the chair a moth flutters out of its folds and beats itself

against the lamp. I slowly turn in a circle, taking in the whole room. Matt's hockey stick is propped against the bookshelf where Wheelock's Latin leans against Peterson's *Field Guide to Birds*. Matt's collection of Hardy Boys on the top shelf. Lucy's Nancy Drews on the middle. Over Matt's bed hangs a pennant for Dartmouth College. I'd forgotten that's where Matt wanted to go to college. He said he liked that it was founded by an Indian.

I look back at the desk and notice a few sheets of stationery with "Exeter" printed on top. The letters from Brian. There, too, are a supply of hairpins. A piece of lined paper, its edges ragged where it was ripped out of its stitched binding, lies under a smooth gray-green rock. I lift the rock and see there's only one line written on the top of the page. It's the last page from my journal. The last line I wrote before going down to the lake to find Matt. *I won't let anyone stand in my way,* I'd written, *not even Lucy.*

As I put the stone down I hear a sound from the back of the house. There's no window facing the back in the attic, so I run down the stairs, through the dark house, thankful there's no furniture to bump into. I unlatch the back door and step into the fog. I can't see more than a few feet in front of me and when I try to listen all I can hear is the drip of melting snow and the rush of moving water somewhere in the woods. It must be the Schwanenkill, thawed out, flowing out of Heart Lake. Then I look down at my feet and see that

I'm standing in a narrow groove, a footpath carved out of the snow, just wide enough for one. And something gleaming in the wet snow. I bend down and pick it up. It's a tiny silver skull earring. A macabre thing, but I recognize it as Athena's. It's impossible, in this fog, to see where the path goes, but I'm already following it into the woods.

Chapter Thirty-three

AT FIRST THE PATH RUNS PARALLEL TO THE Schwanenkill. I know, not because I can see the stream but because I can hear it—a faint watery whisper like the murmuring of an unseen companion passing through the woods beside me. Then it veers abruptly left and plunges into the deep, fog-white woods.

It's like entering a white tunnel. On either side the snow rises steeply and where the snow leaves off the white fog rises, like a curtain being lifted from the ground to shield... shield what? I'm reminded of a slide Tacy Beade showed us in her ancient art lecture of two hand-maidens holding up a draped cloth to shield the goddess at her bath. The face I see staring out behind the curtain now is the wide-eyed

frightened face of a lost child. The awkward little girl we called Albie who used to follow us through the woods. The little girl who's turned the game around and become the leader instead of the follower.

The path loops around tree trunks and meanders through the forest. When I come to the first branch I don't know which way to go and stare hopelessly into the white mist. Then in the stillness of the woods I hear a faint chiming. At first I think I'm imagining it—a tinny bell that might be the ringing of my own blood in my ears—but when I follow the sound to the left branch of the trail I catch the faint glimmer of metal swinging from an over-hanging branch. Three hairpins linked in the shape of a horned animal dangling among the pine needles. I take that trail and from then on, at every divergence, I look for the corniculum like a trail blaze and follow it. I've soon lost any sense of direction or time. The convolutions of the trail seem to grow tighter and more erratic, folding back on themselves like a Mobius strip, until I feel as though I am no longer following a path through the woods but a train of thought in some addled brain. But whose addled brain? Because even though I know it's Albie's path I'm following, I feel as if I'm traveling into my own past, taking the same path I took that night twenty years ago when I went down to the lake to meet Matt at the icehouse.

WHEN I LEFT THE DORM I GRABBED A JACKET ONLY half noticing that it was Lucy's pale blue parka instead of mine. I was halfway down the hall before I remembered that I had left the corniculum on the door. Should I go back and take it down? If I left it on the door, Lucy would no doubt come along to the icehouse when she got back. Then I wouldn't be alone with Matt. I thought of going back, but I felt too impatient, too anxious to be out, breathing the wet, sweet air. I was already past the matron's desk (I told her I'd left a book in the dining hall); I was already on the path heading around the west side of the lake.

Outside the night was even more stirring than it had promised to be. The wind moved through the trees spraying pine-scented water across my face. The lake was still coated with a white layer of ice but its surface was dull and I could hear the water moving restlessly beneath the surface as if trying to break free. Patches of ice, gritty and opaque, still littered the path. When I stepped on them pale air bubbles raced beneath my feet. All around me, the melting snow rose in a pure white mist, like a linen cloth pulled away to reveal some magical transformation: paper flowers, the flutter of pale wings. I kept looking into the woods, expecting something to show itself behind the shredded wisps of fog, but although I heard, once or twice, the snap of a branch or a watery sigh, I saw no one and I dismissed my sense of being followed to my imagination. I thought about

Matt waiting at the icehouse and the thought that I was going to be with him soon moved through my body like the wind moving through the pine trees.

SHE MUST HAVE BEEN WATCHING ME THAT NIGHT, just as she's watching me now. When I have wandered in enough circles to wear myself out will she pounce on me from behind the white fog? Or will she merely leave me in the woods to freeze to death while she makes away with Athena? The thought of Athena sharpens my wits for a moment. What does she have in mind for her? I am beginning to understand why Dr. Lockhart hates me. As she sees it, I killed her two best friends and caused her favorite teacher to lose her job and ultimately kill herself. She spent the rest of her school days in a rigid, loveless place. She must have felt she was in exile. How Heart Lake and the memory of Lucy and *Domina* Chambers must have grown in her mind. It must have infuriated her to see me come back here and take *Domina* Chambers's place. *Think of Helen Chambers when you're dealing with your students,* she said to me at that first meeting. And from that moment on my life has been a replica of what happened to Helen Chambers. That is the punishment she devised for me.

I stop for a moment on the path and stare into the impenetrable fog. I hear, again, the whisper of water on the wind and together with the fog it reminds me of that last night I went

487

down to the icehouse to meet Matt. I think about that last meeting and try to see it through Albie's eyes.

As I rounded the end of the lake, I saw that there was a light coming from the icehouse. I crossed the Schwanenkill carelessly, crashing through the thin ice in the middle. He must have heard me, because as I struggled up the bank I saw him above me, reaching out his arm to give me a hand up. I took off my mitten so I could feel the warmth of his flesh right away.

"I knew you'd come," he said, pulling me up the bank. His voice sounded hoarser and deeper than I remembered. He pushed back the hood of my parka and touched my face.

"Jane!" he said. I couldn't tell if it were surprise or excitement that I heard in his voice. And then I saw the unmistakable look of disappointment in his face and I knew.

"Where's Lucy?" he said. "Why didn't she come?"

I stared at him and tried to keep the tears from coming. After all, just because he'd expected his sister didn't mean he didn't want to see me as well.

"She was with Domina Chambers so I came first. I left the corniculum on the door, though, so she'll be here soon." I was glad, now, that I had left it. "I thought...well, I thought, you might want to see me, too."

Matthew sighed and put his arm around my shoulder. "Of course I want to see you, too. Good old Jane. It's just that I'm worried about Lucy.

I heard about what happened at Christmas and then about what happened to poor Deirdre. And then Lucy sent me a very confusing letter..."

"She told you about what happened at Christmas?"

"Well, I heard from my parents that she tried to kill herself. At first I just couldn't believe it, and then I thought I might understand why..."

"But didn't she write and say she didn't really mean to kill herself?"

"Yes, but don't people always say that after they've tried and failed? That they didn't really mean it? She did cut herself, didn't she? I can't stand the idea of her hurting herself especially when it's probably all my fault."

I saw the look of pain on his face and I thought to myself, well, at least I have the power to do something for him. "She didn't try to kill herself at all, Mattie, it was all a sham."

"A sham?"

"Yes, it was a cover-up. For Deirdre. Not that she appreciated it, although I guess I shouldn't speak ill of the dead."

"What are you talking about, Jane?"

"Look, let's go inside the icehouse and sit down. I'll explain everything."

THE PATH, I NOTICE, IS BEGINNING TO SLOPE DOWN-ward. At one point it becomes so steep I have to hold on to branches to keep from sliding down the icy chute. I hear a soft moaning sound and I strain to hear if it's Athena. *It's me you want*, I say to myself, over and over.

489

And then I call it out. "Albie, it's me you want for letting Lucy die, not Athena."

My own words come back in an echo as if they've bounced off a rock wall. And then I see why. I've come to the end of the path and it ends in sheer ice. I'm at the edge of the lake, on the southern tip, not far from the ice-house. Directly across from the rock wall of the Point. I could have gotten here in fifteen minutes from the Toller house if I'd followed the Schwanenkill instead of following the crazy meandering of Albie's path. She's worn me out and given herself more time and gotten me just where she wants me.

I hear again the sound of bells, louder than the tinny chime of the corniculi, and when I look up I see, hanging like Damocles' sword, twin silver blades. I step out from under them and see that they're skates hanging from a branch by their knotted laces. An index card has been threaded through the laces and on it, in childish scrawl, is written "Lucy's Skates," only the name Lucy has been exxed out and under it there's my name, crossed out as well, then Deirdre's name, crossed out, and then, finally, my name again. Jane's skates, it is then. I take them down and, as I'm meant to, put them on.

They're a little tight (it's a good thing I'm wearing thin stockings), but otherwise they fit well, and, I notice as I stroke out over the slick ice, the blades have recently been sharpened. As tired as I am I seem to be skimming over the surface of the lake effortlessly. I even do

a little spin and land looking back at the ice-house, at the doors left open from the recent ice harvest, creaking in the wash from the channel that's been carved out of the ice. Is that where Albie hid that night, behind the doors? If she had, she would have heard everything I said to Matt.

HE'D LEFT HIS FLASHLIGHT ON THE LEDGE; THAT was the light I'd seen coming from the icehouse. We sat down in the boat and leaned against the stern, next to each other so we could both look at the lake. I remembered the last time I had looked out these doors onto the lake. It was when Lucy and I were putting back the boat. The blizzard had started and the air was so full of snow it had blotted out the lake. Now the air was white from that same snow evaporating back into the sky. I liked the idea of the snow returning to the sky; it was the past rewritten with all its mistakes rubbed clean.

While I talked Matt bowed his head so that I couldn't see his face. I told him everything that had happened the day I came back from Albany, from the moment I walked into the dorm room to the last glimpse I had of the tea tin sinking into the black water. When I finished he asked one question.

"Whose baby was it?"

"Lucy thought it was Ward's because that's who Deirdre was with on May Day."

Matt lifted his head, but he didn't look at me. His eyes were on the lake, as if drawn there by some kind of magnetism.

"Why did she think the baby was conceived on May Day?"

"Because Deirdre hadn't been with...anyone... for weeks before. Because of the rain, remember? And the time before that, well, that would have been too long. Lucy said the baby was small so it was probably early and the time worked with May Day." I was beginning to realize what Matt was afraid of.

"Did you see it?"

I nodded and then realized he still wasn't looking at me. I decided then to say no, but he must have seen me out of the corner of his eye.

"Who did it look like?" he asked.

"Oh Matt, it hardly looked like a person. It was tiny." I remembered the way the skin had glowed like opals and the pale red hair like fire.

Matt turned to me and took me by the shoulders. "Did it look like me, Jane? Tell me the truth."

"Matt," I cried, surprised at how hard he was gripping me. "It couldn't be yours because you weren't with Deirdre on May Day."

"Shut up, Jane."

The words startled me more than the way Matt was hurting me. They came from behind us. Matt got up and stepped out of the boat, which rocked so hard I slid and knocked my head on the stern. When I scrambled to my feet and got out at the front of the boat I saw Matt facing his sister, his hands balled into tight fists. I'd never seen him look so angry. Actually, I couldn't remember ever seeing him angry at all.

"Whose baby was it, Lucy?" he asked his sister.

"It was Deirdre's baby, Mattie. Isn't that what Jane told you?" Lucy looked toward me and the coldness of her look shocked me. "She promised not to tell anyone, but that doesn't matter now. Don't you believe her, Matt? You know Jane would never lie."

"I also know she'd believe anything you told her." Matt came around the boat toward me. He looked so unlike himself that I took a step away from him, but when he took my hand he was gentle.

"You saw it, Lucy. Tell me, what color hair did it have?"

"Babies don't always have hair," Lucy said. I heard an unfamiliar note of panic in Lucy's voice. She came around the other side of the boat and stood next to me. We were all three standing in the doorway facing the lake.

"Did it have hair, Jane?"

I looked from Matt to Lucy. Lucy shook her head and, seeing her movement, Matt dropped my hand and whirled around on her. "Was it red like mine, Lucy?" He took a step toward her and Lucy backed up to the edge of the doorway.

"Your cousin has red hair, too, Matt," I called over his shoulder. "Maybe Deirdre was with Roy on May Day."

Matt looked back at me and laughed. "Oh, Janie... ," he began, but before he could finish what he was going to say he was silenced by a sound that made my whole body go cold. It was a high keening moan, like no sound I'd ever heard a human being make, and yet there was something like human emotion in the sound. We both turned

493

*to the lake and saw that Lucy had run onto the
ice. The moan was coming from the ice itself, buckling under her weight.*

I STAND ON THE ICE NOW, PICTURING LUCY COMING
out of the icehouse onto the melting ice.
She'd run in a straight line from the icehouse
out into the middle of the lake, the ice shuddering and moaning at every step, leaving
black water in her wake. The path she took is
now marked by the channel. When Matt tried
to follow her he had to stay on the east side
of the lake. That's how I go now, making
toward the east cove and the sister stones. I
look down at the ice to see if I can see the mark
of skate blades, but the fog is so thick I can't
even see my own feet. It makes me feel queasy,
as if I've become invisible.

Then I see a figure up ahead, standing still
in the fog. I skate toward it, trying to glide on
each skate as long as I can so as not to make
too much noise. The figure seems not to hear
me and I'm afraid I'll find that it's Athena,
frozen and dead on the ice, but when I reach
it I see it's only one of the statues left over from
the ice harvest. I look around and realize
they're everywhere, standing on the ice like
sentinels before a tomb. I skate from one to
another, looking for some sign that Albie and
Athena have passed this way. I stare into
each face as if it might speak and tell me
where they have gone, and so animate are
they it seems they might at any moment gain

voice. The crudely hewn features have softened, the caverns of their chisel gouged eyes deepening, rough-cut lips separating as if about to speak. I wonder for a moment how these hastily crafted sculptures have become so lifelike, and then I realize what it is. They're melting.

I think of the rain I'd encountered on the Northway. The temperature's been rising steadily since the electrical storm last night. That's why there's so much fog. How long, I wonder, before the lake ice melts and cracks? I listen to the low moan of the ice as if it could tell me, and then I realize the moan I'm hearing isn't coming from the ice, it's coming from the sister stones, which, I now see, are directly in front of me. I skate toward them, stilling inside myself the terrifying impression that the stones themselves are calling out to me. It's just another trick of the ice, I tell myself, and then, when that doesn't work I recite a little Latin to calm myself down.

"*Tum rauca adsidero longe sale saxa sonabat,*" I whisper to myself, choosing the Virgil passage Athena translated only last week in class. It seems fitting—*Far out were heard the growl and roar of the stones where the surf beat unceasingly*—and comforting somehow, to think of Aeneas's ship safely navigating around the Sirens' stones and making its way to the Italian shore and the sibyl's cave.

I've reached the second sister stone where the sound seems to be the loudest and, I can no longer deny, human. But this cry of human

anguish is not coming from the sister stone, but from the rock face of the Point. Someone is in the cave. I shuffle forward on my skates as I approach the entrance to the cave, sure that at any moment Dr. Lockhart will pop out and impale me with one of those horrible ice pikes. I take out my can of de-icer and hold my finger over the spray top. But when I peer into the dark cavern I see only Athena, kneeling gagged and tied on the narrow ledge above the ice.

I take off the gag first.

"Dr. Lockhart," she gasps, "she's crazy."

I nod and put a finger to my mouth to shush her.

"Tace," I say, "I know. Let me untie you and get you out of here."

The ropes around Athena's wrists and ankles are too tightly bound to come undone. The more I pluck at the wet, frozen cords the tighter they seem to grow. Her trembling makes it all the harder to undo the knots.

"I need to cut them," I tell her, as if she could go into the next classroom to borrow a pair of scissors.

"Don't leave me," she cries, swinging her head toward me so that I feel the wet ends of her hair brush my cheek. I look up and see the wild fear in her eyes and the tears that streak her muddy face. "She wants to kill me. First she called me Deirdre, then Lucy, then Jane. She didn't seem to be able to keep straight who I was."

Athena sobs and I pat her shoulder clum-

sily. I tell her I won't leave, but she's got to help me think of a way of getting these ropes off her. I sit back on my heels to consider our predicament and sit down hard on the ends of my skates.

I've got the left skate unlaced and off before I can think through how vulnerable this leaves me if Dr. Lockhart should show up at this moment. What difference does it make though? I'm not leaving here without Athena. I hold the skate by the boot toe, place the blade over the ropes on Athena's ankles, and start to saw. My travels over the ice have dulled the blades slightly, but they still cut through the ropes, one thread at a time. Or so it seems, so slowly does the rope finally unravel and give way under the metal.

I go to work on her wrists next, twice slipping and nicking her skin in the dark of the cave, but Athena doesn't call out or complain. When I've got the ropes off I help her to her feet, but she ends up having to hold me up. My legs have cramped and I'm off balance with one skate on, one skate off.

"I better put the other one on," I say. I stuff my left foot into the skate. It feels like I'm forcing my foot into an iron vise. My feet have swollen and blistered and my stocking has torn, so it's like I'm cramming my bare foot into the stiff leather. I pull the laces tight and try to ignore the searing pain.

"OK," I say, straightening up, "let's try to get across the ice to the mansion." We step out onto the ice and for a moment, after the dark

of the cave, I'm blinded by the white glare of the moonlit fog. I can barely make out the black mass of the second sister standing guard at the mouth of the cave. The looming shape seems to quiver before me and then to split in two as if I'd started seeing double. But then that second shape comes into focus and sprouts a horrible horn.

It's Candace Lockhart, crouched and wielding an eight-foot ice pike like a javelin, its steel tip quivering only a few feet from our throats.

"You run for the shore," I whisper without looking in Athena's direction, "she'll follow me."

"But *Magistra*..."

"Do what I say." I say it in my strictest, no-more-fooling-around-I'm-the-teacher voice and not only does it silence Athena but I see from a slight narrowing in her blue eyes that it momentarily unnerves Dr. Lockhart. I think I know why. For a moment, I sounded just like *Domina* Chambers.

I decide to take advantage of the resemblance. "Alba," I say sternly as I start to back skate along the edge of the Point, heading out onto the lake, "What do you think you are doing with that thing?"

I see out of the corner of my eye Athena making her unsteady way over the ice to the shore and then she disappears in the fog. Dr. Lockhart appears not to notice, she is staring at me. Then she blinks and laughs.

"As if you could ever take *her* place."

"I have taken her place," I say, putting a few more feet between us. I've never been much good at skating backwards, but I remember Matt showing me how to do it. *In and out, little figure eights with your feet, it's all in the inner thighs.* The insides of my thighs feel like melting ice and I can't even feel my feet, but I widen the distance between us while keeping my eyes locked on hers. I'm afraid that when she notices she'll throw the pike or rush me, but instead she starts skating toward me, slowly, as if maintaining a polite conversational distance.

"That's what you wanted to do with Lucy," she says. "You wanted to take her place. First you took her scholarship away, then you wanted Matt."

I lift my shoulders in an attempt at a casual shrug, but it feels more like cringing. "Lucy wanted me to try for the scholarship," I say.

She laughs. I'm surprised at the high-pitched nervousness of it, like a child caught stealing. Something about this conversation is getting to her, unraveling some carefully preserved veil she keeps in place. I have to keep her engaged—entertained, so to speak—or she'll tire of it and I'll end up impaled on that ice pike just like Vesta.

It's a mistake thinking of Vesta. She sees, I think, the fear in my eyes, but instead of attacking me with the pike, she digs in another way. "Poor stupid Jane," she says in a voice that's suddenly not her own. "Thought we were competing for the Iris, as if I wanted it. As if

499

I wanted to be separated from Matt. We picked you that first day as the best one to win it so I wouldn't have to leave Mattie. Didn't realize what a slow study you were, though. Didn't even know what a declension was! Mattie thought that was hilarious."

The mimicry is so precise it almost stops me on the ice. But of course that's what she wants. I keep my feet moving. In and out, little figure eights. Press my thighs together until tears sting my eyes.

"God, what an idiot you were, Janie. You actually thought we were skating those nights we went to the icehouse," the voice has changed, now it's Deirdre's voice. "But we saw you come creeping out on the lake to spy on us, me and Mattie. That's why you wanted to get rid of me, isn't it? So you could have Mattie to yourself?"

"I didn't want to get rid of Deirdre, it was Lucy—"

"Who drove her out onto the Point? You were glad to see her die. Why else didn't you go and pull her out? You let her die there, clinging to the ice."

"That's not how it happened," I say, although I know I can't win an argument with a crazy woman; all I can hope is that as long as I keep her talking she won't throw that spear. "We went down to the hole in the ice where she went in. She wasn't there. She didn't cling to the ice."

Dr. Lockhart shakes her head. "I saw it all." Her voice is small now, the voice of a small,

frightened child. "I hid behind the sister stones and watched her until she couldn't hold on any longer. She said your name over and over again. 'Jane,' she called, 'Jane, you promised.' "

This time her mimicry does stop me dead on the ice. Because it's not Deirdre's voice she's imitating. It's Lucy's.

"You mean Lucy," I say. "You watched Lucy clinging to the ice."

She has stopped, too. She lifts the back of her right wrist, the hand still gripping the lower end of the shaft, to wipe her eyes. The point of the ice pike tilts up and I realize, a moment too late, that it's my best opportunity to rush her, but she sees me coming and lowers the pole again so that I nearly impale myself on it. The metal tip slices through my down parka as I backskate away from it.

"You killed her," she cries, moving forward again. "You left her to die even though you promised you'd come back for her."

MATT FOLLOWED LUCY ONTO THE ICE AND I FOLlowed him. I saw cracks shooting out in all directions from his footsteps and the ice seemed to scream as if it were human flesh being torn. The black water crept between the cracks. But still Matt walked forward as if he didn't notice the ice breaking all around him. For every step he took forward Lucy took one backwards. It was like a dance along an invisible tightrope and I realized they were walking over the same ice that Lucy and

I had broken through with the boat. It was where the underground spring fed into the Schwanenkill and the ice was always the thinnest.

I called to them but they paid no attention to me.

"Matt," I called, desperate to get his attention, "I'll tell you. I did see the baby and his hair was red."

Matt turned to me and in that instant a crack opened up in the ice just behind Lucy. She staggered for a moment, beating the air with her arms. For a moment I thought she had caught her balance. Matt turned back to her. He was so close to her that all he'd have to do is reach out his hand and grab her and she'd be safe. But when he turned to her I saw something change in Lucy's face. It was the first time, I think, that I'd ever seen her truly frightened. She took a step back and fell into the black water.

"It was because you told him," Dr. Lockhart says in a whisper so low I can barely hear it over the scrape of her skates moving steadily toward me. "You should have seen the look on his face when he knew it was his baby. It killed her."

"But how did you see..." and then I understand. She wasn't hiding behind the door of the icehouse. She'd been hiding behind the sister stone. The only part of the argument she'd heard that night was when I told Matt that the baby was his. "But Dr. Lockhart," I say, "*Albie,* I tried to save her. I loved her, too."

She lowers the ice pike and for a moment I think I've gained some ground. I think she's going to drop the pole to the ice, but instead she lifts one knee and, drawing her lips back like a snarling cat, snaps the pole neatly in two. The crack it makes echoes over the ice. "Liar," she hisses, "I saw everything," and then, holding the lighter weapon like a hockey stick, comes at me.

I turn and tear into the ice with my skates. I feel cold metal graze my neck and I fall headlong to the ice, splaying out on the slippery ice. She's on me at once. Her knee digs into the small of my back and she pulls my head up off the ice by yanking my hair back. I can feel the serrated tips of her skate blades grinding into my legs.

"You left her to die," she hisses into my ear. "You promised to save her and you left her on the ice to die." She wraps her hand once in my hair and slams my face to the ice. I hear a loud crack and I think it must be my skull. Before my eyes darkness spreads like a cool green blanket waiting to envelop me. *OK*, I think, *OK*. Somewhere far above me I hear a child crying.

"She said she'd never leave me. She promised, she promised." With every *promise* my head slams into the ice and the darkness spreads, like blood pooling. It is blood pooling. My blood. It's seeping between the cracks in the ice. Dripping into the black water. Through the red-stained blackness I see Lucy's face. Her lips are forming a word but I can't hear what

she's saying because all around us the ice is cracking.

WHEN HE SAW LUCY STEP BACK INTO THE WATER, *Matt froze. I thought he'd go to her, but he stood on the ice as if he'd become a part of it. When I passed him I brushed against his arm and I felt that he was trembling. I saw why. Between him and Lucy the ice had broken into three pieces. The piece that Lucy clung to was loose. When she tried to move her elbow forward on it, the slab tilted toward her. I got down on my hands and knees and held down the other end of the ice.*

"Look," I said to Matt. "If you hold this still, maybe I can help her back up." I looked back over my shoulder to see if he had heard me. His eyes were fixed past me, on Lucy's face, just as her eyes were fixed on his. It was like I wasn't even there.

I tugged on his pant leg and pulled him down to his knees. "Just hold this," I yelled. He didn't move his eyes off Lucy, but he did what I told him to. He crouched on the edge of the unbroken ice and held the slab of ice that lay between us and Lucy. I crawled onto the slab of loose ice and felt it rock in the water, but I also felt Matt adjust his grip to steady it. I got on my belly and crept forward. When I got to Lucy I could see that ice was clinging to her hair and her lips were blue. She was trying to say something, but her teeth were chattering too hard for me to understand her. I tried to move closer, but just as I touched her hand the ice beneath me rocked free and I saw Lucy's eyes widen in fear. I looked over my shoulder and

saw Matt crouched on the edge of the ice. He was still looking at Lucy, but he'd let go of the ice and stretched his arms over his head, his two hands coming together as if in prayer. I tried to remember where I'd seen him in this pose before and then remembered. At the swim club.

He only looked away from Lucy at the last moment to tuck in his chin. He went into the water without a splash. His form perfect.

"Jane," Lucy said, "Jane." I could see she was struggling to control the shaking so that she could speak. "You have to save him."

"I can't," I told her. "He's below the ice. Let me help you." But as I spoke we both saw him surface a few feet away. He got one arm onto the ice, but made no effort to pull himself up. He looked around and when he saw us—or saw Lucy, I should say, because he seemed to look right through me—he shook his head.

I took Lucy's hand and tried to pull her up but she pulled her hand out of mine. "No," she said, "I won't come out until he's safe. Go help him and then me. Promise, Jane. Promise you'll save him first."

I could see it was no good arguing with her. I turned on the ice and crawled toward Matt. I could hear Lucy behind me. Every time I stopped she called my name. "Jane," she said, over and over, "you promised." And so I kept going away from her.

When I was a few inches from Matt I think he finally saw me. He smiled. Like a boy playing keep away. Then he took a deep breath and sank back under the water. I saw his face, like a pale green

star under the black water, grow smaller and smaller and then disappear. I turned back to Lucy, and saw that she'd sunk lower in the water, her lips touching the surface. She was going under. There wasn't time to crawl to her. I threw myself down on the ice and reached for her hand. I felt her fingers under mine—felt them pull away from me and saw her slip into the darkness.

THE ICE FEELS COOL AGAINST MY CHEEK NOW THAT Dr. Lockhart has stopped slamming my head into it. At some point, *she promised* became *you promised*. I picture her—I picture Albie—hiding behind the sister stone and listening to Lucy saying these words to me as I crawled away from her. I can't blame her for thinking I left her to die. Even if I could explain that the promise I made was to save Matt, the truth would be the same. I let her convince me. She knew how I felt about Matt. Knew I would go. And when I reached for Lucy's hand what Albie saw was not Lucy pulling her hand away but me prying her fingers off the ice and sending her to her death.

"You promised, you promised," she whimpers. She sounds like a child and I know she isn't just repeating Lucy's last words. I wonder how long Albie stayed there that night, hiding on the ice because there was no one to come for her. Not even Lucy who had promised always to come for her. When she finally left she stole into our room and found my journal. She'd read the last line I'd written

that night. *I won't let anyone stand in my way. Not even Lucy.*

When they tore up the ice on the lake Albie smashed the fanlight above the doors to Main Hall. She smashed the heart and the words of Lucy's broken promise. I picture shattered glass, like the window in Dean Buehl's office this morning, only instead of light pouring through the cracks there's black water—a blackness that's swallowing me, making it hard to think.

You promised, I hear, and there is something about the childish refrain—*you promised, you promised*—that I think I should remember.

I feel the weight lift off my back and something sharp and metal gnaws into my side. I remember who said that last. Olivia. But you promised, she said on the phone.

The knife in my side is Dr. Lockhart's skate. She's kicking me over, rolling me like a log. I roll once, and feel something dig into my side. It's not Dr. Lockhart's skate though. It's the can of de-icer in my coat pocket. I open my eyes and through a blur of blood see where I'm being rolled. We're inches from the open black water of the ice canal. She only has to roll me once more and I'll be in the water, my heavy skates pulling me to the bottom.

And then I won't see Olivia tomorrow. She'll wait and wait for me and think she wasn't worth coming for. After all, I've already abandoned her once.

I wait for the sharp metal to mash into my skin again and when the searing pain blooms there, I wrap my left arm around her ankles

and pull her down. When her face is close enough I pull out the de-icer and spray it directly into her eyes. She screams and tumbles over me, almost gracefully, and would, I later think, have neatly regained her balance if she'd landed on ice and not the edge of the canal. She teeters for a moment and then slips into the black water.

I lie on the ice for a moment, trying to hear above the sound of my own ragged breath sounds of struggle in the water. But there's nothing. She's dropped as silently as a stone into the lake. After a minute, I turn myself painfully onto my stomach and creep along the ice to the edge of the canal. I'm only an inch or two from the edge when I see the fingernails embedded in the ice. I try to push back, but my hair trails in front of me and she grabs a handful and pulls herself up by it. I see her blue eyes, like painted eyes on a marble statue, just above the surface of the ice, fixed on mine. But then I realize that the chemical spray has blinded her. She can't see me.

I reach out my hand along the ice, and lay it over her other hand, the one not holding onto my hair. She tries to pull away, but I talk softly. "It's OK, Albie," I say, "It's Lucy. I've come to get you. Let me help you." I see her trying to dig her nails out of the ice to take my hand, but she can't. So I move forward another inch and take her hand, prying each finger out of the ice until I've got a good grip. I've never noticed how small and slender her hands are. Just like Lucy's.

And like Lucy she has a grip like a vise. She snakes her hand around my wrist and pulls. I slide forward on the ice and would slide in, except now I feel another pull, someone pulling on my feet. I begin to slide away from the canal, but she won't let go of my hand and she won't try to help herself up onto the ice. A clump of my hair tears away in her hand and she slips down under the water, but still she holds on to my wrist.

"Let go!" I hear someone shout behind me. It's Roy. "You can't save her. The ice is cracking."

I turn my head a little to one side and see dark cracks, like fine veins in marble, radiating out all around me.

"She won't let go of me," I say, so faintly I'm sure he won't hear me, but he does. I feel him creeping up beside me, careful to keep one arm around me so I won't slip into the canal. He must see the dark veins widening under his weight, but he doesn't stop until his face is near mine and we are both looking over the canal's edge into the water. Candace Lockhart's face is a few inches below the water, the whites of her open eyes tinged green by the lake. Roy reaches over me to where she's got my wrist and tries to unpry her fingers from my hand.

"No," I breathe.

"She's gone, Jane. Look at her."

I look back into the water. Her eyes are open, her lips slightly parted, but there are no air bubbles coming from her mouth. Still, I

can feel those eyes watching me, some will rising up toward me through the filter of cold green water, and then I see her, just as I saw Matt's features rise up in Roy's, I see Lucy, her eyes looking out of Albie's blue eyes.

I reach forward with my other hand, but just as I do I feel her fingers, one by one, lifting off my wrist and her small, white hand, relaxed and open, slips below the water, the fingers slightly curled. She sinks, straight and slow, her white hair fanning up around her face, her blue eyes burning like twin stars until they're extinguished by the darkness.

Chapter Thirty-four

●

"WHATEVER MADE THEM PICK MAY DAY FOR the Founder's day Picnic?" Hespera, the eighth grader whose stola I am fixing, complains. "It's too cold up here to frolic half naked around a Maypole."

I try to smile but my mouth is full of hairpins.

Athena answers for me. "It's the founder's birthday, or close to it."

I nod, taking the pins out of my mouth. "Yep, India Crevecoeur was born on May 4, 1886.

So this would be her one hundred and tenth birthday and it's the seventieth anniversary of the school's founding. I actually met her once."

"Really, *Magistra*? You couldn't possibly be that old," Octavia, who's sewing up a seam on Flavia's stola, asks wide-eyed. Flavia rolls her eyes at her sister. When the sisters came back to Latin they demanded a Latin club. To revive our classical spirit, they said. Now they vie with one another to see who has the most classical spirit and who can be nicest to their teacher who valiantly saved the life of one of their classmates. It was their idea to stage a Procession of Floralia for the Founder's Day Maypole dance.

"*Prima,*" I say, "I am that old, and *secunda*, she was ancient. Ninety, I guess, because it was my junior year and the fiftieth anniversary of the school's founding."

"Wow, was she like all senile?" Mallory Martin, although not a Latin student, has volunteered to join in the Procession of Floralia. Mostly because, Athena asserts, she thinks she looks good in a sheet.

"No, actually she was sharp as a tack. She recognized me as the granddaughter of her maid, who'd worked for her fifty years before."

"Your grandmother was a maid here?" Athena asks, pushing her hair, recently dyed sea-green, out of her eyes. I'd been looking forward to seeing its natural shade grow out, but she'd gone to the city last weekend and "caved in to peer pressure" at some East Vil-

lage clip joint. I was disappointed at first, but now that I've gotten used to the color I have to admit that with her green eyes and pale skin it's kind of arresting. Especially today. For her role as goddess of the lake for the Procession of Floralia she's robed in a green satin sheet, a sheet volunteered by, of all people, Gwen Marsh. *Satin* sheets, Gwen? I say every time I see her now. It's just one of the surprising things I've learned about Gwen Marsh in the last few weeks as I've tried to get to know her better. The other is that under those ace bandages are old scars.

"Uh huh," I say absently as I notice the time. "But we're going to be late for our meeting. Hadn't you better change?"

Athena shrugs and pulls on a denim jacket over her sea-green stola. "Why? Is it a formal thing?"

"I don't know what kind of thing it is. Dean Buehl just said it was Heart Lake business and she wants both of us in the Music Room at noon."

"I think they will give you a medal for saving Athena's life," Octavia says.

"And for defeating the evil Dr. Lockhart," Flavia adds.

I could say for the hundredth time that I tried to save Dr. Lockhart and failed, but even I am getting tired of hearing myself say it.

"Well, if that's the occasion," Athena says, "I definitely think I should go as Goddess of the Lake." Athena strikes a pose—one finger to her left temple, her right hand curled in the

air as if holding a scepter—much like a figure of a Greek goddess I once saw on an Attic vase. For not the first time I think there is something regal in Athena's bearing. Maybe that's why her name seems to suit her so well.

"All right," I say. *"Deo parere libertas est."* Before Octavia can get out her book of Latin quotations I provide the source and translation. "Seneca," I say, "To obey a god—or in this case, a goddess—is freedom. OK, then, Octavia and Flavia, I leave it to you to organize the procession. You've got the wreaths and garlands."

"Check."

"Athena and I will meet you outside the mansion at one o'clock then. *Bona fortuna, puellae.*"

We have to stop twice on the path to the mansion to pin closed the seams on Athena's stola which keeps blowing open in the wind. Most of the girls have opted to wear clothes under their stola, but Athena, always a purist, is not even wearing underwear. Luckily I have a pocketful of safety pins. I remember that *Domina* Chambers always kept a supply of pins on hand for errant toga and stola seams. When we get to the foot of the mansion steps she stops and walks a few feet away to the edge of the lake. I think there must be a problem with her outfit again, but when I catch up to her I see that she's started to cry. I sit down on a rock by the edge of water and pat the stone for her to sit next to me.

"We're already late," she says tucking the folds of the sheet up around her knees so she

can sit down on the rock. I'm glad that the stone has been warmed in the sun. Even though Hespera is right about it being too cold to frolic half naked around a Maypole, it is an extraordinarily beautiful day. The lake, under a cloudless blue sky, is so bright it's hard to look at it.

"They'll wait," I tell Athena. "After all, how can they start without the Goddess of the Lake?"

"Maybe that wasn't such a good idea, considering..." Her voice trails off as she stares into the hard glitter of the lake. We both know how much there is to consider. I wonder if Athena will ever look at this lake without remembering the two friends she lost to it. I know I can't.

"It wasn't your fault," I say, something I've said, and had said to me, countless times in the last two months. Still we go on blaming ourselves. Roy and I have gone around and around it. He suspected, as soon as I found the deer's mask, that it must be Albie because she was there on May Day and could have found the mask after he left it in the woods. But he hadn't guessed that Albie was Dr. Lockhart.

The only one who knew that for sure was Dean Buehl and she holds herself accountable for hiring Dr. Lockhart in the first place.

"I felt so awful when the girl was expelled. I told her she'd always have a home here at Heart Lake and she took me at my word. How could I turn her away again? Then she asked me not to tell anyone she'd gone here

and been thrown out. You see, she wasn't really an old girl."

"She took advantage of you," I've said many times to Dean Buehl. "You couldn't have known she was crazy. Maybe she would have been all right if I had never shown up here."

"Well, that certainly isn't your fault." And so it goes—the two of us absolving each other of our sins. Sometimes I wonder if there's any end to this cycle of guilt and retribution. Even Athena has been sucked into the whirlpool of blame.

"But she couldn't have done it without me," she says now. "I told her we'd taken the boat out from the icehouse..."

"You certainly couldn't know she'd use it to take Olivia out to the rock that day," I say trying to keep my voice from shaking. It's still unbearable for me to think of Olivia and Dr. Lockhart in that boat. Or to think of Dr. Lockhart lurking around the preschool, seeding the ground with corniculi.

"I also told her you left your homework folder on your desk." Athena sighs. She's determined, I see, to confess all. Maybe she needs to finally get it all out.

I nod. "That's how she sent me that first journal page, but she would have found another way."

"I told her about Melissa's crush on Brian and she sent her those awful letters from Exeter pretending to be a girl who knew Brian."

"Yes," I say, remembering the Exeter sta-

tionery I saw in the attic bedroom, "and then she must have called Melissa and pretended that she was that girl, to lure her down to the lake." I remember how well she was able to change her voice. A natural mimic.

"And I told her I was mad at Vesta for planning to go skating alone that night and she waited for her out there and killed her."

"Athena, you thought you were talking to a psychologist. You were supposed to tell her things. You couldn't have known what she would do with the information. She used you," I say, "but it was to get at me. She wanted me to relive that whole awful year only, this time, not to survive it."

"But it wasn't your fault what happened twenty years ago."

"From where she stood it was." And she may have been right, I add to myself. Some part of me wanted Deirdre gone so I could have Lucy to myself and some part of me was willing to save Matt at the risk of losing Lucy. The part of me that didn't want to be left out again. In many ways, I was a lot like Albie.

"So why didn't she kill me, too?" Athena asks, shading her eyes from the glare off the lake so she can see my eyes when I answer.

I tuck a strand of sea green hair behind her ear. "I think you reminded her of herself. Her notes on your sessions, she wasn't talking about you anymore, she was telling her own story through you. A girl who had been shuttled from school to school..." Athena looks away and I wonder if I should go on. "Whose par-

ents don't seem to care..." I stop. How many of these girls, I wonder, have a little Albie inside of them?

I shiver at the thought and Athena, as if reading my thoughts, sets me straight. "I'm not that girl," she says. "And neither are you."

THEY'RE WAITING FOR US IN THE MUSIC ROOM. lunch today is a barbecue on the swimming beach, so we've got the room to ourselves. Sitting on one side of the long table, their backs to the long windows facing the lake, are Dean Buehl, Meryl North, Tacy Beade, Myra Todd, Gwendoline Marsh, and one man in a dark suit whom I don't recognize. Roy Corey sits next to two empty chairs on the other side. The long expanse of polished mahogany is bare except for a pitcher of water and some glasses and a manila folder in front of the man, who rises as we come in to introduce himself as the lawyer in charge of the Crevecoeurs' estate. I shake his hand and sit down next to Roy. Athena is still standing.

"And you must be Miss Craven. I know your aunt. She wanted to be here today..."

"But she's got something, somewhere, I know." Athena ignores the lawyer's outstretched hand and plops down in the chair next to me. Two of the pins in her stola pop open, but, much to my relief, the folds of Gwen Marsh's satin sheets stay in place. I notice Myra Todd staring at Athena's outfit, pursing

517

her lips to comment, but before she can the lawyer slaps his hand down on the manila folder.

"Well, since all the principals involved are present," he says, "let's begin."

"I don't see why Jane Hudson is here," Myra says. "She isn't on the board and she isn't a principal."

"A principal in what?" I ask, more confused than insulted. "Would someone please say what this is about."

"India Crevecoeur's bequest," Miss North, the historian answers. "When she turned the property over to be made into a school her relatives were furious. She agreed that she'd give the family a chance to reclaim the property."

"But not until the seventieth anniversary of the founding," Tacy Beade finishes.

"When most of them would be long dead," Dean Buehl adds. "It was her idea of a little joke."

We all instinctively look up at the family portrait that hangs at the end of the room from which India Crevecoeur, dour as Queen Victoria, looks down on us.

"She doesn't look like she would have much of a sense of humor," Roy says.

I'd be inclined to agree, but then I look at Tacy Beade and remember that May Day morning twenty years ago when the old woman escaped from her and Miss Macintosh and found her way into the mansion.

"So, the school could go back into private

hands?" Across the table seven heads nod in agreement.

I am surprised at how bereft I feel at the thought of Heart Lake closing. After Dr. Lockhart's death I told Dean Buehl I'd stay to the end of the term but I just couldn't say for sure what I would do after that. She said she understood the place must have bad memories for me and promised that she would write me a good reference. But now, at the thought of Heart Lake closing its doors forever, I am suddenly enraged.

"That bitch," I say so loudly even Athena looks shocked. "How could she do it? What about all the girls here? Where are they supposed to go?" I imagine all of us—teachers and students—in a procession north to St. Eustace's. I wonder if it still exists. Or has Heart Lake become the last stop, the school of last resort? And if it has, what refuge is left if Heart Lake closes?

"Jane," Dean Buehl says, "I know how you feel. But the school won't close if the Crevecoeur descendants don't want it to." Her eyes slide from me to Roy and Athena. Roy shifts nervously in his chair and Athena slides a little lower down in hers and bites a cuticle.

"Oh, yeah," she says, "my aunt said we were related to those people. That's why she sent me here, because she got a break on tuition or something. Well, if it's up to me, I say, sure, the school should, like, go on."

"Wait a second," I say, "Athena's only just turned eighteen. Shouldn't she have a lawyer

present? She doesn't have to decide right now, does she?"

"Now you're worried about Miss Craven's rights?" Myra Todd asks. "A minute ago you were all upset about the school closing."

"It doesn't matter," Roy says. "I'm the only other descendant, right?"

I look over at him incredulously and he shrugs. I remember then, that May Day, old Mrs. Crevecoeur telling Lucy that the Coreys were related to the Crevecoeurs if you went back far enough. Then it hits me, what any good Latin teacher should have noticed long ago. Craven and Corey. They each derive from one half on the name Crevecoeur.

Myra Todd shifts uneasily in her chair, releasing a whiff of mold into the room. "That settles it then, the bequest becomes permanent and the board now has access to the whole estate—"

"With Mr. Corey and Miss Craven installed as lifetime board members for which they will be paid a stipend..." Dean Buehl is already rising from her seat. All the women on that side of the table are following suit when the lawyer stops them.

"Well, that would be the case," he says, "if not for the codicil."

"The codicil?" Dean Buehl echoes, falling back to her seat. One by one the rest of the women sink down, like sails in a regatta becalmed by a lull in the wind.

"Yes, India Crevecoeur added a codicil to her bequest on May 4, 1976. It was, I under-

stand, prompted by her visit to the school on the fiftieth anniversary of the Founder's Day. If you will all listen patiently now, I will read to you the terms of the codicil." He looks at each of us in turn to see if any one of us will object, but when we all remain silent, he extracts a thick sheet of cream-colored writing paper from a folder and reads, at first in a hurried monotone as he dutifully repeats the legal formulas, and then slowly when he comes to the substance of India Crevecoeur's missive.

"It was my intent, after the death of my youngest daughter, Iris, to transform a scene of grief to one of communal productivity and improvement for young girls. I had some qualms, though, that in providing for strangers I might be impoverishing the children of my children, and so I made my bequest provisional. I confess I was afraid, as well, that a school founded so on grief might founder, and I wanted to give my descendants an opportunity to reclaim their inheritance if such were the case.

"It is not surprising, though, that in my grief-stricken state I overlooked one thing. I'd meant the school to honor the memory of my lost daughter, Iris, and so I should have provided especially for her relations instead of just my own."

Myra Todd clucks her tongue. "She must have been senile. The girl died at twelve! She wasn't old enough to marry. How could she have relations that weren't Crevecoeur descendants?"

The lawyer glares at Myra and resumes. "My daughter Iris was adopted." He pauses a moment for us to take in this piece of information. We all look again at the family portrait at the end of the room. There's little Iris standing off to one side of the group, closer to her nursemaid than the rest of the family. She's small and dark, where everyone else in the family is large and fair.

"She was the natural child of an unfortunate girl who worked in our mill. I'd long wanted a third daughter, but the good Lord had chosen not to bless me with that boon. When I was made aware of the mill girl's predicament I proposed to give the innocent baby a good home—and offered the mill girl a position in my own household. When our little Iris left us, her natural mother chose to leave as well. I could understand her reluctance to remain on the scene of such a tragedy. I tried to make what amends I could, but I'm afraid her daughter's death left the poor woman distracted with a grief that turned to bitter gall in her heart. She even blamed my own two daughters, Rose and Lily, for the death of her child."

I look up at the portrait. Rose and Lily, smiling smugly at the camera. What use would they have had for this strange dark interloper? I remember the story of how the two older girls had taken the youngest out in a boat and she'd fallen in. She'd been saved, but she'd gotten a chill and fallen ill with the flu that was ravaging the country. When I look away

from the picture, I notice that Dean Buehl and Roy are both staring at me.

"When it recently came to my attention that my former servant—Iris's mother—had subsequently married and borne a child of her own, who in turn had her own child, I realized that the chance to make amends had finally arrived. Better late than never, as the girl herself said to me."

It's that phrase, so out of tune with the rest of India Crevecoeur's language, that finally wakes me up. I remember the way the old woman looked at me when I said it. I thought she was appalled at my cheek. Appalled to find her servant's granddaughter attending her school.

Although the lawyer is still reading I get up and walk over to the picture. I look, not at poor, spindly legged Iris, but at the nursemaid, my grandmother, who bends down to fix her charge's ribbon. At least, that's what I always assumed she was doing. Now that I look more closely I see she's giving the girl a little push, trying to send her closer to her sisters so that she'll be part of the family group. Why didn't I ever wonder how the maid got in the family portrait? Was it because Iris would never have been far from her? I look at the maid's face; her brow, dark and plain, is pinched with worry, but under that anxiety, that her child will never really fit in with her adopted family, I think I can read, in the plain brown eyes, familiar to me as my own, something like love.

"And so, Miss Hudson," the lawyer is saying, as I turn back to face the table where everyone is now looking toward me, "Mrs. Crevecoeur left the deciding vote to you. The granddaughter of Iris's mother."

"Well, then I say make the bequest permanent."

"As you told Miss Craven," the lawyer says, "you don't have to decide right now. Certainly you'll want to consider the amount of money you'd be giving up."

Dean Buehl claps her hand to her breast and begins to weep as if she'd been holding back this uncharacteristic flood of emotions the whole time. Athena looks at her and starts to giggle, but stops herself by biting her thumb. Roy gets up and puts his arm around me.

"Are you sure?" he asks.

"Why? Would you like me better if I were an heiress?"

The smile he gives me comes slowly but reaches into someplace deep, someplace that feels as if it's never been touched until now, like the cold bottom of the lake that the sun has never warmed before this moment. "You forget," he says, "you're my heart's true love."

"Oh yeah," I say.

Then the others are around us, all talking at once, but it's Athena I hear.

"You're going to be late, *Magistra*."

"Yikes, you're right." I look down at my watch.

"The procession?" Roy asks.

"Something else," I tell him, giving him a quick, hard kiss on the mouth. "A surprise."

I RUN DOWN THE STEPS OF THE MANSION. MY GIRLS are gathered there, the flowers in their hair trembling in the light breeze coming off the lake. I wave to them and tell them that Athena will lead the procession and I'll join them at the Maypole. Beyond them I see the car parked down by the lake. As I step off the path, the car door opens and she gets out. For a moment, she is only a dark figure silhouetted against the bright fire of the lake; a small girl standing alone in an enormous swirl of atoms. Then she sees me and comes running, arms open wide.